Insight Guides

THAILAND

APA PUBLICATIONS L

Part of the Langenscheidt Publishing Group

THAILAND

Editorial

Project Editor
Tom Le Bas
Art Editor
Richard Cooke
Picture Manager
Steven Lawrence
Series Manager
Rachel Fox

Distribution

UK & Ireland
GeoCenter International Ltd
Meridian House, Churchill Way West
Basingstoke, Hampshire RG21 6YR
sales@geocenter.co.uk

United States
Langenscheidt Publishers, Inc.
36–36 33rd Street 4th Floor
Long Island City, NY 11106
orders@langenscheidt.com

Australia
Universal Publishers
1 Waterloo Road
Macquarie Park, NSW 2113
sales@universalpublishers.com.au

New Zealand
Hema Maps New Zealand Ltd (HNZ)
Unit 2, 10 Cryers Road
East Tamaki, Auckland 2013
sales.hema@clear.net.nz

Worldwide
**Apa Publications GmbH & Co.
Verlag KG (Singapore branch)**
38 Joo Koon Road, Singapore 628990
apasin@signet.com.sg

Printing

CTPS - China

©2010 Apa Publications GmbH & Co.
Verlag KG (Singapore branch)
All Rights Reserved

First Edition 1978
Fifteenth Edition 2010

CONTACTING THE EDITORS
We would appreciate it if readers
would alert us to errors or out-
dated information by writing to:
**Insight Guides, P.O. Box 7910,
London SE1 1WE, England.**
insight@apaguide.co.uk

www.insightguides.com

ABOUT THIS BOOK

The first Insight Guide pioneered the use of creative full-colour photography in travel guides in 1970. Since then, we have expanded our range to cater for our readers' need not only for reliable informa- tion but also for a real understand- ing of a destination and its people. Now, when the Internet can supply inexhaustible (but not always relia- ble) facts, our books marry text and pictures to provide those much more elusive qualities: knowledge and discernment. To achieve this, they rely heavily on the authority of locally based writers and photographers.

How to use this book

Insight Guide: Thailand is structured to convey an understanding of the country and its people as well as to guide readers through its attractions:

◆ The **Features** section, indicated by a pink bar at the top of each page, covers the landscape and history of Thailand as well as aspects of the fascinating Thai culture: its people, religion, arts and crafts, performing arts, cuisine and architecture.

◆ The main **Places** section, indi- cated by a blue bar, is a complete guide to all the sights and areas worth visiting. Places of special inter- est are coordinated by number with the maps. A list of recommended restaurants is included at the end of each chapter in this section.

◆ The **Travel Tips** listings section, with a yellow bar, includes all the practical information you'll need, divided into five sections: transport, accommodation, activities, an A–Z listing of practical tips, and a handy section on the Thai language with suggestions for further reading. A contents list for the Travel Tips is printed on the back cover flap, which also serves as a bookmark.

LEFT: ruins at Si Satchanalai-Chaliang Historical Park, near Sukhothai.

based freelance journalist **Sarah Rooney**, while writer and magazine editor **Howard Richardson**, also based in Bangkok, provided the chapter on Cuisine as well as the Bangkok restaurant listings. The chapters on Performing Arts and Arts and Crafts were the work of **Connelly La Mar**, an arts aficionado who is well known in the Bangkok creative scene. For the 2008 edition, the history chapters were expertly condensed into a digestible read by specialist writer and Insight regular **Andrew Forbes**.

The original Places chapters were largely the work of four writers. Covering Bangkok, Central Thailand, Eastern Seaboard, Northern Gulf Coast, and Ko Samui, Ko Phangan and Ko Tao was Bangkok-based British freelance writer **Steven Pettifor**.

Freelance writer **Lauren Smith**, who moved from the UK and made sunny Phuket her home base, wrote the chapters on the Northern Andaman Coast, Phuket, and Krabi, Ko Phi Phi and Ko Lanta.

The chapter on the Deep South was the work of freelance American writer and photographer **Austin Bush**, who now makes Bangkok his home. Finally, anchoring the North and Northeast regions was well-known Thailand expert **Joe Cummings**, who writes prolifically about his adopted country from his home base in Chiang Mai.

Several talented photographers contributed to the striking photography you see in this book – Insight regular **Peter Stuckings**, **David Henley** and **Austin Bush** plus **Jock Montgomery**, **Jason Lang**, **John W. Ishii** and **Nikt Wong**.

This fifteenth edition was proofread by **Neil Titman** and indexed by **Helen Peters**.

The contributors

This new edition was supervised and edited by **Tom Le Bas** at Insight Guides' London office. Two expert Thailand-based writers were enlisted to rewrite and update this latest incarnation of the book.

The History and Features sections as well as the Places sections on Bangkok, Central and Southern Thailand, were comprehensively updated by Phuket resident **Ed Peters**, a travel writer, journalist and long-standing Insight contributor. North and Northeast Thailand, as well as the bulk of the Travel Tips, were brought up to date by **Peter Holmshaw**, who has lived in Chiang Mai for the past 20 years and contributed to several Insight titles.

Their work builds on the efforts of those involved in previous editions of the guide. The People and Culture chapter was written by Bangkok-

Map Legend

─ ·· ─	International Boundary
─ ─ ─	Province Boundary
─·─	National Park/Reserve
─ ─ ─	Ferry Route
⊖	Border Crossing
✈ ✈	Airport: International/Regional
🚌	Bus Station
Ⓢ	Skytrain BTS
Ⓜ	Metro MRT
❶	Tourist Information
✝ ✝ ✝	Church/Ruins
✝	Monastery
∴	Archaeological Site
∩	Cave
⚊	Statue/Monument
★	Place of Interest
⚑	Beach
🗼	Lighthouse

The main places of interest in the Places section are coordinated by number with a full-colour map (e.g. ❶), and a symbol at the top of every right-hand page tells you where to find the map.

BELOW: dressed up for the Loy Krathong festival.

Contents

LEFT: James Bond Island, near Phuket.

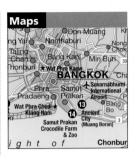

Maps

Travel Tips

6

THE BEST OF THAILAND: TOP SIGHTS

From buzzing Bangkok to mist-shrouded Mae Hong Son, and from the paradisiacal beaches of Phuket to the rambling ruins of Ayutthaya, this is a rundown of the best that Thailand has to offer

△ **Bangkok** is a modern Asian city with an array of hip dining and nightlife options, but thankfully, its more traditional charms – like golden-spired Buddhist temples, serpentine canals and a colourful street life – are still quite evident. *See page 109*

△ **Similan Islands Marine National Park** – easily accessed from Phuket, the crystal-clear waters attract both divers and snorkellers. *See page 225*

◁ **Nakhon Ratchasima (Khorat) Province** in northeast Thailand is a treasure trove of Khmer-era temple ruins and the pristine Khao Yai National Park. *See page 336*

△ With its spectacular white-sand beaches, luxury resort hotels, plentiful seafood and buzzing nightlife, **Phuket** is a natural choice for anyone seeking a relaxing holiday. *See page 231*

◁ Hemmed in by high mountains and bordering Myanmar (Burma), **Mae Hong Son** in the far north is a good starting point for treks to see colourful hill tribes in the surrounding region. *See page 329*

△ Principal rival to Phuket and the west-coast beaches, the white-sand beaches on the resort island of **Ko Samui** are lapped by the clear waters of the Gulf of Thailand. Nearby **Ko Phangan** and **Ko Tao** offer yet more perfect beaches, wild nightlife and fabulous diving. *See page 201*

▽ **Krabi** and its surrounding islands in south Thailand have stunning beaches, lush national parks, excellent diving and snorkelling, and a fiery southern cuisine to sample. *See page 249*

△ The ancient city of **Sukhothai**, to the north of Bangkok, is associated with the golden era of Thai history. This magnificent collection of buildings has been awarded Unesco World Heritage status. *See page 315*

◁ With its distinctive Lanna-style wooden temples, superb handicrafts and gracious people, **Chiang Mai** in north Thailand is an obvious magnet during the cool-season months from December to February. *See page 281*

▷ Another Unesco World Heritage site with a prominent role in Thai history, **Ayutthaya** is easily accessed from the capital by coach or by boat along the Chao Phraya River. *See page 162*

THE BEST OF THAILAND: EDITOR'S CHOICE

Unique attractions, idyllic beaches, lush national parks, ancient ruins, awe-inspiring temples, diving hotspots, treks to see hill-tribe communities, fun festivals... here at a glance are our recommendations on what to see and do

THAILAND FOR FAMILIES

- **Ancient City: Samut Prakan**. See Thailand in a nutshell. Replicas of its most famous sights, some full-size, others scaled down, are strewn around this open-air park. *See page 170*
- **Crocodile Farm & Zoo: Samut Prakan**. Families shriek as handlers wrestle with large crocodiles and stick their heads between the snapping jaws of these giant reptiles. *See page 171*
- **Rose Garden Riverside Resort: Nakhon Pathom**. Traditional dances, Thai boxing and other forms of folk culture are performed in a garden setting near Bangkok. *See page 149*
- **Phuket Fantasea: Phuket**. A stage extravaganza combining dance, drama and acrobatics with pyrotechnics and performing elephants. *See page 237*
- **Siam Ocean World: Bangkok**. A giant aquarium with over 30,000 marine creatures will leave the kids spellbound. They can even ride in a glass-bottomed boat. *See page 130*
- **Sriracha Tiger Zoo: Si Racha**. The world's largest zoo devoted solely to tigers; over 200 Bengal tigers roam here. *See page 178*
- **Thai Elephant Conservation Centre: Lamphun**. Learn how elephants have been used in Thailand's logging industry, then take a ride on elephant back through tropical jungle. *See page 299*

TOP BEACHES

- **Ao Kantiang: Ko Lanta**. No pressing crowds, only pure white sand and clear aquamarine waters. *See page 261*

- **Ao Maya: Ko Phi Phi**. Hordes of day-trippers detract from its ethereal beauty, framed by limestone cliffs. This is where the movie *The Beach* was shot. *See pages 256 and 258*
- **Ao Hin Khok: Ko Samet**. One of Samet's less busy beaches, it has a nice laidback vibe. *See page 183*
- **Hat Kuat: Ko Phangan**. It's easy to see why this lovely beach gets so many repeat visitors. *See page 211*
- **Hat Nai Harn: Phuket**. Scant development and a broad stretch of white sand make this a clear winner. *See page 239*
- **Hat Tham Phra Nang: Krabi**. Utterly gorgeous, this is possibly Thailand's most stunning beach. *See page 254*
- **Ko Nang Yuan: near Ko Tao**. Three islets joined by mere wisps of the softest sand guarantee this island beach top billing. *See page 214*

TOP: beautiful beaches at Ko Tao. **ABOVE:** gruesome masks at the Phee Ta Khon Festival.

BEST NATIONAL PARKS

• **Doi Inthanon National Park: Chiang Mai Province**. This natural reserve is centred around Thailand's highest mountain, Doi Inthanon. *See page 297*
• **Erawan National Park: Kanchanaburi Province**. The seven-level Erawan Waterfall is the star attraction at this national park to the west of Bangkok. *See page 156*
• **Kaeng Krachan National Park: Phetchaburi Province**. Thailand's largest national park is, surprisingly, one of the least explored. *See page 194*

• **Khao Sam Roi Yot National Park: Gulf of Thailand**. Expect varied topography, with beaches, marshes, lush forests and mountains at this vast reserve. *See page 197*
• **Khao Sok National Park: Northern Andaman Coast**. South Thailand's most popular national park is unique in many ways, and has an amazing variety of flora and fauna. *See page 222*
• **Khao Yai National Park: Nakhon Ratchasima**. Although located in northeastern Thailand proper, this popular national park is more usually accessed from Bangkok. *See page 336*
• **Phu Kradung National Park: Loei**. This high-altitude forest and mountain reserve is one of the most memorable escapes in northeastern Thailand. *See page 354*

LEFT: elephant bath time. **ABOVE:** coral formations at Hin Bai, near Ko Tao. **BELOW:** transvestite performer at Simon Cabaret, Phuket.

ONLY IN THAILAND

• **Canal Cruising: Bangkok**. Hop on a longtail boat and glide along the canals for a slice of Bangkok's past. *See pages 119 and 368*
• **Dancing plant: Udon Thani**. The Udorn Sunshine Nursery is famous for the Thai dancing plant, whose leaves sway gently when spoken or sung to. *See page 351*

• **Full Moon Parties: Ko Phangan**. These wild all-night raves are the island's main claim to fame. *See page 206*
• **Lady-boy** *(kathoey)* **cabaret: Bangkok, Pattaya, Phuket, Ko Samui and Chiang Mai**. Is she or isn't she? (a woman). Vegas-style shows by elaborately costumed transvestite performers. *See pages 397–400*
• **Samui Monkey Theatre: Ko Samui**. Monkeys clamber up trees at lightning speed to pluck coconuts. *See page 204*
• **Motorcycle taxis: Bangkok**. Fast and furious, these madmen weave through the city's gridlock with knee-scraping accuracy. *See page 368*
• **Thai boxing: Bangkok, Phuket and Chiang Mai**. Punishing and brutal, this ancient martial art is more than

BEST SNORKELLING AND DIVE SITES

• **Burma Banks**. Three submerged peaks that provide a superlative diving experience. *See page 222*
• **Chumphon Pinnacle**. Famous for frequent sightings of grouper and other large fish. *See page 215*
• **Hin Bai (Sail Rock)**. Rising like an iceberg out of the water, its highlight is a vertical chimney. *See page 212*
• **Hin Daeng and Hin**

Muang. These world-class dive sites are located near Ko Rok. *See page 262*
• **Ko Rok**. Easily Thailand's best site for snorkelling, with colourful corals and fish found in shallow waters. *See page 262*
• **Richelieu Rock**. One of the world's top sites for sightings of whale sharks. *See page 222*

BEST MARKETS AND BAZAARS

- **Chatuchak Weekend Market, Bangkok**. The biggest market of them all. An unbeatable shopping experience; this has everything. *See page 140*
- **Chiang Mai Night Bazaar**. Hundreds of vendors selling everything from cheap trinkets to hand-embroidered hill-tribe clothing. *See page 286*
- **Damnoen Saduak Floating Market: Samut Songkhram**. This century-old market has become a bit of a circus, with tourists clamouring to photograph fruit-laden boats paddled by women in straw hats. Still, it's worth seeking out. *See page 152*
- **Patpong Night Market: Bangkok**. Surrounded by sleaze and neon, its location is as much the attraction as the fake designer watches, bags, clothes and general tourist tat. *See page 133*
- **Trang Night Market: Trang**. One of the largest markets in south Thailand, the offerings run the gamut from handicraft to food, glorious food. *See page 268*

ABOVE: sea canoeing at Ao Phang Nga.

HISTORICAL SITES

- **Bang Pa-In**. The old palaces of the Chakri kings are an interesting hybrid of East-West design. *See page 161*
- **Bridge on the River Kwai: Kanchanaburi**. Thailand's haunting memorial to the POWs who died during World War II. *See page 153*
- **Lopburi**. Explore the ruins of the old summer palace of an Ayutthayan king. *See page 167*
- **Phitsanulok**. Its Sukhothai-era main temple holds Thailand's second-most important Buddha image. *See page 321*
- **Prasat Hin Khao Phanom Rung**. Thailand's largest and best-restored Khmer ruins are in the northeast of the country. *See page 342*
- **Prasat Khao Phra Viharn**. Technically in Cambodia, this magnificent cliff-top Khmer temple is only accessible from Thailand. *See page 344*

ABOVE: vendor at Damnoen Saduak Floating Market near Bangkok. **RIGHT:** Buddha statue and monkey at Wat Tham Seua, Krabi.

FESTIVALS AND EVENTS

● **Chinese New Year: Bangkok**. Firecrackers, lion and dragon dances, and festival foods herald the start of the new year for Bangkok's Chinese community. Jan/Feb. *See page 409*
● **Elephant Round-Up: Surin**. In November, this provincial town becomes a hive of activity when a series of elephant-related events take place. *See pages 58, 343 and 410*
● **Fireboat Festival: Nakhon Pathom**. This northeastern Thai festival sees gaily decorated "fireboats" being launched on the Mekong River. Oct. *See pages 359 and 410*
● **Flower Festival: Chiang Mai**. The city comes alive in glorious colour with floral floats and flower displays. Feb.

See page 410
● **Loy Krathong: nationwide**. Expect a visual treat as Thais honour water spirits by lighting candles and setting them afloat on tiny baskets along the country's waterways. Nov. *See pages 59 and 410*
● **Phee Ta Khon Festival: Dansai**. Possibly Thailand's most raucous celebration, with people dressed up in colourful costumes and wearing grotesque masks. June/July. *See pages 58, 353 and 410*
● **Songkran: nationwide**. Pack water pistols (along with a sense of humour) for a three-day orgy of soaking. The Thai Lunar New Year is the nation's largest and wettest celebration. Apr. *See pages 59 and 410*

ABOVE: wet and wild during Songkran Festival.
BELOW: giant sleeping Buddha image at Wat Pho.

OUTDOOR ACTIVITIES

● **Elephant trekking**. Ride on elephant-back through tropical jungle. *See pages 181, 186, 299, 406 and 409*
● **Diving and snorkelling**. Warm, clear waters and a profusion of marine life make Thailand a diving hotspot. *See pages 405–8*
● **Golfing**. Some of the golfing world's stellar architects have built courses in Thailand. *See pages 404–8*
● **Hill-tribe treks**. Book an organised trek to see and experience a bit of the life of north Thailand's hill tribes. *See pages 56 and 409*
● **Rock climbing**. The sheer limestone cliffs of south Thailand attract climbers from the world over. *See pages 255 and 408–9*
● **Sea canoeing**. The islands and pinnacles of Ao Phang Nga invite exploration by sea canoe. *See pages 226 and 408*
● **Whitewater rafting**. Take an adrenalin-charged ride down one of Thailand's churning rivers. *See page 409*

MOST INTERESTING TEMPLES

● **Tham Khao Luang: Phetchaburi**. More than 100 Buddha images fill this cave temple sanctuary. *See page 193*
● **Wat Chalong: Phuket**. Phuket's largest and most important Buddhist temple. *See page 241*
● **Wat Pho: Bangkok**. The capital's largest temple is best known for its gigantic statue of the reclining Buddha. *See page 116*
● **Wat Phra Kaew: Bangkok**. No one leaves the capital without seeing the Temple of the Emerald Buddha. *See page 111*
● **Wat Phra Mahathat: Nakhon Si Thammarat**. One of six royal temples in Thailand. *See page 274*
● **Wat Phra That Doi Suthep: Chiang Mai**. Stunning mountain-top temple just outside of this northern city. Be prepared to climb 290 steps. *See page 293*
● **Wat Phra That Lampang Luang: Lampang**. This is a masterpiece of northern-style temple architecture. *See page 300*
● **Wat Phumin: Nan**. Most famous for its beautifully rendered 19th-century murals. *See page 311*
● **Wat Ratchabophit: Bangkok**. Stunning for its hybrid mix of Western and Thai architectural styles. *See page 117*
● **Wat Phra Singh: Chiang Mai**. The city's most important temple – and the largest within the old walled city. *See page 284*
● **Wat Tham Seua: Krabi**. Vast temple complex tucked amid Krabi's forests and cliffs. *See page 250*

THE KINGDOM OF THAILAND

Land of the free, land of smiles. The former is a literal translation of Thailand, while the latter is a promotional tourism slogan that is pleasingly truthful. Both define the Thai people and the welcoming nature of their land

Beneath their graciousness, the Thais have a strong sense of self and tradition. It is this pride in themselves, and in their culture and monarchy, that underpins the Thai sense of identity and an ability to smile at the vicissitudes of life.

The Kingdom of Thailand is ruled by an elected government, but retains the tradition of a ruling monarchy – which commands intense loyalty from the people. It has a population of over 66 million and is about the same size as France – twice that of Britain. Its climate is tropical, with three seasons: the hot season (Mar–May), the wet monsoon season (June–Nov) and the cool season (Dec–Feb). The capital city of Bangkok, or Krung Thep in Thai, has at least 10 million people (accurate estimates are, by definition, dubious).

Bangkok is the country's international gateway, and its seat of government, business and the royalty. It is almost a city-state unto itself and bears little similarity to the rest of the nation. When a Thai says, "I'm heading upcountry tomorrow," she or he could mean anywhere outside of Bangkok's city limits. Anywhere is upcountry. Indeed, the second-largest city in Thailand (Udon Thani) has perhaps one-fortieth the population of Bangkok. Most of Thailand is rural, a patchwork of rice fields, villages, plantations and forests.

Thailand is commonly divided into four regions: the Central Plain, of which Bangkok is a part; the north, including Chiang Mai and Chiang Rai; the northeast; and the south, extending from Chumphon down to the Malaysian border. Each region has its own culture and appeal.

Since the East first encountered Siam a millennium ago and Westerners began trickling in during the 16th century, Thailand has been a powerful magnet for adventurers and entrepreneurs. An abundance of resources, a wealth of natural beauty, a stunning cultural tradition revealed in dazzling architecture and art, and a warm, hospitable people have proved irresistible lures.

PRECEDING PAGES: Patong beach, Phuket; harvesting rice near Mae Sariang; Wat Arun and the Chao Phraya River, Bangkok. **LEFT:** Buddha image at Wat Pho, Bangkok. **TOP:** parasailing at Pattaya. **ABOVE RIGHT:** young novice monks. **ABOVE LEFT:** traditional knife and wooden sheath.

Thailand's traditional charms form only one side of the picture, of course. It is a nation in transition, evolving from a developing to a developed country in a rollercoaster of a ride. Since the millennium, economic fortunes have fluctuated, and recent years have seen a great deal of political turbulence. But true to the people's spirit, consistent throughout the country's history, Thailand has tended to recover quickly from any disruption .

Throughout its history, Thailand has shown a stubborn maverick streak and a sense of pragmatism, both of which have created a determination to chart its own course. The result is a country that has never been colonised by a foreign power and one that has intentionally retained its past while moving ahead into the future.

It is hard to ignore the changes taking place, yet there is much that sets Thailand apart from nations on similar paths. The natural beauty is still there in superb beaches, seas of green rice and forested hills, somewhat safe now that logging is illegal (although it still happens). And even in the most modern towns, the past continues to shine through as temples and palaces are preserved. This uniqueness is not always apparent, especially in a chaotic city like Bangkok that pounds on the senses unceasingly. *This is not the exotic Thailand I was promised,* the visitor laments. *This is a nightmare.* True, it is a city that is vibrantly alive, but it is also a repository of some of the world's most exquisite architecture and historical artefacts.

The Thais enjoy life. Something that fails to give personal satisfaction, whether in work or in play, is not worth doing. Any activity must have something of this quality within it. Part of this is distilled from holding on to one's traditions. This may change in Thailand, but for the moment, it is firmly intact. The traveller can't help but notice this.

A note on spellings

The transliteration of Thai pronunciation into a Roman alphabet has proved to be a quagmire of phonemes and good intentions. The traveller will encounter several, not just one or two, possible spellings for a single place name. Leaps of linguistic creativity are in order as one negotiates street signs (often Romanised), maps and guidebooks, including this one. As much as possible, this book has sided with common sense and common usage, along with a dose of consistency.

When the letter *h* follows a consonant, it makes the consonant's sound less explosive, softer. Just as Thailand is pronounced *tai-land*, not *thigh-land*, so too the *ph* sound. The pronunciation of *Wat Po* is the same as *Wat Pho*, and, in fact, they are the same temple in Bangkok. Similarly, the island of *Phuket* is always spelled with *ph*, but it is pronounced, always, like *poo-ket*, not *foo-ket* or in other less gracious ways. Other common variations of place-name spellings include *ratcha* and *raja*, and *chom* and *jom*.

The rule of thumb regarding spellings is to be like a Thai when in Thailand: adaptable and tolerant, and with a sense of humour. ❑

Top: Wat Phra That Doi Suthep, Chiang Mai. **Above Right:** palm trees are a common sight in tropical Thailand. **Right:** Ko Hae, also known as Coral Island, off Phuket.

GEOGRAPHY AND LANDSCAPE

Although Thailand's wild lands have diminished owing to aggressive development over the past few decades, the country is still endowed with some unique flora and fauna

From the forested mountains of the northwest to the beaches and plantations of the southern peninsula, Thailand covers some 513,115 sq km (198,115 sq miles), which makes this tropical land roughly equal in size to France. It can be divided into six geographical regions.

In the north, extending along the borders of Myanmar (Burma) and Laos, parallel mountains run from north to south, generally reaching over 2,000 metres (6,500ft) in height. The valleys have been cultivated for centuries, but since the 1950s, the proliferation of slash-and-burn farming techniques has resulted in considerable loss of forest cover in the higher altitudes.

To the south, the vast valley called the Central Plain stretches 450km (280 miles) east to the Gulf of Thailand. The overflowing tributaries have deposited rich silt that created large areas of rich farmland. These days the farms are supported by intensive irrigation, provided by a network of dams.

The Myanmar border to the west is marked by mountain ranges, the source of tributaries of the Mekong, Chao Phraya and Salween rivers. Sparsely populated, this region harbours a rich repository of wildlife.

The northeastern region, known as Isaan, encompasses the broad and shallow Khorat Plateau, which lies less than 200 metres (656ft) above sea level. This is a land of poor soils, little rain, too many people, and more grass and shrub than forest.

The hilly southeast coast is bordered on the north by mountains which protrude from Cambodia. It includes some 80 rocky, forested islands along the east coast of the Gulf of Thailand.

Endowed with the heaviest rainfall and humidity, the south covers the narrow Isthmus of Kra

all the way to the Malay Peninsula. The south is famous for its beaches on both the Gulf of Thailand (east) and Andaman (west) coasts. Most of the coastal forests have been cleared to make way for rubber and palm plantations; some 275 islands scattered in the Andaman Sea support unique marine species and rich coral reefs.

Flora

In the 1940s, forests still covered about 70 percent of Thailand's land area. By 1960, the figure had dropped to 50 percent. Today, probably only about 15 percent of undisturbed forest remains, although perhaps another 15 percent of it has been replanted, often with non-indigenous species, or else turned into plantations growing palm-oil trees and, especially in the south, rubber and pineapple. Deforestation rates were among the highest in Southeast Asia, but following several fatal landslides, logging was outlawed in 1989, and the situation is now more stable.

Thailand's forests are either evergreen or deciduous. There are many sub-categories, and a single habitat may contain both types of trees. Evergreen forests are most abundant in the uplands of the south and southeast, where rainfall is plentiful and the dry season brief.

However, not all tropical forests are evergreen, and not all evergreen forests are rainforests. A rainforest is a four-layered forest harbouring the

varieties of orchids also proliferate. The leaves of the taller dipterocarps turn yellow and red before shedding in the dry season.

Fauna

Of the world's estimated 4,000 species of mammals, 287 have been recorded in Thailand, including 18 hooved species, 13 species of primates, nine types of wild cats (including tigers and leopards), two species of bear, and two of wild dogs. Bats are abundant, with 107 species identified so far. The tiger population has declined, along with the Asian elephant – Thailand's national symbol. From over 200,000 a

world's densest concentration of species. Herbs, shrubs, ferns and fungi form the bottom layer. Just above ground level is a relatively open layer of palms, bamboos and shrubs. At mid-level are trees, festooned with vines, mosses and orchids, which create a 25-metre (82ft) high canopy. The well-spaced trees of the uppermost forest canopy can soar as high as 60 metres (200ft).

More common than rainforest is the broad-leaved evergreen forest, which is found at higher elevations, especially in the north. It comprises temperate-zone laurels, oaks and chestnuts, along with ferns and rhododendrons. Several

century ago, fewer than 3,000 wild elephants survive in Thailand today. Khao Yai National Park *(see page 325)* or the parks close to the Myanmar border offer the best chance of seeing one.

> On a map, Thailand resembles the head of an elephant, with the narrow southern peninsula forming the trunk. It is sheer coincidence that the elephant is Thailand's national symbol.

Thailand also harbours four types of reptiles and three types of amphibians. Among the 175 species of snakes are deadly cobras, kraits and vipers. Many of the insect species have yet to be

LEFT: brightly coloured tropical bloom.
ABOVE: limestone cliffs at Ao Phang Nga.

identified, but there are 1,200 variegated butterflies. Beetle species may number in the tens of thousands, but have been so little studied that entomologists occasionally discover new ones.

Visitors to national parks will be rewarded with bird sightings. There are around 900 species permanently resident in the region, while about 240 non-breeding and wintering migratory species pass through Thailand annually.

Coastal geography

With over 3,000km (2,000 miles) of coastline and hundreds of islands washed by two seas – the Gulf of Thailand in the east and the Andaman Sea in the west – littoral geography is a significant element in Thailand's environment. Tourists are drawn to the region's powdery sand beaches and clear waters that are rich in tropical marine life *(see panel below and pages 228–9)*.

Geologically, the region is noted for its dramatic limestone karst formations jutting out of the sea. Soft and easily eroded, the limestone once formed the seabed. Spectacular caves carved out by underground streams and lagoons hidden within the limestone karsts make for fun-filled exploration on inflatable kayaks. Ao Phang Nga National Park *(see page*

A DIVER'S HAVEN

With long coastlines skirting either side of the south, Thailand is a major diving and snorkelling destination. The waters are clear and warm year-round, and a plethora of colourful coral reefs attract a huge variety of marine life, including turtles, rays and sharks. With dive shops and live-aboard tours accessing remote dive sites that border Malaysia to the south, Myanmar to the west and Cambodia to the east, Thailand is one of the most affordable places in the world to dive.

The Andaman Sea on the west coast is generally considered better in terms of reef and marine diversity, water clarity and a wealth of idyllic islands to drop anchor at. The remote Similan and Surin island chains (accessed only by live-aboard dive trips from Phuket) are regarded as the country's premier dive sites, but the waters off Phuket, Krabi, Ko Phi Phi and Ko Lanta are also popular dive havens. More intrepid divers head out to Burmese waters to explore the reefs of the Mergui Archipelago and the Burma Banks – all off the Andaman coast.

Off the Gulf of Thailand, Ko Tao is especially popular among would-be dive enthusiasts. This is Thailand's dive capital, with over 50 dive schools. Also popular are dive trips from Ko Samui and Ko Phangan. Pattaya's waters offer little in terms of marine life and water clarity, but this is compensated by a number of interesting wreck dives. Fast gaining in popularity, the Ko Chang Archipelago, with over 50 islands, is still being mapped out as a dive destination.

226) comprises an eye-popping series of crumbly cliffs, jutting islets and karst rocks.

Environment at risk

The country's Forestry Department is underfunded and understaffed. In the past few decades, at least 40 rangers have been murdered in the line of duty. Earning less than a factory worker, many rangers also collude with loggers and poachers. The country's poorest people also inadvertently contribute to environmental degradation by farming on protected lands. The endangered populations of tigers and other wildlife are further threatened by the demand for medicinal products among the Chinese.

The coastal environment has not been spared. Illegal construction, surreptitious land grabs and poor sewage disposal remain a problem at some of the Eastern Seaboard resorts, notably Pattaya. Even national parkland is not sacrosanct. Ko Samet, for instance, is part of a marine national park, but unbridled development along its coast has progressed despite the law. Elsewhere, new legislation, or existing legislation more rigorously applied, is slowly making a difference.

The December 2004 tsunami had some initial positive spin-offs on the affected areas of the Andaman coast. Illegal buildings and ramshackle resorts were literally swept away by the gigantic waves. The Thai authorities tried to prevent illegal rebuilding in the aftermath, but this was met with forceful opposition by many displaced locals. Even on a national park like Ko Phi Phi, illegal construction is once again rife.

The marine life of southern Thailand's coastal waters are similarly menaced by human activities, including dynamite and poison fishing – both now strictly outlawed – as well as anchor drag and over-fishing. An additional threat is rising sea temperatures, which can cause coral bleaching. To counter this, "reef balls" of hollow, reinforced concrete are being sunk to rehabilitate reefs in the Andaman Sea off Phuket, and also in the shallower Gulf of Thailand.

In the mountainous north of Thailand, deforestation and illegal logging have diminished markedly over the past two decades. Unregistered ownership of power chainsaws is now illegal. However, forest fires, often caused by careless burning of fields or casual disposal of

cigarettes, remains a serious problem, and this in turn has led to fire and haze problems during the hot season from March to May.

River flooding can be a problem, with Chiang Mai suffering particularly seriously. In 2006, the Ping River burst its banks four times, a record within living memory.

In the larger Thai cities like Chiang Mai, Nakhon Ratchasima and Bangkok, attempts are being made, with some degree of success, to limit air pollution caused by vehicular traffic. Two-stroke motorbikes have been largely replaced by less noisy and polluting four-stroke models. Random checks on exhaust emissions and the

replacement of old, smoke-belching public transport by newer, greener buses has helped – as has the provision of Bangkok's expanding Metro and Skytrain. All this, however, is undone by the damaging dust caused by constant construction in cities like Bangkok and Chiang Mai.

Tourism undoubtedly plays a part in contributing towards environmental degradation, most visibly when seaside hotels spew untreated sewage. But there are encouraging signs that tourism may become a positive force in the preservation of Thailand's ecology. More enlightened trekking agencies, local green groups and a few progressive politicians are becoming aware that environmental preservation is the key to sustaining the country's booming tourism industry. ❏

LEFT: a school of yellowfin goatfish off Phuket. **RIGHT:** white-faced gibbon, Khao Sam Roi Yot National Park.

DECISIVE DATES

PRE-THAI CIVILISATION

3600–250 BC
Ban Chiang culture flourishes in northeastern Thailand.

AD 4th–8th century
Influence of Mon and Khmer empires spreads into Thailand.

9th–13th century
Khmer empire founded at Angkor. Tai peoples migrate south from China into northern Thailand, Burma and Laos.

SUKHOTHAI ERA

1238
Khmer power wanes. Kingdom of Sukhothai founded.

1281
Chiang Rai kingdom founded in north.

1296
Lanna kingdom founded at Chiang Mai. Mangrai controls much of northern Thailand and Laos.

1280–98
Reign of Ramkamhaeng in Sukhothai. First attempts to unify the Thai people, the first use of the Thai script and the flourishing of the arts.

1298–1347
Lo Thai reigns at Sukhothai. The slow decline of the Sukhothai kingdom starts.

1438
Sukhothai is now virtually deserted; power shifts to the Kingdom of Ayutthaya.

KINGDOM OF AYUTTHAYA

1350
City of Ayutthaya founded by Phaya U Thong (Ramathibodi I).

1390–3
Ramesuen captures Chiang Mai and Angkor.

1448–88
Reign of King Borommat-railokanat.

1549
First major warfare with Mon Kingdom of Bago (Burma).

1569
Burmese capture and destroy Ayutthaya.

1590
Naresuan becomes king and throws off Burmese suzerainty. Ayutthaya expands rapidly at the expense of Burmese and Khmer empires.

1605–10
Ekatotsarot reigns and begins significant economic ties with European traders and adventurers.

1628–55
Reign of Prasat Thong. Trading concessions expand and regular trade with China and Europe is established.

1656–88
Reign of King Narai. British influence expands. Reputation of Ayutthaya as a magnificent city and a remarkable royal court spreads in Europe.

1678
Greek adventurer Constantine Phaulkon arrives at Narai's court and gains great influence; French presence expands.

1733–58
Reign of King Boromakot. A period of peace, and of flourishing arts and literature.

1767
Invading Burmese sack Ayutthaya, before being repelled by General Phaya Taksin. Capital moves from Ayutthaya to Thonburi, near Bangkok.

THE CHAKRI DYNASTY

1767
Phaya Taksin crowned as King Taksin.

1779
Chiang Mai is captured and the Burmese expelled. The Emerald Buddha is brought from Vientiane, Laos, to Thonburi in Bangkok.

1782
Taksin is deposed. General Chao Phaya Chakri founds the Chakri Dynasty and assumes the name Phra Phutthayofta (later Rama I). The capital is moved across the river to Bangkok.

1868–1910
Chulalongkorn (Rama V) ascends the throne. Schools, infrastructure, military and government modernised.

1925–32
Reign of Prajadhipok (Rama VII).

END OF ABSOLUTE MONARCHY
1932
A coup d'état ends the absolute monarchy and ushers in a constitutional monarchy.

1939
The name of the country is officially changed from Siam to Thailand.

1941–5
Japanese occupation.

1946
King Ananda is killed by a mysterious gunshot, and King Bhumibol Adulyadej (Rama IX) ascends the throne.

1973
Bloody clashes between army and demonstrating students bring down the military government; political and economic blunders bring down the resulting civilian government just three years later.

1992
Another clash between military forces and civilian demonstrators; the military then leaves government to the civilian politicians.

1993–7
Years of unprecedented economic growth.

TOP LEFT: a typical Bangkok canal in the late 19th century. RIGHT: there is a strong military presence in Thai politics.

CONTEMPORARY THAILAND
1997
Thailand's banking system and economy in freefall as the baht loses half of its value.

1998
Thailand follows guidelines established by the International Monetary Fund to resuscitate its economy.

1999
Economy returns to growth.

2000
Senators for the Upper House are democratically elected for the first time.

2001
Thaksin Shinawatra and his populist Thai Rak Thai Party win the national polls for the Lower House.

2002
Thai Muslim nationalists step up terror operations in Yala, Pattani and Narathiwat provinces.

2004
In December, a massive tsunami causes devastation along the Andaman Coast. Some 8,000 lives are lost.

2005
The Thaksin administration wins a second four-year term in the general elections.

2006
Thaksin is accused of evading taxes. Mass protests take place in Bangkok. A bloodless military coup then removes his administration from power.

2007
General Surayud Chulanond is appointed interim prime minister by the military while a new Constitution is drafted. In the December elections, the Thaksin-endorsed PPP party triumphs and Samak Sundaravej is appointed as prime minister.

2008
Thaksin returns to Thailand with his wife, but jumps bail before being found guilty of corruption and sentenced to two years in jail in absentia. Anti-government protestors block Bangkok's airports, causing widespread disruption. Abhisit Vejjajiva becomes prime minister.

2009
Protestors disrupt Asian summit in Pattaya, forcing its cancellation. PAD leader Sondhi Limthongkul narrowly survives assasination attempt.

2010
Anti-government protests in central Bangkok are overpowered by the army in May after two months of violence.

EARLY HISTORY

Following on from the earliest Ban Chiang and Indic Srivijaya civilisations, the ethnic Thais migrated from southern China into the region in the 10th century AD. Surrounded by powerful neighbours – the Khmers and Mon – they later established the independent state of Sukhothai

The earliest known civilisation in Thailand dates from around 3600 BC, when the people of Ban Chiang in the northeast of Thailand developed bronze tools, fired pottery, and began to cultivate wet paddy rice and rear domesticated animals. At this time, the Tai people, who have given their name to the country, did not inhabit the region that makes up present-day Thailand, but were thought to have been living in loosely organised groups in what is now southern China. The identity of the original Ban Chiang people, however, remains a mystery. According to archaeological timetables, the Ban Chiang settlement appears to have lasted until 250 BC, after which the people seem to have faded from history.

The Indian influence

As early as 300 BC, Indian traders began arriving in Southeast Asia, including peninsular Thailand, in search of fragrant woods, pearls and especially gold – hence the region became known as Suvarnabhumi, or "Golden Land". These traders brought with them both Hinduism and Buddhism, which became established in southern Thailand by the 1st century AD. By about AD 500, a loosely knit kingdom called Srivijaya had emerged, encompassing the coastal areas of Sumatra, peninsular Malaya and Thailand, as well as parts of Borneo. Ruled by *maharajah*, or kings, its people practised both Hinduism and Buddhism. Sustained by brisk trade with India and China, Srivijaya flourished for almost 700 years.

LEFT: bronze Ganesha, in Sukhothai style. RIGHT: Ban Chiang pottery, northeast Thailand.

From the 10th century onwards, the power of Srivijaya began to decline, weakened by a series of wars with the Javanese, which disrupted trade. In the 11th century, a rival power centre arose at Melayu, a port believed to have been located further up the Sumatran coast, possibly in what is now Jambi Province. (Melayu's influence is indicated by the fact that the name is the origin of the word "Malay".) The power of the Hindu kings was also undermined by the arrival of Muslim traders and teachers who began to spread Islam in Sumatra along the coast of the Malay Peninsula. By the late 13th century, the Siamese kings of Sukhothai would bring much of the Malay Peninsula under their control. Nevertheless, the great wealth of the region, with its rich resources of aromatic timber, sea products, gold, tin, spices and resins, kept Srivijaya prosperous until its eventual demise in the 14th century.

The Mon kingdom of Dvaravati

While the Srivijaya kingdom dominated the southern part of the Malay Peninsula, another group, the Mon, established themselves in the northern part of the Thai Peninsula and the Chao Phraya River valley, centring on present-day Bangkok. The Mon's Dvaravati kingdom flourished from the 6th to the 11th centuries,

with Nakhon Pathom, U Thong and Lopburi as its major settlements. Like the Srivijaya kingdom, the Dvaravati, too, was strongly influenced by Indian culture and religion. Its Mon people played a central role in the introduction of Buddhism to present-day Thailand.

It is not clear whether Dvaravati was a single, unitary state under the control of a powerful ruler, or a loose confederation of small principalities. Either way, the Mon succumbed to pressure from the north by the 12th to 13th centuries as the Tai people moved south, conquering Nakhon Pathom and Lopburi, but absorbing much of Mon culture with its dominant Buddhist religion along the way.

The Khmer empire

Over in the east, another major power – the Khmer empire of Angkor, forerunner of present-day Cambodia – had begun stamping its influence on the area that is now eastern Thailand, covering an area that extends all the

> The term "Tai" is used for the original ethnic group believed to have moved south from China into Thailand (and Laos) some time after AD 1000. The ethnic group is sometimes, incorrectly, called "Thai".

way from the Chao Phraya valley to the Cambodian frontier, as well as northwards to as far as Laos. Strongly influenced by Indian culture, the Khmer civilisation reached its zenith under the reign of Suryavarman II (1113–50), during which time the temple of Angkor Wat in Cambodia was built. Suryavarman united the kingdom, conquering the Dvaravati lands and the area further west of the border with the kingdom of Pagan (Bagan), and expanded as far south into the Malay Peninsula as Nakhon Si Thammarat, dominating the entire coast of the Gulf of Siam.

The next great Khmer ruler was Jayavarman VII (1181–1219), who defeated the Cham people, unified the empire and initiated a series of astonishing building projects. His work finally culminated in the construction of Angkor Thom, probably the greatest city in the world at the time, with a population estimated at around 1 million. Yet this was to be the last flowering of Khmer independence until modern times. Like the Dvaravati and Srivijaya kingdoms, the Khmer empire would fall victim to the emerging power that would become known as Thailand.

Arrival of the Tais

There are several interesting theories to explain the arrival of the Tai people in what would eventually become Thailand. The most persuasive one suggests that from as early as the 10th century, the Tai people living in China's Yunnan region migrated down rivers and streams into the upper valleys of the Southeast Asian

LEFT: elephant on an old temple mural. **RIGHT:** praying deity, c.13th–15th century. **FAR RIGHT:** 14th-century seated Buddha.

river system. There, they branched off. The Shan (also known as Tai Yai) settled in Upper Burma; the Ahom settled Assam in northeast India; while other groups settled in Laos and northern Vietnam.

Within Thailand, the first of these groups settled around Chiang Saen in the far north around 1150. They formed themselves into principalities, some of which later became independent kingdoms. The earliest was established in 1238, at Sukhothai. Then came Chiang Rai in 1281, and then Chiang Mai in 1296. Long after the main group of Tais moved further down the peninsula to establish more power-ful states, Chiang Mai continued to rule more or less autonomously over the northern region, maintaining the distinctive Lanna culture of its own *(see page 32)*.

By the 13th century, the Tai had begun to emerge as the dominant rulers of the region, and slowly began to absorb the weakened empires of the Mon and Khmers.

Sukhothai, the first Tai kingdom

Sukhothai, roughly halfway between Bangkok and Chiang Mai, was part of the Khmer empire until 1238, when two Tai chieftains seceded and established the first independent Tai kingdom.

THE LEGEND OF SUKHOTHAI

Siamese tradition attributes the founding of the kingdom of Sukhothai to Phra Ruang, a mythological hero. Prior to his time, according to historical legend, the Tai people were forced to pay tribute to the Khmer rulers of Angkor. This tribute was exacted in the form of sacred water from a lake outside Lopburi; the Khmer god-king needed holy water from all corners of the empire for his ceremonial rites, a practice later adopted by Thai kings.

Every three years, the water tribute was sent by bullock carts in large earthenware jars. The jars inevitably cracked en route, compelling the tribute payers to make second and third journeys to fill the required quota. When Phra Ruang came of age, he devised a new system of transporting water in sealed woven bamboo containers, which arrived in Angkor intact. This success aroused the suspicion of the Khmer king. His chief astrologer said the ingenious Thai inventor was a person with supernatural powers who constituted a threat to the empire. The king at once resolved to eliminate the Thai menace, and sent an army westwards.

Phra Ruang perceived the danger and went to Sukhothai, where he concealed himself at Wat Mahathat as a Buddhist monk. The Khmers were defeated, and Phra Ruang's fame spread far and wide. He left the monkhood, married the daughter of Sukhothai's ruler, and when that monarch died, he was invited to the throne by popular mandate. Fact and fiction are inseparable in this popular account.

This event is considered to mark the founding of the modern Thai nation, and from this point we can begin to speak of "Thais" rather than "Tais". Rather confusingly, for all of Thai history from this point until the modern era, "Thai" is broadly interchangeable with "Siamese", and "Thailand" with "Siam".

Sukhothai represents the birth of the Thai nation, although other less well-known Tai states, such as Lanna, Phayao and Chiang Saen, were established at about the same time. Sukhothai was able to expanded by forming alliances with the other Tai kingdoms and adopted Theravada Buddhism as the state religion with the help of Sri Lankan monks.

Under the rule of King Ramkhamhaeng (1280–98), Sukhothai enjoyed a golden age of prosperity. During his long reign, the present Thai alphabet evolved, Theravada Buddhism became more entrenched, and the foundations of present-day Thailand were securely established. King Ramkhamhaeng *(see panel, below)* expanded his control over the former Mon and Khmer territories in the south as far as the Andaman Sea and Nakhon Si Thammarat on the Gulf of Thailand coast, as well as over the Chao Phraya valley and southeast into present-day Cambodia.

KING RAMKAMHAENG'S LEGACY

Since the days of Sukhothai, Buddhism has been deeply rooted in the Thai way of life. King Ramkamhaeng (r. 1280–98) was a devout Buddhist of the Theravada school that was practised in Sukhothai. Exchanges were initiated with Sri Lankan monks that resulted in a purification of texts and an adoption of Sinhalese influences in the design of the *chedi*. There remained, however, a trace of animism in Thai Buddhism. Ramkamhaeng wrote about a mountain-dwelling ghost named Phra Khapung Phi. If correctly propitiated, the spirit would bring prosperity to the country. The idea of a superior spirit looking after the Thai nation survives today in the image of Phra Siam Devadhiraj, Siam's guardian angel.

Sukhothai Buddha images, characterised by their refined facial features, fluidity and harmony of form, are perhaps the most beautiful of Thai artistic expressions. The Sukhothai aesthetic is regarded as the high point of Thai civilisation.

One of the keys to King Ramkamhaeng's political success lay in his clever diplomatic relations with China. The Mongol court in China pursued a divide-and-rule policy and supported the Thais' rise, but only at the expense of the Khmers. Ramkamhaeng was said to have gone to China himself – the *History of the Yuan* records seven missions from Sien (Siam) between 1282 and 1323. Chinese craftsmen came to teach the Thais their secrets of glazing pottery, resulting in the beautiful ceramic ware of Sawankhalok, whose products were shipped to China on Siamese junks.

With the creation of the kingdom of Sukhothai, a new political structure came into being across mainland Southeast Asia. A new and vigorous

> King Mangrai of Lanna was struck by lightning in the year 1317. By this time he had founded not just a kingdom, but a dynasty that would rule northern Thailand for the next two centuries.

state subdued the Mon and absorbed broad swathes of territory from both Srivijaya and the

by King Mangrai (1259–1317) in 1296, Lanna's territorial limits extended far beyond present-day northern Thailand, into Burma's Shan State, China's Xishuangbanna region, and western Laos.

For the next two and a half centuries, Lanna flourished as an independent state, trading and exchanging goods and ideas with neighbouring countries. Links were established with distant Sri Lanka via the Burmese port of Martaban, and Theravadan monks travelled between the great Sri Lankan Buddhist centre of Anuradhapura and Chiang Mai. As a result of these links, King Tilokaraja sponsored the Eighth Buddhist Council at Chiang Mai in 1477. Delegates travelled to

Khmer empire. At the same time the Thai newcomers, an ethnically Sinitic people, intermarried with the inhabitants of the states they had supplanted, and adopted their Indianised culture.

The Kingdom of Lanna

Long after the main group of Thais moved further down the peninsula to establish Ayutthaya, Chiang Mai remained independent as the Kingdom of Lanna, or "One Million Rice Paddies", maintaining a distinctive culture of its own. With its capital at Chiang Mai, the "New City" founded

the council from Pegu, Sri Lanka and all over the Buddhist world. Lanna was in its prime, a respected regional power able to deal on equal footing with both Burma and Ayutthaya (*see page 162*).

Inevitably, there were wars too. The kings of Chiang Mai were under constant pressure from the Siamese to the south, and during the century of decline that followed the death of King Tilokaraja in 1487, the Lanna kingdom suffered attacks not just from Ayutthaya, but also from Burma, Laos and even Vietnam. In 1558, King Bayinnaung of Pegu succeeded in occupying Chiang Mai, and for the next two centuries Lanna became a tributary of Burma, although it still remained very much part of the Thai world. ❑

LEFT: Wat Mahathat, Sukothai. **ABOVE:** a 15th-century Lanna gold crown, inlaid with rubies and pearls.
RIGHT: Portuguese map of the region, *c.*1575.

FROM AYUTTHAYA TO THE 1932 COUP

The rulers of Ayutthaya oversaw the increasing influence of
European traders in the region. Brief subjugation by the
Burmese was followed by the emergence of the long-lasting
Chakri Dynasty – before the absolute power of the kings
was brought to an abrupt end by the 1932 coup d'état

The glories of Sukhothai, the first Tai kingdom, were to be short-lived. During the
early 14th century, a rival state began to
develop in the lower Chao Phraya valley, centred on the ancient Khmer city of Lopburi,
close to present-day Bangkok. In 1350, the
ambitious ruler, known as Phaya U Thong,
moved his capital from Lopburi to a nearby
island in the river which would be more defendable, giving the new city the name Ayutthaya,
and proclaiming himself King Ramathibodi
(1351–69). He declared Theravada Buddhism
the state religion, invited Buddhist monks from
Sri Lanka to help purify and spread the faith,
and compiled a legal code based on the Indian
Dharmashastra which would remain largely in
force until the 19th century.

Ayutthaya soon eclipsed Sukhothai as the leading Thai kingdom, and by the end of the 14th
century it had become the strongest power in
Southeast Asia – even though it lacked the man-
power to dominate the region fully. In the last
year of his reign, Ramathibodi seized Angkor
during what was to be the first of many successful Thai assaults on the Khmer capital. The
weakened Khmer periodically submitted to
Ayutthaya's suzerainty, but efforts to maintain
continued control over Angkor were repeatedly
frustrated. Forces were also diverted to suppress
rebellion in Sukhothai and to campaign against
Chiang Mai, where Ayutthaya's expansion was
tenaciously resisted. Eventually, Ayutthaya subdued Sukhothai, and after Ramathibodi died
in 1369, his kingdom was recognised by the
Hongwu emperor of China's newly established
Ming Dynasty as Sukhothai's rightful successor.

Ayutthaya at this time was not a single, unified
state but rather a patchwork of self-governing

AYUTTHAYA'S FOUNDER

Legend has it that the king of Traitrung unhappily discovered that his unmarried daughter had given birth
after eating an aubergine, which a vegetable gardener
had fertilised with his urine. The culprit – Nai Saen
Pom, or Man With a Hundred Thousand Warts – was
banished from the city, along with the princess and
their son. The god Indra took pity on the trio and
granted the gardener three wishes. Saen Pom first
asked for his warts to disappear. Next, he prayed for
a kingdom to rule over. Finally, he asked for a cradle
of gold for his son. The child, named Phaya U Thong
(Prince of the Golden Crib), later became the first ruler
of Ayutthaya, taking the name Ramathibodi I.

principalities and tributary provinces owing allegiance to the king. These states were ruled by members of the royal family of Ayutthaya who had their own armies and warred among themselves. The king had to be vigilant in order to prevent royal princes from combining against him or allying with Ayutthaya's enemies.

During the 15th century, most of Ayutthaya's energies were directed southwards, towards the Malay Peninsula, where the great trading port of Malacca contested its claims to sovereignty. Malacca and other Malay states to the south of Nakhon Si Thammarat had become Muslim early in the century, and thereafter Islam

conflict with the Burmese. The Portuguese had conquered Malacca in 1511, and soon thereafter their ships sailed to Siam. King Ramathibodi II (1491–1529) granted the newcomers permission to reside and trade within the kingdom in return for arms and ammunition. Portuguese mercenaries fought alongside the king in campaigns against Chiang Mai and taught the Thais the arts of cannon foundry and musketry.

In 1569, Burmese forces captured the city of Ayutthaya and exiled the royal family to Burma. A vassal ruler, King Thammaracha (1569–90), was appointed king, before his son, King Naresuan the Great (1590–1605) succeeded in

served as a unifying symbol of Malay solidarity against the Thais. Although it failed to make a vassal state of Malacca, Ayutthaya established control over much of the peninsula, making both the Andaman Sea and the Gulf of Siam coasts definitively Thai as far south as Hat Yai, and extending its authority further south over the Malay regions of Pattani and Kelantan.

Europeans and Burmese

The 16th century was marked by the first arrival of Europeans, as well as by almost continual

LEFT: crypt mural detail, Wat Rachaburana, Ayutthaya.
ABOVE: temple wall painting depicting Thai–Burmese conflict.

restoring Siamese independence for a further century and a half. The reign of Naresuan's brother, Ekatotsarot (1605–10) coincided with the arrival of the Dutch, who opened their first trading station at Ayutthaya, in 1608. Keen to promote commercial relations, Ekatotsarot sent emissaries to The Hague, the first recorded appearance of Thais in Europe.

During the reign of Songtham (1610–28), the English arrived bearing a letter from King James I. Like the Dutch, they were welcomed and allotted a plot of land on which to build.

Europeans were primarily attracted to Siam as a gateway to the riches of China. The nature of seasonal monsoons made direct sailing to China impossible, so Ayutthaya and its ports became entrepôts for goods travelling between Europe, India and the East Indies, China and Japan. The Siamese home market was also quite substantial. The peace initiated by Naresuan had given rise to a surplus of wealth, which created a demand in Thai society for luxury items like porcelain and silk. The Japanese, who had already established a sizeable community of traders at Ayutthaya, paid in silver for local Siamese products such as hides, teak, tin and sugar.

The Dutch established maritime dominance in the East when they drove the Portuguese out of Malacca in 1641. Seven years later, they made a show of naval force in the Gulf of Thailand, thereby persuading the Ayutthaya court to agree to certain trade concessions and giving the Dutch virtual economic control in Siam.

King Narai

The new king, Narai (1656–88), mistrusted the Dutch and welcomed the English as a European ally to counter Holland's influence. But another Dutch blockade, in 1664, this time at the mouth of the Chao Phraya River, won them a monopoly on the hide trade and, for the first time in Thai history, extraterritorial privileges.

PHAULKON THE GREEK

Constantine Phaulkon was a Greek who began his career as a cabin boy with the East India Company. He arrived in Siam in 1678, quickly learnt Thai and rose through Thai society to the rank of Phaya Vijayendra. In this powerful position, he had access to King Narai. The crafty Phaulkon also ingratiated himself to the French by promising to convert the Thais to Roman Catholicism (which, of course, never came to pass). In the meantime, high-ranking Thai court officials became irked by Phaulkon's extravagant lifestyle and his influence on King Narai. When Narai fell ill in 1688, an anti-French faction of the court took over. Phaulkon was arrested for treason and executed.

It was the French who gained the greatest favour in Narai's court. French Jesuit missionaries first arrived at the court of Ayutthaya in 1665. The king's friendliness and religious tolerance were taken by the bishops as a sign of his imminent conversion. Their exaggerated accounts excited the imagination of Louis XIV, who hoped that the salvation of Siamese heathens could be combined with French territorial acquisition. Narai was delighted to receive a personal letter from the Sun King in 1673, but he did not convert and would remain a good Buddhist all his life.

The presence of Europeans throughout Narai's reign – including that of Constantine Phaulkon (*see panel, left*) – gave the West most of its early knowledge of Siam. Voluminous literature was generated by Western visitors to Narai's court. Their attempts at cartography left a record of Ayutthaya's appearance, though few maps exist today. Royal palaces and hundreds of temples crowded the area within the walls around the island on which the capital stood. Some Western visitors called Ayutthaya "the most beautiful city in the east".

The kings who succeeded Narai ended his open-door policy. A modest amount of trade was maintained and missionaries were permitted to remain, but Ayutthaya embarked on a course of isolation that lasted about 150 years.

Siamese state with a capital at Thonburi on the west bank of the Chao Phraya River. In 1768, he was crowned King Taksin, and would posthumously become Taksin the Great. Taksin rapidly reunited the central Thai heartlands under his rule, and in 1769 conquered Cambodia. He then marched south and re-established Siamese rule over all southern Thailand and the Malay States as far south as Penang and Terengganu.

Although a brilliant military strategist, by 1779 Taksin was in trouble. He alienated the Buddhist establishment by claiming to be in the possession of divine powers, and attacked

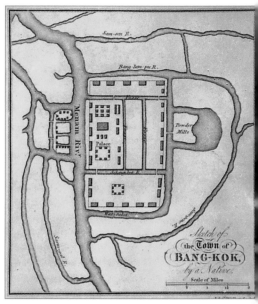

The kingdom of Thonburi

In 1767, the Burmese armies once again invaded, destroying the capital and scattering the defending forces. Ayutthaya's art treasures, the libraries containing its literature and the archives housing its historic records were looted, and the city left in ruins.

Against the odds, Siam made a rapid recovery. A noble of Chinese descent named Taksin led the resistance. From his base at Chanthaburi on the southeast coast, he defeated the Burmese within a year and re-established the

After his abdication, Taksin was executed in the traditional royal manner – with a blow to the neck by a sandalwood club concealed in a velvet bag.

the economically powerful Chinese merchants. In 1782, he sent his armies under General Chao Phaya Chakri to invade Cambodia, and while they were away, a rebellion broke out near the capital. The rebels, who commanded widespread popular support, offered the throne to General Chakri, who accepted. Taksin was subsequently executed, an ignominious end to an able leader.

LEFT: mural image of a 17th-century European adventurer. **ABOVE:** 18th-century illustrated manuscript from Thonburi. **RIGHT:** early map of Bangkok.

The Chakri Dynasty

After ascending the throne on 6 April 1782 – a day commemorated today in Thailand as Chakri Day – Chao Phaya Chakri took the name Phra Phutthayotfa. Later known as Rama I (1782–1809), he became the founding father of the Chakri Dynasty – which continues in place to this day. Uniquely in this part of Asia, the dynasty managed to maintain formal Thai independence (albeit somewhat compromised at times) from the European colonial powers.

During his rule, Rama I would prove to be a strong and far-sighted king who not only laid firm foundations for modern Thailand's secu-rity and prosperity, but also launched an assidu-ous cultural revival programme. One of his first decisions was to move the capital across the Chao Phraya River from Thonburi to a small settlement on the east bank called Bang Makok, the "place of olive plums". Here he built a new grand palace and laid out the ground plan for an artificial island, protected from attack by the river to the west and by a series of canals to the north, east and south. Called Ko Rattanakosin, it would become the heart of the Chakri realm and contain the principal components of the Thai nation: those representing religion, monarchy and administration.

THE LONGEST PLACE NAME IN THE WORLD

When King Rama I established the new capital on a bend in the Chao Phraya River in 1782, he wisely chose an easily defendable site where an old settlement, called Bang Makok – or Bangkok for short – already existed. The name translates as "place of olive plums", and King Rama I deemed it insufficiently noble for a royal city.

Hence, the capital was given a new name (take a deep breath): *Krung Thep Mahanakhon Amon Rattanakosin Mahinthara Yuthaya Mahadilok Phop Noppharat Ratcha-thani Burirom Udomratchaniwet Mahasathan Amon Phiman Awatan Sathit Sakkathattiya Witsanukam Prasit* – officially the longest place name in the world. And yes, it is written in Thai script without a single break.

In English, this may be rendered: "Great City of Angels, City of Immortals, Magnificent Jewelled City of the God Indra, Seat of the King of Ayutthaya, City of Gleaming Temples, City of the King's Most Excellent Palace and Dominions, Home of Vishnu and All the Gods".

How do the Thais get around the verbiage? Quite simply, they style their capital city Great City of Angels, etc in official usage, but quite practically refer to it by just the first two syllables, Krung Thep – City of Angels – in everyday speech.

Whatever you call it, Bangkok or Krung Thep is today the thriving metropolis that dominates Thailand, and is 30 times larger than any other city in the kingdom.

The lofty Wat Phra Kaew, or the "Temple of the Emerald Buddha", was constructed in 1784 to house the country's most revered Buddha image, which was brought from Thonburi earlier. Next on his agenda was the Grand Palace. Rama I also restored much of the social and political system of Ayutthaya, promulgating new law codes, reinstating court ceremonies and imposing discipline on the Buddhist *sangha* (monkhood).

Rama II and Rama III

King Rama I's successors, Rama II and Rama III, completed the consolidation of the

extremely pious Buddhist, he was considered to be "austere and reactionary" by Europeans. One thing he is remembered for is encouraging missionaries to introduce Western medicine, including the smallpox vaccine, to Thailand.

King Mongkut (Rama IV)

King Rama IV (1851–68), loosely represented in the Hollywood film *The King and I*, was a modern-minded and learned scholar who studied English and Latin as well as Pali and Sanskrit. A monk for many years before his accession to the throne – which had given him a unique opportunity to roam as a commoner

Siamese kingdom and the revival of Ayutthaya's arts and culture. Best remembered as an artist, Rama II (1809–24) was responsible for building and repairing numerous Bangkok monasteries. His most famous creation was Wat Arun, or the Temple of Dawn, on the Thonburi side of the Chao Phraya River. He is also said to have carved the doors of Bangkok's Wat Suthat. Rama II also reopened relations with the West, which had been suspended since the time of King Narai.

Rama III (1824–51) continued his predecessor's policy of opening Siam's doors to foreigners. An

LEFT: 18th-century Siamese women. **ABOVE:** Wat Arun, legacy of Rama II.

DEATH OF AN ASTRONOMER

Mongkut's beloved hobby, astronomy, was the indirect cause of his death. From observatories at his favourite palaces, the Summer Palace at Bang Pa-In and the Palace on the Hill, at Phetchburi, he successfully calculated and predicted a total eclipse of the sun in 1868. European and Asian sceptics joined him on the southeastern coast of the Gulf of Thailand to await the event. As the moon blocked the sun's light, both the Europeans and the scoffers among the royal astrologers raised an exclamation of admiration, raising the king's esteem among both parties. But his triumph was short-lived. The king contracted malaria during the trip, and died two weeks later from it.

among the populace – he studied history, geography and the sciences, especially astronomy.

Better known as King Mongkut, Rama IV realised that traditional Thai values alone would not save his country from Western encroachments. Instead, he made the momentous decision to Westernise many of the country's institutions, believing that modernisation would bring Siam in line with the West and reduce hostilities with foreigners.

Britain was the first European country to benefit from this policy, when an 1855 treaty – not gained entirely without coercion by the British – granted extraterritorial privileges: a duty of

only 3 percent on imports, and permission to import Indian opium duty-free. Other Western

> Before the reign of King Rama VI (Vajiravudh) most Thai people did not have surnames, a practice that the king considered to be uncivilised. (Even today, it is common practice to refer to Thai people by their first names only.)

nations, including France and the United States, followed suit with similar treaties.

Together with his son and successor Chulalongkorn, this approach means that he can be considered chiefly responsible for Thailand's

continued independence throughout the colonial period. To this day Thais reserve a special place in their hearts for both these monarchs.

King Chulalongkorn (Rama V)

King Mongkut's son, King Rama V (1868–1910), also widely known as King Chulalongkorn, ascended the throne in 1868 when he was only 15 years old. By the time of his death, 42 years later, he had become the "Beloved Great King", a father-figure for his people and perhaps the most popular Thai monarch ever. A man of remarkable foresight, Chulalongkorn instituted a veritable revolution from above, abolishing serfdom and ending the ancient custom of ritual prostration in the presence of the ruler. He brought in foreign advisers from abroad, and sent his sons to study at universities across Europe.

Chulalongkorn's contributions to the cultural heritage of Bangkok included the construction of Dusit Palace, Rajadamnoen Avenue and the palace and pleasure-gardens of Bang Pa-In. When he died in 1910, a grieving nation posthumously awarded him the title *Phya Maharaj*, or "Beloved Great King".

In the area of foreign relations, however, Chulalongkorn had to compromise and give up parts of his kingdom in order to protect Siam from foreign colonisation. When France conquered Annam (Vietnam) in 1883 and Britain annexed Upper Burma three years later, Siam found itself sandwiched between the two rival powers. It was forced to surrender to France its claims to Laos and western Cambodia. Similarly, in 1909, certain Malay territories were ceded to Britain in exchange for renunciation of British extraterritorial rights in Siam. But that was a small price for maintaining the country's peace and independence. Unlike its neighbours, Siam was never under colonial rule (unless one counts the Japanese occupation of 1941–5).

Rama VI and Rama VII

King Rama V was succeeded by King Vajiravudh (Rama VI), who reigned from 1910 to 1925. Being Oxford-educated and thoroughly Anglicised, he introduced Western-inspired reforms to modernise his country. Primary education was made compulsory throughout the kingdom; Chulalongkorn University, the first in Siam, was founded, and schools for both sexes flourished during his reign. Vajiravudh was, however, criticised as autocratic and lacking in coordination. His extravagance soon emptied the funds built up by Chulalongkorn; near the end of Vajiravudh's reign, the national treasury had to meet the deficits caused by his personal expenses.

Following his brother's early death in 1925, King Prajadhipok (Rama VII) succeeded the throne. Unlike the former, he tried to cut public expenditure by drastically reducing civil service and royal household expenses. Prajadhipok's economic policies, combined with increased revenue from foreign trade, amply paid off for the kingdom.

military and civilian group masterminded by foreign-educated Thais – ended the absolute power of the Thai monarchs. The chief ideologist was Pridi Panomyong, a young lawyer trained in France. On the military side Plaek-Phibunsongkhram (Pibul) was responsible for gaining the support of important army colonels. At the time, King Prajadhipok was in Hua Hin, a royal retreat to the south. Perceiving he had little choice and to avoid bloodshed, he agreed to accept a provisional constitution by which he continued to reign. For the next 14 years, Siam would be without a resident monarch, and power would lie with the military. ❑

The worldwide economic crisis of the 1930s, however, affected Siam's rice export. Prajadhipok dropped the gold standard, linking the Thai baht to the pound sterling, but it was too late to stem the financial crisis. The government was forced to implement further measures, such as cutting the salaries of junior personnel and retrenching the armed forces, which fuelled much discontent in the process.

Coup d'état and World War II

In 1932, a coup staged by the People's Party – a

LEFT: Rama V (King Chulalongkorn) r.1868–1910.
ABOVE: royal barges along the Chao Phraya River at Prajadhipok's (Rama VII) 1925 coronation.

CHAKRI KINGS TIMELINE

Since 1782, the Chakri Dynasty has lorded over Thailand. King Bhumibol, the present incumbent, is currently the longest-reigning monarch and head of state in the world.

Reign	Title	Name	Relationship
1782–1809	Rama I	Chakri	Founder
1809–24	Rama II	Phuttayotfa	Son of Rama I
1824–51	Rama III	Nangklao	Son of Rama II
1851–68	Rama IV	Mongkut	Son of Rama II
1868–1910	Rama V	Chulalongkorn	Son of Rama IV
1910–25	Rama VI	Vajiravudh	Son of Rama V
1925–35	Rama VII	Prajadhipok	Son of Rama V
1935–46	Rama VIII	Ananda Mahidol	Grandson of Rama V
1946–	Rama IX	Bhumibol Adulyadej	Grandson of Rama V

CONTEMPORARY THAILAND

Thailand was under the rule of an absolute monarchy for 150 years, until the 1932 coup d'état. The constitutional monarchy that followed has proved a stabilising anchor amid the upheavals that continue to characterise the country's modern history

The years leading up to World War II were characterised by a number of political power struggles. Following the 1932 coup, the power of Plaek Phibunsongkhram (Pibul) and the army was further strengthened by the decisive defeat of a rebellion in October 1933 led by Prince Boworadet, who had been the war minister under King Prajadhipok. The king had no part in the rebellion, but had become increasingly dismayed by quarrels within the new government. He moved to England in 1934 and abdicated in 1935. Ananda Mahidol (Rama VIII), a 10-year-old half-nephew, agreed to take the throne, but remained in Switzerland to complete his studies.

After a series of crises and an election in 1938, Pibul became prime minister. His rule, however, grew more authoritarian, and he was famous for whipping up sentiment against the Chinese. Borrowing many ideas from European fascism, he attempted to instil a sense of mass nationalism in the Thais. In 1939, Pibul ordered the name of the country to be officially changed from Siam to Thailand, and adopted the current national flag.

Post-World War II

On 7 December 1941, the Japanese bombed Pearl Harbor and launched invasions throughout Southeast Asia. Thailand was overrun – resistance lasted less than a day, despite a decade of military build-up. Pibul acceded to Japan's request for "passage rights", but Thailand was allowed to retain its army and political administration. By 1944, Thailand's initial enthusiasm

LEFT: on the edge of Bangkok, 1950.
RIGHT: King Bhumibol Adulyadej's coronation, 1946.

for its Japanese overlords had evaporated. The country faced runaway inflation, food shortages, rationing and black markets.

In 1946, while on a visit to Thailand from Europe, the now-adult King Ananda was found shot dead in his bedroom. He was succeeded by his younger brother, Bhumibol Adulyadej (Rama IX), the present monarch (see page 46), who returned to Switzerland to complete law studies. He did not, however, take up active duties until the 1950s.

The first few years after the end of World War II were marked by a series of democratic civilian governments. In 1948, under threat of military force, Pibul assumed power again, ushering in a period marked by strife, failed coup attempts and corruption. In 1957 he was overthrown by a clique of one-time protégés. The leader, General Sarit Thanarat, and two crony generals, Thanom Kittikachorn and Prapas Charusathien, ran the government until 1973 under martial law. All three men used their power to amass huge personal fortunes, but they also deserve some credit for developing Thailand. Health standards improved, the business sector expanded, construction boomed and a middle class began to emerge. These socio-economic changes would, in turn, lead to new aspirations among the Thais.

ian demonstrators, dubbed "Bloody May" by the media, took place in Bangkok, near Sanam Luang and the Democracy Monument. Killings, beatings and riots went on for three days and only ended when the leaders of both factions were summoned before King Bhumibol. The military bowed out and an unrepentant Suchinda left the country. In the September 1992 re-elections, the Democrat Party and other prominent critics of the military prevailed.

Democracy is ushered in

Prime Minister Chuan Leekpai, considered honest but ineffectual, held office from 1992

String of governments and coups

On 13 October 1973, a demonstration in Bangkok to protest against the military dictatorship turned violent, and at least 100 students were shot by riot police. With the country in turmoil, the army switched sides and the generals fled into exile. For the next two decades, Thailand was to be chronically unstable: a succession of governments were ousted after periodic clashes with protesting students and a succession of military coups.

In April 1992, public discontent grew when a former coup leader, General Suchinda Krapayoon, assumed the prime ministership without having stood for election. In May 1992, another violent clash between military forces and civil-

to 1995, and can be credited with diluting the power of military officers in many state enterprises. But for many, he was too passive a leader. No one was held responsible for the

> Bangkok's Democracy Monument was built in 1939 to commemorate the 1932 revolution. Since the 1970s it has been the focus of many pro-democracy protests, and the scene of much bloodshed.

1992 clashes, and the numbers and identity of those who died or disappeared are still in dispute. His coalition finally collapsed in 1995 when wealthy members of Chuan's own party were discovered profiting from a land-reform programme.

Two subsequent elections brought a provincial businessman, Banharn Silpa-archa (1995–6), and a former general, Chavalit Yongchaiyudh (1996–98), to the highest office for brief terms. Both were lambasted for their incompetent handling of the economy, which suddenly went into freefall in 1997, setting off an Asian economic crisis and a massive devaluation of the baht.

In 1998, a Democrat government led by former prime minister Chuan Leekpai replaced

interests of his friends and family. He rebuked critics and the press harshly, and ran the government like a private business. However, his populist policies guaranteed large-scale support in the poorer rural areas.

To Thaksin's credit, his government dealt swiftly and decisively with the fallout from the massive tsunami that hit Thailand's southern beaches on 26 December 2004. The tragic natural catastrophe left some 8,000 people dead, including many foreigners.

In January 2006, Thaksin faced another political crisis when his family was accused of tax evasion after they sold their stake in Shin Corp, one

the Chavalit administration. After two years of hard work and changes in banking and investment laws, the economy began to recover.

The Thaksin administration

In 2001, general elections saw the leader of the Thai Rak Thai (TRT) Party, billionaire entrepreneur Thaksin Shinawatra, replace Chuan as premier – amid allegations of vote-buying and rigging. Thaksin's governance proved controversial, and he was routinely accused in the press of corruption and promoting the business

LEFT: anti-government protests in 1975; the banners read "Return my people to me", referring to arrested students. **ABOVE:** ex-premier Thaksin Shinawatra.

of Thailand's largest telecommunications companies, to Temasek Holdings in Singapore for US$1.9 billion. Although the accusation could not be proven, thousands of protesters took to the streets in Bangkok, while the opposition demanded his resignation. In response, Thaksin announced a snap election in April 2006. Opposition parties boycotted the elections, and although Thaksin won again, he resigned as prime minister in the face of mass protests, appointing his deputy, Chidchai Wannasathit, as the new caretaker premier. At the same time, Thaksin was plagued by claims of rigged bids for the new Suvarnabhumi Airport by his critics, *lèse-majesté* against King Bhumibol, and faced a worsening Muslim insurgency in the south.

A Much-Loved Monarchy

After six decades as the Thai monarch, King Bhumibol remains as popular as ever – as well as exercising considerable influence

Thais take the institution of the monarchy very seriously. Ever since the first independent Thai kingdom was established more than seven centuries ago, Thailand has been ruled by kings. Although the 1932 revolution ended absolute mon-

archy and replaced it with the constitutional variety, Thais continue to love and honour their royal family, and especially its father figure, King Bhumibol Adulyadej, with a consuming passion.

The vast majority of Thais are confirmed monarchists, with the throne making up one of the three central pillars of the national polity – in Thai, *chat*, *sat* and *pramahakasat* – Thai Nation, Buddhist Religion and Chakri Dynasty. It would be hard to overestimate the affection and respect Thais feel for their kings, and this applies to non-Buddhist minorities as well. In many Muslim homes, for example, it is common to find a framed print of the king hanging next to a picture of the Kaaba at Mecca in a convincing statement of both spiritual and mundane loyalty.

Thailand's present monarch, King Bhumibol Adulyadej, acceded to the throne in 1946. Born in distant Cambridge, Massachusetts, where his father was studying medicine at Harvard, Bhumibol has proved to be an able leader. Perhaps because of this ability to reach the common man, he enjoys an extraordinary popularity, shared in the past only by his grandfather, King Chulalongkorn.

Although Bhumibol is a constitutional monarch, because of the affection in which he is held by Thais, he does play a political role, occasionally intervening when he feels politicians have got out of hand. In May 1992, when military strongman Suchinda Krapayoon seized power in a coup, the king intervened to end three days of riots and killings when soldiers fired on demonstrators near the Democracy Monument. Suchinda was forced to resign in disgrace, and democracy was restored.

More recently, King Bhumibol made it clear on a number of occasions that he disapproved of ex-Prime Minister Thaksin Shinawatra's executive style of government. In fact, in 2006 – the year he celebrated 60 years on the throne – Bhumibol endorsed the military coup that removed Thaksin from power, while in 2008 Queen Sirikit presided at the funeral of a People's Alliance for Democracy street protestor, which was generally regarded as a tacit admission of support. So great is the king's moral authority that no politician can afford to ignore him. He is the final bulwark against oppression, yet he remains a modest, even diffident man, conscious of his position as *po luang*, the "royal father" of his people.

The monarchy costs the Thai treasury nothing, at least not directly, since the royal family pays its own way with income from vast property holdings and investments built over the years (the king has a fortune estimated at US\$35 billion). The royal family also earns the respect of the people through its own enterprise. For example, the king's mother initiated a series of successful agricultural projects that greatly reduced opium production in the north, while Queen Sirikit works to preserve the traditional arts and crafts of Thailand and spearheads a programme to provide rural folk with the skills to produce these crafts. There are also numerous royal ceremonies, such as the seasonal robing of the Emerald Buddha, and various traditional Buddhist holy days.

As the king ages, fears for his health (he was released from hospital in February 2010 after a five-month stay with pneumonia) have prompted questions about the succession. ❑

LEFT: King Bhumibol and Queen Sirikit.

The 2006 coup and its aftermath

In September 2006, when Thaksin was in New York for a UN meeting, the army led by General Sonthi Boonyaratglin seized power in a bloodless coup. The Thai people rallied behind the decision as the coup was publicly endorsed by King Bhumibol. Thaksin was not allowed to return to Thailand, and he and his family were placed under investigation for various charges of corruption. Retired soldier General Surayud Chulanond was appointed as interim prime minister while a new Constitution was drafted. The military also dissolved Thaksin's TRT party, and banned its executives from contesting in the elections for five years.

In the meantime, Thaksin had been working behind the scenes from exile in London. Led by Thaksin-installed proxy and one-time minister Samak Sundaravej, outlawed TRT officials regrouped under the banner of the People's Power Party (PPP). In the general elections held in December 2007, Thaksin had the final word when the PPP defeated the Democratic Party by winning the majority of the seats in Parliament. While short of the 241 seats needed for a majority of the 480-seat house, Samak was able to get himself elected as prime minister in a parliamentary vote held in January 2008. The following day, he was officially endorsed as prime minister by King Bhumibol. The following month Thaksin returned to Thailand facing charges of corruption.

Turbulent times

The period since 2008 is proving to be one of the most turbulent of recent times – with echoes of comic opera. Dramatic events such as the closure of the international airport in late 2008 by opposition protestors have had some impact on Thailand's status as a tourist destination.

Trouble started brewing in May 2008 when the newly strengthened People's Alliance for Democracy (PAD) took to the streets of Bangkok, demanding Samak's resignation. By August the Thaksins had jumped bail, flying to the United Kingdom, and shortly afterwards the PAD invaded Government House. Street clashes the following month left one dead and 43 injured, and Samak was forced out of the premiership to be replaced by Somchai Wongsawat – Thaksin's brother-in-law. In November

the PAD launched its invasion of Suvarnabhumi International Airport (dubbed, without apparent irony, "Operation Hiroshima"), which

> Foreign media reported the PAD were offering cash to mothers and children to join the 2008 airport protest, though this was strenuously denied by party spokesmen.

severely damaged Thailand's reputation around the world and disrupted travel for thousands of passengers. By the end of 2008 Abhisit Vejjajiva

(Democrat Party) had taken over as prime minister, and the PPP had been officially dissolved.

After further unrest in 2009, pro-Thaksin "red shirt" demonstrators – largely rural poor from the northeast of Thailand – once again took to the streets of the capital in March 2010, with escalating violence. By May, the protestors' bases in the heart of Bangkok had been surrounded by the army and overpowered. The violence – the worst since 1992 – resulted in at least 85 deaths and widespread damage. The events have placed the urban rich/rural poor divide firmly on the political map, and the situation is likely to remain unstable. Meanwhile Thaksin remains at large, although his assets (46 billion baht) were seized by a Thai court in 2009. ❑

RIGHT: "red shirt" anti-government protesters in 2010.

PEOPLE AND CULTURE

Warm-hearted smiles, a pleasant disposition and a sense of calm: these are the qualities which are readily discerned by visitors to Thailand. But Thais can also be fiercely patriotic; criticisms against the Thai monarchy are not easily tolerated

Travellers to Thailand are generally struck by the smiles, warmth and friendliness of the local people. There is always amiable concern – not to be interpreted as nosiness – and an openness seldom found elsewhere in the world. The standard greeting is *pai nai*, or "Where are you going?" But this is not meant to be interpreted literally; rather, it is the approximate equivalent of "Hello" or "How are you?" One of the guiding precepts of Thai life is *sanuk*, which means fun or joy. The quantity and quality of *sanuk* in both work and play will often determine whether something is worth pursuing.

Almost as important is the concept of *sabai*, best translated as "comfortable" or "contented". As far as Thai people are concerned, in the best of all possible worlds, life should be both *sanuk* and *sabai*. The antithesis of sanuk is *seriat* – a borrowing from the English word "serious". Life just isn't meant to be taken too seriously. Underpinning this light-hearted pursuit of happiness are the Buddhist values of tolerance and acceptance.

The Thai jigsaw

Thailand has a population of over 64 million people, more than 90 percent of whom are Theravada Buddhists *(see page 61)*. Muslims make up around 6 percent of the population and, though they live all over the country, are mostly concentrated in the southern peninsular regions.

Around 14 percent of the population are descendants of Chinese immigrants who relocated from China during the 19th and first half of the 20th century. The Chinese have assimilated remarkably well into local society and have intermarried freely with the Thais. There is no deep-rooted anti-Chinese bias, in contrast with some other parts of Southeast Asia. Living mostly in urban areas and involved in trade and commerce, the Chinese knack for entrepreneurial know-how has ensured that much of the country's wealth is controlled by Sino-Thai families. Other, much smaller, immigrant groups in Thailand include Indians, Khmer, Vietnamese and the various hill tribes *(see pages 56–7 and 332–3)* living in the north.

Thailand can be divided into four regions: central, north, northeast and south. Each of the regions has its own language variant, cultural traits and distinctive cuisine. Bangkok is the geographical and commercial heart of the country, home to around one in five Thais. It is located in the Central Plain, Thailand's linguistically dominant region. The central Thai dialect is the language spoken by educated Thais from all over the country.

In the mountainous north, once the seat of the ancient Lanna kingdom, people speak a Thai variant called *kham meuang* and share culinary similarities with neighbouring Myanmar. People in the northeast speak Isaan, a language closely related to Lao, and eat their meals with sticky rice. The northeast also happens to be Thailand's poorest region, often subject to debilitating droughts. Many northeasterners leave to seek work as migrant labourers in Bangkok.

The south is a more prosperous region; its beautiful coastal scenery attracts tourists and there are significant fishing and fruit-growing industries. Aside from a small group of Malay-speaking Muslims, most people in this region speak a southern dialect of Thai. Travellers should be aware that in the three southernmost provinces of Yala, Pattani and Narathiwat, civil unrest between Muslims and the Thai government has been escalating for many years.

A revered monarch

At the heart of Thai society is the kingdom's reverence for the Thai monarch, His Majesty King Bhumibol Adulyadej *(see page 46)*. Visitors will be struck at how the national anthem is played before cinema screenings and the audience will stand as a mark of respect to the king. Even when the anthem is played at 8am and 6pm on radio and TV each day, many Thais stop whatever they are doing and stand erect. At offices, shops and houses throughout the land, the king's portrait is prominently portrayed – such is the measure of respect accorded to the Thai monarch.

> The three colours of the Thai flag represent the key components of the Thai kingdom: red is symbolic of the blood of the Thai people, white is Buddhism and blue is the monarchy.

In fact, when the king celebrated his Golden Jubilee in June 2006, commemorating 60 years on the throne, well-wishers wearing yellow shirts (the colour of Monday, the day he was born) jammed the roads leading to the Royal

PRECEDING PAGES: directing the Bangkok traffic.
LEFT: schoolchildren in Chiang Mai. **RIGHT:** Muslim man outside a mosque in Khao Lak.

Plaza. Millions of people across the country donned yellow T-shirts as a sign of loyalty during the king's 80th birthday celebrations in 2007, and during the civil disturbances the following year HM remained a symbol of stability. Criticism of the king and royal family is extremely rare, and *lèse-majesté* laws prevent public critique of the king in the local media.

Hi-So and Lo-So

Thai society is fiercely hierarchical, with an individual's roles and duties defined by his or her social status. In fact the Thai language uses personal pronouns which indicate whether the

speaker is addressing a younger or elder person, or a person of lower or higher status.

The top end of Thai society is known as "Hi-So", a Thai slang abbreviated from "high society", and comprises Thai nobility and wealthy Sino-Thai families. Being Hi-So is as much about glamour and wealth as it is about pedigree (their ranks were swelled by the *nouveaux riches* created during the economic boom of the 1980s and early '90s, but reduced somewhat in the 2008–10 downturn). The Hi-So scene is confined mainly to Bangkok and is frequently depicted in the society pages of the city's newspapers and magazines, like *Thailand Tatler*, with the immaculately attired women sporting big hair and big jewels.

Thailand's growing middle class is largely made up of educated urbanites living on suburban housing estates and working at corporate jobs in the city. Billboards advertising these housing estates are everywhere; they often depict Western-style houses complete with two children and a dog playing in the garden.

The majority of Thai people make up the agrarian segment who live in villages and farm the land. The village idyll, however, has changed radically over the past few decades as environmental degradation and poverty have forced many villagers to find work in the big cities as taxi drivers, construction workers and

women maintain power behind the scenes as matriarchs and holders of the family purse-strings. For years, women have also been at the helm of large private businesses as men customarily go into government or the military. Today, Thai women are prominent in the hotel trade, tourism, real estate, advertising, the export trade, banking, medicine and the law. The university population is almost equally male and female, while the government bureaucracy attracts large numbers of women.

In relationship stakes, women generally don't fair too well. It is a well-accepted fact that most Thai men are *chao choo*, or adulterers. The

prostitutes. The rural-urban divide is stark, and it is only in recent years that the problems of rural Thailand have been brought to the fore in the capital by coalitions like the Forum of the Poor, which organises protest movements in the capital regularly, striking out at the building of dams and other ruinous government policies.

Women in Thai society

There is an old Thai saying that women are the hind legs of the elephant. And it does hold true to a certain extent; while most of the legal discrimination against women has been largely eliminated, women are still expected to be socially submissive to Thai men. Still, many

law favours male promiscuity; if a women is unfaithful, it is ample grounds for divorce but it is not, however, when a man cheats on his wife. The extra-marital affair is semi-formalised in the practice of keeping a *mia noi*, literally "minor wife" or mistress.

Sexual attitudes

Thailand has unfortunately acquired a reputation as a sexual playground *(see page 126)*, witnessed by its large-scale exploitation and degradation of women and, especially, children. While prostitution attracts unsavoury

ABOVE: four generations of a Thai family.
RIGHT: trendy Thai teenagers in Bangkok.

foreign tourists, visitors are seldom aware that most of the clients are in fact Thais. Outside of a few areas in Bangkok, like Patpong and Nana Plaza, or Pattaya's tawdry sex scene, prostitution in Thailand is similar to elsewhere in the world: brothels exist on the margins of almost every medium-sized town, but the rest of society is usually fairly conservative where sex is concerned.

Tradition still dictates a certain propriety of dress, and public displays of affection are rare. While Western influence has meant that young Thai couples hold hands in public, it is unusual to see anything but very chaste interactions.

Thai people are generally sympathetic in their attitude towards sexuality. Consensual adult homosexuality is tolerated, and this extends to a peculiarly Thai phenomenon: transvestism. Thailand has more than its share of *kathoey*, or "lady-boys" – transvestite men who are accepted for what they are, treated with understanding and some respect, and generally addressed as women.

Socialising and etiquette the Thai way

The Thai love of fun, or *sanuk*, infuses all social gatherings. They enjoy group activities, and it's

THAI SOAP MELODRAMAS

The national obsession with soap operas provides an entertaining window into the Thai psyche. *Lakhorn teewee*, or TV plays, occupy the prime-time slots on national Thai television, and there are over 40 companies producing more than 200 soap operas each year.

The reel-life soaps present an idealised and highly dramatised depiction of Thai life. Important social problems such as HIV/AIDS or extreme poverty are seldom touched upon, and the plots are superficial, mainly revolving around melodramatic love stories and convoluted family sagas. There is always an innocent female heroine who is the personification of the perfect Thai woman – beautiful, demure and diligent, and portrayed quite often these days by a

near-perfect *luk kreung (see page 55)* mixed-race beauty. The male lead will be dashingly handsome and incredibly wealthy. Added to the mix are a plethora of jealous male suitors, evil sisters, mean mothers and overly protective fathers. For comic relief there may be a *kathoey* or "lady-boy" transvestite character or a dark-skinned goofy-looking maid from Thailand's poor northeast region.

This basic mix of characters is repeated through a variety of historical, urban and rural settings. Supernatural tales are popular, and ghosts can make cameo appearances in any genre. Rags-to-riches tales are a sure-fire hit. And, not surprisingly, in the rarefied world of Thai soaps, the hero and heroine almost always live happily ever after.

always a case of the more the merrier. Generally speaking, Thais hate to be alone, and most are puzzled by the average foreigner's need for occasional solitude.

Thais greet each other with a *wai (see panel, below)*, but may use the more intimate *hom kaem* (to smell the cheek), which is simply a sniff against someone's face. Surnames are rarely used, and even relative strangers will refer to each other by their nickname, or *cheu len* (play name). These are most often one-syllable monikers based on animals like Moo (pig), Noo (mouse), or Poo (crab), or are more modern adaptations from English, such as X, Boy or Benz.

THAI-STYLE GREETING

Thais greet each other by raising and clasping their hands together in a prayer-like gesture called the *wai*. While the *wai* may look like a simple movement, it is loaded with social nuances. The hands must be held at certain levels between the chest and the forehead, depending on the relative social standing of each person. When greeting a person of higher rank, for instance, the hands must be raised higher to show respect. In response to a child's greeting, an adult may keep his or her hands at the chest level. Modern-day adaptations include the informal one-handed *wai*, used among friends – and no one bats an eyelid when a mobile phone is held in the other hand.

There is a sense of family about Thai activities, a gathering that does not exclude outsiders. For the visitor invited to join, there is no automatic expectation of reciprocation, although it is always much appreciated. It is not unusual for a visitor to stray into a small city lane and be invited to join a partying group. Such activities are usually accompanied by music, alcoholic drinks and small snacks. Drunkenness is frowned upon, but a certain tipsiness is acceptable in such circumstances.

Aside from *sanuk*, there are a few particularly Thai concepts that are helpful in understanding Thai culture. One key emotion is *kraeng jai*, which denotes an unwillingness to impose on other people. This often means that emotions such as anger or displeasure are hidden away, and tension and conflict avoided at all cost. Thais place a high value on equanimity and will go to great lengths to prevent confrontation. Neither do they like saying "no" too directly for fear of causing offence.

Connected to this is the idea of *jai yen*, or "cool heart". It is imperative for Thais to keep a cool and calm heart in all situations. To lose your temper or to raise your voice in public is seen as a severe loss of face; problems should always be dealt with in a friendly manner and with equanimity. Those unable to maintain this cool veneer are considered to be *jai ron*, or "hot-hearted".

It is difficult to stir a Thai to real anger. A smile and an apology should deflate almost any tense situation. Anger, demonstrated by physical violence or raised voices, can provoke serious hostility, however, and an angry Thai can be aggressive indeed. For example, touching a Thai (especially on the top of the head), shouting, or threatening the strong sense of independence that Thais have may effect an immediate and often hostile response. Visitors should also avoid pointing their feet at Thais, for example, when crossing their legs. The foot is considered unclean, and pointing it at someone is thought to be a great insult.

Closely allied with *jai yen* is a concept that provides the answer to all of life's vicissitudes: *mai pen rai*, a phrase best translated as "never mind." Most Thai would rather shrug their shoulders in the face of adversity than risk escalating a difficult situation. Solutions that contribute to restoring or maintaining calm are welcomed. In fact, one reason the Thais have survived intact as a sovereign nation is by adopting a superb sense of compromise, putting trifling or trivial matters in perspective, or else ignoring them.

Behind those smiles

Beneath the placid and happy-go-lucky surface of Thai society lies a darker underbelly. Organised crime is prevalent throughout the country as powerful mafia clans thrive on illegal gambling, drugs and prostitution. Known as *jao phor*, the godfathers often operate legal businesses as well and may even participate in provincial politics. Gangland-style assassinations by hired hit-men are not uncommon in Thailand.

Corruption is as rife in politics as it is in day-to-

Adapting to new influences

The effects of globalisation have profoundly altered Thailand. Bangkok is in a constant state of renewal. Skyscrapers filled with apartments, offices and shopping malls have sprouted throughout the city with alarming speed. Life in the rural villages, too, is being transformed. Not so long ago, villagers might gather around the communal well at sunset to collect water and catch up on village gossip; now, many have water piped into their homes and they gather instead around their TV sets or chat on mobile phones.

Historically, Thailand has always welcomed outside influences – such as that of Western

day interactions on the street. Government and big businesses have nepotistic values; construction contracts, for instance, will often be offered to favoured companies. At the other end of the spectrum, a policeman can usually be convinced to erase a traffic ticket for a 200-baht bribe.

As traditional family networks are broken down by the rural-to-urban demographic shift, people no longer have the safety net of family and community. The side-effects of rapid modernisation can be seen by the rising number of slum-dwellers and beggars who live in Bangkok.

LEFT: Thai policeman. **ABOVE:** the universal *wai* greeting is loaded with social nuances. **RIGHT:** a resident of Hua Hin.

colonisation in the 19th century – rather than fought them. The Thais have traditionally preferred to adapt or accept, influenced in part by their Buddhist faith. Today, this mentality can be seen all over the country. International chainstores mushroom in the cities, and trends, like the recent nationwide obsession with Korean soap operas, have gripped the population. Even beauty is now personified by the *luk kreung* – literally "half child" – mixed-race children who have one Thai and one Caucasian parent. Their perfectly formed features dominate the world of music, soap operas and advertising today.

As the country hurtles along the road of modernisation, hopefully there will be more *sanuk* and smiles along the way.   ❑

Thailand's Hill Tribes

The colourfully clad minorities who inhabit the forested hills of northern Thailand are a major tourist draw

The tribal people of Thailand – referred to as "hill tribes" or *chao khao* (literally, mountain people) make up less than 2 percent of the total population. There are least 20 distinct hill tribes, which belong to six principal groups: Karen, Hmong, Lahu,

Mien, Akha and Lisu. They mainly originate from Tibet, Myanmar (Burma), Laos and China. Virtually all live in the mountainous areas of Chiang Mai, Chiang Rai, Mae Hong Son and Nan provinces.

Karen

With a population of over 320,000, the Karen are by far the largest hill tribe in Thailand. They comprise two subgroups, the Sgaw and Pwo, whose dialects are not mutually intelligible. The Karen have been settling in Thailand since the 18th century and they are still trickling in, fleeing human-rights abuses in neighbouring Myanmar, where they have been fighting for independence for over 50 years. Early converts to Christianity when Myanmar was a British colony, the Karen place a great

emphasis on monogamy and trace their ancestry on the maternal side of the family.

Hmong

Numbering around 120,000, the Hmong are the second-largest hill tribe in Thailand. The majority arrived in the 1950s and 1960s, fleeing the civil war in Laos. On the alert for communists at the time, the Thai military regarded them as subversives, and Hmong relations with Thai officialdom still remain edgy – despite the fact that in Laos they are known for their anti-communist stance, having been allied with the Americans during the Vietnam War. Kinship is patrilineal and polygamy is permitted. The White Hmong and Blue Hmong can be identified by their dialects and clothing. Blue Hmong women wear indigo pleated skirts and tie their hair up in huge buns, while White Hmong women wear white hemp skirts and black turbans.

Lahu

Some of the 73,000 Lahu in Thailand are Christian, but they are also animists and have a long history of messianic leaders who are believed to possess supernatural powers. The traditional dress of the four groups – Red Lahu, Black Lahu, Yellow Lahu and Lahu Sheleh – are all slightly different, but red and black jackets are common. Lahu are skilled makers of baskets and bags. The Lahu are famed for their hunting prowess with both rifles and cross-bows. Although leopards and tigers no longer roam the northern hills, the Lahu continue to hunt bear, wild pigs, deer, squirrels, birds and snakes.

Mien

Like the Hmong, most Mien (also known as Yao) probably came to Thailand from Laos, but there are large numbers in Myanmar, Vietnam and China's Yunnan Province. Many Chinese elements, such as ancestor worship and Taoism, are evident in their animist religious beliefs. Kinship is patrilineal and polygamy is practised. Though many of Thailand's 40,000 Mien wear modern garments, women traditionally wear black jackets with red fur-like collars and large blue or black turbans. They also create dense, intricate embroideries on bags and clothing.

Akha

Probably the poorest of the hill tribes, the 48,000 Akha have been the most resistant to assimilation with the Thais. Tourists are drawn by the ornate headdress of silver discs, coins, beads and feathers worn by the Akha women. Unlike other tribals who save their finery for ceremonies, Akha women wear their headdress even while tending the fields. Animist beliefs are mixed with ancestor worship, and the Akha can trace their ancestry back 20 generations.

Lisu

The 28,000 Lisu in Thailand are easily identified by their penchant for bright colours. Women wear long green or blue cotton dresses with striped yokes. Men wear baggy trousers of the same colours. Animist beliefs are combined with ancestor worship. The Lisu are good silversmiths and make jewellery for the Akha and Lahu. They are regarded by other

Shan may have been the first Tai inhabitants of northern Thailand in the 9th or 10th century.

The Kayan (also known as Padaung) are a Karennic people residing in Myanmar. Kayan women are famous for the heavy brass neck rings they wear; these typically weigh 5kg (11lbs) and make their necks appear elongated. The money generated from tours to view the so-called "Giraffe Women" is so lucrative that Thai officials have allowed three tourist villages to be set up just west of Mae Hong Son. Though the practice had almost died out in Myanmar, a number of Padaung women there, forced by grinding poverty to chase the tourist dollar, have since donned the coils.

tribes as sharp businesspeople, and have a strong sense of self-esteem.

Other minorities

Two other groups deserve mention as their villages are frequent stops on trekking tours, though strictly speaking they are not Thai hill tribes. The Shan are very similar to the Thais with their settled communities, rice-growing practices and Theravada Buddhist beliefs. They are an ethnic Tai group and their language is close to the northern Thai dialect. Many Shan have immigrated to Thailand in recent times to escape the upheavals in Myanmar. The

LEFT: an Akha man in Chiang Rai Province.
ABOVE: Lisu girls near Mae Hong Son.

Threats to tribes

The cultures of Thailand's hill tribes are threatened by shortage of land, resettlement, lack of land rights and citizenship, illiteracy and poor medical care. Living in villages at higher elevations, most hill-tribe farmers practise slash-and-burn agriculture and traditionally grow opium. The Thai authorities have been discouraging such practices. Some of the crop-substitution programmes sponsored by the Thai government, the UN and foreign governments have been very successful. Tribal people now grow coffee, tea and fruit. The idea is that if villagers can make a living from more profitable crops, they would not need to grow and sell opium in order to buy rice. But some have resisted switching to non-opium cash crops because of the capital investment involved. ❑

A Calendar of Celebrations

Whether religious or secular, national or local, festivals in Thailand are almost always an occasion for celebration

There can be no doubt that the Thais place great importance on their festivals. Some are of venerable vintage, such as Loy Krathong, which began in the 13th century. Others, like Lamphun's Lamyai Fruit Festival, are recent creations. In fact, new festivals are thought up every year, sometimes to promote tourism and often just for a bit of *sanuk* (fun). Some festivals are weighty matters upon which the future of the nation depends. Some are more spiritual, allowing one to make merit and ensure a better karmic rebirth, while others are purely secular celebrations of the joy of living. Note: As Buddhist festivals rely on the lunar calendar, their exact dates vary each year.

LEFT: the Surin elephant festival in northeast Thailand takes place over the third weekend of November, attracting visitors from all over the country.

ABOVE: the three-day Phee Ta Khon festival at Dan Sai in Loei Province takes place each June or July and features devilish masks. It is possibly the most riotous festival in the Thai calendar.

BELOW RIGHT: Magha Puja is observed on the full moon of the third lunar month, to mark one of the Buddha's most important sermons.

Merit-making ceremonies are held at temples across Thailand in a quiet and dignified tradition that goes back centuries. Food is offered to monks, candlelit processions wind around temples, flowers and incense are offered to Buddha images, and caged animals are released.

LEFT: 3 December is the Trooping of the Colours, held outside the old Thai Parliament in Bangkok. The king, queen and members of the royal family review the elite Royal Guard, who are clad in elaborate, brightly coloured dress uniforms and tall plumed hats. The monarch himself arrives in style in his personal yellow Rolls-Royce.

ABOVE RIGHT: the King's Birthday is celebrated on 5 December nationwide, but in most spectacular fashion at Rattanakosin in Bangkok. The Grand Palace is illuminated, and there is a fireworks display.

RIGHT: the Boun Bang Fai, or rocket festival, is celebrated in the northeast. Rockets are fired into the sky to bring rain at the end of the dry season.

BELOW: Thais mark Songkran, the lunar new year, on 13 April with good-humoured water-throwing throughout the country. Don't expect to stay dry for long when in public. Songkran festivities may last as long as four to five days.

RIGHT: perhaps Thailand's most picturesque festival, Loy Krathong is celebrated on the full-moon night in November to pay respects to Mae Khongkha, goddess of the country's life-bringing rivers and lakes. The festival is supposed to have started at Sukhothai, the first Thai capital, during the time of King Ramkhamhaeng, when a court lady prepared a *krathong*, or float, for the king. Banana-stem floats, beautifully decorated with flowers, incense, candles and small coins, are released on waterways across the country.

RELIGION

All over Thailand, the visitor will see saffron-clad Buddhist monks, and hear the soft chanting of Pali scriptures and the tinkling of temple bells. Yet a strong thread of animism and superstition persists, as seen in the use of amulets and the presence of spirit houses and city pillars

Thailand is an overwhelmingly Buddhist nation. More than 90 percent of the population follow Buddhism, and its influence is apparent throughout the country. Only about 6 percent of the Thais are Muslims, and they live mainly in the far south, close to the border with Malaysia, while the remainder is made up of a sprinkling of Christian, Hindu and Sikh communities.

Over the centuries, Buddhism has played a profound role in shaping the Thai character. The Buddhist concept of the impermanence of life and possessions, and of the necessity to avoid extremes of emotion or behaviour, has done much to create the relaxed, carefree charm of the Thai people.

Theravada Buddhism

Most of the Thai population are followers of the Theravada school of Buddhism, which is also the main Buddhist form practised in neighbouring Laos, Cambodia and Myanmar (Burma), as well as Sri Lanka. Nevertheless, even a casual visitor to temples in these countries will quickly notice differences between them. In the same way that they have adapted other external cultural influences – Khmer temple decorations and Chinese food, for instance – into a unique Thai form, the Thais have evolved their own interpretation of Buddhism over the centuries.

Theravada Buddhism is a mixture of Buddhist, Hindu and animistic beliefs. It is the oldest of all Buddhist faiths, and it is the only one to trace its origins directly back to the teachings of Gautama Buddha in the 6th century BC. The central

doctrines are based on the temporary nature of life and the imperfections of all beings.

With the help of a complicated system of rules, each Thai, whether layperson or monk, tries to achieve spiritual merit in the present life so that it will favourably influence their next life – thus permitting an existence that will be characterised by less suffering and ultimately lead to the final goal of *nirvana*, or enlightenment. To this end, almost all the religious activities that a traveller will experience in Thailand have to do with the concept of merit-making. Therefore, a man who spends some part of his life as a monk will earn merit by living in accordance with the strict rules governing monastic life. Similarly, a

LEFT: worshippers at Wat Bowonniwet, Bangkok.
RIGHT: flower garland at the Erawan Shrine, Bangkok.

person who supports the monks on a daily basis by donating food, or who visits a temple to pray for a sick person, gains merit.

The Buddha image in front of which the prayers are offered provides only a formal background for these activities. It is imporant to note that neither the statue, nor the Buddha himself, is worshipped.

Mahayana Buddhism

Mahayana Buddhism is practised mainly by those of Chinese descent, and visitors are most likely to spot Mahayana temples in Bangkok's Chinatown district. Mahayana literally means "Greater Vehicle". The defining belief, according to this doctrine, is that those who have attained *nirvana* return to earth to help others reach the same state. The various Buddhist sects and practices that predominate in countries like China, Tibet, Taiwan, Japan, Korea and Vietnam are classified as Mahayana.

This form of Buddhism is characterised by the use of lucky charms and talismans. The visitor entering a *sanjao*, or inner shrine, of a typical Mahayana temple will have a chance to shake sticks out of a canister, from which their fortune can be told. At funerals, paper money and doll-sized cardboard houses (complete with

INDIAN INFLUENCE

Many of the Thais' non-Buddhist beliefs are Brahman in origin, thanks to Indian influence in early Thai history. Even today, Brahman priests officiate at major ceremonies. The Thai wedding ceremony is almost entirely Brahman, as are many funeral rites, while the rites of statecraft pertaining to the royal family are presided over by Brahman priests. One of the most popular of these, the Ploughing Ceremony (Raek Na), takes place each May in Bangkok. To signal the start of the rice-planting season, sacred oxen are offered a selection of grains. The grains they choose will determine the amount of rainfall to come, and the success or failure of the crops in the year ahead.

paper Mercedes-Benz cars) are burnt to assist the deceased in his or her next life.

Temple life

Most of Thailand's 300,000 or so monks live in *wat* (temples), practising and teaching the rules of human conduct laid down by the Buddha. There are literally hundreds of Buddhist temples in the cities and suburbs, usually sited in serene pockets of densely packed neighbourhoods and serving as hubs for the spiritual and social life of the community.

The term *wat* defines a large, walled compound made up of several buildings, including a *bot* or hall where new monks are ordained, and one or more *viharn* where sermons are delivered. It may also contain a bell tower, a *ho trai* (library) and *guti*, or monks' living quarters, as well as a domed edifice, called *chedi* in Thailand, or *stupa* on the Indian subcontinent. The *chedi* sometimes contains relics of the Buddha, but in most instances the relics are of wealthy donors or holy people.

> Thailand differs from most other Buddhist countries in that women cannot be ordained into the priesthood. It is thus the duty of a son, as a monk, to earn merit on behalf of his mother and other female relatives.

Tradition requires that every Buddhist male enter the monkhood for a brief period before marriage, and companies customarily grant paid leave for male employees wishing to do so. The entry of a young man into monkhood is seen as repayment to his parents for his upbringing, and for bestowing special merit on them, particularly his mother.

Despite the ascetic nature of monastic life, a Buddhist *wat* in Thailand is by no means isolated from the outside world. In addition to the schools that are attached to most *wat* (for centuries, the only schools were those run by monks), the temple has traditionally been the centre of social and communal life. Monks also double up as herbal doctors, psychological counsellors and arbitrators of disputes in the villages. They also play an important part in daily life, such as blessing a new building, or at birthdays and funerals.

Spirits and amulets

It is not known exactly when the Thai people first embraced a belief in spirits, but it was most probably long before their migration south into present-day Thailand, and certainly long before their gradual conversion to Buddhism around AD 800–1200. Even after Buddhism took root in Thailand, the people continued to worship their old deities and spirits to fill in what they saw as gaping holes in Buddhism.

Most Thais widely accept that there are spirits everywhere – spirits of the water, wind and woods, and both locality spirits and tutelary spirits. These spirits are not so much good or

---

LEFT: nearly every Thai male spends part of his lifetime as a monk, regardless of age.
RIGHT: amulets protect from misfortune and evil.

bad, as powerful and unpredictable. Moreover, they have many of the foibles that plague humans, being capable of vindictiveness, lust, jealousy, greed and malice. To appease them, offerings must be made, and since spirits display many aspects of human nature, these offerings are often what people would value themselves.

To counteract the spirits and potential dangers that lurk in life, protective spells are often cast and kept in small amulets, mostly worn around the neck. Curiously, the amulets cannot be bought or sold, but rather rented on an indefinite lease from "landlords", often monks considered to possess magical powers.

Some monasteries have been turned into highly profitable factories for the production of amulets. There are amulets that offer protection against accidents during travel or against bullet and knife wounds; some are even said to boost sexual attraction. All this, however, has no more to do with Buddhism than the intricate blue-patterned tattoos sported by some rural Thais in an attempt to ward off evil.

The city pillar

When the first Thai migrants established themselves in the plains around Sukhothai, their basic unit of organisation was the *muang*, a group of villages under the control and protection of a *wiang*, or fortified town. Of crucial importance was the *lak muang*, or city pillar, located at the centre of each *wiang*. This structure remains a feature of many towns throughout Thailand. Generally a rounded pole – thought to represent a rice shoot – it is the home of the guardian spirits of the city and surrounding district. It is venerated on a regular basis, and an annual ceremony, with offerings of incense, flowers and candles, is held to ensure the continuing prosperity and safety of the *muang*.

Spirit houses

Traditionally, offerings are made when land is cleared for agriculture or building. After all, the spirits of a place are its original owners, and their feelings have to be taken into consideration. At some point, it was decided that an effective way of placating a locality spirit was to build it a small house of its own. That way, it would be comfortable and contented.

Today, no building in Thailand, not even the humblest wooden hut, will be seen without a spirit house, or at least a house altar. In ordinary residences, the small doll-like house may resemble a Thai dwelling; in hotels and offices, it is usually an elaborately decorated mini-temple.

Thai Buddhist temples have also accommodated the practice of spirit worship. There is

CONSECRATING A SPIRIT HOUSE

Setting up a spirit house is not a casual undertaking, but one that requires the services of an experienced professional. Usually this is a Brahmin priest called a *phram* (clad in white, in contrast to the Buddhist saffron robes), or at least someone schooled in Brahmin ritual.

The consecration ritual is commenced by scattering small coins around the site chosen for the new spirit house, and in the soil beneath the foundations. The spirit house is then raised, and offerings are made. These include flowers, money, candles and incense – the last is often stuck into the crown of a pig's head.

The *phram*, together with the householder and his various relatives and friends, then pray to the spirits,

beseeching the local *chao thii*, or lord of the locality, to take up residence in the new spirit house.

Spirit houses are often beautifully decorated with statues of dancers, ponies, servants and other items made of plaster or wood. In more recent times, contemporary offerings like replica cars and other modern consumer desirables have been offered as well, each carefully chosen to placate the resident spirit. In the grounds of Bangkok's Nai Lert Park Hotel is an unusual spirit house that is filled with offerings of phalluses, from tiny to gargantuan, sculpted from wood, wax, stone and cement, and with startling fidelity to real life. These are left by women hoping to conceive a child.

hardly a *wat* anywhere in the country that does not incorporate an elaborate spirit house in its grounds – built at the same time as the consecration of the temple in order to accommodate the displaced locality spirits.

Thais also erect spirit houses along the roads linking their settlements, paying particular attention to threatening or ominous landscapes or features. Even today, every pass or steep section of road is marked by a spirit house to accommodate the inconvenienced locality spirit. Passing drivers beep their horns in salutation, and many stop to make offerings. Spirit houses are also raised in the fields to ensure the safety of the crop.

When the first Muslims arrived, they settled and intermarried with the local Malays, most of whom practised a syncretic Hindu-Buddhist religion. By Islamic law, the children of such unions were raised as Muslims, and over the centuries a combination of intermarriage and proselytising led to the conversion of almost all the indigenous Malay population.

Comprising about 6 percent of the national population, Thai Muslims are dominant in the four southern provinces of Satun, Pattani, Yala and Narathiwat. In this region, most people work as farmers or fishermen, studying the faith in religious schools, and saving up to go on the

Islam in the south

It is only in the southernmost regions of peninsular Thailand, in Malay-speaking territory, that temples and spirit houses disappear, replaced by minarets and mosques. Islam first came to this region in the 8th century. Carried across the Indian Ocean by Arab and south Indian traders, it found fertile ground among the region's Malay-speaking people. The Muslims of Thailand's deep south, as in neighbouring Malaysia, follow the Sunni Islam branch of the Shafi'i school.

FAR LEFT: spirit house. **LEFT:** phalluses at Nai Lert Park Hotel in Bangkok. **ABOVE:** Muslim children from Hat Yai in the far south.

haj, or pilgrimage, to Mecca. The Shafi'i school is not overly rigorous, although in recent times, there has been growing fundamentalist influence from foreign Muslim radicals from Malaysia and Indonesia, fuelling the separatist movements and sporadic unrest in Pattani, Yala and Narathiwat provinces. Satun Province, although largely Muslim, has steered clear of such strife and unrest, and is safe to visit.

A spirit tradition is also practised by some southerners, although it is officially condemned by orthodox Muslim teachers. This tradition is represented by the *bomoh*, or Malay "witch doctor", who can foretell future events, cure physical, mental and spiritual diseases, curse individuals or lift such curses. ❑

IMAGES OF THE BUDDHA

From the gigantic seated Buddhas to tiny Buddhas worn as amulets, these religious icons rank among the world's greatest expressions of Buddhist art

Images of the Buddha are devotional objects and are not considered to be works of art by their makers. When artists create an image of the Buddha, they follow a set of specific rules that have been laid down for generations. The Buddha is defined by a set of peculiar characteristics, a particular monastic garb and a series of *mudra* (attitudes, postures or gestures). The 32 bodily marks, evident at the time of the Buddha's birth, include hands that reach the knees without bending, a lion-like jaw and wheel marks on the base of the feet. Buddhist artists have interpreted these marks according to the era in which they were working and the school of interpretation they had chosen to follow.

Sukhothai school

Thai Buddhist imagery was at its artistic height during the Sukhothai period (early 13th–early 15th centuries), when the smoothness and sheen of cast metals perfectly matched the graceful, elongated simplicity of the basic Buddha form. During this era, the Buddha was usually represented sitting cross-legged or with one foot forward in the "striding" position. One hand is raised in the *abhayamudra* (dispelling fear) action. Slightly androgynous in appearance, the Buddha images also feature a flame-like *ketumula* on the crown of the head, protruding heels, flat soles and toes all of the same length.

ABOVE LEFT: all kinds of Buddhist paraphernalia are on sale outside Thai temples.

RIGHT: Buddha at Wat Ko Loi in Si Racha.

RIGHT: Thai artists simplify anatomical details in their images of the Buddha to emphasise the spiritual qualities of Buddhism and to convey enigma and serenity.

ABOVE: Wat Suthat in Bangok is known for its fine statuary. The large ordination and sermon halls are surrounded by cloisters of gilded Buddha images.

SYMBOLISM OF THE *MUDRA*

The Buddha can be seen sitting, standing, lying or, in Thailand, walking. Every image of the Buddha is represented in a particular *mudra* or attitude. Hand gestures in particular are key iconographical elements in representations of the Buddha:

• *Abhayamudra* is the *mudra* of dispelling fear or giving protection: the Buddha is usually in a standing position, the right hand raised and turned outwards to show the palm with straightened fingers.

• *Bhumisparsamudra (see picture above)*, or calling the earth as witness: this is made by a seated figure, with the right hand on the knee and the fingertips pointing towards the ground.

• *Dharmacakramudra* means spinning the Wheel of Law: both hands are held in front of the body, with the fingertips of the left hand resting against the palm of the right hand.

• *Dhyanamudra* is the meditation *mudra*: the hands rest flat in the lap, one on top of the other.

• *Varamudra*, giving blessing or charity: made by the seated or standing Buddha with the right arm pointing downwards, the palm open and fingers more or less straightened.

• *Vitarkamudra* is the preaching *mudra*: the end of the thumb and index finger of the right hand touch to form a circle, symbolising the Wheel of Law.

RIGHT: a depiction of the meditation *mudra*; the hands are laid flat on the lap.

ABOVE: seated buddha at the feet of the Big Buddha Temple on Ko Samui.

LEFT: the standing Buddha on Khao Takiab (Chopstick Hill) towers 20 metres (66ft) above the southern end of Hua Hin beach.

THE PERFORMING ARTS

Thailand's traditional dance-dramas are an entrenched part of its performing-arts scene. Lesser known, but just as engaging, are its shadow-puppet theatre, a cutting-edge movie industry, contemporary theatre and dance, and a popular music scene

The Thai people have combined a lively imagination and a superb sense of the aesthetic to produce some of the most arresting performing arts found in Asia. Thai dance-dramas, for instance, with their elaborate and colourful costumes, and graceful, enchanting movements, are among the world's most dazzling and stylistically challenging dance forms.

But there's more to Thai performing arts than traditional dance and drama. Several genres of indigenous music and contemporary theatre, as well as a vibrant independent movie scene, contribute to the cultural landscape. Underpinning all this is a strong body of Thai literature that acts as both a creative source and an inspiration for the performing arts.

THAI DANCE DRAMA

Traditional theatre is still the most recognised performing-arts genre in Thailand, and comprises six main forms: *khon*, *lakhon*, *likay*, *manohra*, *lakhon lek* and *nang*. Both dance and drama are inextricably linked in traditional Thai theatre. In effect, the actor is a mime, with the storyline and lyrics provided by a singer and chorus to the side of the stage. A traditional *phipat* orchestra *(see page 71)* creates not only the atmosphere, but also an emotive force.

Khon

The most identifiable form of dance-drama is the *khon*, traditionally performed by a troupe of male dancers, some of whom wear beautifully crafted masks. Originally staged for the royal court, these days a condensed version of several

episodes from the *Ramakien (see page 73)* – based on the Hindu epic *Ramayana* – is adapted into a short medley of palatable scenes for tourist dinner shows in Bangkok, Phuket and Chiang Mai. More elaborate *khon* performances are staged occasionally at Bangkok's National Theatre and the Royal Chalermkrung Theatre, but even these are abridged versions as the entire *Ramakien* would take up to 720 hours to perform.

Four types of characters make up a *khon* performance: men and women, monkeys and demons. Only the monkeys and demons wear masks during the performance. The expressionless masks force the viewer to focus attention on the dancers' movements, whether it's a

LEFT: *khon* dancers in a traditional performance.
RIGHT: a *phipat* orchestra.

dismissive flick of the hand, a finger pointed in accusation, or a foot stamped in anger.

Lakhon

The most graceful Thai dance-drama is the *lakhon*. There are two main forms: *lakhon nai* ("inside" *lakhon*), once performed only within palace walls by women, and *lakhon nawk* ("outside" *lakhon*), performed beyond the palace by both sexes. Resplendent in costumes as elaborate as their movements, the performers glide slowly about the stage, their stylised movements conveying the plot. The dance's rich repertoire includes scenes from the *Ram-*

akien, and Thai folk tales, with their romantic storylines. These days, a simpler version called *lakhon chatri* can be seen at temple festivals and shrines throughout Thailand. A variation of this dance is *lakhon kae bon*, which consists of a 20-member ensemble of dancers and musicians who perform at shrines as a form of thanksgiving. Performances can be seen at Bangkok's Lak Muang (City Pillar) shrine and the Erawan Shrine.

Likay

There have always been two cultures in Thailand: palace and village. The village arts are

OPERA AND CLASSICAL MUSIC

Multi-talented Cambridge graduate Somtow Sucharitkul, writer of Hollywood scripts and several books in English, set up the Bangkok Opera in 2002. Among its three or four yearly productions of mainstream Western classics are Somtow's own works (written in English) such as *Mae Naak*, which is based on a Thai ghost story. His works are mainly staged at the Thailand Cultural Centre in Bangkok.

In addition to providing many of the musicians for the Bangkok Opera, the Bangkok Symphony Orchestra plays regular concerts throughout the year, often at the Thai Cultural Centre. They also perform at Lumphini Park on Sundays during the cool season.

often parodies of the palace arts, but more burlesque, with pratfalls and bawdy humour. *Likay* is the village form of *lakhon*, played out against gaudy backdrops to an audience that walks in and out of the performance at will, eating and talking, regardless of what happens on stage.

Likay has lost some of its audience in recent years, but it still remains a vital art form in some parts of Thailand. It is usually staged by troupes of performers who travel from village to village. The performances could be excerpts from the *Ramakien*, but they are more likely to be stories incorporating elements of melodrama, slapstick comedy, sexual innuendo and the occasional stab at Thai politics and society.

Shadow-puppet theatre

Traditional Thai shadow-puppet theatre is something of a declining art. Two forms still exist, mainly in the south of Thailand. The *nang thalung* form is what visitors will most likely encounter in places like Nakhon Si Thammarat. Originating from Malaysia and Indonesia, *nang thalung* recounts excerpts from the *Ramakien*.

Puppeteers manipulate figures made from *nang* (dried buffalo hide) against a translucent screen, which is backlit by torches, to relate complex tales of good and evil. A rarer version of shadow-puppet play in south Thailand, known as *nang yai*, uses life-size puppets but is seldom practised due to the lack of expertise.

Marionette theatre

Visually mesmerising and based on *khon* masked dance-drama, the art of *hun lakhon lek* requires three puppeteers who manipulate sticks attached to the 1-metre (3ft) tall marionettes to bring them to life. Once only performed for royalty, this endangered art was revived by Sakorn Yangkeawsot, who goes by the moniker Joe Louis.

This revival has updated *hun lakhon lek* by allowing freer movement and more detailed costuming, and also by incorporating contemporary themes and modern speech. You can see these elaborately costumed puppets twist and turn nightly at the Joe Louis Theatre at Suan Lum Night Bazaar *(see page 131)*.

Contemporary dance and theatre

The main venue for quality modern productions is the open-air Patravadi Theatre in Bangkok *(see page 395)*, run by Patravadi Mechudhon, whose adaptations of classic Thai tales meld traditional local dance and theatre with modern Western styling. Some of its works fuse elements of diverse Asian dance forms such as the Japanese *butoh* and Indonesian *wayang kulit*.

The Patravadi Theatre stages its acclaimed shows seasonally in Bangkok. Otherwise, try and catch one of its dinner theatre shows on Friday and Saturday nights at the Supatra River House *(see page 136)*.

LEFT: *hun lakhon lek* puppeteers at Bangkok's Joe Louis Theatre. **RIGHT:** a scene from Patravadi Theatre's *Eclipse*, a portrayal of Buddhist suffering.

> *Patravadi Theatre hosts the annual Bangkok Fringe Festival, which has a varied programme of dance, drama and music. See www.patravaditheatre.com for highlights.*

Thai classical music

To the uninitiated, classical Thai music sounds like a jarring and ear-piercing mishmash of contrasting tones without any fixed pattern. The key is to listen to it as one might listen to jazz, picking out one instrument and following it, switching to another as the mood moves you.

The music is set to a scale of seven full steps, with a lilting and steady rhythm. Each instrument plays the same melody, but in its own way and seemingly without regard to how others are playing it. Seldom does an instrument rise in solo; it is always challenged and cajoled by the other constituent parts of the orchestra.

A classical *phipat* orchestra is made up of a single reed instrument, the oboe-like *phinai*, and a variety of percussion instruments. The pitch favours the treble, with the pace set by the *ching*, a tiny cymbal, aided by the drums beaten with the fingers. The melody is played by two types of *ranat ek*, a bamboo-bar xylophone, and two sets of *khlong wong*, which are tuned gongs arranged in a semicircle around the player.

> *His Majesty King Bhumibol Ayuladej knows how to swing on the saxophone, and has cut several records influenced by the bebop genre. A song that only he could write is entitled "H.M. Blues".*

Another type of *phipat* orchestra employs two violins, the *saw-oo* and the *saw-duang*, which usually accompany a Thai dance-drama. A variation of the *phiphat* orchestra performs at a Thai boxing (*muay thai*) match to spur the combatants to action.

MODERN MUSIC AND FILM

Apart from the vibrant Thai pop scene, full of plastic-looking *luk kreung* (half-Thai and half-Caucasian) stars lisping bubblegum tunes, there are several genres of popular music worth mentioning. Love songs and colloquial storytelling are at the heart of *mor lam* music, which is played on the *khaen* instrument, a type of mouth organ. *Mor lam* music comes from Laos and northeast Thailand and is based on traditional poetry (known as *glawn*), which emphasises local folklore, struggle and political sentiment. The tempo is rapid and accompanied by staccato vocals. Modern versions of *mor lam* use electronic instruments and are more structured, often blending with other traditional forms of

music. Purists have criticised the shift, but the offshoot has its own devout circle of fans.

Luk thung (literally "child of the fields") is Thai country music, peppered with tales of hardship, poverty and despair. It is very popular with working-class Thais. Vocals are usually drenched with vibrato and feature slow, steady tempos and the use of electric guitars, keyboards and drums. This genre of music is so in demand it has spawned several magazines and TV programmes, its own dedicated radio station and even a few films.

Plaeng phua chuwit (songs for life) are protest songs that originated in the 1970s and became the voice of student movements rebelling against the brutal military government of the time. The most famous contemporary practitioner is Ad Carabao.

Cinema

In common with practically everywhere else in the world, Hollywood blockbusters dominate cinemas in Thailand. Of late, however, a few talented Thai directors have been receiving acclaim for their works on the international film circuit. Leading the charge is the new-wave director Apichatpong Weera-sethakul, whose 2002 film *Blissfully Yours* was awarded the *Prix Un Certain Regard* at the Cannes Film Festival, followed by the atmospheric 2004 film *Tropical Malady (Sud Pralad)*, which also picked up a special prize at Cannes.

Apichatpong's 2004 collaboration with Thai-American artist Michael Shaowansai on the hilariously campy *Adventures of Iron Pussy* – about a cross-dressing superhero – is proof that Thai cinema is engaging and provocative to both domestic and international audiences. Another Thai filmmaker to watch out for is Pen-Ek Ratanaruang, who has produced two successful films, *Last Life in the Universe* (2004) and *Invisible Waves* (2006), starring the Japanese superstar actor Tadanobu Asano.

However, many such films do not get the airing they deserve in Bangkok – the only real indie cinema is House on RCA, with occasional screenings at Lido in Siam Square. Many are, however, featured during film festivals, including the World Film Festival, EU Film Festival and, since 2002, the big one, the Bangkok International Film Festival. ❏

LEFT: a scene from the film *Adventures of Iron Pussy*.

Thai Literature

For years accessible to the aristocracy alone, Thai literature did not come of age until the 20th century

The Thai literary tradition is both absorbing and rich in its history, and includes a complex oral tradition of storytelling that dates back centuries and predates written text.

Nearly all forms of early Thai writing were lost in 1767 when Burmese invaders burnt down the old capital of Ayutthaya, along with its wealth of literature. After this tragic event, the rewriting of the old texts became primarily a royal task, as until the mid-19th century all literature was written in verse form – only known to royalty and the aristocratic classes.

The *Ramakien*

The rewrite was further necessitated by the loss of the *Ramakien*, the piece of literature at the heart of all Thai oral and transcribed history which is based on the Indian classical tale *Ramayana*, an enduring story that has found a home in the literature of almost every country in Southeast Asia. In retelling the *Ramayana*, the Thais made it their own and gave a Buddhist spin to what was essentially a Hindu text. Understanding the *Ramakien* allows one to comprehend a wide variety of Thai dramatic forms, including dance-drama, its significance for Thai monarchs (who have adopted the name Rama as their own) and its role as model for exemplary social behaviour. In fact, the *Ramakien* is part of the Thai school curriculum.

Indigenous literature

Exceptional among 19th-century writers is Thailand's best-known poet, Sunthorn Phu *(see page 184).* He was the first commoner to be celebrated as a writer, and he abandoned the verse form used by the aristocratic classes for his works. His epic poem *Phra Aphaimani* follows Prince Aphaimani, a flawed hero, in his adventures in ancient Thailand.

It wasn't until the 1920s that Thai novels were published, with themes touching mainly on social or political issues. In the 1950s, however, censorship became so heavy and writers so harshly persecuted that quality fiction practically disappeared. Since the

RIGHT: *Ramakien* mural, Wat Phra Kaew, Bangkok.

1980s, writers have recovered a measure of political freedom. While they remain social critics, there are efforts to write fiction of literary merit. The late prime minister and cultural advocate Kukrit Pramoj's *Many Lives*, for instance, gives a good introduction to the Buddhist way of thinking. His *Four Reigns* is a fictional, yet accurate, account of court life in the 19th and 20th centuries. Pramoj, who died in 1995, was a hugely influential prose writer and the standard by which all modern literature is measured.

Contemporary Thai writers have shown a tendency to pontificate on societal ills in their writing; among the least sanctimonious is Pira Sudham. His books are available in English, and notable works

include *Tales of Thailand* and *The Force of Karma*.

Perhaps the most significant current Thai writer is Prabda Yoon. Born to a wealthy family and educated in New York, his career was launched with a collection of short stories called *Probability*. This won him the SEA Write award (the highest literary honour for a Thai writer) in 2002. His dry writing style and quiet cynicism have influenced many young Thai writers.

A range of expatriate writers have published novels set in Thailand. Alex Garland's *The Beach* is the most famous, but most are forgettable detective romps replete with CIA agents, conspiracies, enchanting prostitutes and crooked cops. The best of such writing is probably *The Big Mango* by Jake Needham, which keeps most of its indulgences in check. ❑

ARTS AND CRAFTS

With numerous cultural and aesthetic influences from around Asia, it's little wonder that Thailand's traditional arts and crafts have an almost universal appeal. No less absorbing is Thai contemporary art, which is inspired by a heady mix of spiritual and modern metaphors

A s with its architecture, music, religion, and cuisine, the visual arts and handicrafts of Thailand are the result of an inventive amalgamation of various regional influences. Someone with some knowledge in the field may say, "Hmm... that bit's Chinese... and that bit's Indian... and that bit's European," yet it must also be concluded that the total effect, the end-product, is entirely home-grown and uniquely Thai.

Thailand is renowned worldwide as a centre of flourishing arts and crafts – one of the reasons why it's such a shopper's delight. But Thai artistry is found almost everywhere if you open your eyes to it, adorning temple walls in the form of murals and gold and lacquer paintings, and in the palaces filled with ornate furniture and fabrics. It's even found in food, with fruit and vegetables carved into intricate flowers, fish and birds.

Lacquerware and pottery

Thailand's traditional crafts have a rich heritage that dates back centuries. While each region has its own specialities, the largest variety for sale (and the best prices) are found in Bangkok and Chiang Mai, and to a lesser extent in Phuket. The range on offer at both the large malls and street vendors is astounding.

Lacquerware is a Burmese-Chinese import, and much of that made today, mainly in north Thailand, is fashioned by highly skilled and patient artists who laboriously apply layer after layer of a resin to containers most often made from wood or woven bamboo. Some of the finest work may take several weeks or months to complete.

Another craft from China, related to lacquering, is mother-of-pearl decoration. Thai craftsmen are supremely skilled at setting the iridescent oyster shells aglow in black lacquer backgrounds to create scenes of enchanting beauty on boxes, furniture and statuary.

The earliest pottery discovered in Thailand dates back to 3600 BC and was discovered in Ban Chiang in the northeast. While original antiques are rare, most ceramics are still fashioned along the same shapes and designs of their time-honoured counterparts. Among the most well-known pottery are Sawankhalok ceramic plates from the Sukhothai era with their distinctive twin fish design. Celadon is a

LEFT: *mudmee* silk from northeast Thailand.
RIGHT: high-quality lacquerware.

beautiful stoneware with a light jade-green or dark-brown glaze, and is used to make dinnerware, lamps and statuary.

The fine art of *bencharong* ceramics originated in China and was later developed by Thai artists. The five colours of *bencharong* – red, blue, yellow, green and white – appear on delicate porcelain bowls, containers and decorative items. Blue-and-white porcelain, which also originated in China, has been produced in Thailand for centuries.

Woodcarvings

Another distinctly Thai handicraft is ornamental woodcarving. Traditional motifs include the lotus and other flowers, mythological creatures from India, and serpents and dragons from China. Usually, decorative woodwork is found on furniture and in the adornmvnt of religious and royal buildings, royal barges and carriages, and even in the humblest homes, albeit in a more modest style. Teak is seldom used in carving nowadays as it is very expensive; most of the woodwork sold today is made from rattan, bamboo and cheaper woods.

Textiles

The glamour of Thai silk was first recognised in the late 1940s by American entrepreneur

BUYER BEWARE: RELIGIOUS ANTIQUES

Thai and Burmese antiques are among the finest in Asia, but the real thing is hard to come by these days. For the tenacious and well informed, though, treasures can still be unearthed. The centre of Thailand's antiques trade is located in Bangkok's River City shopping centre, which contains a sprawling array of shops selling genuine antiques as well as look-alike objets d'art.

Note that the Ministry of Culture's Fine Arts Department maintains strict control over the export of religious antiques *(see panel, page 402)*. Genuine antiques dealers will be able to obtain the export permits required to take a true antique out of Thailand.

Jim Thompson *(see page 128)*. He promoted it abroad, where it quickly gained favour for its slightly bumpy texture and shimmering iridescence. While Jim Thompson outlets all over Thailand offer an excellent range of silks and ready-made products, better bargains can be had at the lesser-known Jim Thompson Factory Outlet along Thanon Sukhumvit in Bangkok. Most of the Thai silk these days is produced in the northeast, and the northeastern city of Khon Kaen celebrates an annual silk festival each November.

A variation is *mudmee*, a silk from northeast Thailand that is characterised by subtle zigzagging lines and comes in more sombre hues such as dark blue, maroon and deep yellow.

Dazzling embroidery can be found in the modern-day versions of *teen chok* – a method with which women of the ancient Lanna kingdom in the north of Thailand symbolically wove their family histories into their silk or cotton sarongs. The country's northern hill tribes also have their own distinctive patchwork and embroidery designs on cotton, mainly in bright blues, magentas and yellows.

At shops all over Thailand, hand-woven silks and cottons are sold in lengths, or ready-made as cushion covers, tablecloths and clothes. Bangkok and other cities have excellent tailors who can whip up elegant dresses made of Thai silk and embellished with appliqué and beadwork.

Jewellery and gemstones

Thailand is also famous for its gold and silver jewellery and gemstones. It is a major player in the global jewellery market, rivalled only by Sri Lanka and India. In the Ayutthaya and early Bangkok eras, the use of gold in royal household items, such as cosmetic jars and tableware, as well as on thrones and ceremonial objects, brought honour to the artisans who were commissioned by royal families. Today, most of the gold jewellery sold is unimaginative, taking the form of thick and heavy chains purchased mainly as a guarantee against a fluctuating currency.

More affordable (and trendy) is jewellery fashioned from silver. Most of the silver is imported and then pounded into delicate jewellery and ornately crafted trays, boxes, bowls and other containers. The finest pieces are from north Thailand and usually sold at shops in cities like Chiang Mai and Chiang Rai.

Bangkok is home to the world's leading cutters of coloured gems. Both the International Colored Gemstone Association (ICA) and the Asian Institute of Gemological Sciences (AIGS) are based here. Most of the gems sold in Thailand today are imported from neighbouring Myanmar and Cambodia, some of which arrive in Thailand by questionable means. Rubies range from pale to deep red (including the famous "pigeon's blood" rubies); sapphires come in blue, green and yellow, as well as in the form most associated with Thailand – the star sapphire. Thai jewellers can turn gold,

> During the Ayutthaya period, generals would ride into battle on elephants, wearing sashes encrusted with jewels that they believed would give them protection from injuries and strength to wage war.

white gold, silver and platinum into delicate jewellery settings and are able to produce both traditional and contemporary designs.

Be careful when shopping for gems and jewellery; on the streets and in some small shops, the stones may not be of the quality and weight

advertised. The Tourism Authority of Thailand has joined hands with gem-trading organisations to provide quality control through the Jewel Fest Club – look for the ruby-ring logo on shopfronts in the major cities. Border markets in Mae Sot, Mae Hong Song and Mae Sai in the north are also good bets for gems and offer an exciting alternative to the high-pressure Bangkok "factories", where quality is often questionable and the prices can be ridiculous.

Other handicrafts

There is a whole range of handicrafts that do not belong to any of the categories discussed above. Teakwood is carved into practical items such as breadboards and salad bowls, as well as

LEFT: the dazzling colours of Thai silk.
RIGHT: hill-tribe-influenced fashion accessories – pendants at Chiang Mai's vibrant night market.

more decorative trivets and statues of mythical gods, angels and elephants. Bronze statues of classical drama figures, like the recumbent deer from the *Ramakien*, make elegant decorations. Brassware, like the large noodle cabinets which street vendors sling on bamboo poles, can double up as small side tables. Natural fibres woven into products like placemats, laundry baskets and handbags also make great buys.

Street markets all over Thailand sell umbrellas made of *sah* paper (from Chiang Mai), silk fans, linen bedspreads, and mango and coconut wood utensils and receptacles. One of Thailand's lesser-known arts is nielloware, which involves applying an amalgam of black metal onto etched portions of silver or, to a lesser extent, gold.

Thai craftsmanship and creativity extends far beyond the realm of the traditional – and Bangkok is fast becoming a hub for contemporary design, while local designers are also making waves in the area of home decor. Thai cosmetics-makers are busily reinventing natural Thai beauty products like jasmine rice soap and tamarind facial scrubs, and packaging them in elegant rattan baskets. Walk into any of the major malls and you will encounter shops selling trendy home accessories that often use indigenous materials. Bangkok's sprawling shopping mecca, Chatuchak Weekend Market *(see page 140)*, is an alternative treasure trove for all crafts traditional and contemporary (and cheap).

Temple art

The inner walls of the *bot* (ordination halls) and *viharn* (sermon halls) in Thai temples are traditionally covered with murals. In the days before public education, the temple was the principal repository of knowledge for the commoners. The principal themes are the life of Buddha, with the back wall generally depicting stories from the *Maravijaya*, in which all earthly temptations are united to break the meditating Buddha's will and prevent his achieving *nirvana* (*see also page 93*).

The murals at Buddhaisawan Chapel in Bangkok's National Museum are among the finest examples of Thai painting. Others include the murals at Wat Suthat and the 19th-century paintings at Wat Bowonniwet, both in Bangkok. Although restored several times with less than perfect accuracy, the *Ramakien* murals in the walls surrounding Bangkok's Wat Phra Kaew include wonderful scenes of village and palace life.

Traditional art is also executed in the form of lacquer and gold paintings found on the shutters of most Thai temples. The best examples of lacquer painting can be found on the walls of the Lacquer Pavilion at Suan Pakkad Palace in Bangkok. Equally stunning is the intricate mother-of-pearl work by Thai artisans.

Contemporary art

At the turn of the 20th century, King Chulalongkorn commissioned several European artists to embark on art projects in Bangkok, a trend the government continued in 1923 when they hired Italian sculptor Corrado Feroci. The

THE ARTISTRY OF BUDDHA IMAGES

The focal point of the *bot* and *viharn* (ordination and sermon halls) of a Thai temple is the Buddha image. The image is not considered a representation of the Buddha, but is meant to serve as a reminder of his teachings. Buddha images cast in bronze, or carved in wood or stone, constitute the bulk of classical Thai sculpture. They employ some of the finest artistry (and some of the highest prices) of any arts. Superb examples of bas-relief sandstone carving can be seen around the base of the *bot* (ordination hall) of Bangkok's Wat Pho *(see page 116)*. Delicately executed, the dozens of panels depict scenes from the *Ramakien*.

Florentine artist proved catalytic in the development of modern Thai art right through to the 1960s; locals even gave him the adopted name Silpa Bhirasri. He is attributed as being the forefather of modern art in Thailand, and established the country's first School of Fine Arts, which later became Silpakorn University.

Spirituality and Buddhism have been, and still are, major precepts in contemporary art – whether created by neo-traditionalist painters like Thawan Duchanee and Chalermchai Kositpipat, or the meditative installations of the late Montien Boonma. Sakarin Krue-on uses spiritual metaphors as his basis, appropriating traditional ridicules the Thai urbanite's consumerist compulsions with his satirical *Pink Man* series.

The future of contemporary art

Despite having a wealth of talented young artists, Thailand is struggling to find its feet and voice as an artistic centre in Southeast Asia. Lack of funding and proper infrastructure are the primary problems.

The works of Thailand's most famous contemporary artist, Rirkrit Tiravanija – who divides his time between Berlin, New York and Thailand (and was born in Buenos Aires) – have been favourably received in the West

imagery to question the blind adoption of Western trends. Also of note is Bangkok artist Jakkai Siributr, who weaves giant textile pieces using bright silk, which he then pastes, cuts and mutilates using cartoons. The result is a comment on the perversities of modern Buddhism as well as Thai society.

Aside from the spiritual, many local artists question the effects of globalisation on the Thai identity. The artist Vasan Sitthiket blurs his art with faux political campaigning to highlight his contempt for national policies, while conceptual photographer Manit Sriwanichpoom

but, unfortunately, he has not shown locally for many years.

Meanwhile, contemporary art exhibitions are regular and sometimes outstanding at the galleries of the Silpakorn and Chulalongkorn universities and at a small number of private galleries in Bangkok, like H Gallery and Tonson Gallery. Thailand also held the first Bangkok International Art Festival with government and private support in 2007, but unfortunately budget cuts have so far rendered this a one-off. On a brighter note, the long-delayed Bangkok Art and Culture Centre (*see page 135*) finally opened its doors in 2008. It was supposed to have opened in 2005 but construction were delayed due to lack of support and funds. ❑

LEFT: Buddha images, Leng Noi Yee temple, Bangkok.
ABOVE: art for sale at Chiang Mai night market.

CUISINE

Thai cuisine is not just about tongue-numbing and tear-inducing spices. Regional, ethnic-migrant and fusion styles of cooking combine to create a variety of exciting and complex flavours that appeal even to the serious gourmand

Thai food is expanding faster globally than any other cuisine, and it's easy to see why. Less a dining experience than a sensory overload on different levels, it's one of the few cuisines in the world capable of drawing people to a country purely on its own merit.

It may be the explosive spiciness of Thai food that initially overwhelms, but what's most impressive is the extraordinary complex balance of flavours that lie underneath. And contrary to what most people think, Thai cuisine is not all blatantly spicy; most Thai meals will include a sampling of less aggressive dishes, some subtly flavoured with only garlic and mild herbs.

The variety of foods and cooking styles is immense, as each of Thailand's four regions have given rise to distinct cuisine variations. The northeast is influenced by Laos, the south by Malaysia and Indonesia, the central area by the cuisine of the Royal Thai kitchens (the one foreigners are probably most familiar with) and the north by Myanmar and Yunnan (in China).

Tourist centres such as Bangkok, Chiang Mai, Pattaya, Phuket and Ko Samui have restaurants as diverse as Brazilian, French, Japanese and Italian (the country's favourite foreign food). Adding excitement, especially in Bangkok, are restaurants experimenting boldly with Thai and Western ingredients and methods of preparation.

How to eat Thai food

Most Thai meals have dishes placed in the middle of the table to be shared by all; the larger the group, the more dishes you get to try. For novices

to Asian-style dining, the proper etiquette is to dish out a heap of rice onto your plate together with small portions of various dishes at the side (it's polite to take only a little at a time).

Eat with a fork and spoon, using the fork in the left hand to push food onto the spoon. Chopsticks are only for Chinese and noodle dishes. For soupy noodle dishes, use the chopsticks to pile noodles onto the spoon with a little broth.

Rice is the staple (*see page 87*); in the past it sustained workers throughout the day with just small portions of chilli, curry or sauce added for flavour. Even now, many rural Thais eat large helpings of rice with just small morsels of dried or salted fish. Jasmine-scented

LEFT: gourmet Thai cuisine.
RIGHT: chillies add the all-important fire.

Thai rice is one of the most delicious varieties found in Asia.

Condiments on the table usually include such items as dried, ground red chilli, sliced chilli with vinegar, sliced chilli with the ubiquitous *nam pla* (fish sauce), and white sugar. These are mainly used to add extra flavour to noodle dishes.

Northern cuisine

This is the mildest of Thai food. Northerners generally eat *khao nio* (sticky rice), kneading it into a ball to dip into sauces and curries such as the Burmese-inspired *kaeng hanglay*, a sweet-

and-tamarind-sour pork dish. The noodle dish called *khao soi* is also found in Myanmar, but it is possibly of Chinese origin. Usually made with chicken, it has fresh egg noodles swimming in a mild coconut curry, with crispy noodles sprinkled on top.

Other northern Thai specialities include sausages, such as the spicy pork *sai oua* (roasted over a coconut husk fire to impart aroma and flavour) and *naem* (fermented raw pork and pork skin seasoned with garlic and chilli). *Laab* is a popular salad dish of minced pork, chicken, beef or fish served with mint leaves and raw vegetables to reduce the heat of the spices. It's also commonly served in the northeast region.

Northern-style dipping sauces include *nam prik ong* (minced pork, mild chillies, tomatoes, garlic and shrimp paste), and the potent classic, *nam prik noom* (grilled chillies, onions and garlic). Both are eaten with the popular snack called *khaep moo* (crispy pork rind).

> The small but very fiery Thai chillies (prik) come in red or green forms, but both pack a potent punch. When sliced and served in fish sauce (nam pla) *as a condiment, it's called* prik nam pla.

Northeastern cuisine

The food of the northeastern (Isaan) region is generally simple peasant fare, usually spicy, and eaten with mounds of sticky rice kept warm in bamboo baskets. Spicy dishes include the ever-popular *som tam* (shredded green papaya, garlic, chillies, lime juice, and variations of tomatoes, dried shrimp, preserved crab and fermented fish) and a version of *laab* sausage, which is spicier and more sour than its northern counterpart.

But perhaps the most popular Isaan food, *gai yang*, is not spicy at all. This is chicken grilled in an aromatic marinade of peppercorns, garlic, fish sauce, coriander and palm sugar, then chopped into bite-sized pieces and served with both spicy and sweet dipping sauces.

Southern cuisine

The south – notable for some of Thailand's most fiery dishes – also has gentler specialities such as *khao yam*, a mild salad of rice, vegetables, pounded dried fish and a southern fish sauce called *budu*. Slightly spicier is *phad sataw*, a stir-fry usually of pork or shrimp, and *sataw*, a large lima bean look-alike with a strong flavour and aroma. *Khao moke gai* is delicious roasted chicken with turmeric-seasoned yellow tinted rice, like an Indian-style *biryani*, often sprinkled with crispy fried onions.

Spicy southern dishes include *kaeng tai plaa*. Fishermen who needed food that would last for days out at sea are said to have created this dish by blending the fermented stomachs of fish

LEFT: Isaan food featuring *gai yang* (fried chicken) and *som tam* papaya salad. **RIGHT:** *tom yum goong* soup. **FAR RIGHT:** *kaeng massaman*, a southern Thai Muslim-style curry.

with chillies, bamboo shoots, vegetables and an intensely hot sauce. An even hotter dish is *kaeng leuang* (yellow curry), a variant of the central Thai *kaeng som* curry, with fish, green papaya and bamboo shoots or palm hearts.

Central cuisine

Central cuisine, influenced by the royal palaces (*see panel, below*), includes many of the dishes made internationally famous at Thai restaurants abroad. It's notable for the use of coconut milk and garnishes such as grapes, which mellow the chilli heat of the fiery dishes and add a tinge of sweetness. Trademark dishes include *tom kha*

gai (a soup of chicken, coconut milk and galangal) the celebrated *tom yum goong* (hot and sour shrimp soup) and *kaeng khio waan* (green curry with chicken or beef, basil leaves and pea-sized aubergines). Another influence on the regional cuisine is the large Chinese presence – stir-fries and noodle dishes are commonplace.

Local specialities

A lack of rural transport infrastructure until the late 20th century and geographical obstacles, such as the mountains in the north, have resulted in significant local variations within the four regions of Thailand, often forged by

ORIGINS OF ROYAL THAI CUISINE

The so-called Royal Thai cuisine has had an enormous influence on the food of central Thailand, with popular dishes such as green curry or *kaeng khio waan* (made with beef or chicken) and the hot-and-sour shrimp soup called *tom yum goong* originating in the royal kitchens. The great-grandson of King Rama IV, MR Sorut Visuddhi, co-owner of Bangkok's Thanying restaurant, a royal Thai restaurant that serves the recipes of his mother, Princess Sulap-Walleng Visuddhi, explains: "In the palace it was considered bad manners to perspire at the table or to eat foods that had strong smells. So we would use coconut milk to cut down on these tastes. This had a big influence on Central cooking."

The Grand Palace had many residences where *ahaan chawang* (food for the palace people) was prepared. Recipes spread through the wealthy classes via palace finishing schools and publications such as *Mae Krua Hua Baak*, the country's first cookbook, written by a descendant of King Rama II. Later, when the royal families moved out of the palaces, the kitchen hands they had hired began cooking the royal dishes for their own families. A number of royally connected restaurants began to open from the 1980s onwards, but few authentic ones remain today. The intricate fruit and vegetable carving you will see at fine Thai restaurants – like the Sala Rim Naam at the Oriental hotel – is also a legacy of Royal Thai cuisine.

ingredients available locally or the cultural character of village communities. Some towns are celebrated for "the best" version of a particular dish or product.

Phetchaburi, a coastal city south of Bangkok, is reputed to have the best palm sugar in Thailand. Consequently, it is famous for desserts, notably a legendary yellow bean pudding called *khanom mor keng*. Phetchaburi's central market also has stalls selling *khao chae*, which is rice in chilled water flavoured with fragrant herbs. The dish originated from the Mon, who populated areas mainly in the west of Thailand, from around the 6th century AD. Traditional Mon dishes are still found in stalls around Kanchanaburi, and in Bangkok, on the island of Ko Kret.

Close to the borders with Myanmar, near the towns of Sangklaburi, Mae Sot and Mae Hong Son, tea-leaf salads are common, along with a snack called *miang*, consisting of chopped ingredients like grated coconut, dried shrimp and chilli wrapped in tea leaves. By talking to locals while travelling, you will find some hidden culinary gems.

Kaeng is usually loosely translated as curry, but it covers a broad range, from thin soups to near-dry dishes such as the northern *kaeng ho*. Many *kaeng* are made with coconut cream, like *kaeng*

EATING INSECTS

Farmers in Thailand's northeast region make extra income by catching insects to sell to local food stalls. They may look gruesome and even revolting to the uninitiated, but these spiky and multi-legged critters are rich in nutrients. The *takkatan* (grasshopper) has the flavour of deep-fried crispy pork skin, the *mawn mai* (silkworm) is somewhat nutty, and if you fancy a *maeng da* (water beetle), the females displaying bright orange eggs are said to be the tastiest. Be sure to rip off the legs and shell first: they slide down your throat more easily. Insect cuisine is now also found in tourist areas, and insects are even canned for export, mainly to Japan.

pet (red curry), *kaeng khio waan* (green curry) and *kaeng massaman*, a rich, spicy-sweet dish of Persian origin with meat, potatoes and onions. *Kaeng* without coconut milk include what is known as "jungle curries", which are very spicy.

Fish and seafood often feature in Thai cooking. Trang is famous for its soft-shell crab, and if you're visiting Satun, be sure to try the speciality black fried squid cooked in its own ink. Other dishes to try are *hoi malaeng poo op maw din* (mussels in their shells, steamed in a clay pot with lime juice and herbs) and *poo pat pong karee* (steamed chunks of crab in an egg-thickened curry with crunchy spring onions). Mud crabs caught fresh on the Gulf coast beyond Chonburi are said to be the best in Thailand.

Meat

Meat – usually chicken, pork or beef – is cooked in all manner of styles, such as *muu thawd kratiam prik Thai* (pork fried with garlic and black pepper) or the sweet-and-sour pork dish called *muu pad prio waan*, probably of Portuguese origin, although brought to Thailand by Chinese immigrants. *Neua pad nam man hoi* is beef fried with oyster sauce, spring onions and mushrooms. The popular and spicy *pat pet pat bai kaprao* dishes include meat stir-fried with chillies, garlic, onions and holy basil (*bai kaprao*). The main ingredients to note in Thai cuisine are: chicken (*gai*), pork

yai), narrow (*sen lek*) or very narrow (*sen mee*), and with broth (*sai naam*) or without (*haeng*).

Common dishes are *kuay tiaw raad naa* (rice noodles flash-fried and topped with sliced meat and greens in a thick, mild sauce) and *paad thai* (narrow pan-fried rice noodles with egg, dried and fresh shrimp, spring onions, tofu, crushed peanuts and bean-sprouts) – one of the best-known Thai dishes in the West. In *mee krawp*, the rice noodles are fried crispy, tossed in sweet-and-sour sauce and topped with sliced chillies, pickled garlic and slivers of orange rind.

Many lunchtime rice dishes are of Chinese origin. They include the popular *khao man gai*

(*moo*), beef (*neua*), duck (*ped*), seafood (*talay*) and shrimp (*goong*). In remote northern villages you can still find wild foods such as snake, turtles and deer, while in the northeast, frogs, lizards and insects are commonly eaten (*see panel, opposite*).

Noodles and rice

Noodles – a Chinese import – are ubiquitous all over Thailand, and come in two types: *kuay tiaw*, made from rice flour, and *ba mee*, from wheat flour. Both can be ordered broad (*sen*

FAR LEFT & LEFT: street food at a Khon Kaen market, featuring an edible cricket. **ABOVE:** a food stall on Bangkok's Khao San Road.

DINING OPTIONS AND COSTS

Major cities have a range of international cuisine, but elsewhere the options will be almost exclusively Thai. If you're anywhere near the coast, check out the local seafood for the giant prawns, crab and lobster. Eating out is still cheap. Roadside stalls can serve up delicious noodle soup, or *kuaytiaw*, for 30–50 baht, while the bill for a full meal with alcohol at most restaurants will rarely exceed 1,000 baht (around US$30) per head. Expect to pay around 400 baht (around US$12) per head on average. Service charges are sometimes included; if not, a 10 percent tip is appreciated. Most restaurants are open throughout the day, closing around 11pm.

(chicken with rice cooked in chicken broth), *khao moo daeng* (with Chinese red pork) and *khao kaa moo* (with stewed pork leg and greens).

At night and in the early morning, two soup-like rice dishes are favoured by Thais: *khao tom*, which comes in the water it was boiled in (with additions such as garlic-fried pork, salted egg or pickled ginger), and the close relative *joke*, which is porridge-like rice seasoned with minced pork, chopped coriander leaves and slivers of fresh ginger.

Thai desserts

Khanom (desserts) come in a bewildering variety,

lising flavour comes from crisp fried onions. Look out for vendors who sell *khanom beuang*, crispy shells filled with strands of egg yolk

> If you sample nothing else in Thailand, don't miss the heavenly khao niao ma-muand *(sweet mango with sticky rice and coconut cream).*

cooked in syrup with shredded coconut, sweet and spicy dried shrimp, coriander and coconut cream.

from feathery light concoctions with crushed ice and syrup, to custards, ice creams and an entire category of cakes based on egg yolks cooked in flower-scented syrups. After-meal desserts, served in small bowls, are generally light and elegant. *Kluay buat chee* has banana slices in sweetened and salted warm coconut cream. *Kluay kaek* uses bananas sliced lengthwise, dipped in coconut cream and rice flour, and deep-fried until crisp. Another favourite is *taap tim krawp* (water chestnut pieces covered in red-dyed tapioca flour and served in coconut cream and crushed ice), and *sangkhaya ma-praoawn*, a coconut cream custard steamed in a coconut or a small pumpkin.

Many desserts are inventive – you may finish a rich pudding before realising that its tanta-

Refreshments

With meals, Thais drink locally brewed beers such as Singha, Kloster and the stronger Beer Chang. Many city restaurants have a decent selection of wines (although very expensive, due to high taxes), with the wine lists in the top Bangkok restaurants being particularly eclectic.

Among Thailand's working classes, rice whisky brands like Maekhong and Saeng Thip are popular, usually served as a "set" with ice, soda and lime. Fresh fruit juices and iced drinks will often get a good splash of syrup (and salt) unless you request otherwise. ❑

LEFT: rice cakes. **ABOVE:** Thai desserts often feature fruit and a savoury item such as sticky rice.

Culture of Rice

A central pillar of Thai culture, the planting and harvesting of the staple crop has an important unifying role in rural society

The Thai expression *kin khao* is translated as "to eat", but it actually means "to eat rice". Indeed, in this land where rice has been a staple for centuries, the two are synonymous.

Cultivating rice is by necessity a cooperative effort, tightening the bonds of family and community. According to tradition, a farmer can ask fellow villagers to help with the work, and without having to pay for their labour. All that is expected from the host is a meal during the day, and perhaps some rice liquor in the evening. In the countryside, nearly everyone is drafted in to help with the preparation of paddy fields and the sowing of seed. Children are on holiday from school, as they will be when harvesting begins later in the year *(see below)*.

The social importance of this cooperation can hardly be exaggerated. It has a direct influence on individual behaviour, because if there are problems between individuals, families and communities, the work may not get done. Moreover, it is believed that quarrelling will upset the rice spirit and the crop may fail.

The rice-planting season – there is just one harvest each year – begins in May, when the king presides over the ancient ploughing ceremony at Sanam Luang, in Bangkok. This Brahmanic rite *(see panel, page 62, and Travel Tips, page 410)* symbolises the attention that the spirits give to the prospects for the forthcoming rice harvest. Soon after the rice seedlings are transplanted into the paddy fields, villagers leave token packets of rice and other food in the fields, as offerings to the rice spirit.

Another rice-related ceremony is the Boon Bang Fai, or skyrocket festival, which takes place at the start of the monsoon season to encourage abundant rains. It has Buddhist origins, although there are also elements of Brahmanism and animism. The traditional Buddhist account is that Boon Bang Fai began at the death of the Lord Buddha, when one of his grieving disciples, unable to reach his torch to the top of the funeral pyre, hurled it up to the top in a manner similar to the appearance of skyrockets being launched. Villagers make their own rockets with gunpowder, firing them from a ladder-like structure, or from a very tall tree. Monks are involved, and if the rockets do not go off properly, the monks will lose prestige.

The cooperative effort given to the rice crop continues through the growing months. One of the most onerous tasks is keeping birds away from the ripening grain. By early December, the rice is ripe enough for harvesting in the central plains and the north. The harvest comes later in the south. Harvesting schedules are fixed by common consent within each village.

Finally, when the rice has been harvested and is safely stored away, the farmers can relax and enjoy themselves. And it is then that they celebrate Songkran – the most joyous festival of the year, which marks the beginning of the traditional Thai new year, in April.

Yet there are, inevitably, some changes to this age-old ritual. Large-scale commercial farmers and agribusiness companies produce rice on an industrial scale. Chemicals have now supplanted the powers of the rice spirit. Former farmers have left their fields altogether, and instead work on roads, drive trucks and maintain tractors. Rice is no longer the top Thai export, although it is still a vital one – Thailand continues to remain the world's top rice exporter, earning over US$2 billion annually. ❑

RIGHT: the rice harvest near Mae Sariang.

ARCHITECTURE

The stunning temples of Thailand are a microcosm of
the Buddhist world, while the traditional Thai house –
many of which have been turned into museums –
reflects a near-perfect adaptation to the environment

As is the case for much of Thailand's artistic expression, many of the country's
finest temples, palaces and other noteworthy buildings show the influences of several
cultures, yet at the same time are all identifiably
Thai. Indian, Khmer, Burmese and Chinese
architectural styles have all had substantial
impact on Thai design through the centuries,
but there is no mistaking the bright colours, the
swooping multi-tiered roof lines, the ornamental decorations, the stunning interior murals
and the lovingly crafted gold-adorned Buddha
images that define the Thai style.

Temple architecture

Any study of Thai architecture begins with the
temple, or *wat (see also photo feature on pages
92–3)*, which has asumed the traditional role as
school, community centre, hospital and entertainment venue, as well as a place of community worship and where lessons on Buddhism
were taught. There are approximately 32,000
temples in Thailand today.

Temple compounds can be vast like Wat Pho
in Bangkok, or modest, as is the case in most
villages. Whatever their size, temples usually
include a *bot* (ordination hall), a *viharn* (sermon
hall), dome-shaped *chedi*, where relics of the
Buddha or other holy people may be housed,
as well as towering, phallic-like spires called
prang, epitomised by Wat Arun *(see page 119)*
in Bangkok. In addition, there might be ancil-
lary temple structures such as a *sala* (open-sided
pavilions), *guti* (living quarters for monks) and
a *ho trai* (Buddhist scripture library).

Symbolism abounds in the ornate decoration
found in Thai temples. The ends of temple columns are often shaped like water lilies or lotus

buds: the lotus symbolises the purity of the
Buddha's thoughts in the same way it pushes
through the muck to burst forth in extraordinary beauty. The *bot* is always bounded by
eight stones, believed to keep away evil spirits,
an example of how animist beliefs coexist with
Buddhism. Roof peaks are often adorned with
chofa, the curling, pointed extensions at each
end that represent the *garuda*, the vehicle of
Vishnu. Thai palace architecture too is fairly
similar to that of the temple, employing many
of the same motifs and construction materials.

Regional influences

Regional influences have also left their mark
on Thai temples. Northeastern Thailand was

once part of the sprawling Khmer empire of Cambodia. Hence temples like Prasat Hin Khao Phanom Rung *(see page 342)* and Prasat Khao Phra Viharn *(see page 344)* are boldy Khmer in style. In the north, many of the older and less well-known temples are Burmese in style, constructed during the Burmese occupation of what was then the Kingdom of Lanna.

Window panels and murals in Bangkok's old temples cross many cultural and international boundaries, and are often decorated with Chinese dragons, mythological figures from the Indian *Ramayana* and foreign merchants wearing distinctly European garb.

nated village life, with a few rooms or one large divided room elevated on pilings, characterised the earliest homes. The structures were positioned to shed rain and take advantage of the prevailing winds, and many of the components were prefabricated, then fitted together with wooden pegs.

Over time, the houses were raised higher on stilts to protect the home from flooding and unwanted animals, while creating a space beneath the house for keeping livestock or to be used for daily work such as weaving. Such homes are common in villages throughout Thailand today, although in urban areas,

Traditional houses

Homes for ordinary Thai people share the same sensitive treatment as those for the wealthy. Thai-style teak houses, with their inward-sloping walls and steep roofs, seldom fail to impress with their airiness and their adaptation to the tropical climate.

Like the temple, the Thai house has gone through centuries-old evolution. Some trace the style to southern China, the origin of much of today's Thai population. Steep roofs, sometimes multi-layered like the temples that domi-

LEFT: Wat Thammamongkol in Bangkok. **ABOVE:** Jim Thompson's House. **RIGHT:** central *chedi* at Wat Phra Mahathat, Nakhon Si Thammarat.

DOMESTIC DESIGNS

The architectural styles of traditional homes vary from one region to the other, although some characteristics are common throughout. In the flat Central Plain north of Bangkok, an open veranda is often the focus of home life – it becomes an outside living space. In north Thailand, where dry-season temperatures are lower, the ventilation and living spaces are designed to retain warmth. In most traditional dwellings, the central innermost room is both a sleeping area and the abode for any ancestral spirits.

Outside most Thai homes and commercial buildings stands the spirit house *(see page 64)*, varying between plain and modest, or gaudy and large.

nearly all houses are more Western in design and steadfastly anchored to the ground with brick and mortar. Most of the early homes were made of native woods such as teak and bamboo, materials that are rarely used today as teak is expensive and hard to come by. Jim Thompson's House *(see page 128)*, Suan Pakkad Palace *(page 131)* and Kamthieng House *(page 135)* are fine examples of grand Thai houses. Numerous, albeit humbler, examples line the banks of the canals that crisscross Bangkok's Thonburi suburbs.

In south Thailand, a different design evolved, featuring shorter pillars, no exterior veranda, and windows with hinged shutters that closed from the top during torrential monsoon rains.

Western influences

With the arrival of Western traders and missionaries in Bangkok in the 18th century, Western architectural design started to make its presence felt. This was further bolstered by trips to Europe by the Thai monarchy in the 19th century. By the mid-19th century, Western-style buildings were taking root alongside traditional Thai structures on both sides of the Chao Phraya River, the centre of Bangkok's government and commerce.

HOTEL HIGH-STYLE

Thailand is a cut above the rest of Asia when it comes to design and high style, evident in the raft of hotels that have opened in recent years. It's almost impossible to come up with a definitive list of the country's best hotels and resorts, as the choices are just too varied and too many. Most will agree that the ones listed here are worthy of mention, having been lavishly awarded or praised in the international media.

Bangkok: Urbane **The Metropolitan** (www.metropolitan. bangkok.como.bz), resort-like **The Sukhothai** (www. sukhothai.com), chic **Conrad Bangkok** (www.conradhotels. com) and **Peninsula** (www.peninsula.com) are all high-end options. Cheaper but just as stylish is the **Arun Residence** (www.arunresidence.com).

Chiang Mai: **The Four Seasons Chiang Mai** (www. fourseasons.com) has always been a hip outpost. Newer places include **The Rachamankha** (www.rachamankha. com) and **The Chedi** (www.ghmhotels.com).

Beaches: Closer to Bangkok, the best luxury boltholes are **Aleenta** (www.aleenta.com) in Pranburi and **Alila Cha-Am** (www.alilahotels.com) at Cha-am. In Phuket is the much-lauded **Amanpuri** (www.amanpuri.com) and more affordable **Twinpalms** (www.twinpalms-phuket.com). North of Phuket on Ko Racha is the minimalist **The Racha** (www.theracha. com). Other contenders are **Rayavadee** (www.rayavadee. com) in Krabi, **Zeavola** in Ko Phi Phi (www.zeavola.com) and **Four Seasons** in Koh Samui (www.fourseasons.com).

Some of this early architecture still stands today, including the original Author's Wing of the Oriental Hotel (see page 133) as well as the French Embassy, the East Asiatic Company and the Old Customs House, all designed by European architects and found within walking distance of each other along the riverside near Thanon Silom. The Vimanmek Mansion (page 123), in Bangkok's Dusit district, built entirely of teak but decidedly more Western than Thai, the monumental Grand Palace (page 112) with its Western neoclassical features, and the Italianate palace built by King Chulalongkorn at Bang Pa-In (page 161) near Ayutthaya, offer ample evidence of Thailand's passionate embrace of Western styles, which continues to this day.

Another legacy of this era are the shophouses built in the Sino-Portuguese style. These narrow and long two-storey linked buildings with ornate window and roof treatments can still be seen near the Tha Chang boat landing along the Chao Phraya River in Bangkok, as well as Thanon Thalang in Phuket and Thanon Charoenrat in Chiang Mai. As in the past, the ground floor of the structure serves as a shop, while the family lives on the floor above.

Contemporary architecture

Most contemporary architectural efforts show little regard for the past, as hundreds of functional high-rises appear each year in the cities, while cardboard-copy rows of townhouses are erected for the country's growing middle class in the suburbs and small towns. During the building boom of the 1980s and '90s, many architects tried to outdo each other and some fairly quirky designs evolved in Bangkok. Some of the more successful designs include the UOB Building at the corner of Thanon Sathorn and Soi Pikun. Looking more like the creation of a child's fantasy than a stuffy bank headquarters, it was designed by the country's foremost modern architect, Dr Sumet Jumsai, and is affectionately dubbed the "robot building". Complete with eyes and antennae, the robotic appearance is a symbol of modernisation in Thai banking.

Also of note is the 60-storey Thai Wah Tower II on Thanon Sathorn Tai, remarkable for its unusually slim profile and elegant open "sky deck" between the 51st and 54th floors. In the

north Bangkok business district at Soi Pahon Yothin is the whimsical Elephant Tower, which has three towers connected to form the shape of Thailand's national animal.

The end of the building boom came in 1997 with the Asian economic crisis. In the same year, Bangkok's tallest building, the 90-storey Baiyoke Tower II, on Thanon Rajpraprop, was completed. The tower has a revolving observation deck on the 84th floor that provides an eye-popping 360-degree view of the city.

Since 1997, economic stability has to a large extent returned to Thailand, and today, architectural trends lean towards the restoration of

traditional housing, as well as the creation of new buildings clad in steel and glass. Unfortunately, many of these are blights on the cityscape with little or no reference to the surroundings.

More successful are colonial-style residences that are being restored and converted for use as boutique hotels or museums. In Chiang Mai, one fine example, the Lanna Architectural Centre, now houses a museum devoted to Thai architecture. Another trend is the construction of luxurious new hotels (see panel, opposite) consciously designed to recreate traditional Thai aesthetics, or to incorporate these elements into creative modern architecture. This trend indicates a renewed cultural confidence increasingly appreciated by the Thais themselves. ❑

LEFT: Kamthieng House, Bangkok.
RIGHT: Bangkok's landmark Elephant Tower.

TEMPLE ART AND ARCHITECTURE

The temple, or *wat*, plays a vital role in every community, large and small; for many visitors, Thailand's temples are the country's most enduring sights

A typical Thai *wat* (temple) has two enclosing walls that separate it from the secular world. The monks' quarters are situated between the outer and inner walls. In larger temples, the inner walls may be lined with Buddha images and serve as cloisters for meditation. This part of the temple is called *buddhavasa* or *phutthawat*. Inside the inner walls is the bot or *ubosot* (ordination hall), surrounded by eight stone tablets and set on consecrated ground. This is the most sacred part of the temple – ordinations and special ceremonies are held here – and only monks can enter. The *bot* contains a Buddha image, but it is the *viharn* (sermon hall) that contains the principal Buddha images. Also in the inner courtyard are the bell-shaped *chedi* or *stupa* (relic towers), which contain the relics of the Buddha, as well as towering Cambodian-style spires called *prang*, which are a variation of the *chedi*.

Sala (open-sided pavilions) can be found all around the temple; the largest of these is the *sala kan prian* (study hall), used for afternoon prayers. Apart from Buddha images, various mythological creatures are found within the temple compound.

LEFT: Wat Si Sawai, Sukhothai, an example of the Khmer temple style that dominated the region during the years of Khmer hegemony.

BELOW: temple exteriors are often very ornate, such as that of the Bot of the Emerald Buddha at Wat Phra Kaew. Gold tiles, glass mosaic, lacquer and mother-of-pearl are some of the materials used.

LEFT: gilded *chofa* (the curling, pointed roof extensions), intricately carved gables, and green- and ochre-coloured tiles (said to resemble the scales of the *naga*, or serpent) are common features of Thai temple roofs.

ABOVE: a double gallery enclosing the *bot* of Wat Pho houses 394 seated bronze Buddha images. These were brought from Sukhothai and Ayutthaya during the reign of Rama I, and are of assorted periods and styles. The base of the main image contains the ashes of Rama I.

TEMPLE MURALS

Thai temple murals are created on a background that has been prepared and dried before the artist paints on it using coloured pigments mixed with glue. Often featured on the interior of temple walls, such murals depict the classic subjects of Thai painting, including tales from the *Jataka* (Buddha's birth and previous lives) and other Buddhist themes, and also vignettes of local life.

During the reign of Rama III (1824–51), mural painting reached its peak, with artists not only following the principles of traditional Thai art, but also introducing new elements, like Western perspective. The mural illustrated above, from Wat Suthat in Bangkok, is an example of the late 18th-century art style (better known as the Rattanakosin period).

BELOW: the Sri Lankan-influenced 15th-century *chedi* at Wat Sorosak at Sukothai is supported by a parade of elephants. Considered sacred, the elephant is an important motif in Thai (and Khmer) religious architecture.

ABOVE: the gleaming Phra Si Rattana Chedi at Wat Phra Kaew is bell-shaped with a ringed spire and a three-tiered base, a feature of Sri Lankan reliquary towers called *stupa*. Its surface is made up of thousands of tiny gold mosaic pieces.

ABOVE: these towering *chedi* at Wat Pho sit on square bases and have graceful and elegant proportions, reminiscent of the Lanna-style architecture of north Thailand. Decorated with coloured tiles, the *chedi* are memorials to the first four Chakri kings.

ABOVE: Wat Arun features five rounded *prang* – reflecting Cambodian-Khmer influence – encrusted with thousands of broken porcelain pieces, leftover ballast from Chinese ships that visited Bangkok in its early years.

PLACES

A detailed guide to the entire country,
with principal sites cross-referenced by
number to the accompanying maps

Diversity and contrast characterise both Thailand's people and its geography. Within an area of around 514,000 sq km (199,000 sq miles) – roughly the size of France – are an abundance of natural resources, tropical rainforests, broad plains and forest-clad hills.

This tropical bounty extends from the beautiful palm-lined beaches that line much of the 2,600km (1,600-mile) coastline to the 2,565-metre (8,415ft) peak of Doi Inthanon up in the north. Under the canopies of its tropical rainforests is a wide variety of animal life: iridescent kingfishers, parakeets, pheasants, hornbills, flying squirrels and lizards, gibbons, hundreds of species of butterflies, and nearly 1,000 varieties of orchids. A cornucopia of fruit grows wild in the jungles, or tended carefully on small family holdings and in larger plantations.

The northeast is dominated by the arid Khorat Plateau, where farmers struggle to cultivate rice, tapioca, jute and other cash crops. With strong cultural affinities with neighbouring Laos and Cambodia, the region is rimmed and defined by the Mekong River.

The north is a region of hills clad in teak forests and valleys carpeted with rice, fruit trees and vegetables, and bordered by Myanmar (Burma) and Laos.

In the central plains, monsoon rains transform the landscape into a vast hydroponic basin, which nourishes a sea of rice, the country's staple and an important export. Through this region flows the Chao Phraya River, or Mae Nam Chao Phraya (*mae nam* means river), carrying produce and people south to Bangkok, washing rich sediment down from the northern hills and, during the monsoons, flooding the rice fields.

The south of Thailand runs down a long, narrow arm of land leading to Malaysia. An area strongly influenced by Malay culture and Islam, this southern isthmus is peppered by rubber and palm-oil plantations that alternate with rice and fruit trees. ❏

PRECEDING PAGES: the three Khmer-style *prang* of Prang Sam Yot at Lopburi; Wat Phra Kaew detail; view of Bangkok from Sirocco restaurant. **LEFT:** west-coast scenery at Krabi. **TOP:** the triple *chedi* of Wat Phra Sri Sanphet, Ayutthaya. **ABOVE LEFT:** a longtail boat. **ABOVE RIGHT:** Pattaya seafront.

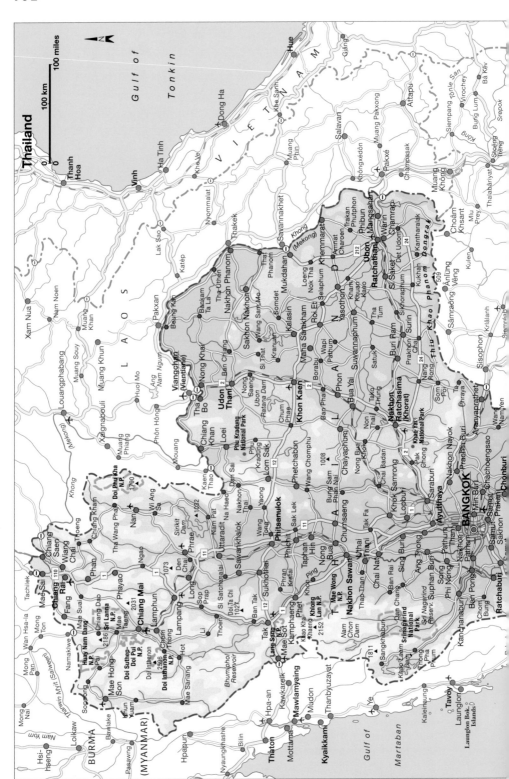

Thailand

100 miles

100 km

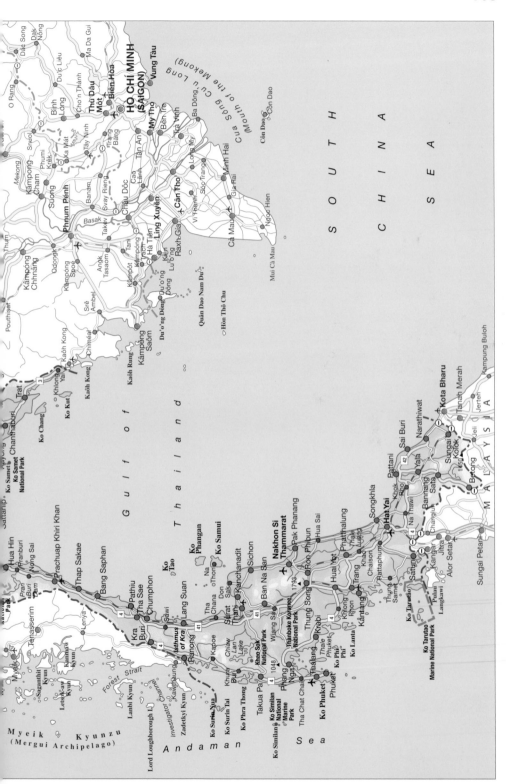

BANGKOK AND SUBURBS

City of Angels, or City of Angles? There's always another twist and turn in steamy yet chic Bangkok, as the Thai capital continues to reinvent itself

As the capital of Thailand, Bangkok may have seen some political ups and downs in recent years, but as a metropolis in its own right, it's been developing in leaps and bounds. Gleaming glass-and-steel towers continue to alter the horizon, the infamous traffic snarls have become slightly less pervasive, thanks to the Skytrain and an underground Metro line, and the pollution is noticeably less smothering. Sure, there are grubby parts and the steamy heat still socks you in the face, particularly if you visit in muggy April. And while the economy has been shaken by domestic and international events, it hasn't dampened Bangkok's reputation as Asia's urban centre of cool.

With hip hotels like the Metropolitan and Sukhothai and a clutch of über-cool nightlife spots led by the white-hot Bed Supperclub, Bangkok is a modish destination for the 21st century. The dining scene hasn't lagged far behind. Stylishly minimalist cafés like Greyhound have become *de rigueur* with the city's fashionable set, and wait until you try Thai food within the rarefied atmosphere of Mahanaga, which mixes North African, Thai and Indian design accents.

With its feet set firmly in the present, Bangkok hardly qualifies as an Asian backwater. The shopping, too, has gone up a notch in the design stakes. The traditional goods for which Thai artisans are so famous are still there – silver jewellery, tribal handicrafts and the like – but young Thai entrepreneurs are fast making a name for themselves with bold designs in clothing and fashion, accessories, furniture and home decor.

Thankfully, Bangkok hasn't become too painfully hip. Many of the traditional markers are still there: the golden spires of Buddhist temples and saffron-robed monks with arms outstretched for offerings, mobile food stalls trundling the streets, and the warm smiles that are the icon of Thailand. Urban life has changed much of Bangkok's sensibilities, but it's a rare Thai who doesn't seek out *sanuk* (fun), whether dining at a chic French restaurant or huddled around a pavement table piled with Singha beer and street food. ❏

LEFT: live jazz performance at The Saxophone. **ABOVE LEFT:** fresh-flower vendor at Thanon Silom. **ABOVE RIGHT:** a frenetic bout of *muay thai* kick-boxing – Thailand's most popular sport.

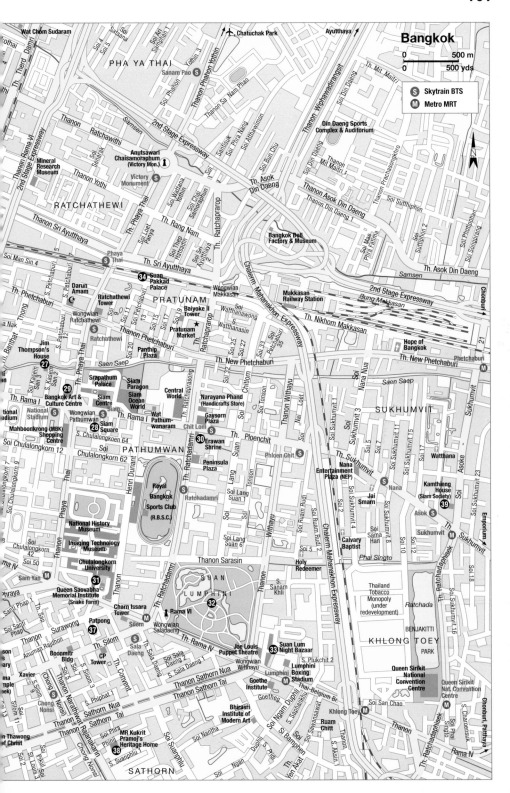

BANGKOK

Thailand's capital offers a mind-blowing array of experiences: royal architecture at Rattanakosin, spirituality at ancient Buddhist temples, shopping at raucous street markets and hip mega malls. Come evening, there are eateries and nightspots galore

A t first glance, this Asian super-city of nearly 10 million people seems like a bewildering amalgam of new, old and indeterminate, as well as exotic, commonplace and indescribable, all tossed together into a gigantic urban maze. It's hardly surprising that Bangkok should convey this impression, considering that only a little more than half a century ago, much of what makes up the Thai capital was farmland. Despite the construction of the Skytrain and Metro mass transit networks which have done much to make this vast city more navigable – and comprehensible – the traveller's mental map of Bangkok needs a few pointers in order to aid orientation.

The long and winding Chao Phraya River is the city's most obvious landmark, and cradles many of the city's most important sites on its eastern bank. On the western side of the river, Thonburi's canals thread through colourful residential neighbourhoods.

In the late 18th century Bangkok's founding king, Rama I, ordered the construction of a canal between two of the river's bends and sliced off a parcel of land into an artificial island called Rattanakosin. This is the location of the glittering Grand Palace and Wat Phra Kaew, an essential part of any city tour.

Just south of Rattanakosin are the enclaves where foreigners originally settled: Chinatown, Little India (or Pahurat) and Thanon Silom. Today, Silom, together with Thanon Sathorn and Thanon Sukhumvit further east, have become important business and commercial centres.

RATTANAKOSIN

The establishment of the royal district of **Phra Nakorn**, centred on the island of **Rattanakosin**, marked Bangkok's rise in 1782 as the new capital of Thailand. Rattanakosin's foundations were based on the former capital of

---

Main attractions

WAT PHRA KAEW AND
   GRAND PALACE
NATIONAL MUSEUM
WAT PHO
WAT ARUN
MUSEUM OF ROYAL BARGES
LOHA PRASAT
VIMANMEK MANSION
WAT BENJAMABOPHIT
CHINATOWN
JIM THOMPSON'S HOUSE
ERAWAN SHRINE
PATPONG NIGHT MARKET
BANGKOK ART AND CULTURE
   CENTRE (BACC)

LEFT: Skytrain station. **RIGHT:** *kinnaree* statue at Wat Phra Kaew.

Yaksha, a half-demon, half-god protector at Wat Phra Kaew.

BELOW & BELOW RIGHT: the Wat Phra Kaew and Grand Palace complex.

Ayutthaya, which was abandoned after being ransacked by the Burmese in 1767 *(see page 37)*. The majestic Grand Palace formed its epicentre, moats and ramparts created a stronghold, while canals were dug to transport people across marsh and swampland.

Rattanakosin brims with architectural grandeur; it contains many government offices as well as two of Thailand's most respected universities – Thammasat and Silpakorn. It is also the religious and ceremonial nucleus of the country. Best explored on foot, the area's proximity to the river means that it can be conveniently accessed by water transport.

Wat Phra Kaew and Grand Palace complex

Jostling among throngs of tourists may not engender the most romantic vision of exotic Thailand, but the dignified splendour of two of Bangkok's principal attractions – Wat Phra Kaew and the Grand Palace – is breathtaking in spite of the pressing crowds. These two structures are an arresting spectacle of form and colour, comprising glistening golden *chedi*, soaring glass mosaic-

studded pillars, towering mythological gods and fabulously ornate temple and palace edifices.

The site originally spread over 160 hectares (400 acres) around this strategic locale by the banks of the Chao Phraya River. It was initiated by King Rama I in 1782, who ordered a new residence built to house the Emerald Buddha, the country's most revered religious image, as well as a palace befitting the new capital of Bangkok. The entire compound is surrounded by high crenellated walls, securing a self-sufficient city within a city.

The only entrance (and exit) to the **Wat Phra Kaew and Grand Palace ❶** complex is along Thanon Na Phra Lan to the north (daily 8.30am–3.30pm; charge includes entry to Vimanmek and several other sights in Dusit; www.palaces.thai.net). Make sure you are dressed appropriately *(see margin tip, page 112)* and disregard touts who linger outside the complex telling you that it is closed for a major festival (unfortunately, many tourists fall for this age-old scam). It's worthwhile hiring the informative audio guide (B100,

with passport/credit card deposit; in eight languages). If you prefer, official guides (B300) are also available near the ticket office.

The complex is loosely divided into two, with the Wat Phra Kaew encountered first to the left, and the Grand Palace and its peripheral buildings to the right. Most of the Grand Palace's interiors are not open to the public, but the exteriors are still nothing short of awesome.

Wat Phra Kaew

Wat Phra Kaew (Temple of the Emerald Buddha) serves as the royal chapel of the Grand Palace. The magnificent temple compound is modelled after palace chapels in the former capitals of Sukhothai and Ayutthaya, and contains typical monastic structures (with the exception of monks' living quarters – a feature found in most Thai temples).

At the main entrance to the temple compound is the statue of Shivaka Kumar Baccha, reputed to be the Buddha's private physician. First to catch the eye on the upper terrace on the left are the gleaming gold mosaic tiles

which adorn the Sri Lankan-style **Phra Si Rattana Chedi Ⓐ** – said to enshrine a piece of the Buddha's breastbone.

In the centre of the compound, **Phra Mondop Ⓑ** (Library of Buddhist Scriptures) is a delicately beautiful building, studded with blue-and-green glass mosaic and topped by a multi-tiered roof fashioned like the crown of a Thai king. The library is surrounded by statues of sacred white elephants.

Next door, **Prasat Phra Thep Bidom Ⓒ** (Royal Pantheon) contains life-size statues of the Chakri kings and is open to the public only on Chakri Day (6 April). Around the building stand marvellous gilded statues of mythological creatures, including the half-female, half-lion *aponsi*. The original pantheon was built in 1855, but was destroyed by fire and rebuilt in 1903. Flanking the entrance of the Prasat Phra Thep Bidom are two towering gilded *chedi*.

Behind Phra Mondop is a large **sandstone model of Angkor Wat**, built during King Rama IV's reign when Cambodia was a vassal Thai state. Just behind this, along the northern edge of the compound, the **Viharn**

TIP

Be sure to keep your admission ticket to the Wat Phra Kaew and Grand Palace (see opposite). This allows you access to many of Dusit's sights for free, like the Ananta Samakhom Throne Hall, Vimanmek Mansion, Abhisek Dusit Throne Hall and the Royal Elephant Museum.

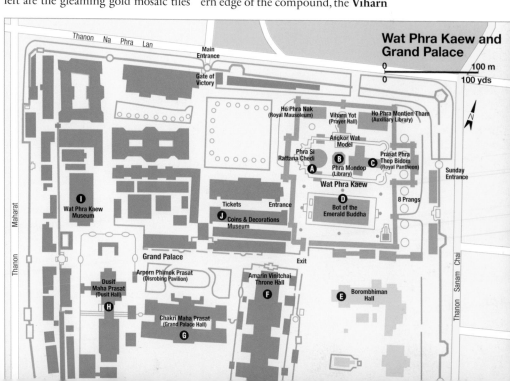

Wat Phra Kaew and Grand Palace

Yot (Prayer Hall) is flanked by the **Ho Phra Nak** (Royal Mausoleum) on the left and **Ho Phra Montien Tham** (Auxiliary Library) on the right.

Be sure to observe the walls of the cloister enclosing the temple courtyard. Painted with a picture book of murals telling the *Ramakien* epic, the Thai version of the Indian *Ramayana*, these were originally created during the reign of King Rama III (1824–50), and have been meticulously restored.

Around the cloisters, six pairs of towering *yaksha* (demons), again characters from the *Ramakien*, stand guard, armed with clubs, protecting the Emerald Buddha. At the complex's eastern edge are eight Khmer-style *prang* structures, which represent Buddhism's Eightfold Path.

The Emerald Buddha

Wat Phra Kaew's most sacred structure is the **Bot of the Emerald Buddha D**. Outside, at the open-air shrine, the air is always alive with suppliants' murmured prayers and heavy with the scent of floral offerings and smouldering joss sticks.

BELOW: gilded *garuda* images encircle the exterior of the Bot of the Emerald Buddha.

At the top of the elaborate golden 11-metre (36ft) altar, in a glass case and protected by an ornate nine-tiered umbrella, sits the country's most celebrated image, the diminutive 75cm (30-inch) tall Emerald Buddha, which, surprisingly, is not made of emerald but carved from a solid block of green jade. Many non-Buddhists are invariably disappointed by the size of the statue (it's hard to get a clear view of it from ground level), but its power and importance should be instantly apparent from the demeanour of the pilgrims inside the hall.

Said to bestow good fortune on the kingdom that possesses it, the statue is of unknown origin; legend claims the Emerald Buddha image was carved in India, but stylistically, its design is more reminiscent of 13th- or 14th-century Thai craftsmanship – the statue was found in Chiang Rai in 1434. Kept hidden in a *chedi*, the story goes that the image was only later revealed when the *chedi* was struck by lightning. It was removed to Luang Prabang and remained in Laos until the Thais seized it back in 1779. King Rama I brought the statue to Bangkok in 1784.

The Grand Palace

Adjoining Wat Phra Kaew, the **Grand Palace** embodies Thailand's characteristic blend of temporal and spiritual elements, and has been added to or modified by every Thai king since it was first built. The result is a mélange of architectural styles, from traditional Thai, Khmer and Chinese to British, French and Italian Renaissance. In the early 20th century, the royal abode shifted to the more private Chitralada Palace in Dusit district (*see page 123*), with the Grand Palace now reserved only for special ceremonies and state visits.

Palace buildings

Exiting Wat Phra Kaew, immediately to the left and tucked behind a closed gate guarded by a sentry is the French-inspired **Borombhiman Hall E**. It was built in 1903 as a residence for King Rama VI but is now reserved as a state guesthouse for dignitaries.

To the right, the **Amarin Vinitchai Throne Hall** ❻ is part of the three-building Phra Maha Montien complex. Originally a royal residence, it contains the bedchamber of King Rama I.

In a large courtyard adjacent to the throne hall stands the triple-spired royal residence, and the grandest building in the complex – the **Chakri Maha Prasat** ❼ (Grand Palace Hall). This two-storey hall was constructed during King Chulalongkorn's reign (1868–1910) to commemorate the 100th anniversary of the Chakri Dynasty in 1882. An impressive mixture of Thai and Western architecture, it was designed by British architects. The Thai spires, however, were added at the eleventh hour, following protests that it was improper for a hallowed Thai site to be dominated by a European-style building.

The top floor contains golden urns with ashes of the Chakri kings; the first floor still functions as an audience chamber for royal banquets and state visits, while the ground floor is now a **Weapons Museum**. Outside, the courtyard is dotted with ornamental ebony trees pruned in the Japanese *bonsai* style.

The next building of interest is the **Dusit Maha Prasat** ❽ (Dusit Hall), built in 1789 by King Chakri (Rama I) to replace an earlier wooden structure. A splendid example of classical Thai architecture, its four-tiered roof supports an elegant nine-level spire. To its left stands the exquisite **Arporn Phimok Prasat** (Disrobing Pavilion). It was built to the height of the king's palanquin so that His Excellency could alight from his elephant and don his ceremonial hat and gown before proceeding to the audience hall.

Opposite, don't miss the collection of small but exquisite Buddha images made of silver, ivory, crystal and other materials at the **Wat Phra Kaew Museum** ❿.

On the way out, next to the ticket office, the **Coins and Decorations Museum** ⓳ has a collection that dates from the 11th century as well as royal regalia, decorations and medals made of gold and precious stones.

Worshipper outside the Bot of the Emerald Buddha.

BELOW: the large grounds fronting the Chakri Maha Prasat.

Lak Muang

Every Thai city has a foundation stone or city pillar, known as the *lak muang (see page 64)*, around which the city's guardian spirits gravitate, protecting and bringing good fortune to worshippers. Bangkok was officially founded in 1782 when King Rama I erected the **Lak Muang ❷** (daily 5am–7pm; free), to mark the official centre of the capital.

Located across Thanon Sanam Chai from the eastern wall of the Grand Palace, the gilded wooden pillar resembles the Hindu Shiva *lingam*, which represents strength and potency. The pillar accompanies the taller Lak Muang of Thonburi, which was moved here when that district (and former capital) became part of Bangkok.

Sanam Luang

North of the Wat Phra Kaew and Grand Palace, the large oval greensward of **Sanam Luang ❸** (Royal Field) is the site of royal cremations as well as other important ceremonies. The field is par-

ticularly lively during the birthdays of King Bhumibol (5 December) and Queen Sirikit (12 August), the Songkran (New Year) festival in April and the Ploughing Ceremony in May. Most of the time, however, the often dusty field is filled with sleeping vagrants and evening soothsayers foretelling your destiny, and from February to April, kite-flyers.

National Museum

To the west of Sanam Luang at Thanon Na Phra That, the **National Museum ❹** (Wed–Sun 9am–4pm; charge; guided tours 9.30am on Wed and Thur; www.thailandmuseum.com) houses a vast collection of antiquities from all over Southeast Asia.

The museum has an interesting history of its own. Its grounds and some of the principal rooms were part of the former **Wang Na** (Front Palace) that belonged to the king's second-in-line, called the Prince Successor – a feature of the Thai monarchy until 1870.

The oldest buildings in the museum compound date from 1782, including the splendid **Buddhaisawan Chapel**.

Bangkok's Lak Muang (or City Pillar) houses the city's guardian spirits.

BELOW & BELOW RIGHT: Wat Pho's main *chedi* are dedicated to the Thai monarchs.

Built by the Prince Successor as his private place of worship, it contains some of Thailand's most beautiful and best-preserved murals (dating from the 1790s) as well as Thailand's second-most sacred Buddha image, Phra Buddha Sihing – which dates back to 13th-century Sukhothai.

To the left of the museum entrance, the **Sivamokhaphiman Hall** was originally an open-sided audience hall, but now houses a prehistoric art collection. The front of the building is devoted to the **Thai History Gallery**, documenting the country's history from the Sukhothai period (13th century) to the present Rattanakosin period (1782 onwards).

Also on site is the **Red House** (Tamnak Daeng), an old golden teak dwelling that once belonged to King Rama I's elder sister. Built in the Ayutthaya style, the house has an ornate wood finish and elegant early Bangkok-style furnishings.

The central audience hall of the Wang Na is divided into rooms (Nos 4–15) containing various ethnological exhibits like elephant *howdah*, woodcarvings, ceramics, palanquins, royal furnishings, weapons, *khon* masks, musical instruments and other treasures. Temporary exhibits are displayed in the Throne Hall.

Wat Mahathat

Nestled between Silpakorn and Thammasat universities, **Wat Mahathat ❺** (daily 7am–8pm; free) is best accessed from Sanam Luang. Founded in the 1700s, the temple also houses the **Maha Chulalongkorn Rajavidyalaya University**, one of the two highest seats of Buddhist learning in the country, where King Rama IV spent almost 25 years studying as a monk before acceding to the throne in 1851.

Wat Mahathat exudes a more genuine, working temple atmosphere than the more ceremonial temples in the area, with locals crowding in to receive spiritual tutelage. Those who are keen to get in tune with their inner selves may do so at the temple's **International Buddhist Meditation Centre** (www.mcu.ac.th/IBMC). The centre conducts regular classes and meditation retreats in English.

Apart from an outdoor herbal medicine mart, a fascinating **amulet market**

Amulets on display at Wat Mahathat's amulet market. These come in myriad forms and serve a variety of purposes, from religious or spiritual to the more practical, such as ensuring sexual potency (see also page 63).

BELOW: the National Museum.

Close-up of whorls on the toes of Wat Pho's Reclining Buddha.

BELOW: the giant Reclining Buddha at Wat Pho.

pitches along Trok Silpakorn alley, right between the temple and Silpakorn University. Amulets are mostly worn around the neck to ward off evil and attract good fortune (*see also page 63*).

Wat Pho

South of the Grand Palace and Wat Phra Kaew complex, on Thanon Thai Wang, **Wat Pho** ➏ (daily 8am–5pm; charge; www.watpho.com) is the city's largest and oldest surviving temple. Apart from its historic significance, visitors come to Wat Pho to pay homage to the monumental Reclining Buddha, and to unwind at the city's best traditional massage centre.

Also known as Wat Phra Chetuphon, the temple dates back to the 16th century. However, it did not achieve real importance until the establishment of Bangkok as the capital. Wat Pho was a particular favourite of the first four Bangkok kings, all of whom added to its treasures. The four towering coloured *chedi* to the west of the *bot* (ordination hall) are memorials to past monarchs, and around the hall are some 90 other *chedi*.

The temple cloisters contain almost 400 bronze Buddha images, retrieved from ancient ruins in Sukhothai and Ayutthaya. One of the most important additions was the Reclining Buddha, donated by King Rama III in 1832, who also converted the temple into the country's earliest place of public learning. The monarch instructed that the walls be inscribed with lessons on astrology, history and archaeology.

Wat Pho's giant Reclining Buddha, 46 metres (150ft) long and 15 metres (50ft) high, depicts the resting Buddha passing into *nirvana*. The flat soles of the Buddha's feet are inlaid with mother-of-pearl designs, illustrating the 108 auspicious signs for recognising Buddha. Also numbering 108 are the metallic bowls that span the wall; a coin dropped in each supposedly brings good luck to the devotee.

Wat Pho massages

Wat Pho became, and still is, the place to learn about traditional medicine, particularly massage and meditation. The temple's medicine pavilion displays stone tablets indicating benefi-

cial body points for massage. Skirting the temple grounds, several small rock gardens contain statues of hermits striking poses; these were used as diagnostic aids. The **Wat Pho Thai Traditional Massage School** (daily 10am–5pm; www.watpomassage.com) offers cheap hour-long massages, as well as courses for students of the art of Thai massage.

Wat Ratchabophit

Located on the opposite bank of Khlong Lord canal on Thanon Fuang Nakhon, **Wat Ratchabophit** ❼ (daily 5am–8pm, chapel 9–9.30am and 5.30–6pm; free), is recognisable for its characteristic amalgamation of Thai temple architecture and period European style; an unusual design fusion places the main circular *chedi* and its circular cloister in the centre. Inaugurated in 1869 by King Chulalongkorn (Rama V), the complex took well over two decades to complete.

The ordination hall is covered in brightly patterned Chinese ceramic tiles, known as *bencharong*, while the windows and entrance doors to the hall are exquisite works of art, with tiny pieces of mother-of-pearl inlaid in lacquer. The doors open into one of the most surprising temple interiors in Thailand – a Gothic-inspired chapel of solid columns that looks more like a medieval cathedral than a Thai temple.

THONBURI

Accessed by ferry or via several bridges across the Chao Phraya River from Rattanakosin, **Thonburi** has a markedly easy-going atmosphere compared with the frenetic neighbourhoods of downtown Bangkok. Life in this residential half of the capital primarily revolves around its serpentine network of canals and the river.

Established by King Taksin after the fall of Ayutthaya in 1767, it served as Thailand's third capital for 15 years prior to the establishment of Bangkok in 1782. Taksin spent most of his reign conquering factions of rebels to protect his throne, leaving time only late in his reign to embellish his city.

Several canals in Thonburi are worth exploring. These include the **Khlong Bangkok Noi**, which winds into

TIP

When having a Thai massage, try to relax completely. The massage will involve some contortionist-like poses, and the natural inclination is to resist when you are sometimes bent into awkward positions. Don't resist – just go with the flow.

BELOW LEFT: longtail boatman.
BELOW: Wat Ratchabophit.

Waterways

The old thoroughfares of Bangkok were water- rather than land- based. Those that remain reward exploration by boat

For centuries, the river and *khlong*, or canal, served as the transportation arteries of Thailand. In a land that flooded whenever the monsoon-swollen rivers overflowed their banks, it made little sense to build roads that would be washed away. Rivers and canals also provided natural defences as moats against invaders.

Engineering feats

At Ayutthaya on the Central Plain, master engineers diverted the local waterways to create a fortified island. Later, in Bangkok, engineers dug a canal across a neck of land between the present site of Thammasat University and Wat Arun, thereby eliminating a long roundabout route to the mouth of the Chao Phraya. Erosion eventually widened the canal, which has now become the river's main course. The original river loop became the *khlong* of Bangkok Noi and Bangkok Yai. When King Rama I established Bangkok, he had three concentric canals constructed, turning the royal city into an island. Other canals were dug to connect them. In the 19th century, it was estimated that more than 100,000 boats plied Bangkok's waterways.

The most extensive rural canal expansion was ordered by King Chulalongkorn. His engineers mapped the Central Plain, and the monarch gave land to whoever would dig the section of canal passing through his property. Within a few years, thousands of miles of canals crisscrossed central Thailand. The magnitude of this enormous project can only be appreciated from the air.

Bangkok's *khlong*

Zipping along at water level in a *reua haang yao*, or longtail boat, is one of the most pleasant ways to see Bangkok. The *reua haang yao* is a particularly Thai invention, born of necessity. In engineering terms, it is simplicity itself: a car or truck engine is mounted on a pivot at the stern of a long, low and narrow boat. A long shaft, or "tail", with a propeller on the end extends into the water, spinning furiously and propelling the boat at rapid speeds. In the narrow canals, the pivot allows the boatman to turn the craft in a very tight radius.

A lovely 90-minute route zips upriver to Khlong Bangkok Noi. A short way beyond the Bangkok Noi Railway Station, the driver, if asked, will stop for a few minutes for a tour of Royal Barge Museum. Continue up the canal, turning left into Khlong Chak Phra, which soon changes its name to Bang Kounsri and eventually to Bangkok Yai.

One of the most scenic *khlong* in the eastern section of Bangkok is Khlong Saen Saep, dug to carry troops to Chachoengsao to fight invaders from the east, and to join the Bangpakong River for a journey into the sea. The canal begins at Pratunam, but the water is filthy and fetid there.

It is better to start at the Ekamai Bridge or at Phrakanong Khlong Tan Bridge. The canal is straight and unshaded, so it's less attractive than the twisting and convoluted Thonburi canals, but nevertheless it passes through lovely rice country. In any case and on any *khlong*, take a look.

Starting around the middle of the 20th century, Bangkok inevitably moved with the times and shifted from water to land transport. Canals were filled in to create roads, and houses were built on solid ground. The result is evident: congested and noisy streets in the hot season, flooded streets in the monsoon season. ❑

LEFT: a *khlong* to the west of Bangkok.

Khlong **Bangkok Yai** downstream, as well as connecting to **Khlong Om** upstream. Once a source of fresh daily produce, the floating markets at **Wat Sai** and **Taling Chan** have become little more than tourist souvenir stops these days. With rickety teak houses, vendors selling produce from boats, fishermen dangling rods out of windows and kids frolicking in the water, the sights along Thonburi's canals are reminiscent of a more peaceful bygone era.

Canal and river cruising

Thonburi's major canals are serviced by public longtail boats. But as services can be erratic at certain times of the day, it is better to hire your own private longtail boat for a more leisurely exploration. Getting from pier to pier along the Chao Phraya River is best done by the **Chao Phraya Express** boats, which operate from the southern outskirts all the way up to Nonthaburi in the north. For shuttling from one side of the river to the other, make use of the cheap cross-river ferries; these can be boarded at the many jetties that also service the Chao Phraya Express boats. *(See pages 368–9 for more details on river and canal boat travel.)*

Wat Arun

When King Taksin first moored at the Thonburi bank of the Chao Phraya River at sunrise after sailing down from the sacked capital of Ayutthaya in 1768, he found an old temple shrine and felt strangely compelled to build a fitting holding place for the sacred Emerald Buddha. Eventually known as **Wat Arun ❽** or the Temple of Dawn (daily 8.30am–5.30pm; charge), the temple was originally attached to Taksin's new palace (Wang Derm).

After Taksin's demise, the new king, Chakri (Rama I), moved the capital (along with the Emerald Buddha) to Bangkok, but the temple kept the interest of the first five kings. Over the years, Wat Arun grew in size and ornamentation. In the early l9th century King Rama II enlarged the structure and raised the central *prang* (Khmer-style tower) to 104 metres (345ft), making it the city's tallest religious structure.

Recycling piles of broken ceramic which were leftover ballast from Chinese merchant ships, Rama III introduced the colourful fragments of porcelain that cover most of the temple's exterior. The great *prang* represents the Hindu-Buddhist mythological Mount Meru, home of the gods with its 33 heavens.

There are four smaller *prang* standing at each corner of the temple with niches containing statues of Nayu, the god of wind, riding on horseback. The entire complex is guarded by mythical giants called *yaksha*, similar to those that protect Wat Phra Kaew.

Museum of Royal Barges

On the north bank of the Khlong Bangkok Noi canal, which was a major waterway during King Taksin's reign, is the **National Museum of Royal Barges ❾** (daily 9am–5pm; charge, photo fee extra). The dry dock displays eight vessels from a fleet of over 50 that are rarely put to sail except

TIP

If you've a night to spare and want to cruise the Chao Praya in style, book a cabin on one of the converted rice barges that sail up- and downriver daily, serving gourmet food to go with the sights.

BELOW: Wat Arun at dusk.

The Giant Swing was the venue of an annual Brahman ceremony in former times. Four men would set the swing in motion, trying to grab with their teeth the bag of coins suspended on a pole.

BELOW: the Museum of Royal Barges.
BELOW RIGHT: the Democracy Monument.

on auspicious occasions, such as the anniversary of King Bhumibol's 60th year on the throne in 2006. The royal barge procession held on 12 June that year saw a flotilla of 52 gilded barges, manned by 2,200 oarsmen from the Thai navy, sweep down the Chao Phraya River while the king watched and entertained visiting royals from 25 nations.

The Royal Barge fleet dates back to 14th-century Ayutthaya, while the present craft were constructed in the early 20th century. In the old days, the royal family, like everyone else, travelled around Bangkok by boat. The king would sit in the largest of the barges, the magnificent *Suphannahongse*, which was made from a single trunk of teak stretching over 46 metres (151ft). The model on display at the museum was built in 1911 and based on the design of its 18th-century predecessor.

OLD CITY AND DUSIT

Dominated by the wide boulevard of Thanon Ratchadamnoen, this section of the "Old City" of Bangkok to the east and northeast of Rattanakosin

contains all the peripheral buildings and temples that lie outside the old royal hub. The area once marked the outskirts of the city, with the canals of Khlong Banglamphu and Khlong Ong Ang ferrying in supplies from the surrounding countryside. Time has drastically altered the area's visual appeal, yet there is still a strong sense of the past, making this is one of the city's most rewarding areas to explore.

Wat Suthat

Standing tall behind the **Giant Swing**, *(see margin, left)* once the venue for a now-outlawed Brahmin ceremony, **Wat Suthat ❿** (daily 8.30am–9pm; charge) is considered one of the country's six principal temples. Begun by Rama I in 1807, it took three reigns to complete. The temple is noted for its enormous *bot*, or ordination hall, said to be the tallest in Bangkok, and for its equally large *viharn* (sermon hall), both of them surrounded by cloisters of gilded Buddha images. The 8-metre (26ft) tall Phra Sri Sakyamuni Buddha is one of the largest surviving bronze images from Sukhothai, and was transported

by boat all the way from the northern kingdom. The temple courtyard is a virtual museum of statuary, with stone figures of Chinese generals and scholars, which originally came as ballast in rice ships returning from deliveries to China and were donated to temples.

Democracy Monument

Behind City Hall, north along Thanon Dinso, the **Democracy Monument** ⑪ was designed by Italian sculptor Corrado Feroci (also known as Silpa Bhirasri) in 1939. The monument is a celebration of Thailand's transition from absolute to constitutional monarchy in 1932. Marked by four elongated wings, the central metal tray contains a copy of the Constitution. Almost every detail of the monument has symbolic relevance.

A rallying point for civil discontent in May 1992, the monument became the scene of a bloodbath after the army violently suppressed peaceful demonstrations against the military dictatorship.

14 October Monument

Just a short walk from the Democracy Monument along Thanon Ratchadamnoen Klang towards the corner of Thanon Tanao leads to another chiselled edifice to the democratic struggle, the **14 October Monument**. While not as grandiose as the Democracy Monument, this granite memorial remembers the victims of the 1973 mass demonstrations against authoritarian rule. The central spire is inscribed with the names of 73 of the victims.

Wat Bowonniwet

North of the 14 October Monument along Thanon Tanao is **Wat Bowonniwet** ⑫ (daily 8am–5pm; free), a modest-looking monastery with strong royal bonds. It was built during the reign of Rama III in 1826, and King Mongkut (Rama IV) served as abbot of the temple for a small portion of his 27 years as a monk. More recently, the present King Bhumibol (Rama IX) donned saffron

robes here after his coronation in 1946. Home to Thailand's second Buddhist university, the temple is known for its extraordinary murals painted by monk-artist Khrua In Khong.

Thanon Ratchadamnoen

Stretching east and then northeast from the Grand Palace all the way to the Dusit Park area, the wide **Thanon Ratchadamnoen** (Royal Passage) splits into three sections and is modelled after the boulevards of Paris. Built at the turn of the 20th century, the tree-lined avenue has some of the city's widest and least cluttered pavements. On royal birthdays, the area is turned into a sea of decorative lights, flags and royal portraits. At night, be a little wary as vagrants sometimes lurk in the shadows.

Loha Prasat and Wat Ratchanatda

At the point where Thanon Ratchadamnoen Klang crosses the Pan Fah canal bridge, veering left into Ratchadamnoen Nok, several noticeable structures dot both sides of the busy intersection. More evocative of

During World War II, the Golden Mount served as a watchtower, with guards equipped with signal flags to warn of enemy invaders.

BELOW: seated Buddha images at Wat Suthat.

Streetside hair-braiding service on Khao San Road.

BELOW: Khao San Road, backpacker central.

Burmese temple structures, the **Loha Prasat** (Metal Palace) shares the same grounds as **Wat Ratchanatda** (sometimes spelt as Rajanadda) and is the main attraction here (both daily 8am–5pm; free).

Originally meant to be the temple's *chedi*, Loha Prasat's unusual architecture is said to draw on an Indian design dating back some 2,500 years. Commissioned by Rama III in 1846, two tiers square the central tower, peaked by 37 iron spires which symbolise the virtues needed to attain enlightenment. Just behind the temple is a thriving **amulet market**, similar to the one found at Wat Mahathat *(see page 115)*.

Golden Mount

Standing tall south of Mahakan Fort, the elevated spire of the **Golden Mount** (Phu Khao Thong; daily 7.30am–5.30pm; charge) was for many years Bangkok's highest point. Started by Rama III as a huge *chedi*, the city's soft earth made it impossible to build on, and the site soon became an artificial hill overgrown with trees and

shrubbery. King Mongkut added a more modest *chedi* to the abandoned hill, and later, King Chulalongkorn completed work on the 78-metre (256ft) high plot.

A stairway curves around the side of the hill to the summit, and is shaded by trees and dotted with small shrines along the way. A part of **Wat Saket** located at the bottom of the Golden Mount, the gilded *chedi* is said to contain a Buddha relic from India.

Thanon Khao San

Since the early 1980s, **Thanon Khao San** (or Khao San Road as it's more popularly known) has been a self-contained ghetto for the back-packing globetrotter. Once a rather seedy gathering of cheap guesthouses, noodle shops and poky bars, as portrayed in Alex Garland's novel *The Beach*, Banglamphu's nerve centre has undergone a significant upgrade in recent years. The arrival of a new breed of trendy boutique hotels, along with new bars, restaurants and international chains like Starbucks may have taken some of its gritty edge away, but

this neon-lit street is still full of character. For gap-year travellers and those watching their budget, Khao San Road makes sense; older and slightly more moneyed visitors may not feel the need to venture near.

Dusit area

Heading east from Khao San Road, Thanon Ratchadamnoen Klang crosses Khlong Banglamphu and turns northeast to become Ratchadamnoen Nok. This pleasant, tree-lined boulevard then leads down to a broad square in front of the old National Assembly building. Known as **Royal Plaza**, the square is watched over by a bronze **Statue of King Chulalongkorn** (Rama V) on horseback. Chulalongkorn was responsible for the construction of much of this part of Bangkok, which was once a rustic royal retreat from the city and the Grand Palace, some 3km (2 miles) away. With the present king residing in nearby **Chitralada Palace** and the day-to-day governance taking place in Parliament House, this area is still very much at the heart of the nation.

Ananta Samakhom

North of the Royal Plaza, the monumental edifice of the **Ananta Samakhom Throne Hall** ⑯ is an ornate Italian Renaissance-style hall of grey marble crowned by a huge dome (daily 9.30am–3.15pm; charge, or free with Grand Palace entrance ticket).

This is the tallest building within the manicured gardens of **Dusit Park**, a rare area of open space enlivened by canals, bridges and fountains. Built in 1907 by King Chulalongkorn as a grandiose hall for receiving visiting dignitaries and other state ceremonies, the highlight of the hall's rich interior is the dome ceiling frescoes depicting the Chakri monarchs from Rama I to Rama VI. The building was also formerly used as a Parliament house.

Vimanmek Mansion

Behind the Ananta Samakhom Throne Hall, the **Vimanmek Mansion** ⑰ is billed as the world's largest golden-teak building (daily 9.30am–3.15pm; charge, or free with Grand Palace entrance ticket; www.thai.palaces.net; compulsory guided tours every 30 minutes;

Bangkok's full name is "Krung Thep Mahanakhon Amon Rattanakosin Mahinthara Yuthaya Mahadilok Phop Nopparat Ratchathani Burirom Udomratchaniwet Mahasathan Amon Phiman Awatan Sathit Sakkathattiya Witsanukam Prasit". Understandably, most Thais just stick to Krung Thep.

BELOW: Vimanmek, the world's largest building made of golden teak.

Fine teakwood decorations at the Abhisek Dusit Throne Hall.

BELOW: Wat Benjamabophit.

visitors dressed in shorts must wear sarongs that are provided at the door; shoes and bags have to be stowed in lockers).

Originally built in 1868 as a summer house for King Chulalongkorn on the east-coast island of Ko Si Chang (*see page 178*), the king had the three-storey mansion dismantled and reassembled on the Dusit grounds in 1901. Made entirely from golden teak and without a single nail used in its construction, the gingerbread fretwork and octagonal tower of this 72-room mansion looks more Victorian than period Thai – reflecting the fascination with all things Western at the time. The king and his large family lived here for only five years; the mansion eventually fell out of favour, lying abandoned until restored for the Bangkok bicentennial 50 years later.

Vimanmek (meaning Palace in the Clouds) offers an insight into how the royal family of the day lived. In the pavilion on the south side of the mansion, Thai dancers and martial arts experts perform free every day at 10.30am and 2pm.

Abhisek Dusit Throne Hall

To the right of Vimanmek, the **Abhisek Dusit Throne Hall** (daily 9.30am–3.15pm; charge, or free with Grand Palace entrance ticket) was constructed in 1903 for King Chulalongkorn as an accompanying throne hall to Vimanmek; the ornate building is another sumptuous melding of Victorian and Moorish styles, but still retains its distinctly Thai sheen. The main hall is now used as a showroom-cum-museum for the SUPPORT foundation, a charitable organisation headed by Queen Sirikit that helps preserve traditional arts and crafts. A shop next door sells the handiworks of village artisans.

Dusit Zoo

To the east, the grounds of **Dusit Zoo** ⓲ (daily 8am–6pm; charge) were originally part of the Royal Dusit Garden Palace, the site of King Chulalongkorn's private botanical garden. The 19-hectare (47-acre) site became a public zoo in 1938. It now holds around 300 different species of mammals, almost 1,000 bird species and around 300 different kinds of reptiles, but conditions at some of the animal enclosures are less than adequate.

Wat Benjamabophit

Southeast of the King Chulalongkorn statue along Thanon Rama V, **Wat Benjamabophit** ⓳, more popularly known as the Marble Temple (daily 8am–5.30pm; charge), is the most recent major temple to be built in central Bangkok and the best example of modern Thai religious architecture.

Started by King Chulalongkorn at the turn of the last century, the *wat* was designed by the king's half-brother Prince Naris together with Italian architect Hercules Manfredi, and completed in 1911. The collaborators

fused elements of the East and West to dramatic effect. The most obvious of these must be the walls of Carrara marble from Italy, the cruciform shape of the main temple building and the unique European-crafted stained-glass windows depicting Thai mythological scenes. The *bot*'s principal Buddha image is a replica of the Phra Buddha Chinarat of Phitsanulok, with the base containing the ashes of King Chulalongkorn.

Behind the *bot*, a fascinating gallery holds some 53 original and copied Buddha images from all over Asia, providing a useful educational display. The temple is most interesting in the early morning, when merit-makers gather before its gates to donate food and offerings to the line of bowl-wielding monks – this is in contrast with other parts of the city, where monks generally walk the streets begging for alms.

CHINATOWN

The area to the southeast of Rattanakosin was settled by Chinese merchants forced to relocate here so that the

Grand Palace could be built. In 1863, King Mongkut built Thanon Charoen Krung (New Road), the first paved street in Bangkok, and Chinatown soon mushroomed from the original dirt track of Sampeng (now officially Soi Wanit 1). Other adjacent plots of land were given to the Indian and Muslim communities.

With narrow roads and lanes teeming with commercial bustle, this is one of the capital's most traffic-clogged districts, but exploring on foot allows you to soak up the area's mercantile atmosphere. Away from downtown's plush mega malls, Chinatown is a raw experience of Bangkok past and present: old shophouses, godowns (warehouses), temples and shrines, all teeming with life and activity.

Sampeng Lane

The **Sampeng** area is considered the old pulse of Chinatown and has a rowdy history. What began as a mercantile enclave soon degenerated into a raunchy entertainment area. By 1900, it had a reputation as "Sin Alley", with lanes leading to opium dens, gambling

Pak Khlong Talad (the Flower Market) in Chinatown.

BELOW: a traditional Chinatown tea shop.

Love for Sale

Thailand's lucrative sex industry is based on the exploitation of women from the poorer regions of the country and elsewhere

There are few greater contrasts in Thailand than Patpong's main street around sunset. Centre stage is the fairly family-friendly night market brimming with every sort of souvenir, an enormous variety of knock-offs, and a veritable orchestra of electronic whistles and bells. And in the wings, raucous bar upon raucous bar dangles the possibility of X-rated fun and frolic. To the Thai way of thinking, there is little wrong with the scene. Shop if you want to shop, there's no need to look anywhere else. And if you have something else in mind, go ahead.

Much of the area belongs to the Patpongpanich family, who bought the initial plots in 1946 and must have seen a substantial return on their investment. Patpong took off with the Vietnam War, when thousands of battle-weary GIs were flown in for R&R. By the mid-1970s, it had secured a worldwide reputation, with sex tourists heading over directly from the international airport.

These days, Patpong consists of two main streets, with two parallel thoroughfares catering to gay and Japanese visitors respectively. There is little that could be described as cheerful about the scene.

NGOs estimate that there are between 100,000 and 300,000 Thai sex workers in Thailand. Most of those in Bangkok come from the poverty-wracked region of northeast Thailand. Those who earn a living in the capital's red-light districts often have the consent of their families, and regularly send money home each month. The pay is infinitely better than working in a factory or on the land. Many sex workers hang on to the Cinderella dream that they will be rescued by a client; indeed, more than a few cross-cultural marriages have had their beginnings in a Bangkok brothel. But these are few and far between, and often overshadowed by stories of abuse and exploitation.

NGOs in Thailand no longer focus on extricating women from prostitution. They have found that few in the business are motivated to get out: the money is too good, or the girls have become entrenched in a way of life. Organisations such as Empower (www.empowerfoundation.org) instead educate them about the dangers of AIDS, and teach them English so that they are less likely to be exploited.

The other end of the sex trade is infinitely more grim. Young women and girls are trafficked from neighbouring Laos, Myanmar and Cambodia, countries far poorer than Thailand. Lured by promises of factory jobs or work as waitresses or hotel receptionists, they unwittingly sell themselves into locked-up brothels in the capital. There, they must work under inhuman conditions until they have earned back the money the brothel-owner paid for them.

All this insalubrious activity has had an effect on Bangkok society, with a backlash against the loose sexual morals of local teenagers. Under pressure from teachers and parents, the government launched a Social Order Campaign to keep under-age Thais away from Bangkok's seedy nightlife. With random drug raids, earlier closing times and frequent ID checks, the campaign has enjoyed a certain measure of success. ❏

ABOVE & LEFT: neon lights and working girls in the infamous Patpong neighbourhood.

houses and brothels. Eventually, however, Sampeng lost its sleaze and became a bustling lane of small shops selling imported goods from China. The stretch of **Sampeng Lane** ❷ that lies between Thanon Ratchawong and Thanon Mangkon sells everything from cheap clothing and footwear to sticky sweet Chinese confectionery, cosmetics and tacky costume jewellery.

Pahurat Market

West of Sampeng Lane, **Pahurat Market** ❷ (daily 9am–6pm) is a two-level bazaar sometimes known as Bangkok's Little India. In the late 19th century Indian migrants converged here, and their presence is still strongly felt today. It is filled with merchants selling all manner of colourful fabrics, including saris, as well as Hindu deities and wedding regalia, together with traditional Thai dance costumes. On Thanon Pahurat and parts of Thanon Chakraphet, cheap curry eateries and Indian tea and spice stalls do a roaring trade. Nearby at Thanon Chakraphet, the golden-domed **Sri Guru Singh Sabha** temple (daily 8am–5pm; free) is the focal point of Bangkok's Sikh community.

Pak Khlong Talad

With floral garland offerings at temples and shrines all over the city, Bangkok needs a constant supply of fresh blooms for its worshippers. Situated on the riverfront by the mouth of Khlong Lord, **Pak Khlong Talad** ❷ (Flower Market) serves as the capital's flower and vegetable garden (daily 24 hours). The bargain-priced bunches of both exotic and familiar flowers are a riot of fragrance and colour. The market is a great place for taking photographs.

Thanon Yaowarat and Nakhon Kasem

Running parallel to Sampeng Lane, **Thanon Yaowarat** is the main drag in Chinatown, and with its forest of neon signs looks much like a busy Hong Kong street. It is best known for its gold jewellery shops.

Between Thanon Yaowarat and Thanon Charoen Krung, at the corner with Thanon Chakrawat, stands **Nakhon Kasem** ❷ or Thieves' Market (daily 8am–8pm). A few decades ago, this was a black market for stolen goods. It later developed into an antiques dealers' area, but today, most of the antiques stalls have disappeared. If you search hard enough among the piles of run-of-the-mill goods, you may chance upon a few old treasures.

Wat Mangkon Kamalawat

On Thanon Charoen Krung near Soi Itsaranuphap, the towering gateway of **Wat Mangkon Kamalawat** ❷ (daily 8.30am–3.30pm; free) is also known as Leng Noi Yee (Dragon Flower Temple). The most revered temple in Chinatown, it is enveloped by a constant swirl of activity and incense smoke. Built in 1871, the *wat* is one of the most important centres for Mahayana Buddhism in Thailand. Elements of Taoist and Confucian worship are also prevalent at the temple.

TIP

It's an armchair on a motorbike – or an alfresco gas oven. *Tuk-tuk* are Bangkok's signature transport, great for short trips but not really a transport of delight. If you do board, bargain hard for the fare before setting off.

BELOW: the Odeon Circle China Gate, with Wat Traimit in the background.

Jim Thompson, the king of Thai silk, disappeared mysteriously in the jungles of Malaysia in 1967.

BELOW: Jim Thompson's House offers respite from the cacophony of the city.

Soi Itsaranuphap

Chinatown's most interesting lane, **Soi Itsaranuphap** (Soi 16), runs south from Thanon Phlab Phla Chai and passes a 19th-century Thai temple called **Wat Kanikaphon** (daily 6am–4pm; free). Around the entrance to Soi Itsaranuphap shops sell "hell money" and miniature houses, cars and other items made of paper for the Chinese *kong tek* ceremony. The items are taken to the temple and burnt as offerings to deceased relatives.

Talad Kao and Talad Mai

Soi Itsaranuphap contains two of the city's best-known markets. Closer to the corner with Sampeng Lane is the two-century-old **Talad Kao** (Old Market), while a little way off Soi Itsaranuphap (closer to Thanon Charoen Krung), **Talad Mai** (New Market) has been plying its goods for more than 100 years. The Old Market wraps up by late morning, while the newer keeps trading until sundown. These fresh markets have a reputation for high-quality meat, fish and vegetables, and overflow with crowds during the Chinese New Year.

Wat Traimit

Just east of the point where Thanon Yaowarat meets Thanon Charoen Krung, across from the Odeon Circle China Gate, stands the unremarkable-looking **Wat Traimit** (daily 8am–5pm; charge). The real treasure – a lustrous **Golden Buddha** – lies within. The story goes that it was discovered by accident in the 1950s: a 3-metre (10ft) stucco figure was being transported to its present site when the crane lifting it snapped and sent the statue smashing to the ground. A crack in the stucco revealed a solid gold image weighing some 5.5 tonnes. The gleaming image is said to date from 13th-century Sukhothai, and was probably encased in stucco during the Ayutthayan period to conceal its true worth from the Burmese invaders.

PATHUMWAN AND PRATUNAM

The commercial heart of downtown Bangkok, **Pathumwan** is a sprawl of shopping malls, all connected by the Skytrain. It's an area mostly identified with retail therapy, yet there are still

Jim Thompson's House

The protected oasis of **Jim Thompson's House** is the principal downtown attraction on most tourist itineraries (daily 9am–5pm; charge includes compulsory guided tours of the museum; www.jimthompsonhouse.com). Its former occupant was the American entrepreneur responsible for the revival of Thai silk. An architect by training, Thompson first came to Thailand at the end of World War II, later returning to Bangkok to live. He became interested in the almost redundant craft of silk weaving and design, which he subsequently (and profitably) reinvigorated. He mysteriously disappeared in the Malaysian jungles in 1967, but his well-preserved house still stands today by the banks of the Khlong Saen Saep canal. Thompson was an enthusiastic collector of Asian arts and antiquities, many of which adorn his traditional house-turned-museum.

The museum comprises six teak structures, which were transported from Ayutthaya and elsewhere to the silk-weaving village of Ban Khrua, just across Khlong Saen Saep, before being reassembled at their present site in 1959. From the windows of the house, it's easy to imagine how scenic the view would have been some 50 years ago, looking across the lush gardens, or "jungle" as Thompson called it. Next to the old house is a pondside café, while opposite the Jim Thompson Art Centre is a contemporary gallery that holds exhibitions of local and international arts and crafts.

plenty of sights harking back to an older and more traditional city – the best-known of which is **Jim Thompson's House** ㉗ *(see panel, opposite)*. Created in the early 19th century, the man-made canal **Khlong Saen Saep** runs east–west through the neighbourhood: it was the construction of this canal that enabled the capital to spread east to **Pratunam** and beyond. This area extends as far as Thanon Withayu (Wireless Road), a major thoroughfare lined by a string of embassies as well as upmarket housing.

Shopping and art along Thanon Rama I

As downtown Bangkok loses character to a growing conglomeration of faceless air-conditioned malls, **Siam Square** ㉘, along Thanon Rama I, retains its maverick air as one of the city's few remaining street-side shopping enclaves. This maze of teen-friendly low-rise shops, cafés and restaurants is a favourite hangout for Bangkok students.

Cross the footbridge over Thanon Phaya Thai from Siam Square and head into the bewildering mayhem of **Mahboonkrong**, better known as MBK. It's always busy with youngsters, especially at weekends when they crowd around shops selling a cluttered variety of teen merchandise.

Across from Siam Square along Thanon Rama I, the **Siam Centre** and **Siam Discovery Centre** are interconnected. The former mall is the turf of Bangkok's younger set, with its local designer wear and sports and surf clothing shops, while the latter is decidedly more upmarket, sporting home accessories and international brand-name outlets.

Close by, on the west side of Thanon Phaya Thai, the huge 11-storey **Bangkok Art and Culture Centre** ㉙ (BACC; Tue–Sun 10am–9pm; free; www. bacc.or.th) has been the place to see some of the city's best contemporary art and multimedia shows since opening in 2008. The retail outlets on the lower floors have been issued to small independent galleries or organisations such as the Thai Film Foundation and Bangkok Opera. Art markets feature regularly on the concourse and performances in a small auditorium.

BELOW: shoppers at the Mahboonkrong shopping centre.

A young volunteer at the Snake Farm gingerly handles a python as he poses for a photograph.

To the east of the Siam Centre, the newest kid on the block is the swanky retail haven called **Siam Paragon**. As well as a glut of chichi designer shops and numerous restaurants and cafés, the mall's basement houses **Siam Ocean World** (daily 9am–10pm; charge; www.siamoceanworld.com). The giant Oceanarium is filled with over 30,000 marine creatures.

At the corner of Thanon Rama I and Thanon Ratchadamri is the **Central World** (formerly Central World Plaza) which opened in 2007 to much hype as Bangkok's largest mall. A large chunk of the complex, which covers a whopping 550,000 sq metres (5.9 million sq ft), was gutted by fire as the anti-government "red-shirt" protests withdrew from the city in May 2010. At least part of the mall is expected to reopen later in 2010.

Thanon Ploenchit malls

Further east, Thanon Rama I morphs into Thanon Ploenchit. There are yet more malls along this stretch, including the **Erawan Bangkok**, a boutique mall connected to the Grand Hyatt

Erawan hotel. Across the street, the **Gaysorn** is a designer mall that is relatively quiet save for the trickle of "Hi-So" spenders and window-shoppers. A large treasure trove of Thai arts and crafts can be found to the north along Thanon Ratchadamri, just opposite Central World, at the three-floor emporia of **Narayana Phand**. At the southeast corner of Ratchadamri and Ploenchit is the atmospheric **Erawan Shrine ㉚** (*see panel, below*).

Snake Farm

For an encounter with dangerous reptiles, visit the **Queen Saovabha Memorial Institute ㉛**, popularly called the **Snake Farm** (Mon–Fri 8.30am–4.30pm, Sat–Sun 8.30am–noon; charge). Located on Thanon Rama IV, it was founded in 1923 as the Pasteur Institute. The institute's principal work lies in the research and treatment of snakebites. Venom-milking sessions (Mon–Fri 11am and 2.30pm, Sat–Sun 11am; slide show 30 mins before) are the most popular times to visit, when the snakes are pulled from the pit and mercilessly goaded for the audience.

Erawan Shrine

The **Erawan Shrine ㉚** (daily 8am–10pm) is a haven of peace and quiet in the midst of the frenetic city. The aromatic haze of incense hits you before you actually see the shrine. Attracting locals and Asian tourists in droves, it is dedicated to the four-headed Hindu god of creation, Brahma. Originally erected on the site of the former Erawan Hotel, which was rebuilt as the present Grand Hyatt Erawan, the initial spirit house *(see page 64)* was deemed ineffective after a spate of unfortunate events (including deaths) slowed the hotel's construction. After an astrological consultation, this plaster-clad 1956 replacement halted the unlucky run, and ever since then the shrine has been revered for its strong talismanic powers. However, in March 2006, the shrine was hacked to pieces by a madman, 27-year-old Thanakorn Pakdeepol, who was subsequently lynched by an angry mob (such is the devotion that Thais accord to this shrine). The shrine has since been restored, and was reopened on 21 May 2006 shortly before noon when the sun was shining directly overhead.

Vendors line the enclosing fence selling floral garlands and wooden elephants (symbols of Brahma's elephant mount, Erawan). Supplicants whose prayers have been answered buy these as offerings, while some hire the resident dance troupe to perform *lakhon* dances on site.

Lumphini Park

Green spots are few and far between in Bangkok, but in the southeast of the downtown area, at the junction of Thanon Rama IV and Thanon Ratchadamri, **Lumphini Park** ❷ (daily 4.30am–9pm; free) is the city's premier green lung. The park was bequeathed to the public in 1925 by King Vajiravudh (Rama VI), whose memorial statue stands in front of the gates. Embellished with lakes (pedal boats for hire) and a Chinese-style clock tower, the park sees elderly Chinese practising t'ai chi and sweaty joggers at sunrise or sunset. The park was used as a base by the anti-government "red shirts" during the violent protests of 2010.

Suan Lum Night Bazaar

Across from the park gates along Thanon Withayu (Wireless Road), **Suan Lum Night Bazaar** ❸ (daily 3pm–midnight) is a more sanitised and cooler alternative to the frenzied Chatuchak Weekend Market *(see page 140)*. Geared towards tourists, the open-air bazaar offers a wide array of clothing, handicrafts, antiques, jewellery and homeware. Also found at Suan Lum Night Bazaar is **Joe Louis Theatre** (one show nightly at 8.00pm; charge; thaipuppet.com). Sakorn Yangkeawsot, who goes by the moniker Joe Louis *(see page 71)*, is responsible for reviving the fading art of *hun lakhon lek*, a unique form of traditional Thai puppetry.

Pratunam area

Northwards, past the Khlong Saen Saep canal and Thanon Phetchaburi, is the somewhat dingy **Pratunam Market**. This bustling warren of stalls is more a lure for residents than tourists, with piles of cheap clothing, fabrics and assorted fashion accessories. The area is shadowed by Thailand's tallest building, **Baiyoke II Tower** (304 metres/ 997ft), whose 84th floor observation deck (daily 10am–10pm; charge) offers eye-popping views of the city and beyond. Across Thanon Phetchaburi from Pratunam, **Panthip Plaza** (daily 10am–9pm) is entirely devoted to IT.

Suan Pakkad Palace

Most tourists make a beeline for Jim Thompson's House *(see page 128)*,

The multicultural makeup of Bangkok includes a quarter of a million mainland Chinese, 5,000 Nigerians and 44,000 Japanese – the largest Japanese population in Asia outside Japan. And that's just those who've registered!

BELOW: Lumphini Park, a rare open space.

missing out on an equally delightful abode, the **Suan Pakkad Palace**
❸ (daily 9am–4pm; charge includes
guided tour; www.suanpakkad.com).
Located a short walk along Thanon
Sri Ayutthaya from Phaya Thai Skytrain station, the name Suan Pakkad,
or "Cabbage Patch", refers to its former
use as farmland before the palace was
constructed here in 1952. The former
residence of the late Prince and Princess Chumbhot, both of whom were
prolific art collectors and garden-
ers, Suan Pakkad comprises five teak
houses set amid a beautiful, lush
garden and lotus pond. Converted into
a museum, the wooden houses display
an eclectic collection of antiques and
artefacts.

BANGRAK AND SILOM

Bangkok's main business district, **Bangrak** lies to the south of
Pathumwan's shopping malls. Gravitat-
ing eastwards from some of the Chao
Phraya River's premier riverfront real
estate, Thanon Silom is the principal
thoroughfare, ending at Thanon Rama
IV with Lumphini Park beyond. Par-

allel to Silom are Sathorn, Surawong
and Si Phraya roads.

Thanon Silom along with **Thanon
Sathorn** are considered the city's
main business arteries, but at dusk, the
shift from day to night trade quickly
becomes apparent when the office
workers depart and a bevy of attractive
females and males (as well as those of
indeterminate sex) begin to converge
in the area.

But it's not all starchy office blocks
and unbridled sleaze that make up
Bangrak. Between the River City shopping centre and the luxury Shangri-La
hotel is what is regarded as the old
farang (foreigner) district. Easily navigable, the lanes in this part of town
still hold a few buildings from its days
as a 19th-century port settlement. This
is one of the city's more interesting
corners, so try to make time to discover
it on foot.

Assumption Cathedral

Close to the **Oriental Hotel** ❸ (*see
panel, opposite*), along Oriental Avenue
and towards the river, a side road on
the left leads to a small square domi-

nated by the **Assumption Cathedral** (daily 6am–9pm; free). Built in 1910, the red-brick cathedral is surrounded by a Catholic mission. Its ornate interior is topped by a beautiful domed ceiling towering over a large sacristy with gilded pillars. Take a breather here and mull over Bangkok's secluded architectural delights.

Maha Uma Devi Temple

Looming behind the Assumption Cathedral at the corner of Silom and Charoen Krung is the ostentatious and faux-classical **State Tower**, worth a mention for its fashionable rooftop drink-and-dine venue, **Sirocco** (*see page 138*).

Continuing further along Thanon Silom, the lively Hindu **Maha Uma Devi Temple** ❸ (daily 6am–8pm; free) makes its presence felt on the corner of Soi Pan. Named after Shiva's consort, Uma Devi, the temple was established in the 1860s by the city's Tamil community, who maintain a strong presence in the area. It is known to Thais as Wat Khaek, meaning "guests' temple" (*khaek* is also a less welcoming term used by locals for people from the Indian Sub-

continent). On holy days, the temple throngs with worshippers – Indians, Thais and Chinese.

Patpong

Come nightfall, the upper end of Thanon Silom transforms to entertain a clientele of varied persuasions. Stall vendors set up a **night market** along Thanon Silom from Soi 2 to Soi 8, commandeering the narrow pavements in either direction, including the shabby fleshpot of **Patpong** ❸ (Soi 1 and Soi 2; *see page 126)*. The market plies mainly tourist tat, including counterfeit watches, fake name-brand bags and clothes, and bootleg CDs.

With its rash of trashy go-go bars and anything-goes strip clubs, Patpong still merits its sleazy reputation, although government clampdowns on nightlife over the years have reduced its wilder excesses to some degree. Developed on the site of a former banana plantation by a Thai-Chinese tycoon, the playground first found favour among affluent locals and foreign airline crews – before American GIs descended here in droves on R&R from Vietnam in the

A T-shirt stall in Patpong.

BELOW: the Authors' Lounge at the Oriental Hotel.

The Oriental Hotel

Founded back in the 1870s, the riverside **Mandarin Oriental Hotel** ❸ has consistently been rated as one of the world's best. A retreat for the influential and wealthy, its grandeur has endured through the years. However, the uninspiring exteriors of two newer extensions, the Garden Wing (1958) and the River Wing (1976), added to the original **Author's Wing**, somewhat detract from its classic feel. To imbibe its old-world atmosphere fully, sit down to afternoon tea in the elegant **Authors' Lounge** and muse over the literary greats who have passed through its doors, such as Somerset Maugham, Noël Coward and Graham Greene. As well as partaking of first-class wining and dining, guests can also ride the shuttle across the river to the Oriental's spa, in a traditional house carved from golden teak.

MR Kukrit Pramoj's Heritage Home – a good example of traditional Thai architecture.

BELOW: motorcycle taxis waiting for passengers.

late 1960s and '70s. Despite incessant touts claiming a freakish assortment of sex shows, today's tamer experience is a blitz of neon, relentless techno beats and gyrating bikini-clad dancers on bar tops.

A few lanes east from Patpong, **Silom Soi 4** attracts throngs of beautiful and young (both straight and gay) revellers to its compact dance clubs and bars. Nearby **Silom Soi 2** is similar in appeal, though designated for gay men. Further on still, the expensive hostess bars along **Soi Thaniya** cater for an exclusively Japanese clientele.

Kukrit Pramoj's Home

Halfway down Thanon Sathorn, **MR Kukrit Pramoj's Heritage Home** ❸ (Sat and Sun 10am–5pm; charge) is tucked away on Soi Phra Phinij. Born of royal descent (signified by the title Mom Ratchawong – MR), the late Kukrit Pramoj had a brief stint as prime minister during the disruptive 1970s, but is better remembered as a prolific author and cultural preservationist.

Surrounded by an ornate Khmer-style garden, this splendid wooden home – now a museum – comprises five stilt buildings that recall the traditional architecture of the Central Plain. The *bonsai* garden adds a sense of serenity, and the home is livened up with displays of beautiful objets d'art, antique pottery and an ornate bed that belonged to Rama II.

SUKHUMVIT

The eastern extension of Thanon Rama I/Ploenchit, **Thanon Sukhumvit** is a bustling and traffic-clogged road which pushes the urban sprawl eastwards. It continues, amazingly enough, all the way to the Cambodian border. The efficient Skytrain provides the fastest means of transport between the plethora of upmarket shops, restaurants, spas and entertainment venues that line this major artery. Although thin on major tourist attractions, Thanon Sukhumvit is where most of the city's growing expatriate community lives.

After dark

Sukhumvit's early blocks burst with a profusion of tailors, pool halls, beer bars, inns and hotels. A **night market**

crowds the pavements from Soi 3 to Soi 19, replaced later at night by make-shift food-and-drink stalls. The area has a lascivious veneer, anchored by the three-storey mall of go-go bars, **Nana Entertainment Plaza** (NEP), on Soi 4. Across the Asoke intersection (Soi 21) is Sukhumvit's other notorious neon strip devoted to pole dancing, **Soi Cowboy**.

Nonetheless, Sukhumvit's overall character is far from sleazy, with many of the city's best nightspots dotted along the area's winding side streets. Leading the charge is **Soi 11**, where both the long-established **Q Bar** and the equally chic **Bed Supperclub** pull in the rich, famous, and those aspiring to one or the other or both. Much of the attraction here is the chic and thoroughly independent Thai design, together with some very novel concepts characterised by a terrific attention to detail.

Kamthieng House

One of Sukhumvit's oldest buildings is the headquarters of the **Siam Society** at Sukhumvit Soi 21 (Soi Asoke), founded in 1904 to promote the study of Thai culture. A fire in November 2009 shut down operations temporarily. There's an excellent library full of rare books on Thai history, old manuscripts and maps.

In the same grounds, **Kamthieng House** ㊴ (Tue–Sat 9am–5pm; charge; www.siam-society.org) is an authentic 150-year-old wooden home transplanted from Chiang Mai and carefully reassembled here as an ethnological museum.

Emporium area

On the corner of Soi 24, near Phrom Phong Skytrain station, stands Sukhumvit's premier shopping magnet, **Emporium** (with an excellent food court on the top floor), a great place to watch Bangkok's moneyed elite parade in their finest togs and splash out at its many designer stores. The side lanes around are home to upmarket furniture and home accessories shops, bakeries, spas, galleries, cafés and restaurants.

Further east, just off the Thong Lo Skytrain station is **Sukhumvit Soi 55** (also known as **Soi Thonglor**), lined with a variety of hip restaurants, cafés and nightspots as well as boutique shopping enclaves. ❏

Possibly one of the world's most eccentric golf courses lies between the runways of Don Muang Airport; run by the Royal Thai Air Force, Kantarat's 18 holes are hardly spectacular but get played, like Mount Everest, "because it's there".

BELOW LEFT: Sukhumvit night market. **BELOW:** the Chong Nonsi intersection in the southern suburbs.

RESTAURANTS AND BARS

Restaurants

Price per person for a
three-course meal
without drinks:
$ = under B300
$$ = B300–800
$$$ = B800–1,600
$$$$ = over B1,600

Rattanakosin
Thai
Coconut Palm
394/3–5 Th. Maharaj.
Mobile tel: 08-1827 2394.
Open: daily 10am–7pm. $
Family-style restaurant
serving far better meals
than its fast-food-esque
interior suggests. The
curries (red and green)
and soups (*tom yam* and
coconut, or *tom kha gai*)
disappear by lunchtime.
For dinner, try excellent
dishes like rice noodles
with spicy-and-sour sauce.

Rub Ar-roon
310 Th. Maharaj. Tel: 0-2622
2312. Open: daily 8am–
6.30pm. $
Chinese shophouse with
coffees, toasted sand-
wiches and not-too-spicy
local food. This was a
pharmacy 80 years ago,
and the herbal display
cabinets are still in place,
adding to the bistro-like
atmosphere (although the
only alcohol is beer).

Thonburi
Thai
Krua Rakang Thong
306 Soi Wat Rakhang, Th.
Arun-Amarin, Sirirat. Tel:
0-2848 9597. Open: daily
11am–11pm. $
This old-style riverfront
restaurant with views of
Wat Arun and the spires
of the Grand Palace is a
good sunset spot to dine

on king prawns in sweet-
and-sour tamarind sauce,
spicy northeastern
salads, and "exploded"
catfish, diced and fried
until crumbly, then added
to coconut soup.

Supatra River House
266 Soi Wat Rakhang,
Th. Arun-Amarin, Sirirat.
Tel: 0-2411 0305. Open:
daily L & D. $$
www.supatrariverhouse.com
Former family home of
owners Patravadi
Mechudhon (of Patravadi
Theatre fame) and her
sister. Good Thai cuisine
served on the riverbank
terrace or in one of two
Thai-style houses.
Traditional music and
dance accompany your
dinner at weekends.

Old City and Dusit
Italian
La Casa
210 Th. Khao San. Tel:
0-2629 1628. Open: daily
noon–midnight. $$
Simple open-fronted trat-
toria with terrace seats
ideal for watching the
Khao San bustle. A few
spicier dishes, such as
the moreish sizzling squid
with chilli, garlic and lime,
enliven the ample menu
of pastas, risottos and
traditional dishes.

Thai
Kaloang Home Kitchen
2 Th. Sri Ayutthaya, Dusit.
Tel: 0-2281 9228. Open:
daily 11am–10pm. $–$$
This restaurant has
retained its rustic charm,
even though much else
around it has careened
into the 21st century.

Serves a good choice of
Thai standards, but most
people go for the grilled
fish and seafood, such as
curried crab.

Kinlom Chon Saphan
11/6 Samsen Soi 3. Tel:
0-2628 8382–3. Open: daily
5pm–midnight. $
Live tanks of fish and
seafood advertise the
speciality at this riverfront
restaurant opposite the
Rama VIII Bridge. Diners
sit on the open-air terrace
for meals of steamed
shrimp in spicy sauce,
curried crab and
charcoal-grilled fish.

May Kaidee
117/1 Th. Tanao. Tel: 0-2281
7137. Open: daily 8am–
11pm. $
www.maykaidee.com
Serving vegetarian food
since 1988, May has a
fine reputation for her
meat-free Thai standards
(second outlet at nearby
33 Th. Samsen). Isaan-
style (from northeast
Thailand) vegetarian
dishes with mushrooms,
tofu and soya beans, and
massaman curry with
tofu, potatoes and pea-
nuts are popular selec-
tions. Dessert of black
sticky rice with coconut,
banana and mango is
heavenly. To find this
place, take the *soi* next to
Burger King, and turn left.

Roti-Mataba
136 Th. Phra Arthit. Tel:
0-2282 2119. Open: Tue–
Sun 7am–10pm. $
An army of women here
make the Muslim-style
breads – flat unleavened

LEFT: Sirocco, 200 metres (650ft) above the city.

roti and meat-stuffed *mataba* – by the hundreds in this busy shophouse. Dip the crisp *roti* into their delicious *massaman* and *korma* curries of fish, vegetable or meat. There are only a few tables inside and on the pavement, so be prepared to wait.

Chinatown
Chinese
Noodle N' More
513/514 Th. Rong Muang. Tel: 0-2613 8972. Open: daily 11am–11pm. **$**
Hong Kong-style noodle restaurant with a good corner location close to Hualamphong station. Serves good range of noodle dishes, plus all-day *dim sum*, rice with mixed dishes and a few desserts, like sesame dumplings with ginger.

Indian
Punjab Sweets and Restaurant
436/5 Th. Chakraphet. Tel: 0-2623 7606. Open: daily 8am–9pm. **$**
Bangkok's Little India (Pahurat) sits at the western edge of Chinatown. Its alleyways are crowded with tiny Indian cafés, of which this is one of the best. Its meat- and dairy-free food includes curries and *dosa* from south India, and Punjabi sweets wrapped in edible silver foil.

Thai Food Stalls
Soi Texas
Th. Padung Dao. No phone. Open: 9am–2am. **$–$$**
Named after its **Texas Suki** restaurant, this atmospheric *soi* (side street) also has several seafood eateries. The best are **Rut and Lek** and **T & K** (from 6pm daily), both at the entrance of the *soi*. You can't go wrong with crab and seafood, either cooked in curry, charcoal-grilled or fried with garlic and chilli.

Pathumwan and Pratunam
French
Cáfe Le Notre
Gnd Fl, Natural Ville Executive Residences, 61 Soi Lang Suan. Tel: 0-2250 7050–1. Open: daily 6am–10.30pm. **$–$$**
This stylish café has a small menu of interesting starters, salads and mains to supplement its lovely cakes and pastries. Great quality and reasonable prices.

Le Café Siam
4 Soi Sri Aksorn, Chua Ploeng Road, Thung Muahamek, Sathorn. Tel: 0-2671 0030. Open: Mon–Sat 6pm–midnight. **$$$$**
www.lecafesiam.com
First, the location, the restored home of a railway official, is superb; and the food, cheffed by Paul Anthony Quarchioni, is exquisite. Take some time to chill in the upstairs lounge, whether over an aperitif or a nightcap or both.

Italian
Biscotti
Four Seasons Hotel, 155 Th. Ratchadamri. Tel: 0-2255 5443. Open: daily L & D. **$$$**
A power dining mecca of terracotta, marble and wood in a stylish Tony Chi-designed outlet. The large and busy open kitchen sets the tone for its excellent Italian cuisine, while the open space is ideal for being seen. Packed with businesspeople for lunch and a who's who list of Thai society for dinner.

Calderazzo
59 Soi Lang Suan. Tel: 0-2252 8108–9. Open: daily L & D. **$$–$$$**
Clever lighting and lots of wood, stone, metal and glass create a warm and stylish atmosphere for homey southern Italian food.

Thai
Coca
416/3–8 Th. Henri Dunant, cnr Siam Square Soi 7. Tel: 0-2251 6337. Open: daily 11am–11pm. **$**
www.coca.com
Part of a chain of restaurants offering communal dining with a pot of hot broth in the centre of the table for cooking morsels of fish, meat and vegetables, fondue-style. Dunk the food into a small bowl of sweet-and-spicy chilli sauce before popping it into your mouth. Delicious.

Curries & More
63/3 Soi Ruam Rudee. Tel: 0-2253 5405–7. Open: daily 11am–11.30pm. **$$**
A branch of the famous **Baan Khanitha** (at 69 Th. Sathorn Tai and 31/1 Sukhumvit Soi 23) serving tasty Thai food with the spices toned down to suit international palates. Charming townhouse setting. The *kaeng leuang* (yellow curry) is excellent. It also has some international dishes (pasta, pies, crepes and excellent apple crumble).

Gai Tort Soi Polo
137/1–2 Soi Polo, Th. Withayu. Tel: 0-2252 2252. Open: daily 7am–7pm. **$**
One of Bangkok's most famous fried-chicken shops. The delicious *gai* is marinated in soy sauce, tamarind and pepper, and served piping hot topped with fried garlic. Eat it with *somtam* (green papaya salad) and dipped in sweet-and-spicy and sour-and-spicy sauces.

Savoury
Gnd Fl, Siam Paragon, Th. Rama I. Tel: 0-2129 4353. Open: daily 11am–10pm. **$$**
Stylish café with high-backed armchairs, bright cushions and marble tables. Lemongrass chicken with mixed fruits in a delicious hot-and-sour *somtam* dressing is typical of the inventive dishes here. Mouth-watering cakes to wash down with a range of teas and fruit juices.

Thai Food Stalls
Mah Boon Krong Food Centre
Top Fl, Mah Boon Krong, 444 Th. Phayathai. Tel: 0-2217 9491. Open: daily 10am–9pm. **$**
Huge Thai food court in a shopping mall. Large variety of local dishes (noodles, rice, salads, desserts, vegetarian). Buy vouchers as you go in, choose from as many stalls as you like and sit down anywhere. Redeem unused vouchers for cash on your way out. If streetside food puts you off, this is a good alternative.

Bangrak and Silom
Chinese
China House
Oriental Hotel, 48 Oriental Ave. Tel: 0-2659 9000. Open: daily L & D. **$$$**
Beautiful 1930s Shanghainese Art Deco interior of red lanterns, carved wood and ebony pillars. Miniature black-and-white photos and Chinese calligraphy cover the walls. It's a wonderful setting for top-quality dishes like hot-and-sour soup filled with fresh herbs and sweet lobster meat.

French
Le Bouchon
37/17 Patpong Soi 2. Tel: 0-2234 9109. Open: Mon–Sat L & D, Sun D. **$$–$$$**

This atmospheric seven-table bistro gains a certain frisson from its location in Patpong – very French and slightly naughty, like a Marseille dockyard diner. Very popular with local French expats for its simple home cooking and friendly banter at the small bar.

La Boulange
2–2/1 Th. Convent. Tel: 0-2631 0355. Open: daily 7am–8pm. **$$**
Enticing French bakery and patisserie that serves freshly baked croissants and brewed coffee to the breakfast crowd, all-day snacks such as *croque monsieur*, pâtés and salads, and daily specials like duck confit.

D'Sens
Dusit Thani Hotel, 946 Th. Rama IV. Tel: 0-2236 9999. Open: Mon–Sat L & D. **$$$$**
This branch of the 3 Michelin-starred Le Jardin des Sens, in Montpellier, France, is full of delicious surprises. Chef Philippe Keller works wonders in his kitchen with dishes like porcini mushrooms and duck-liver ravioli in a frothy truffle *sabayon*. Desserts are equally outstanding.

Indian
Tamil Nadu
Silom Soi 11. Tel: 0-2235 6336. Open: daily 11.30am–9.30pm. **$**
Simple south Indian café whose house speciality is *masala dosa*, a pancake made of rice flour and

urad dal, stuffed with potato and onion curry and served with coconut chutney. You can also order meat and vegetable curries to eat with the plain *dosa*.

International/Fusion
Cy'an
Metropolitan Hotel, 27 Th. Sathorn Tai. Tel: 0-2625 3333. Open: daily B, L & D. **$$$–$$$$**
Serves inspired Mediterranean-Asian seafood amid the cutting-edge minimalism of this hip hotel. Spanish and Moroccan flourishes bring sweet and spicy flavours to dishes like seared tiger prawns, and tortellini with pine nuts, raisins and parmesan.

Eat Me
Fl 1, 1/6 Piphat Soi 2, off Th. Convent. Tel: 0-2238 0931. Open: daily D. **$$$**
Very popular restaurant with art exhibitions often featuring edgy young artists promoted by the nearby H Gallery. The food is modern Australian, featuring dishes such as charred scallops with mango, herb salad, pickled onion and citrus dressing. On cool nights ask for a table on the terrace. Excellent wine list of mainly Australian varietals.

Sirocco
Fl 63, Lebua at State Tower, 1055 Th. Silom. Tel: 0-2624 9555. Open: daily D. **$$$–$$$$**
www.thedomebkk.com
Spectacular 200-metre (650ft) high outdoor rooftop restaurant with magnificent views over the river. Greco-Roman architecture and a jazz band add to the sense of occasion. In the same complex, there's classy **Distil Bar** serving top-quality seafood, the Ital-

ian eatery **Mezzaluna** and the alfresco pan-Asian restaurant **Breeze**.

Italian
La Scala
Sukhothai Hotel, 13/3 Th. Sathorn Tai. Tel: 0-2287 0222. Open: daily L & D. **$$$**
Asian modernist interior of teak, bronze, terracotta and glass brickwork with a central open kitchen where diners sit around to watch culinary theatre. If you don't fancy dishes like roasted fillet of turbot with fennel, black olives and dill, order the thin-crust pizzas fresh from the wood-fired oven.

Zanotti
Gnd Fl, Saladaeng Colonnade, 21/2 Soi Saladaeng. Tel: 0-2636 0002. Open: daily L & D. **$$$**
www.zanotti-ristorante.com
The homey Italian fare from the Piedmont and Tuscany regions includes over 20 pasta dishes, as well as seafood and steaks charcoal-grilled over orange wood from Chiang Mai. The chic wine bar **Vino di Zanotti**, opposite, also serves a full menu and has live jazz.

Japanese
Aoi
132/10–11 Silom Soi 6. Tel: 0-2235 2321–2. Open: daily L & D. **$$**
Black stone walkways invoke a cool calm in this unfussy restaurant serving well-prepared Japanese food. As usual, set meals are much cheaper than the à la carte options.

Thai
The Blue Elephant
233 Th. Sathorn Tai. Tel: 0-2673 9353. Open: daily L & D. **$$–$$$**
www.blueelephant.com/bangkok
Upmarket Thai restaurant

that mixes Thai standards with a few fusion dishes like foie gras in tamarind sauce. The food is excellent, but the flavours are slightly toned down to suit Western palates. Housed in a beautiful century-old restored historic building.

Le Lys
104 Narathiwat Soi 7. Tel: 0-2677 5709. Open: daily 11am–10.30pm. **$**
The Thai-French owners avoid Thai clichés like *tom yum goong* and green curry in favour of dishes like tamarind sour soups (*tom som* with stuffed squid), spicy jungle curries and baby clams in curry sauce. The homey interior resembles a French bistro, with checked cotton tablecloths and ballet posters on the walls.

American
New York Steakhouse
JW Marriott Hotel, 4 Sukhumvit Soi 2. Tel: 0-2656 7700. Open: daily D. **$$$$**
Top-notch restaurant with a relaxed atmosphere, despite the formal trappings of club-like dark woods and high-backed leather chairs. Start with the Manhattan clam chowder before sinking your teeth into the grain-fed Angus beef, sliced at the table from a silver trolley.

Indian
Hazara
29 Sukhumvit Soi 38. Tel: 0-2713 6048–9. Open: daily D. **$$**
www.facebars.com
Tasty north Indian fare, like peppery *khadai kheenga* (shrimps stir-fried with bell peppers), in a setting embellished with Asian antiques and artefacts. The complex also

houses the trendy Face Bar and a Thai restaurant called Lan Na Thai.

International
Bed Supperclub
26 Sukhumvit Soi 11. Tel: 0-2651 3537. Open: Sun–Thur 7.30pm–midnight, Fri–Sat 7.30pm–1am. **$$$**
www.bedsupperclub.com
Extraordinary tubular construction with an all-white interior where diners lie on beds and cushions to eat the brilliant fusion cuisine. Choose from multi-choice three-course set menus. Next door is **Bed Bar**, one of the city's top clubs and popular with Bangkok's trendy.

Greyhound
Fl 2, Emporium, Th. Sukhumvit. Tel: 0-2664 8663. Open: daily 11am–9.15pm. **$$**
www.greyhound.co.th
Trendy modern Thai café serving European-influenced dishes such as the signature Thai anchovy spaghetti with chilli. Meals are chalked up on giant blackboards, and there are glass-fronted displays of mouth-watering cakes.

Kuppa
39 Sukhumvit Soi 16. Tel: 0-2663 0450. Open: Tue–Sun 10am–11pm. **$$**
Bangkok's sophisticated thirtysomethings browse magazines and enjoy their *tête-à-tête* over espressos in a huge room of comfortable sofas, blond wood and brushed metal. Decent international and Thai food.

Italian
Café Buongiorno
22 Sukhumvit Soi 33. Tel: 0-2662 3471. Open: daily 10am–10pm. **$$**
Sipping cappuccino in

this elegant, secluded house in a walled garden, it's hard to believe you're a stone's throw from the hostess bars of Soi 33. The menu culls dishes from the owner's family archives, including great cakes and breads.

Il Tartufo
Sukhumvit Soi 51. Tel: 0-2259 3569. Open: Tue–Sun 11am–2.30pm, 6–11pm. **$$**
www.iltartufobangkok.com
That the set lunch starts at 300 baht is indicative of sensible pricing; and you can expect solid Italian fare with a certain amount of flair at this cosy and well-laid-out eatery.

Japanese
Koi
26 Sukhumvit Soi 20. Tel: 0-2663 4990–1. Open: Tue–Sun 6pm–midnight. **$$$–$$$$**
www.koirestaurantbkk.com
This sister of a celebrity hangout in Los Angeles fuses Japanese and Californian cuisines in a cool interior with scented candles and dark woods.

Thai
Baan Khanitha
36/1 Sukhumvit Soi 23. Tel: 0-2258 4181. Open: daily L & D. **$$**
This first outlet of the well-known Baan Khanitha (also at **69 Th. Sathorn Tai**) is located in a charming old house with a lush garden. Busy with mainly Japanese and Western customers dining on tasty foreigner-friendly flavours ranging from Chiang Mai sausage and spicy salads to various curries.

Basil
Sheraton Grande Sukhumvit, 250 Th. Sukhumvit. Tel:

0-2649 8888. Open: L & D. **$$–$$$**
One of few hotel Thai restaurants that avoids neglecting robust home-grown flavours for the delicate stomachs of tourists. The teak interior has a modern, clean-lined elegance.

Cabbages & Condoms
10 Sukhumvit Soi 12. Tel: 0-2229 4610. Open: daily 11am–11pm. **$–$$**
Renowned for its promotion of family planning (its owner is former senator Mechai "Mr Condom" Viravaidhya, who has done much for AIDS awareness in Thailand). The two-storey restaurant, with mainly outdoor seating, has a pleasant ambience. Free condoms as you leave.

Spring/Summer
199 Soi Promsri 2, Sukhumvit Soi 39. Tel: 0-2392 2747/57/46. Open: daily L & D. **$$**
www.springnsummer.com
Three venues in one. **Spring**, in a glass-and-metal Art Deco house, has tasty modern Thai dishes such as rice noodle rolls with fried sea bass, with lime, chilli, shallots and betel leaf. Opposite, **Summer** serves desserts amid the sublime aromas of chocolate and berries, while in between, there's a bar with beanbag seating strewn on the lawn.

Vegetarian
Tamarind Café
Sukhumvit Soi 20. Tel: 0-2663 7421. Open: Mon–Fri 11am–11pm, Sat–Sun 9am–11pm. **$**
www.tamarind-cafe.com
This stylish all-white Bangkok branch of a Hanoi café holds photography exhibitions and has a flair for European-Asian flavours. Tapas-style starters include tabouleh, falafel coated in sesame seeds and Thai crispy mushrooms with a mild chilli dip.

RIGHT: the extraordinary Bed Supperclub.

BANGKOK'S SUBURBS

Accessible getaways from the big city's relentless pace are sleepy Nonthaburi by the river, delightfully green Rama IX Royal Park, child-friendly Dream World and the sprawling Chatuchak Weekend Market – highly recommended for incurable shopaholics

Main attractions
CHATUCHAK WEEKEND MARKET
NONTHABURI
KO KRET
PRASART MUSEUM

BELOW: souvenir shopping par excellence at Chatuchak Weekend Market.

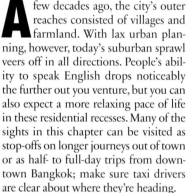

A few decades ago, the city's outer reaches consisted of villages and farmland. With lax urban planning, however, today's suburban sprawl veers off in all directions. People's ability to speak English drops noticeably the further out you venture, but you can also expect a more relaxing pace of life in these residential recesses. Many of the sights in this chapter can be visited as stop-offs on longer journeys out of town or as half- to full-day trips from downtown Bangkok; make sure taxi drivers are clear about where they're heading.

Chatuchak Weekend Market

The final stop on the Skytrain's northern line at Mo Chit station drops you at the **Chatuchak Weekend Market ❶** (Sat–Sun 7am–6pm). Reputed to be the world's biggest flea market, sprawling Chatuchak (sometimes also spelt Jatujak) is a must-see for any visitor; even the least enthusiastic shopper cannot fail to be overawed by the sheer scale and variety of goods available.

With an estimated 400,000 visitors weaving through the market's maze-like interior every weekend, Chatuchak is a heady assault on the senses, so an early start (arrive by 9am) is essential to beat the soaring heat and ensuing feelings of claustrophobia. Navigating your way around Chatuchak is an adventure in itself. Although loosely partitioned into sections, the fun is in stumbling across hidden pockets of culture or kitsch as you meander the web of narrow alleyways. You will find everything from crafts, home decor and clothing to flowers and even pets. Wherever you are, beware of pickpockets, who can spot a distracted cashed-up shopper at 100 paces.

Tip: if you get lost, use the **clock tower** in the middle of the market as a contact point. Free maps of the market are available at the **Chatuchak Information Counter** at the entrance near Section 27 along Thanon Kamphaengphet 3. Some people prefer to wander around, chancing upon things they like until they run out of steam.

Chatuchak aficionados will tell you that it's imperative to know exactly which section to head for to find what you want, otherwise you'll definitely run out of steam!

Numerous cafés, snack and juice bars are dotted throughout the market, with many staying busy long after the stalls pack up for the day. After sunset, the outer edge of the market on Thanon Kamphaengphet comes alive with a string of bars and coffee shops.

If the market is simply too overwhelming, retreat to the nearby **Chatuchak Park** (daily 4.30am–9pm; free). Built on land once owned by the State Railway, the park has a small **Hall of Railway Heritage Museum** (Sat–Sun 7am–3pm; free), with displays of old steam locomotives as well as other forms of transport, including – oddly – London taxis.

Nonthaburi

The riverside town of **Nonthaburi ②**, some 10km (6 miles) north of Bangkok, feels a world away from the hectic city. To get there, take an express boat (around 45 mins) to the end of the line at Tha Nonthaburi pier. The journey passes under bridges and weaves past tiny tugboats, gilded temples and communities of stilted houses. At Nonthaburi, it's worth exploring the streets and markets, or charter a longtail boat to visit the island of Ko Kret (*see below*) or the scenic canal of Khlong Om. A canal trip along Khlong Om will take you past durian plantations and water-bound communities. Five minutes upriver from Nonthaburi pier brings you to the stunning temple of **Wat Chalerm Phra Kiet**, a beautifully restored 19th-century monastery seemingly set in the middle of nowhere.

Ko Kret

Further upstream from Nonthaburi is the car-free island of **Ko Kret ③**. Best reached by chartered longtail boat from Nonthaburi to Tha Pa Fai pier on Ko Kret, the island makes for a laidback half-day tour, allowing tourists to soak up a relaxed pace of life more typical of the rest of Thailand. The island has no roads, and can be circumambulated in less than two hours. While there are no specific attractions, it is famous for

Allow a sufficient amount of time to browse the gargantuan Chatuchak Market.

BELOW: a Mon potter at Ko Kret.

its earthenware pottery studios. The villagers are primarily from the ethnic Mon group, who migrated to central Thailand from Burma and were a strong regional influence from the 6th to 11th centuries.

Dream World

Anyone who has visited other major theme parks around the globe isn't going to be rendered speechless by Bangkok's **Dream World** ❹ (Km 7, Thanon Rangsit Nakornnayok; Mon–Fri 10am–5pm, Sat–Sun 10am–7pm; charge; www.dreamworld-th.com).

Nevertheless, the park, located east of Don Muang Airport, is worthwhile if you have a bunch of youngsters in tow. It comprises Dream World Plaza, Dream Garden, Fantasy Land and Adventure Land. A sightseeing train circles Dream Garden, while a cable car and monorail offer views of the park and surrounding rural areas.

Thrill-seekers should head for Adventure Land, the most stomach-churning section of the park. Along with the rollercoasters, there is a Viking swinging ship, an exciting Super Splash log flume and the Grand Canyon water ride. In Snow Town, locals get to experience frosty weather, with sledge rides down a slope made of artificial snow.

Safari World

Some 45km (28 miles) northeast of Bangkok near Minburi is **Safari World** ❺, a popular destination for Bangkok families (99 Thanon Ramindra; daily 9am–5pm; charge; www. safariworld.com). Animals on view at the 81-hectare (200-acre) park include giraffes, zebras, ostriches, rhinos and camels. The feeding sessions at the tiger and lion enclosures are big attractions here. The wildly popular orangutan boxing shows, however, one of the park's most popular attractions, are questionable to say the least. Its adjoining **Marine Park** features acrobatics performed by sea lions and dolphins, as well as airborne antics by parrots and cockatoos.

Prasart Museum

Little visited, partly because of its rather remote location in Huamak, is the **Prasart Museum** ❻ (9 Soi 4A

Bangkok Suburbs

Thanon Krungthep Kreetha; visits only by appointment – tel: 02-379 3601/7 – Thur–Sun 10am–3pm; charge). Housed within a garden, the antique Thai arts and crafts on display belong to its ardent private collector, Prasart Vongsakul.

The artefacts are contained in several magnificent buildings, all of which are replicas inspired by the region's architectural classics. These elegant structures include a European-style mansion, a Khmer shrine, teak houses from Thailand's north and central regions, as well as a Thai and Chinese temple.

Wat Thammamongkhon

At the easternmost reaches of Thanon Sukhumvit at Soi 101 is **Wat Thammamongkhon 7** (daily 6am–6pm; free), unique for its 95-metre (312ft) high *chedi*, which at 14 storeys is the tallest in Bangkok and offers commanding views of the low-rise eastern suburbs. Built in 1963, the *chedi* is modern in design, containing study rooms for novice monks and a lift to the topmost circular shrine room.

At the *chedi*'s base, the Will Power Institute runs classes in Buddhist meditation. The three-level glass pavilion beside the temple houses a 14-tonne Buddha image and a 10-tonne sculpture of the Chinese goddess Guanyin, both carved from a solid slab of jade.

Rama IX Royal Park

One of the city's largest green spaces, the 81-hectare (200-acre) **Rama IX Royal Park 8** (daily 5.30am–6.30pm; charge) offers a delightful escape from the city. Unfortunately, the park's suburban locale in Sukhumvit 103 entails taking a 20-minute taxi ride from the last Skytrain station at On Nut. In a city desperately thin on public greenery, the park's opening in 1987 as a 60th birthday tribute to the king was a welcome addition.

With a dome-covered botanical garden, canals and bridges, water-lily pond, as well as Chinese and Japanese ornamental gardens, the park is a delight to explore. Pack a picnic lunch, and on a weekday you'll pretty much have the place to yourself. ❏

Enjoying a picnic at Rama IX Royal Park.

BELOW: dolphins in action at Safari World.

CENTRAL THAILAND

When Bangkok overwhelms, easy escapes within a few hours' drive from the city provide welcome relief. Choose from ancient monuments, verdant national parks and a floating market

Residents say that the next best thing to living in Bangkok is being able to leave it – and an array of attractions within a few hours' drive of the city makes this an attractive proposition. Some are strictly day trips but several, especially beach destinations, can be extended into leisurely week-long stays. Getting around in Thailand is relatively easy and inexpensive, with a good network of domestic flights, a regular if rather leisurely rail network, and frequent inter-city buses.

The flat, fertile Central Plain region, with its wealth of sun-ripened rice fields, is the nearest and most accessible area from Bangkok, holding the remnants of former kingdoms as well as several national parks. West of Bangkok are attractions like the Rose Garden, with its tourist-geared cultural shows, and its close neighbour, Samphran Elephant Ground. Beyond the Rose Garden lies Nakhon Pathom with its colossal golden Phra Pathom Chedi and assortment of palaces, where many a Thai royal used to rest on journeys to places further afield. Southeast of Nakhon Pathom, Damnoen Saduak Floating Market ranks as a must-see on every first-time Bangkok visitor's list.

Even further west is Kanchanaburi, site of the legendary World War II bridge across the Kwai River. The surrounding area is an outdoor adventure playground with endless possibilities for river rafting and trekking. West of Kanchanaburi are the ancient Khmer ruins at Prasart Muang Singh, while due north are the rainforests at Erawan and Sai Yok national parks.

Turning north, the ancient city of Ayutthaya is a grand repository for faded ruins, dating to the 14th century when it functioned as Thailand's capital. Some say the best part about Ayutthaya is getting there – on a teakwood barge winding up the sinuous Chao Phraya River. Still further north is Lopburi, the old summer retreat of the Ayutthayan kings.

The area immediately south of Bangkok is scant on tourist sights; the main attractions are the Ancient City, where you can see Thailand in miniature, and the Crocodile Farm and Zoo. ❑

PRECEDING PAGES: Erawan Waterfall at Erawan National Park, Kanchanaburi.
LEFT: Damnoen Saduak Floating Market. **ABOVE RIGHT:** Bang Pa-In Palace.
ABOVE LEFT: Phra Narai Ratchanivet ruins at Lopburi.

WEST OF BANGKOK

Home to the world's tallest Buddhist monument, the historic River Kwai Bridge and spectacular waterfalls in rainforest-clad national parks, this region offers history, culture and nature in equal measure

Main attractions
ROSE GARDEN
SAMPHRAN ELEPHANT GROUND
PHRA PATHOM CHEDI
DAMNOEN SADUAK FLOATING MARKET
KANCHANABURI
PRASAT MUANG SINGH
ERAWAN NATIONAL PARK
SAI YOK NATIONAL PARK

Bangkok's immediate surroundings have a number of attractions that are in range of a day trip or which make a pleasant overnight break. The western provinces are only a short distance from the capital and share a border with nearby Myanmar (Burma). Most people heading in this direction make a brief stop in Nakhon Pathom Province to gawk at the huge *chedi* that dominates the town, before heading on to Kanchanaburi Province, famous for its so-called "Bridge on the River Kwai" and its tragic wartime associations. However, equally fascinating are the seldom-visited coastal provinces of Samut Sakhon and the lush lowlands of Samut Songkhram.

NAKHON PATHOM
Rose Garden
Some 32km (20 miles) west from Bangkok on Route 4 towards Nakhon Pathom is the **Rose Garden Riverside Resort ❶** (daily 8am–6pm; charge; www.rosegardenriverside.com). It features well-landscaped gardens with roses and orchids, as well as a resort-style hotel, a cultural centre, restaurants, tennis courts, an artificial lake with paddleboats, a spa and an excellent golf course.

The most visited attraction here is the Thai Village Cultural Show, held daily in the garden. In a large arena,

costumed actors perform folk dances to the accompaniment of live traditional music and re-enact a traditional wedding ceremony and a Thai boxing match. Outside, after this, elephants put on their own show, moving huge teak logs as they would in the forests of the north. The elephants also carry tourists around the compound for a small fee. Otherwise, spend time browsing at the Cultural Village, with gift shops and demonstrations by weavers creating thread from silkworm cocoons.

LEFT: Phra Pathom Chedi. **RIGHT:** manicured grounds at the Rose Garden Riverside Resort.

Samphran Elephant Ground

Just a stone's throw from the Rose Garden is **Samphran Elephant Ground
& Zoo** (daily 8am–5.30pm; charge;
www.elephantshow.com), another family-
oriented attraction where visitors can
ride on an elephant and learn about its
importance in traditional Thai culture.
Other animals on view here include
gibbons, macaques, pythons, crocodiles
and a diverse collection of local birds.

Phra Pathom Chedi

Some 56km (35 miles) west of Bangkok, beyond the Rose Garden on Route
4, is the town of **Nakhon Pathom ❷**,
known for the colossal **Phra Pathom
Chedi**. Measuring 130 metres (420ft)
tall, this golden landmark is claimed as
the tallest Buddhist monument in the
world, and possibly the oldest Buddhist
site in the country, dating back to the
year 3 BC. The original small Sri Lankan-
style *chedi* was erected to commemorate
the arrival of Indian Buddhist missionaries who supposedly brought Buddhism
to Thailand via Burma in that year.

The town itself was established
between the 6th and 11th centuries by
the Dvaravati empire, a Mon civilisation which flourished in Burma and
Thailand. In the early 11th century the
Khmers invaded from Angkor, overrun-
ning the city and replacing the original *chedi* with a more Brahman-style
prang.

Then, in 1057, King Anawrahta of
Burma besieged the town, leaving the
religious edifice in ruins. When King
Mongkut (Rama IV) visited the old
chedi in 1853, he was so impressed by its
historical significance that he ordered
the restoration of the temple. A new
chedi was built, covering the older one;
the present structure was completed by
King Chulalongkorn (Rama V).

Set in a huge square park, the massive
chedi rests upon a circular terrace and is
surrounded by trees associated with the
Buddha's life. Located in the compound
is the **Phra Pathom Chedi National
Museum** (Wed–Sun 9am–noon and
1–4pm; charge; www.thailandmuseum.
com), which is worth seeing for its artefacts, including tools, carvings and statuary from the Dvaravati period.

In former times, a visit to Nakhon
Pathom was more than a day's journey

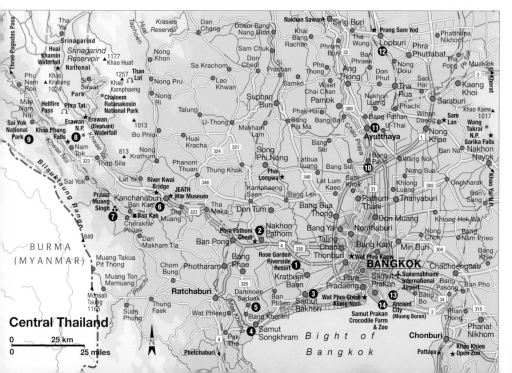

from Bangkok, so it's not surprising that a number of palaces and residences were built for visiting royalty. One of them, **Sanam Chandra Palace** (Thur–Sun 9am–4pm; charge; www.palaces.thai.net), 2km (1¼ miles) west of Phra Pathom Chedi along Thanon Raja-mankha Nai, comprises several buildings: these include a Thai-style pavilion that is now used as government offices, and an idiosyncratic structure built in the English Tudor style. The palace was commissioned by King Vajiravudh (Rama VI) in 1907.

Be sure to see the **Yaleh Monument**, which honours Yaleh, the pet dog of Vajiravudh. The fierce dog, unpopular with the court, was poisoned by the king's attendants. Even as a statue, Yaleh looks insufferable.

Although the grounds are open to the public, the palace buildings are off-limits – apart for one, which serves as a small museum and contains memorabilia of King Vajiravudh.

SAMUT SAKHON

A good way to approach the coastal port of **Samut Sakhon** ❸ (Ocean City), on the coast 28km (17 miles) southwest of Bangkok, is by the Mae Khlong railway line that connects to Thonburi in Bangkok. The line carries passengers on a 40-minute journey through the capital's suburbs, then through thriving vegetable gardens, groves of coconut and areca palms, and rice fields. A busy fishing port, Samut Sakhon (also called Mahachai) lies at the confluence of the Tachin River, the Mahachai Canal and the Gulf of Thailand. The main landing stage on the riverbank is marked by a clock tower and a seafood restaurant.

At the fish market pier, it's possible to hire a boat for a round trip to Samut Sakhon's principal temple, **Wat Chong Lom**, at the mouth of the Tachin River. Most of the temple structures are modern, except for an old *viharn* (sermon hall) immediately to the right of the temple's river landing. The *viharn* dates back about a century. The grounds overlooking the river are laid out with shrubs and flowering trees. There is also a bronze statue of King Chulalongkorn commemorating his visit to the temple.

If you see an elephant being made to beg in the street, don't be tempted to hand over any cash. Your money will be better spent if donated to a registered charity, rather than to a possibly unscrupulous mahout.

BELOW LEFT: Phra Pathom Chedi.
BELOW: rural station on the Bangkok–Samut Sakhon line.

SAMUT SONGKHRAM

From Samut Sakhon, cross the river to the railway station on the opposite side. Here, board a second train for another 40-minute trip to **Samut Songkhram ❹** Province, 74km (46 miles) southwest from Bangkok, on the banks of the Mae Khlong River. The route passes by broad salt flats, with their picturesque windmills slowly being turned by the sea breezes.

The smallest province in Thailand, Samut Songkhram has abundant fruit orchards: pomelo, jackfruit, rose apple, lychee, mango, as well as the ubiquitous banana and coconuts, are harvested here before being sent to Bangkok to be loaded onto the ice-packed vending carts that trundle the streets of the capital. Samut Songkhram itself is just another fishing town; wandering around its wharf is an olfactory and visual experience. Teak barges can be hired for private dinner cruises up the river (ask at riverside restaurants), a trip made more picturesque by the swarms of fireflies that magically illuminate the shoreline of *lamphu* trees in the evenings.

Rose apples harvested in the orchards of Samut Songkhram. Indigenous to Southeast Asia, rose apples have a lovely tart flavour.

BELOW: Damnoen Saduak Floating Market.

King Buddhalertla Naphalai Memorial Park

From Samut Songkhram, you can detour to Amphawa district to visit the **King Buddhalertla Naphalai Memorial Park**, also known as Rama II Historical Park (park daily 9am–6pm, museum Wed–Sun 9am–4pm; admission charge), situated at the birthplace of Rama II. This small museum houses arts and crafts from the early Rattanakosin period in four beautifully reconstructed teakwood stilted houses, illustrating how Thai people lived during the rule of King Rama II. Rare trees, some of which are mentioned in classical Thai literature, flourish in gardens around the museum.

Nearby, the **Amphawa Floating Market** anchors in front of the old Wat Amphawa each morning from 6–8am. It's located about a 10-minute walk from the historical park. The market is smaller and more authentic compared to the one at Damnoen Saduak (*see below*).

Don Hoi Lot

Another option, accessible by either car or longtail boat from Samut Songkhram, is **Don Hoi Lot**, at the mouth of the Mae Khlong River. Don Hoi Lot is, in fact, a bank of fossilised shells that has become a popular attraction with locals. It's a great place to enjoy fresh seafood and tube-like clams (*hoi lot* in Thai, meaning straw clams). In the late afternoon when the tide is low, villagers enthusiastically search the muddy estuary for their quarry.

Damnoen Saduak

From Samut Songkhram, hire a longtail boat for a trip up the Mae Khlong River to the **Damnoen Saduak Floating Market ❺** (daily 7am–1pm) in Ratchaburi Province. An early morning departure is necessary if you want to beat the tour buses from Bangkok that flock to this famous floating market by 10am.

While it is possible to walk along the bankside lined with souvenir stands,

it's advisable to hire a longtail boat to get a better sense of the water-bound commercial bustle. Be prepared to be caught up in a touristic jumble: this 100-year-old market is little more than a tourist sideshow today, with tourists clamouring to snap pictures of the colourful fruit- and vegetable-laden wooden vessels, paddled by smiling sun-beaten women wearing wide-brimmed straw hats.

If you've hired your own longtail boat, it might be worthwhile asking the boatman to take you deeper into the canals where you can get a better glimpse of the lives of the canal-side communities.

KANCHANABURI

Located around 130km (75 miles) west of Bangkok, the sleepy provincial town of **Kanchanaburi** ❻ is well worth the two-hour drive it takes to get there. This can be simply a busy day trip – but it works better as a more relaxing overnight, with an evening spent on the banks of the Khwae Yai River.

Kanchanaburi has achieved widespread fame for its infamous railway,

which was built during World War II by Allied POWs and Asian labourers under the watch of the Japanese. Thousands of lives were lost as the ill-equipped prisoners struggled under appalling conditions to complete over 400km (250 miles) of railway track, called the "Death Railway" *(see panel, page 155)* linking Thailand with Burma.

Despite its association with the war and the railway, modern Kanchanaburi is a laidback provincial town. Situated close to the Burmese border, it is home to several interesting temples, as well as nearby caves, waterfalls, forests and the remnants of a 13th-century Khmer palace.

River Kwai Bridge

Spanning the Khwae Yai River (also known as Kwai Yai), the latticed steel **Bridge on the River Kwai** has become a memorial to the fallen. It can be reached by boat or rickshaw from Kanchanaburi Town. The site may have lost a degree of its sombre symbolism to the rampant commercialisation, but walking across it is still a sobering experience. A steam locomotive used shortly

TIP

Instead of staying at a land-based hotel in Kanchanaburi, opt for a floating guesthouse moored by the riverbank. Be warned, though; while these are atmospheric, they can also get very noisy during weekends, thanks to loud music and karaoke boats packed with young Thais.

BELOW: produce for sale at Damnoen Saduak.

Only the eight curved sections of the Bridge on the River Kwai are original; the rest of it was rebuilt after World War II.

BELOW: the Bridge on the River Kwai.

after the war is displayed beside the tiny Kanchanaburi station platform, along with an ingenious Japanese-designed supply truck that could run on both road and rail. Floating restaurants and hotels line both banks of the river.

The bridge itself was the second of two structures, built side by side across the river; the earlier wooden bridge was completed in 1942, with the sturdier steel structure erected by May 1943. Both bridges became a constant target for Allied bombers and were eventually bombed right out of action in 1945. Only the eight curved segments on each side of the current structure are original; the rest was rebuilt after the war as part of Japan's wartime reparations.

The tragic saga of the bridge was famously represented on celluloid in the 1957 film *The Bridge on the River Kwai*, directed by David Lean and starring Alec Guinness, both of whom were later knighted. The movie won seven Academy Awards, although it contained several historic inaccuracies – most blatant of which was that the bridge was destroyed by commandos, when in fact it was bombed by Allied planes.

Today, most of the old railway tracks have been removed, except for a section that runs from Kanchanaburi to the train terminus at **Nam Tok**. The 50km (30-mile) journey takes about 90 minutes to complete and the train passes over the reconstructed bridge. The railway line north of Nam Tok to the Burmese border was destroyed after the war, but some remnants of the track can still be seen today at **Hellfire Pass**, about 14km (9 miles) from Nam Tok. This was the longest of several mountain cuttings hacked out of the rock by the POWs and Asian labourers. The **Hellfire Pass Memorial Museum** (daily 9am–4pm; donation; www.hellfirepass.com) is a tribute to the thousands who died while toiling on the railway line.

World War II Museum

Located beside the bridge is the rather garish **World War II Museum** (daily 9am–6pm; charge), also known as the Art Gallery & War Museum. It contains an odd mixture of exhibits, most of which have nothing at all to do with the war. But if you are into kitsch, there's

plenty of interest. Around the building's exterior are life-size sculptures of significant figures involved in the war; the likes of Hitler, Churchill, Einstein and Hirohito are among those given an almost comic treatment.

JEATH War Museum

The small but informative **JEATH War Museum** (daily 8.30am–6pm; charge), tucked away in the grounds of Wat Chaichumpol on Thanon Pak Phraek at the southern end of Kanchanaburi Town, grants a better appreciation of the enormous obstacles the prisoners faced. Its peaceful locale on the banks of the Mae Khlong River (the larger river that splits into the two tributaries of Kwae Yai and Kwae Noi), shadowed by a 500-year-old *samrong* tree, provide for a quiet moment of reflection.

The acronym JEATH comes from the first letter of some of the principal countries that were involved in this regional conflict during World War II, namely Japan, England, America, Thailand and Holland. The museum is split into two buildings, the larger of which is a long bamboo hut similar to those that housed the POWs during their construction of the Siam–Burma railway. Inside is a collection of poignant photographs, sketches, paintings, newspaper clippings and other war memorabilia illustrating the harsh conditions the POWs endured during their period of enforced labour and incarceration.

Death Railway Museum

Equally fascinating to visit is the **Death Railway Museum** (daily 9am–5pm; charge; www.tbronline.com), housed in the Thailand–Burma Railway Centre, located adjacent to the Allied War Cemetery *(see below)*. The museum has eight galleries tracing the history and sufferings of the people involved in the Death Railway without making a biased judgement. It even has on display a full-scale replica of the original wooden bridge. The museum was founded by Australian Rod Beattie, the local supervisor of the Commonwealth War Graves Commission.

Allied War Cemetery

The **Kanchanaburi Allied War Cemetery** (daily 7am–6pm; free) opposite

One day the war will be over. And I hope that the people that use this bridge in years to come will remember how it was built and who built it. Not a gang of slaves, but soldiers, British soldiers… even in captivity.

Colonel Nicholson
(Alec Guinness)

Death Railway

The Japanese began work on a railway line between Thailand and Burma in 1942 in an effort to improve the supply lines between Japan and Burma. For most of its 400km (260-mile) length from Bangkok to the Burmese border, the railway followed the valley of the Khwae Yai River, with construction taking place simultaneously in different areas. In the end, nearly 15km (9 miles) of bridges were completed. The Japanese forced some 250,000 Asian labourers and 61,000 Allied POWs to construct 260km (160 miles) of rail on the Thai side, leading to the Three Pagodas Pass on the Thai-Burmese border. It is estimated that 100,000 Asian labourers and 16,000 Allied POWs lost their lives between 1942 and 1945 from beatings, starvation and disease.

BELOW: Allied War Cemetery grave.

Khmer ruins at Prasat Muang Singh.

BELOW: JEATH war museum.

the museum is the last resting place of 6,982 Allied soldiers, representing less than half of the 16,000 soldiers who lost their lives building the railway. Immaculate green lawns planted with colourful flowers add a sense of serenity to the graves of the British, American, Australian, Dutch and other Allied soldiers that are lined up row upon row. Look at the grave markers and you'll notice that most of the young men who died for their countries were under the age of 30. Its location, however, beside noisy Thanon Saengchuto detracts from the solemnity of the place.

Located in a more tranquil setting is the **Chung Kai Allied War Cemetery** (daily 7am–6pm; free), situated across the river just southwest of Kanchanaburi town. Another 1,750 POWs are said to be buried at this site.

AROUND KANCHANABURI

For those who opt to stay overnight in Kanchanaburi, the surrounding countryside holds plenty of interest. The limestone crags on the southern outskirts of town are home to cave temples. Some nimble legwork is required in order to navigate the claustrophobic passageways that lead to the eerily lit meditation cells filled with Buddha images. While generally safe, don't venture into the more remote caves unaccompanied; in 1996 a British female tourist was murdered by a drug-crazed monk at Wat Tham Kao Pun.

One of the most frequently visited cave temples is **Wat Tham Mangkhon Thong** (daily 8am–5pm; charge), primarily known for its "floating nun". An old nun, who has since died, used to float on her back and in sitting position in a large pool of water while in a state of meditation. Today, a young disciple gives her own interpretation of the ritual – in return for a fee – for busloads of tourists.

Prasat Muang Singh

Located 43km (27 miles) west of Kanchanaburi, the Khmer ruins of **Prasat Muang Singh** ❼ (daily 8am–5pm; charge) are situated in a manicured park. The site makes for a great picnic as it is located beside the picturesque Khwae Noi River (a smaller tributary of the Khwae Yai). The central sanctuary of this 13th-century temple complex points east, and is in direct alignment with its more grandiose sister, Angkor Wat in Cambodia. Although nowhere near as impressive or intricate as Angkor Wat, Prasat Muang Singh is still a fascinating testament to just how far west the Khmer empire stretched at the height of its power.

On the same site is a small exhibition hall containing duplicates of Khmer sculptures, while near the river is a Neolithic burial site displaying partially uncovered skeletons.

Erawan National Park

Other trips in the vicinity include the spectacular seven-tiered **Erawan Waterfall**, found in **Erawan National Park** ❽ (daily 6am–6pm; charge) and best visited during – or just after – the rainy season (May–Nov), when the water is at full flow. Situated

some 70km (40 miles) north of Kanchanaburi, it is a popular sight and can become quite congested with locals at weekends and on public holidays.

The route to the waterfall starts from the national park office. The climb up the first few levels is manageable, but getting up to the slippery sixth and seventh levels is not recommended unless you are fit and reasonably agile. You can cool off at the inviting natural pools (don't forget your swimsuit) at the base of each of the tiers. The thundering water flow from the highest level is said to take on the shape of the three-headed elephant Erawan, hence its name.

There are several hiking trails in the park, which covers some 550 sq km (212 sq miles) and comprises mainly deciduous forests with limestone hills rising up to 1,000 metres (3,300ft). One of the most popular hiking options is the 90-minute Khanmak-Mookling trail; the 1,400-metre (1,530yd) circular route starts from the national park office. Also taking approximately 90 minutes, the Wangbadan Cave trail takes you through bamboo and evergreen forest along a 1,350-metre (1,480yd) route.

Sai Yok National Park

Less visited is **Sai Yok Waterfall** in **Sai Yok National Park** ❾ (daily 6am–6pm; charge). The stunning cascade (again best seen in the rainy season, or just after) is a little more remote at 100km (62 miles) northwest of Kanchanaburi and best undertaken on an overnight tour.

The national park covers over 500 sq km (193 sq miles) of forest – predominantly teak – with one side bordering Myanmar. The park is also known as the habitat of the smallest known mammal in the world – the bumblebee bat. Found in Sai Yok's limestone caves in 1974, the creature, which weighs a mere 2 grams (¾oz) – and is hardly larger than a bumblebee – has been declared an endangered species. An interesting sight is **Tham Daowadung**, a cave filled with eerie stalactites.

To the north of the park is **Hin Dat Hot Springs** (daily 6am–6pm; charge), another worthy stop. Just metres away from the cold rushing waters of the river, bathers can soak in the steaming-hot spring mineral waters. ❏

The Erawan Waterfall is best visited after the rainy season.

RESTAURANTS

Nakhon Pathom
Thai & Western
Nakhon Inn
Nakhon Inn Hotel, 55 Ratwithi Road. Tel: 0-3425 1152.
Open: daily B, L & D. **$–$$**
In a town with not too many good dining options, this hotel restaurant and coffee shop serves good central Thai fare and some basic Western dishes.

Damnoen Saduak
Thai
Inn Chan
Rose Garden Riverside Resort, Km 32, Th. Phetkasem, Sampran, Nakhon Pathom. Tel: 0-3432 2544.
Open: daily L. **$$**
There are a number of eateries at Rose Garden,

but the Inn Chan offers the most authentic Thai food. This pleasant restaurant overlooks the pretty Ta Chine River and prides itself on its use of ingredients from the surrounding villages.

Kanchanaburi
Thai
Ya Jai
301/1 Th. Mae Nam Kwai. Tel: 0-3462 4848.
Open: daily L & D. **$**
Delightful garden restaurant known for its excellent Isaan specialities and classic central Thai dishes. Most evenings young musicians perform Thai ballads and northeastern country music.

Thai & International
**Ali Bongos –
Taste of India**
232 Mae Nam Kwai, Tamakan. Tel: 0-811 944 858.
Open: daily L & D. **$$**
www.ali-bongos.com
Excellent variety of dishes from all over the Subcontinent. Very good prices.

Taraburee
Mae Khlong River near the end of Th. Lak Muang. Tel: 0-3451 2944. Open: daily L & D. **$**
There are several floating restaurants south of Kanchanaburi's Rattanakarn Bridge. The Taraburee, one of the best, specialises in freshwater fish and seafood dishes. Their *pla nung khing* or steamed fish with chilli,

ginger and mushrooms is very good.

River Kwai Floating Restaurant
River Kwai Bridge, Kanchanaburi.
Tel: 0-3451 2595.
Open: daily L & D. **$$**
Despite its tourist-trap overtones, the food is generally excellent and relies heavily on locally produced fare, be it fish or vegetables.

Price per person for a three-course meal without drinks:
$ = under B300
$$ = B300–800
$$$ = B800–1,600
$$$$ = over B1,600

A FEAST OF FRUITS

There is a sizeable range of fruits in Thailand, many of which may be unfamiliar. As well as bananas and pineapples, there are all kinds of brilliantly coloured and strangely shaped produce to sample

Thai people love food, and during the afternoon they snack on an incredible variety of fruits. For visitors who are in need of a boost, fruit can be a great source of refreshment and energy. Traditional fruit sellers have glass-fronted carts stacked with blocks of ice and peeled pieces of seasonal fruits. Choose a selection of what you want to eat and the vendor will pop it into a bag for you along with a toothpick for spearing the slices. Some fruits, like pineapple, are eaten with a little salt and ground chilli, a twist of which is supplied separately. Don't be afraid of this combination – the natural sweetness of the pineapple is enhanced by this bitter condiment, surprisingly enough.

One of the best ways to cool down is to drink a delicious fruit juice or *naam phon-la-mai*. To order, say the Thai word for water (*naam*) in front of the name of the fruit, or just point to your selection from the fruits on display. Another favourite drink is fruit juice blended with ice – known as a *naam pan* or "smoothie". You can have syrup mixed in to sweeten your juice (*naam pan*) or salt added (as the Thais like it) to bring out the flavour of the fruit.

Controversial durian

People either love or hate durian. Ask any visitor in Thailand to recall the first time they came across it and they will describe, in detail, its "perfume". To most *farang* (Europeans or Caucasians), the durian's odour is repugnant, but for the Thais the fruit commands the utmost respect.

According to devotees, the rewards of eating durian far outweigh any objections to its smell. The only way to enter the great durian debate is to try it for yourself. If you can't face eating the fruit *au naturel* there is durian cake, ice cream and chewing gum.

ABOVE: rambutan *(ngaw)*. The hairy rambutan (*rambut* means hair in Malay) is a close relative of the lychee, and its translucent, sweet flesh has a similar taste. There is a technique to squeezing it open to avoid squirting yourself with its juices; any Thai can demonstrate this.

LEFT: jackfruit *(khanun)*. The ripe, rich yellow section of the jackfruit are waxy textured and semi-sweet. When green they are used in curries, and the flowers and young shoots are eaten in salads.

BELOW: snake fruit *(ra-gahm* or *salak)*. Easily peeled, this unusual dry fruit has a pleasant flavour. The leathery skin varies from bright red to brown.

RIGHT: durian *(turian)*. The most expensive of Thai fruits has mushy flesh that tastes good with sticky rice and coconut milk. Ignore the smell and you will be rewarded.

CROPS: A GROWING CONCERN

Farming and fishing have always been at the centre of Thai life. Despite rapid industrialisation, this is still the case. Thailand is self-sufficient in food, and agribusiness is an important pillar of the Thai economy, claiming nearly a quarter of GDP and making Thailand the only net food exporter in Asia. Thailand is the world's leading exporter of canned pineapple and has big overseas markets in canned logans and rambutans.

Fruit production is expected to increase as available land and labour resources dwindle and farmers switch from producing staple crops, such as rice and cassava, to cash crops like soya beans, fruits, sugar cane and rubber. Large fruit farmers are starting to process their products before they reach the consumer, and many are now applying for loans to invest in equipment to dry and freeze their produce. Although some of this produce will be sold to Thailand's neighbours, much of it will end up in the snack-food departments of Japanese supermarkets – Japanese businesses have already set up factories in Thailand to process fruits, vegetables and nuts for their home market.

ABOVE: mangosteen *(mangkhut)*. Thais believe durian requires the cool, refreshing sweet taste of the mangosteen as a chaser. See if you can guess how many sections your mangosteen has before you break it open.

BELOW RIGHT: star fruit *(ma feuang)*. This sweet, yellow fruit is native to India. It has a thin waxy skin with a crisp texture and sweet-tart juice. It can be found in fruit salads or can be candied and eaten as a confection. The unripe fruit is bright green and is sometimes added to dishes that require an acidic taste.

BELOW: pummelo (or pomelo) *(som)*. At up to 30cm (12ins) in diameter, this is the world's largest citrus fruit. It is related to the grapefruit, although it has a sweeter flavour. Used in Thai salads.

BELOW: dragonfruit *(gaeo mang gawn)*. The common name for the pitaya, whose bright magenta skin makes it unmistakable. Grows best in dry areas.

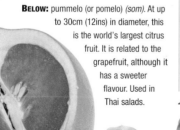

NORTH OF BANGKOK

Ayutthaya – the undisputed capital city of the Thai kingdom more than 600 years ago – is a time capsule that captures the faded grandeur of that violent era. Further north is Lopburi, where the Ayutthayan kings retired to during the hot summers

North of Bangkok in the Central Plain, watered by the Chao Phraya River and a network of tributaries and canals, lie two important sights that played a central role in Thai history. The first is Ayutthaya, Thailand's fabled capital from 1350 to 1767; the second is Lopburi, a former Khmer stronghold and part of the ancient Mon Dvaravati kingdom from the 6th to 10th centuries.

BANG PA-IN

Bang Pa-In  (daily 8.30am–4.30pm; charge; www.palaces.thai.net), some 60km (37 miles) north of Bangkok, is an eclectic collection of palaces and pavilions once used as a royal summer retreat. Most people make a stop here before continuing another 25km (16 miles) north to Ayutthaya.

The palace buildings date from the late 19th- and early 20th-century reigns of King Chulalongkorn (Rama V) and King Vajiravudh (Rama VI), who came here to escape the mid-year rains in Bangkok. Following the wishes of Chulalongkorn, the buildings that are dotted around the manicured grounds feature Italian Baroque, European Gothic, Victorian and Chinese architectural styles. Only part of the royal quarters is open to public view, but it provides a glimpse into Chulalongkorn's penchant for European furniture and decor.

Buildings of note include the two-storey Chinese-style **Wehat Chamrun Palace** and the red-and-yellow **Withun Thatsana** observation tower situated on a nearby islet, as well as the Italianate **Warophat Phiman Hall**. The 1876 Thai-style pavilion in the middle of the lake adjacent to the main entrance, called the **Aisawan Thipphaya-at**, is regarded as one of the finest examples of Thai architecture.

Main attractions
BANG PA-IN
AYUTTHAYA HISTORICAL PARK
LOPBURI

LEFT: golden Buddha at Wat Phra Mahathat, Ayutthaya. **RIGHT:** a mix of Thai and Western-influened architectural styles at Bang Pa-In.

The lookout tower known as Withun Thasana.

Across the river and slightly south of the palace, **Wat Niwet Thammaprawat** is surmounted by a spire and as a result looks more like a Gothic Christian church than a Buddhist temple. The pleasant gardens are embellished with canals, fountains, bridges and quirky elephant-shaped hedges.

AYUTTHAYA

Of central importance to the history of Thailand, **Ayutthaya** ⑪ is one of the country's most rewarding sights. It is difficult not to be impressed by the beauty and grandeur of the city, built over a period of 400 years by a long succession of monarchs. From the ruins, it is easy to appreciate the genius of the kings who built it. A Unesco World Heritage site, Ayutthaya is a must-visit.

Located 85km (55 miles) north of Bangkok, Ayutthaya was laid out at the confluence of three rivers: the Chao Phraya, Pa Sak and Lopburi. Engineers only had to cut a canal across the loop of the Chao Phraya to create an island. A network of canals – few of which

exist today – acted as thoroughfares, and palaces and temples were erected alongside. Europeans dubbed it the "Venice of the East", and, even today, chartering a longtail boat for a trip around the natural moat is the best way to see many of the riverbank ruins. Several boat operators from Bangkok organise regular trips by river from the capital to the historic city, conveying them in either modern express boats or traditional teakwood barges (*see page 405*).

Ayutthaya's foundations

Ayutthaya was founded around 1350 by Prince U Thong (later known as King Ramathibodi I). Thirty years later, the northern kingdom of Sukhothai (*see page 315*) was placed under Ayutthayan rule, which then extended its control east to Angkor and west to Pegu in Burma. By the 1600s, it was established as one of the richest and most cosmopolitan cities in Asia – exporting rice, animal skins and ivory – and had a population of 1 million, greater than that of London at the time. Merchants came from Europe, the Middle

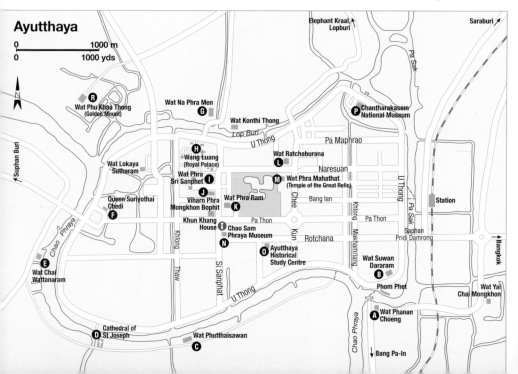

Ayutthaya

0 ————————— 1000 m
0 ————————— 1000 yds

N

Elephant Kraal, Lopburi
Saraburi

R Wat Phu Khao Thong (Golden Mount)

Wat Na Phra Men **G**

P Chantharakasem National Museum

Wat Konthi Thong

Lop Buri
U Thong
Pa Maphrao

Suphan Buri

H Wang Luang (Royal Palace)

Wat Ratchaburana **L**

Naresuan

Wat Lokaya Sutharam

Wat Phra Sri Sanphet **I**

M Wat Phra Mahathat (Temple of the Great Relic)

Chee
Bang Ian

U Thong

Station

Queen Suriyothai Chedi **F**

J
Viharn Phra Mongkhon Bophit

Wat Phra Ram **K**

Khong
Pa Thon

Saphan Pridi Damrong

Bangkok

Chao Phraya

Khun Khang House **i** Chao Sam Phraya Museum **N**

Pa Thon
Kun
Rotchana

Makhamriang

Wat Suwan Dararam **B**

O Ayutthaya Historical Study Centre

E Wat Chai Wattanaram

Thaw
Si Sanphet
U Thong

Phom Phet

Wat Yai Chai Mongkhon

A Wat Phanan Choeng

D Cathedral of St Joseph

Wat Phutthaisawan **C**

Chao Phraya

Bang Pa-In

East and elsewhere in Asia to trade in its markets, with many eventually settling there.

Today, there is a plaque to mark Ayutthaya's former Portuguese settlement and a memorial hall and gate to mark the Japanese settlement. Europeans at the time wrote accounts eulogising the fabulous wealth of the courts, describing, amongst other things, the 2,000 temple spires clad in gold. Thirty-three kings left their mark on the old capital.

Although in ruins, very impressive remnants of Ayutthaya's rich architectural and cultural achievements can still be seen today. As swiftly as it rose to greatness, it collapsed, suffering destruction so complete that it was never rebuilt. Burmese armies had been pounding on its doors for centuries before managing to occupy the city for a period in the 16th century. Siamese kings then expelled them and reasserted independence. In 1767, however, the Burmese triumphed again. In a mad rampage, they burnt and looted, destroying most of the city's monuments, and killing, enslaving and scattering the population.

Within a year, Ayutthaya had been reduced to a ghost town; its population had diminished to under 10,000 as the royal court resettled south near the mouth of the Chao Phraya River in what today is Bangkok. By the time the Burmese were eventually defeated, Ayutthaya was beyond repair, a fabled city left to crumble into dust.

Visiting the site

Today the ruins, collectively known as the **Ayutthaya Historical Park** (daily 8am–5pm; charge), stand on the western half of the island, with the modern city of Ayutthaya on the eastern side. Some of the more centrally located ruins can be visited on foot, but it is best to rent a bicycle or a *tuk-tuk* for the further-flung sights. As several of the major temples are located along the edge of the riverbank or close to it, longtail boats can be hired from the pier outside the Chantharakasem National Museum for a two-hour trip.

By the riverside

Begin close to the junction of the Pa Sak and Chao Phraya rivers, passing

TIP

One of the best ways of exploring the widely spread-out ruins of Ayutthaya is by bicycle. These can be rented for about B50 a day at many guesthouses in Ayutthaya. If you are disinclined to expend your energy, hire a motorised *tuk-tuk* with driver for about B180 an hour. Bear in mind that exploring the ruins can be tiring on hot days – take along sunscreen, a hat or umbrella, as well as something to eat and drink.

BELOW: a European impression of the royal capital of Ayutthaya.

In the 1950s, unscrupulous locals plundered Ayutthaya's hidden treasures and Buddha images. The Thai government recently realised that some of Ayutthaya's most important treasures are now housed in overseas museum collections, and they are trying to reclaim these stolen artefacts. Even today some temple abbots in Ayutthaya are forced to stand guard and sleep beside their precious Buddha images.

BELOW: exploring the ruins of Ayutthaya on elephant back is a novel option.

by the imposing **Wat Phanan Choeng** . Records suggest that the temple was established 26 years prior to Ayutthaya's foundation around 1350. The temple houses the statue of a giant seated bronze Buddha, so tightly pressed against the roof that the statue appears to be holding it up. With an unmistakably Chinese atmosphere, Wat Phanan Choeng was a favourite with the Chinese traders of the time, who prayed there before setting out on their long sea voyages. The temple also holds the Mae Soi Dok Mak shrine, a tribute to a Chinese princess who supposedly killed herself on this spot after receiving an icy reception from her suitor, an Ayutthayan king.

Ayutthaya was at one time surrounded by fortress walls, of which only a few sections remain today. One of the best preserved is at **Phom Phet**, across the river from Wat Phanan Choeng. Nearby is the restored **Wat Suwan Dararam** , built towards the end of the Ayutthaya period. Destroyed by the Burmese in 1767, the temple was rebuilt by Rama I, with the wall murals dating from the reign of Rama III; later

(1925–35), a more unconventional mural depicting King Naresuan's famous battle with the Burmese was added. Still used as a temple, the *wat* is magical when the monks chant prayers in the early evening.

Upstream from Wat Phanan Choeng by the riverbank is the restored **Wat Phutthaisawan** . Seldom visited, it is quiet, and the landing is an excellent place to enjoy the river's tranquillity in the evenings. Further upstream, the Catholic **Cathedral of St Joseph** is a reminder of the large European population that lived in the city in its prime.

Where the river bends to the north stands one of Ayutthaya's most romantic ruins, **Wat Chai Wattanaram** , erected in 1630. Modelled after the Angkor Wat complex in Cambodia, the dramatically placed temple is a photographer's favourite, especially at sunset. Restored in the 1990s, it was built by King Prasat Thong, and has a large central Cambodian-style *prang* fringed by several smaller *chedi*. Perched high on a pedestal in front of the ruins, a Buddha keeps solitary watch. With its rows of headless Bud-

dhas, this extraordinary temple makes a fine contrast to the somewhat less impressive **Queen Suriyothai Chedi**  on the city side of river. The shrine commemorates the life of Suriyothai, an Ayutthayan queen who, dressed as a male soldier and riding an elephant into battle, sacrificed herself by intervening in a duel between her husband King Maha Chakraphet and a Burmese prince. The stuff of legend, her passionate act was immortalised in the 2001 film *Suriyothai*, one of Thailand's most lavish and expensive movies.

Across a river bridge from the palace of Wang Luang *(see below)* stands the restored temple of **Wat Na Phra Men** . Used as a strategic attack post by the Burmese when they descended on the old city, the temple is one of Ayutthaya's few monasteries not to have been ransacked. Here, a large stone Buddha is seated on a throne, a sharp contrast to the yoga position of most seated Buddhas. Discovered in the ruins of Wat Phra Mahathat *(see page 166)*, the statue is believed to be one of five that originally sat in the Dvaravati-period complex in Nakhon Pathom.

The main hall or *bot* contains an Ayutthayan-style seated Buddha in regal attire, which is very unlike the more common monastic dress of Buddha representations.

The palace and surroundings

The palace of **Wang Luang** (Royal Palace) was substantial, if the foundations for the stables of some 100 elephants are any indication. Established by King Borommatrailokanat in the 15th century, it was later razed by the Burmese. The bricks were removed to Bangkok to build the city's defensive walls, so only remnants of the foundations survive today to mark the site.

A part of the original palace grounds, the three Sri Lankan-style *chedi* next door belong to **Wat Phra Sri Sanphet** . The royal temple would have held as much importance in its heyday as the Temple of Emerald Buddha (Wat Phra Kaew) does in Bangkok today. Two of the *chedi* were built in 1492 by King Borommatrailokanat's son, Ramathibodi II, to hold the ashes of his

A stone Buddha at Ayutthaya.

BELOW: Wat Phra Sri Sanphet, Ayutthaya Historical Park.

A fleet of tuk-tuks
at Ayutthaya.

BELOW: Buddha
head entwined
within the gnarled
roots of a banyan
tree at Wat Phra
Mahathat.

father and brother, while the third
was added in 1540 by Ramathibodi
II's son to hold the ashes of his late
father. The three spires have become
the iconic image of Ayutthaya.

For two centuries after Ayutthaya's
fall, a huge bronze Buddha – over 12
metres (39ft) tall – sat unsheltered
near Wat Phra Sri Sanphet. Its flame
of knowledge (on the top of its
head) and one of its arms had been
broken when the roof, set on fire by
the Burmese, collapsed. Based on the
original, a new building called **Viharn
Phra Mongkhon Bophit** ⓙ was built
in 1956 around the restored statue.
As one of Thailand's largest bronze
images, it seems rather cramped in its
new sanctuary.

Across the road to the east, **Wat Phra
Ram** ⓚ is one of Ayutthaya's oldest
temples. Founded in 1369 by the son
of Ayutthaya's founding king, Prince
U Thong, its buildings dating from
the 1400s have been restored twice.
Elephant gates punctuate the old walls,
and the central terrace is dominated by
a crumbling *prang* to which clings a
gallery of stucco *naga*, *garuda* and Bud-

dha statues. The reflection of Wat Phra
Ram's *prang* shimmers in the pool that
surrounds the complex, making it one
of Ayutthaya's most tranquil settings.

Ayutthaya's best temples

Two of Ayutthaya's finest temples
stand side by side across the lake from
Wat Phra Ram. The first is known as
Wat Ratchaburana ⓛ, and was built
in 1424 by the seventh king of Ayutthaya, King Borom Rachathirat II
(1424–48) as a memorial to his brothers who died as a result of a duel for
the throne. Excavations during a 1957
restoration revealed a crypt below the
towering central *prang*, containing a
stash of gold jewellery, Buddha images
and other artefacts, among them a
magnificent ceremonial sword and an
intricately decorated elephant statue
– all likely to have been the property
of the interred brothers. The narrow,
claustrophobic and dimly lit crypt
can be accessed through a doorway in
the *prang*, leading down steep stairs to
some barely visible wall paintings.

The second temple, **Wat Phra
Mahathat** ⓜ (Temple of the Great
Relic) was once one of the most beautiful temple complexes in Ayutthaya,
and one of its oldest, dating from the
1380s. The site, across the road from
Ratchaburana, was the focal point for
religious ceremonies and reverence,
and the residence of King Ramesuan
(1388–95). Its glory was its huge laterite *prang*, which originally stood at
46 metres (150ft) high. The *prang* later
collapsed, but its foundations are still
there, surrounded by several restored
chedi. A much-revered symbol here is
a stone Buddha head that has been
embedded in the gnarled roots of an
old banyan tree. Next door, the government has built a model of how the
royal city may have once looked.

Ayutthaya's museums

While looters quickly made off with
a great deal of Ayutthaya's glories, the
surviving highlights of Thailand's
greatest archaeological treasure chest

are now displayed at the **Chao Sam Phraya Museum** to the south (Wed–Sun 9am–4pm; charge; www.thailand museum.com).

The **Ayutthaya Historical Study Centre** (Mon–Fri 9am–4.30pm, Sat–Sun 9am–5pm; charge) nearby was funded by the Japanese government. Sitting on land that was once part of Ayutthaya's Japanese quarter, the modern building houses excellent hi-tech exhibits that guide visitors through 400 years of the development, trade, administration and social changes of the Ayutthayan period. There are also models of the city in its glory days, a Chinese junk, and small tableaux of village life.

To the east, **Chantharakasem National Museum** was formerly known as the Chantharakasem Palace (Wed–Sun 9am–4pm; charge; www. thailandmuseum.com). It was originally constructed outside the city walls, close to the confluence of the rivers and the canal. King Maha Thammaracha built it for his son Prince Naresuan (later king), and it became the residence for future heirs apparent. In 1767, the Burmese destroyed the palace, but King Mongkut (Rama IV) resurrected it in the 19th century as a royal summer retreat. Today, it looks out on the noisiest part of modern Ayutthaya. The palace's collection isn't notably impressive but it is still worth perusing.

To its rear, the European-style four-storey **Pisai Sayalak** tower was built by King Mongkut for stargazing. Across the street from the palace is the boat pier for trips around the island, and a night market with food stalls set up beside the water.

LOPBURI

Lopburi ⑫ lies 150km (100 miles) north of Bangkok, a two- to three-hour drive through the fertile rice bowl of Thailand. Centuries before it became the favoured summer residence for Ayutthayan King Narai, the strategically located town was known as Lavo and lay within the Mon Dvaravati kingdom (6th–10th centuries). From the 10th–13th centuries, it became an outpost of the Angkor empire, before falling under the influence of the Sukhothai kingdom to the north.

ElephantStay (www. elephantstay.com) in Ayutthaya is a working elephant village where guests can spend a few days and learn more about Asian elephants, a fascinating experience and one that helps the animals, too.

BELOW: Phra Narai Ratchanivet, Lopburi.

Monkeys amid the ruins at Ayutthaya. Be aware that they can be aggressive.

BELOW: headless Buddha image at Prang Sam Yot.
BELOW RIGHT: *prang* at Wat Phra Si Rattana Mahathat.

Lopburi enjoyed its heyday in the mid-1600s when King Narai retreated here each summer to escape Ayutthaya's heat. When the Dutch imposed a naval blockade on Ayutthaya from the Gulf of Siam, King Narai decided to install Lopburi as a second capital, running his court from there. It was said that while his throne was in Ayutthaya, his heart belonged to Lopburi; he spent more and more time here after his new palace was completed.

Wat Phra Si Rattana Mahathat

Just across from Lopburi's main train station, **Wat Phra Si Rattana Mahathat** (daily 8am–6pm; charge) was originally a simple Khmer temple with a tall stucco-decorated laterite *prang*. Around the 12th century, King Narai added a large *viharn* (sermon hall) that infused elements of European and Persian architecture, the latter influence coming from the strong Persian presence at the Ayutthayan court: the Ayutthaya period was notable for the number of influential foreign visitors

arriving in Thailand, including Indians, Chinese, Japanese, Persians and Europeans *(see pages 35–7)*.

Phra Narai Ratchanivet

Just northwest, the grounds of **Phra Narai Ratchanivet** (or Lopburi Palace), built between 1665 and 1677 (daily 8am–6pm; charge), are enclosed by massive walls which still dominate the centre of the modern town. Built in a mélange of Thai, Khmer and European styles, the palace grounds are divided into three sections enclosing the complex of official, ceremonial and residential buildings.

The outer grounds contained facilities for utilities and maintenance. The middle section enclosed the **Chanthara Phisan Pavilion**, the first structure built by King Narai, and later restored by King Mongkut. On the south side is the **Dusit Maha Prasat Hall**, built for the audience granted by King Narai in 1685 to the French ambassador of Louis XIV.

To the left is the **Phiman Mongkut Pavilion**, a three-storey colonial-style mansion. It was built in the mid-

19th century by King Mongkut, who wanted to restore the entire palace. The immensely thick walls and high ceilings went some way to averting the summer heat in the days before air-conditioning.

The mansion, small but full of character, now functions as the **Narai National Museum** (Wed–Sun 9am–4pm; charge; www.thailandmuseum.com). It contains a display of bronze statues, Chinese and Sukhothai porcelain, coins, Buddhist fans and shadow-play puppets. Some of the pieces, particularly the Ayutthaya bronze heads and Bencharong porcelain, are superb. The inner courtyard housed the private chambers of King Narai; not much is left except for the foundations and the **Suttha Sawan Pavilion**, nestled amid gardens and ponds.

Baan Vichayen

North of Phra Narai Ratchanivet are the remains of **Baan Vichayen** palace (daily 8am–6pm; charge), said to have belonged to Constantine Phaulkon (*see page 36 and margin, right*), the Greek adventurer who arrived in Siam in 1678 to work for the British East India Company and gained favour with King Narai. As a foreigner, Phaulkon's mercurial rise aroused a great deal of suspicion and resentment, and he was eventually executed. The period following his demise saw the Siamese court become more xenophobic towards foreign influence.

The palace buildings of Baan Vichayen show strong European influences, with its straight-sided walls and stucco decorations embellishing Western-style windows.

Prang Sam Yot

To the east are the three laterite towers of **Prang Sam Yot** (daily 8am–6pm; charge). This much-photographed sight is of interest as the towers were originally built by the Khmers as a Hindu shrine honouring the gods Brahma, Vishnu and Shiva. It was later converted into a Buddhist shrine, incorporating a hotchpotch fusion of Brahman, Khmer and Buddhist elements that is often dubbed as the Lopburi style. Beware of the persistent and rather aggressive monkeys at this site. ❑

Constantine Phaulkon antagonised many of the other foreign settlers in Ayutthaya, as well as Thai nobles who felt threatened by a foreigner wielding so much influence. He forged strong ties with the French, but when missionary priests started arriving in Siam, local Buddhists believed the Greek was conspiring with King Louis XIV to covert Siam to Christianity. As King Narai lay on his death bed, his successors had Phaulkon arrested and executed for treason.

RESTAURANTS

Ayutthaya

Thai

Bann Kun Pra
48/2 Th. U Thong.
Tel: 0-3524 1978. **$**
Open: daily B, L & D. **$**
With a lovely terrace location overlooking the river, this guesthouse restaurant serves a mix of freshwater fish and seafood. Try the giant barbecued prawns with various chilli dips along with Thai-style steamed mussels.

Phae Krung Kao
4 Th. U Thong, south of Pridi Damrong Bridge. Tel: 0-3524 1555. Open: daily L & D. **$**
Located on the Pa Sak River, where the river hums

with activity, this is one of Ayutthaya's oldest floating restaurants. Specialities include freshwater fish; try the unappetisingly named snakehead fish, either in a curry or deep-fried.

Thai & Western

Chang House
14/10 Soi 8 Th. Naresuan.
Mobile tel: 08-9414 1448.
Open: daily B, L & D. **$**
Bar and restaurant that serves a mix of Thai, Western and Indian dishes. The Indian delights are what sets it apart from other faceless places in the Naresuan Road area. The samosas and *alu palak* – potato and spinach curry – are recommended.

Siam Restaurant
11/3 Th. Pratuchai
Ayutthaya
Tel: 0-3521 1070.
Open: daily L & D. **$$**
Thai food pure and simple, with a range of dishes drawn from around the country. Strongly patronised by the locals.

Lopburi

Thai

Anodard
Sa Kaew Circle, New Lopburi.
Tel: 0-3541 1433. Open: daily L & D. **$**
This is located some way away from the historic part of Lopburi, but it is worth the effort coming here for the very good selection of Thai and Chinese dishes.

Try the *kai phat pet mamuang* or chicken and cashew nuts, or one of the superb *tom yam* soups.

White House Garden
18 Th. Phraya Kamjat. Tel: 0-3641 3085. Open: daily D. **$**
A pleasant spot opposite Lopburi's tourist office. Locals come here for the excellent central Thai food and to listen to the resident guitarist play some relaxing Thai folk classics.

Price per person for a three-course meal without drinks:
$ = under B300
$$ = B300–800
$$$ = B800–1,600
$$$$ = over B1,600

SOUTH OF BANGKOK

This area is scant on sights, and these are mostly visited by travellers en route to the beaches of the Eastern Seaboard. The Ancient City and Crocodile Farm are the two principal diversions

Main attractions
ANCIENT CITY
CROCODILE FARM & ZOO

BELOW: a reproduced monument at Ancient City.

Samut Prakan Province, near the river-mouth town of Paknam, is 30km (20 miles) – or about half an hour's drive – southeast of Bangkok. Although not on every tourist's itinerary, a day trip here from the capital makes for an interesting alternative. Otherwise, it can be visited while on the way to one of the beaches along Thailand's Eastern Seaboard *(see page 177)*.

The province is home to two prime attractions – one of the world's largest open-air museums in Muang Boran, and a much-touted crocodile farm.

Bangkok's **Suvarnabhumi Airport** is also located in Samut Prakan. Officially opened in 2006, after several protracted delays, it has brought an influx of hotels, housing for staff and other peripheral facilities to this area.

Ancient City

One of Bangkok's best-value tourist (and surprisingly under-visited) attractions is the **Ancient City** ⑬ or Muang Boran (daily 8am–5pm; charge; www.ancientcity.com), located 33km (21 miles) southeast of Bangkok. This is the brainchild of a Bangkok tycoon, Lek Viriyaphant, with a passion for Thai art and history. In what used to be 80 hectares (200 acres) of rice fields, designers sketched an area roughly the shape of Thailand and placed the individual attractions as close to their real sites as possible.

There are replicas – some full-sized, most one-third the size of the originals – of famous monuments and temples from all parts of the kingdom. Some are reconstructions of buildings that no longer exist, such as the Grand Palace of Ayutthaya, others are copies of buildings such as the temple of Khao Phra Viharn on the Thai-Cambodian border, while a few are salvaged antiquities.

Experts from the National Museum worked as consultants to ensure the historical accuracy of the reproductions. At present, there are over 100 monuments, covering 15 centuries of Thai history.

There is a lot to see and you could spend a whole day here. The grounds are landscaped with small waterfalls, creeks, ponds, rock gardens and lush greenery, while deer graze among the sculptures representing figures from Thai literature and Hindu mythology. With the monuments spread over such a large area, the best way to get around is on a rented bicycle.

Finish your tour at the Old Market Town, a street of shops disguised as traditional wooden houses, with handicrafts and sculptures for sale. Here you can watch Thai craftsmen carve puppets from buffalo hide and woodcarvers sculpt Khmer idols.

Crocodile Farm & Zoo

Samut Prakan's famous **Crocodile Farm & Zoo** ⓮ (daily 7am–6pm; charge) is located a short distance from the Ancient City on the old Sukhumvit Highway (Route 3). Seeing the reptiles up close is fascinating, even though you know that a good number of the creatures will end up as leather for handbags and wallets, and the meat on restaurant tables (and there is no effort made to hide this fact – *see below*). Almost all wild Siamese and Asian species of crocodiles have been hunted to extinction.

Having started in the 1950s with a paltry initial investment, the owner now runs three farms (two are in the northeast) worth millions of dollars. The Samut Prakan farm is home to more than 60,000 freshwater and saltwater local crocodiles from 28 species, as well as some South American caimans and Nile River crocodiles. Also present is the world's largest captive crocodile (listed in the *Guinness Book of World Records*). Called Chai Yai, the massive creature measures 6 metres (20ft) long and weighs a whopping 1,114kg (2,456lb).

A highlight of the Crocodile Farm is the eight daily shows (hourly from 9am–4pm, reptile feeding 4–5pm), during which handlers wrestle with the crocodiles, even placing their heads in the beasts' mouths. The farm's shops sell handbags, belts and shoes made from their skins, as well as stewed crocodile meat. Used as an ingredient in traditional Chinese medicine, the meat is purportedly a tonic and an aphrodisiac, but is something of an acquired taste. ❑

Suvarnabhumi (pronounced "su-wa-na-poom") Airport opened in 2006 after several protracted delays. It is located 30km (19 miles) east of the city centre, just to the north of the Ancient City theme park.

BELOW: croc handlers perform daring stunts at the Crocodile Farm.

SOUTHEAST AND SOUTH THAILAND

For many, Thailand is synonymous with paradise islands; so the south of the country, with miles of unspoilt beaches by the emerald waters of the Gulf of Thailand and the Andaman Sea, is the place to head

Blessed with some 3,000km (2,000 miles) of stunning coastline and more than 30 beautiful islands washed by the Gulf of Thailand and the Andaman Sea, this is a region that attracts everyone, from gregarious party animals to reclusive honeymooners.

A short way from the capital, the brash coastal resort of Pattaya has been dubbed (somewhat hopefully) the "Riviera of the Eastern Seaboard". Further east, the pretty island of Ko Samet is a favourite weekend escape for young Bangkokians, while Ko Chang, Thailand's second-largest island, is part of an extensive marine national park that's woken up to its tourism potential.

Heading south, the Gulf of Thailand coast is fringed with sandy beaches and backed by mountains. The most accessible and popular is family-friendly Hua Hin, but further south, Pranburi is fast making a name for itself too, with its clutch of design-conscious resorts. Offshore, Ko Samui, the largest of some 80 islands comprising the Samui Archipelago, is the main tourist hub and can be combined with visits to neighbouring Ko Phangan, notorious for its anything-goes full-moon raves, and Ko Tao, a renowned mecca for diving.

Lapped by the blue-green waters of the Andaman Sea on the west coast, Thailand's largest island, Phuket, is the kingdom's premier holiday spot. It hosts some of the world's most luxurious hotels, which contrast with rus-

tic fishing villages and mangrove forests. Further south lie Ao Phang Nga and Krabi, and islands like Ko Phi Phi and Ko Lanta with their amazing limestone towers that teeter skyward above azure waters. The spectacular dive sites near Similan and Surin islands are another major lure.

Heading south, Trang, Satun, Songkhla and Nakhon Si Thammarat are all breathtakingly beautiful but less touched by tourism. For the present, this guides omits the restive Muslim-dominated provinces – Pattani, Yala and Narathiwat – in the deep south of Thailand. Everything else, as they say, is fair game. ❏

PRECEDING PAGES: view of Ko Tao. **LEFT:** soaking up the scene at Ao Maya (Maya Bay), Ko Phi Phi Ley. **ABOVE RIGHT:** Hat Na Ko on the island of Ko Kradan. **ABOVE LEFT:** longtail boat, a common means of transport.

EASTERN SEABOARD

Miles of sandy beaches, dozens of tiny offshore islands, dense forests and hidden waterfalls... all these and more await on Thailand's easily accessible Eastern Seaboard

The Eastern Seaboard is Thailand's most commercially and industrially developed shore, with numerous factories and oil refineries between Bangkok and Rayong. Thankfully, the development has done little to deter tourism's potential, and with miles of sandy beaches and dozens of islands lying just offshore, plus relatively calm seas all year through (*see margin tip, page 185*), it's easy to find your own private oasis. This section of the Thai coast has something for everyone; the beaches around Pattaya and Rayong, along with the islands of Ko Samet and Ko Chang, abound with activities. Speckled with several national parks, the region is also a golfer's paradise, with more than 20 international-standard fairways around Pattaya.

Highway 3 is the principal road that trails its way through the provinces of Chonburi, Rayong, Chantabhuri and Trat, all the way to Cambodia. There is a rail line as far as Pattaya, but services are limited and slow. Two small airports serve the vicinity: U-Tapao, near Pattaya, and Trat, the entry point for passengers from Bangkok en route to Ko Chang.

BANG SAEN

Just south of Chonburi, the 2km (1½-mile) long beach at **Bang Saen ❶** springs to life each weekend as hordes of middle-class Bangkokians arrive in cars and buses. The nearest stretch of beach from the capital, it is covered with a profusion of beach umbrellas and inflatable inner tubes, and the surf is filled with bobbing bodies fully dressed to avoid a tan (in addition to concern about UV rays, many Thais associate tanned skin with working folk who toil in the sun).

SI RACHA

The coastal port town of **Si Racha ❷**, about 100km (62 miles) from Bangkok,

Main attractions
SI RACHA
KO SI CHANG
PATTAYA
KO SAMET
KO CHANG
KO MAK
KO KUT

LEFT: sunset at Hat Kai Bae, Ko Chang.
RIGHT: Sriracha Tiger Zoo.

Wat Atsadang Nimit in Ko Si Chang features a mix of Thai and European architecture.

nestles between two ranges of hills. The town's signature tangy red sauce – *nam prik si racha* – can be enjoyed at waterfront restaurants, where it's used to spice up fresh shrimp and crab.

The nearby **Sriracha Tiger Zoo** (daily 8am–6pm; charge) claims to be the largest tiger zoo in the world, with over 200 Bengal tigers; you can visit the nursery to hold and feed the young cubs. The emphasis here is more entertainment than conservation: tigers star in the daily circus shows, which also feature a large number of crocodiles. There is also an elephant show, a bear show, pig racing and ostrich riding.

KO SI CHANG

A 45-minute boat ride from Si Racha, the island of **Ko Si Chang** ❸ (not to be confused with the far larger Ko Chang, further east) is known primarily as a coastal retreat for the late King Chulalongkorn (Rama V). The king built his summer palace here in the 1890s, only to abandon it after the French briefly occupied the island a few years later. Busy on weekends with Thai day-trippers, the island has a few passable beaches, though certainly not Thailand's best – or cleanest. However, it does provide an interesting slice of island living without the typical tourism onslaught. Ko Si Chang can be visited as a day or overnight trip from Bangkok or en route to Pattaya or beyond.

Sights and activities

Once off the pier and after exploring **Tha Bon**, the island's main fishing town, most visitors head straight for the grounds of Rama V's **Judhadhut Palace** (daily 8am–6pm; free). Recently restored, the grounds double up as an oceanfront public park, with a small pebbly beach beside the rebuilt **Atsadang Bridge**. Once a colonnaded wooden pier used as Chulalongkorn's landing stage, this is now a popular spot for kids to leap off from and swim around the moored fishing boats.

While the main teak palace itself was dismantled and rebuilt in Bangkok as the Vimanmek Mansion (see page 123), several of the palace's other structures

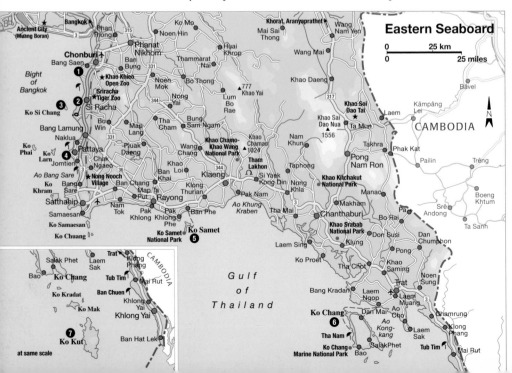

have been remodelled, including the green wooden house **Ruen Mai Rim Talay**, which was used as a convalescent home for infirm Western visitors. The pretty gardens that extend up the hill are worthy of exploration, and the top is marked by the white spire of **Wat Atsadang Nimit**. As with palace buildings of the day, the temple's design was a fusion of Thai and European architecture, with the circular *chedi* featuring unique stained-glass panels.

Continue to the island's principal beach of **Hat Tham Pang** (Fallen Cave) on the west coast. Depending on the tide, the 1km (2/3-mile) long beach can shrink, and is usually crowded with lines of beach umbrellas and food shacks located behind.

Over on steep Kayasira hill, **Sanjao Pho Khao Yai** (daily 8am–6pm; free) is a gaudy Chinese temple perched high on the rock with great views overlooking the town and port below. The temple is a popular stop for Chinese visitors who pay homage at the damp cave shrines before hiking up further to a *sala* (pavilion) said to contain the Buddha's footprint.

PATTAYA

Good or bad, **Pattaya**'s ❹ reputation precedes itself, with most people having formed their own opinion of this resort area even before they set foot here. Pattaya's notoriety dates back to the Vietnam War, when it was an R&R stopover for American troops.

Located 147km (91 miles) from Bangkok, or around two hours by road, Pattaya has long been popular with Thai families. In recent years, Europeans have been outnumbered by Asian and Middle Eastern visitors, along with significant numbers of Russians.

The once-polluted beaches have been cleaned up, but they are nowhere near as pristine as those of Thailand's southern islands. However, what Pattaya lacks, it more than compensates for in other areas. There is a plethora of good-value accommodation and restaurants, a wide range of outdoor and indoor activities,

as well as several cultural attractions. Beyond that, Pattaya's buzzing, if salacious, nightlife scene is something to be experienced or avoided, depending on your sensibility.

Property in Pattaya is being built at an astonishing rate. Many foreigners own beach condos and houses here; Bangkok expats use them as weekend getaways, while European retirees escape the northern winter here. There are some very smart residences on the market, and improvements to infrastructure, especially international schools, are drawing more respectable residents. But the city's seedy reputation also attracts a strong criminal element. Thankfully, the underworld is rarely visible to the average visitor, and most of the time, Pattaya feels as safe as anywhere else in Thailand.

Pattaya's beaches

On the beach front, the 3km (2-mile) long crescent-shaped **Hat Pattaya** ❶ is the least attractive of the three beaches, with only a narrow, umbrella-crammed wisp of yellow sand on offer. It is backed by a palm-lined promenade

TIP

Pattaya has a bad reputation for con artists – collecting donations for spurious causes, selling precious stones at "bargain" prices, or offering "free" trips to touristic sights. Keep your wits about you.

BELOW: out and about in Pattaya.

Pattaya

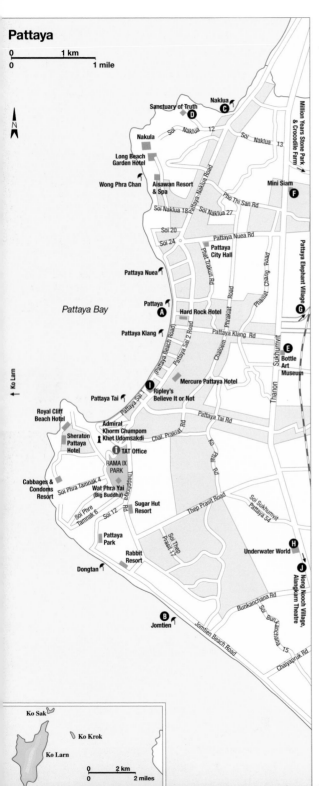

that has unfortunately become a pitching point for working girls. The Phra Tamnak hill area separates the main resort splay from a number of mid- and high-end hotels (like the Sheraton and Royal Cliff) that front several small but pleasant beaches.

Just a short ride south, the 6km (4-mile) long **Hat Jomtien B** is only marginally cleaner and better than Hat Pattaya. The nicest-looking (ie fewer umbrellas) and least populated bays are found in north Pattaya, rounding the **Hat Naklua C** headland towards the fishing village.

Beach activities

Pattaya and Jomtien are good locations for watersports, with windsurfing and sailing equipment available for rent, along with jet skis, waterscooters and waterskiing equipment.

Offshore, **Ko Larn** – identified in brochures as **Coral Island** but whose name actually translates as Bald Island – is one of Pattaya's most popular day-trip locations. Its once-pristine coral reefs have been destroyed by fishermen using dynamite to stun fish. Yet glass-bottomed boats still ferry visitors around its waters, the passengers peering in vain at the dead grey coral in the hope of seeing something alive. Ko Larn, however, has the wide, soft sand beaches that Pattaya lacks and is a great place to spend a day. The shore is lined with seafood restaurants, and there are plenty of watersports facilities.

Several scuba schools run dive trips to Pattaya's outlying islands; the surrounding waters harbour one of Thailand's best wreck dive sites, with four sunken vessels scattered between Pattaya and Satthahip port. Ko Larn and nearby isles like **Ko Sak** and **Ko Krok** see more tourist activity – visibility isn't crystal clear, but the waters are protected from currents, which makes them suitable for beginners. The further-flung islands of **Ko Rin** and **Ko Man Wichai** are better dive spots with clearer visibility and abundant marine life, including sharks and turtles.

Land attractions

Back on land, the **Sanctuary of Truth** **D** (daily 8am–5pm; charge; www.sanc tuaryoftruth.com) is an intricate wood-carved edifice in Naklua Soi 12. This awe-inspiring teak structure, dating from 1981, is intended to revive traditional artisan techniques as well as act as a spiritual beacon. Dramatically perched on the seafront, the fantastical tower blends ancient religious iconography from Thailand and Cambodia.

While many of Pattaya's visitors prefer to quaff bottles of cold beer, others can opt to view a unique collection of delicate miniatures displayed inside some 300 bottles at the **Bottle Art Museum** **E** on Thanon Sukhumvit (daily 8.30am–8pm; charge). The exhibits have been assembled over a period of many years by a Dutchman, Pieter Bij De Leij, and a Thai woman, Prapaisi Thaipanich.

Family-oriented attractions include **Mini Siam** **F** (daily 8am–10pm; charge) at Thanon Sukhumvit in North Pattaya, where you can step around tiny scale models of many of the world's architectural landmarks. The **Pattaya**

Elephant Village **G** on Thanon Sukhumvit (daily 8.30am–7pm; charge; www.elephant-village-pattaya. com) offers a daily elephant show as well as rides into the countryside. For a land-based view of marine wonders, stop by the **Underwater World** **H** (daily 9am–6pm; charge), just after the Thanon Thep Prasit junction with Thanon Sukhumvit. The large aquarium has a 100-metre (330ft) fibreglass viewing tunnel as well as a touch pool for hands-on interaction with small marine animals, and a shark and ray tank. For an extra fee, you can dive with the sharks. There is also a **Ripley's Believe It or Not** **I** (daily 11am–11pm; charge; www.ripleysthailand.com) at the Royal Garden Plaza.

South of Pattaya at Km 163 of Thanon Sukhumvit, **Nong Nooch Village** **J** is a 243-hectare (600-acre) residential landscaped parkland enclosing two lakes (daily 8am–6pm; charge; www.nongnoochtropicalgarden. com). Apart from showcasing an extensive collection of orchids and palms,

Up close and personal with an elephant at Nong Nooch Village.

BELOW: aerial view of Pattaya Bay.

TIP

For those who do not want to get wet, book a trip with the Yellow Submarine (www.thaisubmarine.com). The 2-hour trip involves a boat ride to Ko Sak, southwest of Pattaya, where the submarine is moored. Climb aboard and the vessel will sink up to 30 metres (98ft) for a close-up view of marine life; visibility will vary depending on the time of year.

the park features a butterfly garden, mini-zoo and a daily cultural show with traditional dancing, Thai boxing and an elephant circus.

Pattaya's nightlife

Pattaya's main nightlife zones are clustered around Thanon Hat Pattaya (Beach Road) and Walking Street in **South Pattaya**. There is a staggering range of bars, Irish pubs, German brew houses, live-music venues, nightclubs, as well as an overwhelming number of go-go bars, open-air "beer bars" and massage parlours. The strip called **Boyz Town** (Pattayaland Soi 3) has go-go bars and strip clubs that cater to gay men. Pattaya also has at least three lip-synching Vegas-style cabaret shows that feature a pageant of stunning *kathoey* or "lady-boys" (transsexuals). It's all relatively mild, sort-of-clean fun.

More family-oriented shows at the **Alangkarn Theatre** (Tue–Sun shows at 7pm and 8.45pm; charge; www.alangkarnthailand.com) at Km 155 along Thanon Sukhumvit combine traditional dance and theatre to present a spectacle of historic Thailand, complete with elephant battles, lasers and pyrotechnics.

KO SAMET

Located 200km (124 miles) or three hours by road from Bangkok and a short boat trip across from the fishing harbour of **Ban Phe**, the postcard-perfect island of **Ko Samet** ❺ is a popular weekend getaway for Bangkokians. The island is well known among Thais as the place where Sunthorn Phu (1786–1855), a flamboyantly romantic court poet, retired to compose some of his works. Sunthorn called the island Ko Kaew Phisadan, or "island with sand-like crushed crystal", and it was here that his best-known poem, *Phra Aphaimani*, was set – a tale about a prince and a mermaid.

From a quiet poetic retreat, the island has gained popularity as a laidback resort, helped by its exceptionally fine white sand beaches and clear turquoise-blue waters. The island was declared part of a national marine park in 1981, so technically, most of the resort and bungalow operations are illegal. How-

BELOW: Pattaya's nightlife has a sleazy edge.

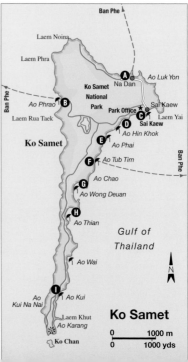

ever, development along the coast has progressed despite the law, though as yet it remains fairly unobtrusive, with single-storey huts and bungalows. A few new boutique resorts have opened on the quieter beaches, while other establishments are upgrading their facilities.

Ko Samet's beaches

Almost all the island's sandy beaches run down the east coast, starting near the larger northern tip with Hat Sai Kaew, and gradually getting more isolated as the island narrows to the southern bay of Ao Karang. Most of the island's infrastructure – school, clinic, temple, market and few shops – are located near **Na Dan** Ⓐ pier and along the paved road to Hat Sai Kaew.

The island is small – only 6km (4 miles) long and 3km (2 miles) wide – and a hike from end to end, passing by the east-coast beaches, can be completed in a few hours, though the coastal track cuts across several rocky headlands. There is a single road running down the centre of the island, which turns into a bumpy dirt track along its outer reaches.

Ao Phrao Ⓑ, the only beach on the west coast, is the most exclusive, with two upmarket hotels nestled into the small scenic bay. On the east coast, **Hat Sai Kaew** Ⓒ (Diamond Sand) – a short walk from Na Dan pier – is the most developed spot on the island and, blessed as it is with powdery white sands, one of the most congested. This is where most Thais and packaged-tour visitors stay, as there is a bigger selection of air-conditioned hotels, bars and seafood restaurants.

Further down the coast, the bay of **Ao Hin Khok** Ⓓ is separated from Hat Sai Kaew by a rocky promontory marked by a weathered statue of a mermaid – inspired by Sunthorn Phu's famous poem. Foreigners tend to nest here and at the next bay, **Ao Phai** Ⓔ, which has an equally nice white sandy beach.

The next white-sand bay is small and intimate **Ao Tub Tim** Ⓕ. There are only two places to stay here, but the noisier attractions of Ao Phai are only a short walk away. There are two more quiet bays, **Ao Nuan** and **Ao Chao**, until you hit the picturesque, crescent-shaped **Ao Wong Deuan** Ⓖ, which is

TIP

While the regular fishing-boat ferries are much cheaper, taking a speedboat across to Ko Samet (around B800) from the mainland port is much faster, drops you on the bay of your choice, and usually means you escape the national park entry fee of B200 per foreign person, which is steep compared to the B20 that Thais are charged.

BELOW: Hat Sai Kaew (Diamond Sand Beach), Ko Samet.

Hat Sai Kaew on Ko Samet is the busiest beach on the island.

becoming increasingly spoilt by boats, noisy jet skis and the clutter of bars and accommodation (mostly middle- to upper-end price range). The facilities are good, with mini-marts, motorcycle rental and internet cafés.

After Ao Wong Deuan, the bays become very peaceful. Scenic **Ao Thian ⓗ** (Candlelight Beach) is actually a series of small beaches separated by rocky outcrops, while the southern **Ao Kui ❶** is little more than a quiet beach and the location of the island's most expensive resort.

Sights and activities

Most activity at Ko Samet is relaxed and beach-bound – sunbathing, beach strolls, swimming and snorkelling – though jet skis and inflatable banana boats do occasionally interrupt the tranquillity. Vendors hawk fruit, beer, ice cream, snacks and sarongs, and there's an army of women offering massage and hair-braiding on the busier beaches. There isn't much by

BELOW: young Thais at Hat Sai Kaew on Ko Samet.

the way of reef around the shoreline and what little there is has been badly damaged, but you will still encounter colourful varieties of fish.

Several resorts offer snorkelling trips by speedboat around Ko Samet and to nearby islets. A few places offer scuba-diving off the beach at Ao Phrao, while boat trips head out to nearby islands such as **Ko Talu**, where visibility is clearer. Off the island's southern tip, **Shark Point** can experience strong currents and is best suited for experienced divers.

Ko Samet is best avoided on public holidays, when visitors outnumber beds, and tents are pitched on any spare patch of land. Evenings are relatively low-key; restaurants set up fresh seafood beach barbecues, while some eateries entertain the impecunious backpacker crowd with the latest pirated Hollywood flicks.

KO CHANG

At 492 sq km (190 sq miles) Thailand's second-largest island after Phuket, **Ko Chang ❻** (Elephant Island) is part of a national marine park that includes

Troubled Troubadour

Poster boy for Ko Samet, Sunthorn Phu was a Byronic hero if ever there was one. Thailand's most famous poet was born a commoner in 1786. He fell in love with a woman named Jun who was related to the royal family. Their affair scandalised protocol, but they were later pardoned and Sunthorn was subsequently appointed court poet. Later, a descent into alcoholism, violence and adultery led to a divorce and a prison sentence. He was stripped of his title, but later won his way back into royal favour.

Sunthorn Phu died in 1855, leaving his historical poems, including the romantic epic *Phra Aphaimani*, as a lasting legacy. Thailand celebrates his poetry every year on 26 June with public recitals, and the cultural significance of his works has been recognised by Unesco.

some 52 islands. Around a five-hour drive from Bangkok (or 45 minutes by air to Trat on the mainland, then a 45-minute transfer by boat), the verdant island is part of Trat Province close to the Cambodian border. Located 20km (12 miles) southwest of Trat town, the mainland pier of **Laem Ngop** is the main jumping-off point to the island.

For years Ko Chang managed to escape the rapid development seen elsewhere on the coast, remaining a firm favourite with backpackers. Things begin to change in the early 2000s when former prime minister Thaksin Shinawatra began actively to promote it as a playground for the rich. This has brought a rapid increase in resort construction and infrastructure, including an upgrade of the road system, and the opening of a domestic airport in Trat.

The availability of quality and stylish accommodation is drawing in a greater number of wealthy Thai vacationers, who, with the increase of car ferries from the mainland, seem intent on bringing their vehicles over to explore the island's one road. This road has

several hazardous hill sections with sharp bends, and exploring on a rented motorcycle should be attempted only by experienced riders.

Ko Chang's beaches

Despite the incursions of the modern world, the island's size means that it has retained its relatively untouched interior, areas of mangrove forest and some lovely beaches. The main beaches are along the west coast, with **Hat Sai Khao Ⓐ** (White Sand Beach) the most developed (and longest) stretch. Its swathe of powdery sands is framed by a backdrop of casuarina trees.

To the south, **Hat Khlong Phrao Ⓑ** is one of the most picturesque and quietest beaches on the island. It is effectively divided into the northern, central and southern sections by canals. Beyond, **Hat Kai Bae Ⓒ** has seen much recent development. Unfortunately, parts of its beach disappear when the tide is high. Next up is the last vestige of Ko Chang's hippie traveller scene, the lovely stretch of **Hat Tha Nam Ⓓ**, or Lonely Beach; it's no longer such a haven of solitude

TIP

Hat Tha Nam (also known as Lonely Beach) is one of Ko Chang's nicest beaches, but beware of the strong undertow and currents at its northern end. A good number of drownings have occurred in these treacherous waters.

BELOW: poolside, Amari Emerald Cove Resort at Hat Khlong Phrao.

*Than Mayom
Waterfall, Ko Chang.*

as plush resorts have edged in. Just over 1km (2/3 mile) long, this fine-sand beach gets a little coarser towards the south. It's the island's best beach for swimming, although there is a steep shelf at the northern tip. Next is **Ao Bai Lan** , a bay with rocks and reef but no beach.

At the southern end of the west coast, the fishing village of **Ban Bang Bao** has become little more than a concrete pier devoted to tourism, with seafood restaurants, dive shops, souvenir shops and guesthouses. This is also the departure point for dive and snorkel trips to surrounding islands. The next bay along the south coast – accessed from the east coast – contains **Salak Phet** fishing village, which has a more authentic and less developed feel than Ban Bang Bao.

Ko Chang's eastern shoreline has few beaches and is largely ignored by most visitors. This makes a leisurely drive along the plantation- and hill-backed road a real pleasure, with few

vehicles and the reward of a seafood lunch at Salak Phet. An alternative route runs east of Salak Phet, where a winding road continues all the way to **Hat Yao** , or Long Beach, on the southern tip.

Sights and activities

The lush forests that clothe the mountainous backbone of Ko Chang are home to many avian species (including hornbills), macaques, pythons and cobras, monitor lizards, deer and boar, as well as striking wild flora.

There are several companies operating elephant treks into the interior. The best one is **Ban Kwan Chang** (book treks with Jungleway, www. jungleway.com), which conducts half-day treks and feeding sessions with the elephants. Other popular activities include kayaking and treks to the island's numerous waterfalls. The two most well trodden are **Khlong Phu** and **Than Mayom**.

Snorkelling and diving trips usually head to the smaller outlying islands off the southern end of Ko Chang. There is fine diving at reason-

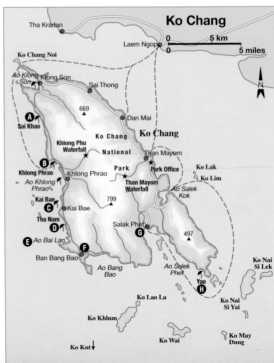

ably shallow depths, at its most enjoyable between November and March, when the sea is calmer and visibility clearer. Some of the best sites include the pinnacles off **Ko Rang**, the reefs around **Ko Wai**, the shallow dives off **Ko Khlum** and **Hin Luk Bat** – a rock pinnacle 30 minutes south by boat from Ban Bang Bao. The **Thonburi Wreck** off Ko Chang's southeastern tip is another highlight.

Nightlife

Ko Chang's nightlife is subdued compared to that of Ko Samui or Phuket, with each beach having its own preferred watering holes. **Hat Sai Khao** hosts the main action. Lying on beach mats is the typical set-up, and live music features at many bars. As a sign of things to come, there is a block of raucous "beer bars" on the road at the southern end of Hat Sai Khao.

Further down the west coast, **Hat Kai Bae** has a small nightlife scene with a couple of unassuming bars along the road. **Hat Tha Nam** has its own pockets of entertainment, with a couple of bars that close by midnight.

Ko Chang archipelago

Around 10km (6 miles) off Ko Chang, the tiny island of **Ko Wai** has limited and basic accommodation, but the views of surrounding islands are spectacular, and there's a lovely coral reef just a short swim from the main beach.

An hour by speedboat from the mainland pier of Laem Ngop, **Ko Mak** is dense with coconut trees and has two lovely, quiet beaches – **Ao Kao** and **Ao Suan Yai**. Both beaches have some basic accommodation and restaurants.

The southernmost island in the archipelago is **Ko Kut ❼**, Thailand's fourth-largest island and 2½ hours away by speedboat. Some 25km (16 miles) long and 12km (7 miles) wide, the island is inhabited partly by people of Khmer origin, with most inhabitants earning a living off fishing or agriculture.

Aside from several fine beaches and clear seas, attractions include **Khlong Chao Waterfall** and the fishing village at **Ao Sa Lad**. Due to its remote location, the island's development has been fairly low-key, and it attracts mainly organised tour groups. ❏

Seashells from the beach at Ko Chang.

BELOW: the island of Ko Wai, off Ko Chang.

RESTAURANTS AND BARS

Restaurants

Price per person for a three-course meal without drinks:
$ = under B300
$$ = B300–800
$$$ = B800–1,600
$$$$ = over B1,600

Ko Si Chang

Thai & Chinese
Sichang View Resort
91 Moo 6. Tel: 0-3821 6210–1. Open: daily L & D. $-$$
www.supatrariverhouse.com
Set on a cliff top with lofty views out to sea, this restaurant's only downside is the rather leisurely service. Serves good Thai and Chinese food. The seafood dishes are especially excellent; try the delicious white snapper and crabs.

Thai & Western
Pan & David
167 Moo 3, Th. Makhaamthaew. Tel: 0-3821 6075. Open: Wed–Mon L & D. $
www.ko-sichang.com/eat.html
Situated beside the quiet road that leads to the summer palace, this ever-popular restaurant is run by American expat David and his Thai wife Pan. The simple open-sided eatery has garden seating and is backed by the sea-view Rim Talay resort. Menu includes breakfast options as well as seafood, Italian, French, Thai and vegetarian dishes.

Pattaya

International
Art Café
285/3 Moo 5, Th. Naklua Soi 16. Tel: 0-3836 7652. Open: daily L & D. $$-$$$
www.artcafe-thailand.com
Tucked behind the beachfront condos of Naklua, this French-Mediterranean restaurant occupies a wooden colonial-style house surrounded by a garden. With lovely alfresco seating at the front, this is the perfect setting to indulge in a fine meal.

Bruno's
306/63 Chateau Dale Plaza, Th. Thappraya. Tel: 0-3836 4600. Open: daily L & D. $$-$$$
www.brunos-pattaya.com
One of Pattaya's most popular expat-friendly bistros, Bruno's offers fine dining at affordable prices. Warm, welcoming vibe. Expect well-presented French-European dishes and an extensive wine list.

Casa Pascal
Th. Pattaya 2, South Pattaya. Tel: 0-3872 3660. Open: daily L & D, Sun brunch. $$$-$$$$
www.restaurant-pattaya.com
Smack in the centre of Pattaya's main drag opposite the Royal Garden Plaza. This Swiss-run place is one of the best places for fine dining in Pattaya. The European menu is mainly French-influenced, although there are some Italian selections thrown in.

Mantra Restaurant and Bar
240 Moo 5, Th. Hat Pattaya. Tel: 0-3842 9591. Open: daily 6pm–1am. $$$-$$$$
www.mantra-pattaya.com
Hot restaurant that serves an interesting mix of Asian (Thai, Japanese, Chinese, Indian) and Mediterranean dishes. Wide-ranging and eclectic menu allows you to pick and match your food. The decor is equally dramatic, with seating on two levels. Later in the evening, it turns into a pulsating nightspot that plays chill-out music.

Thai
Cabbages & Condoms
366/11, Th. Phra Tamnak Soi 4. Tel: 0-3825 0556–8. Open: daily B, L & D. $-$$
www.cabbagesandcondoms.co.th
Its curious name comes from its owner, former Senator Mechai, whose work on birth control has earned him the nickname "Mr Condom". Building on the fine reputation of its older sister outlet in Bangkok, this eatery – which looks out to the ocean – serves excellent Thai standards.

Mum Aroi
83/4 Naklua Banglamung. Tel: 0-3823 4352. Open: L & D. $$
Sensational seafood in sensational surroundings. Great atmosphere, live music, and tables packed with munching Thais who know a good deal (and meal) when they see it.

Nang Nual
Two branches: Th. Hat Pattaya (Walking St) & Jomtien. Tel: 0-3842 8708 (Walking St); tel: 0-3823 1548 (Jomtien). Open: B, L & D. $$-$$$
With two prime waterfront locations on Pattaya Bay and Jomtien beach, this established seafood restaurant is well known. It certainly isn't glam, but for freshly caught fish and shellfish cooked Thai-style, it's unbeatable. The branch on Walking St has a sea view, while the Jomtien eatery is beside the main beach road.

PIC Kitchen
Fl 2, 255 Th. Pattaya 2, Soi 5. Tel: 0-3842 8374. Open: daily B, L & D. $$-$$$
www.pic-kitchen.com
Under the same ownership as Sugar Hut, this long-time favourite in Pattaya offers a real Thai experience with floor seating in a garden-facing *sala* (pavilion), or regular table dining in air-conditioned comfort. Excellent Thai and the odd international dish, like British Raj curry.

Vietnamese
Le Saigon Bayview
Fl 23, Pattaya Hill Resort, 329/245 Moo 12, Th. Phra Tamnak Soi 2. Tel: 0-3825 0329. Open: daily D. $$-$$$
Pattaya's only independent rooftop restaurant offering views of Pattaya Bay and Jomtien. Open from late afternoon for drinks. Choose from the extensive wine list before getting a table on the terrace. Serves good, authentic Vietnamese as well as innovative fusion dishes.

Ko Samet

Thai & Western
Naga Bungalows
Ao Hin Khok. Tel: 0-3864 4034. Open: daily B, L & D. $-$$
A long-time favourite with backpackers, this well-

established restaurant-bar is run by an Englishwoman and is known for its bakery and late-night revelry. The restaurant sits up the hill and serves decent Western breakfasts as well as sandwiches, pizzas, burgers and Thai dishes. Overlooking the beach, the bar gets busy during the evening happy hour.

Samed Villa
89 Moo 4, Ao Phai. Tel: 0-3864 4094. Open: daily B, L & D. **$$**
www.samedvilla.com
Under Swiss ownership, this resort is very popular with Bangkok expats. The restaurant is the usual run-of-the-mill island affair, though it raises the bar just enough to distinguish itself from the crowd. Service is prompt and friendly. Large selection of Thai, seafood and Western dishes.

Sea View Restaurant
Ao Prao Resort, Ao Phrao. Tel: 0-3864 4101–5. Open: daily B, L & D. **$$$**
www.samedresorts.com
If you're hungering for an elegant dining experience away from the string of beach barbies, then this place is about as good as it gets. The selection of Thai food, steaks and international dishes are well presented but by no means a gastronomic epiphany.

Ko Chang
International
Ban Nuna
31/2 Moo 4, Hat Sai Khao. Tel: 0-3955 1230. Open: daily B, L & D. **$$**
This German- and Thai-owned restaurant and bar features a pleasantly

leafy terrace garden and two levels of seating, of which the upper has Thai floor cushions. Open for breakfast, the artistically presented menu covers a broad range, from Thai to pancakes, pizza, pasta, schnitzel and barbecued kebabs.

Invito
Hat Sai Khao. Tel: 0-3955 1326. Open: daily L & D. **$$$**
This is the island's most upmarket independent restaurant, situated in a none-too-ideal location at the southern end of Hat Sai Khao beside a string of trashy bars. The cosy eatery serves fine Italian cuisine including home-made pasta and a wide selection of pizzas cooked in an open wood-fired oven. Portions can be somewhat stingy for the prices.

Thai & Western
Hungry Elephant
Opp Sky Bar, between Hat Sai Khao and Hat Khai Muk. Mobile tel: 08-9985 8433. Open: daily L & D. **$$**
This unassuming street-side restaurant that few tourists venture to is well known among Bangkok expats. Run by a friendly Thai couple (the husband's father was the chef at the French embassy in Bangkok), the menu has Thai staples plus some excellent French dishes.

Kai Bae Marina
Hat Kai Bae. Mobile tel: 08-7044 0385. Open: daily B, L & D. **$$**
Under Austrian ownership, this restaurant has no-frills decor, but it fills up every evening. The appeal is the broad menu that includes a Thai sea-

food section, as well as pizzas, steaks and dishes with a definite northern European bias. Whatever your choice, it's all good.

Kharma
Hat Kai Bae. Mobile tel: 08-6759 7529. Open: daily L & D. **$$**
Run by a Swede and her Thai partner, this simple eatery and bar is located roadside along Kai Bae. It serves a diverse range of good Thai food, some of the island's only Mexican fare, plus Swedish-leaning European dishes.

Rock Sand
White Sand Beach. Tel: 08-4781 0550. Open: daily B, L & D. **$**
Part of a very pleasant resort, Rock Sand is best known for its pizzas and steaks; the switched-on staff are a plus.

Salak Phet Seafood
43 Moo 2, Salak Phet. Tel: 0-3955 3099. Open: daily B, L & D. **$–$$**

www.kohchangsalakphet.com
Considered by many to be the best seafood place on the island, this restaurant and resort on stilts in the southeast of the island is a part of the fishing village of the same name. Great for crabs, squid, shrimp and fish that you can choose yourself from the sunken nets below the pier.

Tonsai Restaurant
Hat Sai Khao. Mobile tel: 08-9895 7229. Open: daily L & D. **$–$$**
On the opposite side of the road from the beach, the novel setting of this restaurant – a banyan tree house – is what initially attracts, but it's the delicious selection of Thai and fusion cuisine at bargain prices that keeps diners coming back for more. Very chilled out; lie back on cushions and sample cocktails from the extensive list before munching on salads and curries.

RIGHT: the Mantra Restaurant at Pattaya.

NORTHERN GULF COAST

This narrow strip of land hosts sandy beaches, good weather, interesting towns and two national parks. Popular destinations include historic Phetchaburi, beach getaways such as Cha-am and Hua Hin, and celebrity-friendly Pranburi

W edged between the Gulf of Thailand and the Andaman Sea, southern Thailand resembles an elephant's trunk snaking down from below the Central Plain to the tip of the Malay Peninsula. The Isthmus of Kra, as this land bridge is named, connects mainland Asia with the Malay Peninsula, and at its narrowest point in Chumphon is only 44km (27 miles) from coast to coast.

The 600km (373 miles) or so from Bangkok to Surat Thani (main jumping-off point for Ko Samui) is blessed with miles and miles of sandy beaches and equable weather (*see margin tip, page 198*), together with lush, forested interiors and historic towns that harbour plenty of attractions worth exploring. The southern rail line and Highway 4, also known as Petchkasem Highway, are the two principal links to the south, although there are also airports in Surat Thani and Hua Hin.

The upper section of the Gulf coast is home to two of the country's best-known national parks: Kaeng Krachan and Khao Sam Roi Yot. Phetchaburi, with its ancient temples, is a worthy stop before travellers continue to Cha-am and Hua Hin, both popular with Bangkokians as weekend beach getaways. Further south, Pranburi has a good reputation as a high-end bou-

tique resort. Prachuap Khiri Khan and Chumphon see few tourists, except those departing from Chumphon's port for the boat ride to Ko Tao (*see page 212*); the latter is more easily accessed from Ko Samui.

PHETCHABURI

Historically rich **Phetchaburi ❶** is one of Thailand's oldest towns and has been an important trade and cultural centre since the 11th century. Lying on the Phetchaburi River some 120km (75 miles) south of Bangkok, the town has

Main attractions
PHETCHABURI
KAENG KRACHAN NATIONAL PARK
CHA-AM
HUA HIN
PRANBURI
KHAO SAM ROI YOT NATIONAL PARK
PRACHUAP KHIRI KHAN

LEFT: tourists making the trek up to Khao Wang, Phetchaburi. **RIGHT:** battle scenes from the *Ramakien* at Wat Mahathat.

Northern Gulf Coast

come under the influence of the Mon, Khmers and Thais at various times, and has over 30 temples that reflect the differing cultures and architectural styles of its past invaders. A pleasant place to while away a day or two, Phetchaburi is easily navigable on foot.

Khao Wang

Just west of town, the 92-metre (302ft) hill called **Khao Wang** (Mount Palace) provides a useful landmark. Commissioned in 1860 as the summer residence of King Mongkut (Rama IV), the complex is known as **Phra Nakhon Khiri Historical Park** (daily 9am–5pm; charge). It is a curious mélange of Thai, Chinese and Western architectural styles taking the form of shrines, temples, pagodas and other structures. Many of these offer fabulous panoramas of the vicinity, especially at sunset.

The hilltop buildings include three throne halls (two of which have been turned into a museum housing furniture and collectables belonging to King Mongkut), a neoclassical observatory (the king was an avid astronomer), a large white *chedi* and the **Wat Maha Samanaram**. The steep cobblestone trail to the peak winds through forest and gardens populated by monkeys. An easier option is to take the cable car (daily 8am–5pm; charge).

Other key temples

The former Hindu **Wat Kamphaeng Laeng** (daily 8am–6pm; free) with its five laterite Khmer *prang* is one of Phetchaburi's key religious sites. Located on Thanon Phra Song, it is thought to have marked the southernmost point of the Khmer kingdom. The temple dates from the 12th century. Although the towers have undergone some restoration, they are still dishevelled enough to look authentic.

Just around the corner on Thanon Phongsuriya, the 17th-century **Wat Yai Suwannaram** (daily 8am–6pm; free) is best known for its fading murals of Hindu gods that date back to the 18th century. The temple's ample grounds hold a lovely teak pavilion, as well as a catfish-filled pond. Jutting out into the pond is a small stilted *ho trai*, or scripture library.

Back across the river and along Thanon Damnoenkasem, five white stucco-covered *prang* make **Wat Mahathat** (daily 8am–6pm; free) the town's most dominant temple. As with any Mahathat (Great Relic) place of worship, the 14th-century site enshrines relics of the Buddha, but is probably better known for the intricate depictions of angels and other mythical creatures in low-relief stucco on the gables of the main buildings.

Tham Khao Luang

Just 5km (3 miles) from town, **Tham Khao Luang** cave (daily 8am–6pm; charge) makes an interesting excursion. Shafts of sunlight filter down from naturally hewn holes in the cave roof, creating a splendid visual effect. The rays illuminate some of the 100 or more Buddha images that rest in the three main chambers of the cave. Beside the entrance, **Wat Bunthawi** showcases wonderfully carved wooden door panels. Unofficial guides wait near the approach to the cave, offering to turn on the cave lights for a fee.

Ban Puen Palace

As the railway line brought greater access to this part of Thailand, a number of palaces were erected for the royal family in times past. Right beside the Phetchaburi River, about 1km (2/3 mile) from the city centre, along Thanon Ratchadamnoen, **Ban Puen Palace** (daily 8am–4pm; charge) would look more at home in Germany's Black Forest than here in the coastal flats of Phetchaburi. Built in 1910 for King Rama V (the same year he died), this stately home was designed by a German architect, a grandiose two-storey palace intended as a rainy-season hideaway. Although little in the way of furniture remains to convey its original splendour, the porcelain-tiled dining room and inner courtyard with its pond and fountain are interesting to explore, as are the expansive gardens by the riverbank.

Avoid feeding the monkeys at Khao Wang, even if they seem tame.

BELOW: Phra Nakhon Khiri.

Hua Hin is known for its fine seafood restaurants.

KAENG KRACHAN N P

Located some 60km (37 miles) southwest of Phetchaburi Town, the vast 3,000-sq-km (1,158-sq-mile) **Kaeng Krachan National Park ❷** (daily 6am–6pm; charge) is the largest in Thailand. It is the source of the Phetchaburi and Pranburi rivers, covers almost half of Phetchaburi Province, and is a haven for numerous species of large mammals, including elephants, leopards, bears, deer, gibbons and monkeys, as well as a few tigers. With around 300 species of resident and migratory birds, it is also a prime bird-watching spot. Considering its proximity to Bangkok, surprisingly few tourists venture here. Trekking is the main activity; guides can be hired at the park's headquarters at the end of the road beyond the dam. Accommodation consists of basic park lodgings, but the easiest way to visit the park is on a tour organised by hotels in Hua Hin.

The topography varies between rainforest and savannah grasslands, and the park harbours both a freshwater lake and rugged mountain ranges. It is possible to ascend the tallest peak, the 1,207-metre (3,960ft) **Phanoen Tung**, for superb views of the lush countryside, or trek to the 18-tier **Tho Thip Waterfall**. Swimming and boating in the vast reservoir created by **Kaeng Krachan Dam** are other popular activities.

On the southern edge of Kaeng Krachan, towards the mountain range that divides Thailand from Myanmar, is the spectacular **Pala-U Waterfall**. Best seen during the rainy season, the falls have 11 tiers and are surrounded by dense forest.

CHA-AM

The long stretch of sand at **Cha-am ❸** is popular as a weekend getaway from Bangkok. Around 40km (25 miles) south of Phetchaburi (178km/111 miles from Bangkok), the beach has a different vibe to that of Hua Hin further down the coast, and is fairly quiet during the weekdays, with plenty of seafood stalls and cheap restaurants along the waterfront Thanon Ruamchit. At weekends, however, the mood becomes more raucous as families and college students arrive in droves, picnicking (and boozing) under the casuarina trees and beach brollies, floating on

rubber inner tubes and riding banana boats. The sand underfoot is a bit rough and the waters are less than pristine, but Cha-am does offer good value for money when it comes to hotels and food. Recently arrived hotels, like the **Veranda** and **Alila Cha-am**, are trying to up the ante with their chic minimalist designs (and high prices).

Maruekhathayawan Palace

Some 10km (6 miles) south of Cha-am heading towards Hua Hin, the seaside **Maruekhathayawan Palace** (daily 8am–4pm; charge) was built in 1923 from teakwood, and served as a retreat for King Vajiravudh during the last two years before his death in 1925. The airy stilted structures were designed by an Italian architect and are European in style – supposedly based on sketches made by King Vajiravudh (Rama VI). Beautifully renovated in summery pastel shades, the three palace wings are interconnected by long raised covered walkways. The magnificent audience chamber is the centrepiece of the palace structure.

HUA HIN

Prachuap Khiri Khan is Thailand's narrowest province and its coast is fringed with mountains and lovely quiet beaches, the most popular of which is the 5km (3-mile) stretch of sand at **Hua Hin ❹**. Located 203km (126 miles) and less than four hours by road or rail from Bangkok, Hua Hin has long had an air of exclusivity, thanks to the private residences maintained by Thai royalty and the capital's wealthy elite. Partly because of this, it retains more of a family ambience than other beach destinations in Thailand.

The royal connection can be seen at the seafront teakwood summer residence called **Klai Kangwon Palace**, which means "Far from Worries". Built in 1926 for King Rama VII, the Spanish-style villa is still used by the royal family and is not open to the public.

One of the country's first rail lines linked Bangkok to Hua Hin at the start of the 20th century, transporting the capital's wealthy to the southern shores. Hua Hin thus assumed the aura of a European spa town, with the royals coming here for the clean air. Today, the coastal town is beginning to reclaim that mantle as several exclusive spa retreats – like the award-winning **Chiva Som** – cater to the needs of moneyed travellers. A string of large brand-name resorts, like **Hilton**, **Hyatt** and **Marriott**, have also opened in recent years, along with local (and equally expensive) concerns like the **Dusit** and **Anantara**.

Hua Hin sights

Today, some visitors still choose to take the train to Hua Hin, and the railway station is a beautiful place at which to arrive: built in the early 1920s, it evokes the romance of a bygone era, complete with a still-intact cream-and-red royal waiting room, once used by King Rama VI.

Thanon Damnoenkasem leads from the railway station directly to the beach and another historic landmark, the colonial-style **former Railway Hotel**. Dating from 1923, the Victorian-

TIP

Despite the road and airport, one of the more pleasant ways of getting to Hua Hin is by train, following the route taken by the royal family who initially popularised the resort.

BELOW: signalling the arrival of the train at Hua Hin's picturesque railway station.

inspired building was Thailand's first resort hotel, and has been restored to its original wood-panelled glory as the **Sofitel Central Hua Hin Resort**. Even if you don't stay here, try to have afternoon tea or dine at one of its eateries, then stroll through its large manicured gardens filled with animal-shaped topiary creations.

The wide sweep of Hua Hin beach is backed by the lavish summer homes of Bangkok's elite, along with a series of faceless condo developments. Some of the beachfront homes, which fuse elements of Thai and Western architecture, date back almost a century, and a few have been restored and converted into unique boutique resorts, like **Baan Bayan** and **Baan Talay Dao**. Hua Hin also enjoys a reputation as a place to retire, with a new generation of condos and beach houses being built to accommodate the upsurge.

The beach, punctuated by occasional boulders that give it some scenic beauty, lacks the character of Thailand's palm-fringed island bays, but is still great for long strolls. The beaches further south of town, **Suan Son** and **Khao Tao**, are nicer and more secluded, but, again, not picture-postcard. While the sea is generally calm during the low season from May to September (with jellyfish an occasional problem), the winds can whip up the water towards the end and start of the year. This is when windsurfers and kite-surfers take to the water.

Outside Hua Hin

For a bird's-eye view of Hua Hin, head up steep **Khao Hin Lek Fai** hill for some of the best panoramas of the beach. Around 3km (2 miles) west of town, turn down Soi 70 and follow the signposts to any of the six viewpoints – dawn and sunset are the best times.

A few kilometres south of town is **Khao Takiab** (Chopstick Hill), a rocky outcrop which marks the end of Hua Hin beach. It is a steep climb to the top, but the views of the surrounding coast are worth the sweat. The hill is split into two windswept peaks; the nearest has several small shrines and a steep staircase that leads down to a towering 20-metre (66ft) tall Buddha image. Standing dramatically just above the crashing surf, the image looks back

towards Hua Hin beach with its hands outstretched. On the other brow is **Wat Khao Lad**, with its lofty pagoda atop a long flight of stairs.

Activities

The town's nightlife has picked up in the last few years, and a number of new restaurants have opened their doors. While Hua Hin was always known as a place for wonderfully fresh seafood, the diversity of culinary options has expanded to Japanese, Korean, Scandinavian, German, French and Italian eateries, reflecting the nationalities of the major tourist arrivals. The restaurants and bars are all clustered into a small area around Thanon Naresdamri and behind on the parallel Thanon Phunsuk. Soi Bintabaht has the highest concentration of beer bars, and the pier area along Naresdamri serves some of the best grilled seafood in town.

Golfers have access to 10 courses within striking distance of Hua Hin, with more on the drawing board. The oldest is the **Royal Hua Hin Golf Course**, built in the 1920s, and used by the Thai royalty.

Hua Hin sees a lot of weekend activities and events catering to the Bangkok crowds. These include the annual **Hua Hin Jazz Festival**, the popular **King's Cup Elephant Polo Tournament**, usually held in September, and more recently, the **Hua Hin Vintage Car Parade**.

PRANBURI

The beaches south of Hua Hin towards **Pranburi** ❺ are gradually being developed. Around a 20-minute drive from Hua Hin, Paknampran, the mouth of the Pranburi River, marks the beginning of a clean but unremarkable beach that runs down towards Sam Roi Yot National Park. Here are some of Thailand's most exclusive beachfront hideaways, including the **Evason** and its newer (and pricier) sister property, the **Evason Hideaway**, along with plush, celebrity-friendly **Aleenta**.

About 63km (39 miles) south of Hua Hin, **Khao Sam Roi Yot National Park** ❻ (daily 6am–6pm;

Limestone pinnacles at Khao Sam Roi Yot National Park.

BELOW: the plush Aleenta resort in Pranburi.

Claim to Fame

When the producers of Roland Joffe's Academy Award-winning movie *The Killing Fields* – depicting Pol Pot's murderous takeover of Cambodia in 1975 – were looking for a suitable location, their eyes fell on the former Railway Hotel at Hua Hin. The hotel's fleeting appearance in the film – it mainly features during the scenes when the foreign correspondents are holed up in the Cambodian capital in the wake of the Khmer Rouge revolution – gave it an added lustre both in the eyes of film buffs around the world and guests who enjoyed its gracious architecture and beautifully manicured grounds.

Hua Hin's other claim to celluloid fame is a short scene in the German film *Devil's Paradise*, which was loosely based on Joseph Conrad's novel *Victory*.

Map on page 192

TIP

The Gulf of Thailand coast covered in this chapter has weather similar to that of the rest of Thailand. However, although the rains here continue well into November, the effects of the monsoon are milder. The best months of the year are from December to March, while April and May are the hottest months. The rainy months stretch from July to November.

BELOW: resort at Phrachuap Khiri Khan.

charge) translates as "Three Hundred Mountain Peaks", referring to the dramatic limestone pinnacles jutting up from the park's mangrove swamps. Carved from the rugged coastline, the 98-sq-km (38-sq-ft) park features beaches, marshes and brackish lagoons, forests, caves and offshore islands. Wildlife includes migratory birds that congregate on the marsh and mudflats, crab-eating macaques and the rare serow (a mountain goat-antelope). At certain times, pods of dolphins also swim along the park's shores.

Reached by boat or by foot along a steep half-hour trail from Hat Laem Sala, **Tham Phraya Nakhon** is the park's most famous attraction; the huge cave has a large sinkhole that allows shafts of light to enter and illuminate the grand Thai-style pavilion or *sala* called **Phra Thinang Khuha Kharuhat**. It was built in the 1890s for a visit by King Chulalongkorn (Rama V). Other noteworthy caves are **Tham Sai** and **Tham Kaew** (Jewel Cave), the latter with glistening stalactite and rock formations.

Most Hua Hin and Pranburi hotels organise day trips to the park, but travellers can also catch a train or bus to Pranburi, and from there take a *songthaew* to the fishing village of Bang Pu. From here, take a short boat ride to the park checkpoint on **Hat Laem Sala** beach. The Forestry Department runs accommodation here, but a better option is to stay at a hotel, like the **Dolphin Bay Resort** (*see page 378*), located at **Hat Phu Noi** beach a few kilometres north of the park.

SOUTH OF PRANBURI

The coastline south of Khao Sam Roi Yot is lined with miles and miles of sandy beaches, yet most foreign tourists go directly to Chumphon for ferry connections to Ko Tao (*see page 212*), or to Surat Thani and then by boat to either Ko Samui (*see page 201*) or Ko Phangan (*see page 208*). While this stretch of the Gulf of Thailand coast may not be geared towards pampering foreign visitors, there is less tourist-oriented commercialism.

Prachuap Khiri Khan ⑦, 85km (53 miles) from Hua Hin, is an interesting town to explore, as are the beaches of **Ao Manao**, 4km (3 miles) south of Prachuap Town, and **Ban Krut**, 70km (43 miles) south. Both beaches have limited facilities by way of accommodation and restaurants. Further south, offshore from the town of **Bang Saphan Yai**, **Ko Thalu** is one of the first islands south of Bangkok that is good enough for snorkelling and diving.

About 184km (114 miles) from Prachuap Khiri Khan, **Chumphon ⑧** is considered by many to be the start of southern Thailand. It has several good beaches, including **Thung Wua Laem**, 12km (7 miles) north of Chumphon Town, and **Ao Thung Makam Noi**, about 25km (16 miles) to the south. Some 20km (12 miles) offshore, the reef-fringed islands of **Ko Ngam Yai** and **Ko Ngam Noi** are popular with divers, while 80km (50 miles) away **Ko Tao** (*see page 212*) is another diving hotspot. ❑

RESTAURANTS AND BARS

Restaurants

Price per person for a three-course meal without drinks:
$ = under B300
$$ = B300–800
$$$ = B800–1,600
$$$$ = over B1,600

Phetchaburi

Thai
Rabieng Rim Nam Guesthouse
1 Th. Chisa-In. Tel: 0-3242 5707. Open: daily B, L & D. $
There are few eateries with English-language menus in Phetchaburi Town, so this rustic restaurant that juts out over the Phetchaburi River is a real find. Part of a guesthouse popular with backpackers, this simple eatery attracts a mix of foreigners as well as locals. Broad menu of decent Thai dishes.

Cha-am

International
Crawford's
252/6 Th. Chad Laird. Tel: 0-3247 1774.
Open: daily B, L & D. $$
Eclectic-looking bar and restaurant tucked back on a parallel road to the Cha-am beachfront. The bar is part of the patio garden, while upstairs is a dining room with a piano. The food has a Brit-Gaelic leaning, but there are also Thai dishes on the menu.

Rabiang Lay
Veranda Resort & Spa, 737/12 Th. Mung Talay.
Tel: 0-3270 9000.
Open: daily L & D. $$$
www.verandaresortandspa.com
Cha-am's most stylish beachfront eatery is a crisp white minimalist affair with design-oriented furniture and both terrace and indoor seating. It specialises in fusion seafood and has a bar mixing up tropical cocktails and innovative smoothies. Part of the Veranda resort and therefore mainly frequented by hotel guests.

Italian
Da Vinci's
274/5 Th. Ruamjit.
Tel: 0-3247 1871.
Open: daily L & D. $$–$$$
Pizza and pasta on an attractive shaded terrace.

Thai
Poom
274/1 Th. Ruamchit.
Tel: 0-3247 1036.
Open: daily B, L & D. $$
With a sea-view patio, this simple outdoor restaurant has been serving some of Cha-am's best Thai-style seafood for over a decade. Advance booking recommended, especially at weekends.

Hua Hin

International
Brasserie de Paris
3 Th. Naresdamri.
Tel: 0-3253 0637.
Open: daily L & D. $$$
This European-flavoured bistro is spread over two floors; the upstairs looks out to sea. The staff are attentive and the Belgian owner Thierry is very personable. The set meals are a great-value option.

Great American Rib Company
8/4 Sailom Pavilion, Th. Damneonkasem. Tel: 0-3252 1255. Open: daily L & D.
$$–$$$
www.greatrib.com
Branch of the hugely popular Bangkok original, this Hua Hin outlet has indoor and terrace seating. The speciality is the wood-smoked ribs in barbecue sauce, but equally good are the combo platters, steaks and burgers. Save room for the huge desserts.

Mamma Mia
19 Th. Damnoenkasem.
Tel: 0-3253 3636.
Open: daily L & D. $$$
Run by Milan native Claudio, this authentic Italian eatery sits beside one of Hua Hin's busiest roads. Spilt over two floors, upstairs is a pizzeria, while downstairs there are plenty of authentic Italian dishes, including handmade pastas and mouthwatering desserts.

Thai
Chao Lay
15 Th. Naresdamri. Tel: 0-3251 3436. Open: daily L & D. $$–$$$
This is the best of all Hua Hin's seafood eateries and is hugely popular with local diners. Set on a jetty over the sea, the Thai-style seafood is very fresh at this no-frills restaurant.

La Mer
111/2 Khao Takiab.
Tel: 0-3253 6205.
Open: daily L & D. $$–$$$
On the side of Khao Takiab hill at the southern end of the beach, this is Hua Hin's best-positioned restaurant for dramatic evening views. Spread over several platforms, it's seafood all the way on its large menu. Not particularly glam, but the food and view packs them in.

Sasi
83/159 Th. Takiab.
Tel: 0-3251 2488.
Open: daily D. $$
www.sasi-restaurant.com
This garden-theatre has a wooden stage over a large pond where a two-hour show of traditional dance and martial arts takes place daily from 7pm. The price includes a set menu of popular Thai dishes. A good place to sample both local culture and food.

Supatra-by-the-sea
122/63 Th. Takiab.
Tel: 0-3253 6561.
Open: daily L & D. $$–$$$
www.supatra-bythesea.com
Right at the end of Hua Hin beach, this lovely restaurant overlooks Khao Takiab hill. A sister of Bangkok's hugely popular Supatra River House restaurant, expect well-executed Thai dishes served on the torch-lit garden terrace or up in the main pavilion.

Prachuap Khiri Khan

Thai
Ma Prow
44 Th. Chai Thaleh.
Tel: 0-3255 1208.
Open: daily L & D. $
Around 150 metres/yds south of the pier, Ma Prow is one of several good seafood restaurants along Thanon Chai Thaleh. There are good views of the bay from the patio.

KO SAMUI, KO PHANGAN AND KO TAO

Ko Samui conjures images of an island paradise, and Ko Phangan is equally idyllic too, except that it's often overshadowed by wild, anything-goes, all-night Full Moon Parties. If you prefer to dive or snorkel, head to the pristine waters off Ko Tao

It's rare that the words "Ko Samui" appear in print without being followed by "paradise". While Ko Samui has changed greatly since the 1960s (when the Peace Corps posted volunteers here), this supremely happy holiday island and its neighbours are still blissfully beautiful in many parts. Some 80km (50 miles) from the mainland town of Surat Thani in the southern Gulf of Thailand, palm-fringed **Ko Samui** is the biggest of 80 islands that make up the Samui Archipelago, which also includes the party isle of **Ko Phangan**, the dive mecca of **Ko Tao** and pristine **Ang Thong Marine National Park**. With only a handful of the islands hosting any significant settlement, much of the area remains unspoilt, with perfect white-sand beaches ringed by colourful coral reefs and rugged forested interiors.

For over a century, the people of the islands – largely immigrant Chinese and Muslim communities – derived their incomes from coconut plantations and fishing. And although tourism dominates today, many of Ko Samui's poorer islanders still make their living from the coconut plantations.

Ko Samui is an hour's flight from Bangkok, 644km (400 miles) away. While Samui increasingly tailors itself to the higher end of the market, Ko Phangan and Ko Tao still gear themselves to backpackers. Convenient ferry connections between the three islands make it easy to sample the unique pleasures of each.

KO SAMUI

When foreign backpackers first began travelling to Ko Samui in the 1970s, travellers' tales of this island paradise soon began to surface – it was only a matter of time before the secret was out. The simple A-frame huts that once sheltered budget travellers can still be spotted on the island's peripheral

LEFT: Ang Thong Marine National Park.
RIGHT: on the streets of Na Thon.

beaches, but nowadays the most scenic bays have been taken over by luxury boutique resorts that blend in with the palm-lined beachfronts.

Covering some 247 sq km (95 sq miles), Ko Samui's raw beauty is still largely intact, and this coupled with a laidback vibe is the reason the island attracts so many repeat visitors. Many have secured their own piece of tropical paradise by buying holiday houses or condos here.

The island is also fast becoming Thailand's hottest spa destination, with a wide variety of extravagant hotel-based pampering spas, as well as independent day spas and retreat centres that claim to restore both physical and spiritual health. For those who tire quickly of the soft sandy beaches, the verdant

jungles and waterfalls of the interior offer a different kind of escape.

Ko Samui still has some way to go before matching the yachting marinas and theme parks of Phuket, but with an 18-hole golf course and two large supermarket chains among its list of amenities, it looks destined to follow in the same footsteps. The rapid rise of tourism has brought some problems, however. Severe water shortages are becoming a regular occurrence during the driest months, while the rainy season sometimes brings flood waters rushing down from deforested hills to many of the island's roads and beachfront properties.

For better or worse, Ko Samui is becoming increasingly cosmopolitan. Dining choices are ever more

Ko Samui is known as "Coconut Island".

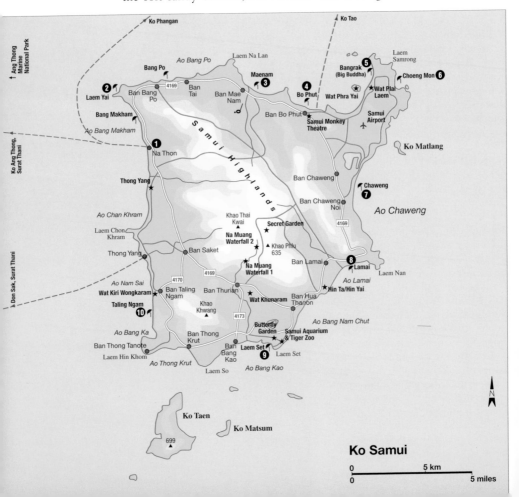

Ko Samui

varied and upscale, with more design-conscious eateries independent of hotels opening by the month. While the nightlife scene is always busy, the island is short on stylish bars and clubs, with most socialising taking place in "beer bars", Brit-style pubs and throbbing clubs.

Getting to Ko Samui

Direct flights link Ko Samui's airport (located on the northeastern tip of the island) with Bangkok, Phuket and Krabi, as well as some international destinations. The tropical escape begins the minute you touch down – with its quaint open-plan buildings and manicured gardens, this is one of Thailand's most picturesque arrival points. Many people also travel by boat from mainland Surat Thani (Ban Don pier) to the busy port town of **Na Thon ❶** on Ko Samui's northwest coast.

Na Thon, which is also the island's commercial centre, has little of interest to visitors, save for a few vintage Chinese-influenced wooden shophouses, souvenir shops for last-minute purchases, banks, restaurants and cafés, travel agents, a few faceless hotels, and an immigration office for visa extensions.

Ko Samui's roads are generally well paved, and the two-lane highway that loops around the island – Route 4169 – is eminently drivable. Yet accidents are frequent (mainly caused by intoxicated drivers), and great care should still be taken if you are driving your own vehicle.

Laem Yai and Hat Maenam

The secluded beach of **Laem Yai ❷**, located on a headland with a steep hillside rising behind it, is home to what is probably Ko Samui's most exclusive resort, the all-villa **Four Seasons Koh Samui**.

The second beach of note on the north coast is **Hat Maenam ❸**, about 13km (8 miles) from Na Thon and 6km (4 miles) from the airport. The 4km (2½-mile) long stretch is fairly isolated and quiet. The golden yellow sand underfoot is a little coarse and the beach is pleasant but quite narrow. Numerous budget hotels have sprung up here in addition to the de luxe-

BELOW: sun, sand and surf on the east coast.

It's obvious how Grandfather Rock and Grandmother Rock at Hat Lamai got their quirky names.

class **Santiburi**. Nights can be quiet in Maenam due to the near-absence of bars and clubs; for that you have to head south to Chaweng.

Hat Bo Phut

East of Maenam is **Hat Bo Phut ❹**. While the beach is nice enough and of similar standard to Maenam, the 2km (1½-mile) strip is better known for the quaint seafront lane of old wooden shophouses, known as **Ban Bo Phut** or **Fisherman's Village**. The old timber shacks have been tastefully converted into restaurants, bars and shops, making this one of the most attractive places on the island to wander around. There are several resorts here, the top-of-the-line place being **Anantara Ko Samui**, a short distance away from Fisherman's Village.

Of all the islands in the Gulf of Thailand, Ko Samui has the most off-beach attractions, many of which are family-oriented. Largely set up for tourists, but a nod to the island's coconut plantation heritage, the trained "monkey work coconut" shows at the **Samui Monkey Theatre** in Bo Phut (daily 10.30am, 2pm, 4pm; charge) reveal how southern Thais use simian labour to assist in harvesting coconuts from towering palms. The expert pig-tailed macaques can gather up to 500 coconuts each a day.

Hat Bangrak

On the headland to the northeast of Bo Phut, **Hat Bangrak ❺** is better known locally as **Big Buddha beach** due to the presence of **Wat Phra Yai**, or Big Buddha Temple (daily 8am–5pm; free) on a small islet across the bay. The 12-metre (39ft) golden Buddha image is linked by a causeway to the end of the beach.

At low tide, the water can retreat quite far out, exposing a swathe of mud. There is some budget accommodation set behind the beach but most of it isn't particularly nice. As the Big Buddha statue is a popular photo stop for island tours of Ko Samui, swarms of vendors hawking souvenirs frequently crowd the path leading to the entrance of the temple.

A short hike and a left turn from the temple entrance is **Wat Plai Laem**, a small temple whose base takes the form of a giant lotus flower and is set in the middle of a large fish-filled pond.

Hat Choeng Mon

On the other side of the headland is **Hat Choeng Mon ❻**, a small but serene white-sand bay backed by casuarina trees. It has a relatively undeveloped ambience, save for a couple of upmarket resorts. There is hardly any nightlife here, but then busy Chaweng beach is only a short drive away. Several of the island's premier beach resorts, like the **Imperial Boathouse**, **Tongsai Bay** and the all-villa luxurious **Sala Samui Resort & Spa** occupy prime positions along this scenic stretch of beach.

Hat Chaweng

The 6km (4-mile) long **Hat Chaweng ❼** on the east coast is by far the busiest beach on Ko Samui. It is roughly divided into three sections: North Chaweng, Central Chaweng and

Spa Horizons

Few aspects of Thailand sum up the national predilection for having a good time and taking it easy *(sanuk* and *sabai)* as a trip to a spa, a pastime that has become an integral part of many Thai vacations. The industry has grown exponentially, partly because many native ingredients are incorporated in spa treatments, additionally because the Thais' gentle nature lends itself naturally to what is universally referred to as pampering, and also because the kingdom's climate and architecture both lend themselves to designing out-of-this-world-class spas.

Tamarind Retreat is a prime example, a bucolic haven that opened in the late 1990s and which now incorporates a swathe of villas where guests can stay just steps away from their next treatment. All over Ko Samui, spas have sprung up in imitation, either attached to hotels or as independent concerns. The real delight of this sybaritic industry is that it's supremely adaptable. Customers can drop in for a quick massage, work out a day-long programme, or go the whole hog and move in for a series of treatments that include several days' fast and come out feeling utterly rejuvenated. First-timers should put aside any doubts – staff are universally considerate and caring, and the sheer delight of lying back and healthily doing nothing for a couple of hours has very few equals.

South Chaweng. The stunning powdery white-sand beach facing clear turquoise waters follows the shore from the headland in the north near the small island of **Ko Matlang**, all the way down to the curving bay and rocky end point of South Chaweng.

North Chaweng beach is sheltered by a coral reef, which means that, while the sea is sheltered from strong winds during the monsoon season, the waters can also be still as a millpond at other times of the year. It is also less crowded than **Central Chaweng**, which is the most built up. Behind the rather cramped line of beach resorts, Chaweng Beach Road is a rather faceless sprawl of somewhat tacky tourist-oriented shops, restaurants and bars. However, recent upmarket shopping arcades like **Iyara Plaza**, **Central Plaza** and **Living Square** are a sign of things to come. Past a tiny spit of land is the relatively quiet **South Chaweng**, which is thinner on accommodation and restaurants.

Hat Lamai

Further south, over a rocky ridge that has stunning viewpoints back towards the Chaweng shoreline, is Samui's second-most populous beach, **Hat Lamai ❽**. The beach is lovely and far less hectic compared to its northern neighbour, with better accommodation choices for budget travellers, although there are also several boutique resorts. Lamai is also the home of the island's original wellness centres, namely **The Spa Samui** and **Tamarind Springs**.

A little beyond the beach's southern tip are two natural rock formations known as **Hin Ta** (Grandfather Rock) and **Hin Yai** (Grandmother Rock). As they resemble male and female genitalia, the rocks are the subject of much photo-taking, and not a little sniggering.

Dining at Lamai doesn't have a patch on Chaweng's breadth and quality, and unfortunately, Lamai gets a bad rap for its slightly lascivious nightlife scene, with its stretch of raunchy girlie bars.

Inland from Lamai

Taking Route 4169 inland from Hat Lamai leads to one of the temples featured on most around-the-island tours, **Wat Khunaram** (daily 8am–5pm; free). The temple is famed as the home of

Famous mummified monk Luang Phor Daeng at Ko Samui's Wat Khunaram.

BELOW LEFT: seated Buddha image at Hat Bangrak.
BELOW: Wat Phra Yai.

Full-Moon Fallout

Ko Phangan has long been known for its wild beach parties. Despite official disapproval, the money they generate has guaranteed survival

An essential stop on any backpacker's tour of Southeast Asia, the Full Moon Party is dubbed the "world's biggest beach party", and, despite the Thai government's intermittent calls for the event to be scrapped, this Ko Phangan cash cow is too vital for the tourism industry to stop milking. The party takes place on Hat Rin Nok, or Sunrise Beach, with the focal point of the all-night rave at the southern end of the beach in front of Paradise Resort.

The event itself builds in momentum from sunset to sunrise, and Paradise Resort is regarded as the main hub of this no-holds-barred party. This is where the party circuit's most popular DJs spin, although there are DJs vying for attention at the main bars all along the beach. Each bar leans towards a different groove, and the dance hotspots shift periodically, depending on who is spinning what, where and when – or on the inclinations of the hell-bent-on-partying crowd in that particular year.

The Full Moon Party (aka F-M) draws thousands of global revellers throughout the year, though the peak season of December and January sees the wildest bounce fests. Guesthouses charge high-season rates and the rooms fill up quickly as the moon waxes, with some places only taking bookings for a minimum of four or five nights. Those craving beauty sleep should choose accommodation well away from Hat Rin Nok as the party scene can be loud on most nights, cranking up to a ear-drum-bursting crescendo on full-moon night.

For those who desire distance from the monthly mayhem, transport from other beaches to the party is plentiful. And if you prefer to nurse a post-party hangover within the confines of a luxury hotel in Ko Samui, numerous boats make the night-time crossing between the two islands.

Anything (and everything) goes

Generally, people spend the night getting wasted on cheap booze concoctions, being painted up in fluorescent ink, and alternating between dancing and passing out on the beach. Aside from all the music, dance, booze and fleeting romances (mostly of the one-night-stand variety), a lot of partygoers are there to sample what first gave F-M its notoriety – illicit substances. However, today's F-M is no longer an open display of magic-mushroom omelettes and teas, Speed and Ecstasy punches, etc. Drug-taking is still prevalent, but with many plain-clothed and uniformed police on patrol, any purveying or indulging of drugs is done with discretion. Penalties for possession of, or being under the influence of, illegal drugs are extremely harsh in Thailand.

The Full Moon Party is a bane for international embassies in Bangkok as, every month, at least one excessive partygoer loses the plot after ingesting some psychotropic cocktail, and officials are left to piece together the patient's fractured mind before shipping him or her back home. The local methamphetamine *yaa baa* (crazy drug) is one of the most common yet most addictive drugs around.

Sunrise is met by triumphant cheers, and the chance to raise the tempo once more for anyone who might have been thinking about collapsing into bed. The beach party winds up late morning, but for those who still have their brain cells and eardrums intact, the traditional after-party kicks off at Backyard Bar up the hill.

For more info and current F-M dates, check out www.fullmoon-party.com. ❑

LEFT: flame-throwing performance at an F-M party.

mummified monk Luang Phor Daeng. His body is still seated in the same meditating position he held when he died more than two decades ago.

Continuing past the village of Ban Thurian is **Na Muang Waterfall 1**: in the wet season, a cascade of water plunges some 20 metres (66ft) into a large pool. Getting to **Na Muang Waterfall 2** (part of the same falls further up) involves a fairly strenuous 1.5km (1-mile) trek; a more novel way would be an elephant ride offered near the entrance to Na Muang Waterfall 1.

Another of Lamai's attractions is the **Samui Aquarium & Tiger Zoo** (daily 9am–6pm, daily show at 1pm; charge; www.samuiorchid.com), located within the Samui Orchid Resort in south Lamai. The aquarium exhibits are nothing to write home about; more entertaining is the daily bird and Bengal tiger show.

South and west coasts

The south- and west-coast beaches aren't as pretty, although a few beautiful resorts can be found along these shores. If you are intent on a secluded holiday, the beach at **Hat Laem Set** ❾ (also sometimes referred to as **Hat Na Thian**) could be the place. There are ample accommodation choices, the most expensive being the luxury spa retreat called the **Kamalaya**. The road to Laem Set Inn also leads to the **Butterfly Garden** (daily 8.30am–5.30pm; charge), where the rainbow-coloured wings of myriad butterflies flutter within its net-covered compound.

Over on the west coast is **Hat Taling Ngam** ❿, the site of the stylish **Ban Taling Ngam**. Occupying a vantage position on a steep hill, the views of the coast here partly compensate for the rather ordinary beach.

Activities

Ko Samui has plenty of options for those who seek more active pursuits. For land-based action, hire a four-wheel-drive jeep, or mountain bike, and explore the dirt trails that lead up into the verdant hills of the interior. There are also a host of watersports – jet skiing, kayaking, windsurfing, waterskiing, parasailing, deep-sea fishing and sailing. Ko Samui is also a popular yachting base; a few companies on the island charter luxury boats.

Although the island has numerous dive shops, the surrounding waters are not particularly good for diving and snorkelling. Most dive trips head out to the nearby **Ang Thong Marine National Park**, **Hin Bai** and **Ko Tao** (see below and page 212).

ANG THONG MARINE NATIONAL PARK

Although Ko Phi Phi's Maya Bay (see page 256) was the chosen location setting for the 2000 film *The Beach*, it was the dramatic scenery of **Ang Thong Marine National Park** that was Alex Garland's original inspiration for his best-selling novel.

Lying some 31km (19 miles) west of Ko Samui, the 42 islands that make up the Ang Thong Archipelago stretch over a 100-sq-km (39-sq-mile) expanse of land and sea. Virtually uninhabited,

TIP

The southwest monsoon brings light intermittent rains to the Samui archipelago from June to Oct. From Nov to Jan, the northeast monsoon takes over: the heaviest rains fall during this period, with Nov being the wettest month. Given the rather unpredictable wet-weather pattern, the best time to visit the islands is from Feb to May – although there are plenty of fine days right through to Sept.

BELOW: island-studded Ang Thong Marine National Park.

Getting to Talay Nai lake involves a 20-minute trek, but the vista of waters encircled by limestone cliffs is worth the effort.

BELOW: sea kayaking at Ang Thong Marine National Park.

the pristine islands are home to a diversity of flora and fauna, including macaques, langurs and monitor lizards. Pods of dolphins are known to shelter in the waters late in the year.

Meaning "Golden Bowl", Ang Thong Marine National Park takes its name from the **Talay Nai** (inland sea), an emerald-green saltwater lagoon encircled by sheer limestone walls that are covered with vegetation. A principal stop on any day trip to the island chain, the picturesque lake can be reached by a trail from the beach on the island of **Ko Mae Ko**.

Several tour companies on Ko Samui operate day trips, including kayaking expeditions to the archipelago, which usually include a stop on the largest island, **Ko Wua Talab** (Sleeping Cow Island). Aside from a beach and the park's headquarters, there is a steep 400-metre (1,300ft) climb up to a look-out point that has unrivalled views of the surroundings. Also involving an arduous climb is Ko Wua Talab's other highlight, **Tham Bua Bok**, or Waving Lotus Cave. It is named after lotus-shaped rock formations.

Diving and snorkelling at Ang Thong are usually best experienced at the northern tip of the island chain around the islet of **Ko Yippon**. Although visibility isn't crystal-clear, the shallow depths make it easy to view the colourful coral beds, which are inhabited by sea snakes, fusiliers and stingrays. There are also shallow caves and archways to swim through.

KO PHANGAN

The second-largest island in the Samui Archipelago, **Ko Phangan** is blessed with numerous seductive white-sand beaches and richly forested mountains, yet the island's current international reputation stems almost exclusively from the infamous Full Moon Party *(see page 206)*, which takes place at Hat Rin Nok on the island's southern tip. With an infamy that rivals that of Ibiza and Goa, the lunar gathering has steadily grown since the first party back in the late 1980s.

Lying around 20km (12 miles) north of Ko Samui, and 40 minutes by boat, Ko Phangan became an outpost on the shoestring traveller's map in the 1980s,

around the same time as Ko Samui. But while the latter rapidly developed into a hub for package holidaymakers and flashy beach homes for the wealthy, Ko Phangan has largely remained an enclave of backpackers, revellers and New Age *nirvana*-seekers. However, pockets of the 193-sq-km (75-sq-mile) island are becoming built up, particularly Hat Rin and its vicinity, which now looks and feels very different to the rest of the island.

While most revellers confine themselves to the southern cape beaches of Hat Rin Nok (Sunrise Beach), Hat Rin Nai (Sunset Beach) and nearby Leela Beach, there are plenty of other more isolated bays that skirt the mountainous interior. Increasingly serviceable roads have made the furthest reaches of the island more accessible, but even so, a couple of coves, such as Hat Kuat (Bottle Beach), can be reached only by boat or on foot.

Located halfway along the west coast, the island's administrative centre and main arrival point is the small town of **Thong Sala ❶**. Apart from fishing boats unloading their daily haul, the port is usually busy with ferries and boats travelling to and from Ko Samui, Ko Tao and Surat Thani. Thong Sala has all the usual tourist-friendly services – internet cafés, banks, shops and a few restaurants and bars, plus a morning and night market mainly patronised by locals.

Ban Tai and Ban Khai

East of Thong Sala, the south coast is endowed with a continuous stretch of white-sand beach running all the way up to the Hat Rin cape, though the shallow reefs make the water often unfavourable for swimming. The most popular beaches here are between the villages of **Ban Tai ❷** and **Ban Khai ❸**. Both basic and more comfortable family-run bungalow accommodation runs along the length to Thong Sala, with Ban Khai, the closest to Hat Rin, the only spot that offers any nighttime activity.

Hat Rin

East of Ban Khai is where all the beach action lies. **Hat Rin** is certainly not Ko Phangan's most serene beach

TIP

There are no official tourism offices in Ko Phangan. Your best source for information is the website managed by the Phangan Batik shop in Thong Sala: www. kohphangan.com. The site has a wealth of information and useful tips on what to do on the island. Phangan Batik also operates a tour agency and an internet café on its premises.

BELOW: the pagoda above Hat Rin Nai Beach, Ko Phangan.

TIP

The advantages of staying on any of the west-coast beaches on Ko Phangan are fewer crowds and beautiful sunset views with the islands of the Ang Thong Marine National Park framed against the horizon.

any more; its original appeal was that it hosted two beaches within easy walking distance – across a flat headland – both with sensational sunrise and sunset views.

Hat Rin Nok ❹, or Sunrise Beach, is the wider, more popular bay, and is where the main nightlife cranks up, climaxed by the monthly Full Moon party. Hat Rin attracts a global melting pot of young clubbers and alternative lifestyle devotees, who find this tiny pocket of Thailand the perfect place to express their inner selves, helped along by alcohol and other substances (*see page 206*).

The less attractive of the two beaches is **Hat Rin Nai ❺**, or Sunset Beach, a thinner stretch of sand lined with beach huts that offer respite from the late-night cacophony over at Hat Rin Nok. The walk between the two beaches is jam-packed with accommodation, shops, restaurants, internet cafés and travel agents.

Further towards the island's southern tip is pretty **Leela** beach. It is around a 15-minute walk from Hat Rin Nai, and has a more peaceful atmosphere.

East-coast beaches

There are several small but fine bays that run north up the east coast from Hat Rin, but a lack of roads means taking a boat (from Hat Rin) is the only way to venture there – and as a result, development is patchy. **Hat Yuan ❻** and **Hat Yao** (not to be confused with the longer Hat Yao on the west coast), and particularly **Hat Thian ❼**, are popular with travellers who seek isolated beaches.

At the top of the east coast are the increasingly popular twin bays of **Ao Thong Nai Pan Noi ❽** and **Ao Thong Nai Pan Yai ❾**, described by many as the island's most beautiful coves. There is a good choice of cheap accommodation at both bays, separated by a headland that can be traversed in about 20 minutes. Getting up here is problematic, though, as the 12km (8-mile) road, actually a dirt track, from Ban Tai in the south is riddled with potholes.

Ao Thong Nai Pan Noi was a favourite stop-off for King Chulalongkorn, who made numerous visits to Ko Phangan between 1888 and 1909, when

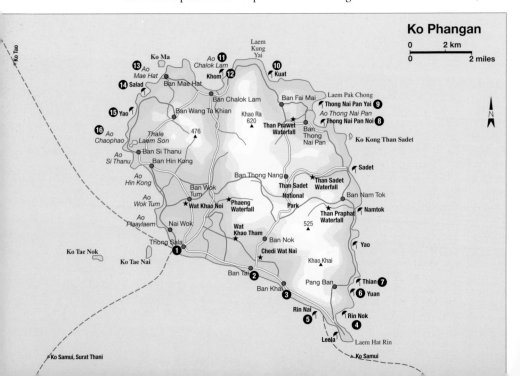

just a few hundred Thai and Chinese islanders eked a living from coconuts, fishing and mining tin.

North-coast beaches

The north coast has two bays that are worth seeking out. The first of these is **Hat Kuat ⑩**, or Bottle Beach. A decent road leads from Thong Sala up to Ao Chalok Lam *(see below)*, from where you can take a boat to Bottle Beach. This is one of Ko Phangan's best bays, the splendid white sands backed by steep hills, but, as elsewhere on the island, accommodation is at the budget end.

The second bay to the west, **Ao Chalok Lam ⑪**, is occupied by a large fishing village which functions as the island's second port. The pier in the centre of the large curving bay is usually busy with fishermen who supply the seafood restaurants here with the freshest catch. The small white-sand cove, called **Hat Khom ⑫**, along this stretch and closer to the headland east, is the best bit of beach here, ringed by a coral reef offshore. The 10km (6-mile) road from Thong Sala in the south to Ao Chalok Lam is one of the island's best roads, so access is not a problem.

West-coast beaches

The west-coast beaches stretching from Ao Mae Hat all the way to Thong Sala in the south are more attractive than those along the southeastern shores, yet see fewer visitors compared to the Hat Rin area.

Starting from the northwest corner is **Ao Mae Hat ⑬**, which has a sandbank at low tide that connects to the tiny reef-fringed island of **Ko Ma** (Horse Island). The reef that runs up the coast from Ao Chaophao all the way to Ko Ma is considered the island's best snorkelling and diving site.

Further down the coast is scenic **Hat Salad ⑭**, with good snorkelling just off the northern edge of the beach. Next is an attractive 1km (2/3-mile) sandy stretch called **Hat Yao ⑮**, or Long Beach. It has become very popular in recent years and is giving Hat Rin a run for its money,

with its range of accommodation, bars, restaurants and other facilities. Further south is a small bay called **Ao Chaophao ⑯**, which has a decent range of facilities. Further down the coast are four more beaches of note: **Ao Si Thanu, Ao Hin Kong, Ao Wok Tum** and **Ao Plaaylaem**.

Inland attractions

Phangan's thickly forested interior has a number of attractions. When King Chulalongkorn used to visit the island *(see opposite)*, one of his favourite haunts was **Than Sadet Waterfall**, which flows out to **Hat Sadet** beach in the next cove down the east coast from Ao Thong Nai Pan Yai, some 12km (7 miles) up from Hat Rin. The island's other cascades are **Than Praphat Waterfall** on the way to the east-coast beach of Hat Namtok, **Than Prawet Waterfall** located near Ao Thong Nai Pan Noi, and **Phaeng Waterfall** found halfway across the island en route from Thong Sala to Ban Chalok Lam village. All these waterfalls come under the umbrella of the 65-sq-km (25-sq-mile) **Than Sadet National Park**.

Lots of vendors offer cheap massages by the beach at Hat Rin Nok and Hat Rin Nai on Ko Phangan.

BELOW: crossing the wooden rope bridge at Chalok Lam beach.

TIP

Ko Tao is too tiny and undeveloped to have a tourism office. Your best bet for information and tips on the island are the following websites: www.kohtao.com; www. on-koh-tao.com.

Diving and snorkelling

Ko Phangan has some coral reefs fringing its shores, but the vast majority of diving takes place at a handful of dive sites some distance from the island at **Ang Thong Marine National Park** (*see page 207*), **Hin Bai** (Sail Rock) and around **Ko Tao** *(see below)*. Snorkelling and diving closer to Ko Phangan is best experienced along the reefs on the northwest tip of the island, around **Ko Ma**, **Ao Mae Hat** and **Hat Yao**. Ko Ma is Ko Phangan's best dive site, with fairly shallow depths of up to 20 metres (66ft). The area is frequented by blue-spotted stingrays, giant grouper and reef sharks.

Located about halfway between Ko Phangan and Ko Tao, **Hin Bai** is regarded as one of the best dive sites in the Samui Archipelago and is suitable for all levels of divers. The rugged rock emerges like an iceberg from the water; most of its bulk is hidden below the surface, reaching depths of more than 30 metres (100ft). The granite pinnacle is circled by large schools of pelagic fish, but the highlight is a dramatic vertical chimney

that can be entered at 19 metres (62ft) underwater, with an exit at 6 metres (20ft) from the surface.

Nightlife and other entertainment

Apart from the notorious Full Moon Party, Ko Phangan has plenty of other regular weekly and monthly party nights to keep the backpackers bouncing until that ultimate night arrives again. Those who like commercial dance music will have to make do with a mix of trance, techno and drum 'n' bass – the music of choice at the island's main nightspots. The so-called **Half Moon** parties shape up twice a month, a week before and after full moon, held at a hypnotically lit outdoor venue in Ban Tai.

For more information on the island's entertainment scene, pick up a copy of *Phangan Info* (www.phangan. info) or see Activities (*page 398*) for nightlife listings.

KO TAO

You don't have to be a diver to enjoy Ko Tao, but it helps. Around 40km (25

BELOW: diving among the coral reefs off Hin Bai (Sail Rock).

miles) northwest of Ko Phangan and 60km (37 miles) from Ko Samui, **Ko Tao**, or Turtle Island, is the northern-most inhabited island in the Samui Archipelago. The remote and tiny 21-sq-km (8-sq-mile) island, topped with tropical forest and fringed with some picturesque secluded bays, is said to draw its name from its rather loose geographical shape of a div-ing turtle; others have attributed its name to the once-abundant turtles that swam in these waters. Today, this laidback outpost might just as well be called "aqualung" island for the density of affordable dive schools that oper-ate expeditions to its coral-abundant waters, making this one of the world's best places to learn diving.

Less than a decade ago, Ko Tao con-sisted solely of rustic backpacker huts. More recent development, however, has seen better accommodation options and entertainment venues. And the bonus of a large percentage of visitors studying in dive schools or out on dive trips is that the island's beaches are relatively peaceful during the day.

West-coast beaches

Ko Tao is accessed by ferries and speedboats from the mainland port of Chumphon (*see page 198*), some 80km (50 miles) to the east, as well as from Ko Samui, Ko Phangan or Surat Thani to the south. The main arrival point is the small but lively village of **Ban Mae Hat ❶** on the west coast. It is little more than a one-street village lined with a post office, banks, shops, cafés, bars and other tourist-related infrastructure.

North of the village is the small, shal-low bay of **Ao Hat Mae**. There is some accommodation here, but it may be too close to the village for some. Much nicer is the 2km (1½-mile) long **Hat Sai Ree ❷**, the island's longest and most popular curve of white sand. Sai Ree is lined with hotels to suit most budgets, getting gradually quieter fur-ther north with the ever-growing **Ban Hat Sai Ree** village backing the beach

just over the halfway mark. Beyond Sai Ree, the road makes an incline up towards the northern tip of the island, with several more out-of-the-way cliff-top resorts, including attrac-tive **Thipwimarn**, whose restaurant offers stunning sunset views.

South-coast beaches

Ko Tao's southern shores are home to a few small, pretty beaches that lie either side of the island's second-busiest beach, **Ao Chalok Ban Kao ❸**, a well-protected bay that is jammed with resorts, dive shops, eateries and bars. The large headland at the eastern end of Ao Chalok Ban Kao features a viewpoint atop the **John Suwan Rock**, which has incredible views in either direction. To the east of the promontory is the long yet quiet **Ao Thian Ok ❹**, and further still is **Hat Sai Daeng**.

Within walking distance to the west of Ao Chalok Ban Kao, several small and scenic bays are located around **Ao Jun Jeua**, **Hat Sai Nuan** and **Ao Jansom**. Unfortunately, the monsoon season from June to October brings

A Ko Nang Yuan dive shop.

BELOW: taking a break at Ko Nang Yuan.

strong winds and heavy seas, causing disruptions to ferry schedules, and a lot of flotsam gets washed up on these beaches.

East-coast beaches

The east coast of the island is characterised by several isolated inlets with scant sleeping options; although none have outstanding beaches, there are plenty of good snorkelling and diving spots here. The dirt trails to the eastern shores can be treacherous (the only other way is by boat) and once you are there, it can be difficult (and expensive) to venture back west. Most lodgings along this coast offer basic facilities. Heading north from Hat Sai Daeng, the bays include the lovely **Ao Leuk** ❺, the scenic horseshoe-shaped **Ao Tanote** ❻, the tiny cape of **Laem Thian**, and eventually the remote **Ao Hin Wong** ❼.

The north coast

A short boat ride off the island's northern tip is the picture-perfect **Ko Nang Yuan** ❽, a gathering of three small

islets joined together by mere wisps of sand that can be walked across at low tide. The setting, both above and below sea level, is incredible, so much so that dive trips and boat tours from around the island, as well as from Ko Samui and Ko Phangan, all converge here, somewhat spoiling the idyll. With simple bungalows spread across the three outcrops, only the **Nangyuan Island Dive Resort** (www.nangyuan.com) has the rights to operate here, with outside visitors charged B100 just to set foot on the island.

Diving and snorkelling

Ko Tao's reputation as a premier dive destination has diminished slightly in recent years, mainly due to the hefty increase in the number of divers; at the more popular sites the undersea human traffic can be annoying. Even so, visibility in the warm water is usually very clear – sometimes over 30 metres (100ft) – and there is a variety of dive sites to choose from. While sightings of giant groupers and turtles are not uncommon, and territorial disputes with toothy triggerfish best

Dive shops are plentiful on Ko Tao, but as most offer more or less the same services, it's best to shop around and ask people for recommendations.

BELOW: taking the plunge off Ko Tao.

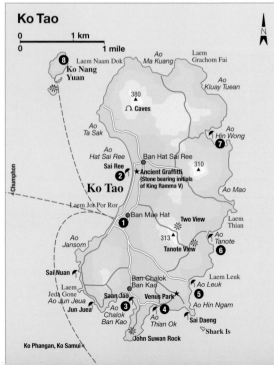

avoided, an encounter with an underwater giant such as a whale shark or a manta ray is still a special event.

Unlike the lengthy journey times to dive sites from Ko Samui and Ko Phangan, Ko Tao has more than 25 dive sites close by that can be reached in less than 30 minutes. Both the proximity and favourable conditions (outside the November–December monsoon) make the island's waters an ideal place to learn diving.

Some of the best dive sites are found off Ko Nang Yuan, including the granite boulder and swim-throughs of **Nang Yuan Pinnacle**. About 5km (3 miles) northwest of Ko Tao, the **Chumphon Pinnacle** is a very popular site, with depths of up to 38 metres (125ft) and regular sightings of large groupers and other sizeable fish. In the opposite direction, the **Southwest Pinnacle**, some 7km (4 miles) from Ko Tao, is rated as one of the best soft-coral reefs in the Gulf of Thailand, with currents that attract large schools of pelagic fish.

Ko Tao has nearly 50 dive schools that offer competitive dive packages that include accommodation; in fact, a few resorts refuse to take in non-divers during the peak season. Advance reservations are advised. The majority of schools offer PADI open-water certification, with rates starting at about B10,000.

Activities and nightlife

Ko Tao's compact size makes the island an ideal place for walking, with the reward of panoramic hilltop views or a hidden pristine cove at the end of your journey. Day-long boat trips around the island can be chartered with longtail boat operators at most of its beaches and piers, or through your guesthouse. Watersports like kayaking, wakeboarding and water-skiing can be enjoyed on Ao Tanote or Hat Sai Ree beaches.

Don't expect much by way of nightlife: the island is an escape for Ko Phangan visitors who seek a reprieve from its wild parties. Unfortunately, as Ko Tao develops, its nightlife is moving from basic beach bars to the fire-jugglers and cheap Thai whisky scene of Ko Phangan. ❏

TIP

Although Ko Tao mainly appeals to divers, those who want to stay on the water can waterski, wakeboard or go on a banana boat ride. Contact **Black Tip Diving & Watersports**, www.blacktipdiving.com.

BELOW: stunning Ko Nang Yuan is a must-see.

RESTAURANTS AND BARS

Restaurants

Price per person for a three-course meal without drinks:
$ = under B300
$$ = B300–800
$$$ = B800–1,600
$$$$ = over B1,600

Ko Samui

International

Betelnut @ Buri Rasa
11/2 Moo 2, Hat Chaweng.
Tel: 0-7723 0222. Open:
daily D only. $$$–$$$$
www.betelnutsamui.net
The tiny street may look unassuming, but it has several of the island's best dining options, including the excellent Betelnut. Owned by American Jeffrey Lord, the restaurant's design is simple but tasteful, leaving the focus on the small but innovative selection of Californian-meets-Thai fusion fare.

The Cliff
Between Hat Chaweng and Hat Lamai. Tel: 0-7741 4266.
Open: daily L & D. $$$
www.thecliffsamui.com
An airy and modern cliff-top restaurant set between the island's two busiest beaches. The view from this vantage point is its main appeal, but the Mediterranean fare is also very good. The menu includes dishes cooked in zesty piri piri sauce, pastas, steaks and burgers.

The Islander
Central Chaweng.
Tel: 0-7723 0836.
Open: daily B, L & D. $$
Always busy, this two-storey restaurant and bar

is on the central stretch of Chaweng Beach Road. Several TVs screen sports, while the menu has an extensive range of international favourites. Look out for the daily specials on the board.

Olivio
Baan Haad Ngam Resort, North Chaweng. Tel: 0-7723 1500. Open: daily L & D. $$$
In the grounds of a resort, this is Italian par excellence, with arresting views, a superb wine list, and service to match.

Prego
North Chaweng. Tel: 0-7742 2015. Open: daily L & D.
$$–$$$
Situated on the quieter north end of Chaweng, opposite the Amari hotel, this stylish Italian restaurant is open and airy, with soothing water elements that add to the mood. The menu, which includes wood-fired oven pizza and fresh seafood, is reasonably priced given the quality of the food and ambience.

Rice
91/1 Moo 2, Hat Chaweng.
Tel: 0-7723 1934. Open: daily L & D. $$$
www.ricesamui.com
Smack in the heart of Chaweng's evening entertainment scene, this fine-dining place is hoping to raise the bar on the island's cuisine credentials. With a contemporary Asian look, the split-level Mediterranean, international and Thai restaurant has a large lily pond in front and a glass elevator to carry

diners up to the third level, where a more exclusive gourmet experience awaits at the rooftop Rice & Stars.

Thai & Western

Chez Andy
Central Chaweng. Tel: 0-7742 2593. Open: daily D.
$$–$$$
www.chez-andy.com
It won't win any awards for decor and ambience, but with staff eager to please and some of the best steaks on Samui, this Swiss-owned steakhouse is a magnet for meat-lovers. The menu has European and Thai favourites, and imported Angus and Kobe beef. A cheaper alternative is the all-you-can-eat international buffet. Kids under 10 eat free.

Montien House
Hat Chaweng. Tel: 0-7742 2169. Open: daily B, L & D. $$
www.montienhouse.com
This is one of the better beach set-ups along the central stretch of Chaweng in the evening. The Thai food at this hotel restaurant is familiar and good, but the Western dishes are quite forgettable. The moonlit beach atmosphere is the main attraction.

Poppies
South Chaweng. Tel: 0-7742 2419. Open: daily 6.30am–midnight. $$$
www.poppiessamui.com
A decade old, this enduring beachfront restaurant has long been an island favourite. Sit under the stars beside the boutique resort's

pool or in the authentic Ayutthaya-style teak pavilion as you dine on well-presented and refined Thai and international dishes.

The Shack Bar and Grill
Fisherman's Village, Hat Bo Phut. Tel: 0-7724 6041.
Open: daily D only. $$$
www.theshackgrillsamui.com
It may look like little more than a shack, but this American-owned place is a firm favourite with the island's expats. Photos of blues legends hang on the wall, and blues is the music of choice here. The chalkboard menu has a selection of local seafood and imported Australian meats, but save room for the homemade ice cream and New York cheesecake.

Zazen
177 Moo 1, Zazen Boutique Resort & Spa, Hat Bo Phut.
Tel: 0-7742 5085. Open: daily L & D. $$$–$$$$
www.samuizazen.com
Stylish and romantic, this restaurant looks out to the sea with Ko Phangan as a backdrop. Sit in an open-sided area with its Balinese-style roof or on the candlelit terrace. The European chef serves up a blend of Asian and European cuisine using healthy organic ingredients. You can order dishes à la carte or choose from one of the four set menus.

Ko Phangan

International

A's Coffee Shop
Thong Sala. Tel: 0-7737 7226. Open: daily B, L & D.

$–$$
Located within the Buakao Inn Guest House, this is a long-time favourite with visitors. It has a great variety of dishes, from traditional Thai to Pacific Rim cuisine, with specialities like pizza baguettes, German, English and American breakfasts, and excellent pastas, all washed down by espresso, cappuccino and large margaritas.

Bamboozle Bar and Restaurant
Hat Rin. Mobile tel: 08-5471 4211. Open: daily L & D. **$–$$**
The island's best (actually, the only) Mexican restaurant and bar is located just off the main drag between the Hat Rin Nok and Hat Rin Nai beaches and set in a garden. The half-price margaritas on Mondays are a real bargain.

Emotion of Sushi
Seagarden Plaza, Hat Rin. Mobile tel: 07-9831 323. Open: daily D only. **$$**
Located just off Hat Rin Nok, this sushi and sashimi eatery has sofas and a bar on the ground floor and a comfortable air-conditioned seating area upstairs.

Nira's Bakery
Hat Rin. Tel: 0-7737 5109. Open: daily B, L & D. **$**
Bakery and café that does great all-day breakfasts and coffees, plus delicious cakes, pastries and breads. The café menu includes sandwiches, pies, pastas and salads.

Om Ganesh
Hat Rin Nai. Tel: 0-86063 2930. Open: daily B, L & D. **$–$$**

Om Ganesh is a reliable and relaxing two-storey restaurant located near the Hat Rin pier. Prepared by a cook with over two decades of experience in New Delhi, the restaurant serves excellent curries and Indian breads.

The Shell
Hat Rin. Tel: 0-7737 5149. Open: daily B, L & D. **$$**
Unbelievably great Italian cuisine is found around the rustic surrounds of Hat Rin Lake (or swamp, rather). The Shell makes its own pastas, pizzas and gelato, and the fresh coffee is excellent.

Thai & Western
Outback Bar
Hat Rin. Tel: 0-7737 5126. Open: daily L & D. **$$**
This expat-run watering hole with a friendly vibe sits towards the pier and attracts a regular crowd who come for the pool tables, sports on the big screen TV, and pub grub. Serves pies, steaks and burgers, as well as Indian and Thai food.

The Village Green Restaurant & Bar
Ao Chaophao. Tel: 0-1078 1670. Open: daily B, L & D. **$$**
www.villagegreen.phangan.info
This two-level restaurant is one of the west coast's best eateries, serving a hearty menu of international and Thai dishes. Full English-style breakfasts, as well as pastas, pizzas, steaks and seafood for lunch and dinner. Located on Ao Chaophao, about 15 minutes' drive from Thong Sala.

Ko Tao
International
Café del Sol

Mae Hat. Tel: 0-7745 6578. Open: daily B, L & D. **$–$$**
This pleasant little eatery serves a broad selection of authentic French, Italian and other international fare, cooked up by a Gallic chef. Tuck into big breakfasts, homemade pastas, bruschettas, tender steaks and smoked salmon. Good wines and coffee too.

Papa's Tapas
Hat Sai Ree. Tel: 0-7745 6298. Open: daily D only. **$$**
www.papas-tapas.net
A sophisticated tapas and cocktail lounge run by a Swedish chef and his mixologist counterpart, this elegant venue serves up inventive tapas and cocktails. There is also a hookah room to enjoy flavoured tobacco and Cuban cigars. The restaurant menu features innovative dishes like teriyaki spare ribs, pan-fried chorizo sausages and a wide

selection of vegetarian dishes.

Thai & Western
New Heaven Restaurant & Bakery
New Heaven Bungalows, Ao Thian Ok. Tel: 0-7745 6462. Open: daily D only. **$–$$**
www.newheavenkohtao.com
This family-run restaurant, bakery and bungalows is famous for its hilltop location that looks out across a beautiful bay. Large menu of simple international and Thai fare, with an emphasis on seafood. The kitchen closes early but the cocktail bar stays open until late.

Chopper's Bar & Grill
Hat Sai Ree. Tel: 0-7745 6641 Open: daily B, L & D. **$–$$**
www.chopperskohtao.com
A sports bar and pub with full-on drinks, food and entertainment menus; hearty fare attracting hearty types. No holds barred and lots of fun.

RIGHT: a classic *phad Thai* with shrimp and rice noodles.

NORTHERN ANDAMAN COAST

This region is well known for its diving and snorkelling hotspots – the Similan and Surin islands – as well as the limestone formations at Phang Nga Bay. Also worth exploring are its land-based waterfalls, hot springs and jungle trails

The spectacular Andaman Coast of western Thailand stretches from Ranong on the Isthmus of Kra all the way south to the Malaysian border. This chapter covers only the land and sea attractions as far south as Phang Nga. Highlights include the renowned scuba and snorkelling hotspots of the Similan and Surin islands, and the dramatic limestone formations towering out of the waters around Phang Nga Bay.

RANONG AND SURROUNDINGS

Ranong Province – some 600km (370 miles) from Bangkok and 300km (185 miles) north of Phuket – is thin on attractions. Despite its coastal location, it is not blessed with beautiful beaches, and the main points of interest lie offshore. The province records the highest rainfall in Thailand, which accounts for the lush greenery and many waterfalls. There are a few inland attractions, as well as the undeveloped islands of Ko Chang and Ko Phayam.

There is not much to see or do in **Ranong Town**, a large port filled with fishing boats. Divers mainly use it as a launch point for dive trips to the **Burma Banks** *(see page 222)*. Because of its proximity to **Myanmar** (25 minutes by boat), many foreigners in south Thailand also use Ranong Town

as a base to leave the country to renew their visas. The harbour is filled with companies offering to make the border run and sort out the paperwork.

Punyaban Waterfall ❶, about 15km (9 miles) north of Ranong Town and off Highway 4, is worth seeing for its cascading waters which plunge down several levels. Access to its base is possible by scaling a few boulders, while a 300-metre (330yd) nature trail leads to an elevated lookout – from here the water below hits the rocks in spectacular fashion before dispersing into a fine mist.

LEFT: a sea gypsy child at Ko Surin.
RIGHT: Punyabun Waterfall in Ranong.

Hot spring pool at the Jansom Hot Spa Ranong Hotel.

About 2km (1½ miles) southeast of town, **Raksawarin Park ❷**, Ranong's most famous attraction, is home to natural **Hot Springs** (daily 8am–5pm; free). Heated to around 65°C (150°F), the water is, however, too hot to bathe in. There are concrete pools circled by stone seats where people can stop, sit and inhale the reviving steam. To experience a hot spring bath, head to either the **Jansom Hot Spa Ranong** or the **Royal Princess Ranong** hotels, where the water is piped directly in from the hot springs.

Ngao Waterfall ❸, located 13km (8 miles) south of Ranong, lies within **Khlong Phrao National Park** (daily 8am–4.30pm; charge). Its source is deep in the dense forest, and the water pouring down the cliff can be seen from a long way off.

Ko Chang

The quiet island of **Ko Chang ❹** is part of **Mu Ko Phayam National Park**, and home to a population who moved here from Surat Thani and Ko Phangan decades ago and now live in small fishing communities. It is acces-

BELOW: hot springs at Ranong.

sible by boat from both Ranong (2½ hours) and Laem Son National Park (1 hour). During the monsoon season from May to October, vessels stop operating as the seas are too dangerous to cross, and accommodation on the island shuts down.

Most of Ko Chang's golden-sand beaches extend along the west coast, the longest being **Ao Yai**, which has most of the basic beach huts. Calm waters and shallow coral reefs mean safe swimming and snorkelling, and as there is no pier, beach access is only possible by long-tail boat, wading through the water on nearing the shoreline. There are no cars on the island, and two concrete tracks lead to Ko Chang's only village, which contains a shop and restaurant. Reaching the smaller beach of **Ao Lek** on the east coast requires a 5km (3-mile) trudge from the village.

Ko Phayam

Smaller but more developed than Ko Chang is **Ko Phayam ❺**, 15 minutes by boat from the former. A backdrop of forested hills shadows white sandy beaches. There is a population of around

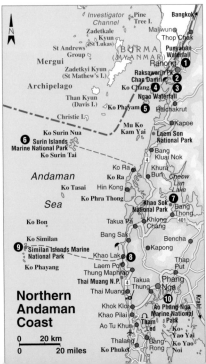

Northern Andaman Coast

0	20 km
0	20 miles

500, who mainly eke a living by growing cashew nuts and coconuts.

The two main beaches are on opposite sides of the island, so the pier is fairly quiet with just a handful of convenience stores and an internet café. As the walk to the other side of the island can take a good hour, motorcycle taxis do a brisk trade. There are no restaurants on either of the beaches, so meals are confined to your hotel.

The most popular beach is **Ao Yai** on the southwest coast. Most of the beach huts are set slightly back from the white-sand beachfront behind a border of palm and pine trees. **Ao Khao Khwai** on the northwest coast is smaller and has fewer lodgings. Nonetheless, it has clear water, a fine stretch of sand and colourful coral close to the shore, making it good for snorkelling. Its nickname, Buffalo Bay, comes from the curvature of its two sides, resembling a pair of buffalo horns.

SURIN ISLANDS

The five islands that make up **Surin Islands Marine National Park ❻** (Nov–May; charge) lie some 55km (34 miles) from the coast and are renowned for their superlative diving and snorkelling. Because of the distance, they are mainly visited by divers on live-aboard boats. The scenery above water is equally spectacular, with numerous sandy bays and coves backed by verdant jungle. The ecology of the islands has suffered badly over the years due to fishermen using dynamite to blast fish up to the water's surface. Mooring posts to prevent anchor damage have helped coral re-growth in recent years, while dynamite fishing has been banned.

The two main islands, **Ko Surin Nua** and **Ko Surin Tai**, are separated by a narrow 200-metre (660ft) channel of small beaches and pockets of mangroves that can be forded at low tide. These islands are largely uninhabited, although Ko Surin Tai is home to a small community of *chao lay* or sea gypsies (*see page 224*), and Ko Surin Nua houses the park's headquarters and the island's only accommodation – rustic bungalows and a campsite. The other three islands, **Ko Ri**, **Ko Khai** and **Ko Klang**, are just small islets covered with sparse vegetation and are not worth exploring.

TIP

From May to October, the southwest monsoon brings heavy rain to the entire Andaman Coast. While this means that some of the islands further away cannot be accessed because of rough seas, it's not unusual to get days of intermittent sunshine even during the peak rainy-season months.

BELOW: a Moken village in the Surin Islands Marine National Park.

TIP

Because the famous
Burma Banks dive site
is located within the
territorial waters of
Myanmar (Burma), the
only way to visit it is by
travelling onboard a
live-aboard dive-cruise
boat that would have
the required papers to
be granted access.

Dive sites

The Surin Islands' most popular dive site, **Richelieu Rock**, is only just exposed at low tide. It is one of the world's top locations for sighting whale sharks, with February to April being the best time. On average, 10 percent of all dives in a year at Richelieu result in an encounter with this 20-metre (65ft) behemoth.

Around 60km (37 miles) northwest of the Surin Islands lie the renowned **Burma Banks**, where the three submerged peaks of **Silvertip**, **Roe** and **Rainbow** rise to within 15 metres (50ft) of the sea's surface before plunging back into the surrounding 300-metre (980ft) deep waters. Encounters with silvertip, nurse and, occasionally, grey reef sharks are a near certainty. The only way to dive these sites is from a live-aboard dive charter arranged out of Khao Lak, Phuket or Ranong.

KHAO SOK NATIONAL PARK

Easily accessible from Phuket and Surat Thani, **Khao Sok National Park** ❼ (daily; charge) is often dismissed as simply another national park. However, alongside the usual flora, fauna, rivers and forests are some features that make Khao Sok unique. It is home to one of the world's oldest evergreen rainforests – approximately 160 million years – and its location on the mountain ridge between the east and west coasts makes it the wettest area in Thailand – rains from both the Gulf of Thailand and the Andaman Sea coasts deposit as much as 3,500mm (138ins) of rainfall annually. Within the park's dense rainforest the world's second-largest flower, the *Rafflesia Kerrii*, grows up to 80cm (31ins) in diameter when in bloom.

Geographically, much of the 740-sq-km (285-sq-mile) park comprises limestone mountains, most in the 400–600-metre (1,300–2,000ft) range, with the highest at 960 metres (3,150ft). Lowland rainforest dominates, but there are also many towering trees, some reaching heights of around 65 metres (215ft). Large mammals, including elephants and leopards, roam free (though they are rarely seen) while cobras, tarantulas and scorpions are common.

BELOW: snorkelling in the clear waters of the Surin Islands.
BELOW RIGHT: scenery at Khao Sok National Park.

Jungle trails

Of the nine trails in the national park, eight follow the same route for the first 5km (3 miles) along the **Sok River**, after which they split. One continues a further 2km (1½ miles) to the **Ton Gloy Waterfall** which is great for a dip, another to the **Bang Leap Nam Waterfall**, which is not as large but easier to reach. **Sawan Waterfall** is the most difficult to access, and involves clambering over the river across slippery and sometimes steep rocks. The ninth trail leads in a different direction altogether, following the **Bang Laen River** all the way to **Sip-et Chan Waterfall**.

You can tackle these jungle trails yourself, but half-day tours booked from Phuket or Krabi are lead by experienced guides who will point out rare flora and signs of animal life that the untrained eye could easily miss.

Another popular day trip takes in **Cheow Lan Lake**, some 60km (37 miles) from the main accommodation area. It is home to over 100 small islands and was formed in the 1980s when the **Ratchprabha Dam** was built to construct a hydroelectric power plant. Activities include boat trips, fishing and canoeing, as well as walks around the lake to locations such as **Tham Nam Talu** cave. The lake is at its most beautiful in the early morning, when gibbons hoot from deep within the mists hanging over the lakes and mountains.

KHAO LAK

Frequented primarily by diving enthusiasts, sleepy **Khao Lak ❽** is the closest access point to the marine-life paradise of the **Similan Islands**, some 60km (37 miles) offshore. Khao Lak has recovered well from the 2004 tsunami, and is seen by many as a pleasant, less frenetic alternative to Phuket, with excellent facilities for families, fewer touts and very little in the way of commercialisation. A prime example is the **Sarojin Hotel**, which opened just before the tsunami hit. Thanks to its highly dedicated owners and staff, following a swift rebuilding programme it is now a leading light of the hospitality industry, running cooking schools, hosting weddings and garnering numerous awards.

Exotic vegetation at Khao Sok National Park.

BELOW: a Khao Lak beach.

Chao Lay: Thailand's Sea Gypsy Community

Outside the mainstream of Thai society, the sea gypsies are content to continue in their traditional ways

The "sea gypsies" of southern Thailand, known in Thai as *chao lay*, or "people of the sea", are divided into three groups, though they sometimes intermarry and generally consider themselves as one kindred people. Numbering between 4,000 and 5,000, they live either in huts by the shore, or on itinerant craft that ply the coastal waters south from Ranong all the way to Ko Tarutao close to the border with Malaysia.

The **Urak Lawoi**, numbering around 3,000, form the largest sea-gypsy group. They live in simple shacks on beaches from Phuket to Ko Tarutao and make a living by fishing and beachcombing. The two largest Urak Lawoi settlements are at Ko Sireh and Rawai in the southeast of Phuket, but smaller communities are also found on the islands of Ko Lanta, Ko Phi Phi, Ko Jum and Ko Lipe. The Urak Lawoi group are fairly well integrated into Thai society and are registered as citizens.

Less numerous than the Urak Lawoi, the 1,000-strong **Moklen** community lives between Ko Phra Tong near Takua Pa and Phuket, including the Surin Islands, while the 500 or so **Moken** live north from Ko Phra Thong to the Burmese frontier. Of the three *chao lay* groups, the Moken are the least adapted to modern life; they still use dugout canoes rather than motorised longtail boats, and avoid all contact with settled people – especially local authorities – as much as possible. They are not registered as citizens and the Thais distinguish them from the other groups by calling them *chao ko tae* or "real island folk". The Moken rarely build huts on dry land, preferring to live a completely nomadic existence on the waters of the Andaman Sea.

Regarded as an indigenous people of Thailand, it seems likely the *chao lay* were among the earliest inhabitants of the region, predating the arrival of the Tais *(see page 30)* from the north by many centuries. They are shorter, stockier and darker than the Tais, and are more closely related to the *orang laut*, or "sea people", of Malaysia, and perhaps also to the Mani or Negrito peoples who inhabit the southern Thai interior. Little is known of the *chao lay's* past as they have no written language or records. Their spoken languages are related to Malay, though the Moken, living furthest from Malaysia, have borrowed a much larger vocabulary from the Thais and Burmese.

Chao lay venerate tutelary spirits, especially those associated with wind, water and islands. The Moken are strictly animist and worship the sea. Twice a year, during the full moon of the sixth and 11th lunar months (usually June and November), they stop working for three days and nights to feast, dance, sing and drink alcohol, often entering into a trance. The Moken believe that their earliest ancestor was washed ashore, but on landing refused to become Muslim or Buddhist, choosing instead to return to the sea. Certainly, the sea gypsies remain a people apart, living on the fringes of southern Thai society, with few material possessions and little inclination to use technology.

Yet, while they may be ill-equipped to deal with modern life, the *chao lay* have some natural advantages. During the December 2004 tsunami, although more than 1,000 sea gypsy households sustained damage and some loss of life, they seem to have instinctively realised the danger better than their Thai neighbours, as many saved themselves by moving early to higher ground. ❏

LEFT: a Mokien Surin islander taking a break.

Khao Lak's beaches

The view over Khao Lak when arriving from Phuket, located 80km (50 miles) to the south, is quite stunning. As the narrow mountain road winds down to the beaches below, turquoise waters lapping against the sand give an impression of a postcard-perfect tropical scene. Khao Lak is, in fact, made up of a string of beaches, each separated by rocky outcrops, keeping them quiet and secluded while also appearing to merge into one another.

From north to south, the beaches run as follows: **Bang Sak**, **Pakarang Cape**, **Khuk Khak**, **Bang Niang**, **Nang Thong** and finally, **Khao Lak**. The last is a relatively small stretch of sand extending 800 metres (2,625ft). Before the tsunami hit, most of the development in the area was centred on Bang Niang, which took the longest to recover. Nang Thong and Khao Lak beaches also have a good number of hotels. Swimming conditions in the high season are excellent on all beaches, but during the monsoon season it is better to keep to the north towards the rocky headland where the currents are not so strong.

SIMILAN ISLANDS

Promoted in nearly every dive shop and diving website and mentioned in countless brochures throughout Thailand is the beautiful **Similan Islands Marine National Park ❾** (Nov–May; charge), 100km (62 miles) northwest of Phuket but most easily accessible from Khao Lak, the nearest mainland point, 60km (37 miles) away.

Similan, derived from the Malay word *sembilan*, means nine, in reference to nine islands that make up this 128-sq-km (50-sq-mile) marine national park. For easy reference, the islands are numbered from north to south in descending order, starting with **Ko Bon** (No. 9), **Ko Ba Ngu** (No. 8), **Ko Similan** (No. 7), **Ko Payoo** (No. 6), **Ko Miang** (collective name for islands Nos 4 and 5), **Ko Pahyan** (No. 3), **Ko Phayang** (No. 2) and **Ko Hu Yong** (No. 1).

With the exception of Ko Ba Ngu and Ko Miang, the Similan group is uninhabited; for years, prior to their rise in popularity among the dive fraternity, the islands were visited only by sea gypsies. Today, the most frequent visitors are day-trippers from Phuket and Khao Lak, and divers on multi-day live-aboard boats.

Like many such sites in Thailand, the reefs have suffered greatly from the effects of dynamite fishing and the indiscriminate anchoring of boats and trawlers. Since 1987, however, fishing has been banned and boundaries set for moorings so that the reefs can return to their former pristine state.

Diving the Similans

There are more than 20 dive sites around the Similan Islands. The eastern side of the archipelago features hard coral gardens where the most popular activity is drift diving along slopes that lean dramatically from the surface down to depths of 30–40 metres (100–130ft). Popular sites include **Christmas Point** and **Breakfast Bend**, both at Ko Ba Ngu, where soft coral growth and

Powder-like beaches and clear aquamarine waters are the hallmarks of the Similan Islands.

BELOW: speedboat on clear water in the Similans.

colourful sea fans are among the largest found in Thailand. The Napoleon wrasse, a rare sight in Thailand, is occasionally glimpsed at Breakfast Bend, along with leopard sharks resting on the sands beneath.

The western side of the Similan Islands offers faster-paced and more exhilarating diving, with currents swirling around huge granite boulder formations, and dramatic holes and overhangs. Colourful soft corals grow so thick on many of these boulders that the rock is no longer visible. Most dive sites on the west coast are best seen with a guide, since navigation can be tricky. Popular sites include **Fantasy Reef** and **Elephant Head** at Ko Similan where clownfish, lionfish and, occasionally, turtles can be seen.

AO PHANG NGA

Less than an hour by road from Phuket Airport, the mainland town of **Phang Nga** has few attractions of interest. There are a few caves and waterfalls nearby, but none are overly impressive. For the main attraction in the area, head south from Phang Nga to reach **Ao Phang Nga**, the site of Thailand's most striking jungle-clad limestone rock formations, monoliths and cliffs. Spread over a coastal area of 400 sq km (155 sq miles) between Phuket and Krabi, the islands are part of the **Ao Phang Nga Marine National Park ❿**.

While impressive by day and very much evocative of a Chinese brush painting, the spectacular vistas of towering karsts are especially captivating on moonlit nights, when the silvery light casts haunting shadows off the eerie rock structures into the watery depths around them. Sheltered from both northeast and southwest monsoon seasons, the blue-green waters around the bay are calm year-round.

Trips to the bay are mostly arranged from either Phuket or Krabi, but they can also be booked in Phang Nga Town itself. A more interesting way of exploring Ao Phang Nga is by sea canoe. At low tide these low-lying craft can slip through sea tunnels beneath the limestone karsts, which shelter hidden lagoons (called "hongs") within. The karsts support their own mini ecosystem, including small troupes of

monkeys, and it has been reported that they even swim from island to island. The hongs are truly magical, lost worlds that seem totally remote from the surrounding area. The better sea-canoe operators run trips in the late afternoon and evening, when there are fewer boats around: check to ensure your trip is to one of the more remote areas, as large tour groups can blight the hongs' serene ambience.

Ko Ping Kan (James Bond Island) and Ko Panyi

Thailand has long been in demand as an exotic film locale, and in 1974, one of the rocky pinnacles of Phang Nga was featured in the film *The Man with the Golden Gun*. As a result, for better or worse, **Ko Ping Kan** is better known today as **James Bond Island**.

The small beach here is perpetually crowded with day-trippers who pose for pictures with the geological oddity called **Ko Tapu**, meaning Nail Island, behind them. Rising from a precariously thin base 200 metres (650ft) out of the water, the rocky outcrop seems destined to tip into the water at some point. Bond

fans are unlikely to care, though; there is something undeniably cool about standing on the same spot as 007.

All tours of Ao Phang Nga also make a stop at nearby **Ko Panyi**, a Muslim village built entirely over the water and nestled against towering cliffs. Come lunchtime each day, it transforms from a quiet fishing community into a bustling hive of restaurants and souvenir shops with the arrival of 3,000 or so tourists on their way to or back from James Bond Island. Overnight tours of Ao Phang Nga stop here for the night, but the accommodation is basic.

Apart from stopping off at James Bond and Ko Panyi islands, most tours will pass by a number of rocks and uninhabited islands named after the strange shapes they resemble. One popular stop is **Khao Khien** (Painting Rock) to see ancient cave art painted on its inner walls. An array of animals, including monkeys, elephants, fish and crabs are depicted alongside human stick figures. Another stop is **Tham Lod**, a narrow sea-cave tunnel filled with strangely-shaped stalactites.   ❑

View of Ko Tapu from James Bond Island.

RESTAURANTS

SUBMARINE SURPRISES

The coral reefs that fringe both of Thailand's coasts are an outstanding wonderland of colour, home to a variety of vivid marine life

Thailand's underwater world is rewarding to explore from both sides of the country, but each coast is quite different in terms of what you can see. The flora and fauna of the Andaman Sea are characteristic of the Indian Ocean, while Gulf of Thailand species are typical of the Pacific. However, the Andaman Sea is deeper and clearer than the Gulf, and overall its coral reefs are more extensive.

The reefs off both coastlines have been only patchily surveyed, but they support at least 400 species of fish and 30 kinds of sea snake. Bottlenose dolphins and the occasional whale are found in Thai waters, but the gentle dugong, or "sea cow", is increasingly hard to find among the sea grasses of Phang Nga, Phuket, Trang and Satun provinces. Thailand's coral species number almost 300, with the Andaman Sea boasting an even greater diversity. Intact reefs, however, survive only in areas far from human habitation, such as the vicinity of the Surin and Similan islands.

ABOVE: Thai waters are home to four species of turtle – green, leatherback, hawksbill and Olive Ridley. All are endangered, and the hawksbill, found in the Andaman Sea, is now very rare.

BELOW: clownfish are found throughout the warm waters of the Indian and Pacific oceans. These colourful fish live in a symbiotic relationship with sea anemones or stony corals. Once an anemone or a coral has been selected as home, the clownfish will defend it aggressively.

TOP: the cuttlefish makes a frequent appearance on Thai menus; in order to meet the demand, these unusual creatures are now reared in large quantities. But species such as the *Sepia pharaonis* can still be observed in their natural habitat in the waters of the Gulf of Thailand. Cuttlefish are among the most intelligent invertebrates in the animal kingdom. Like their close relatives, the squid and octopus, they can expel "ink" when threatened.

BELOW: lagoon triggerfish are frequently seen in Thai waters. The larger titan triggerfish can be very aggressive.

EXPLORING THE REEFS

Thailand has long been considered a great dive destination. Not only does the region offer clear, accessible water and some outstanding coral, it has (in most cases) modern, international-standard dive services at competitive prices.

Phuket is a regional leader in diving. There are extensive, prime dive areas not far from shore, plus an abundance of dive shops competing for business. Any level of diver can enjoy themselves here.

Increasingly, divers are looking to give something back to mother earth. Leading this effort is the Green Fins program *(see page 405)*, which sets out environmentally-sound dive guidelines. The program provides a list of eco-friendly dive operators, as well as beach and coral cleanup programs.

For details on dive companies see pages 405–9.

ABOVE: scuba diving in the Andaman Sea.
BELOW: lionfish, a type of scorpionfish, are equipped with razor-sharp spines on their fins, which are used to inject poison into any perceived threat.

ABOVE: the scorpionfish camouflages itself innocuously on the seabed, but can deliver an extremely poisonous sting if stepped on. Thailand's waters are estimated to support almost 2,000 fish species, including 600–700 freshwater fish.

RIGHT: the poisonous crown of thorns starfish can to grow over 30cm (1ft) in diameter.

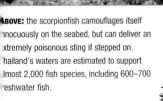

PHUKET

Thailand's largest – and richest – resort island caters to a broad range of holidaymakers. Bars and beaches draw the biggest numbers, but there is a lot more to Phuket's diverse ethnic and geographical make-up, as veering just a short way off the beaten track will show

Phuket is no longer just an island, it's become a brand. In the space of a generation, the country's smallest province (587 sq km/225 sq miles) went from growing coconuts for local consumption to welcoming tourists from all over the world. With tourism came development, driving Phuket's dramatic growth from a sleepy little island in the 1970s to today's full-on resort destination synonymous with hedonism. There are now hotels to suit all budgets, but recent development has seen the construction of boutique properties and upmarket villa-style houses, along with shopping complexes, schools and hospitals of international standard. Not surprisingly, all this has encouraged many foreigners to take up permanent residence in Phuket.

The stunning white-sand beaches along the 48km (30-mile) long west coast are separated by picturesque headlands. Some are small and pristine with intimate hidden coves, while others teem with noisy jet skis and vendors hawking sarongs and souvenirs.

Phuket is a base for dive trips to several renowned sites in the surrounding seas, and a number of operators offer courses, organised dive excursions and live-aboard trips. Phuket is also an excellent base for exploring nearby islands, national parks and mainland areas like Khao Lak and Krabi.

People and economy

The majority of Phuket's 300,000 or so people are Buddhist, with Muslims comprising around 35 percent. A number of locals make their living from the island's rubber and pineapple plantations, but since the 1980s, tourism has overtaken agriculture as the main source of income. When the tsunami hit Phuket and surrounding areas on 26 December 2004 – the peak of the high season – Phuket suffered badly. Some beaches escaped relatively unscathed, while others (like Patong and Kamala)

Main attractions
CHINATOWN (IN PHUKET TOWN)
HAT KAMALA
HAT PATONG
HAT KATA YAI AND NOI
KATA HILL VIEWPOINT
HAT NAI HARN
LAEM PROMPTHEP
WAT CHALONG
KO BON AND KO HAE
KO RACHA
WAT PHRA THONG
KHAO PHRAW TAEW
    NATIONAL PARK

LEFT: beach volleyball at Patong.
RIGHT: extracting rubber latex.

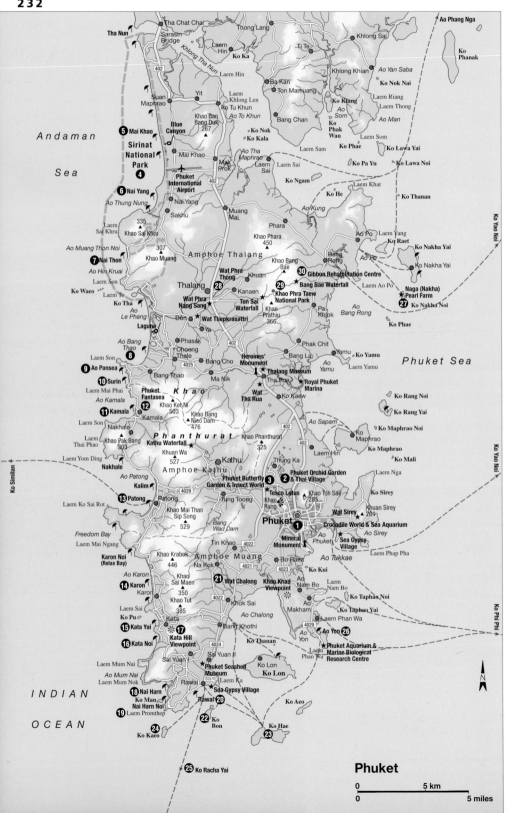

Phuket

0   5 km
0   5 miles

were hit hard. The loss of life, injuries and damage to property were considerable.

Due to rapid rebuilding and focused tourism campaigns overseas, Phuket soon got back on its feet again. Indeed, with beaches swept clean of debris and buildings renovated and given a fresh lick of paint, the island is literally sparkling once more.

PHUKET TOWN

Unsurprisingly, many people head straight for the beaches and give **Phuket Town ❶** a miss. But the town is worth at least a day trip. Only 20 minutes' drive from Patong, the town can seem busy and unattractive, especially given its higgledy-piggledy one-way traffic system. Getting about on foot, with a good map, is the best way to go. There are plenty of sights and shops, as well as a sprinkling of good bars and restaurants.

Chinatown

In the heart of Phuket Town, between Thanon Thalang and Thanon Deebuk, lies the **Chinatown ❹** area, where old colonial houses and Sino-Portuguese-style mansions dominate. Originally built by Europeans, they were designed for Chinese sensibilities. Oddly, the combination of Eastern and Western influence has produced some fine architecture. As many are now privately owned, they can be viewed only from the outside. These residences are easily recognised by their tiled roofs, artistically chiselled exteriors and tall, spiralling pillars at the front.

Chinese temples

Due to the strong Chinese presence in Phuket (*see panel, below*), a number of temples are Taoist in character. A few in particular stand out. **Sanjao Sam San ❸** (daily 8am–6pm; free) at Thanon Krabi, erected in 1853 in dedication to Tien Sang Sung Moo, the patron saint of sailors and goddess of the sea, is recognisable by the gold statues that stand proudly outside and intricate carvings that adorn the inner walls.

Also worth visiting is the **Put Jaw Temple ❸** (daily 8am–6pm; free) on Thanon Ranong, dedicated to Kwan Im, the Chinese goddess of mercy. At a little over 200 years, this is the oldest Chinese Taoist temple in Phuket. It is not overly

TIP

Avoid taxi touts at the airport – their prices tend to be misleading, their navigational and linguistic skills hazy, and they are unlikely to be properly insured.

BELOW: devotees seeking their fortunes at Put Jaw Temple.

Phuket's Chinese

Phuket's Chinese population (35 percent by some estimates) came as labourers, and have now become the island's business leaders. They emigrated mainly from Hokkien in China to work the tin mines and rubber plantations in the 18th and 19th centuries, switched to trading (birds' nests, a highly prized delicacy back home, were an early lure) as soon as they could afford it, intermarried and now play a significant part in the day-to-day life of the island, carrying Thai passports but still very much aware of their ethnic heritage. The Chinese influence on architecture and religion is especially evident in Phuket Town, and if any business is prospering significantly it's more than likely that there's a Chinese hand in it somewhere.

TIP

Inside Put Jaw Temple are two cans filled with numbered sticks. Say your problem aloud and then shake the cans, picking up the first stick that falls out. The number on the stick will correspond to a pigeon hole in the adjacent hall. Inside you will find a piece of paper with your fortune written on it. Fortunes are told for free (you need an interpreter), but you are expected to leave a donation.

impressive from the outside, and is better known for what happens within. In the middle hall, resting before an image of Kwan Im, are some fortune-telling devices, including a pair of wooden divining blocks, which when dropped to the floor by devotees imply a "yes" or "no" answer to a question – depending on which side they fall on. Your fortune can also be told by the aid of divining sticks (*see margin tip, left*).

Jui Tui Temple (daily 8am–6pm; free), right next to Put Jaw, is more ornate. On the altar inside stands the red-faced statue of Kiu Ong Ya, one of the Nine Emperor Gods to whom the temple is dedicated. This temple is the main location for the annual October **Vegetarian Festival**, when the streets come alive with thousands who flock here to witness devotees perform grotesque acts of self-mutilation.

Further east along Thanon Ranong, the **Central Market** hums all day as Thai housewives banter with the merchants among piles of vegetables, fruit and fish. The uninitiated, however, may find the market's olfactory assault somewhat overpowering.

Phuket Orchid Garden and Thai Village

Not quite in Phuket Town but in its outskirts about 2½km (1½ miles) away at Thanon Thepkrassatri is a popular stop on most standard tours of Phuket, the **Phuket Orchid Garden and Thai Village ➋** (daily 8am–9pm; charge).

Apart from its collection of rare orchids, the Thai Village is also a cultural centre hosting traditional dances and elephant shows, a handicraft centre and Thai restaurants. The staged wedding ceremony – while a little kitsch – rivals a Las Vegas show for glitz and glamour, with a ceremony steeped in Thai culture and tradition, and even a grand entry on elephant back.

Phuket Butterfly Garden and Insect World

At the start of Thanon Yaowaraj heading towards Phuket Town centre is the **Phuket Butterfly Garden and Insect World ➌** (daily 9am–5.30pm; charge). Inside are over 40 species of butterfly in a rainforest environment and an enclosure full of rare and native birds of Thailand, an ideal outing for

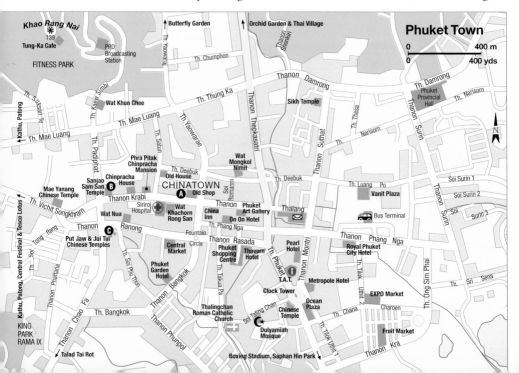

children. Information boards point out the differences between butterflies and moths, and there are educational exhibits of live eggs, larvae and pupa. The adjoining Insect World is where stick insects, tarantulas, scorpions and other creepy-crawlies go about their daily business, unaware of watchful eyes marvelling at them.

Khao Rang

South of the Butterfly Garden is **Khao Rang**. According to tourist brochures, a spiralling road leads to a summit that reveals panoramic views over Phuket Town. In reality, the view is far from spectacular, as roads and traffic are all that can be seen from here. However, the leafy surrounds and the solitude make it a peaceful place to have a picnic. **Tung-Ka** at the peak of the hill serves delicious, cheap Thai food daily for lunch and dinner.

Malls-a-go-go

Slightly at odds with the image of a laidback tropical island, on the main airport road (Th. Chalermprakiet) just outside Phuket Town is a cluster of malls forming Phuket's largest shopping centre-cum-social mecca. Tesco Lotus was the first to appear, but has been trumped by the smarter Central: they're handy for picking up supplies if you are staying for a lengthy period, or to catch a movie or play bowls on a rainy day.

WEST COAST

Phuket's western coastline is its main claim to fame. Over time, the coast has been sculpted by the waves into a string of coves stretching from north to south and covered in sugary white sand.

Sirinat National Park

A large chunk of the northwest cape is given over to **Sirinat National Park ❹**. Formerly Nai Yang National Park, it was renamed in 1992 to commemorate Queen Sirikit's 60th birthday. The 90-sq-km (35-sq-mile) park, of which three-quarters is sea, encompasses the beaches at **Hat Nai Yang** and **Hat Nai Thon** as well as the northern mangrove area at **Hat Mai Khao**.

Casuarinas are the most common tree found in the park, and many

An exotic butterfly at the Phuket Butterfly Garden and Insect World.

BELOW: a Sino-Portuguese-style mansion in Phuket.

BELOW: poolside gardens at JW Marriott Resort & Spa.

species of bird, mammal and insect live in its mangrove forests. The park's marine environment is diverse and its coral reefs are among the most pristine around Phuket. Located in water between 4–7 metres (12–23ft) deep are extensive plate and tree corals, as well as sea fans and sea anemones.

Hat Mai Khao

Despite being the longest of Phuket's beaches at over 17km (11 miles) long, the sands of the secluded **Hat Mai Khao** ❺ are more golden than white and a little coarse underfoot, but the waters are very clean. There is little to do at Mai Khao other than soak up the sun. As the beach is part of the protected Sirinat National Park, development has been low-key, which is perhaps why hundreds of Olive Ridley sea turtles, as well as the odd giant leatherback, come ashore to lay their eggs here between November and February each year.

For years, the only hotel on this beach was the luxury **JW Marriott Resort & Spa**. Initially criticised for encroaching on national park land, the hotel managed to change public perception by

initiating the **Marine Turtle Foundation**. All guests who stay at this hotel are encouraged to donate US$1 a day to support local conservation efforts that help ensure the turtles' yearly return. The Marriott has since been joined by other hotels, and Mai Khao's profile is gradually being raised.

Hat Nai Yang

Despite housing the headquarters of Sirinat National Park and being a protected area, **Hat Nai Yang** ❻ hosts a few hotels. Still, it is very laidback and quiet compared to the beaches further down the coast. In the low season it is virtually deserted, but high season sees a strip of thatched wooden beach huts serving cold beer and seafood. The beach is a beautiful curving bay lined with evergreen trees that provide both visual relief and shade. A large coral reef around 1km (2/3 mile) offshore is home to several different species of fish.

Hat Nai Thon

The smallest of Sirinat National Park's three beaches is **Hat Nai Thon** ❼, which, due to its position at the foot of a series of high hills, is harder to reach and requires a journey along a long and winding road, passing jungle and rubber plantations. The beach is not totally deserted, however, and a few sun beds are available for hire. Nai Thon offers good swimming and snorkelling along its rocky headlands that attract rich marine life year-round. Offshore, the remains of a wrecked tin dredger is a favourite spot with divers.

Ao Bang Thao

The 8km (5-mile) stretch of beach at the gently curving **Ao Bang Thao** ❽ is dominated by the Laguna Resort, a cluster of five luxury hotels, the most exclusive being the **Banyan Tree Phuket**, with its own 18-hole golf course. Bang Thao is one of the loveliest beaches on the island, all the more so for its having once been on the edge of a tin mine which was rehabilitated

to become the luxury resort Laguna is today. Beware of the strong undertow, however, during the monsoon season. All accommodation is found at the northern end of the beach, so a walk south will often lead to a deserted patch of sand.

Ao Pansea and Hat Surin

Thailand's most senior exclusive resort, the luxury **Amanpuri**, occupies prime position at **Ao Pansea ❾**, with Thai-style pavilions interspersed in a coconut plantation on a sea-facing headland. The beach runs for only 300 metres (984ft) and is very private, as it's closed off by headlands on either side of the bay. The other end of Ao Pansea is anchored by the expensive **Chedi** resort.

Beyond the Chedi resort, the beach becomes **Hat Surin ❿**. It is popular with locals, but not as pristine as Phuket's other beaches; again, beware of the undertow during the monsoon season. Vendors frequently set up makeshift stalls at the beach car park and sell freshly grilled prawns and barbecued mackerel.

Hat Kamala

Kamala ⓫ is only a few minutes' drive away from the hustle and bustle of Patong, yet it could not be more different in character; the lovely beach is calm, relaxed and peaceful, with few vendors touting for business. The inhabitants are mainly Muslim, and heavily involved in the tourist industry.

In the heart of Kamala, **Phuket Fantasea ⓬** (daily except Thur 5.30–11.30pm, showtime 9pm; www.phuketfantasea.com) brings a touch of Las Vegas to Phuket. The 57-hectare (140-acre) complex touts itself as a night-time cultural theme park. The show's fun for seven-year-olds of all ages, combining acrobatics, pyrotechnics and illusions, and a vast menagerie of performing animals, including at one point over 40 elephants on stage – all at the same time.

Hat Patong

Love it or hate it, Phuket would not be the successful tourist magnet it is today without **Hat Patong ⓭**. With its multitude of shops, restaurants, street stalls, neon lights, flashy bars and clubs, Patong sums up what many visitors like to see.

Following the catastrophic tsunami of 2004, Phuket is now equipped with an early-warning system and clearly marked evacuation routes in the event of a similar event.

BELOW: tourists flock to Patong beach.

TIP

To see the "lady-boys" at Simon Cabaret without suffering through the show, head to the car park around 11pm when they all come out and line up for photos. This is a better opportunity to see them up close and personal.

But for every punter who is drawn here, there is another who despises it and can't escape quickly enough. The beach is crowded and the constant barrage of hawkers gets annoying, but the location is naturally beautiful. Touts from restaurants and tailors go overboard enticing you into their shops, but at least there is plenty to buy and the variety is good, especially in the new malls like Jungceylon. Restaurants are overpriced, but the range of cuisines on offer is immense and caters for every palate. And while the nightlife in certain areas is seedy and the prostitution blatant (notably along Th. Bangla), you can have a fun and entertaining night out in Patong if you don't take it all too seriously.

The 3km (2-mile) stretch of Hat Patong is strewn with sunburnt bodies sheltering under rows of beach umbrellas, and even in the low season it is virtually impossible to find a quiet spot on the sand. On the plus side, the sea is usually clear outside of the monsoon season, and it is good for swimming or snorkelling, but care should be taken not to get too close to the jet skis and banana boats whizzing by close to the shore.

Patong nightlife

In the heart of Patong is **Thanon Bangla**, the epicentre of the seedy sex trade, with bar after bar of young and not-so-young prostitutes, *kathoey* or "lady-boy" transsexuals, and explicit "ping-pong" sex shows. Despite the blatant commercial trade, the atmosphere is relaxed and feels safe. Single men may get hassled to buy drinks for the bar girls, and families and women on their own may not feel entirely comfortable away from the main street.

Showing how easily Thai men can morph into the opposite sex is **Simon Cabaret** (showtime nightly at 7.30pm and 9.30pm; charge; www.phuketsimon cabaret.com) on Thanon Sirirat, heading south out of Patong. Some people find the show rather dull, with the performing "lady-boys" or *kathoey* miming the lyrics and dancing in an exaggerated manner, but the sight of so many men dressed up as alluring women draws in curious gawkers every night.

Phuket has a fairly large gay district that mainly centres around the network of lanes that make up the **Paradise Complex** near the Royal Paradise Hotel on Thanon Raja Uthit.

Hat Karon Noi and Hat Karon

Beyond Hat Patong is **Hat Karon Noi**, sometimes referred to as Relax Bay. Although it is a public beach, this beguiling crescent of white sand is dominated by a single hotel, **Le Meridien Phuket**, which can make access a little difficult.

The 4km (3-mile) long beach at **Hat Karon** ⑭ is Phuket's second-most popular beach after Hat Patong. The sand is golden in colour and the beach is rarely packed, and it is screened from the road by a line of sand dunes and a grassy embankment. During the rainy season, large waves make Hat Karon excellent for surfing, although unsafe for swimming. There is a good range of hotels, most of which, like in Patong, are tucked behind the beachside Thanon Karon.

BELOW: "lady-boys" perform nightly at Simon Cabaret.

Hat Kata Yai and Hat Kata Noi

Just past the headland from Karon is **Hat Kata Yai ⓯** (mostly referred to only as Kata), arguably one of the most scenic of Phuket's beaches as it looks out towards a small uninhabited hummock-shaped island named Ko Poo (Crab Island). Kata's lovely beach is blessed with white sand and clear waters that are good for swimming and snorkelling, but can get quite busy. The southern end of the beach is home to the **The Boathouse** hotel, which has a well-known fine-dining restaurant. At night, the beach is quiet and romantic, and there are a number of seafood restaurants lit by fairy lights overlooking the waves lapping the shore.

Separated by a rocky headland is **Hat Kata Noi ⓰**, which shares the same white sand and clear blue-green waters as the preceding beach but is even prettier and more peaceful. The sprawling **Kata Thani Resort** has almost complete run of this beach. At the southern end of the beach are some decent corals for snorkelling.

Kata Hill Viewpoint

A sharp, steep mountain road leads out of Kata, one that cars sometimes struggle on and motorbikes splutter trying to crest. On a sunny day, the view from this road is breathtaking. A number of small, reggae-type bars have opened up along the road in recent years, with simple wooden platforms jutting out over the hillside towards the sea; any of them would be good for watching the sunset. At the peak is the **Kata Hill Viewpoint ⓱**, from which the three stunning bays of Kata, Karon and Patong can be seen at one fell swoop. This famous scene appears on postcards island-wide. Photography conditions are better in the morning, as even on a seemingly perfect day the clouds can roll in by mid-afternoon and block the view.

Hat Nai Harn

South of Kata and lying between two ridges is the stunning white-sand **Hat Nai Harn ⓲**, relatively undeveloped despite its charms. For this it can thank the **Samnak Song Nai Harn Monastery**, which occupies a

The view from Kata Hill.

BELOW: fishing boats off Kata beach.

TIP

The views at Promthep Cape Restaurant (tel: 0-7628 8851; daily lunch and dinner) are better than the mostly average food. The fresh oysters, reared in the owner's farm, are far more impressive. Service is slow, but the staff are friendly and the prices reasonable.

large portion of the beachfront land and thwarted development along this beach. Popular with expats who are often seen exercising their dogs along the beach on Sunday mornings, Nai Harn is a quieter alternative to the island's other beaches. It offers some conveniences in the form of a few small bars, restaurants and shops.

SOUTH COAST

The south coast beaches from Laem Promthep onwards are largely mediocre at best and mainly used as a staging point for explorations of the islands off the southern coast.

Laem Promthep

Leading up the mountain from Nai Harn is another viewpoint that features on many a postcard of Phuket, **Laem Promthep** ⓳ (Promthep Cape). This point overlooking a splendid headland stretching into the blue Andaman Sea is packed almost every evening with tourists scanning the horizon to see the mango-hued sun sink slowly over the horizon. When the conditions are right, the sunset vistas here are breathtaking.

Promthep Cape Restaurant (*see margin tip, left*), overlooking the cape and serving cheap Thai food, is an ideal spot for dinner or drinks.

Hat Rawai

A base for a great number of Phuket's foreign residents, **Hat Rawai** ⓴ offers all the attractions of island life but without the intrusive tourist facilities of Kata, Karon and Patong. Rawai is often picturesque with its rows of small fishing and longtail boats waiting to journey to the nearby islands, but at low tide, the exposed rocks make it unsuitable for swimming and snorkelling. Rawai is popular for its street vendors who barbecue freshly caught seafood along the beach road throughout the day, and the fresh seafood restaurants that open in the evenings. To the south of the beach is a small *chao lay* (sea gypsy) village, where visitors can stroll about unhindered.

The most exclusive hotel in the area, the **Evason**, maintains its own private beach in addition to having access to an offshore island, **Ko Bon**, for its guests' use.

BELOW: Laem Promthep at sunset.

Nearby on Thanon Viset the **Phuket Seashell Museum** (daily 8am–6pm; charge), has an interesting display of over 2,000 different species of shells and fossils; some of the latter are reputedly over 380 million years old.

Ao Chalong

North of Rawai is **Ao Chalong**, which is known mainly for an important temple as well as its pier, from which many dive expeditions and boat trips to nearby islands depart daily.

Wat Chalong ㉑ (daily 8am–6pm; free), located inland of Rawai on Route 4021, is Phuket's most important Buddhist temple and the largest of the island's Buddhist monasteries. Architecturally, it's not much different from other Thai temples, but it is one of Phuket's most ornate and among the most visited by both Thais and foreigners. Wat Chalong is associated with the revered monks Luang Pro Chaem and Luang Pho Chuang, famous herbal doctors and bone-setters who tended to the people of Phuket during the tin miners' rebellion of 1876. Far from being just physical healers, they also mediated in the conflict, bringing both parties together to resolve disputes. Today, many Thais visit the temple to pay homage to the two statues that honour the monks.

SOUTHERN ISLANDS

The waters around Phuket's southernmost tip are dotted with islands, all of which can be reached by the longtail boats lining Hat Rawai beach or the pier at Ao Chalong. If you are staying overnight at islands like Ko Racha, the resort will arrange the boat transfers.

Ko Bon

Nearest to shore is the small but pretty **Ko Bon ㉒**. Jointly owned by the five-star Evason on Hat Rawai and by local businessmen, the island can be reached in just 10 minutes. Unfortunately, it has no fresh water or electricity and no accommodation. One side of the island is owned by the

Evason and intended for the private use of its guests (free boat transfers are provided from Hat Rawai). It is possible to hang out at the Evason's side of the beach, and although the beach here is beautiful, the food and drink prices at its clubhouse match those of the resort on the mainland.

Most day-trippers head for the other side where **Sit Lo Chia**, a small Thai and seafood restaurant, is all that rests on the sandy beachfront. There is some coral in the deeper waters offshore, and while the Evason's beach is better for swimming, the water in front of Sit Lo Chia is very good for snorkelling.

Ko Hae and Ko Kaeo

About 20 minutes from Phuket, and often combined on a day trip with Ko Bon, is **Ko Hae ㉓** (Coral Island). Amenities are better than at Ko Bon, with a number of restaurants, a few small shops and some watersports. Overnight stays are possible at the **Coral Island Resort**, the island's only accommodation. The crystal-clear turquoise waters around the island make it particularly good for both swimming

Ko Kaeo is marked by numerous Buddha statues and shrines, hence its name "Buddha Island".

BELOW: scuba-divers at Ko Hae.

Spectacular marine life awaits divers in the waters around Ko Racha Yai and Noi.

and snorkelling, and there is a shallow coral reef within easy swimming distance of the beach.

Known to locals as Buddha Island, **Ko Kaeo ** is by far the least visited by day-trippers due to its lack of facilities, giving visitors the chance to have their own private beach for the day. Only a 10-minute boat ride from mainland Phuket, the island is home to a number of Buddha statues and shrines, hence its name.

Ko Racha

Approximately 20km (12 miles) off the coast of Rawai are **Ko Racha Noi**, a small uninhabited island with more rocks than beaches, and the larger **Ko Racha Yai**. Ko Racha Yai is the site of a stunning luxury resort known simply as **The Racha** on the northeast coast along **Ao Batok**. High season sees the island transform into a bustling hotspot, with day-trippers arriving on longtail boats and filling out the beaches. The shoreline of the beach in front of The Racha is picturesque, the sand almost talcum powder-like and the waters crystal-clear turquoise. Watch out for small corals and rocks, however, when you wade into the waters.

Both Racha islands offer some of the best diving in the Phuket area and are often compared to the waters around the Similan Islands. On **Ko Racha Yai**, the **Bungalow Bay** reef offshore of Ao Batok has clear waters and soft coral gardens, with good visibility and currents that allow gentle drift diving along sloping reefs. Elsewhere on the island are more white-sand beaches and snorkelling spots.

Along the eastern coast is **Ao Kon Kare**, a small sandy beach with **Lucy's Reef** within swimming distance, a nickname given to the staghorn coral found here. Further up the east coast, a submerged wreck lies off **Ao Ter** at depths of 25–35 metres (80–115ft).

On the northern coast is **Ao Siam**, where shallow waters not only make for good snorkelling but also prevent boats from docking, keeping this beach less busy than those on other parts of the island.

The smaller **Ko Racha Noi** also has a few good dive sites for experienced divers; depths here are generally greater and currents stronger. On the southwest side of the island, lots of reef fish are drawn to a 27-metre (88ft) shipwreck, while a large pinnacle at the northern tip attracts stingrays and reef sharks.

Numerous dive sites are scattered around the Andaman Coast (*see pages 222, 225, 259 and 262*).

EAST COAST

The east coast of Phuket was once the bank of a flooded river. Unlike the west, this side of the coastline comprises mainly limestone shoals and virtually no sandy beaches.

Laem Phan Wa

The only decent beach on the eastern coast of Phuket is **Laem Phan Wa**, 10km (6 miles) southeast from Phuket Town. This quiet cape is frequently filled with yachts sailing around **Ao**

BELOW: a sea gypsy mending nets.

Yon **26**, where a totally unspoilt stretch of sand sheltered by headlands on both sides makes it good for swimming year-round. Only a handful of hotels and restaurants are found in the Laem Phan Wa area, and as *tuk-tuk* and motorcycle taxis rarely journey over the winding mountain road to get here, the beach is often deserted.

Khao Khad Viewpoint (reached by following signs along Thanon Sakdidej that lead through Muang Tong village) is one of the island's best-kept secrets and a beautiful spot from which to gaze out to the sea. From this elevated point, Phuket Town lies to one side, Chalong Bay to the other, and the shadowy outline of Ko Phi Phi (*see page 256*) island can be seen in the distance.

On the southernmost tip of Laem Phan Wa on Route 4129 is the **Phuket Aquarium and Marine Biological Research Centre** (daily 8.30am–4pm; charge). Reopened in 2005 after more than two years of renovation, the impressive display of sharks, tropical fish, reefs and a touch pool with starfish and sea cucumbers is an excellent primer before one takes that first diving or snorkelling trip.

Royal Phuket Marina

Roughly in the centre of Phuket's eastern coast, and next to the longer-established Boat Lagoon, Royal Phuket Marina is probably the shape of things to come on the island; there's certainly no budget stuff here, but cashed-up visitors thinking about a pied-à-terre could do a lot worse than start at RPM (*see tint panel below*).

Naga Pearl Farm

The jetty at Ao Po, north of Phuket Town, is the departure point for the 30-minute boat ride to **Ko Nakha Noi 27** island. This is where you will find the **Naga Pearl Farm** (daily 9am–3.30pm; charge), where full-sized South Sea pearls worth thousands of dollars are cultivated. It also displays a replica of the world's largest pearl, the original of which is currently housed at the Mikimoto Pearl Museum in Japan.

Visitors can wander round and see pearls at various stages of cultivation, from the nurturing of the baby oysters

Snorkelling in the waters of Ko Racha.

BELOW: blue skies and clear waters at Ko Racha Yai.

The Royal Phuket Marina

A fair number of holidaymakers have decided that a fortnight a year on Phuket is simply not enough, and either retired to the island or set up in business here. The prime example is Karachi-born mobile-phone tycoon Gulu Lalvani, the brains (and money) behind the Royal Phuket Marina located on the east coast of Phuket. His vision has transformed a muddy backwater into a lifestyle destination, complete with condos, restaurants and shops. The Marina has now become a regular stage for international events as well as a haven for the region's yachties. Not everyone may have the US$49 million required to invest in such a mammoth project, but RPM is a sure indication of both Phuket's allure and growing potential. And there's no harm in starting a bit smaller.

to the extraction of pearls from their shells years later. Longtail boat operators at Ao Po can arrange a boat ride to the island (about B300 per person for a return trip) or else book a guided tour directly with the Naga Pearl Farm.

PHUKET'S INTERIOR

Most visitors confine themselves to Phuket's beaches and see little else of the island. This is a pity, as the interior is filled with lush, jungle-covered hills interspersed with rubber and pineapple plantations. Phuket's compact size and relatively good roads will allow you to access trails through rainforest to take a dip at hidden waterfalls and still be back at your beachside hotel come nightfall.

Thalang

About 12km (7 miles) north of Phuket Town is a large roundabout along Thanon Thepkrasattri (Route 402), with the striking statues of two women encircled by flags. Called the **Heroines' Monument**, these figures stand proud with drawn swords, honouring Lady Chan and Lady Muk, the widow of the

governor of Phuket and her sister, who led the successful defence of the island against the invading Burmese in 1785.

The statues mark the entry into the **Thalang** district. Thalang Town itself is rather run-down, but it is a district steeped in history, having moved from several different locations before taking up its current position in the geographical centre of Phuket in 1894. A short distance northeast of the monument is **Thalang Museum** (daily 9am–4pm; charge). Everything from Phuket's prehistoric cave dwellers and its ethnic diversity as a maritime crossroads, to the island's invasion by the Burmese and the great tin-mining boom of the 19th century are recounted here.

Return to Route 402 and continue to **Thalang Town**. Just a little north beyond the main crossroads is one of Phuket's most famous temples, **Wat Phra Thong** ❷⓼ (daily 8am–6pm; free). Inside is the statue of a golden Buddha that is half buried in the ground. From the chest up it measures about 2 metres (7ft). Over the years, thanks to stories circulating that the Buddha image was cast

in gold, many people, including an invading Burmese army, have tried to dig it out of the ground. To date, none have succeeded in unearthing it, and most have met with grisly deaths, or so the story goes, as a result of a curse associated with the image. The statue is, in fact, made of brick and plaster, with a thin layer of gold covering it.

Khao Phra Taew National Park

East of Thalang Town is **Khao Phra Taew National Park** ❷ (daily 6am–6pm; charge), a pretty but hardly spectacular protected reserve. This is Phuket's largest tract of virgin rainforest and covers an area of 22 sq km (8½ sq miles). A leisurely 20-minute walk from the park's entrance leads to **Bang Bae Waterfall**. It's a nice spot for lunch and a swim, but not overly remarkable as it's neither high nor carries much water, and at certain times of year is totally dry. A further 3km (2 miles) along the same route is **Ton Sai Waterfall**, which, although more impressive, is also at risk of drying up during the summer months.

The rainforest is particularly lush during the rainy season when the greenery is more vibrant. Guides are available at the information centre at the park entrance and should be used for treks; unless you are an expert, the telltale signs of wildlife are easy to miss. Tigers and bears once roamed the park, but today it is far more common to see monkeys, civets and other small animals.

Gibbon Rehabilitation Centre

A 15–20-minute walk from Bang Pae Waterfall leads to the **Gibbon Rehabilitation Centre** ❸ (daily 10am–4pm; free; www.warthai.org). This is a non-profit organisation that aims to stop the poaching of Thailand's gibbons for tourist attractions and the pet trade. The gibbons are kept in large enclosures, but as the whole purpose is to reintroduce them to the wild, it's not possible to see them up close. Although located within the national park, the Gibbon Rehabilitation Centre receives none of the money from park fees and relies solely on donations from visitors. ❑

Gibbons kept as pets are reintroduced to the wild by Phuket's Gibbon Rehabilitation Centre.

BELOW: water buffalos at Khao Phra Taew National Park.

RESTAURANTS AND BARS

Restaurants

Price per person for a three-course meal without drinks:
$ = under B300
$$ = B300–800
$$$ = B800–1,600
$$$$ = over B1,600

Phuket Town

International
Salvatore's
15–17 Th. Rasada. Tel: 0-7622 5958. Open: daily except Mon L & D. $$–$$$
www.salvatoresrestaurant.com
Watching owner/chef Salvatore at work in the kitchen, it is easy to see why *Tatler Thailand* voted this the country's (not just the island's) best Italian restaurant. Begin with the gnocchi with lamb sauce, followed with homemade ice cream and round off with freshly ground Italian coffee. The tables in its rustic interior are fully booked most nights, so reservations are recommended.

Watermark Bar Restaurant
22/1 Moo 2, Th. Thepkasattri. Tel: 0-7623 9730. Open: daily L & D. $$$
www.watermarkphuket.com
Overlooking the yachts at the Boat Lagoon Marina, the atmosphere in this dockside retreat is chic, and although the clientele is a bit pretentious, the food is not. Just about everything on the menu is delicious; the fresh mint and green pea risotto with baby prawns is particularly good.

Thai
Tung-Ka Hill Top Restaurant
Rang Hill, Th. Korsimbi. Tel: 0-7621 1500. Open: daily 11am–11pm. $
Perched on the peak of Rang Hill is this popular restaurant, now in operation for more than 30 years. *Plaa nueng menao* (steamed lemon fish) is particularly good, and although the wine list is limited there is no corkage fee if you bring a bottle. Most impressive at night, when Phuket Town becomes a mass of twinkling lights.

Ao Bang Thao

International
The Red Room
293/25–6 Th. Srisoonthorn. Tel: 0-7627 1136. Open: daily L & D. $$–$$$
Despite the enticing red glow on the outside, giving it an alarming brothel-like appearance, the red candles and red walls within create a rather seductive ambience. Try the fillet of salmon drizzled with champagne lemon dill sauce, or the tuna with capsicum and garlic sauce. Features live jazz on Friday evenings.

The Supper Club
Unit 20/382 Th. Srisoonthorn. Tel: 0-7627 0936. Open: daily 6pm–1am. $$$–$$$$
Chic ambience with food to match. Serves mouth-watering meat dishes including grilled tenderloin of beef and rack of lamb, as well as tasty vegetarian options. The goat's cheese with pesto balsamic dressing is simply divine.

Hat Kamala

International
Rockfish
33/6 Hat Kamala. Tel: 0-7627 9732. Open: daily 8am–late. $$$–$$$$
Trendy food at reasonable prices, considering *Tatler Thailand's Best Restaurants 2005* guide voted this three-storey open-sided house Phuket's top eatery. Despite some flashy dishes such as kingfish wrapped in spinach leaves with red curry sauce, the atmosphere is casual and the sunset beach views are lovely.

Hat Patong

Indian
Baluchi
Horizon Beach Resort, Soi Kep Sap. Tel: 0-7629 2526. Open: daily L & D. $$
Phuket's only award-winning Indian restaurant serves authentic north Indian dishes. Set menus available for lunch and dinner as well as extensive a là carte selection. Mutton *rogan gosh* is the house speciality, although the *tandoori nisa* (barbecued tiger prawns) is also very impressive.

International
Baan Yin Dee
7/5 Th. Muean Ngen. Tel: 0-7629 4104. Open: daily 7am–midnight. $$$
www.baanyindee.com
Grand piano music accompanies an elevated

LEFT: Kang Eang II Seafood restaurant, Ao Chalong.

view of the bay to create an intimate atmosphere inside this elegant restaurant. Serves innovative fusion cuisine such as yellow curry prawns with Cointreau and apples, and good Thai food toned down slightly for delicate palates.

Da Maurizio
223/2 Th. Prabaramee. Tel: 0-7634 4079. Open: daily noon–midnight. **$$$$**
www.damaurizio.com
One of the finest of Phuket's restaurants with waves breaking on rocks close to tables and flickering candlelight bouncing off the interior cave-like walls. Food is exquisite – start with the bacon-wrapped goat's cheese and savour it with a glass of chilled crisp white wine – it simply doesn't get any better. Advance bookings are essential.

Thai
Baan Rim Pa
223 Th. Prabaramee. Tel: 0-7634 0789. Open: daily noon–midnight. **$$$–$$$$**
www.baanrimpa.com
Famous cliff-hugging restaurant in the style of an old teak house. Known for its ambience and quality food. Serves outstanding – and expensive – Royal Thai cuisine, retaining all the flavour but without the chilli kick. Arrive early and have a drink on the terrace while enjoying the sea views. Reservations are essential.

Savoey Seafood
136 Th. Thawiwong. Tel: 0-7634 1171. Open: daily L & D. **$$**
www.savoeyseafood.com
Impossible to miss with its prime beachfront location and elaborate outdoor displays of fresh fish

and ridiculously huge "Phuket lobsters". Selected seafood is whisked away and returned cooked to your liking, whether deep-fried, grilled or steamed with Thai herbs.

International
Las Margaritas Grill
528/7 Th. Patak. Tel: 0-7628 6400. Open: daily L & D. **$$**
www.Las-Margaritas.net
Fusion cuisine from as far across the globe as Mexico, India, Hawaii, the Mediterranean and of course Thailand. Of the extensive selection of dishes, the Mexican offerings are the best. The sizzling chicken *fajitas* go down particularly well with a bottle of Corona.

Wildfire
509 Th. Patak. Tel: 0-7639 6139. Open: daily B, L & D. **$$**
Split-level restaurant combining four dining options in one place: haute cusine restaurant; bar and delicatessen; a Brazilian-style grill; and a pizzeria with a wood-fired oven serving freshly baked pizzas by the beach.

Thai & Western
On The Rock
Marina Phuket Resort. Tel: 0-7633 0625. Open: daily B, L & D. **$$**
Cosy little restaurant within the Marina Phuket Resort, aptly named after the sea-facing rocks on which its elevated deck rests. Menu is predominantly Thai with a few Western dishes. Reservations recommended.

Red Onion
486 Th. Patak. Tel: 0-7639 6827. Open: daily B, L & D. **$**

Although similar in appearance to its competitors on either side of the road, the food is better and the staff friendlier at this open-air eatery. The Western options are mostly on the mediocre side, but Thai classics like *gaeng keow waan gai* (green chicken curry), washed down with Thailand's favourite Chang beer, are all brilliant.

International
Capannina
30/9 Moo 2, Th. Kata. Tel: 0-7628 4318. Open: daily noon–11pm. **$$**
Italian-managed terracotta-and-mustard coloured eatery serving the usual Italian fare: antipasti, fresh breads, homemade pasta and risotto. The real draws, though, are the huge stone-fired oven pizzas. The large measures a whopping 60cm (24ins) in diameter.

Mom Tri's Boathouse Wine & Grill
182 Th. Kata. Tel: 0-7633 0015. Open: daily D only. **$$$–$$$$**
www.boathousephuket.com
This is an internationally acclaimed restaurant with a panoramic view of Kata Bay. It features a fine, if somewhat pricey, wine list, although its zesty vodka sorbet is just as impressive. Serves a selection of well-prepared Thai, European and seafood dishes – try the exquisite Rock Lobster Trilogy.

Seafood
Mali Seafood Restaurant and Bar
20/10 Kata Rd, Kata Beach. Tel: 0-7628 4404. Open: daily 11am–midnight. **$**
The name says it all:

smart location, decor, menu and service. There is a second branch in Karon – both are equally good.

International
L'Orfeo
95/13 Soi Saiyuan. Tel: 0-7628 8935. Open: daily except Wed, D only. **$$**
A wonderfully romantic spot if you can get a table. Sirloin tips are a house speciality, served on wooden chopping boards with a choice of sauce. The desserts change regularly, but keep an eye out for the zesty lemon mascarpone mousse.

International
The Green Man Pub and Restaurant
82/15 Moo 4, Th. Patak. Tel: 0-7628 1445. Open: daily 11am–2am. **$$**
www.the-green-man.net
Owner Howard Digby-Johns's eccentricities, raucous laugh and zest for life keep patrons coming back for more at this English-style pub with a menu so huge it comes in a ring binder. Traditional Sunday roast and Friday curry nights. The giant onion *bhajis* are a meal in themselves.

Thai
Kang Eang II Seafood
9/3 Th. Chaofa. Tel: 0-7638 1323. Open: daily 10am–10pm. **$**
Seafood restaurant directly overlooking the sea where a small fireworks display erupts at 8pm nightly, making it the perfect place for a birthday or anniversary celebration. Mostly seafood either barbecued or steamed and accompanied by a variety of sauces.

KRABI, KO PHI PHI AND KO LANTA

Visually striking, yet still off the beaten track,
Krabi and its islands present one of the more
charming and intriguing facets of Thailand

KRABI PROVINCE

Krabi – a province that embraces
both the mainland and some
idyllic islands – is unique among
Thai destinations. Characterised by
unique limestone formations and
lush vegetation, it sprawls 4,708 sq km
(1,818 sq miles) to the east of Phuket.
Parts of mainland Krabi were once submerged under water millions of years
ago. As a direct result of changing sea
levels, these areas evolved to become
land, while previously flat plains were
sculpted over time into towering limestone peaks. Scattered in the waters
of the Andaman Sea, including at Ao
Phang Nga *(see page 226)*, are hundreds
of these stunning sheer-sided limestone outcrops, known as karsts. As a
result, Krabi is a popular destination
for sports enthusiasts who scale these
challenging rock faces.

Many of the islands around Krabi
Province are tiny or uninhabited, the best
known being **Ko Phi Phi** and **Ko Lanta**,
where the beaches are spectacular.

Krabi mainland is blessed with a
string of white-sand beaches that attract
thousands during the dry season from
November to April *(see margin tip, page
259)*. Inland lush rainforests harbour
rare birds and wildlife. Camera crews
often travel miles to take advantage of
Krabi's stunning surroundings for com-
mercials, television shows and movies.

While Krabi has its own airport, the
area is still less developed than Phuket,
and getting off the beaten track (with
the exception of Phi Phi) is a lot easier
than might be expected.

Krabi Town

Located some 180km (112 miles) from
Phuket, **Krabi Town ❶** is the main
jump-off point for travellers en route
to the beaches and islands of Krabi
Province. Thanon Maharat, which is
the central point in the busy and compact town, hosts both the main market

Main attractions
WAT THAM SEUA
KHAO PHANOM BENCHA NATIONAL PARK
THA POM
THANBOKE KORANEE NATIONAL PARK
HOT SPRINGS WATERFALL
HAT RAILAY WEST
HAT THAM PHRA NANG
KO PHI PHI DON
KO PHI PHI LEY
AO MAYA
KO LANTA
MU KO LANTA NATIONAL PARK

LEFT: scenery on Railay Bay, Krabi.
RIGHT: biker family.

Buddha statue at Wat Tham Seua.

BELOW: rowing through mangroves in Krabi.

and most of the restaurants and shops. A concentration of guesthouses and hotels are to be found on Thanon Chao Fa, a few minutes' walk from **Chao Fa Pier**. The pavements around Chao Fa Pier become a bustling hub in the evenings when grills are fired up and saucepans and woks clatter to whip up a feast of freshly caught seafood.

At the bottom of Krabi Town, **Thara Park** overlooks the **Krabi River**. The river's opposite bank is a thicket of dense mangroves, while a small fishing community lives in wooden huts raised on stilts. Longtail boats can be hired at Chao Fa Pier to explore these mangroves, which shelter many types of fish, crabs, shrimps and shellfish, and are important nesting grounds for hundreds of bird species.

Most tours of the mangroves will stop at the **Khao Khanab Nam ❷**. The two 100-metre (328ft) limestone pinnacles that rise dramatically from the side of Krabi River have come to represent the town, and indeed Krabi Province. Legend has it that two ceremonial *krabi* (swords) were discovered here in ancient times. Inside one of the peaks

a series of caves reveal impressive formations of stalactites and stalagmites. Skeletons – thought to be the remains of people who took refuge here before being cut off by a massive flood – were discovered in one of the caves, though they have long since been removed.

KRABI'S INTERIOR

Wat Tham Seua

More commonly referred to as "Tiger Cave Temple", **Wat Tham Seua ❸** (daily 8am–6pm; charge) was founded by Jamnien Silasettho, a monk and teacher of meditation. The temple is set amid forests and cliffs 9km (6 miles) from Krabi Town and is easily reached by car or motorbike. At the rear of the temple a concrete staircase comprising some 1,272 steps leads to the top of the 600-metre (1,970ft) peak where a small shrine contains a footprint of the Buddha immortalised in a flat rock. The hour-long ascent is exhausting, but the fantastic view of the surrounding area at the top makes up for it. A second staircase, next to a large statue of Kwan Im, the Chinese goddess of mercy, takes you on a different route up 1,237 steps.

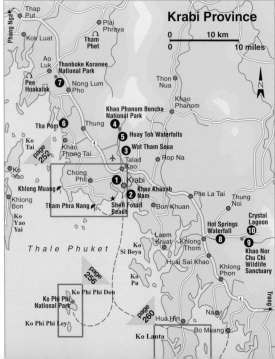

Krabi Province

0   10 km
0   10 miles

Khao Phanom Bencha N P

Covering an area of about 50 sq km (19 sq miles), **Khao Phanom Bencha National Park** ❹ (daily 8am–6pm; charge) lies some 20km (12 miles) to the north of Krabi Town. The park is the site of the dramatic 1,397-metre (4,583ft) limestone karst called **Khao Phanom Bencha**. The reserve lists 218 species of birds and 32 mammals including leopards, Asiatic black bears and even tigers, although sightings of the last are rare. The waterfalls flowing down the mountain slopes are another of the park's attractions, the main one being the 11-tiered **Huay Toh Waterfalls** ❺. Situated near the park headquarters, the tiers are at varying heights, with the highest at 80 metres (262ft).

Tha Pom

Some 34km (21 miles) north from Krabi Town is an unusual canal often referred to as **Tha Pom** ❻ (daily 8am–6pm; charge). On signages leading to this attraction, however, the name appears as **Tha Pom Khlong Song Nam**, which translates as "Canal of Two Waters". A 700-metre (2,300ft) boardwalk takes you on a trail past mangrove and forest, eventually leading to the main attraction, a stream of clear water with two distinct colours. The water will appear colourless in poor weather, but on a good day, when the sun's rays penetrate the water, it creates a seemingly invisible line between its turquoise-blue and emerald-green layers. This phenomenon apparently occurs during high tide when tidal seawater meets fresh spring water running off the mountainside.

Thanboke Koranee N P

About 45km (28 miles) northwest of Krabi Town, **Thanboke Koranee National Park** ❼ (daily 8am–6pm; charge) is popular for its many caves and waterfalls. One of the park's highlights is the cave called **Tham Pee Huakalok**, where an oversized human skull was found over half a century ago. Superstitious locals believe that the ghost of this head dwells within the cave, hence its name – *pee* is Thai for ghost, *hua* means head and *kalok* is skull. The walls of the cave are embellished with hundreds of colourful cave paintings and prehistoric drawings, estimated by archaeologists to

Map opposite

TIP

Longtail boat coxswains tend to be long on boat-handling skills and fairly short on general cheeriness. Don't hesitate to bargain hard for fares, and make sure the coxswain is quite clear about the destination.

BELOW: monks at Wat Tham Seua.

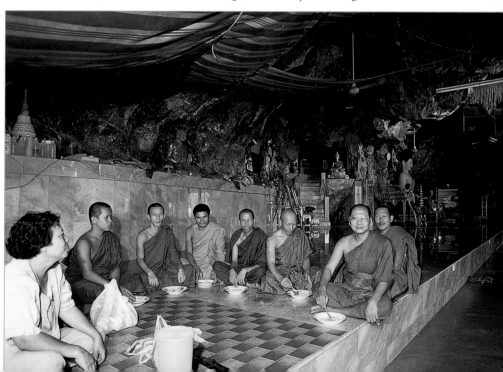

A free back massage at Krabi's Hot Springs Waterfall.

be between 2,000 and 3,000 years old. Accessible by boat from **Bor Tor Pier**, 7km (4 miles) south of nearby Ao Luk, the cave burrows deep into a hill surrounded by water and mangroves.

Hot Springs Waterfall

Some 55km (34 miles) southeast of Krabi Town, past the town of Khlong Thom on Highway 4, is another unusual phenomenon, the **Hot Springs Waterfall ⑧** (daily 8am–5pm; charge). This is where an underground hot spring leaks water through the earth's surface and cascades down smooth boulders. It is quite an experience to let the soothing warm water wash over you before you take a dip in the cool waters of the stream, a sort of a natural hydrotherapy in the middle of the jungle. It's a popular place to relax in but is relatively small and can get crowded around lunchtime when large tour groups arrive.

Khao Nor Chu Chi Wildlife Sanctuary

A 10-minute drive east of the Hot Springs Waterfall, the **Khao Nor Chu Chi Wildlife Sanctuary ⑨** (daily

8am–5pm; charge) is also known as Khao Pra Bang Khram Wildlife Sanctuary. This is said to be the last patch of lowland rainforest in Thailand and one of the few locations in the world where the endangered bird species *Gurneys Pitta* can be found.

A 3km (2-mile) trail from the park leads through a shaded path to **Crystal Lagoon ⑩**. Bacteria and algae living in this emerald-coloured pond cause a variation of colours, ranging from pale green where the temperature is cooler to a greenish blue where the temperature peaks at around 50°C (122°F). It's safe to swim here, but the calcium carbonates in the water make it unsuitable for drinking, and a sign at the entrance asks bathers to refrain from using shampoo or soap. Enter the pond slowly and be careful of slippery moss at the water's edge.

KRABI'S BEACHES

Hat Khlong Muang and Hat Noppharat Thara

Only a handful of small hotels are fortunate enough to share the secluded beach of **Hat Khlong Muang ⓐ**. Rocky

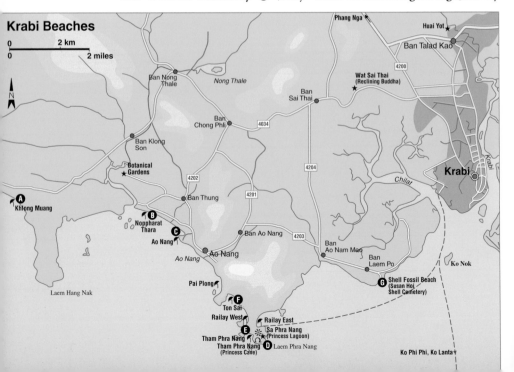

Krabi Beaches

0 ___ 2 km
0 ___ 2 miles
N

in parts and backed by lush vegetation, this beach is very quiet. Set outside Krabi Town (but only a 30-minute drive away), it has clean waters that are pleasant to swim in year-round. Most of the accommodation at Hat Khlong Muang is simple save for the five-star **Sheraton Krabi** (popular for its resident elephant and alfresco cinema shows) and the boutique-style luxury **Nakamanda** resort.

A finger of land called Hang Nak Cape separates Hat Khlong Muang from **Hat Noppharat Thara** ❸, the next beach, which enjoys uninterrupted views out towards a cluster of limestone islands. Shady casuarinas back this 2km (1-mile) long beach, and seafood vendors gather around the car park. The western end of the beach is quiet and, because it is separated by a canal, can only be accessed by longtail boat. The middle section is similarly peaceful, with a visitors' centre and the park headquarters, while the eastern section is the busiest.

Ao Nang

A few minutes' drive from Hat Noppharat Thara, and sharing the same view of the limestone cliffs in the distance, albeit obstructed by a line of longtail boats, **Ao Nang** ❸ is the most commercial and developed beach on mainland Krabi. Located 22km (14 miles) east of Krabi Town, it gets a little crowded in the high season but is not yet so built up as to be totally ruined.

Ao Nang beach is very ordinary, and would be nicer were it not for the longtail boats congesting its shore; at high tide there is very little space to relax. The quiet is also shattered by the piercing drone from the longtail boat engines. North of the beach is a cluster of open-air seafood restaurants, usually owned by the small hotels behind them. Other restaurants serving mostly Thai and Italian food are found along the main beach road.

Laem Phra Nang (Railay Bay)

Surrounded by sheer limestone cliffs on three sides and only accessible by boat, the peninsula of **Laem Phra Nang** ❹,

The Krabi coastline is strewn with islands which make for fun exploration. Most tour agencies sell the well-known "Krabi Four Islands" tour, covering Ko Poda, Ko Tup, Ko Kai and Phra Nang Cave.

BELOW: view of Hat Railay East and West beaches.

TIP

Check the tide before scaling the cliff towards the viewpoint *(see below)* high above Hat Tham Phra Nang. When the tide is at Hat Railay East, it makes for much more stunning views from the top.

better known as **Railay Bay**, feels more like an island paradise than the mainland beach that it actually is. This stunning peninsula has four beaches, each with crystal-clear turquoise waters, powder-white sands and sheer-sided limestone cliffs that seemingly melt into the waters below, making it one of the world's leading rock-climbing destinations.

Hat Railay West and Hat Railay East

Most arriving boats head straight to the western side of the peninsula, to **Hat Railay West**. The absence of a pier demands a short wade to the shore, but this has fortunately also prevented ferryloads of day-trippers landing on its pristine white sands. Although still developing, Railay West is a world away from nearby Ao Nang. Its lodgings are of a better class (no ramshackle guesthouses here), which has helped prevent it from turning into a busy backpacker haunt. Accommodation is more expensive than on the other Krabi beaches, but that is the premium to be paid for direct access to such a lovely beach.

On the opposite side of the peninsula is **Hat Railay East**. Backed by dense mangroves, this is a less scenic beach and is unsuitable for swimming due to the incredibly low tides and the jagged rocks along the foreshore. Still, the lower-priced bungalows here get their fair share of trade. Access between the two Railay beaches is easy – a 5-minute walk along a flat paved pathway takes you from one beach to the other. The same people appreciating the mango-streaked sunsets on Railay West are often seen a few hours later enjoying fire shows and all-night parties at Railay East.

Hat Tham Phra Nang

The prettiest beach on Railay Bay, if not the whole of Thailand, is **Hat Tham Phra Nang ❺**, where the extravagant and ultra-expensive **Rayavadee Resort** occupies prime position (there is no other accommodation here). Set amid 11 hectares (26 acres) of coconut groves and surrounded by towering limestone cliffs, Tham Phra Nang is endowed with the softest of white sands, limpid turquoise-blue waters and beautiful coral reefs offshore. Although staying at the Rayavadee gives you the most direct access to this beach, many day-trippers from Railay West and Railay East flock to Tham Phra Nang to sunbathe, swim and snorkel.

Hat Tham Phra Nang is named after a princess (*phra nang*) who locals believe resides in the area. Near the Rayavadee Resort, at the beach's eastern end, is **Tham Phra Nang** (Princess Cave), where a collection of wooden phallic-shaped objects sit as an offering to her, its supplicants hoping she will bestow the surrounding mountains and sea with fertility. The cave is not as spectacular as it's made out to be, and is actually little more than a series of small overhangs, but a map at its base highlights the way towards a **viewpoint** (*see also margin tip, above left*) and **Sa Phra Nang** (Princess Lagoon), which are both far more impressive.

BELOW: Hat Tham Phra Nang beach, Railay.

The route to each of these sights is straightforward, but neither is suitable for the young, elderly or unfit, and good footwear is a must. The most challenging part of the walk is at the beginning, which involves clinging to ropes to clamber up a fairly steep incline; after this, the pathway becomes easier to follow. Veering to the left as the pathway splits leads to a viewpoint with spectacular vistas of the east and west bays of Railay. Continuing straight leads to a sharp rock face with yet more ropes, this time used almost to abseil down into the Princess Lagoon. The lagoon is suitable for swimming, but it is not crystal-clear and does contain some rocks.

Hat Ton Sai

From Hat Railay West, it is possible at low tide to walk to the nearby **Hat Ton Sai F**. Longtail boats can also be hired to make the 5-minute journey, or if you are feeling energetic, you may simply swim to the beach. Budget travellers are attracted to Ton Sai by its cheaper accommodation and convivial atmosphere. Of all the beaches

on the Laem Phra Nang headland, Ton Sai has the most vibrant nightlife, with beach bars open until the early hours and monthly full-moon parties. The view out to sea is as beautiful as that of Railay's, with limestone monoliths in the foreground and to the sides, but the sand is not as white, and at low tide the beach becomes muddy and makes swimming difficult.

Rock climbing

Sheer limestone cliffs facing mile upon mile of tranquil sea make Railay Bay a favoured spot for rock climbers. Most of the 650 or so routes that have developed since Krabi's cliffs were first scaled by sports climbers in the late 1980s are located in this peninsula. Among the most popular climbs is the challenging yet phenomenal **Thaiwand Wall** on the southern end. There are a range of other climbs suited for beginners right through to professionals, involving limestone crags, steep pocketed walls, overhangs and hanging stalactites.

Any of the climbing operations around Railay will advise on the best

Winches and hooks for rock climbing.

BELOW: rock climbing at Railay Bay.

Rock 'n' Roll

When foreigners started climbing Krabi's extraordinary rock formations for fun, a group of young Thais decided they also wanted to get in on this new, exciting daredevil act. Lead by Somporn "King" Suebhait and Somyod "Tex" Thongkeaw, they learnt as much as they could from the visitors and were soon climbing on their own.

Many of the new local climbers had previously served an apprenticeship in *muay thai*, and the strength, speed and flexibility they had picked up as boxers in the ring stood them in good stead on the cliff face. Some of the early Thai pioneers are now running their very own mountaineering schools in Krabi, passing back the tricks of the trade they acquired from overseas visitors to novice foreigners.

climbs, some of which are accessed by a combination of boat and a hike through the jungle.

Shell Fossil Beach

Approximately 17km (11 miles) from Krabi Town, the entrance to **Shell Fossil Beach ⑥** (also known as Susan Hoi Shell Cemetery) is marked by a small Chinese temple. Extending right to the edge of the sea are the remnants of a 75-million-year accumulation of seashell deposits – which look like large concrete slabs from afar. This phenomenon can only be seen at two other locations worldwide, one in Japan and the other in the US; the one in Krabi is the only coastal site. While it is not extraordinary to look at, many people appreciate how extraordinary it is to witness evidence of life that existed millions of years before man.

KO PHI PHI

Lying in the Andaman Sea between the main hubs of Phuket and Krabi (about two hours by boat from either location) are the twin islands that make **Ko Phi Phi**. The two islands –

the larger **Ko Phi Phi Don** and the smaller **Ko Phi Phi Ley** – are part of the protected **Mu Ko Phi Phi National Park**, but somehow development, especially on Ko Phi Phi Don, seems to have run wild over the years, playing havoc with its natural beauty. From afar though, the islands are still stunning with their mountains and lovely arcs of soft white sand washed by gin-clear waters. Ko Phi Phi Don hosts all the accommodation and facilities, while Ko Phi Phi Ley is uninhabited and mainly visited on day trips.

The islands' rise to fame is characterised by both fortune and tragedy. As recently as in 1998, Ko Phi Phi was still considered a quiet, idyllic retreat. Turquoise waters bordering limestone cliffs and palm-tree-filled interiors made it a postcard-perfect location. Then came the major blockbuster film *The Beach*, which was shot mainly at **Ao Maya** (Maya Bay) on Ko Phi Phi Ley in 1998. Within one year, thousands were flocking to Ao Maya in the hope of seeing this Utopian image of the perfect unspoilt beach. While Ko Phi Phi Ley was spared development,

The Shell Fossil Beach at Krabi.

BELOW:
approaching the pier at Ko Phi Phi Don island.

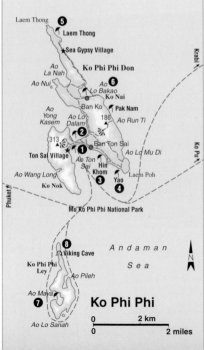

Laem Thong **⑤**
Laem Thong
★ Sea Gypsy Village
Ao
La Nah
Ko Phi Phi Don
Ao Nui
Ao **⑥**
Lo Bakao
Ko Nai
Ban Ko ✦ Pak Nam
Ao
Yong
Kasem
Ao Lo
Dalam
186 Ao Run Ti
②
313 ⌂
Ban Ton Sai
Ton Sai Village
①
Ao Lo Mu Di
Ao Ton
Sai
Hin
Khom
Ao Wang Long
③
Yao
Laem Poh
Ko Nok
④
Mu Ko Phi Phi National Park
⑧
🜄 Viking Cave
A n d a m a n
Ko Phi Phi
Ley
S e a
Ao Pileh
Ao Maya
⑦
Ko Phi Phi
Ao Lo Sanah
0   2 km
0   2 miles

Krabi ➤
Phuket ➤
Ko Phi ➤

it suffered from overcrowding and this took a toll on its ecology. The larger Ko Phi Phi Don also saw a rash of construction – resorts, restaurants and bars built quickly to cater to the constant onslaught of tourists.

There are no roads on the island, so walking is generally the only way to get around. Most dive sites around Ko Phi Phi were unaffected by the 2004 tsunami, and it remains one of Thailand's most popular diving locations.

Ko Phi Phi Don

Ko Phi Phi Don is made up of two elongated islands joined together by a narrow isthmus to create what looks from the air like a giant high-backed chair. Most development is concentrated on the bays found on either side of the isthmus – Ao Ton Sai and Ao Lo Dalam.

Boats to the island dock at the pier at **Ao Ton Sai ❶**, a bay that would be far prettier were it not for the ferries and longtail boats lining it from one end to the other. Information booths cluster at the end of the pier, beyond which **Ton Sai village** comprises a compact area of restaurants, bars, dive shops, internet cafés and stalls selling everything from sarongs and beaded jewellery to sandwiches and banana pancakes. Opposite Ao Ton Sai and only a few minutes' walk away **Ao Lo Dalam ❷** is a quieter and prettier bay with a lovely curve of white sand skimming clear blue waters. What makes it even nicer is that, following the tsunami, reconstruction along Ao Lo Dalam has been slower compared to Ao Ton Sai.

Although **Hat Hin Khom ❸**, located at the western end of Ao Ton Sai, and scenic **Hat Yao ❹** (Long Beach), at the southwestern tip of the island, were similarly hit by the tsunami, the damage was less severe and the hotels were able to rebuild more quickly. Access to Hat Yao is either by longtail boat (10 minutes) from Ton Sai or a 40-minute walk.

All the beaches along the eastern side of Ko Phi Phi Don were left unscathed by the tsunami. The best snorkelling and the most exclusive resorts are found to the northeast of the island on **Hat Laem Thong ❺**, where the majority

TIP

Buying seashells, or taking them from the shore, strips Thailand's ecology, and encourages greedy entrepreneurs. Take a photo instead.

BELOW: beach activity on Ao Lo Dalam.

Harvesting prized birds' nests at the Viking Cave in Ko Phi Phi Ley.

BELOW: magnificent Maya Bay.

of visitors are either honeymooners or those seeking a more isolated beach. The beach is beautiful and quiet, but as boat transportation is scarce in these parts, it is difficult to get to the other parts of the island from here. Hat Laem Thong is also the home of a small community of *chao lay* or sea gypsies *(see page 224)*.

South of Hat Laem Thong, **Ao Lo Bakao ❻** contains mainly upmarket accommodation on its quiet beach, including the luxury all-suite **Zeavola Resort**. Further south is **Hat Pak Nam** and **Hat Ranti**, which are very low key and have scant accommodation.

Inland attractions are limited but many people take the 30-minute hike over to the **viewpoint** located high on a bluff at the southern end of Ao Lo Dalam. To get there, follow the path eastwards towards Hat Hin Khom and turn left when it forks inland. Understandably, the scenic point is at its busiest around sunrise and sunset; from here the vista of the twin bays of Ao Ton Sai and Ao Lo Dalam, separated by a thin band of land with the mountain behind, is simply breathtaking.

Ko Phi Phi Ley

Uninhabited **Ko Phi Phi Ley** is a mere speck at 6.5 sq km (2½ sq miles). It lies about 4km (2 miles) south of Ko Phi Phi Don. Formed entirely from limestone, the island is surrounded by steep karsts rising out of the sea that circle it almost completely. Of the picturesque bays around the island, the most visited are **Ao Pileh** to the east and the aforementioned **Ao Maya ❼** on the west coast. Ao Maya would be a more beautiful spot if not for the day-trippers who descend here in droves and frequently leave their litter behind. It's best to get here very early in the morning, or late in the afternoon.

One of the major draws of Ko Phi Phi Ley is the **Viking Cave ❽** at the northeastern end of the island. The cave walls are inscribed with coloured chalk drawings of various boats, believed to have been sketched hundreds of years ago by pirates who used the cave as a shelter. Today, the pirates have been replaced by hundreds of swifts which build their nests in crevices high up on the steep cave walls. These nests are collected by local villagers who climb the

tall rickety ladders, risking life and limb, to collect the birds' nests, which are so highly prized by Chinese gourmets for their health-giving properties. Swarms of swifts descend on the caves of Ko Phi Phi Ley every year between January and April and build their nests using their saliva as a bonding material.

Diving and snorkelling

Many of the dive sites around Ko Phi Phi are the same ones that can be visited from Phuket, Krabi and Ko Lanta. Around Ko Phi Phi itself, the best diving and snorkelling sites are **Hin Bida** (Phi Phi Shark Point), **Ko Pai** (Bamboo Island), **Ko Yung** (Mosquito Island) and **Ao Maya** on the western side of Ko Phi Phi Ley. The **King Cruiser** wreck between the waters of Phuket and Ko Phi Phi is another favourite dive site.

KO LANTA YAI

Ko Lanta is the most remote, and as a result perhaps the most pleasant, part of Krabi Province. Stretching 27km (17 miles) in length and 12km (7 miles) in width, it is one of only three inhabited islands in an archipelago of over 50. Originally named Pulao Satak, meaning "Island with Long Beaches" by the *chao lay* (sea gypsies) who first settled on the island, the term Ko Lanta generally refers to the largest of these islands, Ko Lanta Yai.

Most backpackers to Ko Lanta travel direct from Krabi, where public ferries leave twice daily on a journey that takes about two hours and terminates at **Ban Sala Dan** village on Ko Lanta's northernmost tip. Running from north to south, the island's single main road passes along the western beaches while a few smaller roads lead inland towards the southeastern coast, where there are small settlements of sea gypsies. Development has mainly been confined to the west coast, where spectacular sunsets viewed from along a number of striking white-sand beaches are a near-daily certainty. The east coast is fringed by long stretches of mangroves and swimming is not advisable.

Ko Lanta will inevitably develop over time, but so far it has managed to retain its sleepy island feel. Phone reception is patchy, internet connections are slow and beach bungalows dominate over high-rise developments. The red-earth dirt tracks are slowly being replaced with tarred roads, making for easier access but invariably attracting more developers.

Ban Sala Dan

Whether arriving by passenger or car ferry, the first stop for most visitors is the main village of **Ban Sala Dan ❶**. Guests at the more exclusive resorts on Ko Lanta have the luxury of being delivered right to the doorstep, or rather shorestep, of their hotel by high-speed private boat transfers. Concrete posts and overhead electrical cables make Ban Sala Dan a rather unsightly place, but for a relatively small island it is well equipped with a police post, clinic, convenience stores, tour agents and internet facilities. Along the pier, a number of seafood restaurants display freshly caught seafood on beds of ice to draw customers.

TIP

The southwest monsoon brings heavy rain from May to Oct to the Andaman Coast, including Krabi, Ko Phi Phi and Ko Lanta. Room rates can drop by as much as half during the wet months, so some people take advantage of this and hope for the best. There can be intermittent days of sunshine between rainy spells.

BELOW: children at Ko Lanta.

Typical beach bar set-up along Hat Khlong Nin.

Hat Khlong Dao

A few kilometres south of Ban Sala Dan, **Hat Khlong Dao** ❷ is the first of the island's westerly beaches. Shallow waters and safe swimming conditions make this 3km (2-mile) stretch of beach a preferred choice with families, and there is plenty of mid-range accommodation. Its proximity to the pier at Ban Sala Dan also appeals to scuba-divers seeking easy access to nearby dive sites. Despite its attractions – white sand, picturesque hilly backdrop and some of the most dramatic sunsets along the western coast – Khlong Dao rarely seems crowded. The beach is wide enough that even in the peak season it's always possible to snag a relatively secluded spot.

Ao Phra Ae

Almost if not equally as popular as Khlong Dao, neighbouring **Ao Phra Ae** ❸ (Long Beach) is slightly longer at 4km (3 miles) and shaded by vast stretches of tall coconut and pine trees. Phra Ae is popular with swimmers and sunbathers, but parts of the seabed are a little steep, so families

with small children should be wary. There are lots of accommodation choices, including the luxury **Layana Resort & Spa**, and an ample variety of restaurants.

Hat Khlong Khong

Just south of Ao Phra Ae is laidback **Hat Khlong Khong** ❹. Although not great for swimming, it is one of the island's best beaches for snorkelling; at low tide the rocky underlay reveals an assortment of fish and other marine life. Accommodation is generally cheaper than on the more northern beaches, with an emphasis on clean but basic beachfront bungalows. Most have attached restaurants and beach bars that spring to life in the evenings, with tables set on the sand.

Hat Khlong Nin and Hat Khlong Hin

Turning right about 4km (2½ miles) from Hat Khlong Khong leads past a few convenience stores and restaurants before emerging at **Hat Khlong Nin** ❺. This lovely beach has a relaxed feel and the atmosphere

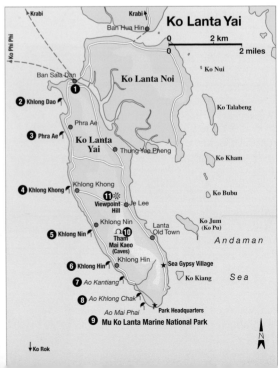

of a small, intimate village. The powdery white sands of Hat Khlong Nin stretch about 2km (1 mile) and calm waters – outside of the monsoon – make it excellent for swimming. Accommodation consists primarily of stylish resorts like **Sri Lanta** and the **Rawiwarin**, most with in-house restaurants and beach bars. At the start of Hat Khlong Nin is the popular reggae-style **Rasta Baby Bar**. A stroll along the beachfront reveals more of the same; at night, the next buzzing bamboo beach bar is never more than a short walk away.

At its southern end, Hat Khlong Nin merges with the much smaller and secluded **Hat Khlong Hin ❻**. Separated from the former by a cluster of trees, the waves here are rough during the monsoon season.

Ao Kantiang

About 6km (4 miles) from Hat Khlong Hin lies the picturesque bay of **Ao Kantiang ❼**. It has a secluded and private feel to it as the bay is framed on both sides and to the rear by jungle-covered hills. To the north and high

up on the hill are a handful of small stilted bungalows; there are lovely views from the top, but it also means climbing up a considerable number of steps. The southern end of this bay is anchored by the luxury **Pimalai Resort and Spa**. This five-star resort is set in 40 hectares (100 acres) of natural tropical surroundings and has direct access to the 1km (½-mile) long stretch of white-sand beach.

Ao Khlong Chak and Ao Mai Phai

Beyond Ao Kantiang, the further south one ventures, the more remote and consequently harder to reach the beaches become. Shortly after the Pimalai Resort, the road comes to an abrupt halt before morphing into a rugged dirt track; navigating it without the assistance of a four-wheel-drive vehicle is a near-impossibility. The reward is a cluster of some of the most scenic and underdeveloped beaches on the island, including **Ao Khlong Chak ❽**, one of the smallest beaches on the island at just 400 metres (1,310ft) long.

TIP

Several companies operate regular ferry services to Ko Phi Phi Don from Phuket and Krabi. The more expensive ones justify their higher prices with indoor air-conditioned areas. However, if the seas are rough, it's better to be on the outdoor decks with the bracing salty air blowing against you.

BELOW: picturesque Ao Kantiang is anchored by Pimalai Resort and Spa at one end.

Sea gypsy (chao lay) fisherman on Ko Jum mending his net.

BELOW: snorkelling near Ko Rok.

Only a small handful of budget to mid-range resorts are found here. During the monsoon season, Ao Khlong Chak is most famous for its waterfall, found 1½km (1 mile) inland.

Beyond this is a short but even bumpier drive leading to **Ao Mai Phai** (Bamboo Bay). This is the last beach before reaching the headquarters of Mu Ko Lanta Marine National Park on the southernmost tip. Its difficulty of access and geography – Ao Mai Phai is backed by mountains on three sides – gives this bay a real sense of isolation. The beach is only 500 metres (1,640ft) in length, but is ideal for swimming; a shallow boulder-strewn stretch at the northern edge is more suited to snorkelling. Only a few resorts are to be found here.

Mu Ko Lanta N P

Declared a national park in 1990, **Mu Ko Lanta Marine National Park ❾** comprises the southern tip of Ko Lanta Yai and 15 small surrounding islands. The southernmost tip of Ko Lanta comprises two beaches: **Laem Tanode** and the rocky **Hat Hin Ngam**; the latter hosts the park headquarters. A 2.5km (1½-mile) hiking trail leading along a cliff begins here and offers the chance of spotting local fauna like fruit bats, deer, wild pigs and reptiles. Also here is a small white lighthouse, from which there are scenic views out to the sea and mountains.

Snorkelling and diving

Some of Thailand's finest spots for snorkelling and scuba-diving are found in the waters off Ko Lanta. The most visited site for snorkelling, and considered by many to be one of Thailand's best, is **Ko Rok**, about 47km (29 miles) south of Ko Lanta. There are actually two islands, **Ko Rok Nai** and **Ko Rok Nok**, graced with powdery white-sand beaches and an extensive patch of coloured coral in between. Visibility is mostly very good, and many interesting types of reef fish can be found in these waters.

Approximately 20km (12 miles) from Ko Rok, the twin peaks of **Hin Daeng** and **Hin Muang** – frequently rated one of the world's top 10 dive sites – pierce the surface of the water.

Ko Lanta Cool

Bangkok's smart set – that is to say, its wealthy rather than merely its famous – has always had a weekend retreat. The location has changed over the years: at one stage it was Hua Hin; Ko Samet has also played its part as A-lister R&R; while Chiang Mai enjoyed a brief period in the top spot. But the popularity of Krabi, and specifically Ko Lanta, has proved enduring. All it takes is a Friday afternoon flight to the airport, followed by a speedboat transfer, and then you can spend a day or more away from the frantic carryings-on in the capital, well out of the gaze of prying paparazzi, and enjoy the luxury of first-rate accommodation and excellent food. Sunday sees an exodus northwards, when Ko Lanta returns to its more usual status as backwater.

An incredible variety of marine life thrives at this site. As the only outcrops in this area of deep open sea, the peaks also attract many pelagics, as well as large tuna and barracuda. Schools of grey reef sharks often approach divers, and the area has one of the highest incidences of whale-shark sightings in the world.

Inland diversions

There are limited attractions on Ko Lanta apart from its stunning beaches. Some 4km (2½ miles) south of Hat Khlong Khong, the road splits into two. The left fork leads all the way to the east coast of the island, where few tourists venture.

A turn-off at the 3km (2-mile) mark to the right leads to **Tham Mai Kaeo ⑩** caves. It is best to get your hotel to organise this trip, as finding the caves on your own is a bit of a challenge – you need to clamber up a steep hill, often with the help of tree branches. The combination of slippery paths, rickety bamboo ladders and confined spaces makes this an inadvisable activity for the physically challenged. The expedition leads through a labyrinth of winding tunnels and caverns, past dramatic rock formations. At the end, after negotiating a steep slope with the aid of a rope, is a deep pool, where you can cool off.

For early risers, a sunrise trip to the central peak referred to simply as **Viewpoint Hill ⑪** is worth the effort. To get there, continue on the road heading east, following the signs that are set at intervals along the way. The near-360-degree panoramic vista amid the crisp morning air is truly breathtaking. The experience can be enjoyed over a "sunrise breakfast" high on the hill at the **Khao Yai Restaurant**. The food is nothing to email home about, but gazing out towards the sea, you will barely realise that.

KO BUBU AND KO JUM

Those seeking an even quieter retreat should consider the smaller islands nearby. At 7km (4 miles) off the east coast of Ko Lanta, tiny **Ko Bubu** takes just 30 minutes to circumnavigate by foot. This uninhabited isle only has a basic restaurant and a few simple bungalows on the western coast, where the small but stunning gently sloping beach is ideal for swimming. Boat transfers can be arranged for guests of **Bubu Bungalows** (tel: 0-7561 2536), the only resort on the island; there is no other regular service. Longtail boats at Krabi and Ko Lanta can, however, be chartered for the journey.

Larger than Ko Bubu, but still small and pleasantly underdeveloped, is **Ko Jum** (Ko Pu) to the northwest of Ko Lanta. The island has powdery white-sand beaches and clear waters with plenty of healthy coral reefs. The best part is that it has yet to sustain any impact from tourism. Some 3,000 permanent residents earn a living mainly from fishing and the island's rubber plantations. Accommodation is limited to basic and mid-range bungalows, but due to the lack of facilities most people visit only for the day. ❑

TIP

If you plan to rent a jeep or a motorbike and explore Ko Lanta yourself, be sure to fill up with enough petrol before leaving the main village of Ban Sala Dan. The few petrol stations on Ko Lanta are expensive, difficult to find and shut annoyingly early.

BELOW: Ko Bubu at dusk.

RESTAURANTS AND BARS

Restaurants

Price per person for a three-course meal without drinks:
$ = under B300
$$ = B300–800
$$$ = B800–1,600
$$$$ = over B1,600

Krabi Town

International

Café Europa
Th. Maharat. Tel: 0-7562 0407. Open: Mon–Sat B, L & D. **$–$$**
This cosy café is something of an institution in Krabi Town. The limited menu is based around a few signature dishes, including pepper steak, meatballs and goulash, all served with salad and bread. Stacks of Thai and international newspapers and magazines.

Thai

Kotung
36 Th. Khong Kha. Tel: 0-7561 1522. Open: daily B, L & D. **$–$$**
Popular with locals, Kotung features a delectable array of Thai dishes with some southern Chinese influences.

Krabi Night Market
Soi 10, Th. Maharat. Open: daily D only. **$**
Probably the best food to be found in in Krabi Town, not to mention the restaurant least likely to burn a hole in your pocket. The *kaab moo* (pork leg), a delicious meaty dish simmered for hours in soy sauce and accompanied by green vegetables and rice, is a good bet.

Ruen Mai
Th. Maharat. Open: daily 11am–9pm. **$–$$**
Vegetarians love this place as staff can prepare, on request, meat-free versions of any dish on the menu. With a wide selection of unusual local vegetables, the adventurous can try stir-fried *sataw* ("stinky beans") in red curry paste, or wing bean spicy salad. Strong flavours and lashings of chilli are not sacrificed to protect sensitive palates; this is the way the locals eat.

Ao Nang (Krabi)

Thai

Aning
Ao Nang. Open: daily B, L & D. **$**
One of the few Thai restaurants that has managed to secure its place along the beach road dominated by Italian eateries. Its orange interior is flamboyant and the food is tasty without being tongue-lashingly fiery. Try the fluffy catfish salad and any of its delicious red or green curries. The seafood *tom yam* soup is fiery but consistently good, too.

Thai & Western

Azura Nova
142 Ao Nang. Tel: 0-7563 7848. Open: daily L & D. **$$**
Italian restaurants dominate Ao Nang's beach road, with this being the best. Owned by Italians, the food is as authentic as it can get. The pizzas, pastas and risottos are all recommended.

Chanaya's Thai-Dutch Restaurant
Ao Nang (opp Krabi Seaview Resort). Mobile tel: 08-9993 3716. Open: daily B, L & D. **$**
Quirky rainforest setting with an interior overflowing with plants, a pebbled floor and colourful birds in wooden cages swinging from the ceiling. Choices include salmon, steak and even ostrich. Delicious baguette sandwiches at lunchtime.

Moon Terrace
154 Moo 2, Ao Nang. Tel: 0-7563 7180. Open: daily D only.
Open-air seafood eatery on a wooden platform just a few feet from the water's edge. Arrive early to catch the setting sun. The seafood and fish served here are freshly caught every day. The white snapper is delicious and, although not on the menu, ask for it steamed with garlic and chilli.

Tanta
Ao Nang. Tel: 0-7563 7118. Open: daily L & D only.
Lovely thin-crust pizzas are the speciality here, but there are also pastas, salads, steaks and also a selection of Thai dishes.

Ko Phi Phi

Only restaurants at Ao Ton Sai beach are listed here. Eating out at the other beaches is largely confined to the hotel cafés and restaurants.

Thai

Pums Restaurant
Ton Sai Village. **$$**
One of Ton Sai's more stylish Thai eateries,

unlike most of the casual set-ups on the island. A large selection of well-presented Thai dishes, including the "Green Lipstick" and "Red Lipstick" (green and red curries).

Thai & Western
Mama's
Ton Sai Village.
Open: daily B, L & D. **$**
One of Phi Phi's mainstays, this French-owned and long-established restaurant, with bamboo walls, thatched roof and art on the walls, serves a mixed menu of Thai and Western favourites. The set menus are good value for money. Good selction of wines and beers. Friendly service.

Restaurant HC Andersen
Ton Sai Village, mobile tel: 08-4846 9010. Open: daily B, L & D. **$$**
www.phiphisteakhouse.com
Long-standing steakhouse with choice cuts of meats and delicious sauces. One of the island's better restaurants, it has a casual and welcoming feel, no doubt aided by the cheerful Matts from Denmark who runs it. Offers a massive choice of breakfasts, everything from Scandinavian to English and American.

Patcharee Bakery and Boulangerie
Ton Sai Village. Open: daily B, L & D. **$**
Less popular than the Phi Phi Bakery situated directly opposite yet just as good, this café serves Thai dishes and baked goods. Service is not as quick, but the atmosphere is far less hectic and there is a greater

chance of getting a table.

Phi Phi Bakery
Ton Sai Village. Open: daily B, L & D. **$**
Popular café with food that comes quickly and in large portions. Given its popularity, the restaurant could do with a facelift but the food is undeniably tasty. The "Phi Phi Bakery Combination" of sausages, sauerkraut, garlic bread, potatoes and salad, is guaranteed to cure hangovers. Sandwiches, pizza and pasta also feature on the menu, apart from cakes and pastries.

Ko Lanta
Only independent restaurants and cafés outside of the guesthouses and hotels are listed here.

Thai & Western
The Brit Café
Ao Phra Ae. Tel: 0-6946 8702. Open: daily B, L & D. **$–$$**
Blatantly British and proud of it, with Union flags on signs everywhere. This basic little café manages to pull in the crowds regularly with its traditional English breakfasts and pies. Packed during English football season as beer-swilling Brits gather around television sets.

Faim De Loup
255 Moo 2, Ao Prae Ae. Tel: 0-7568 4525. Open: daily B, L & D. **$**
Undeniably French in character, with glass cabinets containing pastries and sugar-laden buns served on blue-and-white checked tablecloths. Good coffee,

baguette sandwiches and salads. A great central location, and spoilt only slightly by its roadside location and lack of a view.

The Hut Restaurant
168 Moo 6, Hat Khlong Nin. Open: daily 8am–late. **$**
If the food doesn't captivate you, owner Dang will with her beaming smile. Trained by a Brit, the Thai staff are adept at cooking up Western dishes, and if the extensive menu is not enough, they are happy to cook whatever you fancy.

Lanta Seafood
73 Moo 1, Ban Sala Dan. Tel: 0-7568 4106. Open: daily L & D. **$$**
The seafood eateries along Sala Dan Pier have dishes that look much the same. Locals, however, seem to favour this place, with its snapper, prawns and squid, all served on tables directly overlooking the sea.

Red Snapper
Ao Phra Ae. Tel: 0-7885 6965. Open: daily L & D. **$$**
www.redsnapper-lanta.com
Alfresco-style restaurant with direct beach access from its leafy garden location. Blends European dishes with Thai herbs for an interesting East-West fusion effect. The menu changes every 6–8 weeks, but the seven entrees and eight main courses on offer are always delicious.

Same Same But Different
85 Moo 5, Ao Kan Tiang. Mobile tel: 08-1787 8670. Open: daily B, L & D. **$–$$**
Location is key to the popularity of this laid-back beach restaurant, with many customers strolling in from the neighbouring Pimalai resort. There is a good range of dishes – some slightly overpriced, but for guests staying at the expensive Pimalai resort it's still a bargain.

LEFT: fresh lobsters at a seafood restaurant.
RIGHT: outdoor cooking at Ko Phi Phi.

THE DEEP SOUTH

Here you will find picture-perfect beaches and be able to sample Thai-Muslim culture. Trang and Satun provinces shelter pristine islands, and historic Nakhon Si Thammarat was once capital of an ancient kingdom

Main attractions
TRANG TOWN
HAT CHANG LANG
THAM MORAKOT
KO KRADAN
KO LIBONG
KO TARUTAO MARINE
    NATIONAL PARK
SONGKHLA TOWN
NAKHON SI THAMMARAT

Misconceptions abound when it comes to Thailand's southern-most provinces. Among Thais, the predominantly Muslim residents are regarded as rough and prone to violence. The region is also one of the poorest in Thailand, with scant tourist infrastructure. Therefore, comparatively few outsiders, foreign or Thai, visit the area. Although there are some parts that should be expressly avoided – Narathi-wat, Yala and Pattani, which continue to suffer the effects of a Muslim separa-tist insurgency – the provinces covered in this chapter, especially Trang and Satun, are perfectly safe to visit. Exercise caution in Songkhla, however, as there are signs that the violence has spread there. Bomb attacks and similar vio-lent incidents have plagued the region, including prominent locations such as Hat Yai Airport. While the population in the countryside is mainly Muslim, there are large Chinese communities in the cities of all three provinces.

North of Songkhla along the Gulf of Thailand is Nakhon Si Thamma-rat Province, technically speaking not part of the Deep South and therefore spared from the violence experienced by the more southerly provinces.

TRANG

Trang Province holds what is probably the greatest variety of attractions of any of the provinces in the Deep South, as well as the main urban area, Trang Town. North of the province are pretty beaches and islands with ample accommodation, a wealth of outdoor activities and good food. To the south of Trang, the beaches and islands are more isolated but they do offer some fascinating wildlife and the chance to observe rural island life.

Trang Town

Trang Town ❶ is a pleasant place with a predominantly Chinese population and enough attractions to warrant at

LEFT: intricate designs on a typical fishing boat. **RIGHT:** a coffee shop in Trang Town.

The streets of many towns in the Deep South are lined with elaborate wooden birdcages holding doves. These birds are famous for their cooing. Many contests are organised locally and awards are given out for these birds.

least an overnight stay. While Trang is well known among Thais as the birthplace of Chuan Leekpai, a former prime minister, travellers will be more taken by another legacy – its food. From Chinese-style coffee shops to one of Thailand's best **night markets** – along Thanon Ruenrom – the food in Trang is one of its highlights. Trang Town also has a colourful morning market. Every morning, vendors sell a plethora of fresh produce on Thanon Ratchadamnoen and Thanon Sathani, while seafood stalls line the streets behind the Ko Teng Hotel.

Trang's beaches

A string of secluded beaches along the Trang coast and several islands off the coast are worth seeking out. Trang's 119km (74-mile) coastline from Hat Pak Meng to Hat Chao Mai, plus a number of islands nearby, are part of the **Hat Chao Mai National Park**.

Some 40km (25 miles) west of Trang Town, **Hat Pak Meng** is a shallow beach that gets muddy at low tide. There is a string of seafood restaurants and a pier at the northern end where

boats depart for trips to nearby islands. Apart from these, Pak Meng is very much a local scene, bolstered by Thais picnicking at weekends.

South of Hat Pak Meng, **Hat Chang Lang** ❷ is a lovely and isolated beach with greyish-white sands backed by cas-uarina trees. The beach is only swim-mable at high tide; when the tide is low it exposes large sandbanks, which are great to walk on. When the condi-tions are right, the sunsets can be truly spectacular here, bathing the horizon studded with islands and limestone crags in an orange glow.

Beyond Hat Chang Lang are more beaches – **Hat Yong Ling**, **Hat Yao** and **Hat Chao Mai** – but facilities and accommodation both become very sparse. Nearby Ban Chao Mai is where the harbour is located, a jump-off point for island tours.

Inland from Hat Yao, the caves at **Tham Lod** are best reached by kayak; the journey winds its way past mangrove forests and enters a cave through a tiny gap. A 10-minute paddle in darkness follows until you emerge into a scenic hidden lagoon

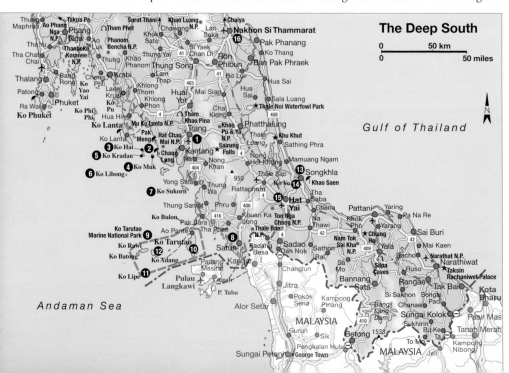

surrounded by mangroves and towering limestone walls.

Trang's islands

Some 16km (10 miles) southwest of Hat Pak Meng is **Ko Hai ❸** (also known as Ko Ngai). It actually lies in Krabi Province, but is more accessible from Trang. Ringed by clear water and coral reefs, it has several low-key resorts and a near-perfect swimming beach on its eastern side.

Approximately 8km (5 miles) south of Ko Hai is **Ko Muk ❹**. Boats to Ko Muk usually arrive at the small fishing village of Hua Laem, on the east side of the island, which is home to a small local population and rubber plantations, giving it a rural atmosphere. Ko Muk's finest beach is the secluded **Hat Farang** on the west coast, a cove-like inlet ringed by limestone cliffs, not unlike Railay Bay in Krabi. The highlight of Ko Muk is **Tham Morakot**, or "Emerald Cave", in the northern part of the island. During low tide, it's possible to swim through this partially submerged cave, the last few metres in complete darkness, to emerge at a hidden beach surrounded by towering limestone cliffs and lush greenery.

Ko Kradan ❺, about 6km (4 miles) southwest of Ko Muk, is considered by some to be the most beautiful island in the area. The beaches are blinding white and there are some nice reefs offshore but, unfortunately, the accommodation on the island is rather ramshackle. The island is mainly visited by day-trippers who come to laze on its beaches, or to snorkel and dive.

Southwest of Ko Kradan are two less frequently visited islands. The first is **Ko Libong ❻**, the largest island in the group and known for its wildlife. The waters around the island constitute one of Thailand's remaining habitats of the dugong. **Libong Nature Beach Resort** (one of only two resorts on the island) offers snorkelling trips to the waters populated by the dugongs.

Ko Sukorn ❼, southeast of Ko Libong, is home to nearly 3,000 people, and just a handful of motor vehicles. The island's beaches are concentrated on the western shore, the most attractive being **Hat Talo Yai**, where there are two budget resorts.

TIP

The southwest monsoon brings heavy rain from May to Oct to the Andaman Coast, including Trang and Satun. Songkhla, which sits on the Gulf of Thailand coast, experiences the worst rains from Nov to Jan. All these regions were vitually untouched by the tsunami in 2004.

BELOW: Amari Trang Beach Resort on Hat Chang Lang.

The National Museum in Satun is housed in the former Kuden Mansion.

BELOW: the dugong is an endangered species.

SATUN

Sharing a border with Malaysia in the far south of Thailand, remote **Satun Province** is a mountainous area, and in many ways is more Malay than Thai in terms of culture. Despite this, Satun has successfully managed to avoid the conflicts of its neighbouring provinces to the east, and is a safe area to travel.

Satun Town

Set in a lovely green valley walled by limestone cliffs, **Satun Town ❽** is pleasant enough for a quick tour. The town's only real tourist attraction is the elegant Sino-Portuguese **Kuden Mansion**, originally built to accommodate King Rama V for a visit that, ironically, never materialised. In 1902, the building become the governor's mansion before it was turned into Satun's **National Museum** (Wed–Sun 9am–4pm; free). The restored building mainly features exhibits on southern Thai life.

Ko Tarutao Marine N P

Ko Tarutao Marine National Park ❾ (mid-Nov–mid-May; charge) is the province's principal claim to fame. It encompasses more than 1,400 sq km (541 sq miles) of the Andaman Sea and comprises 51 islands. Only three of the islands are inhabited, mainly by *chao lay* sea gypsies. Established as a national park in 1974, the forests and seas that comprise Tarutao are home to Thailand's most pristine coral reefs – said to harbour 25 percent of the world's tropical fish species – and an incredible variety of fauna.

The Tarutao islands support creatures such as langurs, crab-eating macaques and wild pigs, as well as aquatic mammals including dolphins and dugongs. Several kinds of turtle lay their eggs on the largest island, Ko Tarutao, and especially along Ao Sone beach on the west coast. This spectacle can be witnessed every January.

The marine park is divided into two parts: the **Tarutao Archipelago** located 45km (28 miles) off the coast of mainland Satun, and the **Adang-Rawi Archipelago**, about 50km (30 miles) west of Ko Tarutao itself. The islands of the latter group are known for their excellent dive spots, and include the

Dugong

Sometimes dubbed "sea cow", reputed to be the origin of legends about mermaids, the dugong is one of the strangest-looking creatures in the ocean.

Found in tropical waters from Australia to East Africa, the vegetarian dugong is sometimes confused with the manatee (both are related to the elephant). Dugongs graze on underwater grasses day and night, and can stay beneath the surface for up to six minutes before coming up for air. Endowed with a certain graceless beauty, these languid animals are often targeted by coastal hunters, and they were long sought for their meat, oil, skin, bones and teeth. Dugongs are now legally protected, but their populations remain endangered. Sighting one while diving or snorkelling is to be transported back to prehistoric times.

park's most popular island, Ko Lipe. The park is only open during the dry season, typically mid-November to mid-May. Boat trips to the islands set off from the fishing town of **Pak Bara**, 60km (40 miles) north of Satun Town.

Ko Tarutao

Imposing **Ko Tarutao** ⑩, the largest of the park's islands, is an excellent place for hiking and exploring caves, or simply relaxing on its wide beach. The 152-sq-km (59-sq-mile) island is home to the park headquarters, behind the vast stretch of powdery white sand on the western shore known as **Ao Phante Malacca**. Behind the park office, at the end of a short path, **Toe Boo Cliff** has great views over the bay from its craggy summit which can be reached in a 30-minute climb.

To the south of Ao Phante Malacca lie two scenic beaches, **Ao Jak** and **Ao Molae**. To get to the next beach, **Ao Sone**, an important nesting ground for endangered turtles from September to May (and especially in January), requires a good two-hour walk.

On the island's eastern side, **Ao Taloh Wow** was a place of exile for Thai prisoners in the 1930s and 40s. Ko Tarutao made the news again in 2002 when **Ao Rusi**, on the northeast coast of the island, was used as the backdrop for the American reality television show *Survivor*. It caused some controversy as Thai environmentalists feared that the virgin environment would be irrevocably harmed. In the end, hard business won out. But to its credit, CBS, the show's producers, left the area more or less in the same pristine condition as when the film crew first arrived.

Ko Lipe and Ko Adang

Tiny **Ko Lipe** ⑪, 40km (25 miles) from Ko Tarutao, is the most popular and also the most developed island. Despite the fact that Ko Lipe lies within the national park boundaries, the 1,000 or so *chao lay* sea gypsies who inhabit the island have gained

the right to develop sections of it. This accounts for the largely disorganised and often unattractive development that has taken root. Fortunately, there isn't enough of it to detract from the natural beauty of the island.

Boats from Pak Bara arrive at **Hat Na Ko** ("front of the island") in the north, where there is some accommodation. A short walk from Na Ko via a dirt path leads to **Sunset Beach**, probably the most beautiful of Ko Lipe's beaches. It plays host to a couple of small-scale resorts and offers a wonderful view of the neighbouring islands.

On the southern side of Ko Lipe is a bay called **Ao Pattaya**. With its long sandy coastline and clear water, this is easily the most popular beach and home to the majority of the island's accommodation.

For those interested in diving and or snorkelling, Ko Lipe's prime position in the middle of the Adang-Rawi Archipelago makes for easy access to nearby dive sites. Popular spots in this area include the reefs surrounding **Ko Rawi**, **Ko Yang** and **Ko Hin Sorn**.

Hornbills on the island of Ko Tarutao.

BELOW: bay view from Toe Boo Cliff on Ao Phante Malacca.

Songkhla Town's Sino-Portuguese architecture.

BELOW: Chinese temple in Songkhla.

Visible from the shores of Sunset Beach and less than 2km (1 mile) away, towering **Ko Adang** ⑫ has a densely forested hilly interior, beautiful white-sand beaches and basic national-park accommodation. It is popular with day-tripping snorkellers, and jungle trails inland lead to waterfalls (during the wet season) and scenic viewpoints.

SONGKHLA

Songkhla Province is often overlooked. Although the flashy border city of Hat Yai draws thousands of Malaysian and Singaporean tourists each year, visitors from other countries typically give the province a wide berth. This is unfortunate, as Hat Yai isn't nearly as seedy as it's thought to be, and offers great food and bargain shopping, as well as a chance to see the southern Thai pastime of bullfighting. Directly east of Hat Yai, the tiny provincial capital, Songkhla Town, is a fascinating melting pot of southern Thai culture, with decent beaches, interesting temples and what is probably the best night market in

the entire Deep South region. There are some security concerns, however, so visitors should be on their guard.

Songkhla Town

Little-visited **Songkhla Town** ⑬, 25km (16 miles) east of Hat Yai, is one of the Deep South's nicer towns. Predominantly Chinese, but with a visible Muslim minority, Songkhla Town is located on a finger of land separating the Gulf of Thailand from the Thale Sap Songkhla, a large brackish lake. On the north coast of this promontory is **Hat Samila**, a long sandy beach marked by a bronze mermaid statue, making it a popular photo spot. While not great for swimming, the beach is nice enough for a stroll to watch the sun set or for a meal at one of the many beachside restaurants.

The town's charming old enclave, found between Thanon Nakhorn Nok and Thanon Nang Ngaam, has a number of Sino-Portuguese buildings, as well as numerous Chinese-style restaurants and old coffee shops that haven't changed in decades. **Songkhla National Museum** (Wed–Sun 9am–4pm; charge), housed in an elegant Sino-Portuguese mansion, is worth seeing for its exhibits of art, sculpture, pottery, ceramics and furniture from all the major periods of Thai history.

Songkhla's most famous temple, **Wat Matchimawat** (daily 8am–6pm; free), is located directly west of the Old Town. Its highlights are the beautiful temple paintings, probably executed in the early Rattanakosin period more than 200 years ago. Another worthwhile temple to visit is the hilltop compound of **Khao Tang Kuan** (daily 8am–7pm; charge). Accessible by air-conditioned tram, the quasi European-style temple complex was originally commissioned by King Rama V. It offers great views over Songkhla Town and Ko Yo island.

Around Songkhla

To the east of Songkhla, in the salty waters of the Thale Sap, is the island

of **Ko Yo** ⑭, which can be visited as a day trip from Songkhla or Hat Yai. In recent years the island has become something of a cultural tourism hotspot. The island is famous for its hand-loomed cotton weaving called *phaa kaw yaw*. The best place to buy this fabric, either in lengths or as clothing, is at the central market.

Also on Ko Yo is the interesting **Thaksin Folklore Museum** (daily 8.30am–5pm; charge), which highlights the history, architecture, traditions and handicraft of the people of south Thailand. The Muslim fishing village of **Khao Saen**, about 5km (3 miles) from Songkhla Town, is also worth seeing for its rows of colourful prawn-fishing boats docked every evening along the beach. The highly decorated boats, embellished with dragon prows, make for great photography.

Hat Yai

Sprawling **Hat Yai** ⑮ is the third-largest city in Thailand, and predominantly Chinese in character. Unfortunately, it has become a tourist destination for all the wrong reasons –

it attracts busloads of Malaysians and Singaporeans who travel across the border from Malaysia to frequent its numerous sleazy massage parlours and nightclubs. There are no real draws in Hat Yai, but the shopping and great food plus ample accommodation options will appeal to those who have just come from an island.

If in Hat Yai during the first Saturday of the month, make sure to catch the colourful southern Thai spectacle of **buffalo fighting**. This is held at **Noen Khum Thong Stadium** (charge), about 10km (6 miles) west of Hat Yai. Unlike the Western, rather more bloodthirsty, version of the sport, Thai buffalo fights involve two bulls locking horns and trying to force the other into submission.

NAKHON SI THAMMARAT

Beyond the Deep South region and north of Songkhla is **Nakhon Si Thammarat Province**. It is home to an excellent national park and Nakhon Si Thammarat Town, the second-largest city in south Thailand and known

Hat Yai is a shopping haven.

BELOW: buying dinner at Songkhla's extensive night market.

Shadow puppetry is an art form that has its roots in nearby Malaysia.

BELOW: some of the ingredients to make fresh curry paste: chilli, garlic, kaffir lime leaves and red shallots.
BELOW RIGHT: Wat Phra Mahathat, Nakhon Si Thammarat.

for its excellent southern food, important Buddhist temples and the art of *nang thalung*, or leather shadow puppets. The terrain is mainly mountainous, but there are some nice beaches to the north of the province.

Nakhon Si Thammarat Town

Nakhon Si Thammarat Town ⑯, usually referred to simply as "Nakhon", has a rich history dating back to the 2nd century when it was known as Ligor, the capital of the ancient kingdom of Tambralinga. It later became an important port and the centre of the Sumatra-based Srivijaya empire, at least until the 10th century. Today, Nakhon is often regarded as a bastion of traditional southern Thai culture. For most tourists, the city is a mere transport hub to Ko Samui or the beaches of Ao Khanom to the north. But Nakhon has several attractions that make it worthy of at least an overnight stay.

The physical aspects of Nakhon's history are extensively displayed in its **National Museum** (Wed–Sun 9am–4pm; charge) at the southern end of Thanon Ratchadamnoen. It houses one of the most important historical collections of Thailand outside of Bangkok's National Museum.

At the northern end of Thanon Ratchadamnoen is **Wat Phra Mahathat** (daily 8am–4.30pm; charge), one of six royally sanctioned temples in the country, and regarded as one of the most important temples in southern Thailand.

Puppet show

Another must-see in this town is **Suchart Subsin's Shadow Puppet Workshop** (daily 8am–4pm; free) along Thanon Si Thammasok. The art of using carved leather shadow puppets to perform tales from the Hindu *Ramayana* epic can be found all over Southeast Asia, including Thailand. Undoubtedly Thailand's most famous *nang thalung* exponent, Subsin has been making puppets and giving performances for over 60 years, and has even performed for King Bhumibol. Puppets can be bought here, and, for a small donation, Subsin may put on a private performance. ❑

RESTAURANTS AND BARS

Restaurants

Price per person for a three-course meal without drinks:
$ = under B300
$$ = B300–800
$$$ = B800–1,600
$$$$ = over B1,600

Trang Town
Thai/Chinese
Raan Khao Tom Phui
Th. Phraram IV. Tel: 0-7521 0127. Open: 5pm–2am. $
This unpretentious restaurant, popular with locals and open only in the evenings, is an excellent place to fill up on spicy Chinese-Thai favourites such as *khanaa fai daeng*, Chinese *kale* flash fried with chillies and garlic, or *hoi lay phat phrik phao*, fresh clams fried with hot chilli paste.

Trang Night Market
Cnr Th. Ratchadamnoen and Th. Phraram VI. Open: daily 5pm–midnight. $
Trang's night market is one of the culinary highlights of the deep south region. Every evening, the small street at the corner of Ratchadamnoen and Phraram VI becomes an endless parade of *raan khao kaeng*, or rice and curry vendors, many of whom have roadside seating. It looks daunting but the food is mostly fresh. Try the local favourite, *khanom jeen*, rice noodles eaten with curry sauce and veg.
Trang is also well known for its old-world Chinese-style coffee

shops, known as *raan kopi*. Try **Yuchiang** on Th. Phraram VI (daily 7am–5pm; $), or the restaurant below the **Ko Teng Hotel** (daily 8am–5pm; $).

Thai & Western
Trang Thana
Thumrin Thana Hotel, 69/8 Th. Trang Thana. Tel: 0-7521 1211. Open: daily 6am–midnight. $$
Basic hotel coffee shop with a good selection of Thai dishes as well as some Western ones. The breakfast and lunchtime buffets are good value.

Hat Pak Meng
Italian
Acqua
Anantara Si Kao Resort & Spa, 198–9 Moo5, Changlang Road, Sikao. Tel: 0-7520 5888. Open: daily noon–11pm. $$$
www.sikao.anantara.com
It's a long way from Italy, but – wow! The setting and the fare at this superb restaurant are awe-inspiring, with the freshest possible ingredients imaginatively served.

Songkhla
Thai
Raan Tae Hiang Iw
85 Th. Nang Ngam. Tel: 0-7431 1505. Open: daily 11am–8pm. $
This Chinese-Thai eatery, known to locals as "Tae", is a local legend. Highly recommended are the *yam mamuang*, a spicy salad of sour mangoes and dried shrimp, and *tom yam haeng*, a delicious "dry" version of the famous *tom yam* soup.

Songkhla Night Market
Th. Wachira. Open: daily 5pm–midnight. $
Songkhla's night market, probably the largest in the region, has Chinese, Thai and Muslim food, all at very low prices. Tell the minivan or motorcycle driver to go to "Wachira", the name of the road where the market is held.

Hat Yai
Thai
Hat Yai Night Market
Th. Montri 1 (near the Pakistan Mosque). Open: daily 5pm–midnight. $
Hat Yai's night market has a mix of Muslim and seafood dishes. A great place to sample local food, such as the Muslim-influenced *khao mok kai*, or rice cooked with chicken and spices.

Sky Buffet
Lee Gardens Plaza Hotel, 29 Th. Prachatipat. Tel: 0-7426 1111. Open: daily L & D. $
www.leeplaza.com
This hotel, the tallest building in Hat Yai, offers a Thai-style buffet lunch and dinner at its 33rd-storey restaurant with panoramic views. Enjoy all-you-can-eat Thai favourites, as well as views over Hat Yai.

Nakhon Si Thammarat
Thai
Krour Nakorn
Bovorn Bazaar, Th. Ratchadamnoen. Tel: 0-75317 197. Open: daily 6am–2pm. $
Sample authentic southern Thai food in a clean and comfortable environment at this well-known no-frills restaurant.

RIGHT: a bowl of *khanom jeen*.

NORTH THAILAND

The north is an area of high mountains, colourful
hill tribes and outdoor adventure. Different from
the rest of Thailand, this is a world unto itself

An extensive region of mountains, valleys and rivers,
northern Thailand straddles an important historical
junction where peoples from China, Laos, Myanmar
(Burma), Thailand and beyond have long traded com-
modities and ideas. The blend was further enlivened by the
migrations of tribes like the Akha, Karen, Lisu, Hmong and
Yao, whose ethnic heritage knows no political boundaries.

Until the early 20th century, the north was accessible
from Bangkok only by a complicated river trip, or by several weeks on elephant back. It is not surprising, then, that
the region has retained a distinct flavour all its own, one still so strong
that tourists from other parts of Thailand come here almost as if to visit
another country. They marvel at the beauty of the temples, with their
splendid teak carvings and intricate Burmese-inspired decorations; the
wild orchids that grow profusely in the hills; the gentle manners of the
people (among whose hospitable habits it is to place a basin of cool water
outside their gates for thirsty strangers); and the novelty
of having to bundle up in a sweater in the cool season.

The north is a region of great natural wealth and
scenic beauty. Although decades of deforestation has
reduced the hardwood forests, a logging ban has ensured
the remainder will survive. The mountains are home to
Thailand's hill tribes, now a tourist industry in their
own right. Still an exotic thread on the fringe
of Thai life, the hill tribes are gradually being
woven into the national fabric, and more and more of them
are migrating to the larger cities of the north.

It is hard for the authorities to patrol this wild terrain ade-
quately, but easy for smugglers to slip back and forth across the
borders with Myanmar and Laos in the notorious Golden Triangle. Although there has been some success in introducing
alternatives to opium as a cash crop, the smuggling of contra-
band drugs is still a major factor in the northern economy. ❑

PRECEDING PAGES: working in the rice paddies. **LEFT:** elephant trekking at Ban Ruam-
mit near Chiang Rai. **TOP:** Hmong children, Mae Sa valley, Chiang Mai. **ABOVE LEFT:**
northern hills as seen from Doi Inthanon. **ABOVE RIGHT:** Sukhothai Historical Park.

CHIANG MAI

Chiang Mai, the capital of north Thailand, is
regarded as the cultural heart of the country.
With its lovely Lanna-style temples, museums and
a market where one can indulge in night-time
shopping, this is a city of diverse charms

It has become trendy to bemoan the supposed demise of **Chiang Mai ❶**, Thailand's "Rose of the North". Noisy *tuk-tuk* replaced silent *samlor* pedicabs years ago, concrete buildings have ousted traditional wooden housing, and high-rise condominiums now mark the skyline. And, above all, the traffic has increased exponentially.

In recent years, however, there has been a revival of sorts. In the beautiful, historically important Old City, new construction is limited to three storeys. Old streets have been cobbled in red brick, concrete lamp standards replaced with ornate Parisian-style lanterns, and the city walls restored. The polluted city moat has been dredged and cleaned up, and is now populated by fish and turtles.

Northern hospitality

Despite rapid urbanisation, 700-year-old Chiang Mai remains a pleasant, balmy escape from Bangkok's humidity. Situated 300 metres (1,000ft) above sea level in a valley divided by the picturesque 560km (350-mile) long **Ping River** (Mae Nam Ping), the city was for seven centuries the capital of the Lanna (Million Rice Fields) kingdom *(see page 33)*. Its remoteness ensured significant isolation from Bangkok – 700km (400 miles) south – well into the 20th century.

This isolation allowed Chiang Mai to develop a culture removed from that of the Central Plain, characterised by its exquisite wooden temples and unique crafts like lacquerware, silverwork, woodcarvings, ceramics and umbrella-making. Although the city is somewhat strained by masses of visitors, the people are more gracious than in other Thai cities.

Thai and foreign visitors alike will find that Chiang Mai has perhaps the strongest sense of place of any Thai city. Keenly aware of its glorious past,

Main attractions
WAT CHIANG MAN
WAT PHRA SINGH
WAT CHEDI LUANG
WAT BUPPARAM
CHIANG MAI NIGHT BAZAAR
WAT SUAN DOK
WAT U MONG
WAT JET YOT
CHIANG MAI NATIONAL MUSEUM

LEFT: at school in Chiang Mai.
RIGHT: Chiang Mai Night Bazaar.

it clings to its northern Thai identity. One obvious manifestation of this are the numerous modern office buildings that bear stylised *kalae* (X-crossed, carved gables typical of traditional northern-style roofs).

Various hill tribes, called *chao khao* (literally "mountain people"), often travel into town from the highlands to trade, adding another element to Chiang Mai culture. One can see their colourful garb and distinctive faces at the Chiang Mai Night Bazaar (*see page 286*), where they have dealt with Thais and foreign traders for centuries.

Northern Thai cuisine will keep gourmets busy with its exciting blend of Thai, Lao, Shan and Yunnanese elements, and an abundance of cookery courses means that Chiang Mai also caters to those who want to learn Thai culinary arts.

Onward travel options from Chiang Mai are plentiful, with good connections to the rest of Thailand by plane, train and bus, while bicycles, motorcycles and cars are easily arranged through rental agencies, hotels or guesthouses.

Buddha statue, Wat Chiang Man.

Origins

Long a major entrepôt along caravan routes from China's Yunnan Province to the port of Mawlamyine (Moulmein) in Myanmar (Burma), Chiang Mai first gained prominence in the 13th century. The northern Thai kingdoms of Lanna and Sukhothai arose in this region and are still widely recognised as sources of Thai nationhood. As Lanna's capital, Chiang Mai became the religious and cultural centre for the entire region.

The city's founder, Mangrai, ruled an empire that ran as far north as Chiang Saen, on the Mekong River. When the Mongol ruler, Kublai Khan, sacked the Burmese city Pagan in 1287, Mangrai formed an alliance with the rulers of Sukhothai to secure his southern boundaries. In 1296, he set up a new base in the Ping valley, and named it Chiang Mai, or "New City". Legend has it that the site was chosen for the auspicious sighting of white deer and a white mouse (with a family of five) at the same time. As the Ping River often floods, Mangrai had 90,000 labourers build his brick-walled city half a kilometre west of the river.

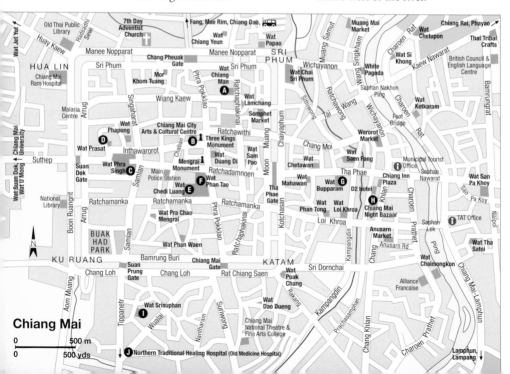

Chiang Mai

0 ___ 500 m
0 ___ 500 yds

Within a century of Chiang Mai's founding, however, Ayutthaya had replaced Sukhothai as the Thai capital. This new kingdom had its own expansionist plans, including designs on its northern neighbour. For 400 years, there was fierce rivalry and sometimes open warfare between the two. In 1515 Ayutthaya crushed an army from Chiang Mai in retaliation for earlier attacks by the Lanna kingdom. And then, in 1556, the Burmese invaded the city – and proceeded to control it for over 200 years.

Under the Thai warlord (and later king) Phaya Taksin, the Thais recaptured Chiang Mai in 1775 and made the Lampang chieftain Chao Kawila the viceroy of Lanna. In 1800, Kawila ordered the massive city walls to be built and began restoring the city to its former prominence. Regional trade also flourished. Chiang Mai continued to enjoy autonomy from Bangkok, at least until the railway facilitated the arrival of central government officials in 1921. In 1932, following the death of the last king of Chiang Mai and the end of absolute monarchy in the country, the north was finally fully incorporated into Thailand.

INSIDE THE GATED CITY

The Old City quadrangle, bounded by canalised moats and crumbling brick city walls, is filled with historic temples, shops, old hotels and guesthouses. Away from the main avenues and tourist districts, the narrow, winding *soi* (lanes) of the moated city draw the visitor into an atmospheric world populated by cobblers and other tradespeople, noodle shops and over 30 Lanna-style temples.

Wat Chiang Man

The city's spiritual history began with **Wat Chiang Man** Ⓐ (daily 8am–6pm; free), which translates as "steadfast city". Located on Thanon Ratchaphakinai in the northeast part of the old walled city, it is the oldest of Chiang Mai's 300-plus temples, and

the first to be built by Mangrai, who lived there during Chiang Mai's construction in 1296. *Lai kham* (gold-leaf stencil designs on red lacquer) on the walls of the main *viharn* (sermon hall) illustrate scenes from the king's life. Two ancient Buddha images are kept in a small sanctuary nearby. The first of these, **Phra Satang Man**, is 10cm (4ins) tall and made of crystal, which Mangrai brought to Chiang Mai from Lamphun, where it had reputedly resided for 600 years. Apart from a short time in Ayutthaya, the image has remained in Chiang Mai ever since. During the Songkran festival in April, the tiny statue is paraded through the city streets.

The second image, a stone **Phra Sila Buddha** in bas-relief, is believed to have originated in India around the 8th century. Both statues are said to bring rain and to protect the city from fire.

The other important structure in Wat Chiang Man worth seeing is the **Phra That Chang Lom**, a 15th-century Lanna-style *chedi* buttressed by rows of stucco elephants.

BELOW: *chedi* and roof details at Wat Chiang Man.

Chiang Mai City Arts and Cultural Centre

Close to Wat Chiang Man, on Thanon Phra Pokklao, is the **Chiang Mai City Arts and Cultural Centre B** (Tue–Sun 8.30am–5pm; charge). It occupies the former Provincial Hall. Built in 1924, this is a good example of European-influenced Thai secular architecture. The centre has interactive displays on Chiang Mai's history and culture and is a useful first stop for visitors wanting to familiarise themselves with the city's heritage.

In a brick plaza in front of the building stands the **Three Kings Monument**, bronze sculptures depicting Phaya Ngam Muang, Phaya Mangrai and Phaya Khun Ramkhamhaeng, the three Thai rulers from whose alliance the Lanna kingdom was formed. Locals still place flowers, incense and candles at the kings' feet in tribute to their powerful spirits.

Wat Phra Singh

Imperiously positioned close to Suan Dok Gate at the head of Thanon Ratchadamnoen – the Old City's principal east–west thoroughfare – is **Wat**

Phra Singh C (daily 8am–6pm; free). Chiang Mai's most important temple, and the largest within the Old City, it was founded in 1345. The magnificent Lanna-style *ho trai* (Buddhist library), on the north side of the compound, is an elaborate wooden affair raised on a high brick-and-stucco base decorated with bas-relief deities. Behind the main *viharn*, built in 1925, is a wooden *bot* (ordination hall); behind that is a *chedi* built by King Pha Yu in 1345 to store his father's ashes.

Wat Phra Singh's most beautiful building is the small **Phra Viharn Lai Kham** to the left of the *bot*. Built in 1811, the wooden building's front wall has *lai kham* flowers on red lacquer. Intricately carved wooden frames accent the doors. Its interior is decorated with murals commissioned by Chao Thammalangka, ruler of Chiang Mai from 1813 to 1821. Focusing on the Buddhist stories of Prince Sang Thong (north wall) and the *Heavenly Phoenix* epic (south wall), they also record in fascinating detail aspects of early 19th-century Lanna society, with clear indications of Burmese cultural influence.

Chiang Mai's Three Kings Monument.

BELOW: street scene on the outskirts of town.

The Phra Viharn Lai Kham houses one of Thailand's most famous bronze Buddha images, the **Phra Singh Buddha**. Thai folk tales claim that the Phra Singh Buddha came from Sri Lanka, but its stylistic features suggest a northern Thai, Lanna-era origin. It is almost identical to two other images, one in Nakhon Si Thammarat *(see page 273)* and the other in Bangkok, whose origins are also shrouded in myth.

Wat Prasat, Wat Chedi Luang and Wat Phan Tao

Across from the north side of Wat Phra Singh stands **Wat Prasat ❶** (daily 8am–6pm; free), whose original *viharn* is a well-kept example of Lanna temple architecture. The walls behind the principal Buddha image depict scenes from the Buddha's life.

Calamity is associated with **Wat Chedi Luang ❷** (daily 8am–6pm; free), built in 1441 east of Wat Phra Singh on Thanon Phra Pokklao. King Mangrai was reportedly killed nearby by lightning. The temple is named after the monumental royal *chedi luang* in the central courtyard. A 16th-century earthquake reduced the 90-metre (295ft) *chedi* to 42 metres (140ft). It was never rebuilt, but the base and reliquary were restored in the 1990s with financing from Unesco and the Japanese government.

Even in its damaged state, the colossal monument is majestic. For 84 years from 1475, the Emerald Buddha was housed in its eastern niche before being moved to Vientiane, and later to Wat Phra Kaew in Bangkok *(see page 111)*. A replica was installed in the same niche in 1995 for the city's 700th anniversary.

Close to the temple entrance stands an ancient, tall gum tree. According to legend, when it falls, so will the city. As if serving as counterbalance, the *lak muang*, or city pillar, in which the spirit of the city is said to reside, stands near its base.

The *viharn* of **Wat Phan Tao ❸** (daily 8am–6pm; free), next to Wat Chedi Luang, was assembled from the teak pillars and panels of a former palace, and is a masterpiece of wooden construction. Its doorway is crowned by a beautiful Lanna peacock framed by *naga*, or

The northern Thai dialect has its own Lanna script, but with the standardisation of central Thai, few northerners today know how to read it, even though they may speak northern Thai as a first language. The northern script is nevertheless commonly used on monastery signs.

BELOW LEFT: *ho trai* (Buddhist library) at Wat Phra Singh.
BELOW: murals inside the Phra Viharn Lai Kam, Wat Phra Singh.

Buddha image at Wat Bupparam.

BELOW: toy stall at the Chiang Mai Night Bazaar.

mythical serpents. The temple has a collection of rare palm-leaf manuscripts and lacquer manuscript cabinets.

OUTSIDE THE CITY WALLS

Thanon Tha Phae, the street running from the Old City's eastern gate to the Ping River, acts as an extension of the Old City, and is lined with travel agencies, antique shops and restaurants. After it crosses the Ping River via Nawarat Bridge, it becomes Thanon Charoen Muang, leading to the main post office and railway station.

Wat Bupparam

Built by Shan and Burmese artisans and financed by Burmese teak merchants who lived in Chiang Mai over a century ago, **Wat Bupparam** **G** (daily 8am–6pm; free), on Thanon Tha Phae about 500 metres (1,640ft) east of the eastern city gate, features a small, ornate Lanna-style ordination hall of carved teak, a larger, modern *viharn* and a Shan-style *chedi*. Guardian deity sculptures surrounding the complex take on whimsical animal forms; look for dogs playing with lions and the mythical *mom*, part-lizard and part-dog.

Chiang Mai Night Bazaar

Once a stopping point for trade caravans travelling between Yunnan and the Gulf of Martaban, and Chiang Mai's best-known tourist epicentre, the **Chiang Mai Night Bazaar** **H** (daily 5–11pm) is a must-see. The evening bazaar covers several blocks of Thanon Chang Khlan between Thanon Tha Phae and Thanon Sri Dornchai. On nearby side streets, such as the Anusarn Market lane (perpendicular to Thanon Chang Khlan), more stalls offer handicrafts and a good selection of restaurants.

Every day, at around 4pm, hundreds of vendors will line the street with their huge steel carts. The carts' upper doors swing open to reveal the vendors' wares, which can range from woodcarvings and inexpensive silk and cotton clothing to elaborate Thai- or hill-tribe-inspired home accessories. Colourfully clad traders from various northern hill tribes are usually present at the market.

Wat Srisuphan

South of the Old City walls on Thanon Wualai is **Wat Srisuphan** **I** (daily 8am–6pm; free). This temple was founded in the early 16th century by the Thai Khün people who migrated to Chiang Mai from Kengtung in Burma's Shan State. Many silversmith workshops established by the Thai Khün can still be seen along Thanon Wualai.

The temple compound houses several structures including a large school, a *chedi* and a large and attractive *viharn*. Most interestingly, the original *ubosot* has been replaced by a strikingly unique example built of pure silver, tin, and silver mixed with aluminium. Silversmiths from the neighbourhood and throughout the country have contributed their labours both in the form of *repoussé* panels portraying scenes from the *Jataka*, as well as intricate silver alloy panels from which the entire structure is fashioned.

Wat Srisuphan is known for its annual Poy Sang Long festival, a Shan-style group ordination of boys as novices, which usually takes place in March. One of the highlights is the colourful street procession, when the boys are garbed in princely regalia before donning the saffron robes of monkhood.

Northern Traditional Healing Hospital

Further along Thanon Wualai, at 78/1 Soi Siwaka Komarat, is the **Northern Traditional Healing Hospital J** (better known as Old Medicine Hospital; www.thaimassageschool.ac.th). This is Thailand's main centre for the healing art known as *nuat phaen bohraan* (traditional northern Thai massage therapy and herbal medicine). Many foreigners enrol here for two-week massage courses.

Wat Suan Dok

About 1km (2/3 mile) west of the western old wall gate on Thanon Suthep is one of Chiang Mai's most impressive temple complexes, **Wat Suan Dok** (daily 8am–6pm; free). The temple dates

back to 1373 and was built by the sixth Lanna king, Phyaa Keu Na. At its northwest corner is a whitewashed *chedi* with the ashes of Chiang Mai's royal family, and a larger central *chedi*, said to hold eight Buddha relics. The monastery grounds also host a branch of the **Mahachulalongkorn Buddhist University** *(see margin, right)* attended by monks and novices from all over Thailand.

Chiang Mai University

Further west just off Thanon Suthep is the sprawling 1,412-hectare (3,490-acre) campus of the **Chiang Mai University K**. Established in 1964, it is the largest educational institution in the north, and has about 18,000 students in 108 departments, including highly rated faculties of medicine, dentistry and engineering. There are several entrances along Thanon Suthep, and a single entrance on Thanon Huay Kaew to the north. Recreational facilities open to the public include a fitness park (free), swimming pool (charge) and sports track (free). The bucolic **Ang Kaew Reservoir**, at the east end of the campus, is a favourite with strollers and joggers.

TIP

Part of Mahachulalongkorn Buddhist University's efforts to spread Buddhism is a forum known as Monk Chat (Mon, Wed and Fri 5–7pm; free; www.monkchat.net). A few rooms have been set aside at Wat Suan Dok so that visitors can discuss Buddhism with monastic residents.

BELOW: Wat Suan Dok dates back to 1373.

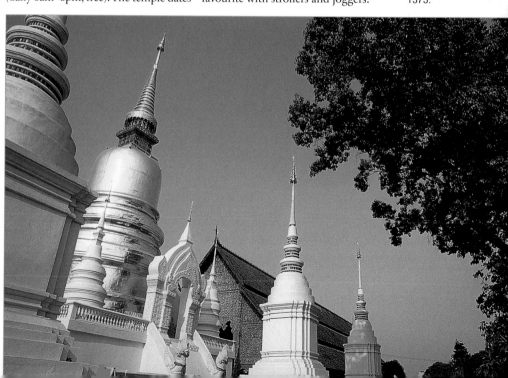

Wat U Mong

South of the university grounds is the 15th-century **Wat U Mong** ❶ (daily 8am–6pm; free), centred on a flat-topped hill honeycombed with underground brick-lined tunnels and meditation cells. A large Lanna-style *chedi* stands on the hill, with a lake on the grounds, surrounded by rustic *guti* (monastic huts). Wat U Mong was all but abandoned for years, but was revived in the 1960s under the late Than Ajahn Buddhadasa, Thailand's famous reformer monk. Amidst grand teak trees, the restored site is one of the few truly quiet spots left in Chiang Mai. Resident foreign monks give free English-language talks on Buddhism at Wat U Mong on Wednesdays and Sundays.

Chiang Mai Zoo and Arboretum

Modern high-rise hotels, shopping centres and apartment buildings line parts of Thanon Huay Kaew, which leads from the northwest corner of the Old City out to Doi Suthep (see page 293). As the road approaches the mountain, the high-rise buildings give way to gently rolling hills and expanses of greenery.

In antiquated facilities spread over a well-landscaped terrain, **Chiang Mai Zoo and Arboretum** ❶ (daily 8am–5pm; charge; additional fee for panda-viewing) on Thanon Huay Kaew houses a wide range of mammals (including two giant pandas), reptiles, birds (over 5,000 birds representing 150 species), a large aquarium and trees – both local and imported.

Wat Jet Yot

Located about 1km (²/₃ mile) northwest of the city walls, **Wat Jet Yot** ❶ (daily 8am–6pm; free) was completed by King Trailokaraja in 1455. As its name "Seven Spires" suggests, its roof is topped with seven *chedi* replicating the Mahabodhi Stupa found in India's Bodh Gaya, where the Buddha gained enlightenment after spending seven weeks in its gardens.

The striking stucco images of the *bodhisattva* (Buddhist saints) that decorate the temple walls are said to bear faces of Trailokaraja's family. Its similarity to a temple in Burma's then-capital of Pagan did not stop invading Burmese from severely damaging it in 1566.

BELOW: flamingos at the Chiang Mai Zoo.

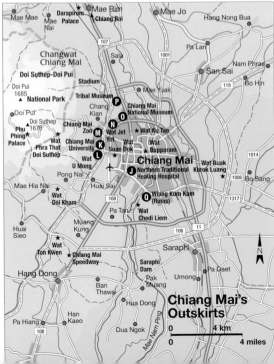

Chiang Mai National Museum

Northeast of Wat Jet Yot is the **Chiang Mai National Museum ⓞ** (Wed–Sun 9am–4pm; charge; www.thailandmuseum.com), established in 1954. The museum has a collection of almost 1 million artefacts, including precious Buddhist art, northern Thai celadon, historic weaponry, costumes and other items of ethnological interest. Most of the collection is labelled in Thai and English. Exhibits are rotated with its sister museums in the nearby northern cities of Lamphun, Chiang Saen and Nan.

Tribal Museum

Ethnology enthusiasts should not miss the smaller but equally fascinating **Tribal Museum ⓟ** (Mon–Fri 9am– 4pm; charge), set in the picturesque gardens of Suan Ratchamangkhala to the north, just off Thanon Chotana. The museum has labelled (in Thai and English) and informative displays of hill-tribe jewellery, costumes, handicraft, household utensils, architecture, tools and musical instruments set out on its three floors.

Video shows on the tribes are presented at regular intervals throughout the day, and the museum is a good first stop for understanding the lifestyles of the various northern hill tribes before setting out on a trek.

Wiang Kum Kam

Close to the southern reach of the Ping River, 5km (3 miles) south of the city, are the partially restored ruins of **Wiang Kum Kam ⓠ** (daily 8.30am–5pm; charge). The Mon people established a satellite capital of the Hariphunchai kingdom here in the 11th and 12th centuries, but heavy flooding led to its abandonment in the 18th century.

The most impressive remains include a rectilinear Mon-style *chedi* (part of the more modern Wat Chedi Si Liam) and the brick foundations of several Mon temples, the most complete of which belongs to Wat Kan Thom. In addition, some 1,300 stone inscriptions have been found here. One of the more interesting is an 11th-century slab of stone, whose proto-Thai script predates the better-known Ramkhamhaeng inscription of Sukhothai by a century or more. ❏

Colourful hill-tribe costume displayed at the Tribal Museum.

BELOW: *chedi* and Buddha image at Wat Jet Yot.

Ethnic Diversity

Chiang Mai's strong sense of identity is apparent to many visitors. While the locals refer to themselves as "Khon Muang" ("people of the principality"), suggesting a homogeneous people, the city's unique character is in fact born of its ethnic diversity. Particularly during the period of Burmese rule (1556–1775), skilled artisans were resettled here. From Pagan in Burma came temple craftsmen who produce the lacquerware found in the Night Bazaar. From the Shan State of northern Burma came the Yong, talented weavers, and the Kheun, skilled silversmiths, who settled in the Wua Lai district of Chiang Mai. The colourful hill tribes such as the Akha and Lisu, as well as the Chinese and Pathan Muslims, add further depth to this ethnic mosaic, which is reflected in the city's festivals, handicrafts and architecture.

RESTAURANTS AND BARS

Restaurants

Price per person for a three-course meal without drinks:
$ = under B300
$$ = B300–800
$$$ = B800–1,600
$$$$ = over B1,600

Chinese

Jasmine
Royal Princess Hotel, Chiang Klan Rd. Tel: 0-5325-3900. Open: daily L & D. $$
Famous for both its dim sum and a wide range of northern and Cantonese dishes, this elegant place offers good value and an accessible location.

Mangkorn Loy (Flying Dragon)
Th. Mahidol. No phone. Open: daily L & D. $$
Although the regulars try to keep it a secret, this unassuming little eatery next to a petrol station near the airport serves the city's best Beijing-style cuisine. You can't go wrong with the Peking Duck, or ask the friendly China-born owner-chefs for their recommendations.

Mit Mai
42/2 Th. Ratchamankha. Tel: 0-5327 5033. Open: daily L & D. $
In a neighbourhood of the Old City once frequented by infamous opium warlord Khun Sa, this simple open-air dining room serves an extensive variety of Yunnanese dishes. Try the delicious Yunnanese ham stew with *mantou* (steamed buns). There is a long list of vegetable-only dishes.

Indian

Le Spice
31 Soi 6, Th. Charoen Prathet. Tel: 0-5323 4962. Open: daily L & D. $$
Recently opened by an Indian Thai family, Le Spice is decorated in saffron tones and Chiang Mai-style teak furniture. The Indian dishes are reasonably authentic, with the fish *tikka* a clear favourite. Excellent Thai dishes are on the menu as well.

International

Art Café
Th. Tha Phae at Th. Kotchasan. Tel: 0-5320 6365. Open: daily B, L & D. $$
Conveniently located outside the moat opposite Tha Phae Gate, Art Café stays busy with a regular and visiting Western clientele who appreciate its air-conditioning and the variety of comfort foods available. The menu ably covers Mexican, Thai, Italian, pizza, pies, pastries and espresso.

Mi Casa
Soi Wat Pa Daeng, Th. Suthep. Tel: 0-5381 0088. Open: Mon–Sat L & D. $$$
www.micasachiangmai.com
Tucked away in a leafy residential neighbourhood between Chiang Mai University and Wat U Mong, this garden restaurant offers a creative menu of original Mediterranean-influenced dishes, tapas and gourmet salads, plus an excellent wine list. The owners, a Spanish chef and his Hong Kong wife, run a restaurant of the same name in Hong Kong as well.

Riverside Bar and Restaurant
Th. Charoenrat. Tel: 0-5324 3239. Open: daily L & D. $$
A favourite among locals and visitors alike for its pleasant riverbank location, cosy wood-floor ambience, consistently good food and live music. The Riverside is so popular that it pays to come early to nail down a good table. The menu covers a good range of Thai, Western and vegetarian options.

Italian

Giorgio Italian Restaurant
2/6 Th. Prachasamphan. Tel: 0-5381 8236. Open: Tue–Sun L & D. $$$
A short walk from the Chiang Mai Night Bazaar is one of Chiang Mai's best Italian restaurants. The pasta choices are broad, and include some made on the premises. The Italian owner often prepares salads at tableside himself. The air-conditioned ambience is a bit formal but still lovely.

Pulcinella Da Stefano
2/1–2 Th. Chang Moi Kao. Tel: 0-5387 4189. Open: daily L & D. $$
The bright, semi-chic interior is complemented by the attentions of the ever-smiling Italian owner. It has a good selection of Italian wines, mouth-watering thin-crust pizzas and a long list of pasta and antipasti dishes.

Pum Pui Italian Restaurant
24 Soi 2, Th. Moon Muang. Tel: 0-5327 8209. Open: daily L & D. $$
One of Chiang Mai's oldest Italian eateries is hidden away in a garden down a very narrow *soi* (lane) near Top North Guest House. Great house wines, an extensive menu, generous servings of complimentary bread and good service are the highlights.

Noodles

Khao Soi Islam
Th. Kaew Nawarat. Tel: 0-5327-1484. Open: daily 9am–3pm. $
Near the Night Bazaar, in the same *soi* as the Chinese Baan Haw Mosque, Khao Soi Islam serves exemplary *khao soi*, the Shan-Yunnanese dish of chicken or beef morsels cooked in a mildly spiced curry broth, and served over thick egg noodles. Their *khao mok*, rice steamed overnight with chicken or goat and Persian-inspired spices, is another dish that is worth trying.

Kuaytiaw Kai Tun Coke
Th. Kamphaeng Din. No phone. Open: daily L & D. $
The idea of marinating chicken in Coca-Cola may not have originated here, but this may well be the most famous "Coke noodles" vendor in Thailand. Cooked into a broth and served in a bowl over thin rice noodles, this dish is basically a fast-food version of Chinese herbal soup – and surprisingly, just as delicious.

Rot Neung

Th. Charoen Prathet. No phone. Open: daily 9am–9pm. **$**
Near the Porn Ping Tower Hotel, Rot Neung is famous for its fishballs (made from ground fish), which are distributed wholesale and used to make the restaurant's famous *kuaytiaw luuk chin plaa* (fishball noodle soup). A vendor in front of the restaurant makes delicious crab spring rolls.

Thai

Aroon (Rai) Restaurant

45 Th. Kotchasan. Tel: 0-5327 6947. Open: daily 8am–10pm. **$**
One of Chiang Mai's oldest and best-known Thai restaurants sits on the east side of the moat just south of Tha Phae Gate. The vast menu focuses mainly on northern and central Thai cuisine. House specialities include *kaeng awm* and *kaeng khae*, soupy dishes made with Thai roots and herbs with distinctive, bitter-hot flavours. The Indian-style chicken curry is one of Chiang Mai's best.

Ban Rom Mai

191/29 Chang Klan Plaza, Chang Klan Rd. Tel: 0-5382-0031. Open: daily 11am-12pm. **$$**
A fairly new place a few blocks south of the Night Bazaar that has acquired a strong following because of the good central and northern Thai (*khantoke*-style) food. Indoor or outdoor tables amidst a tropical-garden atmosphere in an otherwise urban neighbourhood. Live Thai folk music in the evenings.

Baan Rai Yam Yen

Soi Wat Lanka 3, Before Khajow Market Tel: 0-5324 7999 Open: daily L & D. **$**
On the Fa Ham Road restaurant row, this long-running establishment has a cult following for its excellent northern and central Thai food. The *laab gai* (minced chicken with spices) is world-class, or if you're feeling adventurous, try the steamed bee hive (*rang pheung*). Not easy to find, but any *tuk-tuk* driver will know it.

Huen Phen

112 Th. Ratchamankha. Tel: 0-5327 7103. Open: daily L & D. **$$**
Northern Thai cuisine is distinct from the better-known central Thai version, and Huen Phen, set in an old wooden house decorated with local antiques, is generally regarded as serving the best in Chiang Mai. Dishes well worth trying include *laap khua* (spicy minced-pork salad), *kaeng hang-leh* (savoury, Burmese-influenced curry) and the platter of local northern Thai appetisers.

Huen Soontharee

Ban Sanphisua. Tel: 0-5387 2707. Open: daily L & D. **$$**
A little north of the Super Highway, this large but casual open-air restaurant on the banks of the Ping River is owned by famous Chiang Mai folk singer Soontharee Wechayanon. Dishes draw from three regions of Thailand – central, north and northeast – but the main attractions are the riverside ambience and, at weekends, live performances by Soontharee herself.

Palaad Tawanron

Th. Suthep. Tel: 0-5321 6039. Open: daily L & D. **$$**
On the lower slopes of Doi Suthep behind the university and zoo, Palaad Tawanron is run by a local Thai politician, whose winning recipe of good Thai food and live music, combined with superb views, keeps the two-level dining room packed every night.

Vegetarian

AUM Vegetarian Food

65 Th. Moon Muang. Tel: 0-5327 8315. Open: daily L & D. **$**
Just inside the moat near Tha Phae Gate, AUM is a mainstay with Chiang Mai's vegetarian community. The split-level restaurant offers seating both at tables and chairs, and on floor cushions. The place could use some renovation, but the food – mostly Thai or Thai-inspired – is always dependable.

Pun Pun Organic Vegetarian Restaurant

Wat Suan Dok Temple, Suthep Road. Tel: 08-1470 1461. Open: Thur–Tue 9am–6pm. **$**
Serving healthy veggie food using mostly organic produce from local producers. Thai food, salads, pasta, smoothies, fruit drinks and coffee. The restaurant is attractively located in a bodhi-tree-dominated outdoor courtyard within the large grounds of Wat Suan Dok temple.

Vietnamese

Le Gong Kum

Soi Chantarasak, Th. Huay Kaew. Tel: 0-5322 1869. Open: daily L & D. **$$**
In a neo-colonial French-style house full of attractive plants, this quirky restaurant is a good choice for privacy and good Vietnamese fare. The house sits in front of the multi-storey guesthouse Suan Doi House.

RIGHT: pork *kuayteow*, a Chinese noodle dish.

AROUND CHIANG MAI

The area surrounding Chiang Mai provides plenty of opportunities for day trips. There are mountains, lush valleys and national parks, the majestic cliff-top temple of Wat Phra That Doi Suthep and the historic towns of Lamphun and Lampang

Main attractions
WAT PHRA THAT DOI SUTHEP
DOI PUI
BO SANG
BAN THAWAI
WAT PHRA THAT SI CHOM TONG
DOI INTHANON NATIONAL PARK
LAMPHUN
LAMPANG
MAE SA VALLEY
THAM CHIANG DAO

Some of northwest Thailand's most intriguing attractions are found outside the capital in the surrounding mountains and valleys. To the northwest of the city looms the steep escarpment of Doi Suthep and Doi Pui, while further out to the southwest stands Thailand's highest peak, Doi Inthanon. The most striking local mountain scenery can be seen northwards, in the vicinity of the country's third-highest peak, Doi Chiang Dao (also known as Doi Luang), where forested limestone cliffs and caves stand alongside craggy mountain ranges.

The valley plains south of Chiang Mai contain two of northern Thailand's most historic towns, Lamphun and Lampang. Both are endowed with lovely Lanna-period Buddhist monasteries, and are not yet swamped by tourism.

WAT PHRA THAT DOI SUTHEP

A steep series of hairpin curves rise up the flanks of 1,676-metre (5,497ft) **Doi Suthep Ⓐ** – 15km (9 miles) northwest of the city centre via Thanon Huay Kaew – to Chiang Mai's best-loved temple, **Wat Phra That Doi Suthep** (daily 8am–6pm; charge). The legend goes that the site was selected in the mid-1300s by an elephant that was turned loose with a Buddha relic strapped to its back. It climbed halfway up the

mountain, then would climb no more. The temple was built at the spot where it halted, and consecrated in 1383.

The road that climbs up to the temple passes the entrance to the Chiang Mai Zoo (*see page 288*), where red *songthaew* pick-up trucks ply the route from the zoo up to the temple, Phu Ping Palace, and a heavily visited Hmong village. The scenery is spectacular as the road winds through **Doi Suthep/Doi Pui National Park** to a large car park across the road from the entrance to Wat Phra That Doi Suthep. Seven-headed *naga* undulate

LEFT: devotees at Wat Phra That Doi Suthep.
RIGHT: the stairway to the wat.

Wat Phra That Doi Suthep is located near the summit of Doi Suthep mountain.

BELOW: Doi Pui Hmong village.

down the balustrades of a 290-step stairway from car park to temple. For the weary, an enclosed cable car makes the ascent for B30. From Wat Phra That Doi Suthep, Chiang Mai is spread out below one's feet.

From the upper terrace, a few more steps lead through the courtyard of the temple itself. In the late afternoon sunshine, few sights are more stunning than that which will greet you at the final step. Emerging from cloisters decorated with murals depicting scenes from the Buddha's life is a 24-metre (80ft) high gilded *chedi*, partially shaded by gilded parasols. The *chedi* is surrounded by an iron fence with pickets that are topped with praying *thewada*, or angels. At the eastern and western ends of the compound are two sermon halls, or *viharn*. At dawn, the eastern one shelters chanting nuns in white robes. At sunset, monks chant their prayers in the one on the west.

Phu Phing Palace

From the parking area of Wat Phra That Doi Suthep a road ascends 5km (3 miles) to **Phu Phing Palace** (gardens only: Sat–Sun and holidays 8.30am–4pm when the royal family is absent; charge). Constructed in 1972 as the royal family's winter residence, the palace, at an elevation of 1,300 metres (4,265ft), has audience halls, guesthouses, dining rooms, kitchens and official suites. Its beautiful, well-tended gardens are a highlight. It also serves as headquarters for the royal family's agricultural and medical projects in aid of the hill tribes and people living in the nearby villages.

Doi Pui

From the palace entrance, the road continues through pine forests to the commercialised Hmong hilltribe village of **Doi Pui**. Tourism has brought material benefits to the village, including a paved street lined with souvenir stands. Once subsistence farmers, the tribespeople have long since become wise to the tourist dollar, and the sight of a camera automatically triggers a hand extended for a donation. The Hmong, whose population straddles Thailand, Myanmar and Laos, once grew opium for their

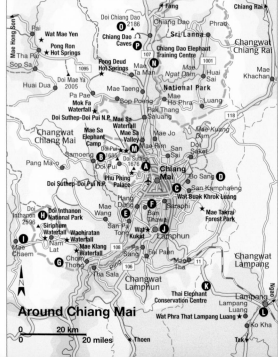

livelihood; despite government efforts to steer them towards other crops, many still cultivate small patches of the lucrative poppy deep in the hills.

For those who lack the time to go deeper into the northern hills, Doi Pui offers an example of hill-tribe life, albeit in rather ersatz form. An interesting insight into opium farming is provided by Doi Pui's **Opium Museum** (daily 9am–5pm; charge), which details the process of cultivation and harvest.

A well-worn hiking trail leads to the summit of 1,685-metre (5,525ft) **Doi Pui ❸**, a much-favoured picnicking spot among Chiang Mai residents. Maps of other hiking trails are available at the Doi Suthep/Doi Pui National Park headquarters (daily 8am–6pm). Two waterfalls, **Sai Yai** and **Monthathon**, can easily be visited in the park.

EAST OF CHIANG MAI

Heading east out of Chiang Mai leads to a handicraft village and a sacred Buddhist cave, but first you will pass **Wat Buak Khrok Luang ❻** (daily 8am–6pm; free) located about 300 metres (330 yards) south off Route 1006, just before the km 4 marker en route to Bo Sang. This is a 19th-century monastery with a charming set of Shan and Lanna murals in remarkably good condition.

Bo Sang

About 9km (5½ miles) east of Chiang Mai on Route 1006 is **Bo Sang ❿** (or Bor Sang), known as the "Umbrella Village" because much of the village is devoted to the crafting of painted paper umbrellas made from the bark of the mulberry tree. But umbrellas are not the only products sold here; there are variety of other handicrafts, including lacquerware, silverware, hill-tribe jewellery, silk, bronze sculptures, woodcarvings and ceramics.

Tham Muang On

Some 28km (17 miles) east from Chiang Mai, off Route 1317, on a scenic country road that parallels Route 1006, is **Tham Muang On**, a sacred Buddhist cave set into a huge limestone cliff. A large stalactite found in the cave's main chamber is worshipped as a natural *chedi* by Buddhist visitors.

Khru Ba Sriwichai (1878–1938) was a charismatic monk who organised the building of a road to Doi Suthep temple as well as many other temple constructions and renovations. Because of his superior ability to organise the local people, he was often in conflict with the Bangkok authorities. Today he is viewed as a nak bun, *or saint, in Chiang Mai, and a shrine dedicated to him at the foot of Doi Suthep is regularly visited by devotees.*

BELOW: umbrella painter at work in Bo Sang.

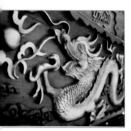

A woodcarving at Baan Thawai village, near Chiang Mai.

Close to the cave are a set of steep cliffs known as **Crazy Horse Buttress**. With 16 crags and over 100 rock-climbing routes, it is very popular with local and visiting rock climbers.

Another 20km (12 miles) to the east in the village of Mae Kompong, lies **Flight of the Gibbon**, a popular new zip-line park.

SOUTH OF CHIANG MAI

Route 108 heads south from Chiang Mai to a cluster of three small towns noted for their handicrafts and antiques.

Hang Dong, Ban Wan and Ban Thawai

About 15km (9 miles) south of Chiang Mai is **Hang Dong ⑤**, a burgeoning centre for ceramics, antiques, wooden furniture and crafts made from woven bamboo, cane and rattan. Shops along Route 108 deal with both retail as well as wholesale business; either way, bargaining is in order.

Ban Wan, to the immediate east of Hang Dong, is a village with a small selection of relatively high-quality antique and furniture shops. A few

kilometres further to the east, its larger and more famous sister village, **Ban Thawai ⑥**, is a mishmash of shops and factories dealing in woodcarvings and made-to-order furniture. Even for those who are not interested in buying, Ban Wan and Ban Thawai are worth visiting to watch artisans at work.

Wat Phra That Si Chom Thong

Some 58km (34 miles) further south-west, Route 108 leads to the district of **Chom Thong ⑥**, the jump-off point for Doi Inthanon National Park (*see opposite*). The pride of Chom Thong, an agricultural centre, is the elegant temple of **Wat Phra That Si Chom Thong** (daily 8am–6pm; charge), where glints of subdued light accentuate a beautiful collection of bronze Buddhas. The gilded *chedi* dates from 1451, and the sanctuary from 65 years later. The large cruciform *viharn* – deeply incised with floral patterns entwined with birds and *naga* serpents – dominates the temple compound. Four standing Buddhas, clothed as celestial kings, flank the *viharn*.

BELOW: Wachiratan Waterfall, Doi Inthanon National Park.

While much of the temple decoration reflects a Shan/Burmese penchant for elaboration, the central Buddha image, with its protective *naga*, seems eminently Lanna, and resembles the image at Wat Phra Singh in Chiang Mai. On either side of the *viharn* are enshrined miniature gold and silver Buddha images, some bejewelled and metallic, others carved from crystal. Behind the main compound, a large **meditation centre** (tel: 0-5382 6869) offers 10- to 26-day courses in *vipassana* (insight meditation).

Doi Inthanon N P

From Chom Thong, the gateway to **Doi Inthanon National Park ⓗ** (daily 8am–6pm; charge), it's another 47km (28 miles) to the summit of **Doi Inthanon**, Thailand's highest peak at 2,596 metres (8,516ft). The steep, forest-clad slopes and mist-shrouded summit of the limestone massif are awe-inspiring. Hmong and Karen villages have been allowed to remain in the reserve since they take part in temperate-weather vegetable farming – part of the Royal Project's opium cultivation eradication program. The ashes of Chiang Mai's last king are enshrined on its summit.

The park admission fee must be paid by all who drive beyond the park entrance near the bottom of the mountain, including visitors to the trio of waterfalls along the way to the summit – **Mae Klang**, **Wachiratan** and **Siriphum**. Mae Klang is the most popular and the most accessible, with a footbridge linking viewpoints at various elevations. By making prior arrangements with park authorities, visitors can take a three- to five-day trek up the mountain on foot or by pony. Several campsites (B40) and bungalows (B800–1,000) provide simple accommodation for trekkers (tel: 0-5328 6730 for reservations).

Mae Chaem

Visitors to Doi Inthanon can take a side trip to secluded **Mae Chaem ⓘ**, famous for the distinctive weaving used to make the *pha sin*, a skirt worn by northern Thai women.

A few kilometres south of Mae Chaem is **Wat Pa Daet** (daily 8am–6pm; free). Thai art historians admire the temple's rare, post-Lanna murals for their velvety blues and reds, accented by bold black outlines that lend a poetic rusticity to the art. The murals provide a rich source of detail on the clothing of the era, with vivid depictions of the loom-woven, horizontal-striped women's skirts, and the intricate waist-to-knee blue tattoos once worn by virtually all northern Thai men. Faded inscriptions below the mural panels record the names of local donors who sponsored the art to earn merit.

LAMPHUN

Straddling the Ping River 25km (15 miles) south of Chiang Mai along tree-lined Route 106, the town of **Lamphun ⓙ** is said to date back to the 8th century. It was a centre of Mon culture until King Mangrai overran the city in 1281. Once sited on the main road from Chiang Mai to Lampang, the newer Highway 11 bypasses Lamphun, which has enabled the town to preserve its mellow

BELOW: giant *yang* trees line the road from Chiang Mai to Lamphun.

Giant gong, Wat Phra That Hariphunchai.

BELOW: Chedi Kukut, Wat Chama Thewi.

upcountry quality. Today, it is famed for its attractive, confident women, succulent *lamyai* fruit and two elegant temples. It has also become a popular place of residence for Thai artists seeking peace from city life.

Wat Phra That Hariphunchai

Lamphun houses two of the most famous temples in Thailand. **Wat Phra That Hariphunchai** (daily 8am–6pm; free) has one of the eight holiest *chedi* in the country. For the best perspective of the temple, enter through its riverside gate, where statues of mythical lions guard its portals. Inside the large compound, monks study in a Buddhist school set amidst monuments and buildings that date back to the 11th century, making this temple one of the oldest in northern Thailand. **Chedi Suwan**, the 50-metre (165ft) high gold-topped tower in the centre of the courtyard dates back to 1418 and may in fact be built over an older, smaller *chedi*.

Six hundred years younger, but still respectably old, the gilt-roofed *ho trai* (library) stands to the left of an open-air pavilion that shelters one of the world's largest bronze gongs. The temple museum contains several styles of old Buddhist art.

Wat Chama Thewi

A kilometre (2/3 mile) west of Lamphun's old moat stands **Wat Chama Thewi** (daily 8am–6pm; free), also known as **Wat Kukut**. It was originally built by the Dvaravati Mon in the 8th or 9th century and rebuilt by the Hariphunchai Mon in 1218. The monastery contains a superb and unusual tower called Chedi Kukut. The rectilinear *chedi* consists of five tiers, each of which has three niches. Each niche houses a Buddha statue, making for an impressive display of 15 Buddha images on each side. The overall plan is very similar to Sri Lanka's Satmahal Prasada, which is approximately a century older, suggesting a Buddhist link between Hariphunchai and Sri Lanka.

Hariphunchai Museum

At nearby Thanon Inthayongyot is the **Hariphunchai National Museum**

Queen Chamadevi

The first ruler of the Mon statelet of Hariphunchai, later to become Lamphun, was a woman called Chamadevi. She ruled the city wisely, and spread the Buddhist faith. Local legend recounts that she received the unwelcome attentions of King Viranga, the ruler of the indigenous Lawa, an uncivilised, animist people from the nearby hills. Protocol demanded that she agree to the marriage, but she added a condition – he must hurl a spear from his native Chiang Mai to Lamphun. His first effort landed just outside her city's walls. Queen Chamadevi then sent him a gift of a hat, which he immediately placed on his head. The hat, however, was made from her petticoat and this sapped Viranga of his supernatural powers and his subsequent efforts fell short of his target.

(Wed–Sun 9am–4pm; charge), which has a very good collection of historical artefacts on the surrounding region. These mainly focus on the Hariphunchai kingdom, along with a number of items from the Dvaravati and Lanna kingdoms.

Thai Elephant Conservation Centre

Off Highway 11, southeast towards Lampang from Lamphun or Chiang Mai, is the royally sponsored **Thai Elephant Conservation Centre**  (daily 8am–3.30pm; charge; www.changthai. com). It stages shows twice a day (three times a day on weekends and holidays) to demonstrate how elephants were once used as work animals for logging and agriculture. The elephants have been trained to play music together on gigantic Thai musical instruments. They can also hold brushes in their trunks and paint colourful scenes on canvases, all of which are available for purchase after the show.

For an additional fee, visitors can take elephant rides through the grounds, lasting from 15 minutes to one hour. An onsite hospital treats sick or injured animals.

LAMPANG

About 30km (18 miles) further to the southeast, Highway 11 enters the provincial capital of **Lampang** ⓛ. Although much of its bucolic tranquillity has disappeared, it retains one relic found in no other Thai city: horse-drawn carriages. These can be hired by the journey or by the hour. There are few more romantic experiences in Thailand than clip-clopping down a moonlit backstreet.

Wat Phra Kaew Don Tao

Several unique temples in Lampang, each showing various degrees of Burmese, Shan and Lanna influence, are worth seeing. On the right bank of the Wang River, **Wat Phra Kaew Don Tao** (daily 8am–6pm; free) is a striking fusion of Burmese and Lanna architecture. In the *mondop* (square pavilion), teak columns soar to a ceiling covered in a kaleidoscope of inlaid enamel, mother-of-pearl and cut glass, depicting mythical animals.

Horse-drawn carts are a feature of Lampang. A 15-minute jaunt around town will cost you B150. They can usually be found near the big hotels in town.

BELOW: Wat Phra Kaew Don Tao.

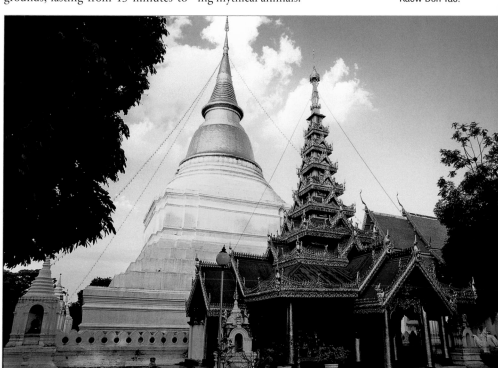

TIP

Don't miss seeing Baan
Sao Nak, or "Many
Pillars House" (daily
10am–5pm; charge; tel:
0-5422 7653). Located
in the northern part of
Lampang town, this
Lanna-style house built
in 1895 is supported by
an astonishing 116 teak
pillars.

Wat Chedi Sao

Surrounded by rice fields 6km (4 miles) north of town, the 20 chalk-white *chedi* of **Wat Chedi Sao** (daily 8am–6pm; free) occupy lovely monastery grounds landscaped with casuarinas and bougainvillea. A 15th-century solid gold Buddha image weighing 1,507kg (3,311lbs) is on display in a glass-encased room built over a pond.

Wat Phra That Lampang Luang

A masterpiece of northern Thai temple architecture, **Wat Phra That Lampang Luang** (daily 8am–6pm; free) is situated 20km (12 miles) south of town in Ko Kha district. Cherished by scholars for its antiquity and delicate artwork, the temple compound is all that remains of a fortress city that flourished more than a millennium ago. The temple's triple-roofed, open-sided main chapel, **Viharn Luang**, was built in 1476 and is thought to be the oldest existing wood building in Thailand. A large gilded and enclosed shrine in the back of the hall displays a venerable 16th-century bronze Buddha image. Other important structures include the 45-metre (147ft) **Phra That Lampang Luang** (a copper-plated, Lanna-style *chedi*) and the diminutive **Viharn Nam Taem**, a 16th-century Thai Lü-style building famous for its surviving pastel-hued murals.

NORTH OF CHIANG MAI

Northwest of Chiang Mai is **Mae Sa** , a valley that was once a thriving agricultural region. Today, a variety of tourist developments have taken hold, including resorts, elephant camps, butterfly farms, orchid nurseries, tiger, snake and monkey exhibitions, even a bungee jump. While most of these fall into the category of "tourist traps", some, especially those with children, report that they quite enjoyed being trapped.

The most visited place is probably the **Mae Sa Elephant Camp** (shows at 8am, 9.40am and 1.30pm daily; charge; www.maesaelephantcamp.com), near the **Mae Sa Waterfall**. Visitors can watch elephants bathing, dragging logs and performing other feats.

The orchid nurseries are nothing to shout about. Of the two options, **Sai Nam Phung Orchid and Butterfly**

BELOW: main *chedi* and Buddha within Viharn Luang at Wat Phra That Lampang Luang.
BELOW RIGHT: northern elephants.

Farm (daily 7am–5pm; charge) is the better bet. About 2km (1½ miles) away are the **Queen Sirikit Botanic Gardens** (daily 8am–5.30pm; charge), developed with the help of Britain's famous Kew Gardens and including a 5km (3-mile) nature trail.

To reach the northern town of **Fang** (see page 303), take Route 107 north from Chiang Mai towards Chiang Dao. The road passes through rice fields and small villages, then climbs past Mae Taeng into the Mae Ping Gorge, which forms the southern end of the Chiang Dao valley. On the left, as one follows the river's right bank through scenic countryside, is the silhouette of Doi Chiang Dao mountain.

Chiang Dao Elephant Training Centre

At the km 56 marker is the **Chiang Dao Elephant Training Centre** Ⓝ (daily 8am–5pm; charge) on the bank of the Ping River. Twice daily, a line of elephants are walked into the Ping River to be bathed by their *mahout* for tourists.

After the show, one can take a short elephant ride, and then hire a small bamboo raft for a 45-minute trip down the river.

Doi Chiang Dao

About 60km (40 miles) north of Chiang Mai on Route 107, a dirt road branches left to **Doi Chiang Dao** Ⓞ, which at 2,186 metres (7,175ft) is Thailand's third-highest peak. A jeep or a trail bike is needed to negotiate this 9km (6-mile) long track up to the Hmong village of Pakkia on the mountain. Entry to the sanctuary is restricted, and permission must be obtained from the wildlife headquarters near **Tham Pha Plong Monastic Centre** at the foot of the mountain.

Tham Chiang Dao

Further north, Route 107 enters the quiet town of **Chiang Dao**, located 70km (45 miles) from Chiang Mai. At the far end of town, a road leads off west and to the left for 5km (3 miles) to the caves at **Tham Chiang Dao** Ⓟ (daily 8am–5pm; charge). Guides lead visitors deep into high caverns that contain Buddha statues. Further down is a large, reclining limestone Buddha. ❑

TIP

A good day trip, either by car or motorcycle, is the so-called "Samoeng Loop", a trip of just under 100km (60 miles), which can be undertaken by heading north towards Mae Rim (Route 107), then following the winding road (Route 1096) up the Mae Sa valley around the back of Doi Pui, where it emerges south of Chiang Mai near Hang Dong, and continuing north to your starting point in Chiang Mai.

RESTAURANTS

Doi Suthep
Thai
Huay Kaew Restaurant
Th. Huay Kaew. No phone. Open: daily L & D. $–$$
The wood-and-bamboo pavilion overlooking Huay Kaew Falls is perfect for a sunset beer or a meal on the way back from Doi Suthep. Good northern and northeastern Thai.

Lamphun
Thai
Kuaytiaw Kai Jaw
Th. Wangsai. No Phone. Open: daily 8am–3pm. $
This corner spot offers a unique dish of rice noodles, steamed chicken sausage, carrots and seaweed. It is an energy-booster, and a good way to begin a day among Lamphun's temples.

Lampang
Thai
Aroy Baht Diaw
Th. Suan Dok. Tel: 08-970 0944. Open: daily 5–11pm. $
The name means "delicious for one baht", and it lives up to the name, making it busy most evenings. Located next to the night market, it's in an old house with a nice garden. Thai dishes such as *tom yam* soups are excellent here.

Thai & Western
The Riverside
328 Th. Tipchang. Tel: 0-5422 7005. Open: daily 11am–midnight. $$
This collection of old teak houses teetering on the edge of the Wang River packs in locals and tourists alike, with a varied menu of Thai, Western and vegetarian fare. The nightly live music performances are a bonus.

Chiang Dao
Western
Chiang Dao Nest
144/6 Moo 5, Chiang Dao. Tel: 0-5345 6242. Open: daily L & D. $$
The Western menu changes daily and can cover items like olives marinated in chilli oil, lime and herbs, pork tenderloin in blue-cheese sauce, thin crust pizzas (baked in an authentic stone oven) or warm chocolate soufflés.

Khao Mao Khao Fang
Ratchapreuk Road, Hang Dong. Tel: 0-5383 8444. Open: L & D $$
Heading south from Chiang Mai, on the right before the turnoff to Ban Thawai, this lovely garden restaurant serves a wide variety of Thai food. A good place to relax after a shopping spree in Ban Thawai.

Price per person for a three-course meal without drinks:

$ = under B300
$$ = B300–800
$$$ = B800–1,600
$$$$ = over B1,600

CHIANG RAI AND EAST

The mere mention of "Golden Triangle" – the point where Thailand, Laos and Myanmar meet – evokes thoughts of uncertain frontiers and illicit smuggling. But there is also much to be enjoyed in this little-visited area of north Thailand

L ike other cities of the north, **Chiang Rai** has undergone rapid development in recent years, not only in the town itself but also in the surrounding hills, where holiday homes for affluent Thais are springing up. Disappointingly for travellers seeking the picturesque, little of Chiang Rai's rich past is still extant. Outside the provincial capital, however, there are many rewarding sights, both historical and natural. To the east, the seldom visited provinces of Phrae and Nan reveal aspects of northern Thai life and culture that only a small percentage of tourists ever encounter.

CHIANG MAI TO CHIANG RAI

For most visitors, the trip to Chiang Rai begins in Chiang Mai. The most direct route between the two cities follows Route 118 (*see page 305*). Taking about three hours, the 183km (114-mile) journey meanders through hills and valleys with little of major interest along the way.

The longer route, via Chiang Dao through Fang and Thaton, is recommended for those with more time. Out of Chiang Mai, Route 107 heads due north past Chiang Dao to **Fang ❷**, 150km (94 miles) from Chiang Mai. Established by King Mangrai in the late 1260s, Fang was destroyed by

the Burmese in the early 1800s and remained uninhabited for several decades before being re-established in the 1880s. During the 1950s, the district witnessed a black-gold rush following a minor discovery of crude oil. Production never matched expectations, but "nodding donkey" pumps still groan and grind in the fields to the west of town. Fang has a rough reputation for *yaa baa* (amphetamine) smugglers, although nothing in its seemingly benign appearance would suggest as much.

LEFT: view of the Kok River from Thaton, Chiang Mai. **RIGHT:** Lahu hill-tribe family.

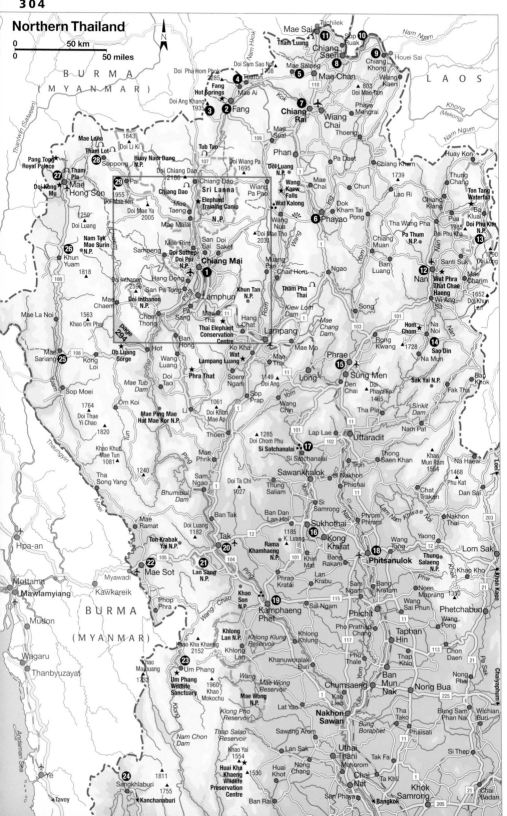

Northern Thailand

0 — 50 km
0 — 50 miles

BURMA
(MYANMAR)

LAOS

BURMA
(MYANMAR)

Andaman Sea

Mae Sai
Tachilek
Sop Ruak
11 Tham Luang
10
Chiang **8** Saen **9** Chiang Khong
Houei Sai
Mae Salong
5 Mae Chan
Doi Pha Hom Phok
Doi Sam Sao Noi 1708
2285
4 Thaton
Wiang Kaen
Doi Mae Tam 803
7 Chiang **6** Rai
Hot Springs
Fang
Doi Ang Khang 1935
3 **2** Fang
Mae Ai
Phaya Mengrai
Chiang Chai
Wiang Chai
Khong (Mekong)
Nam Ngum

Mae Lana
Tham Lot 1843 Doi Li Ki
Huay Nam Dang N.P.
Mae Suai
Thoeng
Pa Daet
Huay Kon
Thung Chang
28 Soppong
Doi Chiang Dao 2186
Chiang Dao
Sri Lanna
Wiang Pa Pao
Phan
Chiang Kham
Ton Tang Waterfall
1739
Chiang Klang
Pua 1895
Doi Phu Kha N.P.
13
Doi Long 1790

Pang Tong Royal Palace
27 Tham Pla
Doi Kong Mu
Mae Hong Son
29 Pai
Doi Mae Yen
Mae Taeng 2005
Elephant Training Camp N.P.
Wang Kaew Falls
Wat Kalong
Dok Kham Tai
Pong
6 Phayao
Tha Wang Pha
Pa Thum N.P.
Doi Phu Kha
Santi Suk
Doi Charim

955
Doi Mae Ya
Mae Malai
Wang Nua
Doi Mae Tho 2031
Chiang Muan
Nan **12**
Wat Phra That Chae Haeng
1250
Doi Luang
San Sai Doi Saket
Mae Rim
26 Khun Yuam 1818
Samoeng
Doi Suthep N.P.
1 Chiang Mai
Muang Pan
Chae Hom
Ban Luang
Wi Ang Sa
1652
Doi Khun Lan

Mae La Noi
1563
Khao Om Phai
Doi Inthanon 2596
Hang Dong
Lamphun
Khun Tan N.P.
Tham Pha Thai
Ngao
Song
Rong Kwang
Hom Chom
Na Nua
Sao Din **14**

25 Mae Sariang
108
Kong Loi
San Pa Tong
Doi Inthanon N.P.
Chom Thong
Pa Sang
Mae Tha
Hang Chat
Kiew Lom Dam
Mae Chang Dam
Na Mun
1728

Mae Sot area... Hot
Ob Luang Gorge
Wang Luang
Doi Tao
Lampang Luang
Phra That
Wat
Mae Mo
Lampang
Phrae
Sung Men **15**
Den Chai
Doi Phaya Fai 1465
Sak Yai N.P.
Fak Tha
Bap Knok

1764
Doi Thae Yi Chao 1820
Mae Tub Dam
Li
Doi Khun Mae Ap
Soem Ngam
Sop Prap
1061
1149
Doi Ang
Long
Wang Chin
Tha Pla
Sirikit Dam
Na Haew

Thaungyin
Khao Khut Mae Tun 1081
Om Koi
Thoen
1285
Si Satchanalai
Doi Chom Phu
Lap Lae
Uttaradit
Thong Saen Khan
1468
Phu Kat
Khao Mun Ram 1564
Chat Trakan
Dan Sai
Loei

Mae Ramat
Mae Phrik
Si Satchanalai
Tron
Si Nakhon
Phichai
Nam Pat

Sam Ngao
Doi Ta Chi
1027
Sawankhalok
Thung Saliam
Si Samrong
Phrom Phiram
Nakhon Thai
203

Mae Ping Mae Hat Mae Kor N.P.
Bhumibol Dam
Ban Tak
Doi Luang 1182
Ban Dan Lan Hoi
1185
Si Samrong
16 Sukhothai
Kong Krailat
Wang Tong
Yaong
Lom Sak

Tha Song Yang
1240
Tak
Rama Khamhaeng N.P.
20
101
Khin Mat
Phran Kratai
18 Phitsanulok
Thung Salaeng Luang N.P.
Khao Kho
1350
21
Phetchabun

Hpa-an
Ton Krabak Yai N.P.
Lan Sang N.P. **21**
104
Lan Krabu
Sam Ngam
Bang Krathum
Noen Maprang
Wang Sai Phun
Wang Pong

22 Mae Sot
Myawadi
Phop Phra
Wang Chao
19 Kamphaeng Phet
Sai Ngam
Pho Prathap Chang
Phichit
Taphan Hin
Chon Daen
113
Pa Sak
Chaiyaphum

Kawkareik
Khao Son N.P.
Khlong Lan N.P.
Khlong Klung Reservoir
Khlong Khlung
Khanuworalak Buri
Pho Thale
Thap Khlo
21

Mottama
Mawlamyaing
Mudon
Khao Kha Khaeng 2152
Khlong Lan
Khao Mamuang 1733
23 Um Phang
Um Phang Wildlife Sanctuary
1960
Khao Mokochu
Mae Wong N.P.
Lat Yao
Chumsaeng
Kao Lieo
Ban Mun Nak
Nong Bua
Tha Tako
Bung Sam Phan Nai
Wichian Buri
225

Wagaru
Thanbyuzayat
Khao Wong
Mae Wong Reservoir
Klong Pho Reservoir
Nakhon Sawan
Bung Boraphet
Phaisali
Si Thep

Ye
24 Sangkhlaburi
1811
1755
Kanchanaburi
1530
Khao Yai 1554
Huai Kha Khaeng Wildlife Preservation Centre
Thap Salao Reservoir
Nam Chon Dam
Sawang Arom
Khao Khot
Nong Chang
Lan Sak
Uthai Thani
Manorom
Huai Khot
San Phaya
Ta Khli
Chai Nat
Ban Rai
Khok Samrong
205
Bangkok
Chai Badan
21
Tavoy

page 294

B U R M A (M Y A N M A R)

T H A I L A N D

Doi Ang Khang

Some 40km (25 miles) west of Fang stands **Doi Ang Khang** ❸, which at an altitude of 1,935 metres (6,348ft) has a pleasant year-round climate (albeit with temperatures that can plummet to freezing in winter). The agricultural station here, supported by the Thai monarchy, specialises in the research of temperate fruit trees, vegetables, herbs and flowers. There are a few accommodation options on the mountain, the most luxurious of which is **Angkhang Nature Resort** (www.amari.com/angkhang), offering rooms with private balconies and mountain views. It makes an excellent base for trekking and biking excursions.

Thaton and Mae Salong

A few kilometres south of Fang, Route 109 cuts east towards Chiang Rai. Alternatively, north from Fang, a rough road leads 25km (15 miles) to **Thaton** ❹, on the banks of the **Kok River**. Here, you can rent a boat for an exciting three-hour journey down the Kok River to Chiang Rai (*see margin, right*).

From Thaton, one can continue north to the unusual hill town of **Mae Salong** ❺ (also known as **Santikhiri**) on a dusty, but wide, paved road. The road climbs a ridge along the Myanmar border, emerging at a small town clinging to the hillside. At first, it seems one has taken a wrong turn and ended up in a Chinese village. The walls of the houses are decorated with red banners covered in gold Chinese characters; everyone speaks Chinese.

Many Mae Salong residents are the descendants of Kuomintang soldiers who were given refuge in Thailand after China's Communist takeover. Unfortunately, many of them became involved in the opium trade, led by infamous opium warlords like the Shan-Chinese Khun Sa, who lived in nearby Ban Hin Taek (now called Ban Thoet Thai). Under pressure from the Thai military, and with incentives provided by the Thai monarchy, the opium farmers gradually converted to other crops, and by the late 1980s large-scale poppy cultivation was finished. Many of the locals now tend tea plantations and brew potent rice wines.

Route 118 via Phayao

Route 118 leads northeast from Chiang Mai via **Doi Saket**, a community whose Thai-style retirement homes have become popular among Westerners. About 74km (44 miles) further on, a detour signposted to Wang Nua (Route 120) leads east for 59km (35 miles) across rolling hills to **Phayao** ❻, focal point of the hugely fertile **Ing River** basin. The province encompasses an extensive area of wetland comprising networks of ponds, swamps and waterways.

Although relatively small (pop. 56,000) and undistinguished, the provincial capital and nearby districts hold considerable interest for archaeologists, who believe that an unbroken series of at least four former settlements existed in the area before the Lanna period. Judging from the remains of a moat and eight city gates that enclose an area of about 2 sq km (¾ sq mile), scholars believe the oldest site here may predate

TIP

It's possible to travel from Thaton to Chiang Rai by boat via the Kok River. Either take the public boat (departure daily 12.30pm; B350 per person) or hire a boat (B2,300 for the entire boat). The ride will take about three hours during the rainy season, but can take longer if water levels are low.

BELOW: an Akha woman picking tea near Mae Salong.

Elephants, which once roamed freely in Thailand, are now an endangered species. There are fewer than 5,000 remining in the country today, and, less than half of these are found in the wild.

BELOW: overloaded pick-up truck at Chiang Rai.

the Bronze Age. Phayao was part of Chiang Mai Province until 1977, when the central government accepted a petition for independent provincial status.

Kwan Phayao and environs

Phayao's landmark **Kwan Phayao**, an 18-sq-km (7-sq-mile) lake stretching out in front of the town's eastern flank, serves not only as a source of livelihood for farmers and fishers, but as the main local source of recreation. Among the fish commonly found in this lake is the sailfin shark (not an actual shark, but related to the carp), which is also found in the Salween and Mekong rivers. A scenic promenade on the lake's east side, a popular gathering place for locals, is lined with restaurants.

On the southern edge of the lake sits **Wat Si Khom Kham** (daily 8am–6pm; free), considered the area's most important temple because it houses a 400-year-old, 16-metre (55ft) high Buddha image called Phra Chao Ton Luang. In a new *bot* (ordination hall) on the lake's edge, modern Thai artist Angkarn Kalayanapongsa's contemporary Buddhist murals use bright col-

ours and modern brush techniques to cleverly reinterpret traditional themes.

Next to Wat Si Khom Kham, the well-designed **Phayao Cultural Exhibition Hall** (Wed–Sun 9am–4pm; charge) contains a collection of historic sandstone sculptures from pre-Lanna cultures in Phayao, along with lacquerware, ceramics, textiles and other handicrafts.

CHIANG RAI

From Phayao, Highway 1 continues north for some 100km (62 miles) towards **Chiang Rai** ❼, the capital of Thailand's northernmost province and situated at an elevation of about 580 metres (1,900ft). King Mangrai, who also established Chiang Mai, founded the city in 1292. He is comemmorated by a much-venerated statue in the northeastern part of the city, by a reconstructed stretch of the old city wall.

Wat Phra Singh and Wat Phra Kaew

Despite its exotic location, the city itself lacks both ambience and historic ruins. Located near the busy streets are two of the town's most important temples:

Wat Phra Singh and Wat Phra Kaew. Both temples share the distinction of having once sheltered famous images.

The *chedi* and *viharn* (sermon hall) at **Wat Phra Singh** (daily 8am–6pm; free) have been restored too many times to allow accurate dating, but documents suggest that construction first took place in the 15th century or earlier.

Founded in the 13th century, **Wat Phra Kaew** (daily 8am–6pm; free), on Thanon Trairat behind Wat Phra Singh, was the original residence of Thailand's holiest Buddha image, now housed in a royal temple of the same name in Bangkok (*see page 110*). Local chronicles say its *chedi* was struck by lightning in 1434, revealing a jadeite Buddha image that became known as the Emerald Buddha. A close copy carved of Canadian jade, commissioned in 1990 and called the Phra Yok Chiang Rai (Chiang Rai Jade Buddha), occupies an ornate shrine, the **Haw Phra Kaew**, on the temple grounds.

Hill Tribe Museum

Another worthy stop is the **Hill Tribe Museum and Education Centre** (Mon–Fri 9am–6pm, Sat–Sun 10am–6pm; charge; www.pda.or.th/chiangrai) on Thanon Tanalai. It provides a useful overview of hill-tribe community life and sells ethnic handicrafts at its gift shop. All proceeds go towards supporting hill tribe community projects.

THE NORTHERN BORDER AND GOLDEN TRIANGLE

The **Mekong River** – the name conjures images of another time, another place, another world. It is the 12th-longest river in the world at 4,000km (2,500 miles), and passes through six countries on its way to the South China Sea. It also defines much of the remote border area between Thailand and Laos.

Chiang Saen

The ancient capital of **Chiang Saen** ❽ – 60km (37 miles) northeast of Chiang Rai – nestles near the point where Myanmar, Laos and Thailand meet. For years this area, known as the Golden Triangle, produced a considerable portion of the world's opium. Thailand's contribution has dropped greatly in the past 25 years, but Laos, and especially Myanmar, continue to produce opium in large quantities.

Scholars believe Chiang Saen was founded around the end of the 13th century and heavily fortified about 100 years later by a grandson of King Mangrai. The Burmese captured it in the 16th century, but Rama I of Thailand retook it in the early 1800s. Fearing history would repeat itself with another Burmese invasion, however, Rama I ordered the town abandoned. It remained deserted for nearly a century. In 1957, the revived town became a district seat. Today, it is a thriving river port for barges from China carrying all manner of Chinese exports. Passengers can now travel up the Mekong by boat on an express passenger boat to the Chinese town of Jinghong (a visa must be obtained in advance at any Chinese consulate, such as in Chiang Mai or Bangkok).

> 66
> *Necessity knows no law. We fight the evil of Communism, and to fight you must have an army, which must have guns that are bought with money. In these mountains, the only money is opium, which is why we deal in it.*
>
> KMT General Duan Shi Wen, interviewed in Doi Mae Salong, Thailand, 1967.
> 99

BELOW: Wat Pa Sak, Chiang Saen.

Chiang Saen's lovely setting on the Mekong River strongly enhances the charm of its old temples. Moreover, it is one of the few ancient towns in Thailand to have retained most of its lovely old trees. The remains of its once-formidable wall and moat can be seen at its perimeter, and the ruins of ancient monuments are scattered everywhere, popping up where one least expects them.

West of Chiang Saen

Just west of town stands **Wat Pa Sak** (daily 8am–6pm; free), whose name is derived from the 300 teak, or *sak*, trunks used for its original enclosure. The temple's foundation was laid in 1295, during the reign of King Mangrai. Earlier Srivijaya and Dvaravati influences, along with the then-prominent Sukhothai style, are evident in the *that* (reliquary), as well as the clothing worn by the deities.

Located about 1km (²/₃ mile) west of the town gate, **Wat Phra That Chom Kitti** (daily 8am–6pm; free) occupies a hill commanding a good view of Chiang Saen. Chronicles suggest that the old *that*, with a leaning top, was first built around the 10th century and restored at least twice. Below it lies a ruined *chedi* of **Wat Chom Chang**. From here, a staircase leads further downhill and back to town.

Chiang Saen National Museum & Wat Chedi Luang

Along the main street Thanon Pha-honyothin is **Chiang Saen National Museum** (Wed–Sun 9am–4pm; charge; www.thailandmuseum.com), with a good assortment of Lanna-period Buddha images and northern Thai ceramics as well as prehistoric and hill-tribe artefacts. Behind are the ruins of ruins of **Wat Chedi Luang**. The 60-metre (200ft) tall, 13th-century *chedi* stands out in style as well as size; its bricks rise from an octagonal base to a bell-shaped top.

Chiang Khong

A scenic excursion from Chiang Saen is to travel via longtail boat down the Mekong as far as **Chiang Khong** ❾, a three-hour trip possible after the rainy season, when the water level is high. The river follows an approximately S-shaped

course, first flowing southeast to the mouth of the Kok River, then curving north between hills and mountains, then finally heading south again for a thrilling 20km (12-mile) ride down deep and narrow sections, through stomach-churning rapids and swirling eddies beneath steep, jungled mountains.

At Chiang Khong, the river widens slightly. The Lao town of **Houei Sai** lies opposite, and ferries carry both passenger and vehicular traffic across the river, including large trucks with shipping containers headed for China, which lies a mere 250km (150 miles) to the north, on what are now quite passable roads. The towns on both sides of the river owe their vibrancy to this border traffic, which will increase when the bureaucratic obstacles are removed and a bridge is built (construction is due to begin in 2011). Visas for Laos are now available on arrival in Houei Sai.

Chiang Khong is also known for its giant Mekong catfish (see panel, below).

Sop Ruak

Head north for around 9km (6 miles) from Chiang Saen to reach the small town of **Sop Ruak** ❿, which proudly promotes itself as the "Heart of the Golden Triangle". In recent years, the town has heavily cashed in on the wild mystique of the area, and is home to several good resorts and hotels. The main street is lined with souvenir shops that sell a variety of local textiles and plastic kitsch, as well as numerous food stalls and restaurants.

Several boat trips are possible from Sop Ruak, including ferries to Chiang Saen and Chiang Khong, as well as round trips on the Mekong and Ruak rivers skirting the Myanmar and Lao frontiers.

Hall of Opium

In reality, Sop Ruak has little to hold the traveller's attention, aside from views of neighbouring Myanmar and Laos. Worth a visit, though, is the impressive **Hall of Opium** (Tue–Sun 10am–3.30pm; charge; www.goldentrianglepark.

The Hall of Opium in Sop Ruak.

BELOW: monument beside the Mekong at Sop Ruak.

com), just opposite the luxury **Anantara Resort and Spa Golden Triangle** to the southwest of town. This small but well-designed museum has multimedia displays and implements relating to the history, cultivation and trade of *Papaver somniferum* – the opium poppy from which heroin is extracted, and which has given the Golden Triangle its notoriety. Most exhibits are labelled in English.

Mae Sai

Continuing 35km (22 miles) northeast from Sop Ruak, the road finally reaches **Mae Sai ⑪**, the most northerly town in Thailand. This busy border town, with **Tachilek** clearly visible on the Myanmar side of the small Sai River, has a real frontier feel to it.

In the shops and stalls along the main streets of Mae Sai, Burmese, Thai, Shan and hill-tribe traders sell a heady mix of gems, lacquerware and antiques – both new and old – along with imported whisky, cigarettes and medicinal herbs.

To the west of the main street, close to the border, is a flight of steps ascending a hill to **Wat Phra That Doi Wao**. This temple was purportedly constructed in memory of several thousand Burmese soldiers who died fighting members of Chiang Kai-shek's Kuomintang army, which in turn was fighting against Mao Zedong's Communists for control of southern China. (Some versions of the story, for those of a different political persuasion, portray the Kuomintang as the heroes.) The temple grounds have splendid views over Mae Sai and Myanmar.

Tachilek (Myanmar)

From Mae Sai, visitors are allowed to cross the small bridge to **Myanmar** for the day to take a quick stroll around **Tachilek** – which really has little to offer except for the claim of visiting Myanmar. Alternatively, longer journeys of up to two weeks or more can be made by those already holding a 28-day Myanmar tourist visa, perhaps travelling as far as **Kengtung**, midway between Thailand and China. Frontier regulations between Thailand and Myanmar are prone to change, so check before crossing. And note that the bridge closes in the evening, so be sure not to get stranded overnight on the wrong side of the river.

Tham Luang

About 6km (4 miles) south of town is **Tham Luang** (daily 8am–5pm; charge), or Great Cave, reached via a turn-off to the west of Route 110 heading back to Chiang Rai. The cave burrows for several kilometres into the hills. Gas lanterns can be hired at the entrance.

NAN PROVINCE

Nan Province – due east of Chiang Mai – may be north Thailand's last great undiscovered tourist territory. The province has lovely mountains, the full complement of hill tribes, a newly designated national park, and a friendly population not yet jaded by exposure to foreign travellers. The principal roads are sealed and offer excellent mountain biking and motorcycling, since they are

BELOW: the bridge to Myanmar.

hilly rather than mountainous and seldom disrupted by traffic. The drawback is that very few people speak English, few signs are romanised, and there is barely any accommodation outside of the provincial capital.

The first Nan Dynasty emerged in the mid-1300s, and later became one of the first 10 Thai-Lao states to merge together to form the first Lanna empire. The town was later conquered by the Burmese and the next few hundred years were tumultuous, but in 1788 Nan allied with Siam. Because Nan's rulers cooperated in the drive by Chulalongkorn to unite a mismatched quilt of vassal states into a modern nation, the province retained its special status as a semi-independent principality until the death of the last Nan prince in 1931.

With its cement-block architecture, the town of **Nan** ⑫, 320km (200 miles) from Chiang Mai, initially appears to be yet another nondescript upcountry backwater. A stroll beyond the downtown area, however, soon reveals plenty of old wooden houses, of which three different upraised provincial styles can be discerned.

Nan National Museum

Exhibits of the three styles of Nan-style houses can be seen at the **Nan National Museum** (Mon–Sat 9am–4pm; charge; www.thailandmuseum.com). Make this your first stop. Located on Thanon Pha Kong, in the 1903 former palace of the last two Nan princes, the museum offers information on the hill tribes, crafts and history of this region – including displays of rare Lanna- and Lao-style Buddha images. A 300-year-old black elephant tusk on display is said to have magical powers.

Wat Phra That Chang Kham

The allegiances and influences of 600 years are evident in the temples of Nan, which display the architectural styles of Lanna, Sukhothai, northern and southern Laos, the Thai Lü people, and combinations thereof. Styles of the Sukhothai period are prominent

at **Wat Phra That Chang Kham** (daily 8am–6pm; free), across the street from Nan National Museum. Elephants, seven on each side, supporting the second tier of the square *chedi*, are a Sukhothai motif. The standing Buddhas in the 15th-century *viharn* are also Sukhothai. The scripture library, with its high ceiling, was once the largest in Thailand, though it is now empty.

Next to the Nan National Museum is the even older **Wat Hua Khuang** (daily 8am–6pm; free), with a wooden veranda in the Luang Prabang (or northern Lao) style. Although it's often closed, lucky visitors may catch the weekend painter who has spent years restoring the murals.

Wat Phumin

Nan's most famous murals are found a short walk south at **Wat Phumin** (daily 8am–6pm; free), which was first constructed in 1596 and features a *bot* with an unusual cruciform layout. The 19th-century murals depict episodes from the *Jataka*, the chronicle of Buddha's previous incarnations. If the great

Monks on the Thai–Burma bridge at Mae Sai.

BELOW: roof formations at Tham Luang cave.

Mural at Wat Phumin.

carved doors of the *viharn* wing are fully open, make sure to peek behind them to see the murals that decorate the front wall: there are rowing boats loaded with bearded foreigners who smoke pipes and wear naval caps, among them a few heavily-dressed *farang* (European) women. At the centre of the hall is a four-sided sitting Buddha in the Sukhothai style.

Wat Phra That Chae Haeng

Standing on a hill about 3km (2 miles) southeast of town and across the Nan River, where large "dragon boats" race for a week every autumn, is **Wat Phra That Chae Haeng** (daily 8am–6pm; free). You'll recognise the temple by the lengthy *naga* serpent snaking down the hill. The striking 55-metre (180ft) gilded *chedi* is classic Lanna. The *bot*, however, shows Thai Lü influences, such as the sweeping, five-layered wooden roof, the low ceilings and the intertwined *naga* carved in stucco over the entrance. Regarded as a minority, but not a hill tribe, the Thai Lü are ethnic Thais who settled in the Nan valley about 150 years ago.

Doi Phu Kha N P

One can arrange one- to three-day hill treks in Nan, but it is also possible to visit tribal (as well as Thai Lü) villages on the 80km (50-mile) journey to **Doi Phu Kha National Park** ⑬ (daily 8am–6pm; charge; www.dnp.go.th). The majestic mountains along this route are some of the most beautiful in Thailand.

The national park has some undisturbed areas, but they are not served by trails. Park rangers can direct you to some scenic spots, such as the 1,300-metre (4,300ft) peak of **Don Khao** and **Ton Tong Waterfall**.

Sao Din

About 60km (37 miles) south of Nan are the strange **Sao Din** ⑭ earth pillars. Carved by the wind, these bare, pointed projectiles form desolate canyons. Getting there by public transport is quite an effort; the easiest way is to rent a motorbike.

Southwest to Phrae

A walled, moat-encircled city like Chiang Mai and Lamphun, **Phrae** ⑮ is a sleepy provincial capital full of old teak mansions and historic temples. Founded in the 15th century, it established itself as an important centre of the teak trade in the 19th and early 20th centuries.

The city's best-known temple, **Wat Phra That Cho Hae**, is an important pilgrimage site. Perched on a low hill 9km (5 miles) southeast of town off Route 1022, it features a 33-metre (108ft) gilded *chedi* at its centre. Just outside the Old City, the towering wooden roofs of 19th-century **Wat Chom Sawan** demonstrate obvious Burmese/Shan influence, a legacy of the once-thriving teak merchants, most of whom hailed from Burma.

The best surviving example of local teak architecture is **Vongburi House** (daily 8am–5pm; charge). Completed in 1907, the two-storey mansion, which once housed Luang Phongphibun, Phrae's last monarch, is now a museum filled with the prince's antique furniture and personal effects. ❏

RESTAURANTS AND BARS

Restaurants

Price per person for a three-course meal without drinks:
$ = under B300
$$ = B300–800
$$$ = B800–1,600
$$$$ = over B1,600

Mae Salong
Chinese
Mae Salong Villa
5 Moo 1, Th. Doi Mae Salong. Tel: 0-5376 5114. Open: daily B, L & D. $$
With a terrific location overlooking the tea terraces, this hotel restaurant serves a nice selection of Yunnanese dishes. Worth trying are the local mushrooms, like *het hawm thawt* (deep-fried shiitake mushrooms).

Halal
Salima
400 Mu 1 Mae Salong Nok. Tel: 0-5370 5088. Open: daily L & D. $
This informal restaurant and tea shop serves excellent halal food (meaning you'll need to go elsewhere for pork or alcohol), including shitake mushrooms stewed in soy sauce, chicken soup with Chinese herbs, stewed beef and a spicy tea-leaf salad.

Phayao
Thai & Chinese
Wiang Tan
17/9 Th. Chai Kwan. No phone. Open: daily 10am–11pm. $
One of the larger and more popular lakeside restaurants in town, Wiang Tan serves a wide range of Chinese, central

Thai and northeastern dishes.

Chiang Rai
Thai
Cabbages & Condoms
620/1 Th. Thanalai. Tel: 0-5374 0784. Open: daily 8am–midnight. $$
Attached to the Hill-Tribe Museum and Education Centre, this garden restaurant is a branch of the Bangkok original, here specialising in northern Thai cuisine. All proceeds go towards HIV/AIDs education.

Salung Kham
384/3 Phaholyothin Rd. Tel: 0-5371 7192. Open: daily L & D. $$
Northern Thai food such as Chiang Rai sausage, Hinlay curry and steamed herbal chicken with bamboo shoots. The indoor section is nicely decorated with Thai handicrafts, and there is also a pleasant garden.

Thai & Chinese
Muang Thong Restaurant
Th. Phahonyothin. Tel: 0-5371 1162. Open: 24 hours. $
Close to the Wiang Inn in the centre of town, this casual eatery has good service, an extensive Thai and Chinese menu and a 24-hour opening policy. In addition to central Thai dishes (its roast duck curry is very popular), there are a few northern specialities.

Western
Golden Triangle Café
Golden Triangle Inn, 590 Th. Phahonyothin. Tel: 0-5371

1339. Open: daily 8am–10.30pm $$
Delicious Thai and Western fare, a number of vegetarian selections at lunch and dinner, plus hearty breakfast sets.

Kae's Casa Burrito
1025/37 Th. Jet Yot. Mobile tel: 08-9755 5225. Open: daily 8am–9pm. $$
Kae, a Thai woman who spent over 40 years in the US, runs this authentic Tex-Mex restaurant. The menu offers standards such as *burritos*, *fajitas*, *tacos* and *quesadillas*. Also on the menu are Thai and American dishes.

Mayura Bakery & Café
Wang Come Hotel. Tel: 0-5371 1800. Open: daily 10am–midnight. $$
Conveniently situated in the centre of town, the hotel coffee shop's lengthy menu covers an adequate variety of Thai and Western dishes.

Chiang Saen
Thai & Chinese
Chom Khong
2km (1 mile) south of town on the Mekong River. No phone. Open: daily 11am–10pm. $
In a simple home near the river (with bungalows for rent at the back), fronted by fruit gardens, a local family cooks up delicious dishes.

Chiang Khong
Thai & Western
Bamboo Riverside
71 Moo 1 Hua Wiang. Tel: 0-5379 1234. Open: daily 8am–9.30pm. $
In a rustic wood-and-bamboo pavilion with stupendous views over

the Mekong River and Laos, the Thai owners serve excellent Thai and Mexican dishes.

Sop Ruak
Thai & Western
Sugar Sugar
Tel: 0-5378 4472. Open: daily 11am–11pm. $$
Undoubtedly serves the best steaks in the north outside of Chiang Mai. Its Thai menu is equally outstanding.

Mae Sai
Thai & Western
Jojo Coffeeshop
233/1 Th. Phahonyothin. Tel: 0-5373 1662. Open: daily 6.30am–4.30pm. $
Decorated with shelves lined with wooden Buddhas, serves good Thai curries and Thai vegetarian dishes, along with Western breakfasts.

Nan
Italian
Da Dario
37/4 Th. Rat Amnuay. Tel: 0-5475 0258. Open: Tue–Sat 3–10pm, Sat–Sun 11am–10pm. $$
This Italian-owned dining room inside the owner's house has a strong local following for its home-made pizzas and pasta.

Phrae
Thai
Ban Fai
57/6 Moo 1, Th. Yantrakit Koson. Tel: 0-5542 3114. Open: daily D only. $
Set in a garden, this restaurant (3km/2 miles north of town) is attached to the Ban Fai Folklore Museum. Extensive menu includes central Thai dishes plus seafood.

SUKHOTHAI AND SURROUNDINGS

Sukhothai was the centre of the first independent Thai kingdom, considered to be the golden era of Thai history. Its magnificent temples, palaces and edifices vie for attention with the nearby monuments at Phitsanulok and Kamphaeng Phet

The ancient city of **Sukhothai ⑯** is set on a broad plain between the mountains of Tak Province and Burma to the west, and the mountains of Phetchabun, facing Laos to the east, depriving potential invaders of an element of surprise. Some 460km (275 miles) north of Bangkok and 330km (200 miles) south of Chiang Mai, the area is well fed by rivers -- ideal for rice cultivation, which allowed Ramkhamheang, the kingdom's most famous monarch, to proclaim, "There is fish in the water and rice in the fields," to describe this bounteous environment. To the Thais, the magnificent site represents the heritage of their people.

The route from Phitsanulok passes through New Sukhothai with its concrete shophouses, hotels and restaurants. About 10km (7 miles) further, the road enters the limits of old Sukhothai through **Kamphaenghak Gate**.

The Sukhothai kingdom was founded in 1238 following King Intharathit's assertion of independence from the Khmer empire. The kingdom, which included most of modern Thailand, parts of the Malay Peninsula and Burma, is synonymous with some of the finest artistic endeavours in Thai history, including the most exquisite Buddha images. Unfortunately, this golden age was relatively short-lived, lasting just two centuries: by 1438, it

had been consumed by the kingdom of Ayutthaya. The most notable of the Sukhothai kings was Ramkhamhaeng *(see page 32)*, who, among other noted accomplishments, reformed the Thai script, promoted Theravada Buddhism and established links with China.

SUKHOTHAI HISTORICAL PARK

The remains of ancient Sukhothai's massive walls reveal that the inner city was protected by three rows of earthen ramparts and two moats. The city was

Main attractions
SUKHOTHAI HISTORICAL PARK
SI SATCHANALAI–CHALIANG
HISTORICAL PARK
PHITSANULOK
KAMPHAENG PHET HISTORICAL
PARK

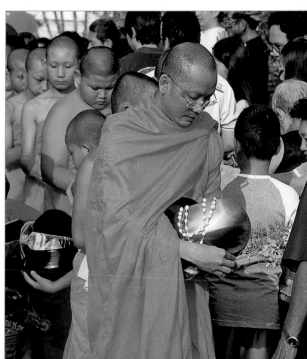

LEFT: Wat Mahathat, Sukhothai Historical Park. **RIGHT:** presenting alms to monks.

Terracotta figure from the landmark Sukhothai period.

originally founded by the Khmers, and the most visible remainder of their presence are the three Hindu *prang*, in the centre of Wat Si Sawai, which the Thais converted to a Buddhist temple. When the Angkor empire began to contract, the Khmers abandoned ancient Sukhothai and the Thais moved in, building their own structures. In place of the intricate Khmer irrigation network, they installed a less complex system – and a lack of water eventually contributed to the city's demise.

The **Sukhothai Historical Park** (daily 6am–6pm; charge) was designated as a Unesco World Heritage site in 1991 – and for good reason. Within the walls of the Old City are the magnificent ruins of 21 temples and monuments. Another 70 monuments are found within a 5km (3-mile) radius of the park. The ruins are divided into five zones – north, south, east, west and central – with the most important sites found within the Old City walls of the central zone. Tickets are sold separately for each zone at a daily price of B100, with an additional B50 charge for motor vehicles.

BELOW: Wat Mahathat at dusk.

Ramkhamhaeng National Museum

A short distance from Kamphaenghak Gate is the **Ramkhamhaeng National Museum** (daily 9am–4pm; charge; www.thailandmuseum.com), a good starting point for a tour of the historical park. The museum has a fine collection of Sukhothai sculpture, ceramics and other artefacts, plus exhibits from other periods.

The entrance hall is dominated by an impressive bronze image of the walking Buddha, regarded as the finest sculptural innovation of the Sukhothai period. Local sculptors were the first to make statues of the walking Buddha. The image also has features that typify the Sukhothai style, including fluid lines, a somewhat androgynous figure, and an interpretation of the 32 *raksana*, or characteristics, by which a Buddha would be recognised, such as wedge-shaped heels, arms down to the knees, and fingers and toes of equal length.

During the Sukhothai period, the Thais definitively embraced Theravada Buddhism and invited monks

from Sri Lanka to teach scripture. Yet, as Buddhism blossomed, Hindu influence remained strong, indicated by the two bronze images of Hindu gods flanking the bronze walking Buddha. The figure on the right, combining the attributes of Vishnu and Siva, is especially fine.

On the mezzanine floor of the museum is a copy of the famous stone inscription of King Ramkhamhaeng; the original is the single most prized exhibit of the National Museum in Bangkok *(see page 114)*.

Central zone: Wat Mahathat

The central zone, contained within the walls of the Old City, covers about 3 sq km (1 sq mile). The sights can be explored on foot, but a bicycle is perhaps the best option.

The largest and most important temple here is **Wat Mahathat**, in the centre of the Old City and surrounded by a moat. It's not certain who founded this temple, the spiritual centre of the kingdom, but it is presumed to be Intharathit, Sukhothai's first king. Wat Mahathat's present form is due

to a remodelling commissioned by Ramkhamhaeng's son King Lo Thai (1298–1347), around 1345.

The original design, before Lo Thai's restoration, was a typical Khmer-style "quincunx", with one central tower and four axial towers resting on a laterite platform. When the structure subsequently collapsed, Lo Thai restored it, adding four brick towers, alternating with the four Khmer laterite towers around a new central "lotus bud" tower, with its distinctive bulbous ornamentation at the top. The brick towers erected by Lo Thai stand at the four corners and look quite different – some experts say they show Lanna influence, others Mon. The entire structure rests upon a square platform with a stucco frieze of walking monks around the base. Scattered around Wat Mahathat are several monumental Buddha images.

Within the central zone

Familiar architectural themes are repeated among the 20 other shrines within the walls of the central zone (and some 70 more scattered in the

TIP

Large open-air ruins like those at Sukhothai and its surroundings are best explored during the cool season from November to February. But even then, either plan for an early morning or evening exploration, when the air is cooler.

BELOW: Wat Si Sawai, Sukhothai Historical Park.

TIP

The annual Loy Krathong festival in Nov, when tiny boats decorated with flowers, incense and small coins are set afloat in the country's waterways, is celebrated in Sukhothai in especially grand fashion. There is a spectacular fireworks display, folk dances and an excellent sound-and-light show highlighting Wat Mahathat. Loy Krathong is said to have originated in Sukhothai.

BELOW: the huge seated Buddha at Wat Si Chum.

other zones). The following monuments found within the central zone are of special interest.

Wat Si Sawai: Southwest of Wat Mahathat, it was originally a Hindu shrine with an image of Shiva. Triple towers built in a modified Khmer style remain, with fine stucco decoration of mythical birds and divinities, added in the 15th century.

Wat Chana Songkhram and **Wat Trakuan**: Located just north of Wat Mahathat, both have notably attractive Sri Lankan-style *chedi*, of which only the lower parts still stand. Wat Trakuan has many bronze images of the Chiang Saen period.

Wat Sa Si: Found to the north on the other side of the highway, on the way to the southern gate, it has a Sri Lankan-style *chedi*. The *bot* (ordination hall) lies on an island to the east of the spire. The ruins of the main shrine consist of six rows of columns, which lead to a well-restored seated Buddha image. As Achille Clarac, author of *Discovering Thailand*, puts it: "The detail, balance and harmony of the proportions and decoration of

Wat Sa Si, and the beauty of the area where it stands, bear witness to the unusual and refined aesthetic sense of the architects of the Sukhothai period."

North zone: Wat Phra Phai Luang

Leave the walled city (or central zone) by the northern San Luang, or Royal Shrine gate, and travel 1km (2/3 mile) or so to to the important shrine of **Wat Phra Phai Luang**. Located within the north zone, it originally consisted of three laterite towers covered with stucco, probably built in the late 12th century when Sukhothai was still part of the vast Khmer empire.

This shrine might have been the original centre of Sukhothai, as Wat Mahathat is of a later period. A fragmentary seated stone Buddha image, dating to 1191 and the reign of the Khmer king Jayavarman VII, was found here. It is now housed in the grounds of the Ramkhamhaeng Museum. During restoration in the mid-1960s, a stucco Buddha image in the central tower collapsed, revealing

many smaller images inside. Some date these images to the second half of the 13th century.

East of the main shrine is a pyramidal brick *chedi* with several seated stucco Buddha images from the late 13th century. The niches, which were walled up with bricks later, were removed during restoration work in 1953.

When heads of the stucco images from this *chedi* appeared in the antique market in Bangkok, authorities realised that the shrine was being pillaged. A government team was sent to the site, but the damage was already done. Those Chiang Saen-style heads that have not left the country are in private Thai collections, and also in the National Museum in Bangkok *(see page 114)*.

North zone: Wat Si Chum

Beyond Wat Phra Phai Luang to the west is **Wat Si Chum**, with one of the largest seated Buddha images in Thailand. The *mondop*, or enclosing shrine, was built in the second half of the 14th century, but the 15-metre (49ft) image itself, called Phra Achana (The Venerable), is believed to be the one mentioned in King Ramkhamhaeng's inscription – which would date it somewhat earlier, as Ramkhamheang reigned from 1280–98.

There is a stairway within the walls of the *mondop* to the roof. The ceiling of the stairway is made of over 50 slate slabs carved with scenes from Buddhist folklore. These turn the climbing of the stairs into a symbolic ascent to Buddhahood. Because of the precarious nature of the stairway, and also to stop people disrespectfully standing above the Buddha's head, climbing is no longer permitted.

There is a story of troops gathered here before a battle who heard an ethereal voice that came from the Buddha. This is attributed to a cunning ploy by a general who hid a man on the stairway and told him to speak through a window concealed by the image; the effect was inspiring, however, and the soldiers routed the enemy.

South zone: Wat Chetupon

South of the walled city is another group of shrines and monasteries. One of the most interesting is **Wat Chetupon**, where the protecting wall of the *viharn* is of imitation wood made from slabs of slate. The gates are also huge plates of slate mined from nearby hills. Some say they resemble the megaliths of Stonehenge, but on a smaller scale.

The bridges over the moat surrounding the temple are also made of stone. The central tower has Buddha images in the standing, reclining, walking and sitting postures. The walking Buddha here is said to be one of the finest of its kind.

Praying at Sukhothai

West zone: Wat Saphan Hin

"To the west of the city of Sukhothai," says Ramkhamhaeng's inscription, "is a forested area where the king has made offerings. In the forest is a large, tall and beautiful *viharn* which contains an 18-cubit image of the standing Buddha." This was identified as **Wat Saphan Hin**, the Monastery of the Stone Bridge, named because it is approached by a stairway of large stone slabs. The 12-metre (40ft) image stands on the crest of a

BELOW: excavations at Si Satchanalai–Chaliang Historical Park.

low hill, and can be seen from a distance. Its hand is raised in the attitude of giving protection, and is almost certainly the image described by Ramkhamhaeng.

Wat Pa Mamuang

There are other monuments in this western area, probably built by Sri Lankan monks, who preferred to locate their monasteries in the forest. Near the road, not far from the western gate of Sukhothai, is **Wat Pa Mamuang**, or Temple of the Mango Grove, where Ramkhamhaeng's grandson King Lu Thai (1347–68) is said to have installed a famous Theravada monk in 1361. Still standing are the shrine foundations and the ruins of the main *chedi*.

SI SATCHANALAI

About 50km (31 miles) north of Sukhothai, just off a highway and on the banks of the Yom River, lies the venerable city of **Si Satchanalai ⓱**. Founded in the 13th century, like Sukhothai, it was the seat of the viceroys of Sukhothai, and has been mentioned in ancient history books as the twin city of the capital. Whereas restoration, the removal of

trees and the installation of lawns have eroded some of Sukhothai's grandeur, Si Satchanalai's setting gives it an aura attained in few other ancient sites. It is a pleasure to wander through the wooded complex, and turn a corner to be surprised by a *wat* or monument.

Si Satchanalai–Chaliang Historical Park

Si Satchanalai and Chaliang, an old city 1km (²/₃ mile) to its east, together form **Si Satchanalai-Chaliang Historical Park** (daily 8.30am–5pm; charge). The most important monument within the 720-hectare (1,780-acre) site is **Wat Chang Lom**. There is little doubt that this is the "elephant-girdled shrine" in Ramkhamhaeng's inscription, which records that construction began in 1285 to house holy relics of the Buddha, and was finished six years later. It is the only surviving *chedi* that can be attributed with certainty to King Ramkhamhaeng. Made of laterite and stucco, its large bell-shaped spire in the Sri Lankan style stands on a two-storey, square basement. The upper tier has mostly empty niches for images, while the lower level has

39 elephant-shaped laterite buttresses.

South of the Elephant Shrine are the ruins of **Wat Chedi Jet Thaew**, which include seven rows of *chedi*, believed to contain the ashes of the viceroys of Si Satchanalai. One *chedi* has a stucco image of the Buddha sheltered by the *naga* serpent, and is in unusually good condition. Further south, close to the massive city walls, are the remains of **Wat Nang Phya**, Temple of the Queen. It has fine stucco decoration on one external wall, which probably dates from the 16th century and is vaguely reminiscent of European Baroque.

Other temples worth visiting include **Wat Khao Phanom Pleung** and **Wat Khao Suwan Khiri**, located on scenic hills linked by a walkway. **Wat Phra Si Rattana Mahathat** in Chaliang, a lovely temple, lies a couple of kilometres southeast of the Old City in a setting overlooking the Yom River.

Si Satchanalai is also associated with the famous Sawankhalok ceramics, which were among Thailand's first exports. The glazed brown or green bowls, with distinctive double-fish designs, were exported to China; remains have been found in sunken ships in the Gulf of Thailand. It's possible to buy antique Sawankhalok ceramics in the area, but most are copies.

PHITSANULOK

Located some 50km (31 miles) east of Sukhothai, **Phitsanulok** ⓲ today has few mementoes of the past; a fire in the 1950s razed most of the old town. The new city is quite dull, although nothing can detract from its superb location along the Nan River, with quays shaded by flowering trees, and houseboats and floating restaurants moored by its steep riverbanks. Phitsanulok is an alternative base to Sukhothai for exploring the region.

Wat Phra Si Rattana Mahathat

Fortunately, the fire spared **Wat Phra Si Rattana Mahathat** (also called Wat Yai), Phitsanulok's main monastery. The **Phra Phuttha Chinnarat** (or Chinnarat Buddha) image in the main *viharn* is considered Thailand's second-most important,

The Phra Phuttha Chinnarat is Thailand's second-most important Buddha image.

BELOW LEFT: Wat Phra Si Rattana Mahathat. **BELOW:** Buddha casting foundry.

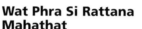

Phitsanulok serves as the economic capital of Thailand's lower north. With its position at the geographical crossroads of three regions – northern, northeastern and central Thailand – it is also of major strategic importance to the kingdom in terms of national communications, transport, trade and defence.

BELOW: laterite Buddha images at Wat Phra Kaew, Kamphaeng Phet Historical Park.

after Bangkok's Emerald Buddha. The seated Sukhothai-style bronze image has a flame-like bronze halo following the outlines of the head and torso and end in *naga* heads near the base.

The temple does brisk business in Chinnarat Buddha amulets and other religious souvenirs. The Lanna-style chapel that enshrines the image comprises a three-tiered roof that drops steeply to head-high side walls, drawing attention to the gleaming image at the end of the nave. Two wooden pulpits of superb late-Ayutthaya workmanship flank the image. The large one on the left is for monks, who chant the ancient Buddhist texts; the smaller pulpit on the other side accommodates a single monk who translates the Pali chants into Thai for the congregation. Note the late 18th-century main doors, inlaid with mother-of-pearl. Behind the chapel is a lofty *chedi* topped by a *prang* (Khmer-influenced tower).

A **bronze foundry** on nearby Thanon Wisut Kasat casts copies of the Chinnarat Buddha, and Buddhas in other styles. Visitors can see photographs of the painstaking process, and watch the

Buddha images being cast and polished (Wed–Sun 8.30am–4.30pm; free).

KAMPHAENG PHET

The city of **Kamphaeng Phet** ⑲, on the Ping River 77km (48 miles) southwest of Sukhothai, was built by King Lu Thai (1347–68), Ramkhamhaeng's grandson, to replace the older town of Chakangrao on the opposite bank. Both served as garrison towns for the Sukhothai kingdom.

Kamphaeng Phet Historical Park

A visit to King Lu Thai's fortifications reveals why the town was called Kamphaeng Phet, or "Diamond Walls": the massive earthen ramparts are topped by laterite walls rising 6 metres (20ft) above the outer moat, once overgrown with water hyacinths but now restored.

The ruins of the Old City are contained within the walled boundaries of the **Kamphaeng Phet Historical Park** (daily 8am–5pm; charge). Of interest here is the **Wat Phra Kaew**, remarkable for its fragile, time-eroded laterite Buddha images. This was the largest

Imperial Diplomacy

The Shiva image in the Kamphaeng Phet National Museum has an interesting history. Early during the reign of King Chulalongkorn, which extended from 1868 until his death in 1910, an insensitive German visitor had removed the image's head and two hands. Too afraid to arrest a *farang* (Westerner), the governor quickly sent word to Bangkok that the priceless fragments were on their way by boat. Officials in Bangkok detained the German, who declared that he was going to give them to the Berlin Museum. King Chulalongkorn managed to placate the German by promising to send an exact copy of the whole Shiva image to Germany, so that the authentic fragments could remain in Thailand. And so it was done. The copy of the bronze is still in Berlin.

and most important temple at this site. Nearby is **Wat Phra That**, represented by a substantial circular Sri-Lankan style *chedi* and laterite pillars. To the southeast is the **Kamphaeng Phet National Museum** (Wed–Sun 9am–4pm; charge), housing one of Thailand's finest bronze statues of the Hindu god Shiva. Other exhibits include pre-Sukhothai bronzes, stucco Buddha heads from local monuments, and some ceramics.

Arunyik temples

Kamphaeng Phet's other monuments are found to the northwest of the walled city. The monks who built them were of a forest-dwelling sect, strongly influenced by teachers from Sri Lanka. These *arunik* (or forest) temples, constructed of laterite, are thought to show Ceylonese influence. Most of them, however, underwent major changes during restoration in the Ayutthaya period.

The familiar themes of Buddhist architecture are repeated in the ordination halls of the two main temples. The first, **Wat Phra Si Iriyabot**, derives its name from Buddha images that are depicted in four postures (*si* mean-

ing four, and *iriyabot*, postures) on the central square *mondop*: walking, standing, sitting and reclining. The standing image is largely intact, with the original stucco coating on its head and lower part of the body. This is an impressive and unaltered example of Sukhothai sculpture. Unfortunately, the other images are in very poor condition. The whole temple stands on a platform that is encircled by the original laterite railing and walls.

The other temple, **Wat Chang Rawp**, comprises the base of a laterite *chedi* surrounded by a row of elephant buttresses, a theme borrowed from Sri Lanka that claims the universe rests on the backs of these beasts. The row of elephants on the south side is almost complete, but several are missing on the other flanks of the *chedi*. The spire of the great monument has vanished, but the ruins of a crypt on the upper level of the *chedi* can still be seen today.

The pillars of the former *viharn* also remain. Sensitive repair work has restored much of the original form and managed to preserve its character. ❏

Elephant detail at Wat Chang Rawp, Kamphaeng Phet Historical Park.

RESTAURANTS

Sukhothai
Thai & Western
The Coffee Cup
Moo 3, Old Sukhothai.
No phone. Open: daily 7am–5pm. **$$**
Convenient for a bracing cup of freshly brewed coffee before an early-morning tour of the Old City ruins. Western breakfasts and sandwiches are also available.

Dream Café
Th Singhawat. Tel: 0-5561 2081. Open: daily 11am–10pm. **$$**
Full of atmosphere, this eatery is housed in a large wooden building, packed with Rama V-period antiques. Offers an

extensive menu of Thai and Western dishes, along with homemade ice cream. Thai-style corn fritters (*thawt man khao phot*) are a speciality.

Phitsanulok
Thai
Fah-Kerah
786 Th. Phra Ong Dam.
No phone. Open: daily B & L. **$**
Famous throughout the northern region for its delicious Thai-Muslim fare, this humble family-owned restaurant serves its own fresh yoghurt, a variety of rich curries (usually ordered with roti – fried, unleavened flatbread) and strong fragrant tea, laced with fresh goat's milk.

Tree House
Near Phitsanulok Thani Hotel.
Tel: 0-5521 2587. **$–$$**
This spacious restaurant has a shaded garden. Try *plaa nung siew* (steamed fish with soy sauce) and *yam mapraw on* (young coconut meat spicy salad).

Thai & Western
Ban Khun Pho
Th. Chao Phraya. No phone. Open: daily 11am–11pm. **$**
Popular with local office workers during weekday lunch hours, this eatery opposite the Amarin Nakhon Hotel serves standard Thai and northern Thai cuisine, along with a smaller selection of Japanese and Western dishes, and good-

value lunch specials. The excellent service is a winner.

Steak Cottage
Lithai Building, Th. Phayalithai.
No phone. Open: Mon–Sat B, L & D. **$$**
Serving the best steaks in town in several styles – try the steak in fresh green peppercorn sauce – this modern establishment also fares well with Thai dishes such as *yam* (spicy Thai-style salads).

Price per person for a three-course meal without drinks:
$ = under B300
$$ = B300–800
$$$ = B800–1,600
$$$$ = over B1,600

TAK AND MAE HONG SON

The remote mountainous provinces of north Thailand provide an opportunity to get off the beaten track. There are Burmese border towns to be visited, fast-flowing rivers to be rafted, national parks to be explored and colourful hill tribes to mingle with

Tucked away along the Thailand–Myanmar border, in the country's northwesternmost corner, Tak and Mae Hong Son are two of Thailand's least populous provinces. Throughout most of Thai history they were covered by the vast teak forests upon which burgeoning northern Thai cities such as Chiang Mai and Lampang later built their economies. Even as recently as 40 years ago, the Thai government classified this region as "remote", an official euphemism for areas over which Bangkok had little control. The 1968–82 communist insurgency movement thrived here, finding ready recruits among impoverished villagers and hill tribes.

For Mae Hong Son and Tak, the sense of separateness was compounded by their shared economy and cultures with neighbouring Myanmar. There is still much exchange, both legal and illegal, between peoples on both sides of the border.

For visitors, these remote provinces offer many opportunities to get off the beaten tourist track, to enjoy the mountains, rivers and forests, and to encounter a multitude of minority hill-tribe communities and their cultures.

TAK TO MYAWADI

On the banks of the Ping River, the quiet town of **Tak ⑳** bills itself as the "gateway to the north". Once called Raheng,

this was a logging town; logs freed from the wild rapids on the upper Ping and the Wang rivers were floated downriver to Nakhon Sawan. During the 19th century, Tak served as a provisioning centre for journeys west into Myanmar and north to Chiang Mai. Until the railway was completed in the 1920s, the only way north was by boat, agonisingly propelled by poles against the swift currents. In those days, Tak was an essential stop for rest and replenishment.

In 1964, the rapids were removed by the construction of **Bhumibol Dam**,

Main attractions
LAN SANG NATIONAL PARK
MAE SOT
UM PHANG
MAE SARIANG
KHUN YAM
MAE HONG HON
PAI

LEFT: scenery on Route 108 near Mae Sariang. **RIGHT:** Karen family.

TIP

When border skirmishes flare up between Karen insurgents and Myanmar's central government, Myawadi (across the Moei River in Myanmar) may be closed to foreign visitors for a few days at a time.

about 60km (37 miles) to the north, although this had the effect of permanently sidelining Tak as a river port. At a height of 154 metres (505ft), the dam is the tallest in Southeast Asia and provides both electricity and irrigation to the surrounding area. Some 62km (37 miles) northwest of Tak, the shores and islands of the reservoir created by Bhumibol Dam are a favourite canoeing, swimming, fishing and picnicking destination for local Thais.

Today, Tak is little more than an administrative and agricultural supply centre for the province, accessed either by Highway 1 from Bangkok, or by an older road that threads through tiny manicured gardens and around a pond near the provincial offices.

Other than views of the Ping River at sunset and the orange suspension bridge spanning the river – resembling a miniature version of San Francisco's Golden Gate Bridge – Tak offers few exceptional sights. A broad esplanade separates the market from the river, and a dyke holds back the river's waters, which are prone to flooding during the rainy season.

Lan Sang National Park

Route 105 leads west from Tak through rugged hills towards Mae Sot, a town on the Thailand–Myanmar border. Around 18km (11 miles) outside of Tak lies **Lan Sang National Park** ㉑ (daily 8am–6pm; charge), with its rugged mountain peaks and waterfalls that are hidden behind a screen of bamboo groves.

Various species of deer, serow (a type of mountain goat), numerous monkeys, golden cats and a few leopards are still present in these hills. If time allows, stop at the *nikhom*, or "settlement", on Doi Musoe to experience the life of the Lisu, Lahu and Hmong hill tribes who live in this area.

Freshly brewed, locally grown coffee is sold on Route 105 to passing motorists, as are wild orchids and forest flowers. The road rises to Doi Phawo mountain, where truck drivers make offerings at the elaborate **Chaopho Phawo Shrine** – named in honour of a Karen warrior – for safe passage. Beyond the pass, the road drops through forest into a peaceful valley dotted with small farmhouses, white *chedi* and ornate Burmese-style temples.

BELOW: Burmese-style pagoda, Mae Sot. **BELOW RIGHT:** the Burmese border at Mae Sot.

Mae Sot

Some 85km (53 miles) from Tak the road reaches **Mae Sot** ㉒, a boisterous border junction inhabited by a diversity of ethnic groups, most of them with family ties and/or business links in Myanmar, which lies just across the Moei River at the town's western limits. Shops around town bear signs in a combination of Thai, Chinese, Burmese and English. With its confusion of narrow streets, sidewalk stalls, Burmese tea shops, bicycles and excited shoppers, Mae Sot has the air of a frontier boom town.

Along with a vigorous smuggling industry (especially in Burmese teak since a 1989 Thai ban on logging), refugee camps on the outskirts of town provide much of Mae Sot's livelihood and contribute to its "not-quite-Thailand" ambience. It is also the centre of the border region's gem trade, specialising in precious and semi-precious stones from Myanmar, particularly jade and rubies.

Wat Wattanaram

From Mae Sot, it's a 5km (3-mile) drive to the Myanmar border. Worthy of a visit is **Wat Wattanaram** (daily 8am–6pm; free), an ornate Burmese-style temple with tiers of red-tiled rectangular roofs fringed with intricate silverwork that are piled skywards into a tower. Within the sanctuary are four Buddha images, one of which has heavy gold jewellery distending its earlobes.

Myawadi

Continue to the Moei River, spanned since 1996 by the **Thai-Myanmar Friendship Bridge**. On the far side is **Myawadi**, a typical Burmese town of dusty streets and glittering pagodas. A riverbank casino here entertains Thai gamblers at weekends.

The border is open from 8am to 5pm, and foreigners are welcome to tour Myawadi for the day upon payment of US$10 (or 500 Baht). A highway from Myawadi leads west to Mawlamyaing (Moulmein) and Yangon, but for now, foreigners are permitted to travel only as far as Myawadi.

During the Thai communist insurgency of the late 1970s and early 1980s the high mountains south of Mae Sot were a formidable stronghold for armed guerrillas, making it an area that few tourists dared venture into. After 1982, an amnesty removed the threat and the mountains enjoyed peace once again.

These western mountains harbour more domesticated elephants than anywhere else in Thailand. Local Karen villages still use the sturdy and clever animals for jungle transport, and for various agricultural tasks.

SOUTH TO UM PHANG

Steep and winding Route 1090 meanders through the mountains to **Um Phang** ㉓, a remote, rural district about 150km (90 miles) south of Mae Sot.

Along the way, the road passes two scenic falls, **Pha Charoen Waterfall** and **Thararak Waterfall**, 26km (15 miles) and 41km (24 miles) respectively from Mae Sot, each with picnic areas and short, steep trails following the cataracts.

A monk at Wat Wattanaram.

BELOW: Thilawsu Waterfall near Um Phang.

*The 150km (93-mile)
road between Mae
Sot and Um Phang
was known as the
"Death Highway"
during the late-1970s
Thai communist
insurgency because
of the frequent
attacks launched on
government transport.*

Um Phang

The sleepy town of **Um Phang**, with its mostly Karen inhabitants, is a centre for elephant treks and whitewater rafting. One of the most popular local rafting-and-trekking trips follows the Klong River to the lofty 400-metre (1,312ft) **Thilawsu Waterfall**, the largest falls in all of Thailand.

The waterfalls are found in **Um Phang Wildlife Sanctuary**, which was declared a Unesco World Heritage site in 1999 and forms part of Thailand's largest wildlife corridor. Combined with the adjacent Thung Yai Naresuan Reserve, Huay Kha Kaeng Reserve, Khlong Lan National Park and Mae Wong National Park, the sanctuary is part of one of the most pristine natural forest zones in Southeast Asia.

Following a trail along the Myanmar border, trekkers can hike all the way from Um Phang to **Sangkhlaburi** ❷ in Kanchanaburi Province (from where it's also accessible). The expedition takes about seven days; experienced guides can be hired through any of the guesthouses in Um Phang. Picturesque Sangkhlaburi is surrounded by high peaks

and remains largely untouched by development. It's also a fascinating cultural meeting point: Thai, Burmese, Mon and Karen all live here, mostly involved in border trade, illegal or otherwise.

NORTH TO MAE HONG SON

From Mae Sot, Route 105 turns north, staying close to the Myanmar border, winding its way for 226km (136 miles) to **Mae Sariang**, where it joins Route 108, the road to Chom Thong and Chiang Mai.

Punctuated by police checkpoints, Route 105 passes the limestone cave complex of **Tham Mae Usu** (daily 8am–6pm; charge), near km 94. The main caverns are open to the public. During the rainy season, the river that runs through the cave seals its mouth, forcing the closure of Tham Mae Usu.

Mae Sariang

Hemmed in by high mountains, **Mae Sariang** ❷ lies along the banks of its namesake Mae Sariang (Sariang River). The district is surrounded by a number of outlying Shan, Karen and Hmong villages. In town, the **Wat Uthayarom** (also called Wat Jong Sung) is worth a brief stop for its Shan-style tin-trimmed teak architecture and 19th-century *chedi*. Mae Sariang also offers several pleasant riverside guesthouses and a few shops selling Karen handicrafts.

Khun Yuam

Route 108 continues north from Mae Sariang, through mountain scenery that is among the most breathtaking in Thailand, reaching **Mae Hong Son** about 170km (100 miles) later. Roughly midway between Mae Sariang and Mae Hong Son, little-visited **Khun Yuam** ❷ has one of the most charming Shan Buddhist monasteries in the province, **Wat To Pae** (daily 8am–5pm; free). Inside the temple and hidden behind curtains is a 150-year-old antique Burmese *kalaga* (embroidered tapestry).

Also in Khun Yuam is the modest **World War II Museum** (daily 8am–

BELOW: wild elephant in the forest near Mae Hong Son.

4pm; charge) which contains artefacts left behind by defeated Japanese troops retreating from Burma at the end of World War II. An estimated 100,000 Japanese soldiers followed the Skeleton Road (named for the many who died en route) from Burma to northern Thailand in August 1945. Many took refuge in Khun Yuam before continuing on to Chiang Mai. The local Shan provided food and medicine to the ailing troops, and turned Wat To Pae into a field hospital. The museum displays a collection of military gear and personal possessions left behind by the Japanese.

Mae Hong Son

Around 75 percent of Mae Hong Son Province consists of forests and mountains. The deep-green peaks that loom over the provincial capital account for **Mae Hong Son Town**'s ㉗ early-morning fogs, and also separate Thailand from neighbouring Myanmar. The presence of Karen, Hmong, Lawa, Shan, Lisu and Lahu tribespeople, who, taken collectively, easily outnumber the ethnic Thais, adds intrigue to the region's worst-kept secret: Mae Hong Son lies smack in the middle of border-smuggling routes.

Wat Phra That Doi Kong Mu

Doi Kong Mu, a hill that rises a steep 250 metres (820ft) above the town, affords a commanding view of Mae Hong Son and the surrounding countryside. At night, two tall *chedi* at **Wat Phra That Doi Kong Mu**, perched atop the hill, light up like timid beacons of civilisation in this remote corner of Thailand. Erected in the 19th century, the temple reflects Shan and Burmese influences.

Wat Chong Klang and Wat Chong Kham

Nong Chong Kham, a serene lake in the south of Mae Hong Son, is flanked by two picturesque Burmese-Shan temples. **Wat Chong Klang** (daily 8am–6pm; free), built two centuries ago, is the older of the pair. **Wat Chong Kham** (daily 8am–6pm; free) is famous for its painted glass panels and carved wooden figures illustrating episodes from the Buddhist *Jataka* tales. The reflection of the graceful, whitewashed *chedi* of the temples in the lake's mirror-like surface is a favourite photo-op.

Lisu hats for sale next to Nong Chong Kham in Mae Hong Son.

BELOW: Mae Hong Son.

Mae Hong Son is famous for its annual Poy Sang Long celebrations, when pre-pubescent boys are temporarily ordained as novice monks. Dressed in mock-royal finery, the boys are paraded on the shoulders of their older family members to a local Buddhist monastery, where they trade their outfits for the ochre-coloured robes of monks.

Tour agencies, hotels and guest-houses in Mae Hong Son can arrange two- to seven-day treks to mountain valleys, caves and hill-tribe villages in the vicinity. Many visitors travel to nearby "longneck villages" *(see panel, below)* to meet Padaung refugees from Myanmar, whose women traditionally wear heavy brass coils around their necks. Of the three Padaung villages in Mae Hong Son Province, **Nai Soi**, 35km (21 miles) northwest of the pro-vincial capital, is the largest.

SOUTHEAST TO PAI

Route 1095 climbs into pine-forested mountains as it heads southeast from Mae Hong Son towards Chiang Mai, yielding spectacular valley views along the way.

Tham Lot

The Shan market town of **Soppong** ㉘, 70km (42 miles) northeast from Mae Hong Son, is a jumping-off point for visits to **Tham Lot** (daily 8am–5.30pm; charge), some 8km (5 miles) away. This is the most famous limestone cavern complex in northern Thailand and

one of the longest in Southeast Asia. When it was first discovered, the huge, multiple chambers of the cave com-plex contained several ancient teak coffins suspended on wooden scaf-folds, suggesting it had been a burial site during prehistoric times. There are eight known coffin caves which are off limits to visitors. Guides carrying gas lanterns are mandatory, and included in the entry fee. A stream runs through all three main caverns, and when the water is high enough, visitors can pass through the caves via bamboo raft.

Pai

Heading southeast, the road arrives at **Pai** ㉙, a picturesque place. Once strictly suitable for the backpacking set, it has now broadened its appeal with many upmarket resorts and res-taurants. The original site of the town is a slightly elevated plateau, known nowadays as **Wiang Neua** (northern walled settlement). It still retains parts of Pai's centuries-old earthen city walls and surrounding moat, which are now used for irrigation. Here, most houses are made of wood and the open-air

BELOW RIGHT:
Padaung girl, Mae
Hong Son.

"Longneck" Villages

Padaung (or Kayan) refugee villages have become a controversial tourist attraction in Mae Hong Son Province because of the tradi-tional brass neck coils worn by many Padaung women. The heavy coils, which typically weigh around 5kg (11lbs) and measure 20–30cm (8 –13ins) in height, depress the collarbone and rib cage, making the neck appear unnaturally long. Despite apocryphal claims that the wom-en's necks will flop over if the coils are removed, Padaung women remove the coils regularly for cleaning and bathing.

The origins of these neck coils are not clear; according to the Padaung, the brass coils are a tribute to a mythical female dragon who consorted with the wind god and produced the first Padaung offspring. Other theories postulate that Padaung women used the neck coils to ward off the attentions of men from other tribes.

The villages charge admission, a portion of which goes to the Padaung women, the rest to village administrators, who are not Thai, as is often assumed, but rather Padaung and Karenni. On the one hand the "long-neck villages" appear to be little more than crass human zoos. On the other, the Padaung have fled an ongoing civil war in Myanmar's border regions, and charging visitors to observe their traditions is one of the few ways they have to make a living in a foreign land.

markets are redolent with Shan spices.

Meanwhile, at a lower level of the valley, the newer **Wiang Tai** (southern walled settlement) contains a colourful selection of cafés, bars, restaurants, travel agencies, galleries, shops and massage centres. The population here is a varied mix of Shan, northern Thai, Chinese Muslim and Lisu, along with a sizeable community of Western expats who relish the peaceful, natural ambience.

Ensconced in a wide, fertile valley, surrounded by low mountain peaks, the town of around 5,000 people has, over the last decade, become a magnet for new-agers, artists and musicians from all over the world.

Wat Mae Yen and Tha Pai Hotsprings

Nearby attractions include a couple of waterfalls, the mountain-top **Wat Mae Yen** (whose buildings have been painted by local Thai artists in a non-traditional but nonetheless inspiring fashion), and **Tha Pai Hotsprings** (daily 7am–6pm; charge), a park with natural mineral springs and freshwater streams, perfect for soaking year-round. Lahu and Lisu villages lie within moderate walking distance of Wiang Tai.

Two-day **river-rafting** trips on the Pai River are popular; the French-owned **Thai Adventure Rafting** maintains the highest standards of any rafting company in Thailand (tel: 0-5369 9111; www. thairafting.com). On the outskirts of Pai Town near the Tha Pai Hot Springs is **Thom's Pai Elephant Camp Tours** (tel: 0-5369 9286), where short elephant treks into the jungle can be arranged.

Huay Nam Dang N P

From Pai, Route 1095 meanders southeast through the mountains for another 90km (54 miles) to **Mae Malai**, a small market town. A stretch of the route bisects the 1,247-sq-km (748-sq-mile) **Huay Nam Dang National Park**, a heavily forested sanctuary famous for the "sea of fog" that blankets the area at dawn. It also has a couple of short nature trails, natural hot springs and several waterfalls. From here, **Chiang Mai** *(see page 281)* is another hour's drive south along Route 107. ❑

A "Welcome to Pai" sign greets visitors. Note that Pai is pronounced as "Bai".

RESTAURANTS

HILL-TRIBE CRAFTS AND CLOTHING

Each hill tribe of Thailand has its own customs, dress, language and spiritual beliefs that are clearly reflected in the crafts they produce

Textiles and silver jewellery play a very important role in the ceremonial activities of Thailand's hill-tribe communities. Hill-tribe women are defined by what they wear, and their choice of clothing and adornment can reveal not only which tribe they are from, but also their social status, age and even where their home town is located. However, the way of life of Thailand's hill-tribe people is changing as they are slowly assimilated into mainstream Thai society, and abandoning many features of their traditional culture. This may be unfortunate for visitors in search of traditional hill-tribe culture, but the process is inevitable and has distinct advantages for these ethnic minorities, as they can now benefit from educational opportunities and medical care.

Hill-tribe crafts

Hill-tribe craft items started to be made commercially available in the mid-1970s when small craft centres were set up in refugee camps. Authentic items are now rare and expensive, but good-quality crafts can be found in craft shops all over north Thailand and in Bangkok.

LEFT: women from the Hmong hill tribe used to hand-weave cloth, but today they use ready-made fabrics for their intricately embroidered clothing. The Hmong are skilled in making indigo-dyed batik which is then embroidered with appliquéd layers of geometrically shaped fabric to make up their skirts.

TOP LEFT: an opium pipe; northwest Thailand lies within the fabled Golden Triangle.

ABOVE: Lisu women make distinctive hats and other clothing. In the past, the cloth was woven by hand but machine-made material is now run up on sewing machines.

RIGHT: Hmong fabrics feature intricate patterns.

IKAT CLOTH

The White Karen tribe *(above)* produce striped-warp *ikat* textiles woven on back-strap looms. *Ikat* is a technique that involves the binding of the cloth with fibre or material, so that in places it becomes resistant to dyeing. Before the cloth is dyed, the weft (yarns woven across the width) or the warp (lengthwise yarns) is pulled tightly over a frame and the threads bound tightly together singly or in bunches. The cloth is then dyed several times using different colours. As a result, beautiful patterns are built up with soft edges on the parts of the cloth not completely covered by the binding materials. The dyeing process is complex, with the dominant colour of the *ikat* dyed first. Cotton yarns are the most suitable for making warp *ikat*, and the dyes used to produce these textiles are natural dyes easily absorbed by cotton. The most popular colours for warp *ikat* are indigo and red. Weft *ikat*, usually made from silk, use mainly yellow turmeric, diluted indigos and a deep crimson red extracted from the lac insect.

BOVE: Padaung women wear brass coils around their arms, legs nd necks. The coils compress the collarbone and rib cage and give e impression that the neck has stretched. Contrary to belief, the moval of the coils is not dangerous.

BOVE: women of the Hmong hill tribe spin cotton into read with a hand spindle, then weave it on a foot-treadle om. The cloth is dyed indigo and is then appliquéd and ecorated with shells, seeds, silver or buttons and made to clothing for the family. The men make a variety of askets and other items from wood, bamboo and ttan.

IGHT: married Akha women are famous for their eaddresses, decorated with silver coins, which they ear all the time. Unmarried women from the tribe tach small gourds to their headdresses.

ABOVE: the Sop Moei Arts shop in Bangkok sells products by Karen villagers. The project was set up in the 1980s with the help of the Swedish International Development Agency.

NORTHEAST THAILAND

This little-visited region of Thailand is economically poor but rich in attractions – from stunning temple ruins dating to the Khmer empire to pristine national parks full of wildlife, and a sweet-natured people

A ccording to official government records, northeast Thailand captures only 2 percent of the country's tourism market. Travellers don't know what they are missing: the northeast is a rich treasure trove of ancient Angkor-era temple ruins, a relatively untouched Lao-Cambodian-Thai culture and pristine national parks. It is a completely different experience to that offered by Phuket or Bangkok, or even Chiang Mai.

Large parts of the northeast (also known as Isaan) were ruled by the Khmers during the golden 10th- to 13th-century period, when they built the remarkable Angkor Wat (in Cambodia). The Khmers established a number of far-flung satellite towns, each with its own majestic temples and shrines, in the lands to the west and north – present-day northeast Thailand; their survival means that the region is studded with magnificent Khmer temples.

Northeast Thailand occupies a high plateau (the Khorat) and is home to around one-third of the country's population. Three out of five of Thailand's largest cities are found here: Khon Kaen, Nakhon Ratchasima (Khorat) and Udon Thani. The region is strongly linked with Lao culture: for long periods in the past, it was part of various Lao kingdoms. Today, most northeasterners can trace their ancestry to Laos, across the Mekong River to the north and east. Northeastern Thais retain the Lao quality of passivity in the face of adversity. This quality is useful, for this is not an easy place to live – the soil is thin, there is either not enough rain, or too much, and the Mekong is prone to floods.

Nonetheless, many travellers find the northeast the highlight of their trip. It is the least "touristy" region of the country – the people are genuine and without wiles, the area abounds with natural beauty, and the cultural attraction of many Khmer sites adds to the interest. It is also possible to make forays into neighbouring Laos at several crossings over the Mekong, either by bridge or by boat. ❑

LEFT: farmers in Loei Province. TOP: central sanctuary, Prasat Hin Phimai, Nakhon Ratchasima Province. ABOVE LEFT: scenery near Phu Kradung National Park, Loei Province. ABOVE RIGHT: pots for sale in Ban Chiang, Udon Thani Province.

NAKHON RATCHASIMA TO UBON RATCHATHANI

Heading in a west-to-east direction takes one from a lush national park that is easily accessible from Bangkok to the magnificent Khmer temple ruins of Prasat Khao Phra Viharn, across the border in Cambodia

Main attractions
KHAO YAI NATIONAL PARK
NAKHON RATCHASIMA
  (KHORAT)
PAK THONG CHAI
PRASAT HIN PHIMAI
PRASAT HIN KHAO PHANOM
  RUNG HISTORICAL PARK
SURIN
PRASAT KHAO PHRA VIHARN
UBON RATCHATHANI
KAENG TANNA NATIONAL
  PARK

The mountainous Khao Yai area gives way to the Khorat Plateau, considered to be the gateway to Thailand's northeast. Further east lie the provinces of Buriram and Si Saket, with a plethora of Khmer sites, and slightly to the north, the elephant capital of Surin. Beyond, Ubon Ratchathani is the gateway to southern Laos.

With its relatively good roads, significant distances between the many out-of-the-way sights, and patchy public transport, the best way to see northeast Thailand is by car.

Khao Yai N P

One of the region's best-known sights is **Khao Yai National Park ❶** (daily 8am–6pm; charge; tel: 0-4424 9305), more frequently accessed from Bangkok than it is from Nakhon Ratchasima Town, the closest northeastern city. The country's oldest and most visited nature reserve, Khao Yai lies about 200km (175 miles) northeast of Bangkok, and there are several routes from the capital; the most popular is Highway 1 to Saraburi, from where Highway 2 leads to the reserve. The drive from Bangkok should take about three hours.

Khao Yai is Thailand's second-largest national park at 2,168 sq km (837 sq miles), and it cuts across four different provinces. Most of the protected area is located at around 400 metres (1,300ft) above sea level, making it a pleasant escape from the hot, humid lowlands of central Thailand. Those hoping to see wildlife should come in the cool and dry season (October–January) when wildlife is at its most active and trails in the jungle passable. Be sure to bring warm clothes during this period as temperatures can plummet to as low as 10°C (50°F) at night. Visiting in the rainy season isn't out of the question, but remember to cover up bare legs and arms, as leeches are common.

Often clad in mist, Khao Yai's highest peaks lie in the east along the edge of the Khorat Plateau. **Khao Laem** (Shadow

LEFT: Prasat Hin Khao Phanom Rung.

Mountain) is 1,313 metres (4,307ft) high, while **Khao Khiew** (Green Mountain) rises to a height of 1,351 metres (4,432ft). Evergreen and deciduous trees, palms and bamboo blanket the park, and unlike much of Thailand, patches of indigenous rainforest can still be seen here. At lower elevations there are areas of dry deciduous forest and some grassland. Gibbons, macaques and langurs are the most commonly spotted wildlife, while black bears, leopards and other big cats, various species of deer, porcupines and wild pigs also roam the reserve. Khao Yai is home to some 200 elephants and a few tigers, but they are rarely seen. In addition, over 320 species of birds have been identified, with regular sightings of great hornbills.

More than 50km (30 miles) of marked trails crisscross the park, most of them originally forged and still used by elephants. In several clearings, there are observation towers where you can watch animals feed. After-dark safaris by tour companies claim to spot tigers and elephants; in reality such spotlighted trucks careering around the park are more likely to yield sightings of deer,

deer, and yet more deer. Guides are available at the park visitor centre, but you'll have a better chance of getting an English-speaking one if you organise a tour of the park through one of the guesthouses in the area.

Other attractions in the park include the 20-metre (66ft) **Haew Suwat Waterfall** – which featured in the film *The Beach* – east of the park headquarters, and the larger three-level **Haew Narok Falls**, rising to a height of 150 metres (500ft) and located further south.

Near the entrance to the park are numerous lodges and bungalows, including the luxury **Kirimaya**, a boutique resort in the vein of African safari lodges with luxury tented villas. Other pursuits include teeing off at internationally designed golf courses and jungle rides on ATVs (All Terrain Vehicles).

NAKHON RATCHASIMA (KHORAT)

Highway 2 continues northeast up the Khorat Plateau, passing the reservoir of **Lam Takhong**, the area's principal

Khao Yai National Park is one of the most accessible of Thailand's protected areas.

BELOW: Haew Suwat Waterfall, Khao Yai National Park.

Khao Yai Wineries

Bacchus has discovered Thailand in the past few years, and local vineyards are beginning to grow in popularity and quality. Khao Yai's climate is quite good for grape cultivation, and a number of vineyards around Pak Chong, like **PB Valley Khao Yai** (tel: 0-3622 6415; www.khaoyaiwinery.com), **GranMonte Family Vineyard** (tel: 0-2653 1522; www.granmonte.com) and **Village Farm & Winery** (tel: 0-4422 8407; www. villagefarm.co.th) have flourished.

The word from connoisseurs is that while these wines are eminently palatable, they still need considerable refinement before they will be ready to compete with international wines. Help from the government – to reduce tax to make local wine significantly cheaper – is also needed. Tours, wine-tastings, meals and even accommodation can all be arranged.

Northeast Thailand

0 ___ 50 km

0 ___ 50 miles

source of water. Soon, the blue lake disappears and scrub brush, typical of the drier northeast, begins to dominate.

The city of **Nakhon Ratchasima ❷** – more popularly known by its older name, **Khorat** – the richest and largest city in the northeast, is located some 260km (162 miles) from Bangkok. The capital of **Nakhon Ratchasima Province**, the city was a base for American bombers during the Vietnam War. It now serves as a trade, communications and military centre for the entire northeast.

City sights

Although a busy and important commercial centre with little of obvious architectural value, Nakhon Ratchasima has not forgotten its past. A statue of national heroine **Thao Suranari** (or Khunying Mo) presides over the town square and the whitewashed old city wall, which dates from around the 10th century. Khunying Mo was the wife of an assistant provincial governor in the early 19th century when Prince Anou of Vientiane led his army here. After taking the city, the prince threat-

ened to enslave its residents. Khunying Mo rallied the women, who enticed the Lao soldiers into a drunken revelry and then killed them whilst they slept. Prince Anou, who meanwhile had gone to attack Saraburi, was forced to withdraw his depleted forces back to Vientiane, to the north. The annual **Thao Suranari Festival**, held over 12 days in late March and early April, pays tribute to her victory with colourful parades, live music, outdoor *likay* performances (bawdy, traditional folk dance-drama) and Isaan food vendors. Local residents still place offerings at her statue's feet.

Another tribute to local and regional history can be found at the **Maha Wirawong National Museum** (Wed–Sun 9am–4pm; charge), on the grounds of Wat Suchinda by Thanon Ratchadamnoen. The museum has a fine collection of Khmer and central Thai art and artefacts, as well as exhibits on archaeology and folkore.

Outside town: Pak Thong Chai

Silk is one of the region's most important industries, and you will see many

"Isaan", the common Thai name for northeastern Thailand, derives from Ishanapura, a Sanskrit name for an ancient, pre-Angkor Mon Khmer Hindu kingdom that once ruled the region. Today Isaan covers 19 of Thailand's 76 provinces.

BELOW: Thao Suranari statue in Nakhon Ratchasima.

Khmer Legacy

Northeast Thailand encompasses a large swathe of former Khmer territory, and over half of the region's Khmer religious sites

Between the 10th and 14th centuries AD, a large part of mainland Southeast Asia, from the Mekong Delta in the east to around Phetchburi in the west, lay under the control of the Khmer empire. The capital at Angkor was connected to the outlying reaches of empire by a system of highways and religio-political strongpoints such as Prasat Khao Phra Viharn, Wat Phu Champasak, Phanom Rung and Phimai.

By the mid-19th century, when the frontiers of present-day Indochina were effectively fixed by the French, the Khmer empire had long since disappeared, leaving Cambodia much reduced in size. It is true that the crowning glory of the Khmer past, Angkor Wat, still lay within Cambodia's confines, as did – just – the magnificent "lofty sanctuary" of Phra Viharn. Yet many other symbolic relics of the Khmer past now lay outside Cambodia's borders, most notably Wat Phu Champasak in southern Laos, and a series of magnificent sites across Thai-

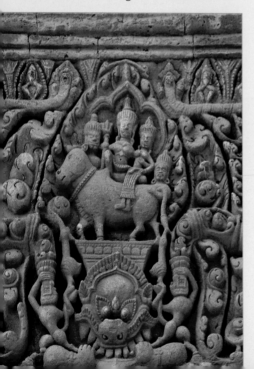

land's northeast, where they are known as *prasat*. In fact, over 200 Khmer religious sites – over half of the total number – are located in this part of Thailand.

Thailand has long valued these unique historic treasures, traditionally considering them to be temporary homes for Hindu deities and, as such, needing to be consecrated regularly in elaborate ceremonies performed by a class of Hindu priests. Yet only very recently have concerted efforts been made to preserve and promote them. Over the past three decades, several of the most important sites have been painstakingly and successfully restored by the government's Department of Fine Arts.

Khorat and Buriram provinces host the major Khmer complexes: Prasat Hin Phimai, Prasat Phanom Rung and Prasat Muang Tam. All three have been carefully restored, though Phanom Rung is perhaps today the most impressive. Like Angkor Wat itself, these temples were all originally constructed as Hindu temples, dedicated to Vishnu and Shiva, and as such the ruins demonstrate, particularly in their carvings, a deistic diversity and Indic sensuality not evident in more recent, Buddhist structures. It was under Jayavarman VII that Hinduism was replaced by Buddhism, and the temples converted to *wats*. Until today, their significance to Thai Buddhists remains strong, weakened neither by memories of foreign powers on what is now Thai soil nor by the slightly unfamiliar iconography. Phanom Rung is indeed a regular and important place of Buddhist pilgrimage.

The structure that most immediately identifies a site as Khmer is the tall tapering tower (called *prang*) with longitudinal ridges. These towers were symbolic of Mount Meru, the mythical mountain at the center of the Hindu universe. Even as far away as Lopburi, Khmer influence is easily recognisable in the three ruined *prang* of Phra Prang Sam Yot, often attributed to Jayavarman VII. And in the vicinity of Phanom Rung are various Khmer *kuti*, or meditation retreats, as well as several other unrestored temple complexes, languishing in the forests and undergrowth.

As recently as 1976, the despotic Khmer Rouge regime was staking a claim to northeast Thailand, promising to "liberate" lost Khmer territories. Fortunately, whilst the local Khmer-speakers are conscious of, and justly proud of, their cultural links with Angkor, they are also loyal Thai citizens. ❑

LEFT: Hindu motifs feature in this ornate stone carving at Prasat Hin Muang Tam.

shops in Nakhon Ratchasima selling the fabric by the metre as well as ready-made clothing and home accessories like cushion covers and tablecloths. To visit a nearby silk production centre, take Route 304 south towards Kabinburi. After 30km (20 miles) is **Pak Thong Chai ❸**, where about 70 factories weave silk, including the Jim Thompson company, Thailand's famous hand-woven silk enterprise. Silk can be bought direct from the factories or at the many silk shops those in the area, although prices are about the same as those in Nakhon Ratchasima or Bangkok.

Dan Khwian

The ceramics made in the village of **Dan Khwian**, about 15km (9 miles) southwest of Nakhon Ratchasima on Route 224 are another interesting local handicraft. The kaolin clay mined from the banks of the nearby Mun River here is of a high iron content and, after firing in the wood-burning kilns, takes on a natural reddish metallic finish. The items are often cut with elaborate lattice patterns and make good lamps.

A wide variety of wares are on offer, but the trip is really made worthwhile for the chance to view Isaan village life at its most traditional. The name "Don Khwian" refers to the two-wheeled carts that are made here. For centuries the village has been a traditional rest stop for travellers from Cambodia.

Prasat Hin Phanomwan

Just northeast of Nakhon Ratchasima, just beyond the city limits is the peaceful monastery of **Prasat Hin Phanomwan ❹** (daily 8am–6pm; free). With its trademark heavy stone galleries, it reveals the Khmer penchant for false windows with stone mullions, a method adopted to imitate lathed wood and also to compensate for the soft stone. Look closely and you will see the zigzag patterns embellished over the carved stones.

An uncommon stillness pervades this 11th-century retreat, broken only by the footsteps of resident monks. Unlike the majority of Khmer-era ruins, this one contains an active temple. Behind its well-preserved vaulted entrance, the original, dark sanctuary is filled with many, more recent, Buddha images of different styles, most of them covered with patches of gold leaf.

Prasat Hin Phimai

Further north are the magnificent 11th-century Khmer ruins of **Prasat Hin Phimai ❺** (daily 8am–6pm; charge, some 50km (30 miles) from Nakhon Ratchasima on the Mun River, a tributary of the Mekong. Renovated with the help of the same experts who restored Angkor Wat across the border in Cambodia, it has been suggested that Phimai may have been a prototype for Angkor Wat itself, which was built in the following century.

The last of the great Angkor monarchs, King Jayavarman VII, who replaced Hinduism with Mahayana Buddhism as the official religion, could travel quite comfortably from his palace to Phimai, which was at the western extent of his expanding kingdom,

A guardian naga *serpent at Prasat Hin Phimai.*

BELOW: Buddha and offering, Prasat Hin Phimai.

on a major trade route. A string of 112 resthouses was constructed along the 240km (150-mile) road to shelter pilgrims and government officials making the long journey to Phimai. During Jayavarman's reign (AD 1181–1201), Phimai prospered within a walled rectangular area of 1,000 by 560 metres (1,090 by 610 yards) on an artificial island created by linking the Mun River and one of its tributaries by a canal. There were four entrances, with serpents, or *naga*, guarding each. The primary entrance faces south. As with the Angkor temples, the monuments at Phimai were never inhabited. Shops, libraries and houses were built of wood, and therefore disintegrated centuries ago.

Phimai National Museum

The Old City gate, likely the main entrance to the sanctuary, still stands at the end of Phimai's present main street. An original 12th-century water tank, called **Sa Kwan**, has also survived.

Facing Sa Kwan, the large, partially open-air **Phimai National Museum** (daily 9am–4pm; charge) displays many of the more beautifully carved lintels

and statues found in the area, inclu[ing] an exquisite, Buddha-like sto[ne] sculpture of King Jayavarman VII.

SOUTHEAST TO BURIRA[M]

Backtracking to Nakhon Ratchasim[a] continue eastwards via Highway 24, ru[n]ning roughly parallel to the Cambodi[an] border, for a good look at rural Isa[n] country and two significant, but rare[ly] visited, Khmer temple sites in **Burira[m] Province**.

Prasat Hin Khao Phanom Rung Historical Park

Three full ponds – essential eleme[nts] of Khmer monumental architecture and scenic farmland surround **Pras[at] Hin Khao Phanom Rung Histo[ri]cal Park ❻** (daily 6am–6pm; charg[e]) – easily accessed from either Nakh[on] Ratchasima, Buriram or Surin. H[is]torians believe this temple was [an] important rest stop between Angk[or] and Phimai during the 11th and 12[th] centuries. Many generations must ha[ve] elapsed during its initial constructio[n], since several of the stone lintels rese[m]ble the mid-11th-century Baphu[on] style, while the *naga* (serpents) da[te] from the later Angkor Wat period. [A] stone inscription in Sanskrit mentio[ns] King Suryavarman II, the ruler behi[nd] the construction of Angkor Wat.

The largest and best-restor[ed] Khmer monument in Thailand, P[ra]sat Hin Khao Phanom Rung includ[es] a Vishnu lintel, which was spirited o[ut] of Thailand by art thieves in the ea[rly] 1960s. It later surfaced in the US, [in] a private museum collection. Aft[er] protracted negotiations, the lin[tel] was returned to Thailand in the ea[rly] 1990s and placed in its original po[si]tion over one of the entrances.

The main *prang* of Phanom Ru[ng] and its galleries and chapels, refle[ct] the geometric precision of Angk[or] architecture: symmetrical doors a[nd] windows face the four cardinal poi[nts]. The monumental staircase, reliev[ed] by landings, exudes a sense of m[ajesty] and power typical of Khmer desi[gn].

Look for the sandstone bas-reliefs of elephants and enthroned Hindu deities. Monks of the strict Dhammayuti sect maintain the temple. During April's Phanom Rung festival there is a spectacular night-time sound-and-light show.

Prasat Hin Muang Tam

Further east, and downhill a couple of kilometres, is **Prasat Hin Muang Tam** ➐ (daily 6am–6pm; charge), or Lower Temple, sitting on a mossy lawn like an art historian's daydream. Older than Prasat Hin Khao Phanom Rung, its cornerstones were laid in the 10th century, with the temple finished about 100 years later. A Shiva lintel suggests it may originally have been devoted to Hindu worship, and later converted into a Buddhist temple.

Five *prang* – surrounded by galleries, protected by walls and now shaded by trees – constitute Muang Tam, which has been beautifully restored and is considered the third-most significant Angkor-period site in the northeast (after Phanom Rung and Phimai). Once-haphazard blocks of masonry

and fallen lintels are back in place, and the monumental tank now rebuilt and filled with water lilies.

The huge rectangular stone blocks that form the outer walls contain drilled circular holes, probably used for stone figures shaped like lotus buds. The rims of the ponds are lined with *naga* serpents, whose many heads rise at the corners, marking the outer boundary of the temple.

SURIN AND SI SAKET

Located on an old Khmer site, the provincial capital of **Surin** ➑ was primarily known for its silk production until 1960, when the first **Elephant Round-Up** was organised. Originally a festival held by the local people, who are known for their abilities in training the animals, the round-up has now been transformed into an elaborate spectacle that takes place on the third weekend of November. These days about 400 elephants will take part in the event, which includes an impressive re-enactment of the famous battle between King Naresuan of Ayuthaya (r. 1590–1605) and the Burmese,

The remote temple complex of Prasat Ta Muan Tot is located close to the Cambodian border.

BELOW: elephants enthral the crowds in Surin.

It's a long climb up to the Khmer ruins at Prasat Khao Phra Viharn.

BELOW: Prasat Khao Phra Viharn overlooks the Cambodian countryside.

which took place in Suphanburi and is a mainstay of Thai patriotic lore. Both men and beasts are elaborately costumed, and the event puts any elephant show you've ever seen to shame. In addition, more prosaic events take place, such as elephant soccer and the obligatory "Miss Elephant Festival" beauty pageant.

The village of **Ban Ta Klang**, located 60km (40 miles) north of Surin, is the true home of elephant culture in Thailand. It is populated by a people known as the Suay (also called Gui), who are originally from Central Asia and settled in this area before the rise of the Khmer empire. They are Thailand's master mahouts and travel throughout Asia as elephant tenders – originally in logging, now in tourism. A visit to Ban Ta Klang is worthwhile for those with a serious interest in elephants and is best arranged with a knowledgeable guide. The elephants taking part in the Surin Elephant Round-Up are trained here, so the best time to visit is in early November – shortly before the event takes place.

Prasat Ta Muan Tot

South of Surin Town in Ban Ta Mia district, on the Cambodian border, **Prasat Ta Muan Tot** ❾ (daily 6am–6pm; free), one of the most remo and atmospheric Khmer temple si in Thailand. Part of a "healing statio on the route to Angkor Wat, the ma sanctuary stands in line with an orna gate *(gopura)* and prayer hall *(mandap* built of sandstone and surrounded a laterite wall.

Prasat Khao Phra Viharn

Route 226 and a direct rail line conne Surin with the next province east, **Saket** ❿, which borders Cambodia.

Si Saket Province's former ma attraction no longer lies in Thailar In the early 1960s, the World Cou awarded Cambodia the splendid te ple complex of **Prasat Khao Ph Viharn** ⓫ (daily 7.30am–4.30p charge), located about 100km (miles) southeast of the provinc capital and easily reached from the or from Surin or Ubon Ratchatha on the Thai side. It is, however, alm inaccessible from Cambodia. Wheth due to Thai dissatisfaction with t (seemingly odd) World Court ruli or wider political animosities, troul has regularly flared between Thai a Cambodian soldiers stationed near t disputed site, and it is not always op to visitors *(see margin tip, opposite)*.

Prasat Khao Phra Viharn sits on 500-metre (1,650ft) perch of the D grak Mountains overlooking the Ca bodian plains. From Si Saket, it i 60km (40-mile) drive to the near town, Kantharalak, then another 40k (25 miles) to the visitor centre at **P sat Khao Phra Viharn National Pa** The visitor centre marks the entra to the Khmer monument, about 1 (2/3 mile) away. Pay a fee of B10 fo border pass on the Thai side; once y reach the Cambodian side, a fee of B2 is collected by the Cambodian offici This is on top of the B400 entrance

Stretching for almost 1 km (½ mi Phra Viharn was first constructed in early 11th century. Its stairs alternate between hewn bedrock and stones put there about 100 years before the days of Angkor Wat. Each layer is marked by an increasingly large *gopura*, or gate, and ends at the topmost sanctuary honouring the god Shiva.

To the east of the first *gopura*, a precarious trail descends through the jungle to the Cambodian plains. The second *gopura*, shaped like a Greek cross, is superbly carved in 11th-century Khmer style. Its lintels show Vishnu in the Hindu creation myth. The stairs continue in a symbolic ascent to heaven, past another purificatory basin, to the first courtyard with its two palaces and *gopura*, and finally up to the second and third courtyards and the main sanctuary. At the end of the long ridge is a breathtaking precipice above the Cambodian countryside, turning a natural site into a stunning work of art.

UBON RATCHATHANI

Called "Ubon" for short, the sleepy northeastern provincial capital of **Ubon Ratchathani** ⓬ lies 700km (430 miles) east of Bangkok and about 60km (40 miles) east of Si Saket. In the 1100s, the area around Ubon belonged to the Khmers, until the Ayutthaya empire supplanted them. Ubon itself is a rather young town, founded in the late 1700s by Lao immigrants. Much of the town's 20th-century growth coincided with the American build-up during the Vietnam War – and the military link is still in evidence today, with many of Ubon's 115,000 inhabitants working for the Thai military. The town's strong trade links with nearby Laos and Cambodia has earned Ubon the moniker "Capital of the Emerald Triangle". A rash of new construction and some of the region's prettiest temples rise behind the banks of the Mun River, which flows east into the Mekong 100km (62 miles) from Ubon.

City sights

Established by King Rama III, **Wat Thung Si Muang** (daily 8am–5pm; free) at Thanon Luang is noted for its scripture library, which is sturdily built of teak and raised on stilts in the middle of a lotus pond.

TIP

On several occasions in 2009, clashes between the Thai and Cambodian militaries resulted in fatalities at Khao Phra Viharn. Although both sides declared it a "misunderstanding", the area was closed to visitors in early 2010. Hopefully this will have changed by the time you plan to visit. To check on the current status call the TAT office in Ubon at 045-243 770.

BELOW LEFT: Mahabodhi Stupa replica at Wat Phra That Nong Bua.
BELOW: rock formations at Kaeng Tenna National Park.

Decorative containers for sticky rice.

Ubon Ratchathani National Museum is Isaan's finest museum (Wed–Sun 9am–4pm; charge; www.thailandmuseum.com). Housed in King Vajiravudh's (Rama VI, r. 1910–25) former country residence, it houses a collection of fine artefacts of Thai, Lao, Khmer, Vietnamese and Indian origin.

On the outskirts of town is **Wat Phra That Nong Bua** (daily 8am–5pm; free), which contains a tall *chedi* that is a close replica of the Mahabodhi Stupa in Bodh Gaya, India. **Ko Hat Wat Tai**, a sandy island in the middle of the Mun River, southeast of the town, is a favourite picnic spot during the hot, dry months of March and April when the river recedes and exposes a temporary "beach".

Two temples in nearby **Warin Chamrap** district are well known for their association with the late Ajahn Cha, a famous meditation master. His original monastery, **Wat Nong Pa Phong** (daily 6am–6pm; free), lies 10km (6 miles) north of the Ubon train station. This peaceful spot has a small museum dedicated to the famous monk, as well as a

chedi enshrining his ashes. Many Western monks ordained and spent time at this monastery studying under Ajahn Cha.

Nearby **Wat Pa Nanachat Bung Wai** (daily 6am–6pm; free) houses another unique Buddhist monastery. Founded by an American monk under Ajahn Cha's tutelage, the tidy, highly disciplined monastery welcomes day visitors for meditation and religious talks, although it is always best to call (tel: 08-1470 9299) before visiting.

Kaeng Tanna N P

From Ubon, it's possible to visit **Kaeng Tanna National Park** (daily 8am–6pm; charge), some 90km (56 miles) to the northeast, near the Mekong River. It has prehistoric cave paintings and rapids where the Mun River squeezes through a gorge before joining the Mekong. The park is also known for its abundance of submerged cave systems. There is basic bungalow accommodation available.

Ubon Ratchathani is also the jump-off point for visiting the scenic peninsula of **Khong Jiam** (*see page 361*) at the confluence of the Mekong and Mun rivers. ❑

RESTAURANTS AND BARS

Restaurants

Price per person for a three-course meal without drinks:
$ = under B300
$$ = B300–800
$$$ = B800–1,600
$$$$ = over B1,600

Nakhon Ratchasima

Thai

Cabbages & Condoms
86/1 Th. Seup Siri.
Tel: 0-4425 8100.
Open: daily L & D. $$
This branch of the humorously named non-profit restaurant chain serves Bangkok-style Thai cuisine, along with a few mandatory Isaan offerings. The foliage-filled garden seating area is very popular.

Kai Yang Seup Siri
Th. Seup Siri. Tel: 0-4426-1493. Open: daily 11am–4pm. $
Northeastern Thailand is famous for *kai yang* (spicy grilled chicken), and this modest roadside eatery grills up Khorat's best. The *som tam* (shredded green papaya and chilli salad) is also excellent.

Thai Pochana
142 Th. Jomsurangyat.
Tel: 0-4424 2840.
Open: daily 7am–2am. $$
One of the oldest restaurants in town, this eatery ranks high on the must-do lists of many Bangkokians visiting the city. The lengthy menu covers all the usual mainstream Thai options, along with such local specialities as *mee khorat* – "Khorat

noodles", a spicier version of *pad thai*.

Thai & Western

Chez Andy
5–7 Th. Manat. Tel: 0-4428 9556. Open: Mon–Sat 11am–midnight. $$
www.chezandy.com
Operated out of the Swiss owner's house, Chez Andy offers an astonishingly varied menu of salads, schnitzel, beef stroganoff, steaks, pasta and Thai dishes.

Ton Som Restaurant
Th. Wacharasarit. Tel: 0-4425 2275. Open: daily 10am–10pm. $$
The faux-biker-bar decor and rock oldies on the sound system offer no hint of the delicious Thai and Western dishes served here. From Isaan *laab* (spicy minced-meat salad) to American-style steak, Ton Som caters to residents as well as tourists just passing through.

Phimai

Thai

Baiteiy Restaurant
Th. Chomsudasadet.
Tel: 0-4428 7103.
Open: daily 8am–10pm. $
A short walk from the entrance to Prasat Hin Phimai Historical Park, humble Baiteiy (named after *bai toei*, the Thai pandanus leaf) has been a choice for legions of visitors. Though the kitchen won't win any awards, it offers the widest variety of Thai dishes in town, from *pad thai* to *tom yum*, and observes conveniently long hours.

Surin

Thai

Laap Lak Muang
Th. Lak Muang.
Open: daily 3–9pm. $
The most authentic source of Isaan fare in town, the small, open-air Laap Lak Muang is renowned for its namesake *laab*, spicy minced duck, beef or pork seasoned with lime juice, fish sauce, scallions and dried red chilli. Absolutely delicious.

Surin Chai Kit
Next to the Sangthong Hotel, Th. Tanasan. Tel: 0-4429 7299. Open: daily B & L. $
Because it opens at 6am, this is one of the town's favourite breakfast spots. The house speciality is *khai ka-ta*, eggs baked and served in a small metal pan with northeast Thai sausage. Chicken stir-fried with holy basil (*khao phat bai ka-phrao kai*), topped with a fried egg, is another good bet.

Ubon Ratchathani

Thai

Kai Yang Wat Jaeng
Th. Suriyat. Tel: 0-4526 3496. Open: daily 9am–5pm. $
This humble, clean open-air eatery a block north of Wat Jaeng is famous for *kai yang* (Isaan-style grilled chicken). Order *som tam* (spicy green papaya salad), *sup naw mai* (shredded fresh bamboo shoots in a spicy sauce) and a basket of sticky rice for a tasty, filling meal. The chicken usually runs out by 2pm, after which a variety of curries are available.

Samchai Gai Yang
Samchai Gai Yang
282/1 Palochai Rd
(near Toh Sang Hotel).
Tel: 0-4520 9118.
Open: daily L & D. $
The most famous restaurant in town for local northeastern Thai food, starting with but not limited to *gai yang* (roasted chicken). Try also the duck or fish *laab*, spicy papaya salad, and Isaan sausage, all of which go well with sticky rice. It's a spacious place with both a/c and non a/c sections.

Thai & Western

Chiokee
307–317 Th. Kheuan Thani.
Tel: 0-4525 4017.
Open: daily 8am–10pm. $
This Ubon mainstay continues to be popular for its Thai, Chinese and Western food, attentive service, long business hours and affordable prices. Whether it's *joke* (rice porridge, a house speciality) or ham and eggs, the kitchen performs with aplomb.

Vietnamese & Thai

Indochine
168–170 Th. Saphasit. Tel: 0-4524 5584. Open: daily 10am–midnight. $$
True to its name, Indochine serves Lao and Vietnamese food, along with a few Thai and Isaan dishes. The most popular item on the menu is Vietnamese *naem nuang*, a large platter of pork meatballs, thin rice noodles, fresh lettuce, sliced starfruit and condiments.

NORTH TO LOEI

Delve deep into the heart of Isaan country at Khon Kaen and Roi Et. Then head to Udon Thani, where excavations at nearby Ban Chiang have yielded traces of Thailand's Bronze Age. Further north, Loei is known for its rugged mountain scenery

From **Nakhon Ratchasima** (Khorat), travellers can continue north on Highway 2 to the heart of the Isaan region in Khon Kaen Province. From Khon Kaen, you can either head east to Roi Et or continue north on Highway 2 to Udon Thani and further until it reaches the northernmost Mekong River town of Nong Khai. Diverting west from Udon Thani leads to the tranquil and mountainous region of Loei.

KHON KAEN AND ROI ET

With a population of 150,000, **Khon Kaen ⓲** is the Isaan region's second-largest city after Nakhon Ratchasima. It is the only large centre in the eponymous province – an overwhelmingly rural part of Thailand, with farming and textiles being the main livelihoods. Aside from serving as a trade and supply centre for these industries, Khon Kaen is also an important commercial, financial and educational centre.

With its good restaurants and hotels, Khon Kaen makes a fine spot to take a rest from travel in Isaan. Travellers continuing to Laos or Vietnam can also obtain visas from the Lao and Vietnamese consulates in town.

City sights

There are a few attractions in town worth checking out. The well-curated

Khon Kaen National Museum (Wed–Sun 9am–4pm; charge; www. thailandmuseum.com) at Thanon Lang Sunratchakan has an impressive collection of Dvaravati-period (6th–10th-century) Buddhist art, and ancient Ban Chiang artefacts of bronze and ceramic from the Sukhothai and Ayutthaya periods.

Also of interest is **Wat Nong Wang Muang** (daily 8am–6pm; free) at the southern end of town. The temple is surprisingly grand for the Isaan region; its beautiful nine-tiered

Main attractions
KHON KAEN
ROI ET
UDON THANI
UDORN SUNSHINE NURSERY
BAN CHIANG
LOEI
DAN SAI
PHU KRADUNG NATIONAL PARK

LEFT: the Phee Ta Khon festival, Dan Sai.
RIGHT: rural scene near Khon Kaen.

The khaen *is the principal musical instrument played in the* mor lam *music of northeast Thailand.*

BELOW: Khon Kaen's night market.

pagoda is said to be designed after the famous Shwedagon Pagoda of Yangon in Myanmar.

Khon Kaen town's two large, shallow lakes, **Beung Kaen Nakhon** (Kaen Nakhon Lake), found at the southern limits of the city and **Beung Thung Sang** (Thung Sang Lake) to the northeast, are favourite venues with strollers seeking cool evening breezes and snacks sold by itinerant vendors.

Around Khon Kaen

Many visitors to Khon Kaen also use the city as a base to make a day trip to **Chonabot** ⓮, some 57km (34 miles) southwest. This is a well-known centre for the high-quality, traditional northeastern silk fabric known as *mudmee*. At the small workshops in Chonabot, you can see the silk being woven and dyed, as well as buy the fabrics.

Around 70km (43 miles) southeast of Khon Kaen, via Routes 23 and 2297, **Prasat Peuay Noi** ⓯ (known locally as That Ku Thong) is a little-visited 12th-century Khmer temple site much admired for its large sand-

stone sanctuary topped by a *prang*. Parts of the original temple walls and gates still stand, along with carved stone pediments and lintels.

East to Roi Et

From Khon Kaen, Route 213 heads east 76km (47 miles) to the small farming centre of **Kalasin**, while Route 214 leads 115km (71 miles) southeast to **Roi Et** ⓰, a worthwhile side trip for anyone interested in Isaan culture, particularly music.

Several villages in the province specialise in the crafting of a type of mouth organ known as the *khaen*, the lead instrument in *mor lam*, a bawdy and occasionally political northeastern music form *(see page 72)*. Consisting of thick, hollow reeds bound in two rows to a carved Asian redwood sound chamber, the *khaen* produces a sound reminiscent of an organ or large harmonica. The rhythmically churning *khaen*, allied with hand percussion and two stringed instruments (the bowed *so* and plucked *phin*), yields a hypnotic sonic brew that inspires all-night dancing among *mor lam* devotees. The most convenient village to see *khaen*-making is **Si Kaew**, approximately 15km (9 miles) northwest of Roi Et City.

Roi Et City

The city of Roi Et itself is centred on an artificial lake called **Beung Phlan Chai**. Although once an independent kingdom with 11 city gates, the local architecture today offers little of historic interest.

The **Wat Burapha** (daily 7am–7pm; free) is a popular pilgrimage point because of its 68-metre (223ft) standing Buddha. A staircase in its base reaches the level of the figure's knees, from where one can take in views of the surrounding townscape.

Nearby **Wat Neua** (daily 7am–7pm; free) contains a very old *chedi* that may date to the Dvaravati period. Dvaravati-style stone ordination markers surround the ordination hall. A stone

pillar inscribed in Khmer suggests the site was also occupied by the Khmers around the 11th or 12th century.

UDON THANI

From Khon Kaen, Highway 2 continues 115km (71 miles) north to **Udon Thani** ⓱ (Udon for short, often spelt "Udorn"), a town that grew quickly with the arrival of American airmen during the Vietnam War in the 1960s. Today, instead of military convoys, noisy motorcycles and packed pick-up trucks fill the busy streets. The city plan is unusual for Thailand in that several of the major avenues are laid out diagonally against a street grid, complete with large traffic circles that might be more at home in a French city.

Aside from the artificial lake, **Nong Prajak**, there is little to see in town. However, just outside the city limits to the northwest, off Route 2024, is a novelty. The **Udorn Sunshine Nursery** (daily 7am–6.30pm; free; www.udorn-sunshine.com) is famous for creating the Thai dancing gyrant, a plant whose leaves sway gently when spoken or sung to. The nursery also blends natural perfumes, using aromatic extracts from orchids it grows on site.

Among Udon's many restaurants, several have earned a reputation for serving the best Isaan cuisine in the northeast, while several shops sell high-quality Isaan handicrafts, particularly hand-woven cotton and silk textiles.

Around Udon Thani

In Nong Han district in the eastern part of Udon Thani Province lies what is probably the most famous archaeological site in Thailand. The people of **Ban Chiang** ⓲, long used to encountering fragments of pots, beads and even human bones when digging around their houses or working on their farms, have paid scant attention to such finds. Then, in 1966, a University of Pennsylvania anthropology student visited the area, some 50km (31 miles) east of Udon Thani. He showed his finds to the archaeology authorities in Bangkok. More comprehensive analysis of the artefacts led to a surprising conclusion; they were much older than had been believed – between 3,500 and 7,500 years old.

The unique dancing gyrant plant at Udorn Sunshine Nursery.

BELOW LEFT: textile-weaving. **BELOW:** Wat Burapha, Roi Et.

Khit *hand-loomed fabric with its distinctive diamond-shaped motifs.*

BELOW: pottery display at the Ban Chiang National Museum. **BELOW RIGHT:** devilish masks used at the Phee Ta Khon Festival in Dan Sai.

Bronze artefacts were also discovered, and dated to around 3600 BC. This places the appearance of bronze in Thailand centuries earlier than in the Middle East, until then thought to be the earliest location of bronze usage. Equally intriguing is that this dating of Ban Chiang bronze suggests that bronze may have been transmitted from Thailand to China, rather than the other way round, which had hitherto been the theory. Some experts, however, maintain that the dating of 3600 BC for the appearance of bronze is too early, suggesting that 2000 BC, or even 2500 BC, is more accurate. This would put the appearance of bronze in Southeast Asia later than the Middle East, but at around the same time as China.

Even if its antiquity were not authenticated, the beautiful whorl designs of its pottery and the intricacy of its bronze jewellery and implements would make the Ban Chiang culture rather more advanced than most of the early peoples of the earth. In recognition of this, Ban Chiang achieved Unesco World Heritage status in 1992.

Many of these artefacts can be seen at the **Ban Chiang National Museum** (daily 8.30am–4.30pm; charge), established with the help of the US-based Smithsonian Institute. One of the original excavation pits, on display at nearby **Wat Pho Si Nai** (daily 8.30am–4.30pm; charge) contains 52 human skeletons that were interred with ceremonial pottery.

Two weaving villages, **Ban Na Kha** and **Ban Thon**, 16km (10 miles) and 18km (11 miles) respectively north of Udon Thani and off Highway 2, are well known for their hand-loomed textiles called *khit*. Diamond-shaped motifs woven into weft brocade are *khit* hallmarks. Several shops in the two villages offer the textiles for sale.

Towards Loei

Route 210 runs 150km (100 miles) west of Udon Thani to the ruggedly beautiful **Loei Province**, and the town of the same name. But first, stop midway at **Tham Erawan**  (daily 8am–5pm; donation), the Triple-Headed Elephant Cave, about 50km (30 miles) before Loei and a couple of

kilometres (1 mile) off the road. The cave, ensconced in the side of large and beautiful limestone cliff, is considered sacred and is part of Wat Tham Erawan, a small complex of shrine rooms and monastic cells in front of the cave. A large sitting Buddha near the mouth of the cave is visible from the plains below. A life-size statue of Erawan, the triple-headed elephant of Hindu-Buddhist mythology, marks the steep 700-step stairway and rocky path to the cave's entrance. The climb is rough, but the views are worth the effort. Prehistoric artefacts have been found here. Besides the occasional cobra emerging from the rocks, and an elephant's skull, there is little to see inside the actual cave, however.

LOEI

The city of **Loei** ⑳ is a flourishing centre for the province's cotton trade and its low-level commerce with neighbouring Laos. The usually placid Loei River flows through the centre of town. Until the 1980s, communist insurgents hid in the surrounding forests. What is now a traveller's delight was once the civil servant's nightmare – in Thai bureaucracy, being assigned to Loei was like going to Siberia: it was an isolated jungle outpost with fever, cold weather and poor security.

Loei is somewhat scant on sights, but the surrounding province makes up for this with several lush national parks, rugged mountainous scenery and the chance to witness a unique festival at Dan Sai.

Phu Rua N P

From Loei, Route 203 plunges west into the wilderness to **Phu Rua National Park** ㉑ (daily 8.30am–5pm; charge). The 50km (30-mile) road slices through heavy banks of red laterite, past a sawmill and fields of *kenaf* and cotton, the latter being the area's primary source of income. The summit of Phu Rua mountain is 1,370 metres (4,495ft) high. A smooth, winding road leads to the top, from where there are spectacular views

of the national forest. Be warned that in winter, the temperature at the summit can drop to freezing point.

Dan Sai

Around 80km (50 miles) southwest of Loei is **Dan Sai** ㉒, famous for its annual **Phee Ta Khon Festival**, possibly Thailand's most raucous celebration. The townspeople don outlandish, clown-like costumes and huge masks with devilish-looking eyes, an oversized wooden nose and a wide, toothy grin.

The festival celebrates the *Mahavessantara Jataka*, a tale in which the Buddha travels to heavenly realms to preach to his deceased mother. The costumed figures represent members of the spirit world who follow the Buddha back to earth after his visit. The figures – women as well as men, children as well as adults – carry large wooden hand totems, carved into graphic phallic shapes (possibly a syncretic blending with a pre-Buddhist fertility festival).

Most of the activities of the three-day festival centre around **Wat Phon Chai**, where the "spirits" circumambulate the main *viharn* (sermon hall) numerous

Loei Province experiences the most extreme weather in Thailand – both hot and cold. In the winter, the province consistently records temperatures below freezing, and in the summer months temperatures often top the nation's maximum temperature list. Enterprising locals have taken advantage of this – in the hot dry months they grow cotton, and in the cooler seasons, at higher altitude, Loei's temperate-species cut flowers are shipped to sweltering Bangkok.

BELOW: scenery near Phu Kradung National Park.

Making Vietnamese spring-roll skins in Si Chiangmai.

BELOW: old wooden houses at Chiang Khan.

times, dancing to live *mor lam* music. Inspired by copious consumption of *lao khao* (home-distilled moonshine), the circumambulations last hours, reaching a frenzied crescendo after midday. The exact date of the festival changes each year, but it falls in either June or July.

Around Dan Sai

Just outside Dan Sai is **Phra That Si Songrak**, a highly venerated *chedi* constructed in the four-sided, curvilinear style of Laos and northeastern Thailand. The 30-metre (98ft) monument was erected in 1560 to commemorate the friendship between Thailand and Vientiane, and to mark the border between the two kingdoms.

Northeast of Dan Sai on Route 203 is **Chateau de Loei Vineyards** (daily 8am–5pm; free; www.chateaudeloei.com), the first vineyard in Thailand to produce French-style wines; it has earned a modest reputation for its Chenin Blanc in particular. Self-tours of the vineyards, as well as wine-tasting, are available.

The tiny town of **Na Haew**, about 30km (20 miles) northwest of Dan Sai, is a de facto border crossing between Thai-land and Laos for Lao and Thai nationals, who cross the Huang River by raft.

Phu Kradung N P

No experience in the Loei area can match the beauty of **Phu Kradung National Park** ㉓ (daily 8am–6pm; charge), the most memorable escape in this region, some 100km (60 miles) south of Loei. Phu Kradung is a 60-sq-km (24-sq-mile) plateau located between 1,200 and 1,500 metres (4,000–5,000ft) high and with over 50km (30 miles) of marked trails.

The park entrance is along Route 201; about 3km (2 miles) further is the park office, where one can arrange for porters and equipment. The park provides bedding and blankets (temperatures in Dec and Jan can reach freezing point) in cabins that hold up to 11 people. The principal trail ascends 6km (4 miles) and takes three hours to climb. It's by no means an easy ascent, but ladders enable you to negotiate the steepest boulders, and it's well worth the effort. During the March to May hot season, it's best to begin the ascent before dawn to avoid the midday heat.

Atop Phu Kradung, clear and mostly level paths crisscross the tableland. Rare birds, including various hornbills, woodpeckers and pheasants, may be seen. Even wild elephants and the occasional tiger make their home on the mountain, along with gibbons, sambars, barking deer and the Asiatic black bear, although few of these species are likely to be seen. As the surrounding forests have been logged indiscriminately in recent years, the authorities close the park in the summer months to permit the ecology to recover.

Chiang Khan

From Loei, the road north leads 50km (30 miles) to the Mekong River – where it once again forms the border between Thailand and Laos – and the charming riverside town of **Chiang Khan** ㉔. Many of the homes lining the riverbank are built of wood in French-Lao style, and the town's Buddhist temples show a dominant Lao influence. Cycle or catch a taxi about 5km (3 miles) east of town to the **Kaeng Khut Khu** rapids, worthwhile for its raging beauty.

East to Nong Khai

From Chiang Khan, Route 211 follows the Mekong east to **Sangkhom** ㉕ village, which has modest accommodation and excellent river views, along with two falls, **Than Thip Waterfall** and **Than Thong Waterfall**, both local picnic spots. Further on along Route 211 beyond Sangkhom, **Wat Hin Mak Peng** is a meditation monastery perched on cliffs overlooking the Mekong. Visitors are welcome to visit the temple if they dress modestly.

Around 20km (12 miles) before Nong Khai, Route 211 passes the town of **Si Chiang Mai** ㉖, directly opposite Vientiane, the capital of Laos, on the other side of the Mekong. Most of its population is of either Lao or Vietnamese descent, mainly engaged in making the translucent rice-flour skins for Vietnamese-style spring rolls, exported all over the world. All around town, one can see the spring-roll wrappers drying on bamboo-lattice racks before being sealed in plastic bags and shipped to wholesalers. A small church serves the town's many Vietnamese Catholic residents. ❏

RESTAURANTS

Khon Kaen
Thai
Bualuang Restaurant
Th. Rop Beung Kaen Nakhon. Tel: 0-4322 2504. Open: daily 10am–11pm. $$
A pleasant lakeside setting, open-air dining areas and an extensive menu of northeastern and central Thai dishes make this eatery a popular choice for locals and visitors.

Em Ot
71/22 Th. Klang Muang. Tel: 0-4324 1382. Open: daily 9am–11pm. $
Opposite the Roma Hotel, this local favourite serves good brewed coffee and *kai ka-ta* (fried eggs and sausage served in a hot

pan), along with some Isaan dishes.

Namai Restaurant
42/14 Ammart Rd. Tel: 0-4323 9958. Open: daily L & D. $
A wide variety of Thai food served in a cosy two-storey house in the centre of town. Try their stir fried roasted duck with chili and coconut hearts or deep fried fish with green mangos.

Udon Thani
Thai
Udon Phochana
244/5 Th. Pho Si. Tel: 0-4222 1756. Open: daily 8am–6.30pm. $
A classic Thai-Chinese eatery, this place has been

around for over 30 years. The cooks can whip up practically an Thai dish.

Western
Steve's Bar and Restaurant
254/26 Th. Prajak Silpakorn. Tel: 0-4224 4523. Open: daily 8am–11pm. $$
www.udonmap.com/stevesbar
This friendly air-conditioned restaurant is popular with the expat community for its Sunday roast, pie 'n' chips and other Western dishes.

Loei
Thai & Vietnamese
Loei Danang
22/58 Th. Chumsai. Tel: 0-4283-0413. Open: daily L & D. $

A delicious mix of Vietnamese and Thai dishes.

Dan Sai
Thai
Restaurant Je-Boy
Route 2114, just north of Dan Sai. No phone. Open: daily 10am–10pm. $
The best place to eat in Dan Sai is this open-air roadside eatery, owned by a Thai-Chinese woman who cooks everything from Isaan to Bangkok fare.

Price per person for a three-course meal without drinks:
$ = under B300
$$ = B300–800
$$$ = B800–1,600
$$$$ = over B1,600

ALONG THE MEKONG RIVER

Follow the winding curve of the Mekong River, from Nong Khai in the far north all the way to Khong Jiam in the southeast to experience some of Thailand's most remote sights

From Udon Thani *(see page 351)*, Highway 2 continues north for some 50km (30 miles) to **Nong Khai ㉗**, on the southern bank of the Mekong River. Alternatively, it's also possible (and more exciting) to approach Nong Khai along the Mekong River east from Chiang Khan *(see page 355)*.

NONG KHAI

In 1994, the 1.2km (¾-mile) **Friendship Bridge** – just 3km (2 miles) west of Nong Khai – opened, connecting Nong Khai with Vientiane, the capital of Laos across the river. This first bridge over the lower Mekong boosted development in the city. The long-awaited rail link across the Mekong via the Friendship Bridge is now operational. Daily departures from Bangkok (one can also board in Nong Khai) connect the Thai and Lao capitals.

Long and narrow, the entire length of Nong Khai Province parallels the Mekong River. From 1353 to 1694, this part of Thailand belonged to the independent Lao kingdoms of Lan Xang and later Vientiane, only becoming a Siamese protectorate in the late 18th century. Nong Khai kept close ties with French-colonised Laos throughout the 19th century, and influences from that period remain in the provincial capital's appealing remnants of Lao-French architecture.

Sunset cruise

To experience the Mekong River fully, take a cruise on the *Nagarina*, a lovingly restored riverboat operated by the Mutmee Guest House, which sails from their premises daily at 5pm. Dinner is available – and highly recommended. Alternatively, rough-and-ready grass-topped vessels can be hired throughout the day at Tha Sadet Market.

During the dry season, when the Mekong shrinks, the "beach" at **Hat Jommani**, 3km (2 miles) west of Nong Khai, transforms into a local picnic spot.

Main attractions
NONG KHAI
SALA KAEW KU SCULPTURE PARK
PHU PHRABAT HISTORICAL PARK
WAT PHU THOK
NAKHON PHANOM
RENU NAKHON
THAT PHANOM
MUKDAHAN
KHONG JIAM

LEFT: Sala Kaew Ku Sculpture Park. **RIGHT:** fish farm on the Mekong River at Nong Khai.

Arresting rock formation at Phu Phrabat Historical Park.

BELOW: Buddha images, Phu Phrabat Historical Park.

Sala Kaew Ku Sculpture Park

Nong Khai's most popular attraction is the **Sala Kaew Ku Sculpture Park** (daily 7.30am–5.30pm; charge), about 4km (2½ miles) southeast of town via Route 212. Founded by Boun Leua Sourirat, a Hindu-Buddhist guru of Lao descent, the religious park is filled with surreal cement sculptures of Shiva, Vishnu, Buddha and other figures from Hindu and Buddhist mythology.

Born in Laos, Boun Leua fled when the communists took over Vientiane in 1975. Moving to Nong Khai, he began building the giant figures with funds from local donors. The guru died in 1996, but his followers still maintain the park today, along with a small shrine and museum dedicated to the man and his philosophical hybrid fusion of Hinduism and Buddhism.

Wat Phra That Bang Phuan

Another temple worth visiting in this area is **Wat Phra That Bang Phuan** (daily 7am–6pm; free) located about 12km (7 miles) south of Nong Khai on Highway 2, and then 11km (7 miles) further west on Route 211. This temple is

well known for its elegant 16th-century Lao-style *chedi*, built by King Jaychettha of the Vientiane kingdom. The *chedi* toppled from rain damage in 1970, but was restored a few years later.

Phu Phrabat Historical Park

About 70km (42 miles) southwest of Nong Khai, in Ban Pheu district, is the **Phu Phrabat Historical Park** (daily 8.30am–4.30pm; charge). This park contains a blend of fascinating prehistoric cave paintings, strange natural rock formations and Buddhist temples. The best way to experience it all is on foot, via a marked trail that takes about two hours to traverse.

ALONG THE MEKONG

It is an exciting journey that few travellers undertake, but it's possible to follow the winding curve of the Mekong River, first northeast, then south all the way to Khong Jiam in Ubon Ratchathani Province. At Khong Jiam, the Mekong first diverts east into Laos and then later south into Cambodia and eventually Vietnam before emptying into the South China Sea.

Beung Kan

The first stop is **Beung Kan** ㉘, a long and winding 185km (111 miles) northeast of Nong Khai. Although there is little of historical or cultural note in this small agricultural backwater, it makes for a convenient stopover for long road trips along Thailand's Mekong rim. From Beung Kan, it's possible to take a side trip to **Wat Phu Thok** (also called Wat Chedi Khiri Viharn; daily 10am–4pm; free). This is a meditation monastery perched atop a huge sandstone outcrop – an amazing sight. Wooden stairs (best avoided by anyone who suffers from vertigo) lead from ground level to the flat top of the outcrop, 200 metres (650ft) above the surrounding plain, past a number of meditation caves and monastic cells.

Nakhon Phanom

Following the Mekong River southeast along Route 212, one arrives in **Nakhon Phanom** ㉙ – 270km (162 miles) from Nong Khai and 175km (109 miles) from Beung Kan – the most remote province in northeast Thailand. The Thai name means "city of hills", a reference to the chain of jagged, powder-grey mountains in the distance, across the Mekong River in Laos.

Apart from the pretty views, there is not much to see or do here. Come late October, however, the town is turned into a hive of activity with the onset of the Fireboat Festival (*see panel, below*).

Nakhon Phanom is also an official Lao–Thai border crossing. On the opposite bank of Nakhon Phanom stands **Tha Khaek**, a former French colonial outpost. Boats ferry passengers back and forth between the two countries, but make sure you have a Lao visa.

Renu Nakhon

From Nakhon Phanom, Route 212 winds gently southwards parallel to the Mekong, at times revealing inspiring views of the Khammuan limestone massif across the river in Laos. Some 44km (26 miles) from Nakhon Phanom, the small town of **Renu Nakhon** ㉚ is home to the Phu Thai minority, who are much admired for their weaving. Best-known for *mudmee* patterns loom-woven in cotton or silk, the Phu Thai hold a handicraft market every Saturday near

TIP

Just east of Nakhon Phanom, in the village of Baan Na Chok, it is possible to visit the 1920s home of Ho Chi Minh, who was one of many Vietnamese exiles to seek refuge in this part of Thailand. His desk has been preserved, and there is good exhibition of archival photographs. Ironically, during the Vietnam War, Nakhon Phanom was a major US Air Force base.

BELOW: Mekong River near Renu Nakhon.

Fire Boat Festival

At the end of the annual three-month Phansa (Buddhist "rains retreat", during which Buddhist monks are required to reside in their home monasteries), usually in late October, Nakhon Phanom becomes the focus of the striking Bun Heua Fai (Fire Boat Festival). In addition to making offerings at Buddhist temples throughout the city, local residents launch homemade "fire boats" on the Mekong River at night. Measuring up to 10 metres (33ft) in length, the elaborate frames and non-functioning "sails" of the curved prow craft are lined with elaborate lanterns, creating a spectacular visual display. The decks are decorated and piled with flowers, balls of sticky rice and cakes, meant as offerings to the Buddhist Devaloka (deity realm).

The river known to most Thais as Mae Nam Khong is sometimes shortened to Mae Khong, whence the Western name "Mekong" is derived.

the town's main Buddhist monastery.

Wat Phra That Renu Nakhon (daily 7am–6pm; free) in town is worth a quick stop to view its centuries-old and highly revered Lao-style *chedi*. At weekends during the cool season (December–February), the Phu Thai people perform folk dances at the temple.

That Phanom

About 10km (6 miles) further south via Route 212 is a turn-off onto Route 2031, which leads east another 7km (4 miles) to the town of **That Phanom** ㉛, home to the most famous *chedi* in all of Isaan. **Wat Phra That Phanom** towers 57 metres (187ft), and is visible from several kilometres away. The *chedi* was built half a millennium ago, when the province was still part of a Lao kingdom. The four-sided, curvilinear style reflects Lao Buddhist architecture and is similar to several major *chedi* found on the opposite side of the Mekong today.

The short road that leads from the temple into That Phanom Town passes through the **Pratu Chai** (Victory Gate), inspired by Paris's Arc de Triomphe, albeit far smaller and decorated with Lao motifs. Towards the Mekong riverfront, many of the town's worn but quaint shophouses date to the French Indochina colonial period.

Most days, a large **Lao Market** convenes at a spot on the riverbank north of the main ferry pier. Note: the crossing between Laos and Thailand here is open only to Lao and Thai nationals.

Mukdahan

Continuing south on Route 212 along the Mekong leads to the district town of **Mukdahan** ㉜ on the banks of the Mekong and opposite the Lao town of Savannakhet. Mukdahan is a trading centre for Lao timber, agricultural products and gems. Its **Indochina Market** and **Danang Market**, named after the port city of the same name in Vietnam, deal in goods from Laos and Vietnam: the main route into Vietnam runs east from Savannakhet to Danang.

Near the river, the skyline is punctuated by the modern **Mukdahan Jewel Hall** shopping centre, which resembles a tall needle. Take the road to the river, turn right and visit **Wat Si Nongkran**, built by Vietnamese refugees in 1956.

BELOW: Lao-style Wat Phra That Phanom.

The gates present a curious mixture of Thai contours, Vietnamese writing and Chinese-inspired dragons. A new bridge opened here in 2006.

Mukdahan National Park (daily 8am–6pm; charge) – also known locally as **Phu Mu National Park** – is located off Route 2034, about 16km (10 miles) south of Mukdahan. The park is famous for its peculiar rock formations, many in the shape of jagged mushrooms.

Around Khong Jiam

At Mukdahan, Route 212 turns inland towards **Ubon Ratchathani** (*see page 345*). From here, head east on Route 217 to the village of **Ban Khon Sai**, where you will find local men forging heavy bronze gongs for temples and traditional Thai music ensembles. Look for open-sided shelters along Route 217, where artisans sit hammering the bronze discs, and then hardening the metal in wood fires.

Several waterfalls can be found in the same general area, the most accessible and unusual of them being one that cascades in front of a cave monastery called **Wat Tham Hew Sin Chai** off Route 2222, southwest of Khong Jiam.

Further west the confluence of the Mekong River and Mun River (or Mae Nam Mun) forms a scenic peninsula on which **Khong Jiam ③** sits. Each river has its own colour (the Mun being muddier than the Mekong), so Thais refer to this section of water as the "Two-Colour River". Longtail boats can be chartered by the hour (B400), with stops at various small river islands.

To the north of Khong Jiam is the **Pha Taem National Park ③** (daily 8am–6pm; charge), famous for its 200-metre (650ft) cliff that bears murals of fish, elephants and human figures thought to be at least 3,000 years old. A 500-metre (1,640ft) rock trail leads to two platforms for viewing the paintings.

Chong Mek

To the south, Route 217 ends at **Chong Mek ③**, the only official land crossing between Thailand and Laos. Another 5km (3 miles) west of Chong Mek is the 288-sq-km (111-sq-mile) **Sirinthorn Reservoir**. A secluded but famous meditation monastery, **Wat Pa Wana Phothiyan**, sits on an island in the reservoir. ❏

Hats, including Vietnamese conical hats, for sale at the Indochina Market in Mukdahan.

RESTAURANTS

Nong Khai
Thai
Udom Rot
Th. Rimkhong. Tel: 0-4242 1084. Open: daily 10am–10pm. **$$**
One of Nong Khai's oldest restaurants and overlooking the Mekong River. The menu includes *plaa sam rot* ("three-flavour fish"), fried and topped with chillies, garlic and coriander leaves.

Thai & Western
Mutmee Guesthouse
1111/4 Th. Kaeworawut. Tel: 0-4246 0717.
Open: daily 8am–10pm. **$$**
www.mutmee.net.
In a quiet, peaceful garden alongside the river, Mutmee serves healthy Thai and Western cuisine, including a variety of vegetarian dishes.

Nakhon Phanom
Thai
Golden Giant Catfish
259 Th. Sunthon Wijit.
Tel: 08-1421 8491.
Open: daily 7am–midnight. **$**
This place no longer serves its namesake giant Mekong catfish (due to near-zero harvests), but other fish dishes include a bracing *plaa neung ma-nao* (fish steamed in lime juice, garlic and chillies).

View Khong Restaurant
527 Sunthornvijit Rd.
Tel: 0-4252 2314.
Open: daily L & D. **$$**

Located on the bank of the Mekong River with a beautiful view of the mountains in Laos, this breezy restaurant offers a variety of Thai foods but specialises in fresh river fish. Try their *laap plaa* (minced fish) or the sour fish soup.

Mukdahan
Thai
Wine Wild Why
Th. Samron Chaikhong.
Tel: 0-4263 3122.
Open: daily L & D. **$$**
Lanterns add ambience to this cosy eatery overlooking the Mekong. Mostly Thai menu, with spicy Isaan fare, along with "steak Lao", grilled beef served with Thai/Lao condiments.

Khong Jiam
Hat Mae Mun
No phone. Open: daily 7am–10pm. **$**
Attractively perched on the banks of the Mun River, this is the best restaurant in the Khong Jiam area. Be sure to try the delicious *yam met mamuang saam suan*, a roasted cashew-nut salad made with tomatoes, chillies and fresh green peppercorns.

Price per person for a three-course meal without drinks:
$ = under B300
$$ = B300–800
$$$ = B800–1,600
$$$$ = over B1,600

INSIGHT GUIDES **TRAVEL TIPS**

THAILAND

T RANSPORT

GETTING THERE
AND GETTING AROUND

GETTING THERE

By Air

Bangkok is not only a key gateway between Asia and the West, but also a major transportation hub for the rest of Southeast Asia. More than 35 international airlines fly into the city's Suvarnabhumi Airport. Thailand has four other international airports at **Chiang Mai, Hat Yai, Phuket** and **Ko Samui**.

The national airline, **Thai Airways International** (THAI) (www.thaiairways.com), flies to more than 60 cities worldwide. **Bangkok Airways** (www.bangkokair.com), **AirAsia** (www.airasia.com) and **Orient Thai** (www.orient-thai.com) operate routes between Thailand's major tourist centres and other Asian cities.

Flying from the UK, US & Australasia

Even if you don't plan to spend any time in Thailand, Bangkok is the most convenient (and sometimes the only) way to connect to neighbouring countries like Laos, Cambodia and Myanmar. The advent of low-cost airlines in the region means that domestic and regional flights to nearby destinations like Malaysia and Singapore, as well as southern China, have become incredibly cheap – if booked in advance.

Passengers from the UK and Europe can fly direct to Bangkok in about 12 hours, though it is usually cheaper to fly via the Middle East. Airlines that fly non-stop include British Airways, Qantas, THAI and EVA Airways. Many travellers to Australia and New Zealand choose Bangkok as a transit point on their journey.

Travel time from the US is considerably longer. Flying from the West Coast usually takes around 18 hours (not including transit time) and often involves a connection in North Asia – Japan, Korea or Taiwan; the East Coast route via Europe takes about 19 hours in the air. THAI operates the only direct flights from New York and Los Angeles to Bangkok.

From Australia (Sydney, Melbourne) the flight to Bangkok takes about 9 hours, while Perth is 7½ hours away. Flight time from New Zealand (Auckland) is 11½ hours.

Bangkok

Suvarnabhumi Airport
Bangkok's **Suvarnabhumi Airport** (www.bangkokairportonline.com) opened in September 2006 after several protracted delays. It is located 30km (19 miles) east of the city centre. Pronounced "su-wa-na-poom", and meaning The Golden Land, the airport handles all international flights to Bangkok as well as many domestic connections.

Suvarnabhumi has one main passenger terminal with seven concourses. In the months after it opened, there were numerous problems ranging from cracked runways to inadequate toilet facilities and a congested arrival hall, but most of these have now been ironed out.

For details, check the airport website or call any of the following numbers for assistance:
Airport Call Centre: 0-2132 1888
Departures: 0-2132 9324–7
Arrivals: 0-2132 9328–9
Note: In line with major airports all over the world, you are no longer required to pay the airport tax in cash when taking an international flight out

of Suvarnabhumi. This is now incorporated into the price of your air ticket.

Don Muang Airport
The old **Don Muang Airport** (tel: 0-2535 1111; www.donmuangairport online.com) reopened in March 2007 following the teething problems at Suvarnabhumi. A small number of THAI domestic flights and all domestic flights operated by One-Two-Go and Nok Air use Don Muang Airport. As it is yet unclear whether the status of Don Muang will change, travellers should check the airport website or call the airline directly to find out from which airport their flights operate.

Don Muang is about 30km (19 miles) north of the city centre. It takes about 40 to 45 minutes by taxi, depending on traffic, to get from the airport to the city centre.
Note: If making a flight connection between Suvarnabhumi and Don Muang airports, be sure to allow sufficient time, as taxi travel time between the two airports could take up to 1½ hours.

Phuket
Though some visitors to Phuket stop off in Bangkok for a few days at the start of their trip, many also fly in direct. There are flights from Cambodia (Siem Reap Airways), Hong Kong (Dragonair), Kuala Lumpur (Malaysia Airlines, AirAsia and THAI), Sydney (THAI) and Singapore (SilkAir, Jetstar Asia, Tiger Airways and THAI).

Ko Samui
Bangkok Airways is the only airline that serves Ko Samui internationally. Currently, it operates direct flights from Singapore and Hong Kong.

Chiang Mai

Several international airlines fly direct to Chiang Mai from other Asian cities, such as Kuala Lumpur (AirAsia), Rangoon (Air Bagan), Luang Prabang (Lao Airlines), Seoul (Korean Air), Taipei (China Airlines) and Singapore (Silk Air and Tiger Airways). Flights to Kunming no longer operate.

By Rail

Trains operated by the **State Railways of Thailand** (tel: 0-2222 0175; www.railway.co.th) are clean, cheap and reliable, if rather slow. There are only two railroad entry points into Thailand, both from Malaysia on the southern Thai border. The trip north to Bangkok serves as a scenic introduction to Thailand.

Services depart from **Butterworth**, the port opposite Malaysia's Penang Island, at dawn and midday, crossing the border into Thailand and arriving in Bangkok the following day. There are second-class cars with seats that are made into upper and lower sleeping berths at night. There are also air-conditioned first-class sleepers and dining cars serving food. Prices from Butterworth to Bangkok are US$35 and up, depending on the class you book.

From Bangkok's **Hualamphong Railway Station**, trains leave in the early morning and mid-afternoon for the return journey to Malaysia. If you want to take a more adventurous, but less convenient, route, another train travels from Kuala Lumpur up Malaysia's east coast to the northeastern town of Kota Bharu. Take a taxi from here across the border to catch the Thai train from the southern Thai town of Sungai Kolok. Trains leave Sungai Kolok at 11am and 2.05pm, arriving in Bangkok at 9.05am and 11.10am the following day.

If you like to travel in style but prefer not to fly, try the **Eastern & Oriental Express**, Asia's most exclusive travel experience (www.orient-express.com). Travelling several times a month between Singapore, Kuala Lumpur, Chiang Mai and Bangkok, the 22-carriage train with its distinctive green-and-cream livery passes spectacular scenery. It's very expensive, but worth it.

It is now also possible to take a train from **Vientiane** (Laos) to Bangkok via Nong Khai and Khorat.

By Road

Malaysia provides the main road access into Thailand, with crossings near Padang Besar and Sungai Kolok.

ABOVE: Suvarnabhumi Airport.

In north Thailand, there are crossings at Chiang Khong (in Chiang Rai Province) and Huay Kon (in Nan Province).

From **Cambodia**, the most commonly used border crossing is Poipet, which connects to Aranyaprathet, east of Bangkok. Officially, one is only allowed to fly in from **Myanmar**. Land crossings are sometimes allowed from places like Mae Sai and Mae Sot, but these are subject to restrictions and the rules are always in a flux. Thais are permitted entry, but foreigners are usually only allowed into Myanmar territory for the day.

GETTING AROUND

From Major Airports

Suvarnabhumi Airport

The new Suvarnabhumi Airport City Rail Link (see page 366) is due to open in 2010 and will cut airport–city journey times to just 15 minutes.

Taxis take about 45 to 60 minutes to cover the 30km (19 miles). Bangkok's traffic is not as bad as it used to be, and the airport is linked to the city by a system of elevated highways. The time taken depends, of course, on traffic conditions; the worst period is between 4 and 9pm.

Negotiating an exit from the arrival hall, however, can be more daunting. If you are on a business trip, you'll understand why it is the norm for Bangkok hosts to deploy a personal greeter or escort. Emerging in the arrival hall, you may be harangued by touts both inside and outside the barriers. Avoid giving your name or destination. If you already have a reservation at a hotel, a representative will have your name written on a sign,

or at least a sign bearing the name of your hotel. If you haven't made prior arrangements, use one of the following modes to get to the city.

Taxi

Operating 24 hours daily, all taxis officially serving the airport are air-conditioned and metered. When you exit from the arrival hall, take the lift or travellator one level down to the taxi counter. Join the queue and tell the clerk at the counter where you want to go to. A receipt will be issued, with the licence-plate number of the taxi and your destination in Thai written on it. The clerk will also tell you the fare. If not, make sure the driver turns on the meter. At the end of your trip, pay the prescribed fare (which will include the B50 airport surcharge and highway toll fees) or pay what is on the meter plus the B50 airport surcharge and the highway toll fees (about B40–80). Depending on traffic, an average fare from the airport to the city centre is around B450 (including toll fees and airport surcharge).

Limousine Service

There are two limousine operators stationed at the arrival hall. **Airports of Thailand Limousines** (AOT; tel: 0-2134 2323–6) operates a variety of vehicles that can take you to the city centre for about B1,000. Luxury cars like a top-end 7-series BMW will cost B1,900. Rates to Pattaya start at around B2,900, depending on the vehicle used. **THAI Limousines** (mobile tel: 081-652 4444) also operates a premium car service. Prices are similar to that charged by AOT.

Airport Express Bus

If you don't have much luggage, consider using the Airport Express Bus, which passes the main hotel

(see page 366)

locations in downtown Bangkok. Tickets can be bought on the bus or at the desk outside the arrival hall of the terminal. Buses depart every 15 minutes from 5am to midnight, and the fare is B150 per person.

Bus Routes:

AE-1 to Thanon Silom via Pratunam, Thanon Ratchadamri, Thanon Silom and Thanon Surawong.

AE-2 to Banglamphu via Thanon Phaya Thai and Thanon Lan Luang.

AE-3 to Soi Nana via Thanon Petchaburi and Thanon Sukhumvit.

AE-4 to Hualamphong Railway Station via Thanon Ploenchit, Thanon Rama, Thanon Phaya Thai and Thanon Rama IV.

Rail

Construction on the overhead 28km (17-mile) **Suvarnabhumi Airport City Rail Link**, connecting the airport to the city, is expected to cut travel time between the airport and the city centre to 15 minutes. Scheduled for completion in 2010, this high-speed electric train service will connect Suvarnabhumi Airport with eight stations: Ladkrabung, Bantubchang, Huamak, Ram-kamhaeng, Makkasan/Asoke, Phayathai and Ratchaprarop. The service will be integrated with the Skytrain and MRT, allowing passengers to switch lines in order to get to other parts of the city.

Phuket Airport

Phuket International Airport (www. phuketairportonline.com) is about 32km (20 miles) from Phuket Town. Travel time is about 40 minutes, while Patong beach can be reached in around half an hour.

Taxi

In the arrival hall, airport taxis and limousines can be hired at the fixed rates displayed on a board. After paying the fare, you are issued a coupon which is then given to the driver. Prices start at B200 to B400 for the nearby northern beaches, rising to B550 to B650 for locations further afield. The flat fare for Kata and Karon is B650.

Minibus

If you are part of a large group, book an 8-seater minibus. The fares are around B900 to Phuket Town, B1,200 to B1,500 to Patong and B1,300 to Kata and Karon. Tickets are sold next to the airport limousine counters.

Airport Bus

Tickets for the airport bus can be bought on boarding or from

designated booths in the arrival hall. Passengers to Phuket Town are usually dropped off first, so if you are staying at one of the beaches it can take a while to get there. At around B300 to Phuket Town, it is a cheaper option than taxis. A larger airport bus, route 8411, also runs daily between the airport and town.

Ko Samui Airport

Taxi

Ko Samui International Airport (www. samuiairportonline.com) is located in the northeast of the island. Fixed taxi fares from the airport typically cost B150 to Bo Phut and Bangrak, B200 to Mae Nam, B300 to Chaweng, B400 to Lamai and B400 to B500 to Na Thon.

Minivan

Private minivans also carry passengers to different beaches, though they usually wait until the van is full before leaving. Typical minivan fares are B70 to Bo Phut, B100 to Chaweng and Maenam, and B120 to Nathon and Lamai.

Chiang Mai Airport

Taxi

Chiang Mai International Airport is about 3km (2 miles) southwest of town. The airport authority operates its own fleet of large, comfortable air-conditioned taxis (or limousines as they are referred to), which cost B150 to most destinations in the city (a 10-minute drive away). These can be booked at counters near the arrival areas in both the international and domestic terminals. Public green-and-yellow metered taxis are also available at the airport. The meter charge plus mandatory B50 airport surcharge amounts to roughly the same as the airport limousines.

Domestic Travel

By Air

Thai Airways International (THAI) operates a network of daily flights to 11 of Thailand's major towns using a fleet of 737s and Airbuses.

The frequency and number of flights change with the seasons – the peak season being November to February. From Bangkok, there are flights to Hat Yai, Phuket, Surat Thani, Ko Samui and Krabi in the south; Chiang Mai, Chiang Rai, Mae Hong Son and Phitsanulok in the north; and Khon Kaen, Ubon Ratchathani and Udon Thani in the northeast. Check its "Discover Thailand" fares, which allow you to fly to three domestic destinations for around US$200.

Another major carrier is **Bangkok Airways**, which flies from Bangkok to Ko Samui more than a dozen times daily. It also operates flights from Bangkok to Chiang Mai, Krabi, Phuket, Sukhothai and Trat, as well as flights from Ko Samui to Pattaya, Krabi and Phuket.

In recent years, a number of low-cost domestic and regional carriers have appeared in Thailand. **Nok Air** is partly owned by THAI and serves Chiang Mai, Chiang Rai, Hat Yai, Krabi, Nakon Si Thammarat, Phuket, Trang, Ubon Ratchathani and Udon Thani. **One-Two-Go** operates flights from Bangkok to Chiang Mai, Chiang Rai, Krabi, Phuket and other places around Thailand. **AirAsia** connects Bangkok with various domestic destinations. **SGA Airlines**, or Nok Mini, is a small outfit that runs flights in the north of Thailand, using Chiang Mai as its hub.

For detailed route information, check the airline websites listed below. All these airlines allow you to book tickets and pay online via their websites. The phone numbers given below also allow you to place bookings directly with reservations staff.

AirAsia: tel: 0-2215 9999; www.airasia.com.

Bangkok Airways: tel: 0-2265 5555; Call Centre: 1771; www.bangkokair.com.

Nok Air: tel: 0-2627 2000; Call Centre: 1318; www.nokair.com.

One-Two-Go: tel: 0-2229 4100; Call Centre: 1126; www.fly12go.com.

SGA Airlines: tel: 0-2664 6099; www.sga.co.th.

Thai Airways International: tel: 0-2356 1111; www.thaiairways.com.

By Rail

The **State Railways of Thailand** (tel: 0-2222 0175; www.railway.co.th) operates five principal routes from Bangkok's **Hualamphong Railway Station** at Thanon Rama IV.

The **northern line** passes through Ayutthaya, Phitsanulok, Lampang and terminates at Chiang Mai.

The **upper northeastern line** passes through Ayutthaya, Saraburi, Nakhon Ratchasima, Khon Kaen, Udon Thani and terminates at Nong Khai. The **lower northeastern line** branches east at Nakhon Ratchasima and passes through Buriram, Surin, Sisaket and terminates at Ubon Ratchathani.

The **eastern line** runs from Bangkok to Aranyaprathet on the Thai–Cambodian border.

The **southern line** crosses the Rama VI bridge and stops at Nakhon

Pathom, Phetchaburi, Hua Hin and Chumphon. It splits at Hat Yai; one branch runs southwest through Betong and continues to the western coast of Malaysia to Singapore. The southeastern branch goes via Pattani and Yala to the Thai border opposite the Malaysian town of Kota Bharu.

Another railway line leaves **Bangkok Noi Station** (tel: 0-2411 3100–2) in Thonburi, on the western bank of the Chao Phraya River, for Kanchanaburi and other destinations in western Thailand.

Express and rapid services on the main lines offer first-class air-conditioned (or second-class fan-cooled) carriages with sleeping cabins or berths and dining carriages. There are also special air-conditioned express day trains that travel to key towns along the main lines. Rail passes (B1,500–3,000) valid for 20 days are available.

Train tickets and rail passes can be bought at Hualamphong Railway Station or at a travel agency.

By Car

Thailand has a good road system, with over 50,000km (31,000 miles) of highways and more being built every year. Road signs are in both Thai and English, and you should have no difficulty following a map. An international driver's licence is required. In Thailand, driving is on the left-hand side of the road.

Unfortunately, driving on a narrow but busy road can be a terrifying experience, with right of way determined by size. It is not unusual for a bus to overtake a car despite the fact that the oncoming lane is filled with vehicles. In addition, many long-distance truck drivers consume pep pills and floor the throttle because they are paid for beating schedules. It is little wonder that, when collisions occur, the consequences are often tragic. You are strongly advised to avoid driving at night for this reason. When dusk comes, pull in at a hotel and get an early start the next morning.

Avis, Budget and numerous local agencies in major tourist centres like Bangkok, Chiang Mai, Pattaya and Phuket offer rental cars with or without drivers, and with insurance coverage. The international companies are more expensive, but they are also more reliable. Car-rental rates range from B1,500 to B2,000 per day, but be sure to double-check that insurance is included.

A safer option is to hire a car or a van with driver. A driver will cost another B300–500 per day, plus a

surcharge if an overnight stay is included.

Recommended car-rental agencies in Bangkok are:
Avis: 2/12 Thanon Withayu, tel: 0-2255 5300–4; Suvarnabhami Airport (arrival hall), mobile tel: 08-4700 8157–9; Reservation Centre, tel: 0-2251 1131–2; www.avisthailand.com.
Krungthai Car Rental: 233–235 Thanon Asok-Din Daeng, tel: 0-2291 8888; www.krungthai.co.th.
You can get to several places outside Bangkok, like Pattaya and Hua Hin, by simply flagging a taxi along a Bangkok street or booking one beforehand. Be sure to negotiate a flat rate before boarding; don't use the meter in such instances.

By Bus

Air-conditioned 42-seater express buses service many destinations in Thailand. VIP coaches with 24 seats and extra leg room and refreshments served on board are best for long overnight journeys.

There is a vast network of both private and government-operated buses in Thailand. The govenment-run buses are operated by the **Transport Company Ltd** (www.transport. co.th). Known locally as Bor Kor Sor (BKS), its terminals are found at every town in Thailand. Bus tickets can be purchased directly with any BKS station or with a travel agency. Private buses, which are usually more expensive, depart either from BKS terminals or their own stations. In Bangkok, many private buses depart from Thanon Khao San.

In Bangkok, BKS terminals are found at the following locations:
Eastern (Ekamai) Bus Terminal: Thanon Sukhumvit opposite Soi 63 (Soi Ekamai), tel: 0-2391 8097.

Northern and Northeastern Bus Terminal: Thanon Kampaengphet 2, Northern: tel: 0-2936 2852–66 ext. 311; Northeastern: tel: 0-2936 2852–66 ext. 611.
Southern Bus Terminal: Thanon Boromrat Chonnani, Thonburi, tel: 0-2435 5605.

City Transport

Bangkok
Taxi

Taxis abound in Bangkok. They are metered, air-conditioned, inexpensive, and comfortably seat 3 to 4 persons. Taxis can be hailed anywhere along the streets; taxi stands can also be found at major hotels and shopping centres.

The flag-fall charge is B35; after the first 2km (1¼ miles), the meter goes up by B4 to B5.50 every kilometre, depending on distance travelled. If your journey involves using a highway to save time, the driver will ask your permission as the toll fee will be borne by you. Note: The toll fee of B20 to B50 is given to the driver at the payment booth, not at the end of the trip.

Before starting any journey, check whether the meter has been reset and turned on; many drivers conveniently "forget" to do so and charge a lump sum at the end of the journey. On seeing a foreign face, some drivers may quote a flat fee instead of using the meter. Unless you're desperate, don't use such taxis. Fares, however, can be negotiated for longer distances outside Bangkok: for instance, Pattaya (B1,200), Koh Samet (B1,500) or Hua Hin (B1,500–2,000).

Drivers don't speak much English, but all should know the locations of major hotels. Foreigners frequently

BELOW: Bangkok's Skytrain system is fast and efficient.

mangle Thai pronunciation, so it's a good idea to have a destination written on a piece of paper. Thai drivers can usually understand street addresses written in capital Roman letters.

These taxi companies will pick up for a B20 surcharge.

Siam Taxi: Tel: 1661 (hotline)
Julie Taxi: Mobile tel: 081-846 2014; www.julietaxitour.com. Slightly more expensive than metered taxis, Julie's drivers are polite and speak some English. It has a range of car and minivan options.

Tuk-Tuk

Tuk-tuk are the brightly coloured three-wheeled taxis whose name comes from the incessant noise their two-stroke engines make. Once synonymous with Bangkok, tuk-tuk have been increasingly losing favour with both locals and visitors, and are much less common than they were a dozen years ago. The heat, pollution and noise have become too overwhelming for most passengers. Few tuk-tuk drivers speak English, so make sure your destination is written down in Thai. Unless you bargain hard, tuk-tuk fares are rarely lower than metered taxi fares. Some tuk-tuk drivers loitering around hotels will offer a B10 fare "anywhere". The hitch is that you must stop at a tourist shop where the driver will get petrol coupons in exchange for bringing you in.

Expect to pay B30 to B50 for short journeys of a few blocks or around 15 minutes or less, and B50 to B100 for longer journeys. A B100 ride should get you a half-hour ride across most parts of downtown. Be sure to negotiate the fare beforehand.

Motorcycle Taxi

Motorcycle taxi stands (with young men in fluorescent orange vests) are clustered at the entrances of most soi (small side streets) and beside any busy intersection or building entrance. The drivers are experts at weaving through Bangkok's heavy traffic and may cut travel time in half, but do so at your peril.

Hire only a driver who provides a passenger helmet. Fares must be negotiated beforehand, and they are rarely lower than taxi fares for the same distance travelled. Hold on tight and keep your knees tucked in as drivers tend to weave precariously in and out of traffic. Their goal is to get you there as quickly, not as safely, as possible. If the driver is going too fast, ask him to slow down in Thai: cha-cha. Females wearing skirts must also

cope with sitting side-saddle.

A short distance, like the length of a street, will cost B10 to B20, with longer rides at B50 to B100. During rush hour (8–10am and 4–6pm), prices are higher. A B80 to B100 ride should get you a half-hour trip across most parts of downtown.

Bus

Bus transport in Bangkok is very cheap but can also be equally arduous, time-consuming and confusing. Municipal and private operators all come under the charge of the **Bangkok Mass Transit Authority** (tel: 184 or 0-2246 0973; www.bmta.co.th).

With scant English signage and few conductors or drivers speaking English, boarding the right bus is an exercise in frustration. Public buses come in four varieties: microbus, Euro II bus, air-conditioned and non-air-conditioned "ordinary". In theory, the routes of both air-conditioned and ordinary buses appear on standard bus maps. In practice, however, routes change and many air-con bus routes have been added in recent years, rendering bus maps out of date.

Skytrain

The **Bangkok Transit System**'s (BTS) elevated train service (BTS Tourist Information Centre: tel: 0-2617 7340; hotline: tel: 0-2617 6000; www.bts. co.th), better known as Skytrain, started operations in December 1999. It is the perfect way of beating the city's traffic-congested streets.

It consists of two lines. The **Sukhumvit Line** runs from Mo Chit station in the north to On Nut in the southeast. The **Silom Line** runs from National Stadium, near Siam Square, south to Saphan Taksin near Tha Sathorn (or Central Pier), and then across the river to Wongwian Yai in Thonburi. Both lines intersect at Siam station, and also connect with the Metro system.

The Skytrain is fast, frequent and clean, but suffers from overcrowding during peak hours. Accessibility, too, is a problem for the disabled and aged as few stations have escalators and lifts. Trains operate from 6am to midnight (3 minutes peak; 5 minutes off-peak). Single-trip fares vary according to distance, starting at B15 and rising to B40. Self-service ticket machines are found at all station concourses. Tourists may find it more useful to buy the unlimited ride 1-Day Pass (B120) or the 30-Day Adult Pass (which comes in two types: B440 – 20 rides and B600 – 30 rides) – all

available at station counters.

BTS Tourist Information Centres are found on the concourse levels of Siam, Nana and Saphan Taksin stations (daily 8am–8pm).

Metro (MRT or Subway)

Bangkok's Metro line (Customer Relations Centre, tel: 0-2624 5744; www.mrta.co.th or www.bangkokmetro.co.th) was launched in July 2004 by the **Mass Rapid Transit Authority** (MRTA). The line has 18 stations, stretching 20km (12 miles) between Bang Sue in the northern suburbs of Bangkok and the city's main railway station, Hualamphong, near Chinatown. The line is variously referred to as the MRT, Metro or subway.

Three of its stations – Silom, Sukhumvit and Chatuchak Park – are interchanges, and passengers can transfer to the Skytrain network at these points.

Operating from 6am to midnight, the air-conditioned trains are frequent, with never more than a few minutes' wait (2–4 minutes peak, 4–6 minutes off-peak). Fares start at B16, increasing by B2 for every station, with a maximum fare of B41, though there are concessions for children and the elderly.

Unlike the Skytrain, coin-sized plastic tokens are used instead of cards, with self-service ticket machines at all stations. Also available at station counters are the unlimited ride 1-Day Pass (B150), 3-Day Pass (B300) and the stored-value Adult Card (B200 – includes B50 deposit).

Boat

The most common waterborne transport is the **Chao Phraya River Express Boat** (tel: 0-2623 6143; www.chaophrayaboat.co.th), which travels from Tha Nonthaburi Pier in the north and ends at Tha Wat Rachasingkhon near Krungthep Bridge in the south. Boats run every 15 minutes from 6am to 7.55pm, and stop at different piers according to the coloured flag on top of the boat. Yellow-flag boats are fastest and do not stop at many piers, while the orange-flag and no-flag boats stop at most of the marked river piers. If unsure, check before boarding. Fares cost B9 to B15 and are purchased from the conductor on board or at some pier counters.

The **Chao Phraya Tourist Boat** (www.chaophrayaboat.co.th) operates daily from 9.30am to 3pm and costs B100. After 3pm, you can use the ticket on the regular express boats. A useful commentary is provided on board, along with a small guidebook and a bottle of water. The route begins at Tha Sathorn (Central Pier) and travels upriver to Tha Phra Arthit, stopping at 10 major piers along the way. Boats leave every 30 minutes, and you can get off at any pier and get onto another boat later on this hop-on-and-off service.

The **cross-river ferries** can be boarded at the jetties that also service the Chao Phraya River Express. Costing B2 per journey, cross-river ferries operate from 5am to 10pm or later.

Longtail boat taxis ply the narrow inner canals and carry passengers from the centre of town to the outlying districts. Many of the piers are located near traffic bridges; remember to stand back from the pier's edge to avoid being splashed by the foul-smelling water. Choose a seat away from the spray, and be sure to tell the conductor your destination, as boats do not stop otherwise. Tickets cost B5 to B30, depending on distance, with services operating roughly every 10 minutes until 6 to 7pm.

If you wish to explore the canals of Thonburi or Nonthaburi, private **longtail boat rentals** can be negotiated from most of the river's main piers. A 90-minute to 2-hour tour will take you into the quieter canal communities. Ask which route the boat will take and what will be seen along the way; try to avoid major tourist attractions that can be visited independently later. Ask to pull up and get out if anything interests you. Negotiate rates beforehand; an hour-long trip will cost B400 to B500, rising to B900 for 2 hours. The price is for the entire boat, which seats up to 16 people, not per person.

Phuket

Taxi
There are few metered taxis and those that have meters rarely use them. Taxi fares have to be negotiated, except for taxis boarded from taxi stands at major shopping centres and some beaches, where prices are fixed.

Songthaew/Tuk-Tuk
The most common form of transport are small pick-up trucks with a roof over the back and two parallel padded benches. Increasingly, these days, minivans are replacing the older-style trucks. These songthaew (often also called tuk-tuk here in Phuket) are plentiful, but prices are among the highest in Thailand, costing nearly as much as taxis. Agree on a price before getting into a songthaew, and be aware that prices will rise at night and

ABOVE: transport in Patong, Phuket.

during rainy spells. Expect to pay about B200 to B250 for a trip between Phuket Town and Patong, and about B150 to B200 between Patong and Kata or Karon. The final rate depends on your negotiating skills.

Motorcycle Taxi and Bus
Motorcycle taxis are a cheaper but more risky way to travel, with at least one accident per week from road collisions during the high season.

Small and slow blue public buses mainly used by locals shuttle from the market on Thanon Ranong in Phuket Town to the main beaches. They leave every half-hour between 8am and 6pm. Those to Rawai and Nai Harn depart from Thanon Bangkok. There are no bus connections between beaches, so this would require unnecessary travelling to and from the town departure point.

Car Rental
Car rental ranges from B1,200 to B2,000 a day. Use a reputable company, because many of the independent beachfront businesses do not provide insurance.
Avis, Phuket Airport, tel: 0-7635 1243; www.avisthailand.com.
Budget, 36/1 Moo 6, Thalang, tel: 0-7620 5398; www.budget.co.th.

Ko Samui

Songthaew/Tuk-Tuk
Songthaew trucks (sometimes also called tuk-tuk) are the island's principal mode of public transport. Drivers always try to overcharge, so make sure you hand over the correct fare. A journey down the length of Chaweng beach is B20, from Na Thon to Chaweng B50, with no journey costing more than B50. Late at night they operate more like taxis, and the fare should be agreed on beforehand.

Taxi
Metered taxis are becoming prevalent on the island but drivers rarely turn on the meter, preferring to quote extortionate rates for relatively short distances.

Motorcycle Taxi
Motorcycle taxis are cheaper, with fares ranging from B20 to B30 for a short journey, and B150 to B200 for a longer ride from, say, Chaweng to Na Thon. A variety of motorcycles, from mopeds to choppers (B200–500), as well as jeeps (B800–2,000), can be hired at all the main beaches. Motorcycle accidents are frequent, so wear a helmet.

Chiang Mai

Songthaew/Tuk-Tuk
Chiang Mai's fleet of songthaew – small red pick-up trucks with roofs over the back and two parallel padded benches – plies the city streets day and night, stopping for passengers who flag them down at kerbside. If the driver is going in the direction you want to go, the fare is B20 per person and you will ride with other passengers. If the songthaew is empty, the driver may offer the option to charter the truck to your destination. In such cases the fare will vary from B50–150, depending on the distance.

Three-wheeled tuk-tuk operate on a charter basis only and cost B50 to B150, depending on the distance.

Taxi
There are small number of air-conditioned, green-and-yellow metered taxis. These are mainly booked by telephone (tel: 0-5327 9291). Rates start at B30 for the first 2km, and B4 for each km travelled.

Car Rental
North Wheels (tel: 0-5387 4478; www.northwheels.com) and **Journey** (tel: 0-53271-579; www.journeycnx.com) are recommended. Both agencies will deliver rental cars to your hotel or guesthouse. Rates run around B1,000 to B1,500 for economy cars, and B2,000 for luxury models. Discounted weekly and monthly rates are also available.

Bicycle
Most of the city is easily accessible by bicycle. Kiosks and guesthouses around the city rent bicycles for B30 to B50 per day. Real mountain bikes are rented by Velocity Bikes (tel: 0-5341 8561) on Th. Manee Nopparat.

A CCOMMODATION

HOTELS IN THAILAND

Choosing a Hotel

The top-end hotels in Thailand's major tourist centres are equal to the very best, anywhere in the world. The facilities in luxury hotels may include as many as six or more different restaurants serving Western and Asian cuisines, bars, swimming pools, fitness centres, spas, business centres, banquet halls, shopping arcades, WiFi internet access and cable television. Service is second to none. Indeed, most of Thailand's moderately priced lodgings rival what in the West would be considered first-class hotels. Even the budget and inexpensive hotels in Thailand will often have a swimming pool and more than one food outlet.

A range of new hotels, high on the design and style quotient, both luxury chains as well as independent boutique properties, have opened in recent years, in Bangkok and also at popular destinations like Hua Hin, Phuket, Ko Samui, Krabi, Ko Lanta and Chiang Mai. Many have won awards or lavish praise in international surveys and magazines.

The following pages contain a selection of hotels of different price ranges in the five regions covered in this guidebook: Bangkok; Central Thailand; Southeast and South Thailand; North Thailand; and Northeast Thailand. Hotels are listed by area first, then price bracket, and then in alphabetical order within each price bracket. The hotels have been picked for their quality of accommodation, level of service and range of facilities, as well as design and architecture. A few properties have been included because they are quirky and unusual in some aspect.

Budget hotels have been included where they represent good value for money.

Note: A resort hotel does not always have the same connotation in Thailand that it might in the West; often it means nothing more than the fact that the hotel is located in the countryside or by the beach. The term is used rather loosely in Thailand, so if you find a "resort" hotel in some remote corner of Thailand and room rates are a real bargain, don't have too high expectations!

Guesthouses

Travellers on a tight budget will find numerous guesthouses offering clean and decent accommodation. Once of primary interest only to backpackers because of their scant facilities, many have been upgraded to include air-conditioning and en suite bathrooms.

In Bangkok, these are mainly found along Thanon Khao San, Soi Ngam Duphli (off Thanon Rama IV) and Sukhumvit Soi 1–15. In Chiang Mai, guesthouses are strewn along the Ping River and in the Thanon Moon Muang area. In Pattaya and Phuket, guesthouses are less common. In most small towns, guesthouses are generally family-run, and mostly found in the vicinity of bus and railway stations, and along main streets.

Rates and Bookings

Thailand has plenty of good-value accommodation, but as more hotels and guesthouses upgrade to compete with new boutique and design-oriented hotels, prices have begun to creep up. Hotel rates can range widely, even among the luxury hotels.

Depending on the season, discounts can exceed 50 percent or more off the published rack rate. It pays to shop around. Relative price categories are used in this section because hotel rates can be quite elastic in Thailand. In Bangkok especially, where there is a glut of rooms, rates can be highly discounted during non-peak periods.

During peak holiday periods (holidays, Christmas, New Year, Chinese New Year, Songkran, etc.), generally between November and April, hotels tend to be full and prices are high. Booking well in advance is advisable. For the rest of the year, it is always worth asking for a discount. Alternatively, check online hotel sites, like **Thailand Hotels Association** (www.thaihotels.org) and **Hotels.com** (www.hotels.com) for better rates.

Many hotels include a compulsory gala dinner in the room rate at Christmas and New Year; some charge exorbitant prices in return for what is little more than a fancy buffet dinner.

Whether a room rate is quoted in US dollars or in Thai baht, it will be billed on your credit card in baht; the final rate can therefore vary, depending upon the prevailing exchange rates.

Note: Most hotels also charge a value added tax (VAT) of 7 percent to the bill, and at the mid- and top-end hotels, a service charge of 10 percent as well.

PRICE CATEGORIES

Prices are for a double room without breakfast and taxes:
Luxury = over B8,000
Expensive = B4,000–8,000
Moderate = B2,000–4,000
Budget = under B2,000

BANGKOK

Bangrak and Silom

Luxury

Banyan Tree Bangkok
21/100 Th. Sathorn Tai
Tel: 0-2679 1200
www.banyantree.com
Located in the precariously narrow Thai Wah II Tower, Bangkok's second-tallest hotel features large and stylishly appointed luxury suites with separate living and working areas, plus the latest technological add-ons. Vertigo restaurant on the roof of the tower and the pampering Banyan Tree Spa (the highest in the city) offer spectacular views of the capital. (216 suites)

Dusit Thani
946 Th. Rama IV
Tel: 0-2200 9000
www.dusit.com
The first high-rise hotel in Bangkok, this classic example of fashionably retro 1950s architecture is located across Lumphini Park, near Silom's many corporate headquarters and the nightlife of Patpong, with both the Skytrain and Metro stations right outside its doors. It has lost out a little to younger and more stylish hotels, but still retains its place among Bangkok's top digs. Enjoy a massage at its exquisite Devarana Spa and then float on to top-floor D'Sens restaurant for impeccable French dining. The Thai and Vietnamese restaurants are highly rated too. (517 rooms)

Mandarin Oriental
48 Oriental Avenue
Tel: 0-2659 9000
www.mandarinoriental.com
Part of the history of East meeting West, the Oriental, established in 1876, is the most famous hotel in Bangkok, and well known for its attention to detail and grand setting along the Chao Phraya River. The Authors' Wing is the only

original surviving structure and its lounge is a delight to sit in and enjoy afternoon tea, while Le Normandie French restaurant is the only place in town that requires a tie for dinner. (395 rooms)

The Metropolitan
27 Th. Sathorn Tai
Tel: 0-2625 3333
www.metropolitan.como.bz
Sister to The Metropolitan in London, Bangkok's younger twin is set among a row of top-end hotels on Thanon Sathorn. Its drink and dine outlets, Cy'an and Met Bar, are among the city's top nightspots. This designer hotel is cool and contemporary, blending East and West minimalist chic in equal measures. A 10-minute walk to Saladaeng Skytrain and Lumphini Metro stations. (171 rooms)

The Sukhothai
13/3 Th. South Sathorn
Tel: 0-2344 8888
www.sukhothai.com
This stunning contemporary Asian hotel draws architectural inspiration from the ancient Thai kingdom of the same name. One of the top five hotels in Bangkok, this class act has well-appointed rooms, the excellent La Scala Italian restaurant and chic Zuk Bar, tropical gardens and a reflecting pool. An 8-minute walk to Lumphini Metro station. (210 rooms)

Expensive

Lebua at State Tower
State Tower, 1055/111 Th. Silom
Tel: 0-2624 9999
www.lebua.com
Located on the corner of Thanon Silom and Thanon Charoen Krung, these de luxe serviced apartments are within the gigantic State Tower building. Just a 10-minute walk to Saphan Taksin Skytrain station, State Tower has established itself as a Bangkok

landmark, with its opulent 64th-floor rooftop dine and drink outlets collectively called The Dome. The contemporary-style apartments have 1–3 bedrooms with kitchenettes. (462 suites)

The Montien
54 Th. Surawong
Tel: 0-2234 8070–9
www.montien.com
This 1960s throwback is one of the city's oldest modern hotels, and located just a stone's throw from the nightlife of Patpong and Soi Thaniya. A short walk to Saladaeng Skytrain station, this grand airy hotel with three restaurants retains a strong Thai atmosphere. (475 rooms)

Moderate

Holiday Inn Silom
981 Th. Silom
Tel: 0-2238 4300
www.bangkok-silom.holiday-inn.com
Located right next to the Jewellery Trade Centre towards the river end of Thanon Silom, this large, comfortable hotel is of much higher quality than its Holiday Inn branding would suggest. Only an 8-minute

walk to Surasak Skytrain station. (700 rooms)

Sofitel Silom
188 Th. Silom. Tel: 0-2238 1991
www.accorhotels-asia.com
This 38-storey hotel located in the quieter part of busy Thanon Silom is only a short walk to Chong Nonsi Skytrain station. Stylishly refurbished to a chic modern style, it caters to both business and leisure travellers. Wine bar V9 has stunning city views from its 37th-floor perch, while one floor above is the excellent Shanghai 38 Chinese restaurant. (502 rooms)

Budget

La Residence
173/8–9 Th. Suriwongse
Tel: 0-2233 3301
www.laresidencebangkok.com
A boutique hotel near – yet far enough away from – the pulse of Patpong, with funky

BELOW: the resort-style swimming pool at the Peninsula.

individually decorated rooms of different sizes. All the expected room amenities and very nicely decorated, plus a friendly vibe. (26 rooms)

Unico Grande Silom
533 Th. Silom
Tel: 0-2237 8300
www.unicograndesilom.com

Halfway down Thanon Silom towards the river and within walking distance of Chong Nonsi Skytrain station, this well-located high-rise hotel has large executive rooms, a swimming pool and a great rooftop terrace with views. There is also a business centre and function rooms, a lobby bar and restaurant. (175 rooms)

Chinatown

Moderate

Shanghai Mansion
479–481 Th. Yaowaraj
Tel: 0-2221 2121
www.shanghaimansion.com

A classy boutique hotel in a part of town that's often written off as lacking in any decent lodgings. The rooms have lovely over-the-top Chinoise-inspired furnishings, four-poster beds and bright colours. Free internet, and a spa on site. (55 rooms)

Budget

River View Guest House
768 Soi Phanurangsi, Th. Songwad
Tel: 0-2234 5429
www.riverviewbkk.com

Few places offer cheap accommodation in the city with river views, but this one does. While basic inside, its location and Chinatown ambience are the main draws. The better rooms have air-con, fridge and TV, and there's a top-floor restaurant. Finding this place is an adventure in itself. (45 rooms)

Old City and Dusit

Moderate

Buddy Lodge
265 Th. Khao San
Tel: 0-2629 4477
www.buddylodge.com

This is Khao San's best hotel, with a rooftop swimming pool and even a well-run spa. The original Buddy guesthouse was located further down the strip, but the owner's business has taken off and he now owns half of Khao San's entertainment. From the outside, the brick building resembles a European municipal hall, albeit with a McDonald's downstairs. (76 rooms)

Old Bangkok Inn
607 Th. Phra Sumen
Tel: 0-2629 1787
www.oldbangkokinn.com

One of Bangkok's newest boutiques, this lovely eco-friendly inn exudes plenty of old-world charm. With just 10 rooms decorated with antique dark-wood furniture and named after local herbs and flowers, this family-run place has all the mod cons and yet is situated in the heart of the historic district. (10 rooms).

Budget

D&D Inn
68–70 Th. Khao San
Tel: 0-2629 0526–8
www.khaosanby.com

Right in the middle of Khao San, this is more of a hotel than guesthouse, with a rooftop swimming pool, bar and an open pavilion for traditional massage. Rooms are well equipped with bathroom, air-conditioning, TV, fridge and IDD phone. (200 rooms)

Peachy Guest House
10 Th. Phra Athit. Tel: 0-2281 6659

This guesthouse occupies a converted school and has a bit more old-world charm than most of Khao San's concrete box digs. The rooms are basic but clean and comfortable, with most facing the garden. A short walk to Khao San, but still removed from all its mayhem. (57 rooms)

Pathumwan and Pratunam

Luxury

Conrad Bangkok
All Seasons Place, 87 Th. Withayu
Tel: 0-2690 9999
www.conradhotels.com

Oozing class, this top-notch hotel is located near embassies and next door to the All Seasons Place shopping centre. Spacious and contemporary rooms are furnished with Thai silk and woods, while large bathrooms sport rain showers. Excellent choice of eateries, as well as chic 87 Plus nightclub and jazzy Diplomat Bar. The serviced apartments here are a better deal for longer stays. Ploenchit Skytrain station is a 6-minute walk away. (391 rooms)

Four Seasons
155 Th. Ratchadamri
Tel: 0-2250 1000
www.fourseasons.com/bangkok

From the magnificent lobby decorated with Thai murals by renowned local artists and hand-painted silk ceilings, to the city's best hotel swimming pool and highest staff-to-guest ratio, the Four Seasons is consistently excellent. And it has the accolades and awards to prove it. Located right in the heart of downtown, a few minutes' walk from Ratchadamri Skytrain station. Some of the city's best dining outlets are found here. (256 rooms)

Grand Hyatt Erawan
494 Th. Ratchadamri
Tel: 0-2254 1234
www.bangkok.grand.hyatt.com

It's all about location, and the Hyatt is smack in the middle of downtown shopping and beside the Erawan Shrine. Decorated in a tasteful contemporary style, and definitively upmarket in style. The basement restaurant-nightclub Spasso is a top nightlife spot. Connected to the Erawan Bangkok mall and a short walk to Chit Lom Skytrain station. Excellent range of eateries. (387 rooms)

Expensive

Amari Watergate
847 Th. Petchaburi
Tel: 0-2673 0966
www.amari.com/watergate

This large tower isn't very attractive on the outside, but has been stylishy refurbished within. Excellent facilities, including a great gym and the basement Americana pub Henry J. Beans. Located just across from Pratunam Market and the main shopping district around Central World. The closest Skytrain station is Chit Lom, about 12 minutes' walk from the hotel. (569 rooms)

Swissôtel Nai Lert Park
2 Th. Withayu
Tel: 0-2253 0123
www.swissotel.com

Set within beautiful gardens with a landscaped pool and jogging track, this hotel is located in Bangkok's central business and diplomatic district, and sports a contemporary edge. The hip lounge bar, Syn, sums up the hotel's ambience. The curious should check out the phallic totems at the Nai Lert Shrine, located at the rear of the hotel, beside the canal. (338 rooms)

Moderate

Luxx
6/11 Th. Decho
Tel: 0-2635 8800
www.staywithluxx.com

The studios and suites (the latter cross over to the "Expensive" price category) are luxurious and come with large bathrooms, hi-tech entertainment systems and picture windows that look out over a tranquil courtyard. The standard rooms and studios are stylish yet functional with comfy beds and the usual mod cons. All the rooms come with quaint wooden barrel bathtubs. (13 rooms)

Novotel Bangkok on Siam Square
Siam Square Soi 6
Tel: 0-2209 8888
www.accorhotels-asia.com

Tailored towards the business traveller, this hotel is tucked among the maze of shopping alleys in Siam Square and is a short walk to the main Siam Skytrain station. At least four cinemas are nearby, and its massive basement entertainment complex, Concept CM2, is frequently packed. (429 rooms)

Pathumwan Princess
444 Th. Phaya Thai
Tel: 0-2216 3700
www.pprincess.com
This centrally located hotel is joined to huge Mahboonkrong mall, making it ideal for shoppers. It is also a family-friendly place with a large saltwater pool, a gym, plus comfortable rooms. It offers good value for money. (462 rooms)

Budget

A-One Inn
13–15 Soi Kasemsan 1, Th. Rama I
Tel: 0-2215 3029
www.aoneinn.com
Located beside Siam Square and with easy access to the National Stadium Skytrain station, the narrow lane where it's located has become a downtown bargain-hotel area, with lots of options nearby. Offers fair-sized rooms with all the mod cons plus friendly service. (20 rooms)

Rattanakosin

Expensive

Chakrabongse Villa
396 Th. Maharat
Tel: 0-2225 0139
www.chakrabongsevillas.com
A beautiful early 20th-century residence with gardens, a swimming pool and superb views of Wat Arun opposite. A short walk to the Grand Palace. Each of the five villas is designed in traditional Thai style: Garden Villa, Riverside Villa, Chinese House, B&B and Thai House. (5 villas)

Moderate

Arun Residence
38 Soi Pratoo Nok Yoong, Th. Maharat
Tel: 0-2221 9158-9
www.arunresidence.com
This tiny boutique hotel,

housed in an old Sino-Portuguese mansion along a residential street just off Thanon Maharat, is a gem. One side perches on the banks of the Chao Phraya River and offers views of Wat Arun. The French-Thai restaurant, Deck by the River, is the perfect place for a sunset cocktail and dinner afterwards. (6 rooms)

Sukhumvit

Luxury

The Eugenia
267 Soi Sukhumvit 31
Tel: 0-2259 9011-7
www.theeugenia.com
A deliciously renovated 19th-century mansion, with just a dozen suites but endless grandeur and style. There's no lift, of course, but plenty of staff on hand to help with luggage. A trip in one of the hotel's Jaguars or Mercedes Benz is practically compulsory. (12 rooms)

Grand Millennium Sukhumvit
30 Th. Sukhumvit Soi 21 (Asoke)
Tel: 0-2204 4000
www.grandmillenniumskv.com
A distinctive landmark along the busy Soi 21 (Asoke junction), its soaring glass sail-like facade glows from afar at night. Perfect location, with easy walking distance to both the Asoke Skytrain and the Sukhumvit Metro station. Large and luxurious rooms feature all the latest high-tech mod cons and contemporary

furnishings. The hotel facilities are excellent, featuring a resort-like 25-metre lap pool, well-equipped gym, rooftop putting course, business centre plus five restaurants (Japanese-Italian, Asian, noodle café, Spanish and a deli/bakery). The in-house spa, Antidote, is on hand to massage away tight shoulders and sore calves after a day's shopping. (325 rooms)

JW Marriott
4 Th. Sukhumvit Soi 2
Tel: 0-2656 7700
www.marriotthotels.com
This classy five-star hotel is just around the corner from Bangkok's risqué Nana Entertainment Plaza, but don't let that deter you. All the usual amenities, plus one of Bangkok's largest fitness centres, efficient business facilities and spacious well-appointed rooms make this one of the best hotels in the city. It has some of the city's best dining in the New York Steakhouse. It also has a convenient location between the Nana and Ploenchit Skytrain stations. (441 rooms)

Expensive

Davis
88 Th. Sukhumvit Soi 24
Tel: 0-2260 8000
www.davisbangkok.net
Boutique hotel with a mélange of style influences. There are different theme

rooms all with the latest mod cons, plus 10 large villas with their own swimming pools. As if that wasn't enough, there is a rooftop pool with bar, and Club 88, a live music venue. Adjoining Camp Davis is a complex of more bars and restaurants. Phrom Pong Skytrain station is a 12-minute walk away. (238 rooms and 10 villas)

Moderate

Landmark
138 Th. Sukhumvit
Tel: 0-2254 0404
www.landmarkbangkok.com
Good location on Thanon Sukhumvit, with easy access to Nana Skytrain station and the girlie bar enclave of Nana Entertainment Plaza. Geared toward the business traveller, with a busy business centre. (415 rooms)

President Park
95 Th. Sukhumvit Soi 24
Tel: 0-2661 1000
www.presidentpark.com
Great for families or business executives, this modern apartment complex is tastefully designed. Spacious studios come with kitchenettes. Three large pools and full leisure facilities in its Capitol Club. Daily, weekly and monthly rates available, with breakfast included. Short walk to Phrom Phong Skytrain station. (228 rooms)

BELOW: the sail-like exterior of Grand Millennium Sukhumvit and its stylish Antidote spa.

Budget

Atlanta
78 Th. Sukhumvit Soi 2
Tel: 0-2252 1650
www.theatlantahotelbangkok.com
A Sukhumvit legend, this
1950s throwback is rich in
character and is a real
treasure among faceless
modern structures. The first
hotel along Sukhumvit, its
pool is set in landscaped
gardens and it has a great
Thai restaurant. Quirky
extras include Thai dancing
at weekends, and classic
roll-top desks in the rooms.
Closest Skytrain station is
Ploenchit. (59 rooms)
Sukhumvit 11
1/33 Th. Sukhumvit Soi 11

Tel: 0-2253 5927
www.suk11.com
Located in the heart of the
Sukhumvit area and within
walking distance of Nana
Skytrain station, this
personable, family-run Thai-
style guesthouse is a gem of
a find, and often full. (67
rooms, en suite and with
shared facilities)

Thonburi

Luxury

Peninsula
333 Th. Charoennakorn
Tel: 0-2861 2888
www.peninsula.com
Standing proud on the
opposite bank of the Chao

Phraya River, this
distinguished hotel has the
city's most entrancing river
views. It has earned the
reputation of being one of
the world's best hotels.
Stylishly contemporary but
still Asian in character, it has
some of the best dining
options in the city, plus
impeccable service. Free
shuttle boats (6am–
midnight) cross the river to
Tha Sathorn Pier and Sapha
Taksin Skytrain station.
(370 rooms)

Expensive

**Bangkok Marriott
Resort & Spa**
257 Th. Charoennakorn

Tel: 0-2476 0022
www.marriotthotels.com
With verdant grounds and
a wonderfully landscaped
pool that fronts the river,
this resort truly feels like an
escape from the frenetic
city. Located on the
Thonburi side, it is located
quite far down the river
almost to the edge of town,
but the free 15-minute boat
shuttle to Tha Sathorn Pier
is part of the novelty of
staying here. Self-contained,
with six restaurants, three
bars, a Mandara spa and
a full-service business
centre, the hotel is also
part of a shopping complex.
(413 rooms)

CENTRAL THAILAND

Ayutthaya

Budget

Krungsri River Hotel
27/2 Moo 11, Th. Rojchana
Tel: 0-3524 4333
www.krungsririver.com
A decent provincial hotel in
a town with few options
(mainly because most
people visit Ayutthaya on
day trips from Bangkok).
Modern facilities but short
on ambience. The rooms
have air-conditioning and
cable TV, and there's a pool,
fitness centre, sauna,
restaurant and bar. (202
rooms)
River View Place Hotel
35 Th. U-Thong
Tel: 0-3524 1444
One of Ayutthaya's better
options, with large rooms,
kitchenettes and spacious
balconies. Feels more like a
condo than a hotel because
it was originally built as
apartments. Ask for a room
with view of the river and
Wat Phanon Choeng. (28
rooms)
U Thong Inn
10 Th. Rojchana
Tel: 0-3524 2236
www.uthonginn.com
This is a popular tourist
hotel in town, close to most
of the attractions and
offering reasonably nice
rooms and modern

facilities. Thai/international
and Japanese restaurants,
plus a swimming pool and
fitness centre are on site.
(209 rooms)

Kanchanaburi

Moderate

**Comsaed River Kwai
Resort**
18/9 Moo 5 Ladya, Kanchanaburi
Tel: 0-3463 1443–9
www.comsaed.com
Many of the area's better
hotels lie some way outside
the main town in the rolling
countryside, which is also
true of the Comsaed. With
manicured lawns, wooden
bridges and riverline views,
it is geared up for outdoor
activities like canoeing and
biking. Huge variety of
accommodation available,
from the basic mountain
wing to suites and family
bungalows. (110 rooms)
**Felix River Kwai
Kanchanaburi Resort**
9/1 Moo 3 Thamakham,
Kanchanaburi
Tel: 0-3451 5061
www.felixriverkwai.co.th
Comfortable resort-style
riverside hotel in a pretty
garden setting near the
bridge. The Felix has been
around for a long time but is
well maintained. The de luxe
rooms face the river and are

worth the premium rates.
Large free-form swimming
pool is perfect for lounging.
(255 rooms)
River Kwai Resotel
55 Moo 5 Tambol Wangkrajae,
Amphur Saiyoke, Kanchanaburi
Mobile tel: 08-1734 5238
www.riverkwairesotel.net
Good riverside location with
basic but clean rooms in
rustic thatched-roof
bungalows scattered among
lots of greenery. Nice pool to
relax. Offers plenty of
activities (rafting, canoeing,
hiking, village excursions,
etc.), although the food
served at its buffet
restaurant is a little boring.
(93 rooms)

Budget

Apple Guest House
52 Th. Saengchuto, Kanchanaburi
Tel: 0-3451 2017/3457
www.applenoi-kanchanaburi.com
This friendly and well-run
place has quiet bungalows
just a stone's throw from
the river, and is locally
famous for its outstanding
food and Thai cooking
courses. The guesthouse
also runs a tour company
that specialises in bicycle
tours of the province's
national parks. (18 rooms)
River Kwai Jungle Rafts
Office: River Kwae Floatel Co. Ltd,
133/14 Th. Ratchaprarop, Bangkok

Tel: 0-2642 6361–2
www.riverkwaijunglerafts.com
For a truly unique
Kanchanaburi experience,
stay on a floating jungle raft.
Eat and drink on the
adjoining floating restaurant
and bar. Aside from the
quaint lodgings, you can
also swim or fish in the river,
ride elephants and visit
nearby tribal villages. (100
rooms)

Lopburi

Budget

Lopburi Inn Resort
144 Th. Paholyothin
Tel: 0-3642 0777
www.lopburiinnresort.com
Probably the poshest hotel
in town, which doesn't say
very much for it. Range of
de luxe and superior rooms,
all with air-conditioning,
and a restaurant serving a
mix of Thai and Western
dishes. There is a decent-
sized swimming pool to
relax by. (100 rooms)

EASTERN SEABOARD

Ko Chang

Expensive

Amari Emerald Cove Resort
88/8 Moo 4, Ao Khlong Phrao
Tel: 0-3955 2000
www.amari.com
A part of the successful Amari chain, this is one of the island's biggest and best options. The rooms are tastefully decked out in a stylish blend of contemporary and Asian design. There is a large beachfront pool and an excellent spa, plus three good restaurants and a lobby bar to relax in. (165 rooms)

Barali Beach Resort
77 Moo 4, Ao Khlong Phrao
Tel: 0-3955 7238
www.baraliresort.com
These contemporary Asian-style villas are representative of the recent upmarket development on Ko Chang. The cosy, private villas come with TV, CD system, hairdryer and safe; some have beautiful sunken bathtubs. The infinity pool is a perfect spot to relax. (40 rooms)

Nirvana Resort
12/4–5 Moo 1, Ban Bang Bao
Tel: 0-3955 8061
www.nirvanakohchang.com
With only a wisp of dark sand at the southern tip of the island near the village of Ban Bang Bao, this is not the best of beaches, but the resort more than compensates with fresh- and seawater swimming pools and tasteful, individually styled rooms. The 1- and 2-bedroom bungalows are

backed by jungle. Paths from the hotel lead to secluded viewpoints. (11 rooms)

Moderate

Bhumiyama Beach Resort
Hat Tha Nam
Tel: 0-3955 8067
www.bhumiyama.com
The only upmarket resort to be set up on the backpacker retreat of Lonely Beach, this pleasant resort is built around a lovely tropical beachfront garden with ponds and a central swimming pool. Away from the main building, the better rooms occupy two-storey houses with Thai accents. (46 rooms)

Koh Chang Kacha Resort & Spa
88–9 Moo 4, Hat Sai Khao
Tel: 0-3955 1421
www.kohchangkacha.com
This is one of Hat Sai Khao's best hotels in this price range. The new extension includes a lovely pool and spa with the main hotel building and sea-view villas, while the older section has more verdant gardens and some large split-level family bungalows located right on the beach. (80 rooms)

Koh Chang Tropicana Resort & Spa
17/3 Moo 4, Ao Khlong Phrao
Tel: 0-3955 7122
www.kohchangtropicana.net
Located right next to the Barali (see above), this resort charges much lower rates for similar facilities. In an effort to meld the resort with nature, the rooms have large picture windows that

look out onto lush grounds embellished with canals, fountains and wooden bridges. There is a large circular pool by the oceanfront and a good spa beside the restaurant. (74 rooms)

Mac Resort Hotel
7/3 Moo 4, Hat Sai Khao
Tel: 0-3955 1124
www.mac-resorthotel.com
One of Hat Sai Khao's original bungalow backpacker flops, Mac has come a long way and now represents the new face of the island. While somewhat squeezed by neighbouring developments, the small resort centres round a nice pool, with bungalows skirting one side and the newer (and more expensive) hotel rooms above the restaurant and lobby area. (24 rooms)

Budget

Saffron on the Sea
13/10 Moo 4, Hat Khai Muk
Tel: 0-3955 1253
Email: info@saffrononthesea.com
A small, low-key resort with a welcoming atmosphere and nestled in a garden on the rocks just south of Hat Sai Khao. There are just seven tastefully-styled rooms with air-conditioning or fan. Said to serve the best breakfasts on the island. (7 rooms)

Treehouse Lodge
Two locations: Hat Tha Nam and Hat Yao
Mobile tel: 08-1847 8215
Amid the ongoing upmarket developments on the island, this long-running backpacker magnet on the southern headland of Hat Tha Nam is a rarity. The rustic hideaway, with its hotchpotch collection of grass-roof shacks, is for the hardened traveller. The rooms don't have electricity, and all share bathrooms. Jutting into the sea, the eatery and bar on stilts is where most people choose to hang out. A second, more remote lodge is found on the island's southernmost tip of Hat Yao. (40 rooms)

Ko Kut

Budget–Moderate

Away Resort
Hat Klong Chao
Mobile tel: 08-1835 4517,
Bangkok: 0-2696 8239
www.awayresorts.com
Simple and rustic but trendy at the same time, this island hideaway is perfect for getting away from it all. Accommodation ranges from basic huts to stylish beachfront bungalows. There is no pool, but the setting and the beach make up for it. Its Escape restaurant serves good Thai and Western food. (42 rooms)

Shantaa
Ao Ta Pao
Mobile tel: 08-1826 4077
www.shantaakohkood.com
Small family-run gem of a resort perched on the cliff overlooking Ao Yai Kee beach. Its lovely sea-view villas with open-air bathrooms will make you want to stay longer. Enquire about its packages, which come with transfers, sightseeing trips and meals. (15 villas)

Ko Mak

Budget

Monkey Island Resort
Mobile tel: 0-1535 9119
www.monkeyislandkohmak.com
This funky resort with a primate theme was built by the same people who own the popular Monkey Shock restaurants in Bangkok.

PRICE CATEGORIES

Prices are for a double room without breakfast and taxes:
Luxury = over B8,000
Expensive = B4,000–8,000
Moderate = B2,000–4,000
Budget = under B2,000

BELOW: fireworks display over Amari Orchid Resort & Tower.

Located in the middle of Ao Kao Bay, the accommodation consists of 2-bedroom large air-conditioned Gorilla Huts, smaller fan-cooled Chimpanzee Huts with outdoor showers, and the overpriced shared-bathroom Baboon Huts. The restaurant serves mostly Thai food. In the evenings, head to the beachfront Orangutan Bar for sundowners. (29 rooms)

Ko Samet

Luxury

Paradee Resort
Ao Kui. Tel: 0-3864 4283–8
www.paradeeresort.com
The island's most expensive all-hotel resort is the only hotel of note on quiet Ao Kui beach at the southern tip of the island. Accessible by a 10-minute speedboat ride from Ban Phe Pier (on the mainland), this is the perfect getaway for honey-mooning couples. The tropical-themed villas have separate bedroom and living areas, capacious bathrooms, DVD players, small private swimming pool and even the services of a personal butler on hand. (40 villas)

Expensive

Ao Prao Resort
60 Moo 4, Ao Phrao
Tel: 0-3864 4100–3
www.samedresorts.com
One of the island's most upscale resorts nestles on the only beach on the sunset side of Ko Samet. It therefore sees fewer visitors, adding to its exclusivity. The elegant bungalows come with modern conveniences, including cable TV. Also has the most upscale restaurant on the island, though don't expect too much. (48 rooms)

Le Vimarn
Moo 4, Ao Phrao
Tel: 0-3864 4104–7
www.samedresorts.com
Under the same ownership as nearby Ao Prao Resort, this teakwood resort with sea-facing infinity pool is

located on the more secluded sunset side of the island. Decked out in an elegant blend of the traditional and contemporary, there are three types of cottages and villas to choose from. A spa and a restaurant are centred around a pond. (31 rooms)

Moderate

Sai Kaew Beach Resort
8/1 Moo 4, Hat Sai Kaew
Tel: 0-3864 4195–7
www.samedresorts.com
Decked out in summery blues and whites, this is one of a new breed of small-scale contemporary resorts on Ko Samet, a part of the growing Ao Prao Resort group. Situated at the northern tip of Hat Sai Kaew, the resort has three types of rooms and a swimming pool. Ask about their long-stay promotions. (40 rooms)

Samed Villa
89 Moo 4, Ao Phai
Tel: 0-3864 4094
www.samedvilla.com
Located at the end of Ao Phai beach on a headland with nice views out to sea, this popular family-run resort is under Scandi-navian management. Most weekends it fills with Bangkok expats, so book ahead. It was recently upgraded and is now one of the island's best places to stay. The bungalows are good value with air-conditioning, hot shower and TV. The restaurant does great Thai and international food. (30 rooms)

Budget

Tubtim Resort
13/15 Moo 4, Ao Tub Tim
Tel: 0-3864 4025
www.tubtimresort.com
This rustic resort is a long-time favourite with Bangkok's hip set, and has a gay-friendly vibe. Family-run, the resort has both cheap wooden huts and concrete air-conditioned bungalows. The beach is one of the prettiest, and the evening barbecue by the bar fills up fast. (75 rooms)

Ko Si Chang

Budget

Sichang Palace
81 Moo 1, Th. Asdang
Tel: 0-3821 6276–9
Slightly over-the-top in decor, this is as upmarket as it gets on the island. Near the pier in town. All rooms have air-conditioning, TV and hot water, and there's also a swimming pool, coffee shop, nightclub and billiards room. (60 rooms)

Sichang View Resort
91 Moo 6. Tel: 0-3821 6210–1
On a hilltop with great sunset and sea views, this well-kept resort in a lovely tropical garden has rooms with TV and air-conditioning or fans; more expensive rooms have hot water. The restaurant serves good seafood. (10 rooms)

Pattaya

Expensive

Amari Orchid Resort & Tower
Th. Hat Pattaya (Beach Rd) North Pattaya
Tel: 0-3841 8418
www.amari.com
Offering two options, the older 4-star Garden Wing and the newer 5-star Ocean Tower Wing. The latter, which features oversized 50-sq-metre (555-sq-ft) ocean-view rooms, opened in 2007. Whatever option guests choose, they will have access to a wealth of facilities, including two swimming pools, fitness centre, spa and various restaurants. (529 rooms)

Dusit D2 Baraquda
Th. Pattaya 2
Tel: 0-3876 9999
www.dusit.com
A very real and similarly stylish move upmarket for Pattaya, D2 incorporates the best of modern design with impeccable service and a cool vibe. Expect a lot of hi-tech add-ons, and some deliciously inviting bath-rooms. (72 rooms)

Hard Rock Hotel Pattaya
Th. Hat Pattaya (Beach Rd)
Tel: 0-3842 8755
www.hardrockhotelpattaya.com

Beachside fun in a contemporary setting. The rooms are fairly standard, with the flashy pop colours and music memorabilia typical of all Hard Rock outlets. The vast hotel pool comes complete with thatched pavilions for you to lie beneath, while Hard Rock's health club is the perfect foil to Pattaya's entertainment scene. (320 rooms)

Pullman Pattaya Aisawan
445/3 Moo 5, Wongamart, Th. Naklua
Tel: 0-3841 1940
www.pullmanhotels.com
Set right on Wongamart beach at Naklua Bay, this large, modern-looking hotel – recently renovated and under new management – is popular with well-heeled Asian travellers. A stylish blend of traditional and contemporary Asian design, the well-equipped hotel features two swimming pools and three restaurants plus conference facilities. (374 rooms)

Sugar Hut
391/18 Moo 10, Th. Thappraya
Tel: 0-3825 1686
www.sugar-hut.com
While its location off a main road away from any beach isn't ideal, this verdant tropical resort is a world in itself. The traditional 1- or 2-bedroom Thai bungalows are very rustic, with indoor garden bathrooms. There's an excellent Thai restaurant and a lovely pool. (28 villas)

Moderate

Cabbages & Condoms
366/11 Th. Phra Tamnak Soi 4
Tel: 0-3825 0556–8
www.cabbagesandcondoms.co.th
Taking its name from owner, former Senator Mechai, whose campaigning on AIDS awareness has earned him the title "Mr Condom", this rustic retreat feels far removed from Pattaya's notorious nightlife. The ocean and treetop suites all have teak decks and private jacuzzis, and there's a large sea-view pool surrounded by a pretty garden. Staying here means you also

contribute money to help Thailand's less fortunate. (60 rooms)

Rabbit Resort
Dongtan, Jomtien
Tel: 0-3830 3303–4
www.rabbitresort.com
Set slightly back from Dongtan beach in Jomtien, Rabbit is a Thai-style resort set in pretty gardens. Popular with Bangkok weekenders,

the rooms are decorated with traditional local furniture and fabrics, giving the place a homely feel. There are two swimming pools, a restaurant and a beach grill. (45 rooms)

Budget

Dynasty Resort Pattaya
378/3–11 Moo 12, Th. Phra Tamnak
Tel: 0-3825 0721
www.dynastyinn.com
This resort on a quiet street in the pleasant Phra Tamnak hill area has no sea view but is good value, with a secluded stretch of beach just a short walk away. Rooms are spacious, though a little characterless. There's a large pool and friendly staff. (69 rooms)

Mercure Pattaya
484 Soi 15, Moo 10, Th. Pattaya 2
Tel: 0-3842 5050
www.mercurepattaya.com
Large new outlet in the heart of downtown Pattaya is elegant considering its low rates. The rooms are equipped with modern conveniences. Large swimming pool and four dining outlets. (245 rooms)

NORTHERN GULF COAST

Cha-am

Luxury

Alila Cha-am
115 Moo 7, Tambol Bangkao, Amphur Cha-am
Tel: 0-3270 9555
www.alilahotels.com
Cha-am's first truly de luxe resort is an expression of tasteful design. Using natural materials, its clean minimalist design manages to feel both contemporary and tropical at the same time. Rooms and villas are capacious, with oversized bathrooms and rain showers. Two restaurants, a stunning lap pool, spa and fitness centre complete the scene. (70 rooms and 7 villas)

Expensive

Casuarina
284 Moo 3, Hat Puk-Tien
Tel: 0-3244 3080
www.casuarinathailand.com
Named after the casuarinas that line much of the beach here, this luxury boutique resort has garden and beachfront villas decked out in modern minimalist design. Its avant-garde style may not

appeal to some, but it's popular among Bangkok's style mavens. Located on Puk Tien beach to the north of Cha-am. (32 rooms)

Dusit Resort & Polo Club
1349 Th. Petchkasem
Tel: 0-3252 0009
www.huahin.dusit.com
Located along Cha-am's main beachfront and around a 10-minute drive to Hua Hin, this is a large beachfront hotel with expansive gardens and plenty of water elements. The decor is a blend of colonial style and traditional Thai design. (300 rooms)

Veranda
737/12 Th. Mung Talay
Tel: 0-3270 9000
www.verandaresortandspa.com
Veranda is highly respected for its contemporary elegance and style. The large pool and pond elements are the central features of this boutique-style resort, and its trendy beachfront brasserie is unique in the area. The regular rooms are slightly cramped, but the sea-view villas are very spacious. (97 rooms)

Moderate

Casa Papaya
810/4 Th. Petchkasem
Tel: 0-3247 0678
www.casapapayathailand.com
A cute family-run boutique resort just south of the main Cha-am beach. Done in peachy pastel shades, it's more evocative of the Mediterranean than Thailand. Options include beachfront and garden-view rooms or sea-view bungalows with hammocks out front. (12 rooms)

Hua Hin

Expensive

Anantara Hua Hin
43/1 Th. Petchkasem
Tel: 0-3252 0250
www.anantara.com
Luxurious hideaway tucked among verdant gardens and fronting the beach. Rooms are spacious and have strong Thai accents, with the more expensive ones facing the beach and lagoon. Highly rated spa, plus Italian and Thai restaurants. (187 rooms)

Baan Bayan
119 Th. Petchkasem
Tel: 0-3253 3540
www.baanbayan.com
Set in a century-old beachfront residence, this place is a real gem, evoking a bygone era yet replete with all the mod cons of a boutique resort. The lovely wooden house is surrounded by a large garden. Both sea- and garden-view rooms, plus a pool and bar. Popular for weddings and private parties. (21 rooms)

Hua Hin Marriott Resort & Spa
107/1 Th. Petchkasem
Tel: 0-3251 1881
www.marriott.com
This chain hotel has more style and ambience than its American counterparts and prides itself on impeccable service. A 5-minute drive into town. Right on the beach and with four dining options, guests have little reason to leave the resort. Rooms are spacious and equipped with all modern amenities. (216 rooms)

Hyatt Regency Hua Hin
91 Hua Hin–Khao Takiab
Tel: 0-3252 1234
www.hyatt.com
This low-rise property with sprawling gardens is popular with families. Comes with all mod cons and facilities, including a free-form swimming pool (one of the largest in Hua Hin) as well as Italian and Thai restaurants. The Khmer-inspired Barai Spa is exquisite, so be sure to have a massage here. (204 rooms)

PRICE CATEGORIES

Prices are for a double room without breakfast and taxes:
Luxury = over B8,000
Expensive = B4,000–8,000
Moderate = B2,000–4,000
Budget = under B2,000

BELOW: symmetrical simplicity at the luxurious Alila Cha-am.

Sofitel Central Hua Hin
1 Th. Damnoen Kasem
Tel: 0-3251 2021
www.sofitel.com
Historic colonial-style hotel nestled in a tropical garden. Although in the heart of Hua Hin beach, it feels very private. As well as six swimming pools, there's a spa and fitness centre, plus several international dining options. (207 rooms)

Moderate

Baan Talay Dao
2/10 Soi Takiab
Tel: 0-3253 6024
www.baantalaydao.com
Centred round a 90-year-old teakwood beach house, this resort lies on a nice stretch of Hua Hin beach towards Khao Takiab. Mainly studio rooms, but there are also several nice villas and suites that are arranged around the pool and jacuzzi area. (32 rooms)

Veranda Lodge
113 Soi 67. Tel: 0-3253 3678
www.verandalodge.com
A short distance from the main drag, this elegantly furnished mid-range hotel has a small pool and restaurant that fronts the beach. The one- and two-bedroom suites come with kitchenettes, and the roof-terrace Veranda Grill is popular. (18 rooms)

Budget

City Beach Resort
16 Th. Damnoen Kasem
Tel: 0-3251 2870
www.citybeach.co.th
This centrally located high-rise hotel and feels dated, but is still good value for money. There's a pool, and most rooms have sea views. (162 rooms)

Phetchaburi

Expensive

Fisherman's Village
170 Moo 1, Hat Chao Samran
Tel: 0-3244 1370
www.fishermansvillage.net
Phetchaburi's only upmarket boutique resort, this getaway on the nearby beach at Hat Chao Samran promotes the merits of its undeveloped location as an alternative to Hua Hin. Built in classic Asian style, with a pool and spa. (34 villas)

Moderate

Rabiang Rua & Village Wing Resort
80/1–5 Moo 1, Th. Anamai, Hat Chao Samran
Tel: 0-2967 1911–2
www.rabiangrua.com
Located on the beach at Hat Chao Samran, this is a popular weekend getaway for Thais. The Boat House rooms, which resemble boats, are the nicer option.

Budget

Rabieng Rim Nam Guesthouse
1 Th. Chisa-In
Tel: 0-3242 5707
This popular backpacker haunt is centrally located beside a busy bridge over the river. Cheap, but with small box-like rooms and shared bathrooms. Also has one of the best restaurants in town. (9 rooms)

Pranburi

Expensive

Aleenta
Pak Nam Pran
Tel: 0-2519 2044
www.aleenta.com
One of the best resorts along this stretch of coast. Private and intimate, the Aleenta resort is all about simple and clean lines. Equipped with a pool, restaurant, bar and spa. Romantic dinners can also be set up on the beach with advance notice. (10 suites, 3 villas plus 5 suites)

Evason Hua Hin Resort and Evason Hideaway
Pak Nam Pran
Tel: 0-3263 2111
www.sixsenses.com
Evason is a contemporary retreat with 185 tastefully designed Asian-accented rooms, a large pool and two beachfront restaurants. Its

Six Sense Spa is set among lily ponds with an outdoor pavilion for treatments. Next door is the luxury retreat called **Evason Hideaway**, with 55 private villas (over US$400 a night), each with pool and butler service.

Moderate

Huaplee Lazy Beach
Pak Nam Pran
Tel: 0-3263 0555
www.huapleelazybeach.com
This small boutique-style resort has six maritime-accented rooms and one 2-bedroom villa. Its sister resort (called **Brassiere Beach** – no kidding) contains a clutch of villas near Sam Roi Yot National Park. (9 rooms)

Sam Roi Yot N P

Budget

Dolphin Bay Resort
227 Moo 4, Hat Phu Noi, Sam Roi Yot
Tel: 0-3255 9333
www.dolphinbayresort.com
Located north of Sam Roi Yot National Park, this well-managed resort lies on a beach whose waters are a playground for dolphins. The family-oriented resort has two swimming pools, regular rooms and bungalows as well as apartments. (72 rooms)

KO SAMUI

Hat Bo Phut

Luxury

Anantara Ko Samui
Hat Bo Phut
Tel: 0-7742 8300–9
www.anantara.com
Plush boutique resort along a quiet stretch of Bo Phut beach, with Fisherman's Village a short walk away. The rooms and suites either overlook the beautifully landscaped gardens or the beach. Huge bathrooms come with terrazzo tubs for two. A 30-metre (98ft) infinity pool, spa, fitness centre, and Italian and Thai restaurants are on site. (106 rooms).

Expensive

Bandara Resort & Spa
Hat Bo Phut
Tel: 0-7724 5795
www.bandararesort.com
Stylish resort right on Bo Phut beach with contemporary and Thai-style design elements. Both rooms and villas available, plus a good in-house spa and a beachfront restaurant. (151 rooms)

Zazen Boutique Resort
Hat Bo Phut
Tel: 0-7742 5085
www.samuizazen.com*
Forget about spare lines and minimalist design. This boutique resort has a very

tropical and Thai feel with its lush gardens and Thai-style architecture and decor. The villas are spacious and well appointed. Inventive East-West fusion cusine at the restaurant. (28 villas)

Moderate

Peace Resort
Hat Bo Phut
Tel: 0-7742 5357
www.peaceresort.com
This long-standing resort on Bo Phut beach has a relaxed family vibe and, despite being fairly large, still retains an intimate atmosphere. There's a nice pool, and all the bungalows

have their own balconies. (102 rooms)

Budget

The Lodge
Hat Bo Phut
Tel: 0-7742 5337
www.apartmentsamui.com
Right in the heart of Fisherman's Village, this place has cosy rooms with

wooden floors and balconies with sea views. The two upper-floor Pent Hut rooms are more expensive. The beachfront bar does great breakfasts and evening cocktails. (10 rooms)

Hat Chaweng

Expensive

Amari Palm Reef Resort
Chaweng Beach. Tel: 0-7742 2015
www.amari.com/palmreef
On the quieter northern end of popular Chaweng Beach, this Thai-style beach resort has a delightful seaside restaurant and two free-form pools. The stylishly outfitted rooms either face the beach or verdant gardens. Italian and Thai/Asian restaurants, plus the highly regarded Sivara Spa. (187 rooms)

Buri Rasa Village
Hat Chaweng. Tel: 0-7723 0222
www.burirasa.com
This lovely boutique resort, just south of Chaweng's busiest stretch, is a real tropical haven. Tastefully designed with a Thai village ambience, the rooms and suites feature DVD players and Wi-fi access but retain an old-world charm with four-poster beds. Features a stylish, pool perfect for lazing, plus a restaurant and beach bar. (32 rooms)

Muang Kulaypan
Hat Chaweng. Tel: 0-7723 0849
www.kulaypan.com
One of the island's stand-outs, this boutique hotel designed in Zen-inspired minimalist style has one of the largest beach frontages on Chaweng. Has a stylish black-tiled swimming pool and a Thai restaurant with traditional dance and music in the evenings. (41 rooms)

Moderate

Chaweng Villa
Hat Chaweng. Tel: 0-7723 1123
www.chawengvilla.com
Set a little close to the main nightlife activity, this beachfront resort with its tropical garden setting and vine-covered roofs is good value. Small pool, plus three beachfront eateries and a busy bar. (48 rooms)

Budget

First Residence
119/6 Moo 1, Th. Taweeratpakdee
Tel: 0-7742 7103
A basic, no-frills hotel with clean and modern furnishings. Each room comes with a balcony with either sea or pool views. Less than five minutes to the beach and shopping centre. In-house restaurant serves international and Thai cuisines. (44 rooms)

Hat Choeng Mon

Luxury

Sala Samui Resort & Spa
Hat Choeng Mon
Tel: 0-7724 5888
www.salasamui.com
This recent addition to the island's de luxe resorts scene has raised the bar with its lavish and impeccably appointed Thai-style villas, most of which have their own private pool. The main pool is fringed by a lily pond and has pavilions for outdoor massage. (69 rooms)

Expensive

Imperial Boat House
83 Moo 5, Hat Choeng Mon
Tel: 0-7742 5041
www.imperialboathouse.com
Almost everything is boat-shaped (or inspired) in this hotel, including its swimming pool. Luxury rooms and suites are set in two-storey converted rice barges as well as the main building. Extensive use of wood gives this hotel a very tropical feel. Spa, two restaurants and fitness centre on site. (210 rooms)

Hat Laem Set

Luxury

The Kamalaya
Hat Laem Set
Tel: 0-7742 9800
www.kamalaya.com
The is Ko Samui's ultimate spa and wellness retreat. Hugging a hillside over-looking the sea, it has a range of accommodation options, from hillside rooms to sea-view villas. Most guests at this exclusive hideaway are booked on

several-day retreats that focus on yoga, detox or spa programmes. The food focuses mainly on organic and vegetarian produce. (60 rooms)

Hat Laem Yai

Luxury

Four Seasons Resort
Hat Laem Yai
Tel: 0-7724 3000
www.fourseasons.com/kohsamui
Various options, from a one-bedroom villa nestled in the hillside to a five-bedroom beach residence, all with indulgent outdoor rain showers and private infinity pools. Teak and rosewood furnishings add to this resort's southern Thai charm. (74 villas)

Hat Lamai

Expensive

Pavilion Samui
Hat Lamai
Tel: 0-7742 4030
www.pavilionsamui.com
The Pavilion has been on Lamai for years but was upgraded into an upmarket resort, with prices and facilities to match. Lovely pool, spa and an attractive beachfront. More expensive rooms have bathtubs on the balcony. (58 rooms)

Tamarind Villas
Hat Lamai. Tel: 0-7723 0571
www.tamarindvillas.com
Known primarily as a spa and wellness centre, this hillside retreat features nine villas aimed at families or couples who want a healthy holiday. In a large tree-shaded setting, the residences vary from a cave-cum-tree house to the magnificent hilltop house with panoramic views. (9 villas)

Moderate

Jungle Park
Hat Lamai
Tel: 0-7741 8034
www.jungle-park.com
Situated at the northern tip of Lamai beach, this French-run outfit has a pool and garden, and beachfront bungalows with air-conditioning, TV and

minibar. Also a bar, massage area and a busy seafront restaurant serving Thai-French cuisine on site. (24 rooms)

Long Island Resort
Hat Lamai
Tel: 0-7742 4202
www.longislandresort.com
Located on the northern stretch of Lamai, this mid-range resort keeps a firm grip of its laidback vibe. Offers a range of rooms (priced from budget to moderate) and there's a nice pool, bar area and spa. (40 rooms)

Budget

The Spa Resort
Hat Lamai
Tel: 0-7723 0855
www.spasamui.com
This retreat is one of the island's first and best health-spa resorts, plus it's affordable. Set around a pool, the rooms vary in standard and rate, and generally have to be booked weeks in advance. Guests come mainly for the detox programmes. (32 rooms)

Hat Maenam

Luxury

Santiburi Resort
Hat Maenam
Tel: 0-7742 5031
www.santiburi.com
Touts itself as the island's first golf resort, but even if the rolling greens don't entice you, the luxury resort has plenty else to offer. Located on quiet Maenam beach, it has a huge oval-shaped pool with suites in the main building, and villas set in the large gardens. (71 rooms and villas)

Expensive

Paradise Beach Resort
Hat Maenam
Tel: 0-7724 7227
www.samuiparadisebeach.com

PRICE CATEGORIES

Prices are for a double room without breakfast and taxes:
Luxury = over B8,000
Expensive = B4,000–8,000
Moderate = B2,000–4,000
Budget = under B2,000

This has spacious bungalows, de luxe rooms and Thai-style suites, all set around a lush garden and two pools on Maenam beach. A bit worn in places, the resort is quiet and more suited to older couples and families. Slightly overpriced for what you get. (95 rooms)

Hat Taling Ngam

Luxury

Baan Taling Ngam Resort & Spa
Hat Taling Ngam
Tel: 0-7742 9100
www.baan-taling-ngam.com
Located on a steep hill on the quiet southwest side of the island, this grand resort has five swimming pools and several restaurants, which make up for its rather inadequate beach and isolated location. The stunning villas are capacious and embellished with traditional Thai antiques and furnishings. (70 rooms)

KO PHANGAN

Expensive

Panviman Resort
Ao Thong Nai Pan Noi
Tel: 0-7744 5101
www.panviman.com
This is one of Ko Phangan's few upscale sleeping options. It is perched atop the headland that divides the pretty northeastern bays of Thong Nai Pan Yai and Thong Nai Pan Noi. Clustered around the pool, the stylish cottages and hotel rooms have modern amenities. (75 rooms)

Santhiya Resort & Spa
Ao Thong Nai Pan Noi
Tel: 0-7723 8333
www.santhiya.com
This resort on idyllic Thong Nai Pan Noi Bay is decked out in a blend of traditional and modern Thai style with teakwood finishes. Rooms have floor-to-ceiling windows and verandas with great views of the pool and gardens. Villas are even more luxurious. (59 rooms)

Moderate

Cocohut Village
Ban Tai (Leela Beach)
Tel: 0-7737 5368
www.cocohut.com
Located on quieter Leela beach, yet within walking distance of Hat Rin, this popular resort sprawls over an area of prime beachfront. Rooms range from the simple guesthouse with shared bathrooms to expensive pool-facing executive suites. (67 rooms)

Green Papaya Resort
Hat Salad
Tel: 0-7737 4230
www.greenpapayaresort.com
Set around a pool, the wooden bungalows come in five price ranges, with the executive suites featuring private terraces and outdoor jacuzzis. The unique restaurant is built like a boat. (18 rooms)

Sarikantang
Ban Tai (Leela Beach)
Tel: 0-7737 5055
www.sarikantang.com
Situated on the tip of Hat Rin at pleasant Leela beach, this small, modern boutique resort has a modern Asian minimalist feel to it. Pick from the basic but comfy wooden bungalows, or if you feel like splurging, plump for the ocean-view suite with separate living room, DVD player and outdoor bathtub. (37 rooms)

Vimarn Samut Resort
Hat Rin
Tel: 0-7737 5027
www.vimarnsamut.com
A small mid-range hotel with rooms over two floors, balconies that look out to the sunset side of Hat Rin, and a restaurant right on the beach. Rooms are modern and clean. (18 rooms)

Budget–Moderate

Haad Son Resort
Hat Son
Tel: 0-7734 9103
www.haadson.net

Occupying the rocky headland at the end of an uninhabited pristine white-sand beach, this is one of the best resorts on the west coast. A variety of rooms, from thatch-roof huts to air-con poolside villas. The sunset views are gorgeous, and the executive penthouse suites come with private pools. (47 rooms)

Milky Bay Resort
Ban Tai (Leela Beach)
Tel: 0-7723 8566
www.milkybay.com
Good-value-for-money resort with stylish rooms and bungalows. Restaurant, small swimming pool and gym on site. (25 rooms)

KO TAO

Expensive

Jamahkiri Resort & Spa
Ao Thian Ok
Tel: 0-7745 6400
www.jamahkiri.com
This lovely top-end resort – probably Ko Tao's most expensive digs – is perched over huge boulders and houses the island's most pampering spa. Decorated in dark woods and Thai silks, there are four room sizes, all equipped with flat-screen TVs, DVD players and bathtubs. Terrace restaurant on site, plus a pool and fitness centre that opened in 2006. (12 rooms)

Moderate

Charm Churee Villa
Ao Jansom
Tel: 0-7745 6393
www.charmchureevilla.com
Perched on pretty Ao Jansom, this eclectic mix of bungalows is one of the island's better mid-range options. Variety of hillside cottages and villas, all with air-conditioning. Seafood restaurant has great views. (30 rooms)

Koh Tao Grand Coral Resort
Hat Sai Ree. Tel: 0-7745 6431
www.kohtaocoral.com
These salmon-pink cottages are clustered around a free-form swimming pool and located on the far end of Sai Ree beach. All have nice wooden interiors and private terraces. Small restaurant on site. (45 rooms)

Ko Tao Resort
Ao Chalok Ban Kao
Tel: 0-7745 6133
www.kohtaoresort.com
Located on a lovely crescent-shaped beach in the south, Ko Tao Resort is an efficient Thai-run dive-oriented hotel with a swimming pool, restaurant and a variety of rooms. (51 rooms)

Thipwimarn Resort
Hat Sai Ree
Tel: 0-7745 6409
www.thipwimarnresort.com
This tastefully designed cliff-top resort is a cosy private retreat with 11 rooms and private access to a small beach below. The bonus is the spectacular sunset view from its circular restaurant. (11 rooms)

NORTHERN ANDAMAN COAST

Ao Phang Nga area

Note: The options in the luxury and expensive categories are on the island of **Ko Yao Noi**, ideally located to enjoy the panoramas of Phang Nga Bay.

Luxury
Six Senses Hideaway
Ko Yao Noi
Tel: 0-7641 8500
www.sixsenses.com
This is the ultimate romantic getaway. Live like Robinson Crusoe but with every conceivable comfort at hand at your infinity-edged pool villa, including a personal butler to cater to your every whim. The gorgeous views of ethereal Ao Phang Nga will keep you spellbound, but when you tire of that there are other diversions – two restaurants, spa, gym and a variety of activities, including dive trips and tours of Ao Phang Nga. (54 villas)

Expensive
Ko Yao Island Resort
Ko Yao Noi
Tel: 0-2673 0966
www.koyao.com
Eco-friendly property with a small number of 1- and 2-bedroom villas along a short stretch of beach. Villas are either ocean-facing or tucked away in a tropical garden. Restaurant serves Mediterranean and Thai dishes. Has a bar but no pool. Prices drop by half during the off season. The resort can arrange transfers from either Phuket or Krabi. (15 rooms)

The Paradise Koh Yao
Ko Yao Noi
Tel: 0-2233 1399
www.theparadise.biz
This beautiful resort is nestled in a secluded spot adjacent to a stretch of private beach. Rooms have semi-outdoor bathrooms, open living areas, air-conditioning and postcard-perfect views of lovely Phang Nga Bay. The resort can arrange transfers from either Phuket or Krabi. (70 rooms)

Budget
Phang Nga Bay Resort
Ko Panyi
Tel: 0-7641 2067
www.thaihotel.com/
phangnga/phangngabay
Accommodation in the Phang Nga Bay area is scarce; this one is found on nearby Ko Panyi island. Rooms are a bit dated, but are clean and spacious. (88 rooms)

Khao Lak

Luxury
The Sarojin
60 Moo 2, Khuk Khak
Tel: 0-7642 7900
www.thesarojin.com
Arguably Khao Lak's most luxurious resort, The Sarojin is the ultimate embodiment of indulgence, with direct access to a secluded 11km (7-mile) stretch of private beach. Rooms are situated in low-rise buildings, and each is appointed luxuriously with strong Thai accents. Ground-floor rooms have access to private gardens while the ones upstairs have capacious terraces. Two restaurants, a bar, a pampering spa and an exquisite infinity pool. (56 rooms)

Expensive
Khao Lak Merlin Resort
7/7 Th. Petchkasem
Tel: 0-7642 8300
www.merlinphuket.com/khaolak
With three swimming pools, a fitness room, spa and tennis courts, this resort caters to more than just the sedentary sun-worshipper. For children there is a kids' club and playground, and for adults a pool bar, beach bar and lounge. Rooms are large yet homely in appearance, many with high ceilings that add to the sense of spaciousness. (209 rooms)

La Flora
59/1 Moo 5, Khuk Khak
Tel: 0-7642 8000
www.lafloraresort.com
A series of small low-rise buildings set among tropical gardens house the villas

and guest rooms in this lovely resort. Marble floors and contemporary artwork on the walls accentuate the modern Asian ambience, and a beautiful mosaic-tiled sea-facing pool adds a touch of luxury. (70 rooms)

Le Meridien Khao Lak Beach and Spa Resort
9/9 Moo 1, Khuk Khak
Tel: 0-7642 7500
www.lemeridien.com
Set within 20 hectares (50 acres) of sandy beach and tropical gardens. Rooms are luxurious and large, with lounge areas and flat-screen TVs. Bathrooms have separate baths and rain showers with glass panelling that allows an unobstructed view of the living and balcony areas. Three restaurants, two bars and one excellent spa. (243 rooms)

Moderate
Best Western Palm Galleria Resort
43/1 Moo 2, Khuk Khak
Tel: 0-7623 6378
www.khaolak-hotels.com/palmgalleria
This four-star resort is in an ideal location, with easy access to both the town and the beach. Guest rooms are clean and spacious, and have private balconies, separate shower stalls and bathtubs. A reasonably good deal considering that most of Khao Lak's resorts are rather upmarket. (74 rooms)

Khaolak Bhandari Resort
26/25 Moo 7, Nang Thong
Tel: 0-7642 0751
www.khaolak-hotels.com/bhandari
Set slightly back from the beach amid tropical gardens, the romantic Thai-style pavilions that form this resort twist around palm trees and a large, curved swimming pool. Has a good restaurant serving Thai and Western options, and an open-air bar. (58 rooms)

Budget
Jai Restaurant and Bungalows
5/1 Moo 7, Khao Lak
Tel: 0-7642 0390
One of the few budget

places to stay at in Khao Lak. Rooms are clean and service is friendly, considering the low prices. Bungalows with small private terraces are set behind Jai Restaurant, just off the main road and a few minutes' walk from the beach. (15 rooms)

Khao Pilai

Luxury
Aleenta Phuket-Phang Nga
Khao Pilai. Tel: 0-2508 5349
www.aleenta.com/phuket
Between Khao Lak and Phuket (but closer to Phuket Airport, only 16km/10 miles away) is this luxury property on Khao Pilai beach – also known as Natai beach. Flanked by pristine beach on one side and lush national park on the other, you'll be blown away by this contemporary bolthole. Choose between a pool villa, beachfront suite or ocean villa. The floor-to-ceiling glass brings the outdoors in. Perfect for honeymooners. (30 suites and villas)

Khao Sok N P

Budget
Bamboo House
Khao Sok
Tel: 0-1787 7484
www.krabidir.com/bamboohouse
Basic but clean and comfortable stilted wood bungalows with separate bathroom and hot showers.

Its restaurant serves Thai and Western food. Staff are very friendly and in high season there is a monthly full-moon barbecue by the Sok River. It also organises trekking tours of Khao Sok and other activities. (17 rooms)

Khao Sok Rainforest Resort
Khao Sok
Tel: 0-7739 5135
www.krabidir.com/khaosokrainforest
Fantastic location right by the river and just 100 metres/yds from the main bridge. Incredibly tall stilted bungalows sit among the treetops, and even the restaurant has a jungle feel to it, with vines creeping over its open walls. It's a bit of a walk up there, but definitely worth it for the spectacular mountain views. Various jungle activities and trekking tours can be booked at the resort. (12 rooms)

Ko Chang

Budget

Cashew Resort
Ao Yai
Tel: 0-7782 0116
Ko Chang's first and largest resort has a variety of bungalows made from wood and bamboo to solid stone. There are more facilities here

than at many other resorts, including a dive school and a beach bar with pool table. Open from mid-October to May only. (25 rooms)

Sunset Resort
Ao Yai
Tel: 0-7782 0171
Shaded beach bungalows with a pleasant attached restaurant. Beach volleyball is played daily at sunset in front of the resort and the staff are happy to advise on fishing and other activities. Open from mid-October to May only. (15 rooms)

Ko Phayam

Budget

Baan Suan Kayoo
Ko Phayam
Tel: 0-7782 0133
www.gopayam.com
Thatched-roof cottages built on a gentle slope where winding paths lead through a cashew-nut garden towards the beach. Cottages range from simple to superior; the latter have larger beds and Western-style toilets. Ask about the packages, which include transfers and tours. (17 rooms)

Bamboo Bungalows
Ko Phayam
Tel: 0-7782 0012
www.bamboo-bungalows.com
This popular cluster of

bungalows open year-round is one of the livelier places in the evenings, when guests from nearby hotels come to enjoy the music on the beach. Nestled about 100 metres/yds back from the beachfront. (25 rooms)

Phang Nga Town

Budget

Phang Nga Guest House
99/1 Th. Petchkasem
Tel: 0-7641 1358
Basic but comfortable rooms with choice of fan or air-conditioning. This is one of the better budget options in town, conveniently situated and with friendly staff. (12 rooms)

Ranong

Moderate

Jansom Beach Resort
Hat Chan Damri
Tel: 0-7782 1611
As the only hotel on Chan Damri beach, the Jansom is peaceful and quiet, with lovely views of Myanmar (Burma) from your room. The downside is the long walk up a lot of rocky steps to reach your room, but the sea breezes at the top make it bearable. (42 rooms)

Jansom Hot Spa Ranong
2/10 Th. Petchkasem

Tel: 0-7781 1510
www.jansomhotsparanong.net
Despite being the best known, this hotel is by no means the best. From the paintwork to the lifts, this 1960s throwback appears old and run-down and the staff are less than welcoming. The hotel justifies its prices by the hot spring-water baths on site. (220 rooms)

Royal Princess Ranong
41/144 Th. Tamuang
Tel: 0-7783 5240
www.royalprincess.com
Easily the best hotel in Ranong Town. Rooms are clean and decently appointed and the staff are friendly. Hot spring water is provided in all guest rooms as well as in the swimming pool and jacuzzi areas. (138 rooms)

Budget

Woodhouse Guest House
Near Royal Princess Hotel,
Th. Tamuang
Tel: 0-9866 3672
This guesthouse may be one of Ranong's cheaper options, but its atmosphere is far more welcoming than some of the more expensive options. There are two rooms per floor, with each pair sharing a bathroom. Everything is clean, and the guesthouse never feels crowded. (16 rooms)

PHUKET

Ao Bang Thao

Luxury

Banyan Tree Phuket
33 Moo 4, Th. Srisoonthorn
Tel: 0-7632 4374
www.banyantree.com
The most exclusive of the five hotels within the Laguna Phuket complex. Luxurious Thai-style villas with landscaped gardens and private outdoor pools. Excellent spa on site. Perfect for honeymooners. (108 rooms)

Expensive

Dusit Thani Laguna
390 Th. Srisoonthorn
Tel: 0-7636 2999

www.dusit.com
Low-rise, modern Thai-style buildings contain bright and airy rooms with wooden floors. Part of the Thai-owned luxury Dusit group, it's located right on Bang Thao beach. All rooms have balconies, and there are six restaurants to chose from. (226 rooms)

Sheraton Grande Laguna Phuket
10 Moo 4, Th. Srisoonthorn
Tel: 0-7632 4101
www.sheraton.phuket.com
It's water everywhere at this large and luxurious Sheraton. Sits on its own small island in the centre of a lagoon, with Bang Thao

beach at the front and forests at the back. Lagoon-style pools wind through the entire property. (252 rooms and 83 villas)

Ao Pansea

Luxury

Amanpuri
118/1 Moo 3, Pansea
Tel: 0-7631 6100
www.amanpuri.com
Without a doubt Phuket's most exclusive retreat, situated on a headland with its own private beach and a fleet of luxury boats. The Amanpuri is all about understated elegance. The beach is located at the

bottom of a long flight of steps. (40 rooms and 31 villas)

Trisara
60/1 Moo 6, Th. Srisoonthorn
Tel: 0-7631 0100
www.trisara.com
Money no object? Then this is the place to stay. Superlative design, dining, management and staff. The private beach is superb, the

infinity pool views to be reincarnated for. An exhilarating property. (39 villas, suites and rooms)

Expensive

The Chedi
118 Moo 3, Pansea
Tel: 0-762 1579
www.ghmhotels.com
Overshadowed by the nearby Amanpuri, rooms here are simple thatched cottages, each with private veranda and teakwood floors. As the cottages hug a cliff, expect to climb a lot of stairs which sometimes take a circuitous route. It has one of Phuket's most inviting swimming pools and a gorgeous beachfront. (108 rooms)

Hat Karon

Expensive

Hilton Phuket Arcadia Resort & Spa
333 Th. Patak
Tel: 0-7639 6433
www.hilton.com
Phuket's largest hotel is housed in this rather odd-looking circular structure set in a prime location at the centre of Karon. The beach itself is located a short walk across the road. The inside is far more appealing and there are excellent facilities, including pool and spa, tennis and squash courts, jogging and walking tracks and a putting green. (679 rooms)

Le Meridien Phuket Beach Resort
Karon Noi
Tel: 0-7637 0100
www.lemeridien.com
Located in a sheltered bay with a private beach on its doorstep. Facilities are top-rate: two massive adjoining swimming pools, spa, numerous restaurants, bars and shops, golf driving range and one of the island's largest and most

PRICE CATEGORIES

Prices are for a double room without breakfast and taxes:
Luxury = over B8,000
Expensive = B4,000–8,000
Moderate = B2,000–4,000
Budget = under B2,000

modern gyms. Rooms are spacious and tastefully furnished. (407 rooms)

Moderate

Central Karon Village
8/21 Moo 1 Karon
Tel: 0-7628 6300
www.centralhotelsresorts.com
Perched on a hill with sweeping views of the beach, the trade-off is no direct beach access. As the hotel is located at the northern end of Karon, it in fact has easy access to Patong beach. Rooms are contemporary in look with pure white linens contrasting against bold, brightly coloured walls and cushions. (72 rooms)

Hat Kata

Expensive

Kata Thani Beach Resort
Kata Noi
Tel: 0-7633 0010–4
www.katathani.com
Located on quiet and stunning Kata Noi beach, the resort is so large and spread out it never seems overcrowded. Rooms (the standard ones feel cramped) have been given a makeover in teakwood and sandstone. (479 rooms)

Mom Tri's Boathouse
Kata Yai. Tel: 0-7633 0015
www.boathousephuket.com
Prime beachfront location along the broad Kata Yai beach. All rooms (albeit on the smallish side) have sunset-facing sea views. Award-winning Boathouse Wine & Grill on site. (33 rooms and 3 suites)
Note: South of the Boathouse and located on the cliff just above the headland is the **Villa Royale**. Under the same management as the Boathouse, its Thai-style villas and suites have stunning sea views and are only a short walk to the smaller and more intimate Kata Noi beach. Prices here are in the luxury category. (35 suites and villas)

Moderate

Kata Beach Resort
Kata Yai
Tel: 0-7633 0006-7
www.katagroup.com/katabeach
Blessed with a prime position on Kata Yai beach, this large low-rise concrete block projects a smaller, more intimate feel than its size would imply. Good facilities make it an excellent family choice, although couples will also benefit from an adults-only swimming pool and a romantic sea-facing restaurant. (273 rooms)

Hat Mai Khao

Luxury

Anantara Phuket
Mai Khao
Tel: 0-7636 6100
www.anantara.com
This boutique resort chain is known for its de luxe properties in Thailand. Anantara Phuket, featuring individual pool villas scattered among lush tropical gardens, is a very special place – well up to the standards set by its sister resorts. (83 villas)

Expensive

JW Marriott Phuket Resort & Spa
Moo 3, Mai Khao
Tel: 0-7633 8000
www.marriott.com
Located a few minutes from the airport, this self-contained sanctuary has extensive facilities including seven restaurants, fitness centre, spa and watersports.

Set in sprawling landscaped grounds, this property on Mai Khao beach sits just adjacent to a national park and a turtle-nesting sanctuary. Some people like the isolation, while others feel it's too far away from the town and the main beaches. (246 rooms and 13 suites)

SALA Phuket Resort and Spa
333 Moo 3 Mai Khao Beach
Tel: 0-7633 8888
www.salaresorts.com
SALA is typical of the latest generation of Phuket accommodation – all villas, very exclusive and with nothing left to chance. Equally adaptable for families or romancing couples, most of the villas have their own "bathing-suit-optional" pool and open-air bathrooms. (79 villas)

Hat Nai Harn

Luxury

The Royal Phuket Yacht Club, Puravarna
23/3 Moo 1, Th. Vises
Tel: 0-7638 0200
www.lemeridien.com
As the only hotel with direct access to Nai Harn beach, Le Royal Meridien, with the sparkling sea to its front and a lagoon at its back, is in high demand year-round. Rooms, all with private terraces, are spacious and tastefully furnished. All have sea views, most overlooking the bay and nearby Promthep Cape. Popular with those seeking a quiet beach away from the

BELOW: the Millennium Resort Patong in Phuket.

hustle and bustle further up the island. (110 rooms)

Hat Nai Yang

Expensive

Indigo Pearl
Nai Yang
Tel: 0-7632 7006
www.indigo-pearl.com
Located within Sirinat National Park and by the beach, the hotel design mixes contemporary and Thai accents, all inspired by Phuket's tin-mining past. (292 rooms)

Hat Patong

Luxury

Ban Yin Dee
7/5 Th. Muean Ngen
Tel: 0-7629 4104-6
www.baanyindee.com
A boutique-style resort with the ambience of a private villa. Distinct Thai-style design with triangular arching roofs and extensive use of teak, marble and rattan throughout. Three swimming pools and a 12-person jacuzzi with a bird's-eye view of Patong beach. (21 rooms)

Expensive

Burasari Resort
31/1 Soi Ruamjai
Tel: 0-7629 2929
www.burasari.com
Burasari is a maze of exotic plants, flowers and waterfalls set around a swimming pool. It's perfectly located just a minute's walk down a quiet street off the main beach road. (90 rooms)
Millennium Resort Patong
199 Th. Rat-U-Thit 200 Pee
Tel: 0-7660 1999
www.millenniumpatong.com
Centrally located hotel, right in the heart of Patong beach and close to shopping and nightlife, with the beach only a 5-minute walk away. Rooms (in both the Lakeside and Beachside wings) are spacious, the restaurants are good and facilities excellent. (421 rooms)

Moderate

Mercure Patong Phuket
239/14 Th. Rat-U-Thit 200 Pee

Tel: 0-7630 2100
www.mercurephuketphuket.com
New hotel (opened in September 2007) only a 10-minute walk to Patong beach. Convenient location for the shops, restaurants and nightlife of Patong. Rooms are contemporary in style, and the facilities are all top-notch for this price category. (249 rooms)
Novotel Phuket
282 Th. Prabaramee
Tel: 0-7634 2777
www.accorhotels-asia.com
Set slightly up a hill on the far end of Patong, the Novotel is popular because of its friendly service and international reputation. It could do with some renovations, but it is comfortable and clean, with spacious rooms and rates that are lower than other hotels in the same category. (215 rooms)

Budget

Stoney Monday Oasis Hotel
35/1 Th. Rat-U-Thit
Tel: 0-7629 0363
www.stoneymonday.com
Australian-owned budget hotel with clean, spacious rooms and free Wi-fi for guests. Relaxed and friendly atmosphere, with a ground-floor restaurant, a rooftop garden and very informative staff. A 5-minute walk from the main shopping district, and under 10 minutes' walk from the beach. (76 rooms)

Hat Rawai

Expensive

The Evason Phuket
100 Th. Viset
Tel: 0-7638 1018
www.sixsenses.com
Popular with couples and honeymooners, the romantic and stylish Evason is secluded and set back from the main road. It has two beachfront restaurants, its own pier and exclusive access to the island of Ko Bon for its guests, partly to make up for its smallish but nonetheless pleasant beachfront. (260 rooms)

The Mangosteen Resort & Spa
99/4 Moo 7, Soi Mangosteen
Tel: 0-7628 9399
www.mangosteen-phuket.com
Intimate resort with a sea view to one side and mountains to the other. Rooms are octagonal in shape and many have private jacuzzi baths. The saltwater swimming pool bends and twists its way around the resort's buildings and restaurant. No direct beach access, but a shuttle bus is offered to Nai Harn beach and takes only 5 minutes. (40 rooms)

Hat Surin

Luxury

Twinpalms Phuket
106/46 Moo 3, Surin
Tel: 0-7631 6500
www.twinpalms-phuket.com
Modern and stylish resort only a 5-minute walk from Surin beach. Contemporary decor with white walls and bed linen contrasting with dark wooden floors and furniture. All the usual amenities expected from a luxury resort, plus the hip Oriental Spoon restaurant serving innovative Western and Thai dishes. (76 rooms)

Expensive

Treetops Arasia
125 Moo 3, Th. Srisoonthorn
Tel: 0-7627 1271
www.treetops-arasia.com
Aptly named due to its elevated positioning high on the tree-covered Surin hill, this boutique resort has a perfect, uninterrupted view of the bay and is within walking distance of the beach. This is a great place to be during the monsoon season when massive storms over the open sea light up the sky. (48 rooms)

Ko Hae

Moderate

Coral Island Resort
Ko Hae (Coral Island)
Tel: 0-7628 1060
www.coralislandresort.com
The only choice on this island. All cottages are air-

conditioned, with terraces overlooking the sea. The resort has the island's only swimming pool. Diving and snorkelling trips. (64 rooms)

Ko Racha Yai

Luxury

The Racha
Ko Racha Yai
Tel: 0-7635 5455
www.theracha.com
The Racha has a chic, modern style with its minimalist white-on-white toned villas and luxurious open-air garden bathrooms with rain showers. If the budget allows, go for the villas with private pools, or at the very least, the large de luxe rooms. A dramatic rooftop glass-edged infinity swimming pool overlooks the turquoise bay. (70 villas)

Laem Panwa

Moderate

Cape Panwa Hotel
27 Moo 8, Th. Sakdidet
Tel: 0-7639 1123
www.capepanwa.com
Located among palm trees and set slightly to the back of a quiet beach. Rooms are sea-facing and are large and comfortable. Holds weekly Thai cooking classes. (246 rooms)

Phuket Town

Moderate

Metropole Hotel
1 Soi Surin, Th. Montri
Tel: 0-7621 5050
www.metropolephuket.com
Large and ugly from the outside, but nicer inside and in a great location close to the town's main shops and attractions. Staff are friendly, and service is of a high standard. (228 rooms)
Royal Phuket City Hotel
154 Th. Phang Nga
Tel: 0-7623 3333
www.royalphuketcity.com
This centrally located hotel is large yet welcoming and easily the best in town. Facilities include a sandwich corner, café, fitness centre and swimming pool. (251 rooms)

KRABI TOWN AND BEACHES

Ao Nang

Expensive

Pavilion Queen's Bay
56/3 Moo 3, Ao Nang
Tel: 0-7563 7612
www.pavilionhotels.com
This four-star hotel is perched atop a hill just 350 metres (1,150ft) from the beach. Views of both mountain and sea are stunning, and the swimming-pool area has elegant white umbrellas and tall, white columns. (106 rooms)

Moderate

Ao Nang Villa Resort
113 Ao Nang
Tel: 0-7563 7270
www.aonangvilla.com
Great location only a minute's walk from the beachfront, with two large free-form swimming pools resting at the foot of Krabi's limestone mountains. The Villa Spa is located in a Thai-style house. (79 rooms)

Cliff Ao Nang Resort
85/2 Moo 2, Ao Nang
Tel: 0-7563 8117
www.krabi-hotels.com/thecliff
Small, elegant and located in the hills a 10-minute walk from the sea. The mountain views from this elevated position are stunning; if one is content to relax around the pool, this is one of Ao Nang's most peaceful retreats. (22 rooms)

Krabi Resort
232 Moo 2, Ao Nang
Tel: 0-7563 7030
www.krabiresort.net
A 5-minute walk from the beach, this resort sprawls over 7 hectares (18 acres) and offers a choice of bungalows or cheaper rooms in the main hotel block. One of the few hotels in Ao Nang to have tennis courts. Huge swimming pool. (95 rooms)

Hat Khlong Muang

Luxury

Nakamanda Resort & Spa
126 Moo 3, Hat Khlong Muang
Tel: 0-7564 4388
www.nakamanda.com

Classy and elegant is a good way to describe this boutique resort. The large and elegant 56-sq-metre (600-sq-ft) villas have Thai-style pointed roofs and are linked by shaded wooden walkways. Sandstone sculptures are scattered on the grounds, and the artistically designed pool is stunning (and makes up for the average beach). The most romantic hotel in the area. (36 rooms)

Expensive

Sheraton Krabi Beach Resort
155 Moo 2, Wat Khlong Muang
Tel: 0-7562 8000
www.sheraton.com/krabi
Set directly on Khlong Muang beach, this large resort is spread across a sprawling area but fits in so well with the natural surroundings that it appears smaller. Beautiful sea-facing pool and all the facilities expected of a Sheraton hotel, including a spa and restaurants. (246 rooms)

Hat Railay East

Moderate–Expensive

Sunrise Tropical Resort
Hat Railay East
Tel: 0-7562 2599
www.sunrisetropical.com
Located on Railay East, this place is blessed with dramatic morning sunrises. Prettier Railay West beach is only a 5-minute walk away. Rooms have been stylishly refurbished with wooden floors, and the resort pool is surrounded by palm trees and faces towering limestone pinnacles. Restaurant, internet and massage facilities on site. (28 rooms)

Hat Railay West

Expensive

Railay Village Resort
Hat Railay West
Tel: 0-7562 2578
www.railayvillagekrabi.com
Perfectly situated for sunsets on scenic Railay

West beach, but be warned that this popular beach gets very crowded. This newly refurbished hotel offers a choice of bungalows that are set close to the beach and among coconut groves. Swimming pool, restaurant and tour desk on site. (48 rooms)

Moderate–Expensive

Railay Bay Resort & Spa
Hat Railay West
Tel: 0-7562 2570
www.krabi-railaybay.com
The only resort on Railay Bay to spread from Railay West beach and inland all the way to Railay East beach. A variety of cottages, beachside restaurant and swimming pool on site, plus the Sunset Bar on Railay West where you can have a drink while watching the sun set. (126 rooms)

Moderate

Sand Sea Resort
Hat Railay West
Tel: 0-7562 2574
www.krabisandsea.com
A pleasant hotel with a variety of room styles (and prices). Restaurant serving Thai and Western food, beachfront swimming pool, minimart and internet facilities on site. (42 rooms)

Hat Tham Phra Nang

Luxury

Rayavadee
Hat Tham Phra Nang
Tel: 0-7562 0740
www.rayavadee.com
One of the most exclusive resorts in Krabi Province, and lavishly praised by just about everyone who visits. Tucked away in a headland alongside spectacular Tham Phra Nang beach on one side and the more prosaic Railay East beach on the other. The well-designed villas all but melt into the surroundings. Includes several restaurants and a spa. Very expensive, but a truly magical location. (103 rooms)

Hat Ton Sai

Budget

Krabi Mountain View Resort
Ao Ton Sai
Tel: 0-7562 2610
www.krabidir.com/krmtnviewres
Pleasant bungalow-style huts situated between the cliffs and the waters of Ton Sai beach, with Railay West just a 10-minute walk away at low tide. Rooms are clean and modern, and offer good value for money. The best accommodation on this beach. (46 rooms)

Krabi Town

Moderate

Maritime Park & Spa
1 Th. Tungfah
Tel: 0-7562 0028
www.maritimeparkandspa.com
About 10 minutes' drive from Krabi Town, this is one of the better resorts away from the beaches. Within its tropical-style setting is a large free-form swimming pool. (221 rooms)

Budget

Krabi City Seaview Hotel
77/1 Th. Kongha
Tel: 0-7562 2885
www.krabidir.com/krabicityseaview
Located on the waterfront with good views of Krabi River and just 2 minutes' walk from the pier to the nearby islands. Quite basic, but all rooms have cable TV, air-conditioning and fridge. (29 rooms)

PRICE CATEGORIES

Prices are for a double room without breakfast and taxes:
Luxury = over B8,000
Expensive = B4,000–8,000
Moderate = B2,000–4,000
Budget = under B2,000

KO PHI PHI

Ao Lo Bakao

Expensive

Phi Phi Island Village Resort & Spa
Ao Lo Bakao
Tel: 0-7623 6616
www.ppisland.com
This attractive resort is situated on 800 metres/yds of private beach, perfect for those who wish to get away from it all. Rooms are tastefully appointed, but it is the idyllic location above all else that keeps guests coming back. Three restaurants, two bars and a spa. (104 rooms)

Ao Ton Sai

Moderate

Phi Phi Banyan Villa
Ao Ton Sai
Tel: 0-7561 1233
www.phiphi-hotel.com
If location is everything, then this place, right in the centre of Ao Ton Sai, wins hands down. The beach, restaurants, shops and pier are just 5 minutes' walk away. Rooms are comfortable and have air-conditioning, cable TV and hot water. (40 rooms)

Budget–Moderate

Chao Koh Phi Phi Lodge
Ao Ton Sai
Tel: 0-7562 0800
www.chaokohphiphi.com

Set on the beachfront 2 minutes from the busiest part of Ao Ton Sai. Rooms are comfortable, with air-conditioning and satellite TV. Facilities include a minimart and a small sea-facing swimming pool. (44 rooms)

Phi Phi Hotel
Ao Ton Sai
Tel: 0-7561 1233
www.phiphi-hotel.com
Smaller and not quite as upmarket as its sister property, Phi Phi Banyan Villa, but sharing the same prime location, this low-rise property has rooms with either sea or mountain views. (64 rooms)

Hat Hin Khom

Moderate

Bayview Resort
Hat Hin Khom
Tel: 0-2677 6240
www.phiphibayview.com
Split-level bungalows set on a hillside and encircled by a thick tree-filled grove. Restaurant and small pool on site. Rooms enjoy panoramic views across the sea towards Ko Phi Phi Ley. (70 rooms)

Budget

Phi Phi Andaman Resort
1 Moo 7, Hat Hin Khom
Tel: 0-7560 1111
www.krabidir.com/ppandamanresort

Located a 10-minute walk from Ton Sai pier and set in a tropical garden backing onto the beach. Mix of bungalows with fan or air-conditioning and basic white walls and tiled floors. All pleasant, bright and spotlessly clean. One of the better options for accommodation in this price range. (50 rooms)

Hat Laem Thong

Luxury

Zeavola Resort
Hat Laem Thong
Tel: 0-7562 7000
www.zeavola.com
Situated on Ko Phi Phi Don's far northern tip. The oversized suites – ranging from the cheaper Village Suites to the mid-range Garden and Hillside ones to the more expensive Beachfront Suites – are housed in wooden thatched bungalows, each with separate bedroom and living room. Huge picture windows face either the gardens or the beach. Two restaurants, a spa and pool. Its isolation will suit those looking for a romantic getaway. (52 rooms)

Expensive

Holiday Inn Resort
Hat Laem Thong
Tel: 0-7562 7300

www.phiphi.holidayinn.com
Nice resort, albeit a little isolated from the island's thriving centre at Ao Ton Sai. Its seclusion, however, makes it a popular location for honeymooners. If a quiet island resort is what you are after, then this is the perfect hideaway. All the usual facilities expected of a high-end resort, including a large free-form pool and a good selection of restaurants and bars on site. (80 rooms)

Hat Yao

Moderate

Paradise Resort
Hat Yao
Mobile tel: 08-1968 3982
www.paradiseresort.co.th
Set on relatively quiet Hat Yao beach, this place is accessed by a 10-minute boat ride from Ao Ton Sai. Variety of rooms, from cheaper fan-cooled ones to more expensive air-conditioned options. Restaurant, bar and internet access. (25 rooms)

KO LANTA

Ao Kantiang

Luxury

Pimalai Resort and Spa
Ao Kan Tiang
Tel: 0-7560 7999
www.pimalai.com
A luxurious five-star resort that cleverly mixes Thai and contemporary styling. Highly rated spa, plus restaurants, dive centre, infinity-edge pool and direct access to a stunning 900-metre (2,950ft) beachfront. Undeniably exclusive, but a bit far out if you like to be close to the busier beaches.

If it's isolation you crave, this is the perfect place to chill out. (79 rooms and 39 villas)

Ao Phra Ae

Luxury

Layana Resort and Spa
Ao Phra Ae
Tel: 0-7560 7100
www.layanaresort.com
Warm and welcoming boutique resort more suited to couples than families. Both the swimming pool and oversized jacuzzi have the sea in front and a

backdrop of forested hills behind. All rooms are equipped with broadband and internet connection. (50 rooms)

Expensive

Lanta Sand Resort & Spa
Ao Phra Ae
Tel: 0-7568 4633
www.lantasand.com
Everything spells tropical at this lovely resort, with its swimming pool, spa and guest rooms tucked in between luscious greenery and coconut palms. All rooms have open-air,

natural garden bathrooms. (48 rooms)

Moderate

Lanta Garden Hill Resort
38/2 Moo 2, Ao Phra Ae
Tel: 0-2673 0966
www.lantagardenhill.com
There is a variety of

ABOVE: poolside at the Pimalai Resort, Ao Kantiang.

accommodation options available at this resort, from standard to de luxe bungalows. On a hillside about 300 metres (900ft) from the beach. (60 rooms)

Hat Khlong Dao

Expensive

Twin Lotus Resort & Spa
Hat Khlong Dao
Tel: 0-7560 7000
www.twinlotusresort.com
Minimalist and ultra-modern both inside and out, this resort uses clever lighting and solid blocks of colour to good effect throughout the guest rooms, spa and reception. (78 rooms)

Budget

Southern Lanta Resort
Hat Khlong Dao
Tel: 0-7568 4174–7
www.southernlanta.com
Largest of the resorts on Hat Khlong Dao. Each bungalow has its own private balcony and garden area. Not the most modern compared to some of the island's other developments, but prices are keen and there is a range of facilities. (100 rooms)

Hat Khlong Nin

Luxury

Langham Place Eco Resort
Hat Khlong Nin
Tel: 0-7560 7400
www.krabi.langhamplacehotels.com
This luxury resort is situated at the foot of a series of hills and overlooking a lovely beach; it has four swimming pools, including one that is built into the sea. Complete range of facilities and even a mini cinema. (163 rooms)

Expensive

Sri Lanta
Hat Khlong Nin
Tel: 0-7569 7288
www.srilanta.com
Well-regarded beachside property with charming thatch-roofed bungalows that are simple yet stylish. Its restaurant is built almost completely from wood and grass and supported by tree-trunks. (49 rooms)

Budget

The Narima
99 Moo 5, Hat Khlong Nin
Tel: 0-7560 7700
www.narima-lanta.com
Three rows of sea-facing wooden huts, all with air-conditioning, as well as fans and mosquito nets should you choose to open the windows and listen to the ocean during the night. Good value. (32 rooms)

DEEP SOUTH

Hat Chang Lang

Expensive

Anantara Si Kao Resort & Spa
Hat Pak Meng, Th. Changlang
Tel: 0-7520 5888
www.anantara.com
The only international-class hotel in the area, the Anantara took over from Amari (which ran this property for many years) and added its own distinctive gloss. Expect excellent design, superb food and facilities, and service that is good even by Thai standards. (138 rooms)

Hat Yai

Moderate

Novotel Hat Yai Centara
3 Th. Sanehanusorn
Tel: 0-7435 2222
www.novotel.com
Located in the heart of Hat Yai, above the Central Department Store, this imposing hotel, easily the best in town, offers comfortable rooms plus the usual four-star facilities. (200 rooms)

Budget

New Season Hotel
106 Th. Prachathipat
Tel: 0-7435 2888
Relatively small but clean and well-designed budget hotel. Excellent location in downtown Hat Yai. Good value for money. (119 rooms)

Ko Hai

Moderate

CoCo Cottage
Ko Hai. Tel: 0-7521 2375
www.coco-cottage.com
Features Balinese-style wooden bungalows with open-air bathrooms, steps from the beach. Rooms with air-conditioning or fan available. (28 rooms)

Fantasy Resort
Ko Hai. Tel: 0-7521 5923
www.kohhai.com
Features spacious air-conditioned bungalows and suites at a range of prices. The resort also provides a decent variety of services, including a pool, internet access, a spa and movie nights at weekends. (40 rooms)

Ko Kradan

Budget

Koh Kradan Paradise Beach
Ko Kradan. Tel: 0-7521 1391
www.kradanisland.com
This resort, the only accommodation on Ko Kradan, is rather basic. Its setting, however, on Hat Na Ko beach is idyllic. (100 rooms)

Ko Libong

Budget

Libong Nature Beach Resort
Ko Libong. Tel: 08-1915 7537
Email: natureresorts@thailand.com
Located on the secluded western shore of Ko Libong, it offers no-frills accommodation on a nice palm-lined beach. Best known for its nature-oriented tours. (15 rooms)

Ko Lipe

Budget

Lee Pae Resort
Ao Pattaya, Ko Lipe
Tel: 0-7472 4336

Located in the middle of Pattaya beach, this operation is one of the biggest on the island and offers several comfy bungalows in a shady wooded area. (70 rooms)

Moderate

BP Samila Beach Hotel & Resort
8 Th. Ratchadamnoen
Tel: 0-7444 0222
www.bphotelsgroup.com
This grand-looking hotel is

PRICE CATEGORIES

Prices are for a double room without breakfast and taxes:
Luxury = over B8,000
Expensive = B4,000–8,000
Moderate = B2,000–4,000
Budget = under B2,000

located at the end of Hat Samila, near the famous mermaid statue. It offers clean, comfy rooms, the more expensive of which have views over the Gulf of Thailand. There's a pool, fitness centre, spa and restaurants. (228 rooms)

Ko Muk
Budget
Koh Mook Charlie Beach Resort
Ko Mook. Tel: 0-7520 3281
www.kohmook.com
This immensely popular resort, the largest on Hat Farang, has nice rooms at a range of prices, internet access, movie screenings, and a wonderful location among the cliffs and coconut trees. Good restaurant on site. (80 rooms)

Ko Sukorn
Budget
Sukorn Beach Bungalows
Tel: 0-7521 1457

www.sukorn-island-trang.com
A low-key resort with a family atmosphere. Fan-cooled as well as air-conditioned rooms. (20 rooms)

Ko Tarutao
Very basic lodgings on **Ao Phante Malacca** and **Ao Taloh Wow** are available from November to May. Book with the park authorities on the island (tel: 0-7478 3485). Electricity is available only from 6pm to 6am.

Nakhon Si Thammarat
Budget
Grand Park Hotel
1204/79 Th. Phanakorn, Nakhon Si Thammarat
Tel: 0-7531 7666–73
The pickings are slim in this town, so this is as good as it gets. A bit sterile, but clean and comfortable and located just outside the heart of downtown Nakhon

Si Thammarat. Rooms in the new building are slightly more expensive but are larger and more modern. (164 rooms)

Satun Town
Budget
Pinnacle Tarutao Hotel
43 Th. Satun Thani
Tel: 0-7471 1607–8
www.pinnaclehotels.com
Satun's only "upmarket" hotel lies slightly outside the town centre, but is a comfortable place to stay. The downtown hotels are really not worth considering. (108 rooms)

Songkhla
Expensive
Pavilion Songkhla Hotel
17 Th. Platha
Tel: 0-7444 1850–9
www.pavilionhotels.com
One of the taller buildings in Songkhla, the Pavilion is one of only two higher-end hotels in the town. It has the

amenities one would expect in a hotel of this category, as well as a snooker room and Thai massage. (179 rooms)

Trang Town
Moderate
Thumrin Thana Hotel
69/8 Th. Trang Thana
Tel: 0-7521 1211
www.thumrin.co.th
Largely oriented towards business travellers, this is Trang's poshest hotel. It has a convenient downtown location and all the amenities one would expect from a hotel of this size. Internet bookings are a steal and can dip into the budget range. (289 rooms)

Trang's Islands
The island hotels, except on Ko Hai, are simple budget affairs with basic facilities (the ones on Ko Hai are in the moderate range). So if it's luxury you want, you should look elsewhere.

CHIANG MAI

Luxury
The Chedi
123 Th. Charoen Prathet
Tel: 0-5325 3333
www.ghmhotels.com
This is an unrivalled haven of luxury right in the middle of town. Expect clean lines and a modern minimalist feel, with muted tones and plenty of wood. Large balconies, open-air bathrooms and objets d'art in the rooms add to the ambience. A stunning lap pool, well-equipped fitness centre and a restaurant serving Thai and inventive Asian-Western cuisine make it hard to leave this property. (84 rooms)
The Four Seasons Chiang Mai
Th. Mae Rim-Samoeng Kao
Tel: 0-5329 8181
www.fourseasons.com
Chiang Mai's first luxury property, located north of the city in Mae Rim district, is still one of Chiang Mai's premier resorts. Its

capacious suites and 2- and 3-bedroom residences are surrounded by rice terraces and gardens. Its Lanna Spa is a masterpiece of contemporary Lanna architecture. Also features a highly regarded cookery school in addition to the usual facilities one would expect from a resort of this class. (64 rooms)
Mandarin Oriental Dhara Dhevi
51/4 Th. Chiang Mai-San Kamphaeng. Tel: 0-5388 8888
www.mandarinoriental.com
This huge complex set in the eastern outskirts of Chiang Mai is a sight to behold. In addition to the replicas of famous Buddhist temples, the public areas are filled with beautiful artworks, including Chiang Mai silverwork and Burmese paintings, from the owner's private collection. The teak-floored suites and villas are clustered around ponds and

are tastefully appointed. (123 villas)
The Rachamankha
6 Th. Ratchamankha
Tel: 0-5390 4111
www.rachamankha.com
Partially hidden in a lane behind Wat Phra Singh, the Rachamankha is the brainchild of local architect Ongard Satrabhandhu and interior designer Rooj Changtrakul. Based on the design of a Buddhist monastery in the ancient Lanna kingdom, expect simple, pared down elegance, both in the rooms and the public spaces. (24 rooms)

Expensive
Amari Rincome Hotel
1 Th. Nimanhemin
Tel: 0-5322 1130
www.amari.com
One of the first hotels built on Thanon Huay Kaew, the Amari has been a comfortable and reliable

business hotel for over a decade. On the premises is a good Italian restaurant called La Gritta, plus coffee shop and bar, a swimming pool and tennis court. Soi 1, Thanon Nimanhemin, behind the hotel, is lined with art galleries, designer boutiques, cafés and bars. Within walking distance of Kad Suan Kaew, the city's second-largest shopping mall. (162 rooms)
dusitD2
100–101 Th. Chang Khlan
Tel: 0-5399 9999
www.d2hotels.com
Stylish contemporary-style hotel with chic and functional rooms with

plasma-screen TVs and high-speed internet. Off the lobby, the Moxie restaurant is one of city's best hotel eateries. The Chiang Mai Night Bazaar is only a few steps away. (131 rooms)

Tamarind Village
50/1 Th. Ratchadamnoen
Tel: 0-5341 8898
www.tamarindvillage.com
Designed by the same people responsible for the Rachamankha, the Tamarind Village takes its name from the tamarind orchard that occupied the land before the hotel was built. In fact a large 200-year-old tamarind tree has been left intact in one courtyard. The hotel is set well away from the busy intersection known as Klang Wiang (walled city centre),

and offers a quiet and elegant retreat from city traffic. (45 rooms)

Moderate

Chiang Mai Plaza Hotel
92 Th. Si Donchai
Tel: 0-5390 3161
www.cnxplaza.com
Five minutes' walk from the Chiang Mai Night Bazaar, this multi-storey hotel has a relaxing ambience despite its size. The large lobby features a live northern Thai musical ensemble each evening. Facilities include two restaurants (one Thai, one Chinese), a lobby bar, a large swimming pool, and a fitness centre with wood-panelled saunas. (450 rooms)

Karinthip Village
50/2 Th. Chang Moi Kao

Tel: 0-5323 5414
www.karinthipvillage.com
Located on a *soi* off busy Thanon Chang Moi, which leads to Chiang Mai's oldest market as well as the city's small Chinatown, Karinthip Village occupies a quiet landscaped corner opposite Wat Chomphu. The three guest wings contain identically sized rooms, differentiated by decor: Chinese, Thai or colonial. A sizeable swimming pool offers the only recreation. The old city quadrangle is only a short walk away. (64 rooms)

Budget

Galare Guest House
7/1 Soi 2, Th. Charoen Prathet
Tel: 0-5381 8887
www.galare.com

A well-managed place that has spacious rooms, the Galare is popular with repeat visitors for its Ping River location and proximity to the Chiang Mai Night Bazaar. The traffic at nearby Saphan Nawarat can be a bit noisy. Discounts are readily available in the low season. (35 rooms)

Lotus Pang Suan Kaew Hotel
99/4 Th. Huay Kaew
Tel: 0-5322 4444
www.lotuspangsuankaew.com
Tucked away behind Kad Suan Kaew shopping centre. Has extensive facilities for this price range: three restaurants, coffee shop, bar, fitness centre, nightclub, massage centre, tennis courts and swimming pool. (420 rooms)

CHIANG RAI AND THE EAST

Chiang Rai

Expensive

Dusit Island Resort
1129 Th. Kraisorasit
Tel: 0-5371 5777
www.dusit.com
This multi-storey resort offers large, comfortable rooms in a quiet garden setting on a large island in the Kok River to the northwest of the town centre. It's a bit isolated for those who don't have their own vehicle, but the staff can arrange transport at hotel rates. Facilities include a swimming pool, a spa and four restaurants, including the city's only steakhouse. (271 rooms)

The Legend of Chiang Rai
124/15 Ko Loy. Tel: 0-5391 0400
www.thelegend-chiangrai.com
The Legend brings a touch of elegance to Chiang Rai's hotel scene. The resort sits on nicely landscaped grounds featuring small canals and ponds. Individual garden bungalows, decorated with Lanna-inspired furniture, and with semi-outdoor bathrooms, a sitting room and a spacious veranda. A

highlight is the infinity swimming pool overlooking the Kok River. (78 rooms)

Moderate

Wangcome Hotel
869/90 Th. Premawiphat
Tel: 0-5371 1000
www.wangcome.com
A middle-class mainstay in the city's hotel scene, the Wangcome offers comfortable air-con rooms, a swimming pool, an international restaurant, a coffee shop and a karaoke bar. (200 rooms)

Wiang Inn
893 Th. Phahonyothin
Tel: 0-5371 1533
www.wianginn.com
The hotel is within walking distance of the city's night bazaar. Rooms are large and comfortable, though not luxurious. On the premises are a coffee shop with Thai, Chinese and European cuisines. (260 rooms)

Budget

Golden Triangle Inn
590/2 Th. Phahonyothin
Tel: 0-5371 3981
Sprawling over tropically landscaped grounds, the rooms are nicely trimmed

with wood and bamboo. Unlike most Thai hotels, the rooms don't come with TVs, a blessing for those seeking peace and quiet. A coffee shop and restaurant round out the offerings. Good value. (39 rooms)

Naga Hill Resort
83 Mu 8, Ban Pha-U
Tel: 0-8181-89684
www.nagahill.com
On a hilltop behind Rajabhat University, Naga Hill is owned by a French journalist and his Thai-German partner, who have designed and built a handful of rustic yet tasteful bungalows amid tropical gardens. Each features an outdoor bathroom, ceiling fan and mosquito net. A 25-metre (82ft) swimming pool enhances the value considerably. Wi-fi access throughout. (9 rooms)

Chiang Saen

Moderate

De River Boutique Resort
455 Moo 1, Th. Sop Ruak
Tel: 0-5378 4466
www.deriverresort.com
With just 18 tastefully designed rooms (all with

river views), this hotel is located between Chiang Saen and Sop Ruak. Overlooking the Mekong and only a short distance from both the historical sights of Chiang Saen and the natural beauty of the Golden Triangle. The hotel restaurant serves a mix of northern and central Thai delights. (18 rooms)

Budget

Chiang Saen Guest House
45/2 Th. Sop Ruak
Tel: 0-5365 0196
Email: csgsthse@hotmail.com
Chiang Saen's most popular backpacker establishment

PRICE CATEGORIES

Prices are for a double room without breakfast and taxes:
Luxury = over B8,000
Expensive = B4,000–8,000
Moderate = B2,000–4,000
Budget = under B2,000

overlooks the Mekong River. It's been around for years and the family that runs the place is friendly and helpful. Accommodation is basic A-frame bungalows and a few rooms with fan and hot water. (12 rooms)

Chiang Saen River Hill Hotel
714 Moo 3, Th. Sukhapibansai 2
Tel: 0-5365 0826
www.chiangsaenriverhill.net
Slightly away from the main town, but still within easy walking distance of all the main sights, this well-appointed hotel is certainly not the usual Thai budget digs. Rooms are nicely decorated with northern Thai handicrafts and *sah* paper umbrellas hanging on the walls. (63 rooms)

Doi Ang Khang

Moderate
Angkhang Nature Resort
1/1 Moo 5, Baan Khum
Tel: 0-5345 0110
www.amari.com/angkhang
Situated close to the Royal Agricultural Research Project (RARP) high up in the hills overlooking Fang, this lovely resort consists of 74 luxury teak pavilions, all with their own balconies. The large lobby is perfect for relaxing after a day's trekking in the surrounding countryside. Good restaurant. (74 rooms)

Budget
Angkhang Villa
2 Moo 5, Baan Khum
Tel: 0-5345 0010
Email: pimpaka_h@hotmail.com
With a number of solid, A-frame bungalows strung

out across the hillside, the Angkhang Villa fits snugly and unobtrusively into its environment. Well located for exploring the nearby hill-tribe villages. Rooms are basic, with large, comfortable beds and TV. (12 rooms)

Mae Sai

Budget
Mae Sai Guest House
Th. Wiengpangkam
Tel: 0-5373 2021
There are a number of guesthouses next to the Sai River and most of them are good, but the Mae Sai Guest House is a winner. The attractive bungalows are right on the banks of the river, so close to Myanmar that you can actually watch the women washing clothes on the opposite bank each morning. (14 rooms)
Wang Thong Hotel
299 Th. Paholyothin
Tel: 0-5373 3389
One of Mae Sai's oldest hotels is still a good standby for anyone not wishing to make their way down to the river. It's situated just a few metres from the bridge and a stroll into Myanmar. The swimming pool is a welcome addition and the rooms facing the border afford great views. (149 rooms)

Mae Salong

Moderate
Mae Salong Flower Hill Resort
779 Moo 1, Th. Doi Mae Salong
Tel: 0-5376 5496
www.maesalongflowerhills.com

Located about 2km (1 mile) east of the main town on Highway 1130, this resort overlooks a stunning valley filled with tea fields. Beautifully manicured gardens with a riot of flowers cover the slopes around the property. Facilities include a pool and restaurant. Good deals on rooms in the low season.

Budget
Khum Nai Phol Resort
58 Moo 1, Th. Doi Mae Salong
Tel: 0-5376 5001
Slightly south of town on the road to Thaton, the Khum Nai Phol has a mix of wooden bungalows and standard hotel rooms. The cosy bungalows are much nicer and overlook a tea plantation. (12 bungalows)
Mae Salong Villa
5 Moo 1, Th. Doi Mae Salong
Tel: 0-5376 5114
Email: maesalongvilla@thaimail.com
As far as views go, this is the pick of the bunch in Mae Salong. Wooden bungalows, all with huge picture windows and a balcony overlooking the hillside to the north. Rooms are well furnished and include satellite TV, fridge and hot-water bathrooms, a must up here in the wintertime. (52 rooms)

Nan

Budget
The City Park Hotel
99 Th. Yantrakitkosol
Tel: 0-5474 1343
www.thecityparkhotel.com
Slightly away from the centre of town, but nevertheless a worthwhile option. Amenities here include an outdoor swimming pool and tennis court. Attractively furnished rooms, all air-conditioned, with satellite TV. (129 rooms)
Dhevaraj Hotel
466 Th. Sumonthavaraj
Tel: 0-5475 1577
Email: inq@dhevarajhotel.com
Nan's best hotel, this longstanding favourite was renovated recently. Good value for the rates you pay. All rooms have cable TV, air-

conditioning and minibar. Other facilities include a pool and sauna. Breakfast is included in the rate.

Phayao

Budget
Gateway Hotel
7/36 Th. Pratu Klong 2
Tel: 0-5441 1333-5
Email: phayaogateway@hotmail.com
A standard Thai provincial hotel, but nevertheless the best in town, the Gateway is situated quite close to Phayao's lovely lake. All rooms have attached bathroom, TV and air-conditioning. (108 rooms)

Phrae

Budget
Maeyom Palace
181/6 Th. Yantrakit Koson
Tel: 0-5452 1028
Email: wccphrae@hotmail.com
This well-run and friendly place is easily Phrae's top hotel. All rooms are air-conditioned with satellite TV and minibar. Other amenities include an attractive pool and two restaurants. (104 rooms)
Nakhon Phrae Tower
3 Th. Muang Hit
Tel: 0-5452 1321
Email: nakornphrae@yahoo.com
A large tower block that looks quite ugly, but the rooms are well furnished and rather comfortable. Most rooms are air-conditioned, but they do have a few fan-cooled rooms available. (140 rooms)

Sop Ruak

Luxury
Anantara Golden Triangle
229 Moo 1, Mae Sai–Chiang Saen Road
Tel: 0-5378 4084
www.anantara.com
One of the north's best

PRICE CATEGORIES

Prices are for a double room without breakfast and taxes:
Luxury = over B8,000
Expensive = B4,000–8,000
Moderate = B2,000–4,000
Budget = under B2,000

BELOW: luxury at the Anantara Golden Triangle.

hotels, the Anantara boasts elegance, style and superb service. Every detail is a reminder of the region you're in, from carved wooden panels and murals in the corridors to beautiful silk and teak furnishings in the

bedrooms. The rooms are spacious, and offer satellite TV, minibar and glass-walled bathrooms. The infinity pool set amidst a bamboo forest is breathtaking. Also runs its own elephant camp on site. (77 rooms)

Moderate

The Imperial Golden Triangle
222 Golden Triangle
Tel: 0-5378 4001
www.imperialhotels.com
The Golden Triangle's original luxury hotel, but it

doesn't reach the standards of its close neighbour, the Anantara. Spacious rooms with great views, plus a pool, massage centre, jogging track, restaurant and beautifully landscaped gardens. (73 rooms)

SUKHOTHAI AND SURROUNDINGS

Kamphaeng Phet

Budget

Chakungrao Riverview Hotel
149 Th. Tesa 1
Tel: 0-5571 4900
www.chakungraoriverview.com
Kamphaeng Phet's top hotel, recently renovated and upgraded, offers exceptional value. Situated on the Ping River, the Chakungrao's amenities include a small business centre in the lobby area, karaoke lounge and spa. Thai-style furnishings lend an authentic local touch to the spacious bedrooms.
(115 rooms)

Three J Guest House
79 Th. Rajwithee
Tel: 0-5571 3129.
Email: threejguesthouse@yahoo.com
Well located just to the south of the historical park, these bungalows are well maintained. Few facilities, but the owner is a mine of information. It's possible to hire a bicycle to explore the temple ruins.
(12 bungalows)

Phitsanulok

Moderate

Grand Riverside Hotel
Th. Phra Ruang
Tel: 0-5524-8333
www.tgrhotel.com.
As the name suggests, the location on the Nan River makes this a good choice, and some of the rooms have great views. It's a new seven-storey building with a spa, and the staff do their best. (79 rooms)

La Paloma Hotel
103/8 Th. Sithamatraipidok
Tel: 0-5521 7930
A large hotel popular with business travellers, the six-storey La Paloma features plain but comfortable rooms and a 24-hour coffee shop. (250 rooms)

Budget

Lithai Guest House
73/1–5 Th. Phayalithai
Tel: 0-5521 9626
Looking more like an apartment block than a guesthouse, the Lithai offers a range of accommodation spread over three

floors. Rates vary depending on whether the rooms have air-conditioning, mini-fridge or TV. (60 rooms)

Sukhothai

Expensive

Tharaburi Resort
113 Th. Srisomboon
Tel: 0-5569 7132
www.tharaburiresort.com
Stands out because it is Sukhothai's most expensive resort. Chic, stylish and decorated with Thai crafts, silks and teakwood, expect spacious villas set amid gardens, a swimming pool and a tour desk. Conveniently located close to the Sukhothai Historical Park. (12 rooms)

Moderate

Pailyn Sukhothai Hotel
Old Th. Sukhothai
Tel: 0-5561 3310–2
www.pailynhotel.com
Popular with tour groups, this large hotel stands roughly halfway between the Sukhothai National Historical Park and the New Town. Features include good-

sized, comfortable rooms, a restaurant, coffee shop and fitness centre. (230 rooms)

Budget

Ban Thai
38 Th. Prawet Nakhon
Tel: 0-5561 0163
Email: guesthouse_banthai@yahoo.com
The family-owned Ban Thai is one of the most popular guesthouses in Sukhothai because of its convenient location near the town centre and bus stop for Old Sukhothai. Expanded over the years to include a choice of rooms in a motel-like building as well as rustic bungalows set around a garden. Friendly service, a good open-air restaurant and useful travel advice from the Belgian owner add further value. (16 rooms)

MAE HONG SON AND THE NORTHWEST

Mae Hong Son

Moderate

Fern Resort
64 Moo 10, Tambon Pha Bong
Tel: 0-5368 6110
www.fernresort.info
About 7km (4 miles) south of town off Route 108, the environmentally friendly Fern Resort has 30 wooden bungalows inspired by traditional Shan architecture and spread out over landscaped grounds.

Walking trails link the resort with national parklands. Facilities include a swimming pool and a large open-air restaurant serving Thai and local specialities. Shuttle vans into town and to the airport and bus station are free. (30 rooms)

Imperial Tara Mae Hong Son Hotel
149 Moo 8, Pang Moo
Tel: 0-5368 4444
www.imperialhotels.com
Part of the Imperial chain of

mid-range hotels, this hotel is popular with tour groups and visiting Thais. Rooms are trimmed with wood and bamboo in a nod to local architecture but are otherwise utilitarian. Restaurant, pool and the usual facilities. (208 rooms)

Budget

The Dai
158 Toongkongmoo Village
Tel: 0-5361 3964
www.the-dai.com

Owned by a Shan family proud of its ethnic roots, The Dai is a lovely property that offers several Shan-style houses spread across lushly landscaped grounds.

Contained within the houses are spacious rooms warmly decorated with bamboo-thatched walls and wood trim. (11 rooms)

Mae Sariang

Budget

Mitaree Garden House Resort
34/1 Th. Wiang Mai
Tel: 0-5368 1109
Email: pakinsit@mitareehotel.com
This is the newer, more comfortable sister to the long-standing Mitaree Guest House. The wooden bungalows are all air-conditioned with satellite TV, and hot water in the bathrooms. Located away from the older part of town and close to the main post office.

River House Resort
6/1 Moo 2, Th. Laeng Phanit
Tel: 0-5368 3066
www.riverhousehotels.com
Modern three-storey hotel. Upstairs rooms are air-conditioned and have balconies with views of the tranquil Yuam River. A few fan rooms on the ground floor overlook the garden and river. Ask for a riverside room. (42 rooms)

Mae Sot

Moderate

Centara Mae Sot Hill Hotel
100 Asia Hwy
Tel: 0-5553 2601

www.centarahotels.com
Just outside of town on a highway bypass between Tak and the Burmese border, this is Mae Sot's most comfortable accommodation. Rooms are spacious and well appointed. Facilities include a lakeside Thai restaurant, a coffee shop with Thai, Chinese and Western cuisines, a cocktail lounge, a swimming pool, a fitness centre and tennis courts. The hotel also provides a free shuttle bus to town and to the Moei River border market. (120 rooms)

Budget

Ban Thai Guest House
740 Th. Intharakhiri
Tel: 0-5553 1590
Email: banthai_mth@hotmail.com
A collection of old houses serves as a guesthouse that has become popular with foreign volunteers working with Burmese refugees in the area. Rooms are clean and quiet. Several inexpensive Thai restaurants can be found within walking distance. (20 rooms)

Pai

Expensive

Pai River Corner
94 Moo 3, Wiang Tai
Tel/Fax: 0-5369 9049
www.pairivercorner.com
Scenically located on a bend in the Pai River and

close to the heart of the tiny town, this hotel offers a selection of tastefully designed air-conditioned apartments with large balconies overlooking tropical gardens. Villa Spa (Room 7), the highlight of the hotel, has its own private jacuzzi. (9 rooms)

Moderate

Baan Krating Pai Resort
119 Th. Wiang Neua
Tel: 0-5369 8255
www.baankrating.com/pai
Well-designed, spacious and comfortable Lanna-style bungalows set amidst rice fields and mountain views make Baan Krating a very popular hotel choice in Pai. (32 rooms)

Belle Villa Resort
113 Moo 6, Th. Huay Poo-Wiang Nua. Tel: 0-5369 8226
www.bellevillaresort.com
Located on a quiet stretch of Pai River, the Belle Villa is one of the nicest hotels in Pai. Bungalows are equipped with cable TV, minibar and well-designed bathrooms – all without forgoing rural Thai charms. Will organise local tours. (26 rooms)

Budget

Pairadise
98 Moo 1, Ban Mae Yen
Mobile tel: 08-9431 3511
www.pairadise.com
Perched on a ridge offering perhaps the best valley and

mountain views of any resort in Pai, this place is a study in efficiency and simplicity. The wooden bungalows are well maintained and have verandas. In the middle of the complex is a spring-fed swimming pond, which is a nice relaxing spot on a warm afternoon. (14 bungalows)

Tak

Moderate

Viang Tak Riverside Hotel
236 Th. Chumphon
Tel: 0-5551 2507
www.viangtakhotel.com
The Ping River works its way lazily past this rather good mid-range provincial hotel. Rooms are airy, clean and comfortable, and the swimming pool offers a quiet place to sit and relax. (144 rooms)

Budget

Suansin Lanna Garden Resort Two
8 Moo 8, Th. Paholyothin
Tel: 0-5589-1333
www.suansin.com
The resort sports a tastefully designed exterior with a blend of Thai and Balinese styles. Set amidst swaying palm trees, it is tucked away in a quiet residential area away from the town centre. Rooms are adequate and comfortable. (74 rooms)

NAKHON RATCHASIMA TO UBON RATCHATHANI

Khao Yai N P

Expensive

Kirimaya
1/3 Moo 6, Th. Thanarat
Tel: 0-4442 6099
www.kirimaya.com
This is one of the plushest hotel options in northeast Thailand. Draws inspiration from African safaris with four luxury tented villas nestled among plantation-style buildings (housing the rooms and suites), all overlooking the lush foliage of the national park. There's

also an infinity pool, spa and golf course. (60 rooms)

Budget

Khao Yai Garden Lodge
Th. Thanarat, Km 7, Pak Chong
Tel: 0-4436 5178/5167
www.khaoyai-garden-lodge.com
Rooms range from fan-cooled to air-conditioned, all with traditional Thai decor and attached bathrooms. Spacious grounds include a bird garden, a 40-year-old tortoise and many botanical wonders. Also has a herbal sauna and a swimming pool

with a waterfall. Offers a range of tours. (35 rooms)

Nakhon Ratchasima

Moderate

Dusit Princess Korat
1137 Th. Suranari
Tel: 0-4425 6629
korat.royalprincess.com
Dusit's mid-priced Royal Princess chain hotel stands at the northeastern edge of town. Large, comfortable rooms are popular with business travellers and tour groups. Chinese restaurant

and a café serving Thai, Chinese and Western dishes. Facilities include a business centre, a fitness centre and a swimming pool. (186 rooms)
Sima Thani Hotel
2112/2 Th. Mittaphap

Tel: 0-4421 3100
www.simathani.com
Well-appointed rooms decorated with Thai and Khmer motifs. Chinese and Thai restaurants plus a café serving Thai, Japanese and Western dishes. A fitness centre, a sauna and a swimming pool fill out the amenities. (265 rooms)

Budget
Korat Hotel
191 Th. Atsadang
Tel: 0-4434 1345
Email: korathotel@hotmail.com
Set back from the road, this pleasant option offers comfy rooms and cheery

welcomes. And if you can't sleep, you can always go for a late-night Chang beer at its Arthur Bar.

Surin

Budget
Surin Majestic Hotel
99 Th. Jit Bamrung
Tel: 0-4471 3980
www.surinmajestichotel.com
This is Surin's best hotel, with clean spacious rooms and a good array of facilities, including free internet, restaurants and swimming pool. Conveniently located near the bus and train

station. (71 rooms)

Ubon Ratchathani

Moderate
Tohsang City Hotel
251 Th. Phalo Chai
Tel: 0-4524 5531
www.tohsang.com
A valiant attempt to create a modern, semi-hip hotel, the Tohsang combines contemporary architecture with local touches such as Isaan silk upholstery. Occupying three buildings on sprawling landscaped grounds, the rooms are comfortable, but there is only one restaurant serving

Thai and international cuisines, and there is no swimming pool or fitness centre. (76 rooms)
Ubonburi Hotel & Resort
1 Th. Si Mongkhon
Tel: 0-4526 6777
www.ubonburihotel.com
The Ubonburi is located south of the city limits in Warin Chamrap District, not far from the Ubon railway station. Tropical gardens enhance the spacious grounds considerably. On hand are a business centre, a swimming pool, a jogging track, a coffee shop and a Chinese restaurant. (110 rooms)

NORTH TO LOEI

Chiang Khan

Budget
Chiang Khan Guest House
282 Th. Chai Khong
Tel: 0-4282 1691
www.thailandunplugged.com
No frills, but clean rooms with shared bathrooms. Restaurant, bicycle rentals and tour desk on site. (14 rooms)

Dan Sai

Moderate
Phunacome Resort
Route 2013, Baan Doen
Tel: 0-4289 2205
www.phunacomeresort.com
Located just 2km (1 mile) from the centre of town, this new addition changes Dan Sai's otherwise basic accommodation

scene. The views are superb, the atmosphere tranquil and the cuisine organic. Nice pool, too. (20 rooms)

Khon Kaen

Moderate
Charoen Thani Princess
260 Th. Si Chan
Tel: 0-4322 0400
www.royalprincess.com
Part of the Dusit hotel group's mid-priced Royal Princess chain, the Charoen Thani courts business travellers, conference attendees and tour groups. Rooms are comfortable. Good range of facilities. (320 rooms)
Sofitel Raja Orchid Khon Kaen
9/9 Th. Prachasamran

Tel: 0-4332 2155
www.sofitel.com
Large, well-appointed rooms in a building with a temple-inspired entry facade. The Sofitel is probably one of the northeast's finest hotels. There is a full range of facilities, including an authentic Chinese restaurant and a German brew pub. The excellent spa offers both Western- and Thai-style treatments (along with a fitness centre, sauna and outdoor swimming pool). (300 rooms)

Budget
Khon Kaen Hotel
43/2 Th. Phimphaseut
Tel: 0-4333 3222
This clean, no-frills hotel with friendly, attentive service is a bargain. The

restaurant serves Thai, Chinese and Western fare. Its Pong Lang Music House is one of the few hotel clubs in the northeast where you can hear authentic Isaan pop and folk music, mixed with occasional Western tunes. (120 rooms)

Loei

Moderate
Loei Palace Hotel
167/4 Th. Charoenrat
Tel: 0-4281 5668
www.amari.com/loeipalace
The most expensive hotel in Loei, and not often busy, the Loei Palace is located in a quiet area outside the town centre and has a nice interior garden. The rooms are clean and comfortable and have cable TV and other

BELOW: a spacious suite at the Sofitel Raja Orchid Khon Kaen.

PRICE CATEGORIES
Prices are for a double room without breakfast and taxes:
Luxury = over B8,000
Expensive = B4,000–8,000
Moderate = B2,000–4,000
Budget = under B2,000

modern conveniences. Other facilities include an outdoor swimming pool, jacuzzi and fitness centre. (156 rooms)

Budget

King Hotel
11/8-12 Th. Chumsai
Tel: 0-4281-1701
Centrally located but quiet; the rooms are clean if

simple. It has been recently renovated, and the attached restaurant is quite good. (50 rooms)

Udon Thani

Moderate

Centara Hotel & Convention Centre
Charoensri Complex, Th. Prajak Silpakorn

Tel: 0-4234 3555
www.centarahotels.com
Attached to the city's largest shopping mall, Charoensri Complex, this decent provincial city hotel offers large, comfortable rooms, a restaurant specialising in northeastern Thai dishes, a Cantonese restaurant, a karaoke lounge and a spa. (234 rooms)

Budget

Udon Hotel
81-89 Th. Mak Khaeng
Tel: 0-4224 8160
Although quite old, regular maintenance and periodic renovations have made this the most popular lower-priced large hotel in Udon. A massage and sauna centre is available for guests. (90 rooms)

ALONG THE MEKONG RIVER

Khong Jiam

Moderate

Tohsang Khong Jiam Resort
68 Moo 7, Baan Huay-Mak-Tay
Tel: 0-4535 1174
www.tohsang.com
With some of the best accommodation this side of Bangkok, the Tohsang presents a selection of beautifully designed rooms in a mix of Thai, Khmer and Balinese styles. All rooms are air-conditioned, have cable TV and overlook the confluence of the Mun and Mekong rivers. Other amenities include a pleasant pool surrounded by tall tropical trees and a riverside spa. (55 rooms)

Budget

Banrimkhong Resort
37 Th. Kaewpradit
Tel: 0-4535 1101
www.banrimkhongresort.com
This lovely little resort with wooden chalets surrounded by pretty gardens is great value for money. There are two chalets overlooking the river and these are the pick of the crop, although all the rooms are clean and comfortable, and feature large wooden balconies – the perfect place to sit back and relax by the Mekong River. (7 chalets)

Mukdahan

Moderate

Ploy Palace Hotel
40 Th. Pitak Phanom Khet
Tel: 0-4263 1111
www.ploypalace.com

This flashy hotel was built when it looked like business would boom in Mukdahan with the opening of the Thai-Lao Friendship Bridge. Unfortunately business did not boom, but it does mean there are some excellent rooms on offer at very reasonable rates. Facilities include a nice large pool, karaoke lounge, traditional massage outlet and a rooftop restaurant. (154 rooms)

Budget

Mukdahan Grand Hotel
78 Th. Songnang Sathit
Tel: 0-4261 2020
An incongruous-looking place in the middle of this quiet low-rise Mekong town. The hotel makes up for it with its great views across the Mekong River to the Lao city of Savannakhet from the rooms on the upper floors. Bedrooms are rather ordinary, but comfortable. Trips to Laos can be arranged by the helpful tour desk. (191 rooms)

Nakhon Phanom

Budget

Nakhon Phanom River View Hotel
9 Th. Sunthorn Wichit
Tel: 0-4252 2333
Nakhon Phanom's most luxurious accommodation is almost 2km (1 mile) south of the town centre and overlooks the Mekong River and neighbouring Laos. All rooms are air-conditioned and attractively decorated with local Isaan furnishings. (122 rooms)

Viewkong Hotel
527 Th. Sunthorn Wichit
Tel: 0-4251 3564
www.mgvhotel.com
At one time the best place in Nakhon Phanom, unfortunately standards have slipped a little recently. Rooms are still adequate, with cable TV and spacious balconies overlooking the river and Laos. If you can get up in time, the Mekong sunrises can be beautiful. (114 rooms)

Nong Khai

Moderate

Nongkhai Grand
589 Moo 5, Th. Nongkhai Poanpisai
Tel: 0-2642-0033
www.nongkhaigrand.com
A favourite with local business-related conferences, the Grand was built during the mini-development boom when the Friendship Bridge was opened in 1994. The decor tends towards chintz and gilt wood in a rather out-dated Thai style, but the rooms are comfortable enough. Restaurant serving Thai, Chinese and Western dishes, a karaoke lounge, a swimming pool and a night-club. (130 rooms)

Budget

Khiang Khong Guest House
541 Th. Rim Khong
Tel: 0-4242 2870
Not as atmospheric as some, but new and clean with private balconies overlooking the Mekong. (14 rooms)

Mut Mee Guest House
1111/4 Th. Kaew Worawut
Tel: 0-4246 0717
www.mutmee.net
This well-known guesthouse sits on the banks of the Mekong, with a view of Laos across the river. The rustic bungalows and wooden houses offer everything from inexpensive dorm beds to comfortable air-con rooms. A pleasant riverside garden restaurant serves some of the best Western food in town. (29 rooms)

That Phanom

Budget

Krisada Rimkhong Resort
90-93 Th. Rimkhong
Tel: 0-4254 0088
Email: ksdresort@thaimail.com
Fairly basic resort to the north of the temple and near the Thai-Lao market has a mix of large fan-cooled and air-conditioned rooms. The owners can organise trips around the area. (50 rooms)

A CTIVITIES

THE ARTS, NIGHTLIFE, SHOPPING, OUTDOOR ACTIVITIES/TOURS AND FESTIVALS

THE ARTS

With pop culture having gained ascendancy over the traditional arts all over Thailand these days, there are few venues in the country that host traditional dance and theatre. Most of these shows are geared towards tourists, and are therefore found in the major tourist centres. The contemporary art scene in Bangkok is more dynamic, with numerous art galleries throughout the city. See also the **Performing Arts** chapter *(page 69)*.

Bangkok

Performing-Arts Venues

Joe Louis Theatre, Suan Lum Night Bazaar, 1875 Th. Rama IV, tel: 0-2252 9683; thaipuppet.com. Responsible for reviving the fading art of *hun lakhon lek*, a unique form of puppetry. Three puppeteers move on stage manipulating expressive marionettes. One show nightly at 8pm.
National Theatre, Th. Ratchini, tel: 0-2224 1342. A grossly underused facility, with few productions or performances ever staged in this grand old theatre. Traditional music and dance performances every month.
Patravadi Theatre, 69/1 Soi Wat Rakhang, Th. Arun Amarin, Thonburi, tel: 0-2412 7287; www.patravaditheatre. com. The nucleus of the contemporary theatre scene, melding traditional and modern dance and drama. Dinner shows on Friday and Saturday at 7.30pm. Also hosts the annual Bangkok Fringe Festival.
Sala Chalerm Krung, 66 Th. Charoen Krung, tel: 0-2222 1854; www.

salachalermkrung.com. Built in 1933, this is one of the country's oldest movie theatres. It was renovated in 1993 and hosts special screenings as well as occasional traditional Thai dance-drama shows for tourists.
Thailand Cultural Centre, Th. Ratchada Phisek, tel: 0-2247 0028; www.thaiculturalcenter.com. Stages everything from pop concerts to works by the Bangkok Opera (www.bangkokopera. com). This is also where the Bangkok Symphony Orchestra plays and where the International Festival of Dance & Music stages its annual show.

Dance and Drama Dinner Shows

For free traditional *khon* dance-drama performances, head to either **Lak Muang** *(see page 114)* or the **Erawan Shrine** *(see page 130)*, whose resident troupes are paid by devotees to dance in thanksgiving when their prayers are answered. Surprisingly, there is nowhere else in Bangkok to view the lavish dance-drama spectacles except in a condensed form at a few restaurants: catering to the average guest's short attention span, they present an hour-long show of bite-sized dance and drama performances after a Thai dinner.
Ruen Thep Room, Silom Village, 286 Th. Silom, tel: 0-2234 4581. A large hall of dark wood and Thai paintings and sculptures creates the right ambience for the nightly hour-long performance at 8.30pm.
Sala Rim Nam, opposite Oriental Hotel, 48 Oriental Avenue, tel: 0-2437 6211. Set on the opposite riverbank, the Oriental's riverside restaurant offers a set dinner menu accompanied by an entertaining dance and drama performance at 8.30pm nightly.

Siam Niramit, 19 Th. Tiamruammit, tel: 0-2649 9222; www.siamniramit.com. A beautifully costumed extravaganza that traverses the country's history and diverse cultures in three acts. Nightly performance at 8pm. Pre-show buffet dinner is served at its restaurant.
Supatra River House, 266 Soi Wat Rakhang, Th. Arun Amarin, Thonburi, tel: 0-2411 0305. This pleasant riverside restaurant in an old renovated Thai house hosts traditional musicians performing classic and contemporary dance. From 8.30am to 9pm on Saturday.

Art Galleries

Most contemporary art on view in the capital is created by home-grown artists, several of whom are gaining significant international exposure. Check the monthly free cultural map *Art Connection*, as well as the *Bangkok Post*, *The Nation* and local magazines for details.
100 Tonson Gallery, 100 Soi Tonson, Th. Ploenchit, tel: 0-2684 1527; www.100tonsongallery.com. Attracts some of the country's best artists and holds high-profile exhibitions that create a lot of media buzz.
Chulalongkorn Art Centre, 7th Floor, Centre of Academic Resources, Chulalongkorn University, Th. Phayathai, tel: 0-2218 2964. Attracts some of the country's most prolific artists, as well as influential foreign creatives.
H Gallery, 201 Soi 12 Th. Sathorn, tel: 0-1310 4428; www.hgallerybkk.com. Located in an old converted wooden school building, H Gallery promotes a stable of young and eclectic artists.
Queen's Gallery, 101 Th. Ratchadamnoen Klang, tel: 0-2281 5360; www.queengallery.org. Five-floor

gallery with a steady exhibition schedule of modern and contemporary art, most of which is locally produced. **Silpakorn University Gallery**, 31 Th. Na Phra Lan, opposite the Grand Palace, tel: 0-623 6120 ext 1418. Thailand's oldest and most prestigious arts university; three galleries display works by students, teachers and visiting artists.
Thavibu Gallery, Suite 308, Silom Galleria, Th. Silom, tel: 0-2266 5454; www.thavibu.com. Promotes a mixed bag of Thai, Vietnamese and Burmese art.

Phuket

Dance and Drama Dinner Shows

There are not very many venues staging traditional dance or theatre, but the few that do are so extravagant they virtually have a monopoly on this form of entertainment.
Phuket Fantasea, 99 Moo 3, Hat Kamala, tel: 0-7638 5000; www.phuket-fantasea.com. Winner of the Thailand Tourism Best Attraction award for three consecutive years, this huge theme park hosts a show featuring acrobatics, dance, drama and even animals and pyrotechnincs. It's more of a Las Vegas-style spectacle than a traditional form of entertainment, but many people find it enjoyable. Daily except Thursday 5.30pm to 11.30pm; showtime at 9pm.
The **Phuket Orchid Garden and Thai Village** (see page 234) is another venue for traditional Thai dance.

Art Galleries

For quality reproduction paintings head to Patong's Thanon Phrachanukhro, which has rows of shops all bearing canvases. All hold similar stock, but the **Manu Art Gallery** (53–57 Th. Phrachanukhro) is one of the few to display prices, and staff are not as pushy. Elsewhere, original pieces can be found at significantly higher prices.
Phuket Art Gallery, 74 Th. Talang, Phuket Town, tel: 0-7625 8388. Located inside a historic Sino-Portuguese house, it has photographs, watercolours and oil paintings featuring both abstract and contemporary work by Thai and Asian artists.

Chiang Mai

Dance and Drama Dinner Shows

Cultural shows where diners sit on the floor and are served a traditional northern-style khantoke dinner are the standard offering. Recommended are:
Khum Khantoke, near Carrefour, off Doi Saket Rd, tel: 0-5330-4121.

A khantoke dinner followed by an excellent performance of Thai classical dance at 7.30pm nightly.
Old Chiang Mai Cultural Centre, 185/3 Th. Wualai, tel: 0-5327 5097. A khantoke dinner is served followed by a hill-tribe dance performance from 7pm to 10pm nightly.

Art Galleries

Galerie Panisa, 189 Th. Mahidon, tel: 0-5320 2779. Large collection of contemporary northern Thai art.
HQ Gallery, 3/31 Th. Samlan, tel: 0-5381 4717. Conveniently located in the Old City, near Wat Phra Sing, the art here hails mainly from Thailand and Myanmar.
La Luna Gallery, 190 Th. Charoenrat, tel: 0-5330 6678; www.lalunagallery.com. At this relatively new gallery near the east bank of the Ping River, the collection includes works from all over Southeast Asia as well as from artists living in Chiang Mai.

NIGHTLIFE

Bangkok

Bangkok's reputation as a centre for sex of every persuasion tends to obscure its other night-time offerings. While there has been no reduction in the number of massage parlours and bars, there has been an upsurge in other activities to meet the needs of the new breed of travellers. Jazz clubs, cool bars and chic clubs are aplenty, attracting young Thais and visitors in droves.
The only downer in Bangkok's nightlife scene is the intrusive Social Order Campaign, which forces establishments to close early and allows the police to raid bars and clubs to conduct random urine tests on patrons for drugs. Be sure to bring along your passport (even a photocopy will do) to be allowed entry at some nightspots.
More sleazy nightlife exists at Patpong (see page 133) and Sukhumvit (see page 134).

Dance Bars and Clubs

Entry fees for clubs in Bangkok were almost unheard of not so very long ago, but in order to keep out the riff-raff (particularly working girls) and keep the crowd chic and trendy, several spots now impose a cover charge.
Bed Supperclub, 26 Sukhumvit Soi 11, tel: 0-2651 3537; www.bedsupperclub.com. This striking,

Two good sources of information on Bangkok nightlife are the Bangkok Post and The Nation, both of which have daily listings sections and weekend entertainment supplements. Other sources of information include websites such as www.bangkokrecorder.com and www.bkmagazine.com, along with weekly magazines like BK, which is found in nearly every coffee shop in town.

elliptically shaped eatery and lounge bar has diners literally eating from beds. Laidback music is played by resident DJs while diners mull over their meal. The other half of the venue operates as a bar/club.
Club Culture, Th. Sri Ayutthaya, tel: 0-2653 7216; www.club-culture-bkk.com. A firm favourite on Bangkok's ever-evolving club scene, this refurbished old Thai theatre venue attracts international DJs with a certain funky edge. Eclectic music ranges from electro, garage and drum 'n' bass to hip hop, house and disco.
Escudo, 4–5/F Dutchess Plaza Sukhumvit 55 (Soi Thonglor), tel: 0-2381 0865. Features a sleek interior that is packed at weekends with Bangkok's fashionable set. The club also hosts one of Bangkok's most popular models' nights, which brings in the heaving crowds.
Q Bar, 34 Sukhumvit Soi 11, tel: 0-2252 3274; www.qbarbangkok.com. Modelled after a New York lounge bar, this dark and seductive two-floored venue hosts some of the city's coolest dance music. The nightly line-up of mix maestros at the bar is well known and the drinks list is impressive, with 50 brands of vodka alone.
Tapas Café & Tapas Room, Soi 4 Th. Silom, tel: 0-2632 0920–1. A true survivor on the city's party scene, this compact two-floor stylish dance bar is packed with beautiful young locals and expats downing jugs of icy margaritas. Choice of two music genres with different DJs on the downstairs deck and above.

Bars and Pubs

Bacchus, 20/6–7 Soi Ruam Rudee, tel: 0-2650 8986. Located in the pleasant restaurant enclave of Ruam Rudee Village, this elegant four-storey wine bar sees a steady flow of creative and media types.
Bull's Head, Soi 33/1 Th. Sukhumvit, tel: 0-2259 4444; www.greatbritishpub.com. Tucked away on a street

dominated by Japanese eateries, this is as English as a pub can be. Attracts a loyal group of regular expats.
Distil, State Tower, Th. Silom, tel: 0-2624 9555; www.thedomebkk.com. Located higher than any of the city's other nightspots, Distil is part of the opulent Dome complex on the 64th floor of the State Tower building. Choose your poison from the 2,000-bottle wine cellar, lie back on the comfy outdoor sofas and enjoy the spectacular panorama.
Face, Soi 38 Th. Sukhumvit, tel: 0-2713 6048–9; www.facebars.com. Part of a small chain of restaurants and bars (branches in Shanghai and Jakarta), Face is located in a Thai villa housing Indian and Thai restaurants. Expect a mellow vibe in the beautiful antique-filled lounge.
Met Bar, Metropolitan Hotel, Th. Sathorn, tel: 0-2625 3399. The Metropolitan is one of the capital's most exclusive yet friendly nightspots. The dark, intimate members-only bar has resident and international DJs.
Sunset Street, Th. Khao San, tel: 0-2282 5823. Halfway up Khao San, Sunset comprises three adjoining bars under the same ownership. Fronting the main street is Sabai Bar, tucked behind is Sanook Bar, and right at the end of the alley is a renovated old house that functions as Kraichitti Museum & Gallery.
Syn Bar, Nai Lert Park Hotel, 2 Th. Withayu, tel: 0-2253 0123. This former hotel lobby bar has been dramatically transformed into a retro-chic cocktail lounge by a New York designer. The stunning bartenders mix up some devilishly tasty cocktails and Martinis.
V9, Sofitel Silom Hotel, Th. Silom, tel: 0-2238 1991. With awesome views from the 37th floor, this stylish wine

bar and restaurant is a fine spot to sip great-value wines.

Live Jazz Venues

Bamboo Bar, Oriental Hotel, 48 Oriental Avenue, tel: 0-2236 0400. The perfect place to soak up jazz, this cosy, intimate bar with its wicker furnishings evokes a bygone era. The band plays laidback jazz classics and backs distinguished guest singers.
Brown Sugar, 231/20 Th. Sarasin, tel: 0-2250 0103. Long established and intimate two-floor jazz bar. The music here is more mod than traditional; expect stellar performances by talented musicians.
Diplomat, Conrad Hotel, 87 Th. Withayu, tel: 0-2690 9999. One of the city's best bars, this is a great warm-up spot for the hotel's other hip hangout spot, the **87 Plus** club. Sit at the circular bar in the middle and be mesmerised by seductive jazz singers.
Saxophone Pub & Restaurant, 3/8 Th. Phayathai, Victory Monument, tel: 0-2246 5472; saxophonepub.com. This lively venue has been packing them in for close to two decades. This two-floor bar hosts great resident bands (at least two a night), who get the whole place jumping and jiving to jazz as well as R&B, soul and funk.

Kathoey Cabaret

For a night of camp fun, see a Vegas-style lip-synching show performed by transsexuals – "lady-boys" – or *kathoey*.
Calypso, Asia Hotel, Th. Phayathai, tel: 0-2216 8937–8; www.calypsocabaret.com. One of the city's best cabarets is staged twice nightly at 8.15pm and 9.45pm. Tickets include a free drink.
Mambo, Washington Square, Th. Sukhumvit, tel: 0-2259 5715. Daily shows at 8.30pm and 10pm.

Gay Venues

A variety of clubs and bars around Silom Soi 2 and Soi 4 cater to gay men. Soi 2 is exclusively gay, while Soi 4 caters to a mixed gay and straight crowd. More sleazy gay pick-up joints with go-go boys are located around Thanon Surawong, Soi Tawan and Duangthawee Plaza.
70's Bar, 231 Soi Sarasin, Lumphini, tel: 0-2253 4433. Retro-chic gay venue along Soi Sarasin. Packed wall-to-wall most weekends with a young crowd moving to thumping rock and pop.
Balcony, 86–88 Soi 4 Th. Silom, tel: 0-2235 5891; www.balconypub.com. Longstanding bar with a mixed gay and straight party crowd that often spills out onto the street.

DJ Station, 8/6–8 Silom Soi 2, tel: 0-2266 4029; www.dj-station.com. Bangkok's most popular gay club, packed throughout the night. The atmosphere is electric and patrons often dress outrageously.
Dick's Café, 894/7–8 Soi Pratuchai, Duangthawee Plaza, tel: 0-2637 0078; www.dickscafe.com. Taped jazz music and paintings by local artists create a mellow mood.
Telephone Pub, 114/11–13 Silom Soi 4, tel: 0-2234 3279; www.telephonepub.com. Popular with expats and locals, this is Bangkok's original gay pub, established back in 1987.

Pattaya

Dance Bars and Clubs

Classroom, Pattayaland Soi 2, tel: 0-3842 0185; www.classroom1.com. A tame go-go bar sans nudity, where girls dress in kinky schoolgirl uniforms. Has a less in-your-face ambience that approaches normality in this town.
Lucifer, Th. Hat Pattaya (Walking Street), tel: 0-3871 0216. A fresh-faced sister establishment to the Bangkok club on Patpong. Opens onto Walking Street with a Latin bar in front drawing a slightly older clientele, while in the back is the pumped up, hell-themed club playing mainstream R&B and hip hop.
Marine, Th. Hat Pattaya (Walking Street), tel: 0-3842 8583. Trashy and loud, this is where everyone gravitates to once Pattaya's girlie bars start winding down. The music is mainly Euro-dance and techno.

Bars and Pubs

Hopf Brew House, 219 Th. Hat Pattaya (Beach Road), tel: 0-3871 0653. Popular microbrewery that sees a steady flow of Pattaya's more respectable types who come for the wood-fired pizzas and Italian and European dishes. In-house band livens things up.
The Kilkenny, Th. Hat Pattaya (Walking Street), tel: 0-3871 1094; www.kilkennypattaya.com. Another of Pattaya's Gaelic watering holes, this pub has a lively atmosphere with quality beers on tap, a daily specials board of pub grub, and all the latest sports on TV.
Mantra Restaurant & Bar, 240 Moo 5, Th. Hat Pattaya, tel: 0-3842 9591; www.mantra-pattaya.com. Sleek new spot that functions both as an eatery (see page 188) and a nightspot. The ambience is evocative of a Bedouin tented camp, with day beds and cosy nooks where you can chill out and

BELOW: Calypso cabaret performer.

order cocktails from its innovative drinks list.

Live Music Venues

The Blues Factory, 131/3 Moo 10, Soi Lucky Star (off Walking Street), www.thebluesfactorypattaya.com. One of Pattaya's best music venues and suitable for all, including families. Features live blues and rock by resident bands.
Hard Rock Café, Th. Hat Pattaya (Beach Road), tel: 0-3842 8755; www.hardrockhotelpattaya.com. This global brand differs little from place to place but it's all good fun. House bands play from 10pm.
The Jazz Pit, 2nd Floor, 255 Th. Pattaya 2 Soi 5, tel: 0-3842 8374; www.pic-kitchen.com. With a logo claiming "It's not for everybody", this music bar has a cool, laidback vibe adjoins the popular PIC Kitchen restaurant. Live bands and jam sessions feature resident bands and overseas acts.

Kathoey Cabaret

Tiffany's, 464 Moo 9, Th. Pattaya 2, tel: 0-3842 1700–5; www.tiffany-show.co.th. Pattaya's most famous *kathoey* or "lady-boy" (transsexual) cabaret routine, with three nightly shows (6pm, 7.30pm and 9pm) in the 1,000-seat auditorium.
Alcazar, 78/14 Th. Pattaya 2, tel: 0-3841 0225; www.alcazar-pattaya.com. Offers a spectacular show in a 1,200-seat venue. Three nightly shows at 6.30pm, 8pm and 9.30pm.

Gay Venues

It's hard to miss Pattaya's main concentration of gay activity, with a big neon sign across the width of Pattayaland Soi 3 flashing "Boyz Town". For more information, visit www.pattayagay.com.
Le Café Royale's Piano Bar, 325/102–9 Pattayaland Soi 3, tel: 0-3842 3515; www.caferoyale-pattaya.com. Smack in the heart of Pattaya's gay nightlife, this piano bar is attached to the hotel of the same name.

Ko Samet

Naga Bungalows, Hat Hin Kok. tel: 0-3864 4034. Perched on a hillside looking down onto the beach, Naga has one of Ko Samet's busiest beach bars, though its popularity ebbs and flows somewhat depending on what its competitor, Silver Sand, is doing at the same time. Daily happy hour and upbeat music.
Silver Sand, Ao Phai, mobile tel:

08-1996 5720. With little else on offer late at night, the beach bar here is usually crammed to the hilt. Sprawling with beach mats, with the decibels cranked high to the ire of those trying to rest at the nearby hotels. Nightly fire-juggling entertainment draws the crowds.
Talebure Bed & Bar, Ao Wong Deuan, mobile tel: 08-1762 3548. This modern minimalist place – with whitewashed timber and dark-wood floors – is a marked difference from your average ramshackle Ko Samet bar hut. Popular with weekending Bangkok trendsters, the bar and resort sit at the southern end of the beach.

Ko Chang

Lek Bar, Kai Bae Beach Resort, Hat Kai Bae, tel: 0-7065 4231. Also known as Nick and Lek's bar, this popular hangout on Hat Kai Bae is run by a Brit and his Thai partner. Has a rustic island look with a garden, nightly live music, a pool table and sports programmes on TV.
Oodies, 7/20 Hat Sai Khao, mobile tel: 08-1835 1271. Situated opposite the beach on Hat Sai Khao, this open-fronted music bar gets busy with a more mature set who gather here in the evenings to enjoy the live blues, folk, rock and Thai music. Thai and French food served here is good too.
Sabay Bar, 7/10 Moo 4, Hat Sai Khao, tel: 0-3955 1098. Whether you come here for sundowners, or later in the night to catch the live band while lying out on beach mats, Sabay is easily the busiest bar on Hai Sai Khao. Nightly fire-juggling shows on the beach keep customers entertained.

Hua Hin

Jungle Juice Bar & Restaurant, 19/1 Th. Selakam, tel: 0-6167 7120. Claiming to be voted "Best Expat Bar" in Hua Hin, this friendly low-key place with a menu of Brit-style pub grub is a regular haunt for local residents.
Monsoon, 62 Th. Naresdamri, tel: 0-325 1062. This charming old two-floor wooden bar sits just behind the seafront. Upstairs is a restaurant, while on the ground floor, tapas and cocktails are served in the evening.
Sasi's Bar, 83/159 Th. Takiab, tel: 0-3251 2488; www.sasi-restaurant.com. The bar sits on the ground floor of an old converted wooden house. Inside is a long bar with sofa seating, while out front there is alfresco seating around a pond.

Ko Samui

Dance Bars and Clubs

Gecko Village, Bo Phut, tel: 0-7724 5554; www.geckosamui.com. This happening beach bar on Bo Phut beach features some of Ko Samui's best DJ-spun dance beats, with international names making guest appearances.
Green Mango, Soi Green Mango, Chaweng, tel: 0-7742 2148. Ko Samui's best-known club, this huge barn of a venue is crammed most nights.
Mint, Soi Green Mango, Chaweng, tel: 0-7089 8726; www.mintbar.com. A loud pumping bar aimed at a dance crowd with a more discerning music sense. Occasionally hosts international DJs.
Reggae Pub, Chaweng Lagoon, tel: 0-7742 2331. A Samui mainstay, it's become more tired than trendy, but still stays busy with cruising single men and the working girls they hope to meet. Mainstream dance sounds with a touch of Bob Marley.

Bars and Pubs

Ark Bar, Chaweng, tel: 0-7742 2047; www.ark-bar.com. On the central stretch of Chaweng beach, this is a bar and restaurant with a mainly Brit clientele. The dance music picks up from early evening onwards.
Sweet Soul Café, Soi Green Mango, Chaweng, tel: 0-7741 3358. The warm-up spot for those moving on to Green Mango just opposite, but with better music and more intimate vibe.
Tropical Murphys, Chaweng, tel: 0-7741 3614; www.tropicalmurphys.com. The island's premier Gaelic haunt is a two-level pub and restaurant with appetising dishes, local and imported beers on tap and live band music.
Unique, Chaweng, tel: 0-7741 3388. A stylish entrant to the bar scene, this split-level minimalist bar is more discerning in its choice of music.

Kathoey Cabaret

Christy's Cabaret, Chaweng, tel: 0-7741 3244. Packing them in every night for the 11pm free show, Christy's is Ko Samui's most popular (but not the only) *kathoey*, or transsexual, cabaret act.

Ko Phangan

Backyard Bar, Hat Rin Nok, tel: 0-7737 5244. A long-established Ko Phangan favourite and the home of the Full Moon Party after-bash, this bar is located up the hill behind Hat Rin Nok. Generally quiet outside its regular parties.

Cactus Club, Hat Rin Nok. Popular mainstay on this beach. It also organises fun day trips to interior waterfalls and nearby beaches.
Drop-In Club, Hat Rin Nok, tel: 0-7737 5444. Located between Cactus Club and Paradise, this long-established bar has the usual beach-mat-and-cushion set-up on the sand, and plays more listener-friendly commercial music.
Pirate's Bar, Ao Chaophao. This bar takes the form of a boat built into the rock face at the end of the beach. To cash in on the Full Moon Party phenomenon, it hosts the monthly Moon Set Party a few days before the real McCoy starts.
Sheesha Bar, Ao Chalok Lam, tel: 0-7737 4161; www.sheesha-bar.com. Positioned near the fishing pier in the sleepy village of Chalok Lam, Sheesha's modern Asian design sets the scene for a relaxing night out with beachfront day beds and hookah pipes to puff away on.

Ko Tao

AC Bar, Hat Sai Ree, tel: 0-7745 6197. One of the island's original night-time hangouts, this is a loud pumped-up dance bar.
Dragon Bar, Mae Hat Centre, tel: 0-7745 6423. One of the island's hippest hangouts. Inventive cocktails, a pool table and DJs playing great music.
Dry Bar, Hat Sai Ree. A chilled-out bar with customers lying on beach mats from sunset until late.
Pure, Hat Sai Ree, tel: 0-7891 2796. Fringed by the large rocks at the southern end of Hat Sai Ree, this lounge bar with glowing red lighting is built over a wooden deck.
Whitening, Mae Hat, tel: 0-7745 6199. Stylish beach bar offers innovative cocktails, cool dance beats and Friday night parties.

Phuket

Phuket, although falling under the same Social Order laws as Bangkok, shows rather less restraint. Bars at some of the quieter beaches may close early, but Patong in particular always has more than its fair share of all-night offerings. The scene in Phuket Town, Karon and Kata beaches is more subdued; elsewhere on the island, it's almost non-existent.

The choice of entertainment in Patong is diverse, with heaving clubs and sex shows on one street contrasting with chic cocktail bars on the next. Most of the scene in Patong takes place along **Thanon Bangla**

and the tiny streets that radiate off it (like Soi Eric, Soi Easy, etc.) all the way past the Thanon Rat-U-Thit junction and also **Soi Sunset**. Most common are raucous "beer bars", simple open-air bars with wooden tables and stools, and hordes of young women in skimpy dress beckoning to customers. Listed here are less sleazy spots more suitable for couples.

Dance Bars and Clubs

Banana Disco, Th. Thawiwong, Patong, tel: 0-7634 0301. This busy venue is air-conditioned and so is never uncomfortable despite the heaving crowds. Plays Top 40 hits and has a large dance floor.
Safari Pub and Disco, 28 Th. Siriat, Patong, tel: 0-7634 1079. Outdoor safari-themed disco surrounded by trees, waterfalls and jungle vines. Several dance floors and intensely loud music. Doesn't shut until daylight.
Tai Pan Disco, Th. Rat-U-Thit, Patong, www.taipan.st. Located on the back road running parallel with Patong beach. Has both DJ music and live bands. Full of young Thai bar girls and may get a bit sleazy, but generally a fun night out.

Bars and Pubs

Angus O'Toole, 516/20 Th. Patak, Karon. Popular Irish bar located at the end of a plaza, slightly off the main road. Shows live sports matches on TV and serves decent pub grub to go with your Guinness.
Dino Bar, Karon, tel: 0-7633 0625. Roadside bar with a rather kitschy Stone Age theme, attached to the Dino Park mini-golf course. Perfect for watching the world go by.
Joe's Downstairs, 223/3 Th.

BELOW: dance bar in Patong, Phuket.

Prabaramee, Patong, tel: 0-7634 4254. Opened in 2006, Joe's is one of Phuket's trendiest drinking spots. Contemporary in design and mostly white, from the long white cocktail bar to the white walls, tables, chairs and silk cushions.
Molly Malone's, 68 Th. Thawiwong, Patong, tel: 0-7629 2774; www.mollymalonesphuket.com. Popular Irish pub at the centre of Patong with both an indoor bar and outside drinking and dining area. Features live music nightly.
Ratri Jazztaurant, Kata, tel: 0-7633 3538; www.ratrijazztaurant.com. Relatively new addition to the Phuket jazz scene, having opened in December 2005. Features an oyster bar with sunset views. Live jazz performed nightly.
Scruffy Murphy's, 5 Th. Bangla, Patong, tel: 0-7629 2590; www.scruffymurphysphuket.com. Another popular Irish pub with a nice party atmosphere and Celtic Rock bands playing nightly. Serves standard but tasty range of pub grub.

Kathoey Cabaret

Simon Cabaret, 8 Th. Sirirat, Patong, tel: 0-7634 2114; www.phuket-simoncabaret.com. Draws in the crowds both for its exaggerated theatrical performances and for the chance to have photos taken with Phuket's most convincing *kathoey* or transsexual "lady-boys".

Gay Venues

Phuket's gay scene isn't as hot and happening as in Bangkok or Pattaya, with most of it taking place around the **Paradise Complex** along Thanon Rat-U-Thit. Here, bars, clubs and saunas cater to a colourful gay clientele. Phuket also has its very own gay festival (www.gaypatong.com) that takes place in February each year.
Boat Bar, Soi 5, Paradise Complex, Patong, tel: 0-7634 1237; www.boatbar.com. Located near the main entrance of the Royal Paradise Hotel. Popular and trendy gay dance club – the place to be seen at.
Galaxy, Soi Sunset, Patong. Plays good music and exudes a happy-go-lucky atmosphere. Mixed venue, but with a large gay clientele.

Krabi

Bobo's, Bobo Plaza, Hat Railay West. This quiet beach bar with its candlelit tables is the only purpose-built bar on Railay West to watch the setting sun. All other places are restaurants that happen to serve drinks.

Gecko Bar, Hat Railay East. Hip and happening beach bar set on the rocks of Railay East. Often has parties lasting late into the night; a favourite spot to gather after all the other beach bars wind down.

Irish Rover Bar and Grill, 247/8 Moo 2, Ao Nang, tel: 0-7563 7607. Irish-style pub just off a side street from the main beach road. Convivial atmosphere with Guinness flowing all evening and sports on overhead TVs.

Luna Beach Bar, Ao Nang. Bar with pool tables, DJs and lively atmosphere; doesn't get going until after midnight. Nightly fire shows on the beach.

Ko Phi Phi

Nightlife on Ko Phi Phi is predictably all concentrated on **Ao Ton Sai**, with mainly small open-air bars making up the scene.

Apache. This huge sea-facing bar is a popular place to relax and chat. Features one-for-one deals on "buckets" of whisky, gin, vodka and cocktails all night long.

Carlitos. Small but very popular bar that goes quite insane after midnight, with crowds spilling onto the beach. Great party atmosphere.

Reggae Bar. The island's biggest, and many would argue best, party venue, with a huge Thai boxing ring on the ground floor and a dance floor on the open-air at the upper level.

Rolling Stoned Bar. Tucked away behind the Reggae Bar is this two-tiered bar with pool tables, hammocks swinging from beams and modern dance tunes that get crowds up and dancing every night.

Ko Lanta

Most of the action takes place on Ao Phra Ae, centred around bars set up along the beach.

Funky Fish, Ao Phra Ae. Nice ambience and a beachfront setting tucked away from the road behind a cluster of dense trees.

The Laughing Leprechaun, Hat Khlong Dao. Irish Bar on the main road fronting Hat Khlong Dao. Serves Guinness and cider, and shows live Premiership football.

Opium, Ao Phra Ae. Popular British-owned bar. Stylish with a chilled-out ambience but only open in the high season.

Rasta Baby Bar, Hat Khlong Nin. Reggae bar with a relaxed island vibe. Has straw mats and low wooden tables inside, although many sit on the sand outside – under the stars.

Chiang Mai

While Chiang Mai can't compete with Bangkok after the sun goes down, in recent years the town has seen a rise in the number of bars and pubs.

Le Brasserie, 37 Th. Charoenrat, tel: 0-5324 1665. On the banks of the Ping River, this restaurant-bar is popular with live music fans who enjoy reggae, blues and classic rock.

Guitarman, 68/5–6 Th. Loi Kroh, near the Chiang Mai Night Bazaar, tel: 0-5381 8110; www.myspace.com/ guitarmanchiangmai. Guitarman hosts two live bands nightly in a bistro atmosphere. The kitchen serves good burgers and pizzas.

Riverside Bar & Restaurant, 9–11 Th. Charoenrat, tel: 0-5324 3239. The sprawling complex on the Ping River has two stages, with three bands playing rock, funk and R&B rotating nightly. This is one of the longest-running and most popular bars in Chiang Mai, as much for the food and ambience as the live music.

Sudsanan, Th. Huay Kaew, tel: 08-5038 0764. This large wooden bar is one of Thailand's best venues for local and visiting *plaeng phua chuwit* ("songs for life", ie Thai folk rock) musicians. Blues and reggae bands also make guest appearances.

UN Irish Pub, 24/1 Th. Ratwithi, tel: 0-5321 4554. This popular watering hole has two floors, plus garden tables out the back. The upper floor hosts live jazz or folk 2 to 3 nights a week, while the ground floor has large-screen cable TV for sport fans.

Warm-Up, Th. Nimanhemin, tel: 0-9993 2963. One of the most popular clubs in Chiang Mai, it has a large dance-oriented space that alternates between DJs and live Thai bands, a smaller DJ lounge and an outdoor area in the centre. The crowd tends to be students from nearby universities.

Kathoey Cabaret

Playhouse Entertainment Complex, 177 Th. Chang Pheuak, tel: 0-5341 0671; www.playhousechiangmai.com. Transvestite cabaret shows are held nightly at 8 pm and 10 pm in this large venue near the Novotel.

SHOPPING

Whatever part of your budget you have allocated for shopping, keep a tight grip on your wallet or you will find yourself being seduced by the low prices and walking off with more than you can possibly carry home.

The range of Thai handicrafts for sale is stupendous (see the **Arts and Crafts** chapter, *page 75*). While regional products were once found only in the towns that produced them, today, due to ease of distribution, it's possible, for instance, to buy Chiang Mai umbrellas in Phuket. The widest range of handicrafts is found in Bangkok, Phuket and Chiang Mai. If you don't have a chance to leave Bangkok, despair not; nearly everything you might want to buy in small towns can be found in Bangkok.

In Bangkok especially, shopping has become an obsessive leisure activity for many. Teenagers, young couples and families love meandering through the new mega malls and department stores. At weekends it all gets extremely crowded.

Most malls and department stores in the large cities open daily from 10am to 10pm. Every June to July and December to January, major department stores and malls take part in the Thailand Grand Sales, though many also offer a 5 percent tourist discount year-round – simply show your passport at the point of purchase. Alternatively, you can claim the 7 percent VAT refund at Suvarnabhumi Airport *(see text box, opposite)*.

Bangkok

Shopping Areas

Chinatown. With its maze of crowded streets, Chinatown will give you a taste of Old Bangkok without the tacky tourist goods. Open-air markets and small family businesses predominate, selling everything from antiques and jewellery to fresh produce and even car parts.

Pratunam. Around the corner from Central World is a bargain-hunter's paradise with shops selling cheap clothes, shoes, handicrafts and cosmetics at Nai Lert and Pratunam markets. Nearby Panthip Plaza sells computers, bootleg software, games and DVDs.

Thanon Khao San. Young backpackers have been descending on Khao San for years, so expect to find shops specialising in tattooing, hair-braiding, funky clothes, used books and silver jewellery, plus a good assortment of travel agents and internet cafés.

Thanon Rama 1 and Thanon Ploenchit area. Gaysorn and Erawan Bangkok along Thanon Ploenchit are havens for designer labels, while adjacent Narayana Phand is a Thai handicrafts paradise. The jewels in

ACCOMMODATION

VAT Refunds

It is possible to get the 7 percent VAT refunded from your shopping if you purchase goods from stores displaying the "VAT Refund for Tourists" sign. Refunds can only be claimed on single purchases of B2,000 or more, with a minimum overall expenditure of B5,000. At the time of purchase, present your passport and ask the sales assistant to complete the VAT refund form. Before departure at Suvarnabhumi Airport, present your goods with the VAT refund form and sales invoice to the Customs officers for inspection. After approval, present your claim to the Revenue officers at the airport's VAT Refund Counter.

Refunds not exceeding B30,000 will be made in cash (in Thai baht) or by bank draft or credited to your credit-card account. Refunds over B30,000 cannot be made in cash. In addition, there is an administrative fee of B100 for cash refunds; bank drafts and credit-card refunds will incur extra charges. See www.rd.go.th for more details.

the shopping scene are Siam Paragon and Central Plaza, the city's two largest shopping centres. Along Thanon Rama 1, Siam Centre, Siam Discovery Centre and teenage hangouts Siam Square and Mahboonkron are all within striking distance.

Thanon Silom. In the evenings, Silom's street stalls (Soi 2 to 8) sell cheap souvenirs, T-shirts and fake Rolexes. Patpong, notorious for its go-go bars, also sports a night market of tourist goods.

Thanon Sukhumvit. Soi 5 to 11 is a street bazaar for fake designer gear, souvenirs and handicrafts where haggling is the norm. Further east is upmarket Emporium mall. Nearby side streets fanning out from Emporium are good for home-decor shops. Soi Thonglor is the city's trendiest street for design-oriented shopping.

Shopping Malls

Central World, Th. Ratchadamri, www.centralworld.co.th. Bangkok's largest mall. It was badly damaged by fire in the anti-government protests in 2010; at the time of going to press it appeared likely to reopen later in the year.

Emporium, 622 Th. Sukhumvit (cnr Soi 24); www.emporiumthailand.com.

Mainly brand-name stores, as well as more practical electronics stores. Exotic Thai section on the 4th floor has a tasteful selection of handicrafts and jewellery, plus a good food court.

Erawan Bangkok, 494 Th. Ploenchit, www.erawanbangkok.com. Behind the Erawan Shrine and connected to the Grand Hyatt Erawan, this boutique mall has a collection of chic shops and eateries.

Gaysorn, 999 Th. Ploenchit; www.gaysorn.com. Another glitzy mall for high-fashion labels; the 3rd floor has elegant home-decor shops.

Mahboonkrong (MBK), 444 Th. Phayathai. This is one of Bangkok's most popular malls, hence the heaving crowds. In general, most goods and services are aimed at Thai youth or bargain-hunting tourists. Great for cheap leather luggage, jewellery and electronics. Bargain hard here. Also has restaurants, a large food court and a multi-screen cinema on the top floor.

Playground, 818 Soi Thonglor, Sukhumvit 55; www.playgroundstore.co.th. Bangkok's hippest boutique mall combines art installations with home decor and fashion shops, trendy cafés and a cookery school.

Siam Centre, 989 Th. Rama I; www.siampiwat.com. Several tailors and numerous clothing stores, a video-games arcade for kids and home-decor stores. Restaurants and sports shops zone on the top floor.

Siam Discovery Centre, 989 Th. Rama I. Packed with imported brands with prices to match. On the 5th floor is Kids' World, a whole floor devoted to youngsters. Top floor has the Grand EGV cinema.

Siam Paragon, 991/1 Th. Rama I, www.siamparagon.co.th. Glitz and glam are the hallmarks of this huge mall which opened in 2006. All the famous international brands are represented, plus many local ones too. Wide range of restaurants, plus Siam Ocean World aquarium for kids.

Department Stores

Central Chidlom, 1027 Th. Ploenchit, tel: 0-2655 7777. The best of the chain and one of Bangkok's top department stores. The Loft food court on the top floor is a great place to eat.

Emporium, 622 Th. Sukhumvit (cnr Soi 24), tel: 0-2664 8000–9. Emporium is one of the classiest department stores (part of the mall of the same name).

Isetan, Central World, Th. Ratchadamri, tel: 0-2255 9898–9. Japanese department store with high-

quality international goods at slightly above-average prices.

Robinson, Soi 19 Th. Sukhumvit, tel: 0-2252 5121. The chain's biggest and most popular branches are on Thanon Silom, Thanon Sukhumvit and Thanon Ratchadaphisek and in Seacon Square mall. While not as high quality as Central, the goods are cheaper.

Siam Paragon, 991/1 Th. Rama I, tel: 0-2610 9000. A sprawling department store having the same name as the mall itself. Vast array of clothing, electronics and housewares.

Zen, Central World, Th. Ratchadamri, tel: 0-2255 9667–9. With a similar look and feel as Isetan, Zen has a wide range of both international and local products.

Markets

Despite the proliferation of air-conditioned shopping malls in the city, markets (both day and night) and street vendors still cater to the majority of Bangkok's ordinary people with their cheap goods and basic necessities. They are also colourful places to observe the more visceral aspects of Bangkok. The following places covered in the Bangkok chapter are worth seeking out: **Pratunam Market** *(see page 131)*; Chinatown's **Sampeng Lane** and **Pahurat Market** *(page 127)*; **Suan Lum Night Bazaar** *(page 131)*; **Patpong** *(page 133)*; **Sukhumvit** *(page 134)* and **Chatuchak Weekend Market** *(page 140)*.

Antiques

O P Place, Soi 38 Th. Charoen Krung, tel: 0-2266 0186. Just across from the Oriental hotel, this upmarket antiques mall stocks goods that are

BELOW: Mahboonkrong shopping mall.

ACTIVITIES

A – Z

LANGUAGE

as expensive as you'd expect for the location. Worth a browse if only to see what you cannot afford to buy.

River City, 23 Trok Rongnamkaeng, tel: 0-2237 0077–8; www.rivercity.co.th. Bangkok's main art and antiques centre, with the second to fourth floors selling art and antiques goods. Antique auctions are held monthly in the Auction House, but beware of pilfered artefacts from historical sites. Prices can be alarmingly high and the merchants are not fond of bargaining, but it can be done. Keep in mind too that some of the "antiques" found here are cleverly aged reproductions.

Books

B2S, 7th Floor, Central Chidlom Dept Store, Th. Ploenchit, tel: 0-2655 6178. Major bookstore retail chain with several outlets downtown.

Basheer Graphic Books, 998 Sukhumvit Soi 55, tel: 0-2391 9815; www.basheergraphic.com. Wide range of art and design-oriented books.

Bookazine, 286 Th. Rama I, tel: 0-2255 3778. Another large bookstore chain with branches all over the city.

Dasa Book Café, 710/4 Th. Sukhumvit (between Soi 24 and 26), tel: 0-2661 2993; www.dasabookcafe. com. Second-hand books in a cosy environment with drinks and desserts to fuel your page-thumbing.

Kinokuniya, 3rd Floor, Emporium, Th. Sukhumvit, tel: 0-2664 8554–6. Japanese chain store with well-organised and comprehensive selection of books on all topics.

Electronics

Panthip Plaza, 604/3 Th. Petchaburi, tel: 0-2251 9724–8. The biggest marketplace for computer gear in Thailand, plus virtually every piece of PC software in existence (much of it pirated); 150 shops spread over five floors selling hardware and software.

Fashion and Clothes

Thais follow fashion trends closely and are quick to copy the latest collections from foreign design houses and flog them at a fraction of the cost. The only downside is they fit the Thai physique, ie small and slim. There aren't many international Thai fashion houses, but **Fly Now** and **Greyhound** are making major inroads. The **Nagara** label is the Jim Thompson's line of contemporary women's clothing.

Fly Now, 2nd Floor, Gaysorn Plaza, Th. Ploenchit, tel: 0-2656 1359; www. flynow.co.th. One of the country's few

home-grown fashion labels to grace the world's catwalks.

Greyhound, 2nd Floor, Emporium, Soi 24 Th. Sukhumit, tel: 0-2664 8664; www.greyhound.co.th. This trendy domestic fashion brand can sometimes be hit or miss, with branches (and great cafés) in several malls around Bangkok.

Inspired by Inner Complexity, 235/3 Soi 31 Th. Sukhumvit, tel: 0-2258 4488. Chill in the tearoom downstairs or browse hip streetwear and accessories upstairs.

It Happened to Be a Closet, 266/3 Soi 3 Siam Square, Th. Rama I, tel: 0-2658 4696. Stocks mainly vintage female clothes and accessories.

Jaspal, 2nd Floor, Siam Centre, Th. Rama I, tel: 0-2251 5918; www.jaspal. com. Local fashion chain with branches in most shopping malls. Influenced by British and European style trends. Unlike most Thai labels, sizes go up to XL.

Tailors

There are nearly as many tailors as noodle shops in the capital, and while the craftsmanship isn't a stitch near to Savile Row, prices are a bargain. There is a proliferation of cheap tailors around Sukhumvit's early *soi* and also at Thanon Khao San.

Embassy Fashion House, Th. Withayu, tel: 02-251 2620. Most tailors give you the hard sell, but this place stands out for its relaxed service. Nearby embassy staff patronise this shop, and many big-name hotels recommend it too.

Textiles

Almeta Silk, 20/3 Th. Sukhumvit Soi 23, tel: 0-2258 4227. Made-to-order hand-woven silk designs in stunning colour combinations that can be turned into home furnishings.

Jim Thompson Thai Silk, 9 Th. Surawong, tel: 0-2632 8100–4; and **Jim Thompson Factory Outlet**, 153 Th. Sukhumvit Soi 93, tel: 0-2332 6530; www.jimthompson.com. With several branches around the city, this famous silk company has had a contemporary makeover in recent years. Specialises in clothing, accessories and home furnishings. Not cheap, although slightly keener prices are to be found at its factory-outlet store in Sukhumvit.

Mae Fah Luang Foundation, 4th Floor, Siam Discovery Centre, Th. Rama I, tel: 02-658 0424–5; www. doitung.org. This royally initiated craft foundation has been acclaimed for its traditional weaves infused with contemporary designs.

Export Permits

The **Thai Department of Fine Arts** prohibits the export of all Thai Buddha images, images of other deities and fragments (hands or heads) of images dating from before the 18th century. All antiques must be registered with the department. The shop will usually do this for you. If you decide to handle it yourself, take the piece to the office at Thanon Na Prathat (tel: 0-2226 1661/224-2050; www.finearts.go.th) together with two postcard-sized photos of it. The export fee ranges from B50 to B200 depending on the antiquity of the piece. Fake antiques do not require export permits, but airport customs officials are not art experts and may mistake it for a genuine piece. If it looks authentic, clear it at the Department of Fine Arts to avoid problems later.

Gems and Jewellery

Bangkok is well known for its gemstone scams. Buy only from reputable shops endorsed by the Tourism Authority of Thailand and the Thai Gem and Jewellery Association. These shops carry the Jewel Fest logo and issue a certificate of authenticity that comes with a money-back guarantee.

Ki-Ti's Jewellery, 2nd Floor, Playground, Sukhumvit Soi 55 (Soi Thonglor), tel: 0-1821 1275; www. kittijewelry.com. Khun Ittipol's stylish take on the ethnic look has given him a well-deserved following. Apart from this main outlet, there is also the Ki-Ti's Gallery at Baan Silom on Soi 19 Thanon Silom.

Uthai's Gems, 28/7 Soi Ruam Rudee, tel: 0-2253 8582. Foreign residents like the personal touch and approach of this reputable jeweller.

Handicrafts and Home Decor

Apart from Chatuchak Market and Suan Lum Night Bazaar, the shops below are worth a browse though. Expect prices to be higher though.

L'Arcadia, 12/2 Soi 23 (Soi Prasanmit), Th. Sukhumvit, tel: 0-2259 9595. Thai and Burmese wood and lacquer items.

Asian Motifs, 3rd Floor, Gaysorn Plaza, Th. Ploenchit, tel: 0-2656 1093. Unique, elegant, contemporary spin to traditional celadon, lacquerware, silks and the like.

Cocoon, 3rd Floor, Gaysorn Plaza, Th. Ploenchit, tel: 0-2656 1006. A modern take on traditional Thai and Asian fabrics and home decor.

Exotique Thai, 4th Floor, Emporium, Soi 24 Th. Sukhumvit, tel: 0-2664 8000–9 ext. 1554. Well-presented display of handicrafts within the mall.

Narayana Phand, 127 Th. Ratchadamri, tel: 0-2252 4670. One-stop shop for all Thai crafts. Spread over several floors, there's everything from traditional musical instruments to ornamental headpieces.

Propaganda, 4th Floor, Siam Discovery Centre, Th. Rama 1, tel: 0-2658 0430; www.propagandaonline. com. Quirkily designed home-decor items (think a Thai version of Alessi) like funky tableware and molar-shaped toothbrush holders. Second outlet at Emporium.

Rasi Sayam, 82 Sukhumvit Soi 33, tel: 0-2262 0729. Sells fine traditional Thai handicrafts and objets d'art, with many one-of-a-kind pieces.

Pattaya

Pattaya is the Eastern Seaboard's best shopping option, with several malls and a couple of outdoor tourist markets. Beyond the usual high-street brands, choices are basically limited to market-stall counterfeits and tacky tourist bric-a-brac, though there are replica antiques and collectables shops, as well as several art galleries.

Ko Samui

As Samui's development continues unabated, shops geared to both tourists and residents have sprung up all over the island. By far the greatest concentration is in and around Chaweng, with at least two major supermarket chains as well as small boutique arcades like **Iyara Plaza**, **Living Square** and **Central Plaza**. In addition, market stalls and shops along Chaweng's main drag peddle the same counterfeit clothing, bags, sports shoes, CDs and DVDs you find in Bangkok.

There are also numerous "copy art" studios that churn out replicas of your favourite masterpieces, as well as handicrafts and homeware stores.

Phuket

The emergence of large shopping malls such as Central Festival on the outskirts of Phuket Town has increased the opportunities to go on a spending spree in Phuket. These malls often have small stalls displaying local goods such as jewellery and beachwear, while the

ABOVE: handicraft shop in Silom.

larger shops within sell international brand names like Levi's and Nike.

All the beaches are lined with stalls selling designer knock-off T-shirts and handbags as well as bootleg CDs and DVDs. DVD prices are usually fixed at B100, but try checking the quality first.

Generally, prices can double or even triple during the high season, so always bargain and never accept the first price you hear. A huge open-air clothing and souvenir market facing Karon beach is one of the few places that indicates prices on its goods. While you may end up paying a little bit extra, many are glad to avoid the hassle of bargaining for better deals.

Shopping Malls

Central Festival, 74–75 Moo 5, Th. Vichit; www.centralfestivalphuket.com. This popular shopping venue opened in late 2004 on the outskirts of Phuket Town. The mall contains numerous shops, the large Central Festival Department Store and several restaurants. On the fourth floor is a huge 7-screen cineplex and a bowling alley.

Jung Ceylon, Patong; www.jungceylon. com. Phuket's first beachside mega mall opened in December 2006. Located in the heart of Patong, it has a range of shops, restaurants, a supermarket and even a cineplex.

Ocean Shopping Mall, 38/1–15 Th. Tilok-U-Thit, Phuket Town. This mall has a supermarket, cheap clothes, cosmetics and many craft stalls. It has two branches in Patong.

Antiques

Chan's Antiques, 99/42 Moo 5, Th. Chalermprakit, tel: 0-7626 1416. Home to Phuket's largest collection of

antiques from Thailand and neighbouring countries. Even if not shopping, with so many displays, it is fascinating to walk around this old Thai-style building on the outskirts of Phuket Town.

Soul of Asia, 37–39 Th. Ratsada, Phuket Town, tel: 0-7621 1122; www.soulofasia.com. Elegant gallery converted from two old Chinese shophouses. Over 700 sq metres (7,535 sq ft) of paintings and antiques.

Fashion and Clothing

The best and widest range of clothes is found in the **Central Festival Department Store**, in the Central Festival mall. Local brands are excellent value for money should you be small enough to squeeze into them, and international labels such as Nike and Levi's are considerably cheaper here than in Europe and the US. Cheaper clothes, however, can be found at streetside stalls and markets.

Tailors

Most of Phuket's tailors are situated around Patong and Kata beaches. Many have overbearing touts who try to cajole you into going inside, which unfortunately often acts as a deterrent to doing just that. Prices are competitive, so it is best to look at the quality and design of the garments in shop windows. The following are recommended.

King's Fashion, 146 Th. Thawiwong, Patong, tel: 0-7634 0192.

Mr Singh's Fashion Gallery, 26/2 Th. Rat-U-Thit, Patong, tel: 0-7634 5038.

Handicrafts and Home Decor

Art and Gift Gallery, Canal Village, Laguna Shopping Unit 16, 390/1 Moo 1, Th. Srisoonthorn, Bang Thao, tel: 0-7627 0616; www.artandgiftgallery. com. Reputable shop that sells an interesting array of handicrafts and home-decor items. Goods can be personalised with name or company logo. Lots of gift ideas here.

Jim Thompson, Central Festival Phuket, tel: 0-7624 9615. This brand, which is synonymous with quality Thai silk, has three stores in Phuket alone, the largest of which is found at the Central Festival mall. Wide range of fabrics, clothing, accessories and home-decor items.

Chiang Mai

Chiang Mai has long been the main centre for Thailand's well-known handicraft cottage industries, which produce everything from the clichéd

TRANSPORT · ACCOMMODATION · ACTIVITIES · A–Z · LANGUAGE

painted umbrellas to a range of stunning modern home-design accessories inspired by Lanna or hill-tribe traditions.

Markets

Sunday Walking Street, Th. Ratchadamnoen and adjacent streets. Every Sunday (and, during the December to March high season, Saturday as well) from 2pm to 10pm, this area to the west of Tha Phae Gate in the Old City is closed off to vehicles for a pedestrian-only market. Vendors line the streets, laying out handicrafts, clothing and souvenirs that generally are of higher quality than comparable offerings at the famous Chiang Mai Night Bazaar. A similar event takes place on Th. Wualai on Saturday evenings.

Chiang Mai Night Bazaar. The city's number-one tourist attraction extends for several blocks along Thanon Chang Khlan and consists of row upon row of steel carts bearing a vast variety of merchandise geared towards tourists. Most goods are made in Thailand, but imports from China, Nepal, Laos, Cambodia and Myanmar are also plentiful. Some of the best buys are home-decor items such as locally crafted lamps with colourful saa (mulberry bark) paper shades, wooden carvings, tribal wall hangings and the like.

Chiang Mai Night Bazaar Building, Th. Chang Khlan near the middle of the street. Has three floors of shops (daily 5–11pm) displaying high-quality antiques, furniture, textiles, jewellery, ceramics as well as inexpensive clothing. Two of the more intriguing shops inside are **The Lost Heavens** (2nd floor, tel: 0-5327 8185) and **Under the Bo** (2nd floor, tel: 0-5381 8831). The former specialises in rare Mien ritual artefacts, the latter in unique furniture, sculpture and textiles from Africa and Asia.

Warorot Market, Th. Chang Moi. Chiang Mai's oldest market is housed in a huge ramshackle building stuffed with everything native to Chiang Mai and northern Thailand, from preserved fruits to loom-woven textiles. The market is open daily from 5am to 6pm.

Shopping Malls

Central Airport Plaza, Th. Mahidon, near Chiang Mai International Airport. Anchored by Robinson department store, Chiang Mai's newest and largest mall boasts a wide selection of shops offering electronics, mobile phones, designer clothing and pharmaceuticals, along with dozens

of restaurants and fast-food outlets, a cineplex and a Tops supermarket.

Kad Suan Kaew, Th. Huay Kaew. The city's first multi-storey shopping mall is centred around the large Central Department Store.

Pantip Plaza, corner of Th. Chang Khlan and Th. Sr Donchai, near the Chiang Mai Night Bazaar. A modern three-storey building filled with shops selling computers and computer-related supplies and accessories.

Handicrafts and Home Decor

Aka Gallery, Neimanheiman Road Soi 1. Tel: 0-5389 4425. Ceramics, furniture and a wide but eclectic gathering of home-decor items. The owners describe their design style as "contemporary oriental functionalism".

Fai Thong, 39/2 Th. Kuang Maen, tel: 0-5323-3419. Hidden in a tiny lane near Warorot Market, the owner, Jei Peng, has the most extensive collection of traditional northern Thai textiles we've seen in Chiang Mai. High-end seamstresses and boutiques are the usual customers.

Laan Pai Lin, Nantawan Arcade, 6/12 Th. Nimanhemin, tel: 0-5322 2026. This small shop sells an impressive variety of essential oils and spa products made from extracts of lemongrass, Thai bergamot and other local herbs.

Mengrai Kilns, 79/2 Th. Arak, tel: 0-5327 2063. In the Old City near Buak Hat Park, Mengrai Kilns specialises in the famous northern Thai-style ceramics made of celadon.

Studio Naenna, 138/8 Soi Chang Khian, Th. Huay Kaew, tel: 0-5322 6042. Owned by Patricia Cheeseman, a renowned expert on Southeast Asian textiles, this workshop-cum-gallery not only sells hill-tribe-inspired silk and cotton fabrics and clothing but offers free weaving and dying demonstrations.

Thai Celadon, 112 Th. Chotana, tel: 0-5321 3541. Another excellent source for celadon, a type of pottery with light-green or dark-brown glaze.

Jewellery

Sipsong Panna, Nantawan Arcade, 6/19 Th. Nimanhemin, tel: 0-5321 6096. Chiang Mai has long been famous for the quality and detail of silverwork, most of it made by second- and third-generation Thai Khün immigrants from Myanmar's Shan State. Here traditional tribal designs, updated for modern tastes, are made from high-quality silver rather than the nickel-diluted cheaper stuff found in other shops.

OUTDOOR ACTIVITIES AND TOURS

Bangkok

Golf

Thais are big golfing buffs, going so far as to employ some of the golfing world's stellar architects to design international-class courses. At around B500 to B2,000, green fees are low and clubs are not snooty about letting guests play. Check www.thaigolfer.com for more details.

Green Valley Country Club, 92 Moo 3, Th. Bangna-Trad, tel: 0-2316 5883–9; www.greenvalleybangkok.com. Beautifully landscaped with a grand clubhouse, this 18-hole course was designed by Robert Trent Jones Jr.

Panya Indra Golf Course, 99 Moo 6, Km 9 Kannayao, Th. Ramindra, tel: 0-2943 0000; www.panyagolf.com. About 30 minutes from downtown, this well-kept course has a challenging 27-hole course.

Thana City Golf & Country Club, Th. Bangna-Trad Km 14, tel: 0-2336 1971–8. The Greg Norman-designed 18-hole course has played host to numerous competitions.

Thai Boxing

Bangkok has two principal places to view Thai boxing, or muay thai.

Lumpini Boxing Stadium, Th. Rama IV, tel: 0-2251 4303. Matches at 6pm on Tuesday, Friday and Saturday. Tickets at B500, B800 and B1,500. Note: This stadium hasn't relocated despite several attempts to move in recent years.

Ratchadamnoen Boxing Stadium, 1 Th. Ratchadamnoen Nok, tel: 0-2281 4205. Matches at 6pm on Monday, Wednesday and Thursday, and 5pm on Sunday. Tickets: B500, B800 and B1,500.

Sightseeing Tours

Unfortunately Bangkok has very little by way of organised sightseeing tours. What little is out there is often directed at the domestic market with guides speaking Thai only. However, all the major hotels have tour desks that can arrange visits (with private guide and car with driver) to the major tourist sites.

The **Chao Phraya Tourist Boat** (see page 368) is more of a shuttle service than a tour proper, but you do get a running commentary on board of the sights along the Chao Phraya River. For those wishing to explore the canals of Thonburi or Nonthaburi, private **longtail boats** (see page 369) can be rented from most of the river's main piers.

Dinner cruises (or evening cocktails) on board an atmospheric teakwood barge are a nice way of spending the evening and soaking up the sights along the river. **Grand Pearl Cruises**, tel: 0-2861 0255; www.grandpearlcruise.com. This company operates day trips to Bang Pa-In and Ayutthaya. Depart by coach at 7.30am and return by boat onboard the *Grand Pearl*, arriving in Bangkok by 4pm. **Loy Nava Dinner Cruise**, tel: 02-437 4932; www.loynava.com. A teakwood barge was refurbished and converted into the *Tahsaneeya Nava*. Its 2-hour dinner cruise (daily 6pm and 8pm) starts with a traditional welcome by hostesses. Dinner is a Thai set menu accompanied by live traditional music. Cost: B1,375 per person. **Manohra Cruises**, tel: 0-2477 0770; www.manohracruises.com. This option uses either the *Manohra* or *Manohra Moon*, both rice barges restored for dining and cocktail cruises. Dinner cruises from 7.30pm to 10pm cost B1,990 per person while cocktail cruises (a drink and light snacks) at 6pm cost B900. Departs daily from the pier at the Bangkok Marriott Resort but can also pick up from Tha Sathorn or Tha Oriental piers. **Oriental Escape**, 187 Soi Ratchawithie 21, tel: 0-2883 1219; www.orientalescape.com. Offers a wide range of tours (including Thai boxing and Thai dance and dinner shows) of Bangkok and its surroundings (Damnoen Saduak floating market, Ayutthaya, Kanchanaburi, etc.), as well as other parts of Thailand, like Chiang Mai and Phuket. **Real Asia**, 10/5–7 Soi Aree, Th. Sukhumvit Soi 26, tel: 0-2665 6364; www.realasia.net. Offers 1-day cycling tours (including a ride on a longtail boat) into the capital's more scenic and traffic-free countryside (B1,500 per person). Also has walking and canal-boat tours plus an interesting train tour into the countryside at Samut Sakhon.

Kanchanaburi

Trekking and Kayaking

AS Mixed Travel, Th. Saengchuto, tel: 0-3451 2017; www.applenoi-kanchanaburi.com. Owned by the Apple Guesthouse, this agency offers tours of the surrounding attractions as well as the chance to trek through Erawan National Park, ride on an elephant and raft on the river. **Safarine**, 4 Th. Tawan, tel: 0-3462 4140; www.safarine.com. Specialises in

ABOVE: Thai boxing is a popular sport.

kayak tours of the Kwae Yai and Kwae Noi rivers. Packaged 1- and 2-day trips are available; longer custom-made trips can also be organised.

Pattaya

Diving

Aquanauts Dive Centre, 437/17 Moo 9, Th. Hat Pattaya (Beach Road) Soi 6, tel: 0-3836 1724; www.aquanautsdive.com. A British-owned operation with over a decade's experience in Pattaya. In addition to its basic courses, it offers several speciality courses, as well as wreck dives and cave dives for the more experienced divers. **Mermaid's Scuba Diving Centre**, 75/124 Moo 12, Th. Hat Jomtien, tel: 0-3823 2219; www.mermaiddive.com. A large, well-managed dive centre with three boats offering regular courses and fun dives, as well as speciality courses such as the PADI National Geographic Diver Course.

Bungee Jumping

Jungle Bungy Jump, Th. Boonkanjana Soi 5, Jomtien, tel: 0-6378 3880; www.thaibungy.com. Claiming to operate the original and safest bungee jump in Thailand, this company offers a 50-metre (165ft) launch over a fishing lake behind the beach. A jump costs B1,900 (inclusive of insurance, 24 photos, souvenir cap and a "courage" certificate), with additional jumps getting progressively cheaper; the fourth jump is free.

Golf

Bangphra International, 45 Moo 6, Bangphra, Si Racha, tel: 0-3834 1149. This venerable par-72 course is one of the area's oldest, dating back to 1958, but the first nine holes were redesigned in the 1980s.

Laem Chabang International Country Club, 106/8 Moo 4, Si Racha, tel: 0-3837 2273; www.laemchabanggolf.com. Rated one of the region's best, this 27-hole course (par 72) was designed by Jack Nicklaus. **Phoenix Golf Club**, Th. Sukhumvit Km 158, Pattaya, tel: 0-3823 9391. With sea views, this 27-hole course (par 72) was designed by Denis Griffiths and is ideal for long hitters. Large clubhouse with excellent facilities.

Go-Karting

K.R. Go-Kart Grand Prix, 62/125 Moo 12, Th. Thepprasit, tel: 0-3830 0347. Burn some rubber at this 1,100-metre (1,200yd) track. There are different engine sizes (80–110cc) to suit both novice and experienced drivers, and a clubhouse. A 10-minute ride costs B300 to B700.

Sailing

Ocean Marina Yacht Club, 274/1–9 Moo 4, Th. Sukhumvit Km 157, Sattahip, tel: 0-3823 7310; www.oceanmarinayachtclub.com. Those with very deep wallets might want to charter their own yacht or catamaran for a half-day or overnight cruise.

Skydiving and Parachuting

Pattaya Airpark, 108/1 Moo 9, Hui Yai, Pattaya, tel: 0-86374 1718–9; www.pattayaairpark.com. Located south of Pattaya, it offers tandem skydives every weekend (weekday dives can also be arranged). A single jump in the drop zone costs B10,000, or B15,000 with a video of your jump recorded on DVD. Also has hour-long Ultralight flights for B3,500. Advance bookings required.

Water Theme Park

Pattaya Park, 345 Hat Jomtien, tel: 0-3825 1201–8; www.pattayapark.com. Centred around Pattaya Tower, this water theme park and amusement ride area called "Funny Land" has plenty to thrill both kids and adults. Ascend the tower for panoramic views, then descend by either the Sky Shuttle cable car, Speed Shuttle, or

Dive Green

Green Fins (www.greenfins-thailand.org) is a United Nations-backed scheme to protect Thailand's coral reefs. Dive companies that adhere to strict environmental regulations receive a stamp of approval from the organisation. Since its founding in 2004, it has played a key role in raising conservation awareness.

TRANSPORT
ACCOMMODATION
ACTIVITIES
A – Z
LANGUAGE

the adrenalin-pumping Tower Jump. The water park also has slides and a whirlpool.

Wind- and Kite-Surfing

Blue Lagoon Water Sports Club, 24/20 Moo 2, Na Jomtien Soi 14, Sattahip, tel: 0-3825 5115–6. This is one of Thailand's few professional kite-surfing schools. Also rents out kayaks and windsurfing boards.

Ko Samet

Diving

Samed Resorts PADI Dive Centre, Ao Prao Resort, Ao Phrao, tel: 0-3864 4100; www.aopraoresort.com. This expensive resort-linked dive centre is well run and offers basic, open-water and advanced dive courses.

Ko Chang

Diving

Dolphin Divers, 38/7 Moo 4, Ao Khlong Phrao, mobile tel: 08-7028 1627; www.scubadivingkohchang.com. A small and friendly company with multilingual courses. Diving is done around the main island, as well as nearby islands like Ko Wai, Ko Rang, Ko Mak and Ko Kut. **Ploy Scuba Diving**, 36 Moo 1, Baan Bang Bao, tel: 0-3955 8033; www. ployscuba.com. Part of a reputable chain of dive shops. Professionally managed, with courses in several languages. **Water World Diving**, Ko Chang Plaza, 17/3 Moo 4, Hat Chai Chet, mobile tel: 08-6139 1117; www. waterworldkohchang.com. Professional and well-equipped outfit with a comfortable boat to get to the dive sites. Competitive prices and multilingual courses.

Catamaran Sailing

Sea Adventures, Hat Sai Khao, mobile tel: 08-4728 6387. For a unique experience, book a seat on a 13-metre (40ft) British-owned catamaran. There are day-long tours of Ko Chang and several of the outer islands. For B1,500 per person, you get an English-speaking crew, snorkel and mask, a barbecue lunch on a deserted beach, and hotel pick-up.

Trekking

Mr Anong, mobile tel: 08-6152 5271. A one-man trekking outfit. Led by the knowledgeable Mr Anong, full-day treks cost B1,200 per person. **Trekkers of Ko Chang**, tel: 0-3952 5029, mobile tel: 08-1578 7513. Selling itself as an eco-friendly company, it has several full-day treks

into Ko Chang's jungled interior, all led by experienced guides.

Elephant Treks

Jungleway, mobile tel: 08-9223 4795; www.jungleway.com. Offers a half-day tour where you get to see elephants bathing and feeding at Ban Kwan Chang camp, followed by a 90-minute trek on elephant back into the forest (B900 per person).

Hua Hin

Adventure Tours

Hua Hin Adventure Tour, 69/8 Th. Petchkasem, tel: 0-3235 0314; www.huahinadventuretour.com. Offers a variety of adventure tours into Kaeng Krachan and Sam Roi Yot national parks. Trips range from 1-day excursions to 3-day camping, trekking, kayaking and rock-climbing tours.

Boat Cruises and Fishing

Mermaid Cruises, 77/5 Moo 1, Pak Nam Pran, Pranburi, mobile tel: 08-4800 7400; www.huahincruises.com. Board its teakwood pleasure boat, the *Peacock*, and embark on one of several trips – evening squid fishing, all-day fishing, or cruises to Monkey Island and Sam Roi Yot National Park.

Thai Boxing

Grand Sport Stadium, Th. Petchkasem (next to Grand Hotel). Usually stages matches two nights a week at 9pm. The norm is five to six bouts per night, with Thai and international boxers (including women).

Golf

Majestic Creek Country Club, 164 Moo 4 Tambon Tabtai, tel: 0-3252 0162. Opened in the early 1990s, this 18-hole par-72 course is one of the country's longest and was designed by Thailand's leading golf architect. **Royal Hua Hin Golf Club**, tel: 0-3251 2475. Opened in 1924, this is Thailand's oldest golf course and is located close to town. The course follows the undulating topography and is fringed by large mature trees.

Kite-Boarding

Hua Hin Kite Centre, Soi 75/1, mobile tel: 08-1591 4593; www. kiteboardingasia.com. Offers 1- to 3-day training in kite-boarding.

Ko Samui

Safari Tours

Mr Ung's Magical Safari, Moo 3, Chaweng, tel: 0-7723 0114; www. ungsafari.com. Mr Ung runs three tours

– a full- and half-day "safari", as well as a day of deep-sea fishing. The full-day safari includes an optional elephant ride, plus four-wheel-drive jeep tours into the lush jungled interior and a waterfall swim.

Diving

Discovery Dive Centre, Amari Palm Reef Resort, Chaweng, tel: 0-7741 3196; www.discoverydivers.com. A small but well-equipped dive centre with its own speedboat. As well as offering courses and fun dives, it rents out underwater video and photography equipment, in addition to kayaks, windsurfing boards and catamarans. **Dive Indeep**, 162/8 Chaweng, tel: 0-7723 0155–6; www.diveindeep.com. This PADI dive centre has been on Ko Samui for over 15 years. Apart from the usual courses, it also organises snorkelling trips to Ko Tao and has introductory dive courses for kids.

Go-Karting

Samui Go-Kart, 101/2 Moo 1, Bo Phut, tel: 0-7742 7194. Open from 9am until late, this jungle-fringed track has three types of karts, the slowest of which are suitable for kids.

Cable Ride

Canopy Adventures, Best Beach Bungalow, Chaweng, tel: 0-7741 4150–1; www.canopyadventuresthailand. com. Suspend from the trees above and glide through the forest canopy in Ko Samui's lush interior. The 2- to 3-hour trip includes six treetop rides, a swim in a waterfall and a drink at their jungle bar.

Golf

Santiburi Samui Country Club, 12/15 Moo 4 Maenam, tel: 0-7742 1700; www.santiburi.com. Opened in 2004, this lush 18-hole (par-72) course, the only one on the island, lies on the hills behind the quiet Maenam beach on Samui's northern coast.

Kayaking

Blue Stars, Chaweng, tel: 0-7741 3231; www.bluestars.info. This outfit runs 1- and 2-day kayak trips around Ang Thong Marine National Park. The 2-night trips feature a barbecue dinner and overnight camping on a desolate beach. The departure point on Ko Samui is Na Thon Pier.

Sailing

Samui Boat Charters, tel: 08-7276 7598; www.samuiboatcharter.com. Has a small fleet of luxury sporting yachts that are professionally crewed and have full waiter service on board.

Ko Phangan

Diving

Hat Yao Divers, Sandy Bay Bungalows, Hat Yao, mobile tel: 08-6279 3085; www.haadyaodivers.com. Located on the island's west coast, this reputable European-run outfit has its main office at Hat Yao beach, another branch on Ao Chaophao and a retail centre in Thong Sala. It offers all the main PADI and speciality courses.

Phangan Divers, Hat Rin, Hat Yao, Ko Ma and Ao Thong Nai Pan, tel: 0-7737 5117; www.phangandivers.com. With four branches on Ko Phangan alone, this is one of the island's first and most comprehensive dive schools. As well as PADI courses, fun dives and snorkelling equipment rental, it operates an Instructor Development Centre for professional certification.

Ko Tao

Diving

Big Blue Diving, Hat Sai Ree and Mae Hat, tel: 0-7745 6050–2; www.bigbluediving.com. One of Thailand's best dive companies, with a well-deserved reputation.

Planet Scuba, Mae Hat, tel: 0-7745 6110; www.planet-scuba.net. One of Thailand's most reputable dive outfits, with over two decades of experience.

Scuba Junction, Hat Sai Ree, tel: 0-7745 6164; www.scuba-junction.com. Located halfway up Hat Sai Ree beach, this outfit has its own boat and runs a wide range of courses.

Watersports

Black Tip Diving & Watersports, Ao Tanote, tel: 0-7745 6488/9; www.blacktipdiving.com. In addition to dive trips, it has wakeboarding and waterskiing lessons, plus operates banana boats and hires out kayaks.

Khao Lak

Golf

Thai Muang Beach Golf and Marina, 157/12 Moo 9, Th. Limdul, tel: 0-7657 1533. This 18-hole course is just a 30-minute drive from Khao Lak or Phuket. Has an interesting placement of bunkers and water hazards, but it is most popular for its scenic beachside location.

Diving

Several dive sites are easily reached from Khao Lak, making it a major haven for scuba enthusiasts. In addition to being the main gateway to the Similan Islands, the wreck-diving sites of *Boonsong* and *Premchai* are easily accessible from here.

Divers Land, 4/56 Moo 7, Khuk Kak, tel: 0-7642 3710; www.diversland.com. Khao Lak's first integrated diving resort, with accommodation, restaurant, fitness and training centres as well as dive equipment sales and service centres all on one site. Organises diving and snorkelling trips.

Sub Aqua Diver Centre, 5/21 Moo 7, Khao Lak, tel: 0-7642 0165; www.subaqua-divecenter.com. Professional and well-established multilingual dive outfit offering daily excursions to the Similan Islands on board one of three modern speedboats. Offers a range of PADI courses.

Phuket

Adventure Tours

Siam Safari, 45 Th. Chaofa, Chalong, tel: 0-7628 0116; www.siamsafari.com. One of Phuket's longest-running tour companies, offering a range of land-based tours incorporating jeep safaris, elephant trekking, canoeing and visits to Thai villages and national parks.

Bungee Jumping

Jungle Bungee, Th. Vichitsongkram, tel: 0-7632 1351; www.phuketbungy.com. Fully licensed, insured and with a good reputation for safety, having opened in June 1992. Jumps overlook a beautiful wooded area surrounding a lagoon. A breathtaking site – if you can keep your eyes open long enough to enjoy it!

Deep-Sea Fishing

Aloha Tours, 44/1 Th. Visit, Chalong, tel: 0-7638 1215; www.thai-boat.com. Experienced crew take boats out daily in search of the massive tuna, marlin and King mackerel that all thrive in Phuket's surrounding waters.

Diving and Snorkelling

Phuket's only notable snorkelling spots are around the headlands at Kata Yai and Kata Noi beaches. Shacks along the sand rent out snorkelling gear by the day or hour. Better snorkelling can be found on trips to nearby islands, and most dive operators offer a cheaper snorkelling-only option. Phuket is a popular base for many day trips and live aboard excursions. Conditions are best during the dry season (Dec–Apr), when seas are calm and the water is at its clearest. Most dive shops offer everything from introductory dives to advanced dive master certification. The following are recommended.

Dive Asia, 24 Th. Karon, Kata, tel: 0-7633 0598; www.diveasia.com. Offers numerous training programmes in different languages as well as day trips and all-inclusive dive live aboards.

Scuba Cat Diving, 94 Th. Thawiwong, Patong, tel: 0-7629 3120; www.scubacat.com. Phuket's first National Geographic dive centre is Canadian-owned and English-managed. The most prominent on Patong due to its central location and outdoor training pool.

Golf

Blue Canyon Country Club, 165 Moo 1, Th. Thepkasattri, tel: 0-7632 8088; www.bluecanyonclub.com. Beautifully landscaped on a 290-hectare (720-acre) green with two award-winning 18-hole courses. First golf course to ever hold the Johnny Walker Classic twice, and has played host to such greats as Nick Faldo and Tiger Woods.

Laguna Phuket Golf Club, 34 Moo 4, Th. Srisoonthorn, Bang Thao, tel: 0-7627 0991; www.lagunaphuket.com/golfclub. An 18-hole course that trails around scenic lagoons, coconut groves and rolling fairways. Water features loom over 13 holes, making this one of Phuket's more challenging golf courses.

Go-Karting

Patong Go Kart Speedway, 118/5 Th. Vichitsongkram, tel: 0-7632 1949; www.gokartthailand.com. This 750-metre (2,460ft) racetrack has go-karts capable of speeds up to 110km (70 miles) per hour. Open daily and floodlit to enable night rides. Situated at the foot of Patong Hill in the Kathu district, next to Jungle Bungee.

Sailing

SY Stressbreaker, mobile tel: 08-1894 3966; www.thailand-sail.com. Offers adventure sailing in the Mergui Archipelago aboard a 19-metre (63ft) ketch that comfortably sleeps eight. Experienced British skipper along with his qualified scuba instructor and sailor wife arrange everything from diving and kayaking to the food and drinks. In constant demand and highly recommended.

Meroja, 86 Th. Patak, Kata, tel: 0-7633 0087; www.meroja.com. Offers the *Meroja*, a 26-metre (85ft) ketch for charter into the waters of the Andaman Sea. The well-equipped boat sleeps 11 people and is manned by a competent European skipper, a Thai chef and two deck hands.

Shooting

Phuket Shooting Range, 82/2 Th. Patak, tel: 0-7638 1667; www.phuket-shooting.com. Indoor and outdoor ranges with choice of rifles, handguns and shotguns. Price depends on the calibre and quantity of ammunition purchased. Open: daily 9am to 6pm.

Sea Canoeing

Phuket is the best base to book tours to see the magnificent limestone karsts of Ao Phang Nga (see page 226). Cruises are the usual way of visiting Phang Nga Bay. The **June Bahtra** (www.asian-oasis.com), an old Chinese junk, offers day and evening sunset cruises with dining options.

The more novel way to explore Ao Phang Nga, however, is by sea canoe. These low-lying craft enable you to enter the area's limestone karsts when the tide is low enough to explore hidden islands. The following companies are recommended.

Andaman Sea Kayak, tel: 0-7623 5353; www.andamanseakayak.com. Tours by inflatable canoe start early in the morning, visiting a number of caves and lagoons as well as Naka and James Bond islands.

John Gray Sea Canoe, 124 Soi 1 Th. Yaowarat, Phuket Town, tel: 0-7625 4505-7; www.johngray-seacanoe.com. The original and best sea-canoe operation, run by the charismatic John Gray.

Sea Canoe Thailand, 367/4 Th. Yaowarat, Phuket Town, tel: 0-7621 2252; www.seacanoe.net. Staff are well trained and the specially designed kayaks are more sturdy than the inflatable ones used by other operators.

All of the above also run expeditions to Krabi.

Thai Boxing

Muay Thai Stadium, Saphan Hin, Phuket Town, tel: 0-7639 6591. Thai boxing matches every Friday night. Tickets can be bought at the door or from any travel agency.

Patong Boxing Stadium, Soi Kebsap 2, Th. Sai Nam Yen, tel: 0-7634 5578. Fights are staged at 8pm every Monday, Thursday and Saturday between sinewy Thai fighters and foreigners who usually give a good account of themselves.

Krabi

Golf

Pakasai Country Club, Ban Lik Nai, Nua Klong, tel: 0-7561 1984; www.pakasaicountryclub.com. This 9-hole course with lake views is currently Krabi's only golf course.

Rock Climbing

Krabi's iconic limestone cliffs were made for rock climbing. There are over 150 pegged routes both inland and offshore in the Phra Nang Bay area. Operators in Ao Nang and Railay can advise on the best courses to suit people of different ages and levels of skill and fitness. Most routes are challenging, but there are also several beginner climbs. Equipment rentals, instruction and guides are all available. The following companies are recommended.

Hot Rock Climbing School, Bobo Plaza, Hat Railay West, tel: 0-7562 1771; www.railayadventure.com.

King Climbers, Hat Railay East, tel: 0-7563 7125; www.railay.com. Reputable outfit with many years' experience. Has even published the well-regarded Kings Climbers Route Guide Book.

Deep-Sea Fishing

Ao Nang Fishing and Snorkelling, 31/4 Moo 2, Ao Nang, tel: 0-7569 5408. Offers fishing day trips off the coast of Krabi aboard longtail boats.

Sea Canoeing

Krabi's limestone cliffs and beautiful bays make it a favoured location for sea canoeing enthusiasts. Tours from mainland Krabi usually depart from Ao Thalane or Ao Luk, where monkeys, otters and tropical birds are a common sight. Away from the main Krabi beaches, one of the prime canoeing areas is around the Railay Peninsula (Ko Hong and Ko Bileh are favoured spots). The popularity of this site is not without good reason – aside from the cluster of rocky peaks and hidden caves, the peninsula is accessible only by longtail boat, meaning there are no large boats or noisy jet skis sharing the water with you.

Sea Kayak Krabi, 40 Th. Maharat, Krabi Town, tel: 0-7563 0270; www.seakayak-krabi.com. Offers both half- and full-day guided canoeing trips to Ao Thalane, Ao Luk and Ko Hong. Lunch is provided on the full-day tours.

Phuket-based operators also run tours to Krabi.

Ko Phi Phi

Diving and Snorkelling

Aquanauts Scuba, mobile tel: 08-1898 1838; www.aquanauts-scuba.com. One of the first dive centres on the island, with friendly and experienced staff. Strong emphasis is placed on personal instruction, with a maximum of four divers per instructor.

Island Divers, mobile tel: 08-9873 2205; www.islanddiverspp.com. Friendly

Cookery Schools

Bangkok

Blue Elephant Cookery School, Blue Elephant Restaurant, 233 Th. Sathorn, tel: 0-2673 9353; www.blueelephant.com. Located in an old mansion, the school offers half-day classes that begin with a trip to a Thai produce market. Up to four dishes are taught in the hands-on classes.

Oriental Cookery School, Oriental Hotel, 48 Oriental Avenue, tel: 0-2659 0000; www.mandarinoriental.com. The legendary hotel runs pricey cooking demonstrations rather than hands-on classes, but even this is a fascinating gastronomic experience.

Thai House, tel: 0-2903 9611/ 2997 5161; www.thaihouse.co.th. Combines Thai cookery lessons with a stay in a rustic Thai-style house in the suburbs of Nontha-buri; 1-, 2- and 3-day courses available with lodging included.

Ko Samui

Samui Institute of Thai Culinary Arts (SITCA), Hat Chaweng, tel: 0-7741 3172; www.sitca.net. A professionally run school that conducts hands-on morning and late afternoon courses. Budding chefs learn to cook three to four dishes, and end up eating them. The school also runs 3-day fruit- and vegetable-carving courses.

Phuket

Mom Tri's Boathouse, Hat Kata, tel: 0-7633 0015; www.boathouse.net. One of Phuket's acclaimed cookery schools is managed by the boutique Boathouse resort on Kata beach. The 1- and 2-day courses are taught by Chef Tummanoon Punchun, the executive chef of the acclaimed Boathouse restaurant.

Chiang Mai

Chiang Mai Thai Cookery School, 47/2 Th. Moon Muang, tel: 0-5320 6388; www.thaicookeryschool.com. One of the oldest and most reputable centres for Thai cooking instruction, offering 1- to 3-day hands-on courses.

and professional staff offer PADI dive courses, day trips and live-aboard diving, as well as snorkelling and kayaking tours.

Viking Divers, mobile tel: 08-1970 3644; www.vikingdiversthailand.com. Offers training for all PADI courses, as well as trips to local dive sites.

Ko Lanta

Diving and Snorkelling

The waters around **Mu Ko Lanta Marine National Park** are home to some of Thailand's best snorkelling and diving sites (see page 262). Most dive operators are found at Ban Sala Dan, while upmarket resorts usually have a dive centre on their premises. **Blue Planet Divers**, Ban Sala Dan, tel: 0-7568 4165; www.blueplanetdivers. net. Qualified instructors offer extensive courses and dive trips aboard a modern air-conditioned boat. Multilingual staff.
Lanta Diver Co. Ltd, Ban Sala Dan, mobile tel: 08-1271 9050; www. lantadiver.com. A five-star IDC dive centre. Keeps diver numbers limited on visits to nearby sites, with a maximum of four per instructor.

Chiang Mai

Rock Climbing

Chiang Mai Rock Climbing Adventures, 55/3 Th. Ratcha-phakhinai, tel: 0-5320 7102; www. thailandclimbing.com. Focusing on Crazy Horse Buttress, the limestone cliffs in Mae On district east of Chiang Mai, this outfit offers guided rock climbs, caving and bouldering instruction.

River Cruises

Mae Ping River Cruises, Th. Charoen Prathet, tel: 0-5327 4822; www.maeping rivercruise.com. At a river pier directly behind Wat Chaimongkhon, 2-hour day cruises of the Ping River can be booked (B400 per person). A separate dinner cruise runs from 7pm to 9.15pm (B500 per person, including food and non-alcoholic beverages).

Thai Boxing

Kawila Boxing Stadium, Soi Sanpakhoi, Th. Charoen Muang, no phone. Every Wednesday and Friday night at 8.30pm, locally trained fighters collide in the ring for up to 10 authentic *muay thai* matches in this small stadium.
Lanna Muay Thai, 161 Soi Chiang Khian, tel: 0-5389 2102; www. lannamuaythai.com. Northern Thailand's well-known Thai kickboxing training camp offers instructions on a daily, weekly and monthly basis. Open to all nationalities.

Trekking

Eagle House, 16 Th. Changmoi Gao, Soi 3, tel: 0-5387 4126; www. eaglehouse.com. Owned by a Thai and Irish husband and wife team (Pon and Annette). Eagle House is a reputable outfit that organises hill-tribe treks in north Thailand.
Trekking Collective, 3/5 Th. Loy Kroh, tel: 0-5320 8340; www.trekking collective.com. Established in 1988, its trekking tours are more expensive than the norm but well worth the price. Treks last from 1 to 6 days and cater to all levels of fitness. Part of its profits goes towards the funding of community projects in the region.

Sightseeing Tours

Journey CNX, 283 Th. Tha Pae, tel: 0-5320 8787; www.journeycnx.com. A well-run company that caters to all palates, with over 20 packages to choose from.
Maeping Riverside Tours, 101 Th. Lampoon, tel: 0-5330 2121; www. tours-chiangmai.com. Offers an extensive range of sightseeing and trekking tours of Chiang Mai and northern Thailand. It also operates a bed and breakfast by the Ping River.

Chiang Rai

Trekking

Dozens of local travel agencies can arrange 3- to 7-day treks to nearby mountains that allow you to enjoy the scenery, learn about natural history and visit hill-tribe villages. Prices range from B2,000 to B3,000 per person per day, including all transport, lodging, food and guide services. The best place to learn about hill-tribe cultures before a trek is the **Hill Tribe Museum & Education Centre** (620/1 Th. Thanalai, tel: 0-5374 0088), which is run by the non-profit Population & Community Development Association. The PDA also works with its own travel agency, specialising in environmentally friendly and culturally sensitive tours.

Mae Sot

Guided trips to Um Phang district, four hours south of Mae Sot, can be arranged at any guesthouse or hotel in town, or through the following tour agencies.
Eco-Trekking, No. 4 Guest House, 736 Th. Intharakhiri, tel: 0-5554 4976; email: no4gh@cscoms.com.
Max One Tour, Mae Sot Square, Th. Intharakhiri, tel: 0-5554 2942; www. maxonetour.com.

Mae Hong Son

Trekking

Famous for its natural beauty and ethnic diversity, Mae Hong Son Province arguably offers northern Thailand's best trekking options. Typical treks take in limestone caves and visits to Lisu, Lahu and Karen villages. Several local agencies arrange 3- to 5-day programmes for around B1,000 per person per day, including all transport, lodging and food.
Nam Rim Tours, Th. Khunlum Praphat, Mae Hong Son, tel: 0-5361 4454.
Rosegarden Tours, 86/4 Th. Khunlum Praphat, Mae Hong Son, tel: 0-5361 1681; www.rosegarden-tours.com.

Pai

Rafting

The Pai River is popular for white-water rafting. Although day trips are available, the best programmes spend a night in the jungle along the way. Most raft trips operate out of Pai itself, although Mae Hong Son agencies can also make the necessary arrangements.
Thai Adventure Rafting, Th. Rongsianoon, Pai, tel: 0-5369 9111; www.thairafting.com. A Frenchman who has been rafting in Pai for 20 years runs incredible trips of 60km (40 miles), taking in 60 rapids on the Pai River, with a night in a jungle camp. Day trips as well.

Elephant Treks

Thom's Pai Elephant Camp Tours, Th. Rangsiyanon, Pai, tel: 0-5369 9286. Three-hour elephant treks through nearby forest, ending with a romp through the Pai River and a hot-springs soak. On request the agency can combine elephant rides with trekking and rafting trips.

FESTIVALS

Thais need little excuse for a party, and the kingdom celebrates festivals aplenty. As it's impossible to list every festival and fair, only the highlights of the calendar are mentioned here. As many events are determined by the lunar calendar, it's best to verify exact dates with the TAT in Bangkok (tel: 0-2250 5500) or check www.tourism thailand.org. (See also pages 58–9.)

January

Bor Sang Umbrella Fair (Bor Sang, Chiang Mai): Celebrates the tradi-tional skill of making gaily painted umbrellas and other handicrafts.

January/February

Chinese New Year (nationwide): Mainly celebrated by the Chinese who visit temples seeking good fortune for the coming year. Shops close and family celebrations go on for 3 days.

February

Flower Festival (Chiang Mai): This annual event features flower displays, floral floats and beauty contests. It coincides with the period when the province's flowers are in full bloom.

Magha Puja (nationwide): Takes place during full moon in February, and marks a spontaneous gathering of 1,200 disciples to hear the Buddha preach. In the evening, devotees gather at temples. Then, when the moon is rising, they clasp their hands in prayer, and armed with candles, incense and flowers, follow the chanting monks around the temple's ordination hall three times before placing their offerings in trays at the front of the temple.

April

Songkran (nationwide): 13–15 April. Thailand's official New Year. In days gone by, people would celebrate by visiting temples and sprinkling water on each other's heads. Nowadays it's a different story, as everyone gets wet and wild on the streets with water pistols the size of machine-guns. No one is exempt as revellers career around the streets in open trucks with barrels of water, drenching everyone in sight. It's best to leave your valuables at the hotel. Thanon Khao San in Bangkok is a popular Songkran destination, as many young Thais converge on the backpacker enclave to douse visitors. In the north of Thailand, particularly in Chiang Mai, Songkran is fervently celebrated over several days and attracts many people from Bangkok.

That Phanom Festival (That Phanom): Celebrated by Buddhist pilgrims who make their way to That Phanom in the northeast to honour one of the country's most sacred Buddha images.

May

Rocket Festival (Boun Bang Fai) (Yasothon): Held in early May, this festival is celebrated in the northeast, especially the town of Yasothon near Mukdahan. It's worth the trip to witness the launching of these locally made missiles. They come in all shapes and sizes, some as tall as a person.

Royal Ploughing Ceremony (Bangkok): Held at Sanam Luang in early May. The king presides at this Brahman ritual which marks the start of the rice-planting season. Crimson-clad attendants lead buffaloes

drawing a plough over specially consecrated ground.

Visakha Puja (nationwide): A public holiday at full-moon night in May that commemorates the birth, enlightenment and death of Buddha. Visakha Puja is celebrated in a similar fashion to Magha Puja.

June/July

Phee Ta Khon (Dan Sai): Possibly Thailand's most riotous festival *(see page 353)*, Phee Ta Khon is celebrated in this northeastern town near Loei.

July/August

Asalaha Puja (nationwide): The full moon in July witnesses the third-most important Buddhist holiday of the year, marking the occasion when Buddha preached to his first five disciples. It is celebrated in similar manner to Magha Puja and Visakha Puja. It also marks the beginning of the three-month "Buddhist Lent", when Thai monks begin a season of prayers and meditation.

Khao Phansa (nationwide): Celebrated immediately after Asanha Puja and marks the start of the annual three-month "Rains Retreat". This is when young Buddhist novices are ordained at the temple.

Candle Festival (Ubon): The Candle Festival takes place during Khao Phansa *(see above)* in this northeastern town. It celebrates the start of Khao Phansa with a lovely spectacle, during which beautifully embellished beeswax candles are paraded along the streets before being presented to temples.

Bangkok International Film Festival (Bangkok): This is a much-anticipated event in the region and showcases more than 100 films from around the world, including the best of Southeast Asian cinema.

September

Moon Festival (nationwide): On the first day of the eighth lunar month, Chinese place small shrines laden with fruit, incense and candles in front of their houses to honour the moon goddess, and eat cakes shaped like a full moon stuffed with bean paste and an egg yolk.

International Swan Boat Races (Bangkok): Held in mid-September and draws an international crowd to the Chao Phraya River.

October

Vegetarian Festival (Bangkok and Phuket): Held in mid-October, and marked by heaps of vegetarian food,

Chinese operatic performances, and elaborate offerings at various Chinese temples in Bangkok and Phuket. In Phuket, devotees go into trance and subject themselves to all kinds of tortuous punishments. Only those wearing all-white attire are allowed in the area of the altar, so dress appropriately.

Ok Phansa (nationwide): Marks the end of the three-month Buddhist Lent, and the beginning of the Kathin season when Buddhists visit temples to present monks with new robes and other necessities. This is also a day of feasting and fun.

Fireboat Festival (Nakhon Phanom): Marking the end of the Ok Phansa period, this northeastern festival launches a series of gaily decorated "fireboats" *(see page 359)*.

Buffalo Races (Chonburi): Held in late October amid much excitement (and betting on the sidelines).

November

Loy Krathong (nationwide): One of the most beautiful festivals in Asia is held at full moon in November. Thais everywhere launch small candle-laden boats into the rivers and canals to seek blessings, forming a beautiful illuminated mini armada.

Elephant Round-Up (Surin): Thailand's iconic elephants are the subject of this popular festival, attracting visitors from far and wide.

Khon Kaen Silk Fair (Khon Kaen): Silk-weaving demonstrations and a chance to buy silk at this major centre of production in the northeast.

December

River Kwai Bridge Week (Kanchanaburi): A sound-and-light presentation recaptures this dark period of recent history, when thousands of Asians and Europeans died at the hands of the Japanese while building the infamous Death Railway during World War II.

Trooping of the Colours (Bangkok): On 3 December, the royal regiments dressed in brilliantly coloured uniforms march in review before the king on the plaza in front of the old National Assembly building.

King's Birthday Celebrations (nationwide): On 5 December (a public holiday), King Bhumibol celebrates his birthday with a ceremony at Wat Phra Kaew for invited officials and guests. This special day is also regarded as Thailand's very own Fathers' Day.

King's Cup Regatta (Phuket): This long-distance yacht race held off Phuket draws competitors from around the world.

A – Z

A HANDY SUMMARY OF PRACTICAL INFORMATION, ARRANGED ALPHABETICALLY

A ddresses

Since most of Bangkok developed with little central planning, getting around can be confusing at first, given the size (and flatness) of the city and its many twisting alleyways.

Bangkok is mostly laid out using the *soi* system – smaller streets leading off a main road of the same name, with each *soi* having a number after the name. For example, Sukhumvit Road (or Thanon Sukhumvit) has numerous streets branching from it in sequence such as Sukhumvit Soi 33, Sukhumvit Soi 55, etc. Most hotels provide business cards with the address written in Thai to show to taxi drivers. Fortunately, taxis are inexpensive, so if you do get lost, it won't cost you too much to find your destination.

Thailand's smaller cities and towns are a lot easier to work out. A typical address might be preceded by the word Moo (referring to the residential estate) before the name of the road or *soi*, as in 23/3 Moo 1. But many

places don't have complete addresses and will just state the beach or general area where they are located.

B udgeting for Your Trip

By Western standards Thailand is a bargain. Five-star hotels cost half or a third of what they would in New York or London, and at the other end, budget (if a bit dingy) accommodation can be as cheap as B100 per night. Street food can be excellent, and you can have a filling and tasty meal for B30 to B40. Transport is cheap, with bus fares priced from B4 to B16, a ride on the Skytrain and Metro from B15 to B40. Taxis are inexpensive as well *(see page 367)*. Drinks in bars cost from B60 to B100 and in clubs from B180 to B300. If you live frugally, you can get by with B1,000 a day, but the sky is the limit here if you want to live it up at luxury hotels and eat at fine-dining restaurants.

As a general rule of thumb, destinations that attract a lot of tourists will entail higher costs of living.

Phuket and Ko Samui, for instance, are the most expensive islands, while Ko Phangan, Ko Lanta and Ko Chang are gradually moving up on the cost of living scale. On the other hand, largely untouched places like Trang and Satun offer the best bargains.

Apart from Chiang Mai, the north and northeast regions have the lowest cost of living in Thailand. In most of these places, you would be hard-pressed to find hotels beyond the moderate category.

Business Hours

Government offices in Thailand operate 8.30am to 4.30pm Monday to Friday. Most businesses are open 8am to 5.30pm Monday to Friday, while some are open 8.30am to noon on Saturday. Banks are open 9.30am to 3.30pm Monday to Saturday.

Department stores are open 10.30am to 9pm daily, though larger stores open as late as 10pm. Ordinary shops open at 8.30am or 9am and close between 6pm and

8pm, depending on location and type of business.

Small open-air coffee shops and restaurants open at 7am and close at 8.30pm, though some stay open past midnight. Large restaurants generally close by 10pm. In Bangkok, most hotel coffee shops close at midnight; some stay open 24 hours, and the city has several outdoor restaurants that are open as late as 4am.

Bangkok's nightlife venues generally close by 2am, but in many resorts – mainly Phuket, Ko Samui, Ko Samet, Ko Phangan and Ko Tao – they don't close until much later.

Generally, outside of Bangkok, opening times are more flexible at small family-run shops, eateries and bars. Knowing that most people are out having fun, businesses located near beaches tend to open later in the day and stay open all evening.

Business Travellers

As Thailand strives to become a regional business hub, Bangkok hosts an increasing number of business travellers from all over the world. Most city hotels have business centres with communications and secretarial services. Outside the capital, such services are scarce, limited only to places like Pattaya, Phuket, Ko Samui and Chiang Mai, all of which are popular as venues for business conferences and seminars.

Children

Travelling with children is a breeze in Thailand. Thais love kids, and those with blond hair will receive special attention. It can be a bit overwhelming, but people are just being friendly and it is part of the Thai sense of community.

Footpaths in Bangkok and most Thai cities and towns are not pedestrian-friendly. They are often in disrepair, and inevitably something or somebody obstructs them: leave the buggy at home and bring back- or chest-mounted baby carriers. Children should never approach dogs, monkeys or other small animals; those seen in the streets are more feral than back at home, and rabies is still a risk.

The tropical sun is intense, so high SPF sun-block lotion and hats are important. Make sure the kids keep their hands clean, as they can easily pick up stomach bugs.

Climate

There are three main seasons in Thailand: hot, rainy and cool. But to the

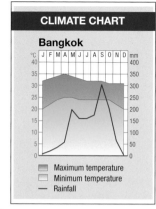

CLIMATE CHART

Bangkok

- ☐ Maximum temperature
- ☐ Minimum temperature
- — Rainfall

tourist winging in from more temperate regions, Thailand has only one temperature: hot. To make things worse, the temperature drops only a few degrees during the night, and is accompanied by humidity levels of above 70 percent. Nights during the cool season, however, can be pleasant.

The following guideline is a rough indication of Thailand's weather patterns (although you can, and should, expect regional variations in weather). Also, with global warming and erratic weather patterns these days, it's hard to predict with near-certainty the onset (and the end) of the rainy season.

- Hot season (Mar to May): 27–35°C (80–95°F)
- Rainy season (June to Oct): 24–32°C (75–90°F)
- Cool season (Nov to Feb): 22–30°C (72–86°F), but with less humidity.

The countryside is somewhat cooler, but the north and northeast can be hotter in March and April than Bangkok. During these months, the north can also be affected by smoke and haze, no thanks to farmers who clear agricultural land by setting entire fields ablaze. Generally, Chiang Mai enjoys a cooler, less humid climate. In the cool season, temperatures in Chiang Mai range between 13°C and 28°C (55°F and 82°F). In the northern hills, however, temperatures can plummet much lower, occasionally reaching single digits. As in Bangkok, the heaviest rain falls in September.

There are regional variations along Thailand's coastline, but generally the Eastern Seaboard and northern Gulf of Thailand coast have a weather pattern similar to that of Bangkok. The southern Gulf of Thailand coast around Ko Samui is a little different: it receives light intermittent rain from June to October; from November to January, however, the northeast

monsoon brings the heaviest rains, with November being the wettest month.

Phuket and the Andaman Coast experiences its wettest months from May to October. November can be a bit unstable.

Thailand's peak tourist season runs from November to March and, not surprisingly, roughly coincides with the country's cool season.

Clothing

Clothes should be light and loose; fabrics made from natural fibres are definitely more comfortable than synthetics. During the height of the rainy season, sandals are preferable to shoes. Sunglasses, hats and sunscreen are recommended for protection from the tropical sun.

Suits are sometimes worn for business in Bangkok but in general Thailand does not have the formal dress code of Hong Kong or Tokyo. A shirt and tie is expected for business appointments, and advisable for any visit to a government office.

Shorts are taboo for both women and men who wish to enter some of the more revered temples. Women wearing sleeveless dresses and short skirts may also be barred from some temples and mosques. Improperly dressed and unkempt visitors will be turned away from large temples like the Wat Phra Kaew (Temple of the Emerald Buddha) and from the Grand Palace in Bangkok.

In some parts of south Thailand, Muslims are in the majority, so dress in deference to the religion and to Thai sensitivities. Although topless sunbathing is common at some beaches in Pattaya, Phuket and Ko Samui, it makes locals uncomfortable. Nudity in public is seen as degrading and generally frowned upon.

Crime and Security

Thailand is a relatively safe country in terms of violent crime. The biggest risk to travellers is from scams and con artists. If you do run into trouble, there are **Tourist Police** (TP) units at the major destinations, which are specially assigned to assist travellers. However, much of the time, there is little they are able to do other than record the details of the crime and provide a report (for insurance purposes). Most members of the force speak some English.

Tourist Police

TP National Hotline: 1155; www. tourist.police.go.th
Bangkok Tourist Assistance Centre, 4 Th. Rachadamnoen Nok, tel:

TRANSPORT

0-2225 7612-4. In Bangkok TP booths can also be found in tourist areas, including Lumphini Park (near the intersection of Th. Rama IV and Th. Silom) and Patpong (at the Th. Silom intersection).

Drugs

Both hard and soft drugs are easy to procure in Thailand, but it is illegal to possess, consume or trade in them. If caught, the penalties are harsh and the death sentence can apply. Stay clear of drug dealers. Police raids are common at tourist destinations and at the infamous full-moon parties at Ko Phangan (see page 206); both plain-clothed and uniformed police will be on the prowl.

Insurgent Activity

Over the past three decades, a low-level insurgency has been brewing in the southern provinces closest to the Malaysian border, ie Pattani, Yala and Narathiwat. Fuelled by foreign Muslim fundamentalists, this has given rise to a violent separatist movement and sporadic unrest. You are advised to stay clear of these provinces.

Common Scams

• Touts at Bangkok's Patpong who offer live sex shows upstairs. Once inside, you are handed an exorbitant bill and threatened if you protest. Pay, take the receipt, and go immediately to the Tourist Police, who will usually take you back and demand a refund.
• Don't follow touts who offer to take you to a gem factory for a "special deal". The gems are usually synthetic or of substandard quality, and there is no way to get your money back.
• Tuk-tuk drivers who offer to take you on a free tour and then stop at every gem, silver and tailor shop along the way where they will collect a commission for wasting your day. A common ruse is to pretend that the attraction you want to visit is closed for a special ceremony. Don't believe them.
• People on buses or trains offering sweets, fruits or soft drinks. The items may be drugged and the passenger is robbed while unconscious.

Keep in mind that in Thai culture, strangers rarely approach and engage foreigners in conversation, so if you find yourself on the receiving end, be on guard no matter how polite and innocent they appear to be. Feel free to walk away, even if it goes against the rules of polite behaviour.

Women Travellers

Thailand is generally safe for women travellers, even those travelling alone.

Thais tend to be non-confrontational, so violent and sexual crimes towards foreign women are not common. That said, like anywhere, it isn't a great idea to be walking alone on quiet streets or beaches late at night. Also, there is a perception (probably a by-product of Hollywood films) that foreign women are "easy", so be careful in your associations with local men, because they may have the wrong idea about you. Reasonably modest dress will certainly help.

Customs Regulations

The Thai government prohibits the import or export of drugs, dangerous chemicals, pornography, firearms and ammunition. Attempting to smuggle heroin or other hard drugs in or out may be punishable by death. Scores of foreigners are serving very long prison terms for this offence.

Tourists may freely bring in foreign banknotes or other types of foreign exchange up to a value of US$20,000. For travellers leaving Thailand, the maximum amount permitted to be taken out in Thai currency without prior authorisation is B50,000. Foreign guests are allowed to bring in without tax 200 cigarettes and 1 litre of wine or spirits.

Buddha images, antiques and art objects cannot leave Thailand without a Department of Fine Arts permit (see page 402).

For more details check the Thai **Customs Department** website at www.customs.go.th, or call the hotline: 1164.

D isabled Travellers

Thailand falls short on accommo-dating the disabled, though this is slowly improving. Pavements are often uneven, studded with obstructions, and there are no ramps. Few buildings have wheelchair ramps. In Bangkok, some major roads have textured brickwork on the paths for the blind. A few Skytrain stations have lifts, but not nearly enough; the Metro has lifts at every station. Getting to many of Thailand's smaller islands often entails taking small boats that are moored at poorly designed piers. It would be a challenge for a disabled traveller on his/her own to get around Thailand – a companion is essential.

E lectricity

Electrical outlets are rated at 220 volts, 50 cycles and accept flat-pronged or round-pronged plugs.

Adaptors can be purchased at department or hardware stores.

Embassies and Consulates in Bangkok

Australia, 37 Th. Sathorn Tai, tel: 0-2344 6300. Visas: Mon–Fri 8.15am–12.15pm.
Canada, 15/F, Abdulrahim Place, Th. Rama IV, tel: 0-2636 0560.
New Zealand, M Thai Tower, 14th Floor, All Seasons Place, 87 Wireless Road, tel: 0-2254 2530.
Singapore, 129 Th. Sathorn Tai, tel: 0-2286 2111.
UK, 14 Wireless Road, tel: 0-2305 8333. Visas: Mon–Thur 8–11am, Fri 8am–noon.
US, 95 Wireless Road, tel: 0-2205 4000. Visas: Mon–Fri 7.30–10am.

Entry Requirements
Visas and Passports

Travellers should check visa regulations at a Thai embassy or consulate before starting their trip, as visa rules vary for different nationalities. For an updated list, check the Thai **Ministry of Foreign Affairs** website at www.mfa.go.th.

All foreign nationals entering Thailand must have a valid passport with at least six-month validity. At the airport, nationals from most countries will be granted a visa on arrival valid for up to 30 days. Officially you need an air ticket out of Thailand, but this is rarely checked.

Longer tourist visas, obtained from the Thai consulate of your home country prior to arrival, allow for a 60-day stay. People seeking a work permit can apply for a non-immigrant visa which is good for 90 days. A letter of guarantee is needed from the Thai company you intend to work for, and this visa can be obtained from a Thai consulate at home.

The on-arrival 30-day visa can be extended by 7 to 10 days for a fee of B1,900 in Bangkok or at the regional immigration offices, or you can leave the country (even for half an hour) and return to receive another free 30-day visa. The 60-day visa can be extended for another 30 days at the same price.

Overstaying your visa can carry a daily fine of B200 to a maximum of B20,000. If the police catch you with an expired visa, life can get very complicated, and you can get thrown into the immigration prison.

In Bangkok, the Thai **Immigration Bureau** is at 507 Soi Puan Plu, Thanon Sathorn Tai, tel: 0-2287 3101–10; www.immigration.go.th (open

Mon–Fri 8.30am–4.30pm). Check the website for contact details of other offices.
Phuket, tel: 0-7634 0477/221 905.
Ko Samui, tel: 0-7742 1069.
Chiang Mai, tel: 0-5320 1755.

Etiquette

Thais are remarkably tolerant and forgiving of foreigners' eccentricities, but there are a few things that are liable to upset them *(see also Clothing, page 412)*.

The Royal Family
Thais revere the monarchy, and any disrespect directed towards members of the royal family will be taken personally. At movies the national anthem is played before the movie starts and it is bad manners not to stand when the others do.

Buddhism
A similar degree of respect is accorded to the second pillar of Thai society, Buddhism. Disrespect towards Buddha images, temples or monks is not taken lightly and, as with the monarchy, public expressions against the institution are considered illegal.

Monks observe vows of chastity that prohibit being touched by (or touching) women, even their mothers. When in the vicinity of a monk, a woman should try to stay clear to avoid accidental contact.

At temples, the scruffy and the underclad are frequently turned away, so dress appropriately.

Terms of Address
Thais are addressed by their first rather than their last names. The name is usually preceded by the word *khun*, a term of honour, a bit like Mr or Ms. Following this to its logical conclusion, Silpachai Krishnamra would be addressed as Khun Silpachai.

Thai Greetings
The common greeting and farewell in Thailand is *sawadee* (followed by *khrap* when spoken by men and *kha* by women). In more formal settings this is accompanied by a *wai* – raising the hands in a prayer-like gesture, the fingertips touching the nose, and bowing the head slightly. However, don't make the mistake of giving a *wai* to all hotel staff, children or the people at the corner shop – it embarrasses them. In these cases, a nod is sufficient. Almost all Thais understand that this is not a part of Western culture. In business

meetings, the *wai* is often followed by a handshake.

Head and Feet
Thai Buddhism regards the head as the wellspring of wisdom and the feet as unclean. For this reason, it is insulting to touch another person on the head, point one's feet at anything or step over another person. In formal situations, when wishing to pass someone who is seated on the floor, bow slightly while walking and point an arm down to indicate the path to be taken, and a path will be cleared.

Public Behaviour
A few decades ago, Thai couples showed no intimacy in public. That has changed due to modernisation and foreign influence on the young, but even these days, intimacy rarely extends beyond holding hands. As in many traditional societies, displaying open affection in public, such as kissing and passionate cuddling, is a sign of bad manners.

Gay and Lesbian Travellers

Gays quickly discover that Thailand is one of the most tolerant countries in the world. The gay nightlife scene in Bangkok, Pattaya and Phuket is huge. Bangkok also hosts the annual Bangkok Gay Pride Festival (www.bangkokpride.org), while similar events take place in Pattaya (www.pattayagayfestival.com) and in Phuket. Chiang Mai has a small gay scene as well, but it's a bit more discreet.

Utopia at 116/1 Soi 23 Sukhumvit, tel: 0-2259 9619; www.utopia-asia.com is Bangkok's centre for gays and lesbians. It's a good place to make contacts and to find out what's going on.

Purple Dragon is a Utopia-affiliated travel agency that caters exclusively to gay travellers. It is located at Tarntawan Place Hotel, 119/5–10 Thanon Surawong, tel: 0-2238 3227; www.purpledrag.com.

Health and Medical Care

Visitors entering Thailand are not required to show evidence of vaccination for smallpox or cholera. Check that your tetanus boosters are up to date. Immunisation against cholera is a good idea, as are hepatitis A and B innoculations. Malaria and dengue persist in remote and rural areas outside Bangkok. When in the countryside, especially in the monsoon season, apply mosquito repellent on exposed skin at all times

– dengue mosquitoes are at their most active during the day. At night, be sure to sleep under mosquito netting.

With its thriving nightlife and transient population, Bangkok is a magnet for sexual diseases. Aids and other sexually transmitted diseases are not confined to "high risk" sections of the population in Thailand, so practise safe sex.

Many first-time visitors take a while to adjust to the heat. It is important to drink plenty of water, especially if you've drunk alcohol. Avoid too much sun when out and about and use sun block with a high SPF – the sun is far more powerful at this latitude than in temperate regions.

Tap water in Bangkok has been certified as potable, but take no chances anywhere in Thailand and drink bottled water instead, which is widely available throughout the country. In Bangkok and at reputable hotels and restaurants at Thailand's major tourist centres, ice is clean and presents no health problems.

Stomach upsets are sometimes caused by over-indulgence rather than contaminated food. Many foreigners over-eat and their stomachs react negatively to the sudden switch to a different cuisine. Stick only to freshly cooked food. Establishments catering to foreigners are generally careful with food and drink preparation. They do not, however, always place such a high priority on keeping the environment clean.

Buy travel insurance before travelling to Thailand. Evacuation insurance is not really necessary, as hospitals listed below are of international standard.

Hospitals

The level of medical care in Bangkok and some of Thailand's regional centres is very good. The hospitals listed here all have specialised clinics as well as standard medical facilities. In fact, there has been a growing business in "medical tourism" over the past 10 years, with people coming to Thailand to have procedures performed (including cosmetic and sex-change surgery) that would cost many times more at home or require waiting in a months-long queue. Equipment is up to date and the doctors are usually trained overseas and speak English. By Thai standards, these are considered expensive, but the fees are a fraction of what they are in most Western countries. Note: Most of the hospitals listed here also have dental clinics.

Bangkok

BNH Hospital, 9/1 Th. Convent, Silom, tel: 0-2686 2700; www.bnh hospital.com. This squeaky-clean hospital offers comfortable rooms, top-notch equipment and a large team of specialists. Service is efficient and English is widely spoken.

Bumrungrad Hospital, 33 Soi 3, Th. Sukhumvit, tel: 0-2667 1000; www.bumrungrad.com. This one is at the top of the heap, and looks more like a five-star hotel than a hospital. Offers a huge range of specialised clinics, excellent staff and a selection of rooms from basic four-bed wards to luxury suites.

Ko Samui

Samui International Hospital, 90/2 Moo 2, Chaweng, tel: 0-7742 2272; www.sih.co.th. The best on the island and on a par with the best in Bangkok.

Pattaya

Bangkok Pattaya Hospital, 301 Moo 6, Th. Sukhumvit Km 143, tel: 0-3825 9999; www.bph.co.th. Part of a network of well-equipped modern private hospitals that also has a branch in Phuket.

Pattaya International Hospital, Pattaya Soi 4, tel: 0-3842 8374–5; www.pih-inter.com. This hospital is equipped to deal with emergencies and elective surgical procedures, including sex changes.

Phuket

Bangkok Hospital Phuket, 21 Th. Hongyok Utis, Phuket Town, tel: 0-7625 4425; www.phukethospital.com. Popular with foreign tourists who come for health checks and surgical procedures.

Phuket International Hospital, 44 Th. Chalermprakiat, tel: 0-7624 9400; www.phuket-inter-hospital.co.th. Probably the best healthcare facility on the island and familiar with the needs of international patients.

Chiang Mai

Chiang Mai Ram Hospital, 8 Th. Bunruangrit, tel: 0-5322 4851, emergency tel: 0-5389 5001; www. chiangmairam.com. The city's premier hospital, with efficient staff and modern faciliies.

Lanna Hospital, 1 Th. Sukkasem, tel: 0-5399-9777; www.lanna-hospital.com. Another hospital with a fine reputation.

McCormick Hospital, Th. Kaew Nawarat, tel: 0-5392-1777; www.mccormick.in.th. Former missionary hospital with a good reputation.

Medical Clinics

In Bangkok, for minor problems, head to the **British Dispensary**, 109 Thanon Sukhumvit (between Soi 3 and 5), tel: 0-2252 8056. It has British doctors on its staff. All the major hotels in Bangkok and at Thailand's main tourist centres have doctors on call, or clinics they can recommend. Some international hotels also have an on-premises clinic.

Badalveda (www.badalveda.com) is a network of dive medicine centres, with branches in Phuket, Ko Tao, Surat Thani and Bangkok. As well as having hyperbaric chambers, they are experienced in treating other dive-related ailments.

Dental Clinics

Apart from the dental clinics at the international hospitals listed here, the

Dental Hospital at 88/88 Soi 49 Thanon Sukhumvit, tel: 0-2260 5000, is recommended in Bangkok. It looks more like a hotel than a dental hospital and has the latest equipment.

In the major tourist centres, head to the recommended hospitals, all of which offer dental services; otherwise grit your teeth if you can and get it fixed when you return to Bangkok.

Pharmacies

These are found everywhere in downtown Bangkok, as well as at most island and beach destinations. In recent years, official control on prescription drugs has been more strongly enforced and requires the presence of a licensed pharmacist on the premises, especially in Bangkok. Nonetheless, most antibiotics and many other drugs that would require a prescription in the West are still available without one in Thailand.

Check the expiry date on all drugs you buy, and wherever possible, purchase them from an air-conditioned pharmacy. There are several branches of **Boots** and **Watsons** pharmacies in central Bangkok.

I nternet

Wireless surf zones (Wi-fi), at Bangkok Airport and in hotels, malls and some branches of Starbucks in Bangkok, are a growing trend.

All major hotels in Thailand offer broadband/Wi-fi internet services, including in the rooms, though these are generally more expensive than at the public internet cafés. These days, even the smallest bungalow outfits in relatively remote towns and beaches have internet terminals for guests to use. Connection speeds at such places, however, can be slow.

In Bangkok, internet cafés usually charge B30 per hour for broadband services. Be warned, though, that – in Bangkok at least – they tend to be full of teenagers playing violent games online and can be quite noisy. The Khao San area has more internet cafés than in any other area in Bangkok, but the Silom and Ploenchit areas have some internet cafés as well. Ask your hotel reception desk for advice.

BELOW: Khao San Road in Bangkok has a high concentration of internet cafés.

L eft Luggage

There are two left-luggage facilities at Suvarnabhumi Airport. One is on Level 2 (near Exit 4) of the arrival hall, and the other is on Level 4 (near Entrance 4) of the departure hall. The fee is B100 per bag per day. The airports at

Phuket, Ko Samui and Chiang Mai also have left-luggage facilities; enquire at the information desks at the respective airports.

All hotels and guesthouses offer a left-luggage service; usually it is free, but some may levy a small daily fee.

Lost Property

If you lose any valuable property, report it as soon as possible to the **Tourist Police** (see page 412) to get an insurance statement.

Suvarnabhumi Airport: For property lost at Bangkok Airport, contact tel: 0-2535 1254.

Public Transit: BMTA city bus service, tel: 0-2246 0973;
BTS Skytrain, tel: 0-2617 6000;
MRTA Metro, tel: 0-2690 8200,
Hualamphong Railway Station, tel: 1690.

Taxis: Bangkok taxi drivers frequently listen to two radio stations that have lost-property hotlines; it's surprising how often forgetful passengers get their lost items back: **JS100 Radio 100FM hotline**: 1137, and **Community Radio 96FM hotline**: 1677.

Maps

Basic maps of Bangkok are available free at the offices of the **Tourism Authority of Thailand** (TAT) offices (see page 418) and at big hotels. More detailed ones can be found at bookshops. The Insight Fleximap map of Bangkok and Thailand is probably the best. Other more useful and off-beat insights to Bangkok's attractions can be found in Nancy Chandler's Map of Bangkok and Groovy Map's Bangkok by Day and Bangkok by Night. In addition, Groovy Map also publishes Phuket Day & Night, and Pattaya Day & Night. At the major tourist centres like Phuket, Ko Samui and Chiang Mai, free maps are available at hotels and tour agencies.

Media

Newspapers

Thailand has two longstanding English-language dailies, the Bangkok Post and The Nation. The Bangkok Post is more conservative than The Nation, which is more maverick and has had a few run-ins with the current government for its often biting coverage. Many big hotels furnish one or the other for free with the room, or they can be purchased at newsstands for B20.

Regional, advertisement-driven newspapers include the weekly Phuket Gazette (www.phuketgazette.net), Pattaya Mail (www.pattayamail.com), Pattaya Today (www.pattayatoday.net) and Chiang Mai Mail (www.chiangmai-mail.com), and the monthly Hua Hin Today (www.huahintoday.net).

Magazines

There are several "what's on in Bangkok" type publications in English, covering events, nightlife, art galleries, restaurants, etc., though most of the free ones are advertisement-riddled and out of date. The best two of the paid glossies are Untamed Travel (www.farangonline.com), a monthly that provides listings and well-written stories about Thailand, Cambodia and Laos, with a comprehensive Bangkok section, and Metro Magazine (www.bkkmetro.com), aimed more at residents than visitors and focusing more exclusively on Bangkok. Both cost B100 each. Also worth picking up is the BK Magazine (www.bkmagazine.com), distributed free at major restaurants and nightspots.

New regional magazines geared towards the tourist market are constantly appearing on the scene. Recommended are the monthly Hua Hin Observer (www.observergroup.net), Ko Samui's Community (www.c-publishing.com), Phuket's Benjarong (www.travel-phuket.com) and Chiang Mai's City Life Magazine (www.chiangmainews.com).

Radio

AM radio is devoted entirely to Thai-language programmes. FM frequencies include several English-language stations with the latest pop hits. Some frequencies have bilingual DJs and play a mixture of Thai and English songs in the same programme.
• **97 MHZ**: Radio Thailand has 4 hours of English-language broadcasts each day.
• **105.5 MHZ**: Tourism Authority of Thailand offers useful tips to tourists every hour.
• **Fat FM 104.5**: Has the latest on Thailand's thriving indie music scene.
• **Eazy FM 105.5**: As the name suggests, mostly easy-listening middle-of-the-road music.
• **FMX 95.5**: Contemporary dance and pop hits.

Television

Thailand has six Thai-language television channels. ITV or Independent Television specialises in news and documentaries. The rest mainly air soaps and game shows with a sprinkling of mostly domestically oriented news. There is also UBC, a cable television network that provides subscribers with a choice of about 24 international channels, including BBC, CNN and CNA.

Money

The baht is the principal Thai monetary unit. Though it is divided into 100 units called satang, this is becoming outdated; only 50 and 25 satang pieces are used.

Banknote denominations include 1,000 (light brown), 500 (purple), 100 (red), 50 (blue) and 20 (green). There is a 10-baht coin (brass centre with silver rim), a 5-baht coin (silver with copper edge), a 1-baht coin (silver), and two small coins of 50 and 25 satang (both brass-coloured).

In early 2010, US$1 was worth B32.7, £1 sterling B48.8, and 1 Euro equalled B44.3.

Changing Money

Banking hours are from 9.30am to 3.30pm Monday to Friday, but nearly every bank maintains money-changing kiosks in the tourist areas of Thailand. Better hotels almost always have exchange facilities at their reception desks, but generally give poor exchange rates when compared to banks.

Credit Cards

American Express, Diner's Club, MasterCard, JCB and Visa are widely accepted throughout Bangkok and major resort towns like Phuket, Ko Samui, Hua Hin and Pattaya. Smaller establishments, however, may impose a 3 percent surcharge on card transactions. Credit cards can be used to draw emergency cash at most banks. If you lose your credit card, contact your card company as soon as possible so that your card can be cancelled.

American Express, tel: 0-2273 0022–44.
Diner's Club, tel: 0-2238 3600.
Visa, tel: 0-2273 7449.
MasterCard, tel: 0-2260 8572.

Warning: Credit card fraud is a major problem in Thailand. Don't leave your credit card in safe-deposit boxes. When making a purchase, make sure that you get the carbon slips and dispose of them. When your card is swiped through the machine, make sure it is done in your presence, and **never** let the card out of your sight.

Travellers' Cheques

Travellers' cheques can be cashed at all exchange kiosks and banks, and generally receive better exchange rates compared to cash. There is a nominal charge of B25 for each travellers' cheque cashed.

P hotography

With more than 10 million visitors per year, Thailand gets its photo taken an awful lot. The country and its people are very photogenic, and everything the photographer may need is readily available.

Postal Services

The Thai postal service is reasonably reliable, though mail seems to go astray more frequently outside Bangkok and at Christmas time. The odds for domestic mail can be improved by registering or sending items by **EMS** for a fee of B20 for a business-sized letter. EMS is supposed to guarantee that a letter reaches a domestic destination in one day, and it generally does, particularly in Bangkok. If you wish to send valuable parcels or bulky documents overseas, it is better to use a courier service.

In Bangkok, the **General Post Office** at Thanon Charoen Krung, tel: 0-2233 1050, is open from Monday to Friday 8am to 8pm, and Saturday, Sunday and holidays 8am to 1pm.

Post offices elsewhere in Bangkok and Thailand usually open at 8am and close at 4pm on weekdays. Postal services are found at all tourist centres, even on small islands like Ko Samet.

In Bangkok, you can find mini post offices in some office buildings and hotels. Look for a red sign in English. These outlets offer basic mail services and accept small packages, but have no telecommunications services.

Courier Services

The usual global courier services are available in Bangkok. You can call direct or book online.
DHL: www.dhl.co.th; **Bangkok**, tel: 0-2345 5000; **Phuket**, tel: 0-7625 8500; **Chiang Mai**, tel: 0-5341 8501.
Fedex: www.fedex.com/th; **Bangkok**, tel: 0-2229 8900; hotline: 1782; toll free: 1800-236 236; **Phuket**: tel: 0-7652 3219; **Chiang Mai**: tel: 0-5330 5212.
UPS: www.ups.com/th; **Bangkok**, tel: 0-2712 3300; **Phuket**, tel: 0-7626 3987; **Chiang Mai**, tel: 0-5375 5030.

Public Holidays

1 Jan: New Year's Day
Jan/Feb: (full moon) Magha Puja.
Note: Chinese New Year is not an

official holiday, but many businesses close for several days.
6 Apr: Chakri Day
13–15 Apr: Songkran
1 May: Labour Day
5 May: Coronation Day
May: (full moon) Visakha Puja
July: (full moon) Asalaha Puja
12 Aug: Queen's Birthday
23 Oct: Chulalongkorn Day
5 Dec: King's Birthday
10 Dec: Constitution Day

R eligious Services

Though it is predominantly Buddhist, Thailand has historically been tolerant of other religions. According to government census, 94 percent are Theravada Buddhists, 3.9 percent are Muslims, 1.7 percent Confucians, and 0.6 percent Christians (mostly hill-tribe people living in the north).

Buddhists will find no lack of places of worship. In Bangkok, there is a handful of Christian churches (both Catholic and Protestant), one major Hindu temple and a mosque, and at least one synagogue. Outside the capital, the options are fewer. The further south you venture the more mosques you will find. Check with your hotel reception desk for addresses of places of worship and timings of services.

T axes

Thailand has a Value-Added Tax (VAT) of 7 percent. This is added to most goods and services (but not goods sold by street vendors and markets). You can get the VAT refunded if you purchase at least B5,000 worth of goods (see panel on page 401).

All major hotels add 10 percent tax plus 8 percent service charge to the room rate. At top-class restaurants, 10 percent service charge is added to the bill.

Telephones
Public Phones

Even though Thais are heavy users of mobile phones, there are still plenty of coin- and card-operated telephone booths in the city. Public telephones accept B1, B5 and B10 coins. Phone cards for local calls in denominations of B50, B100 and B200 can be purchased at 7-11 convenience shops throughout the city.

Local Calls

The prefix 0 must be dialled for all calls made within Thailand, even

when calling local numbers within the same city. Therefore when in Bangkok, dial 0 first, followed by the local 8-digit number; if you need local directory assistance, dial 1133.

International Calls

The **country code** for Thailand is 66. When calling Thailand from overseas, dial your local international access code first, followed by 66 and then the number (without the 0 prefix) in Thailand.

To make an international call from Thailand, dial 001 before the country and area codes, followed by the telephone number. If you need international call assistance, dial 100. Peak-hour calls made from 7am to 9pm are the most expensive, so it pays to call during non-peak hours from 5am to 7am, and 9pm to midnight. The lowest call rates are from midnight to 5am.

Prepaid international phone cards (called Thaicard) of B300, B500 and B1,000 value can be used to make international calls. These can be bought at post offices, certain shops that carry the Thaicard sign or the office of the **Communications Authority of Thailand** in Bangkok, tel: 0-2950 3712; www.cat.or.th.

Mobile Phones

Any local telephone number that begins with the prefix 08 denotes a mobile phone. Just like fixed-line phones, dial the prefix 0 for all calls made within Thailand but drop the zero when calling from overseas.

Only users of GSM 900 or GSM 1800 mobile phones with international roaming facility can hook up automatically to the local

BELOW: Wat Phra That Renu Nakhon.

Thai network. Check with your service provider if you're not sure, especially if coming from the US, Korea or Japan. Your phone will automatically select a local service provider and this enables you to make calls within Thailand at local rates. However, if someone calls your number, international call rates will apply. Charges will be billed to your account in your home country.

If you're planning to travel in Thailand for any length of time, it's more economical to buy a local SIM card with a stored value from a mobile-phone shop. You will be assigned a local number, and local calls to and from the phone will be at local rates. International rates will apply to overseas calls.

Time Zone

Thailand is 7 hours ahead of GMT. Since it gets dark between 6pm and 7pm uniformly throughout the year, Thailand does not observe daylight savings time.

Tipping

Tipping is not a custom in Thailand, although it is becoming more prevalent. A service charge of 10 percent is included in the more expensive restaurants and is usually, though not always, divided among the staff. Do leave a small tip when service charge has not been included. Do not tip taxi or tuk-tuk drivers unless the traffic has been particularly bad and he has been especially patient. Porters are becoming used to being tipped, but will not hover with their hand extended.

Toilets

There are not a great deal of public toilets in Thailand, though Bangkok is beginning to address this issue in tourist areas. Public restrooms are usually dirty and sometimes of the squat-toilet variety, a tricky experience for the uninitiated. Your best bet is to make use of the facilities at fast-food outlets, which are very easy to find. Shopping malls usually have clean toilets as well, particularly near the food courts. Sometimes a small fee of a few baht applies.

Tourist Offices

The **Tourism Authority of Thailand** (TAT) spends billions of baht every year to promote tourism domestically and abroad. They have information outlets in several countries and service kiosks within Thailand that offer maps and other promotional materials as well as advise on things to do and places to see. The main website www.tourismthailand.org has dozens of pages of information.

Bangkok

TAT Call Centre, tel: 1672. Open daily 8am–8pm.
Tourism Authority of Thailand Main Office, 1600 Th. Phetchaburi, Makkasan, Bangkok, tel: 0-2250 5500. Open daily 8.30am–4.30pm.
TAT Tourist Information Counter, Arrival Hall, Suvarnabhumi Airport, tel: 0-2132 1888. Open daily 8am–10pm.
TAT Tourist Information Counter (Ratchadamnoen), 4 Th. Ratcha-damnoen Nok, tel: 0-2283 1500, ext. 1500. Open daily 8.30am–4.30pm.

Regional Offices

Ayutthaya, 108/22 Moo 4, Th. Pratuchai, tel: 0-3524 6076–7.
Chiang Mai, 105/1 Th. Chiang Mai-Lamphun, tel: 0-5324 8604/8607.
Chiang Rai, 448/16 Th. Singhaklai, tel: 0-5371 7433.
Hat Yai, 1/1 Soi 2, Th. Niphat Uthit 3, tel: 0-7424 3747/7423 8518.
Kanchanaburi, Th. Saengchuto, tel: 0-3451 2500.
Khon Kaen, 15/5 Th. Prachasamoson, tel: 0-4324 4498–9.
Loei, Old District Office, Th. Charoenraj. tel: 0-4281 2812.
Lopburi, Th. Ropwat Phrathat, tel: 0-3642 2768–9.
Nakhon Phanom, 184/1 Th. Sunthornvichit, tel: 0-4251 3490–1.
Nakhon Ratchasima, 2102–2104 Th. Mittraphap, tel: 0-4421 3666.
Nakhon Si Thammarat, Sanam Na Muang, Th. Ratchadamnoen, tel: 0-7534 6515–6.
Pattaya, 609 Moo 10, Th. Phra Tamnak, tel: 0-3842 8750.
Phetchaburi, 500/51 Th. Phetchkasem, tel: 0-3247 1005–6.
Phitsanulok, 209/7–8 Surasi Trade Center, Th. Boromtrailokanat, tel: 0-5523 9907.
Phuket, 191 Th. Thalang, tel: 0-7621 1036/7138.
Rayong, 153/4 Th. Sukhumvit, tel: 0-3865 5420–1.
Songkhla, 1/1 Soi 2, Th. Niphatuthit 3, tel. 0-7423 1055/8518.
Surat Thani, 5 Th. Talat Mai, tel: 0-7728 8818–9.
Surin, 355 Th. Thessaban, tel: 0-4451-4447.
Tak, 193 Th. Taksin, tel: 0-5551 4341.
Trat, 100 Moo 1, Th. Trat-Laem Ngop, tel: 0-3959 7259–60.

Ubon Ratchathani, 264/1 Th. Khuan Thani, tel: 0-4524 3770.
Udon Thani, 16/5 Th. Mukmontri, tel: 0-4232 5406–7.

Overseas Offices

UK, 3rd Floor, Brook House, 98–99 Jermyn Street, London SW1 6EE, tel: 44-20-7925 2511.
US, 61 Broadway, Suite 2810, New York, NY 10006, tel: 1-212-432 0433; and 611 North Larchmont Blvd, 1st Floor, Los Angeles, CA 90004, tel: 1-323-461 9814.
Australia, Level 2, 75 Pitt Street, Sydney 2000, tel: 61-2-9247 7549.

Websites

Thailand

www.tourismthailand.org
The official website of the Tourism Authority of Thailand.
www.dininginthailand.com
A guide to the hundreds of restaurants and bars in Bangkok, plus Phuket and Pattaya.
www.bangkokpost.com
Daily news from the Bangkok Post daily newspaper.
www.nationmultimedia.com
Daily news clips from The Nation newspaper.
www.farangonline.com
Listings and articles on Southeast Asia and beyond.
www.circleofasia.com
Reliable hotel and tour bookings with lots of feature stories and articles on activities and culture.

Bangkok

www.bkkmetro.com
What's on and what's hot in Bangkok, plus nightlife and restaurant listings from one of the city's best lifestyle magazines.
www.stickmanbangkok.com
An often humorous and insightful look at Bangkok through the eyes of a somewhat embittered expat.
www.EnglishThai.com
Interpreter and translation services in Bangkok.
www.bangkoktourist.com
Information on Bangkok from the Bangkok Tourist Bureau.
www.bkmagazine.com
Nightlife and restaurant listings, plus what's new and hot in Bangkok.

Weights and Measures

Thailand uses the metric system, except for their traditional system of land measurement (1 rai = 1,600 sq metres) and the weight of gold (1 baht = 15.2 grammes).

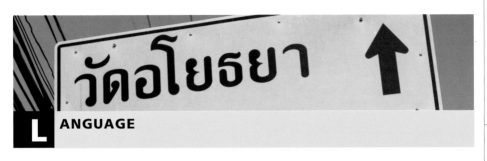

UNDERSTANDING THE LANGUAGE

Origins and Intonation

For centuries, the Thai language, rather than tripping from foreigners' tongues, has been tripping them up. Its roots go back to the place Thais originated from in the hills of southern China, but these are overlaid by Indian influences. From the original settlers come the five tones that seem designed to frustrate visitors. One sound can have five different tones: mid, high, low, rising and falling, and each of these means a different thing from the other *(see panel below)*.

Therefore, when you mispronounce a word, you don't simply say a word incorrectly: it is another word entirely. It is not unusual to see a semi-fluent foreigner standing before a Thai and running through the scale of tones until suddenly a light of recognition dawns on his companion's face. There are the misinformed who will tell you that tones are not important. These people do not communicate with Thais – they communicate at them in a one-sided exchange that frustrates both parties.

Pronunciation

The way Thai consonants are written in English often confuses foreigners. An *h* following a letter like *p* and *t* gives the letter a soft sound; without the *h*, the sound is more explosive. Thus, *ph* is not pronounced *f* but as a soft *p*; without the *h*, the *p* has the sound of a very hard *b*. The word *thanon* (street) is pronounced *tanon* in the same way as *Thailand* is not meant to sound like *Thighland*. Similarly, final letters are often not pronounced as they look. The letter *j* at the end of a word is pronounced as *t*, while *l* is pronounced as an *n*. To complicate matters further,

many words end with *se* or *r*, which are not pronounced; for instance, *Surawongse*, one of Bangkok's main thoroughfares, is simply pronounced *Surawarong*.

Vowels are pronounced as follows: **i** as in *sip*, **ii** as in *seep*, **e** as in *bet*, **a** as in *pun*, **aa** as in *pal*, **u** as in *pool*, **o** as in *so*, **ai** as in *pie*, **ow** as in *cow*, **aw** as in *paw*, **iw** as in *you*, **oy** as in *toy*.

In Thai, the pronouns *I* and *me* are the same word, but it is indicated differently for males and females. Men use the word *pom* when referring to themselves, while women say *di chan*. Men use *khrap* at the end of a sentence when addressing either a male or a female to add politeness, or in a similar manner as "please" (the word for "please", *karuna*, is seldom used directly), ie *Pai nai, khrap* (Where are you going sir?). Women add the word *kha* to their statements, as in *pai nai, kha*.

To ask a question, add a high tone *mai* to the end of the phrase ie *rao pai* (we go) or *rao pai mai* (shall we go?). To negate a statement, insert a falling tone *mai* between the subject and the verb ie *rao pai* (we go), *rao mai pai* (we don't go). "Very" or "much" are

The Five Tones

Mid tone: Voiced at the speaker's normal, even pitch.
High tone: Pitched slightly higher than the mid tone.
Low tone: Pitched slightly lower than the mid tone.
Rising tone: Sounds like a questioning pitch, starting low and rising.
Falling tone: Sounds like an English-speaker suddenly understanding something: "Oh, I see!"

indicated by adding *maak* to the end of a phrase ie *ron* (hot), *ron maak* (very hot), or *phaeng* (expensive), *phaeng maak* (very expensive), and the opposite *mai phaeng* (not expensive).

Thai Names

Thai names are among the longest in the world. Every Thai person's first name and surname has a meaning. Thus, by learning the meaning of the name of everyone you meet, you would acquire a formal, but quite extensive, vocabulary.

There is no universal transliteration system from Thai into English, which is why names and street names can be spelled in three different ways. For example, the surname Chumsai is written Chumsai, Jumsai and Xoomsai, depending on the family. This confuses even the Thais. If you ask a Thai how they spell something, they may well reply, "How do you want to spell it?" So, Ratchadamnoen is also spelled Ratchadamnern. Ko Samui can be spelled Koh Samui. The spellings will differ from map to map, and from book to book.

To address a person one has never met, the title *khun* is used for both male and female. Having long and complicated surnames, Thais typically address one another by their first name only, preceded by the title *khun* for formality, ie Hataichanok Phrommayon becomes *Khun* Hataichanok. Thais usually adopt nicknames from birth, often accorded to their physical or behavioural attributes as a baby, ie *Lek* (small), *Yai* (big), etc. If the person is familiar – a friend, relative, or close colleague – then according to the age relationship between both persons, they are addressed *Pii* (if older), or

Nong (if younger). So an older friend would be addressed *Pii Lek*, and if younger *Nong Lek*.

Numbers

0 *soon*
1 *nung*
2 *song*
3 *sam*
4 *sii*
5 *haa*
6 *hok*
7 *jet*
8 *bet*
9 *kow*
10 *sip*
11 *sip et*
12 *sip song*
13 *sip sam* and so on
20 *yii sip*
30 *sam sip* and so on
100 *nung roi*
1,000 *nung phan*

Useful Words and Phrases

Days of the Week

Monday *Wan Jan*
Tuesday *Wan Angkan*
Wednesday *Wan Phoot*
Thursday *Wan Pharuhat*
Friday *Wan Sook*
Saturday *Wan Sao*
Sunday *Wan Athit*
Today *Wan nii*
Yesterday *Meua wan nii*
Tomorrow *Prung nii*

Basics

Yes *Chai*
No *Mai chai*
Hello/goodbye *Sawadee* (a man then says *khrap*; a woman says *kha*: thus *sawadee khrap* or *sawadee kha*)
My name is... *Pom cheur...* (man); *Di chan cheur...* (woman)
How are you? *Khun sabai dii, mai?*
Well, thank you *Sabai dii, khopkhun*
Thank you very much *Khopkhun maak*
Sorry *Kor toet*
Can you help me? *Chuay pom noy dai mai?*
Never mind *Mai pen rai*
Do you speak English? *Kun poot par sar ang grit dai mai?*
I don't understand *Pom mai kow jai*

Directions and Travel

Go *Pai*
Come *Maa*
Where *Thii nai*
Right *Khwaa*
Left *Sai*
Turn *Leo*
Straight ahead *Trong pai*

Stop here *Yood thii nii*
Fast *Raew*
Slow *Cha*
Hotel *Rong raem*
Street *Thanon*
Lane *Soi*
Bridge *Saphan*
Police Station *Sathanii Dtam Ruat*
Ferry *Reua*
Longtail boat *Reua haang yao*
Taxi *Taihk see*
Train *Rot fai*
Bus *Rot may*
Skytrain *Rot fai faa*
Metro/subway *Rot fai tai din*
Pier *Tha reua*
Bus stop *Pai rot may*
Bus station *Sathanii rot may*
Train station *Sathanii rot fai*
How do I get to...? *Pom ja pai tee... pai yang ngai?*
Can you show me on the map where I am? *Chuay chee nai pairn tee hai doo noy war torn nee pom yoo tee nai?*
Where's the tourist office? *Sam nak ngarn torng teaw yoo tee nai?*

Accommodation

The air-conditioning doesn't work *Air mai tam ngarn*
The light doesn't work *Fai far mai tam ngarn*
There's no hot water *Mai mee narm rorn*

Shopping

Do you have...? *Mii... mai?*
How much? *Thao rai?*
Expensive *Phaeng*
Do you have something cheaper? *Mii arai thii thook kwa, mai?*
Can I try it on? *Kor lorng noy dai mai?*
Too big *Yai kern pai*
Too small *Lek kern pai*
I'll take it *Pom ow an nee la*
I don't want it *Mai ao*
Do you have another colour? *Mii sii uhn mai?*

Colour (sii)

White *sii kao*
Black *sii dum*
Red *sii daeng*
Yellow *sii leung*
Blue *sii num ngern*
Green *sii keeow*
Orange *sii som*

Eating Out

May I have the menu, please? *Kor doo rai garn ar harn noy dai mai?*
Nothing too spicy, please *Mai ow rot jat na krap (ka)*
I'm vegetarian *Pom pehn mang sawi rat*

Hot (heat hot) *Ron*
Hot (spicy) *Phet*
Cold *Yen*
Sweet *Waan*
Sour *Prio*
Delicious *Aroy*
Water *Narm*

Other Handy Phrases

Do you have...? *Mi... mai?*
Can I pay by credit card? *Jai duay bat krey dit dai mai?*
Where's the toilet? *Horng narm yoo tee nai?*
I do not feel well *Mai sabai*
Can you get me a doctor? *Chuay dtarm mor mar hai noy dai mai?*
Is it safe to swim here? *Tee nee plort pai por tee ja wai narm dai mai?*
Is it all right to take pictures? *Tai roop tee nee dai mai?*

Glossary of Terms

ao gulf/bay
baat alms bowl used by monks
baht Thai unit of currency
bai sema boundary stones marking the ground surrounding a *bot*
ban house or village, short for *mooban*
bot ordination hall in a Thai temple
chao lay indigenous sea gypsies
chedi relic tower, also called *stupa*
chofa curling temple roof extensions
doi mountain (in the north)
farang Westerner
garuda half-eagle half-man demi-god
guti monks' living quarters
hat beach
ho trai Buddhist scripture library
Isaan a term for northeast Thailand
kathoey "lady-boy" or transvestite
khao hill or mountain
klong/khlong canal
ko/koh island
laem cape
lak muang city pillar
lakhon form of classical dance drama
likay village folk-dance-drama
mae nam river
mor lam northeastern music tradition
muay thai Thai boxing
mudmee northeastern Thai silk
namtok waterfall
phipat classical Thai music
prang Khmer-style tower
sanuk fun or enjoyment
soi lane or small street
songthaew covered pick-up truck with two rows of padded seats behind
tham cave
thanon street
tuk-tuk motorised three-wheeled taxi
viharn sermon hall in Buddhist temple
wai palms clasped together in a Thai-style greeting
wat temple or monastery

FURTHER READING

General

Bangkok Found: Reflections on the City by Alex Kerr. River Books, 2009. An incisive look into the traditions underpinning Bangkok as well as the often quirky results of mixing old and new in this city of fusion.
Bangkok's Waterways by William Warren and R. Ian Lloyd. Asia Books, 1989. A heartfelt guide to the essence of Bangkok – the canals and rivers that wind through the city, beautifully written and photographed.
Travelers' Tales Thailand edited by James O'Reilly and Larry Habegger. Travelers' Tales Inc., 2002. A stimulating collection of observations and true stories contributed by some 50 writers.

Fiction

Bangkok 8 by John Burdett. Vintage, 2004. A best-selling story about a half-Thai, half-American policeman who avenges his partner's death. Sequels **Bangkok Tattoo** and **Bangkok Haunts** recount further rough-and-tumble tales of the protagonist.
Big Mango by Jake Needham. Asia Books, 1999. This enjoyable thriller exudes a perceptive understanding of the Big Mango, Bangkok.
Fieldwork: A Novel by Mischa Berlinski. Picador, 2009. A thriller set in the north, refreshingly free of bar-girl subplots.
A Killing Smile by Christopher G. Moore. Heaven Lake Press, 2004. A gripping thriller set in the capital city of Thailand. Moore has written many books based on his experiences with Bangkok's seamier side.
Many Lives (Lai Chiwit) by Kukrit Pramoj. Silkworm Books, 1996. Insight into Buddhist thought from the famous Thai polymath.
Monsoon Country by Pira Sudham. Breakwater Books, 1990. One of the best books to come out of Thailand in recent times gives a unique glimpse of rural Thai life.
Probability (Kwam Na Ja Pen) by Prabda Yoon. Typhoon Books, 2002. The collection of short stories that launched the career of this highly rated Thai author.

History and Society

Borderlines by Charles Nicholl. Picador, 1989. The British author roams Thailand, initially interested in Buddhism but also raising questions about the nature of travel itself. Shot through with some highly comic episodes.
The King Never Smiles by Paul Handley, Yale University Press, 2006. A serious but controversial analysis of the monarchy's role in Thailand. Unavailable in the kingdom.
Thailand: A Short History by David K. Wyatt, Silkworm Books, 2003. This scholarly work is considered the best history of the country.
Thaksin: The Business of Politics in Thailand by Dr Pasuk Phongpaichit and Chris Baker. Silkworm Books, 2004. A carefully researched study of Prime Minister Thaksin Shinawatra and his impact on the nation's economy, society and democracy.

Send Us Your Thoughts

We do our best to ensure the information in our books is as accurate and up-to-date as possible. The books are updated on a regular basis using local contacts, who painstakingly add, amend and correct as required. However, some details (such as telephone numbers and opening times) are liable to change, and we are ultimately reliant on our readers to put us in the picture.

We welcome your feedback, especially your experience of using the book "on the road". Maybe we recommended a hotel that you liked (or another that you didn't), or you came across a great bar or new attraction we missed.

We will acknowledge all contributions, and we'll offer an Insight Guide to the best letters received.

Please write to us at:
Insight Guides
PO Box 7910
London SE1 1WE
Or email us at:
insight@apaguide.co.uk

Art and Culture

Architecture of Thailand by Nithi Sthapitanonda and Brian Mertens. Editions Didier Millet, 2005. Explores Thailand's unique architectural lineage, from the simple bamboo hut to teak mansions and religious edifices.
Bangkok Inside Out by Daniel Ziv and Guy Sharett. Equinox Publishing, 2005. A peek into the chaotic city's urban landscape.
Flavours: Thai Contemporary Art by Steven Pettifor. Thavibu Gallery, 2005. Brimming with colourful illustrations of Thailand's burgeoning contemporary visual arts scene.
The Grand Palace by Nngnoi Saksi, Naengnoi Suksri and Michael Freeman. River Books, 1998. A beautifully illustrated and detailed account of Bangkok's Grand Palace.
Very Thai: Everyday Popular Culture by Philip Cornwel-Smith. River Books, 2005. If you've ever wondered why every compound in Thailand has a spirit house or why insect treats are such a hit, this book is for you.

Religion

A History of Buddhism in Siam by Prince Dhani Nivat. Siam Society, 1965. Written by one of Thailand's most respected scholars.

Cookery

Green Mangoes and Lemongrass: Southeast Asia's Best Recipes From Bangkok To Bali by Wendy Hutton. Tuttle Publishing, 2003. Presenting the rich diversity of Southeast Asian cuisine, accompanied by striking photographs.

Other Insight Guides

Titles that highlight Thailand include:

Insight City Guide Bangkok surveys the capital city with insightful text and stunning photography.
Insight Step by Step Guide: Bangkok offers walking tours of the city.
Insight Fleximaps are portable companions. Text and maps are designed for maximum practicality.

ART AND PHOTO CREDITS

akg-images 33R
APA 30
Aleenta Resorts 197
Alila Cha-am 377
Amari Resorts 185, 269, 375
Anantara Golden Triangle 390
avlxyz on flickr 291
AWL Images 172/173, 186
Adam Baker 168T
Austin Bush/APA 267, 268, 270T, 271&T, 272&T, 273&T, 274T
Calypso Cabaret 397
Corbis 31L&R, 44, 70
CPA 35, 38, 40
Joe Cummings/APA 327
Joe Cummings/CPA 348, 350T
Dominique Dalbiez 340
Francis Dorai/APA 101L, 113T, 115T, 120BL, 122T, 175R, 415
Hans Fonk 89L, 128R
Fotolia 8C, 346BL
Kevin Foy/Rex Features 211
Yutaka Fujii 319T
Getty Images 9TR, 11T, 42, 45, 46, 196, 206, 212, 280, 343
A.Good/IBL/Rex Features 248
Grand Millennium Sukhumvit 373L&R
Oliver Hargreave/CPA 181, 183, 187
David Henley/APA 2/3, 7BL, 9TL, 20T, 279(all), 282, 283, 284T, 285L&R, 286T, 287, 288, 289, 292, 293, 294&T, 295, 296, 297, 298&T, 299&T, 300L&R, 302, 303, 305, 306&T, 307, 308, 309&T, 311, 312&T, 314, 315, 317, 319, 320, 321(all), 322, 323, 325, 329T, 330, 331, 335(all), 336, 339, 342, 343T, 344&T, 345L&R, 349, 351T, 352 (all), 353, 354&T, 356, 357, 358&T, 359, 360, 361
David Henley/CPA 7BR, 29, 73, 89R, 128T, 163, 223T, 251, 266
Hans Hofer 62
Jeremy Hou/APA 369
John W. Ishil/APA 7CR, 10BR, 19T, 21, 25, 51, 55R, 65, 126B, 174, 175L, 177, 178, 179, 182, 184&T, 186T, 194BL, 195, 197T, 198, 200, 201, 202, 203, 204T&B, 205L&BR, 208&T, 211T, 213&T, 214&T, 215, 219, 220&T, 222L, 223, 224, 225&T, 241T, 242, 245T, 249, 250&T, 252T, 253T, 254, 255&T,

256&T, 258&T, 259, 260&T, 261&T, 263, 265
iStockphoto.com 6BR, 7TR&CBL, 8T, 24, 32, 39, 100, 124, 144/145, 157, 165T, 207, 217, 222R, 270, 274R, 318
JW Marriott Resort & Spa 236
The Kobal Collection/Kick The Machine 72
Jason Lang/APA 10L, 50, 52, 53, 54, 60, 64L&R, 88, 90, 94/95, 104, 105L, 116T, 117L, 120R, 129, 132, 134&T, 142, 143T, 147L, 148, 151T, 152T, 153, 154T, 156T, 167, 168BL&R, 170, 187T, 190, 193T, 194T&R, 367, 401
Boo Lee 275
Kriang Lerdsuwanakij 143
Mandarin Oriental Hotel Group 133
Millennium Resort Patong 383
Jock Montgomery 253
onAsia 141, 151BR, 218, 221, 274BL
OzMark17 on flickr 171T
Patravadi Theatre 71
Peninsula Hotel 371
Photobank 34, 316T
Photolibrary 209
Pimalai Resort & Spa 261, 387
private archives 43
M.C. Piya Rangsit 26, 41
Scala Picture Library 28, 33L, 37L
Sipa Press/Rex Features 47
Sofitel Raja Orchid Khon Kaen 393
Chrisada Sookdhis 189
Starwood Hotels & Resorts 370
Peter Stuckings/APA 4B, 6CT&BL, 7CTL, 14/15, 16/17, 18, 48/49, 55L, 56, 57, 61, 63, 68, 69, 74, 75, 77, 79, 80, 81, 82, 83L&R, 84L&R, 85, 86, 87L&R, 91, 96/97, 98/99, 105R, 108, 109, 110R, 112, 114R, 117R, 118, 119, 120T, 122, 125&T, 127, 131, 133T, 135L&R, 136, 139, 140, 141T, 146, 147R, 151L, 152, 154, 155, 156, 160, 161, 162, 164, 165, 166&T, 276/277, 278, 281, 284, 286, 289T, 296T, 310, 311T, 324, 326L&R, 327T, 328, 329, 334, 337&T, 341&T, 346T&R, 350, 351L&R, 362, 364, 365, 395, 411, 419
SuperStock 176, 191, 193, 244L
Luca Invernizzi Tettoni 27, 36, 37R, 316

Marcus Wilson-Smith/APA 11B, 19R&B, 22, 76, 78, 101T&B, 110T&BL, 113, 114T&BL, 116, 121&T, 123, 124T, 130L&R, 171, 181T, 205T, 235T, 242T, 245, 257, 403, 405, 417
Nikt Wong/APA 1, 3B, 4T, 5T, 6/7T, 9B, 10TR, 12/13, 20B, 23, 226, 227, 230, 231, 233, 235, 237&T, 238, 239&T, 240, 241, 243&T, 244R, 246, 264, 399
Jason Wesley Upton 126T

PHOTO FEATURES

58/59: Daniel Axelson 59TR; Fotolia 58CR; Michael Freeman 59CR; Getty Images 58BR, 59CL; David Henley/CPA 58/59; Rainer Krack/CPA 59BR; Peter Stuckings/APA 58BL

66/67: John W. Ishil/APA 66CR, 67BL; iStockphoto.com 66BL&BR, 67BR; Peter Stuckings/APA 66TL, 66/67; Marcus Wilson-Smith/APA 67TR

92/93: Francis Dorai/APA 93CL; Fotolia 92CR; iStockphoto.com 93BR; Derrick Lim/APA 93CR; Peter Stuckings/APA 92BL; Marcus Wilson-Smith/APA 92BR, 92/93, 93TR&C

158/159: all images iStockphoto. com except 159TR Peter Stuckings/APA

228/229: all images iStockphoto. com except 228TL Fotolia

332/333: iStockphoto.com 333TR&BC; onAsia 332TL&BR, 332/333, 333CL&CR; SuperStock 332CR; Marcus Wilson-Smith/APA 332BL

Map Production: original cartography Berndtson & Berndtson

© 2010 Apa Publications GmbH & Co. Verlag KG (Singapore branch)

Production: Linton Donaldson, Mary Pickles

INDEX